The Long Journey

BY

JOHANNES V. JENSEN

WITH AN INTRODUCTION BY

FRANCIS HACKETT

The Nobel Prize edition of the world-renowned epic novel that was the basis for the award of the Nobel Prize for Literature to its author in 1944.

three volumes in one:	FIRE AND ICE
	THE CIMBRIANS
	CHRISTOPHER COLUMBUS

Kristin Lavransdatter

BY

SIGRID UNDSET

WINNER OF THE NOBEL PRIZE FOR LITERATURE IN 1928

A new and handsome edition of the great historical novel of medieval Norway.

In three volumes:

I. THE BRIDAL WREATH
II. THE MISTRESS OF HUSABY
III. THE CROSS

THESE ARE BORZOI BOOKS

published in New York by Alfred A. Knopf

Independent People

AN EPIC

Independent People

AN EPIC

BY

HALLDÓR LAXNESS

TRANSLATED FROM THE ICELANDIC BY

J. A. THOMPSON

1 9 4 6

NEW YORK ALFRED A KNOPF

THIS IS A BORZOI BOOK

PUBLISHED BY ALFRED A. KNOPF, INC.

[v]

CONTENTS

BOOK I

PART I *ICELANDIC PIONEER*

PART II *FREE OF DEBT*

BOOK II

PART I *HARD TIMES*

PART II   *YEARS OF PROSPERITY*

PART III   *CONCLUSION*

BOOK I

PART I
Icelandic Pioneer

1. KOLUMKILLI

IN early times, say the Icelandic chronicles, men from the Western
Islands came to live in this country, and when they departed,
left behind them crosses, bells, and other objects used in the practice of sorcery. From Latin sources may be learned the names of
those who sailed here from the Western Islands in the early days
of the Papacy. Their leader was Kolumkilli the Irish, a sorcerer
of wide repute. In those days there was great fertility of the soil
in Iceland. But when the Norsemen came to settle here, the Western sorcerers were forced to flee the land, and old writings say
that Kolumkilli, determined on revenge, laid a curse on the in-
vaders, swearing that they would never prosper here, and more
in the same spirit, much of which has since, to all appearances,
been fulfilled. Later in history the Norsemen in Iceland began to
stray from their true beliefs and to embrace the idolatries of unrelated peoples. Then there was chaos throughout the land; the
gods of the Norsemen were held to derision and new gods and
new saints were introduced, some from the east and some from
the west.

The chronicles tell how at this time a church was built to Kolumkilli in the valley where later stood the bigging Albogastathir on
the Moor. This in the old days had been the residence of a chief-
tain. Much information relating to this moorland valley was col-
lected by Sheriff Jon Reykdalin of Rauthsmyri after the bigging
was last destroyed in the great spectral visitations of the year 1750.
The Sheriff himself both saw and heard the sundry unnatural
happenings that took place there, as is shown in his well-known
Account of the Albogastathir Fiend. The ghost was heard chanting aloud in the bigging from Mid-Thorri to well past Whitsun-
tide, when the folk fled; twice he named his name in the Sheriff's

ear, but answered all other questions with "odious Latin verses
and shameless obscenities."

Of the many stories that have been told of this lonely bigging
in its moorland valley, the most remarkable is undoubtedly one
which dates back to long before the days of Sheriff Jon, and it
may not be out of place to recall it for the pleasure of such people
as have not fared along the level stretches by the river, where the
centuries lie side by side in unequally overgrown paths cut by
the horses of the past; or of those who may wish to visit the old
site on the hillock in the marshes as they make their way through
the valley.

It could not have been later than towards the end of Bishop
Gudbrandur's ministry that a certain couple farmed Albogastathir
on the Moor. The husband's name is not chronicled, but the wife
was called Gunnvor or Gudvor, a woman of a most forceful nature, reputed to be skilled in occult lore and capable of changing
her form. Her husband, who appears to have been the most
craven-hearted of wretches, had little freedom, being kept completely under her domination.

They did not prosper greatly in their husbandry to begin with,
and few indeed were the work-people they kept. Legend says that
the woman, because of their poverty and their many offspring,
forced her husband to carry their new-born children out into the
desert and leave them there to die. Some he laid under flat rocks
on the mountain; their wails may still be heard in early spring
about the time when the snow thaws. To others he tied stones,
then sank them in the lake, whence their weeping may yet be heard
in the mid-winter moonlight, especially in frost or before a storm.

But as the mistress Gunnvor grew older in years, says the story,
she began to thirst greatly for human blood. And she hungered
for human marrow. It is even said that she took the blood of her
surviving children and drank it with her mouth. She had a scaffold
built for incantation behind the house, where in fire and reek she
used to chant to the fiend Kolumkilli on autumn evenings. It is
said that her husband tried to escape and publish her evil doings
abroad, but she pursued him and, overtaking him on Rauthsmyri
Ridge, killed him with stones and mutilated his corpse. She carried his bones home to her scaffold, but the flesh and the bowels
she left behind for the ravens, and had it given out in the district
that he had perished while searching the mountains for sheep that
had strayed.

From that day forward the mistress Gunnvor began to prosper, and everyone believed that it was due to her evil compact with Kolumkilli, and soon she was the owner of many good horses.

There was much journeying through the district in those days, both in the summertime when men went to the fishing under Jokull, and in the springtime, when men journeyed from afar to Jokull to buy their stockfish. As time went on, however, it was rumoured throughout the district that the more horses Gunnvor acquired, the less hospitable towards these travellers did she grow, and though she was a woman who attended church regularly, as was the custom in that age, it is told in the Annals that on Whit Sunday she could not see the sun in a cloudless sky after the service at Rauthsmyri Church.

Rumours now began to be whispered abroad concerning the fate of Gunnvor's husband, and how she murdered men, some for their possessions, others for their blood and marrow, and rode after some on the mountains. Now, there lies in the valley, to the south but not at a great distance from the bigging, a stagnant lake called Igulvatn, which name it bears to this day. The mistress killed her guests in the middle of the night, and this was the manner of their death: she attacked them with a short sword as they slept, bit them in the throat and drank their blood, then, after dismembering their bodies, used their bones as playthings for herself and the fiend Kolumkilli. Some she pursued over the moors and assailed with her sword, and brightly flashed the blade as she made an end of them. In strength she was the equal of any man, and she had in addition the help of the Devil. Clots of blood may still be seen in the snow on the ridges, especially before Yule. She bore their carrion down into the valley and sank it in the lake, after tying stones to it. Then she stole their possessions, their clothes and horses and money, if any. Her children were idiots all and would bark from the housetop like any dog, or squat in imbecility on the paving and bite men, for the Fiend had deprived them of common sense and human tongue. To this very day this lullaby is sung in districts on both sides of the high moors:

> *Guest of Gunnvor was one man,*
> *With pony of price,*
> *Through his heart her sword she ran,*
> *Lullabalulla,*
> *Running blood reddens the blade,*
> *Lullababalulla.*

Guest of Gunnvor was no man
With God or good grace,
She has broken my rib-bone, my leg-bone, my hip-bone,
Lullabalulla,
Running blood reddens the blade,
Lullababalulla.

If Kolumkilli call me should,
This is what he'd say:
Bones and red blood, bones and red blood,
And dododo,
Runs the blood in a flood,
So lullababalulla.

But in the end it came to pass that Gunnvor's vile practices
were unmasked. She had been the bane of many — men, women,
and children alike — and had chanted at night to the fiend Kolumkilli. She was condemned at the district moot and broken at the
lich-gate of Rauthsmyri Church on Trinity Sunday. Then she
was dismembered, and last of all her head was cut off; and she
took her death well, but cursed men with strange curses. Her
trunk, head, and limbs were gathered into a skin bag, which was
borne up to the ridge to the west of Albogastathir and buried in a
cairn at the highest point. The cairn may be seen to this day, now
overgrown with grass below and called latterly Gunnucairn. The
people say that there will be no misfortune if the traveller cast a
stone on to the cairn on the first occasion that he crosses the ridge,
but some throw a stone each time they pass that way, and hope
therewith to buy themselves immunity.

Troublesome as the mistress Gunnvor may have seemed in living life, she far surpassed her former evil conduct after her burial;
she was considered to rest ill in the barrow and walked again at
home on her farm. She woke up with her those several men whom
she had destroyed, and folk at home in Albogastathir had little
rest from disturbance once the nights took to darkening. She resumed her former practices, tormenting living and dead alike, so
that always there might be heard in the croft at night a loud yelling and howling as though flocks of tortured souls held lament on
the roof and at the window because of their great misery and little
rest. Sometimes it was as if the most powerful stench of brimstone
erupted from the earth, filling the house with its gust so that men
lay suffocating and dogs thrashed about as though mad. Some-

times Gunnvor rode the roof so that every timber shook, and in the end no building was thought safe from her evil pounding and shameful night-riding. She would climb on men's backs and on the backs of livestock and crush the cows; she would drive women and children mad and frighten old people, yielding neither to signs of the cross nor to magic spells. The story relates that finally the priest of Rauthsmyri was brought to lay her and that she fled before his most admirable learning into the mountain, splitting it where a cleft is now to be seen. Some people say that she took up her habitation in the mountain, in which case it is not unlikely that it was in the form of a troll. Others believe that she lives much in the lake in the form of some kind of serpent or water-monster; and indeed it is on all men's lips that a monster has now for many generations inhabited the lake and appeared to countless witnesses, who have testified to it upon oath, even those without second sight. Some people say that this monster has destroyed the bigging Albogastathir thrice, others seven times, so that no husbandman had any peace there longer and the farm was laid waste because spectres in various likenesses continually disturbed it. So in the time of Sheriff Jon Reykdalin it was added to the lands of Rauthsmyri first as sheep-cotes for the winter, whence its later name of Winterhouses, but afterwards as a lambs' fold.

2.　THE HOLDING

ON a knoll in the marshes stand the ruins of an old croft-house. This knoll is perhaps only in a certain sense the work of nature; perhaps it is much rather the work of long dead peasants who built their homes there on the grassy bank by the brook, generation after generation, one on the other's ruins. But for over a hundred years now it has been a lambs' fold; here ewes and their lambs have bleated for more than a hundred springs. Out from the fold and its knoll, mainly to the south, spread miles of marshland dotted here and there with islets of ling, and through Rauthsmyri Ridge a little river runs down into the marsh, and another from the lake in the east through the valleys of the eastern moors. To the north of the knoll towers a steep mountain, its lower slopes scarred with landslides, and the tongues between covered with heather. The crags soar up from the landslides in sheer castellations, and in one place above the fold the mountain is cloven by a gully in the basalt, and down from this gully in spring cascades a waterfall, long and slender. Sometimes the south wind blows the spray up over the brink again, so that the waterfall flows backwards. At the foot of the mountain boulders lie, scattered here and there. This lambs' fold, where once stood the bigging Albogastathir on the Moor, has for the past few generations been known as Winterhouses.

A little brook runs down past the fold, runs in a semicircle round the home-field, clear and cold, and never fails. In summer the sunbeams play in its merry stream and the sheep lies chewing on the bank and stretches one foot out into the grass. On such a day the sky is blue. The sun shines brightly on the lake with its swans; and on the smooth flow of the trout river through the marshes. Heath and marshes hum with blithe song.

Ridges and high moorland enclose the valley on all sides. To the west lies a narrow ridge, and the first farm beyond it is called Utirauthsmyri, Rauthsmyri, or simply Myri, the seat of the local Bailiff; this moorland valley has until now been part of his possessions. Broad lands, widely farmed, open beyond Myri. The high heath in the east, over which lies the road down to the market town on the fjord, is considered a five hours' crossing with packhorses. In the south, low undulating moors gradually rise in height until the Blue Mountains close the horizon, melting into the sky, it seems, in pious meditation, and rarely free of snow before St. John the Baptist's Day. And what lies beyond the Blue Mountains? Only the deserts of the land.

And the spring breezes blow up the valley.

And when the spring breezes blow up the valley; when the spring sun shines on last year's withered grass on the river banks; and on the lake; and on the lake's two white swans; and coaxes the new grass out of the spongy soil in the marshes — who could believe on such a day that this peaceful, grassy valley brooded over the story of our past; and over its spectres? People ride along the river, along the banks where side by side lie many paths, cut one by one, century after century, by the horses of the past — and the fresh spring breeze blows through the valley in the sunshine. On such a day the sun is stronger than the past.

A new generation forgets the spectres that may have tormented the old.

How often has the bigging Albogastathir on the Moor been destroyed by spectres? And rebuilt, in spite of spectres? Century after century the lone worker leaves the settlements to tempt fortune on this knoll between the lake and the cleft in the mountain, determined to challenge the evil powers that hold his land in thrall and thirst for his blood and the marrow in his bones. Generation after generation the crofter raises his chant, contemptuous of the powers that lay claim to his limbs and seek to rule his fate to his dying day. The history of the centuries in this valley is the history of an independent man who grapples barehanded with a spectre which bears a new and ever a newer name. Sometimes the spectre is some half-divine fiend who lays a curse on his land. Sometimes it breaks his bones in the guise of a norn. Sometimes it destroys his croft in the form of a monster. And yet, always, to all eternity, it is the same spectre assailing the same man century after century.

"No," he said defiantly.

It was the man who was making for Albogastathir on the Moor a century and a half after the croft had last been destroyed. And as he passed Gunnvor's cairn on the ridge, he spat, and ground out vindictively: "Damn the stone you'll ever get from me, you old bitch," and refused to give her a stone.

His movement was a response to the breeze, his gait in perfect harmony with the uneven land beneath his feet. A yellow dog was following him, a farm labourer's dog with a slim muzzle, and full of lice, for she often threw herself down and bit herself passionately, rolling over and over between the tussocks with the strange, restless yelp peculiar to lousy dogs. She was starved of vitamins, for she stopped every now and again to eat grass. It was equally obvious that she was wormy. And the man turned his face into the fresh wind of spring. The sun shone on the flaunting manes of ancient horses and in the wind was the clopping of long gone hoofs; they were the horses of the past in the bridle-paths along the river, century after century, generation after generation, and still the road was travelled — and now he, the newest land-owner, Icelandic pioneer in the thirtieth generation, was treading it, dauntless as ever, with his dog. Halting on the path of the centuries, he ran his eyes over his valley in the sunshine of spring.

As soon as he halted the dog came fawning upon him. She stuck her slim muzzle between his hard paws, resting it there and wagging her tail and all her body, and the man gazed at the animal philosophically for a while, savouring, in the submissiveness of his dog, the consciousness of his own power, the rapture of command, and sharing, for a second, in human nature's loftiest dream, like a general who looks over his troops and knows that with a word he can send them into the charge. A few moments passed thus, and now the dog was squatting on the withered grass on the bank before him, watching him with questioning eyes, and he replied: "Yes, whatever a man seeks he will find — in his dog."

He went on discussing this subject after he had left the path and was making his way over the marshes towards the home-field, repeating it in various forms: "The things a dog seeks he finds in a man; seek and ye shall find." Bending down, he felt at the spring grass of the marshes with his thick fingers and measured its length; then he uprooted a few blades from a boggy patch, and after wiping the mud from them on to his trousers, put them into his mouth, like a sheep, and thinking as he chewed, began thinking like a sheep. The taste was bitter, but he did not spit; he smacked his lips and savoured the rooty taste of it. "This stuff has saved many a life after a long winter and little hay," he said to himself; "there is a sort of honey in it though it tastes strong. It is this young swamp grass that gives the sheep new life in the spring, you see; and the sheep gives man new life in the autumn." And he went on talking about the swamp grass and mixing it up with philosophy and playing variations on the theme till he had reached the home-field.

Standing on the highest point of the knoll, like a Viking pioneer who has found his high-seat posts, he looked about him, then made water, first to the north in the direction of the mountain, then to the east, towards the marshy tracts and the lake and the river flowing smoothly from the lake through the marshes; then towards the moors in the south, where the Blue Mountains, still coated with snow, closed the horizon in meditation. And the sun shone from a cloudless sky.

Not far from him two Rauthsmyri sheep were cropping the green of the home-field, and although they were his master's sheep, he chased them off, cleared his own home-field for the first time. "This land is mine now," he said.

And then it seemed as if some misgiving gripped him; perhaps the land was not all paid for. Instead of allowing the dog to pursue the sheep, he called her to heel. And went on viewing the world from his own enclosure, the world he had just bought. Summer was just rising over this world.

It was for that reason that he said to the dog: "Winterhouses is no name for a farm like this, no name at all. And as for Albogastathir on the Moor — that's no name either; it's just another of these relics of old popery. Damn me if I'll have names that are bound up with spectres of the past on my farm. I was christened

Bjartur, which ought to mean 'bright.' So the farm shall be called Summerhouses."

And Bjartur of Summerhouses walked round his own home-field, inspecting the grass-grown ruins, scrutinizing the stonework in the walls of the lambs' fold, and pulling down and building up again, in imagination, the same sort of croft-house as he had been born and bred in across the eastern heaths.

"Size isn't everything by any means," he said aloud to the dog, as if suspecting her of entertaining high ideas. "Take my word for it, freedom is of more account than the height of a roof beam. I ought to know; mine cost me eighteen years' slavery. The man who lives on his own land is an independent man. He is his own master. If I can keep my sheep alive though the winter and can pay what has been stipulated from year to year — then I pay what has been stipulated; and I have kept my sheep alive. No, it is freedom that we are all after, Titla. He who pays his way is a king. He who keeps his sheep alive through the winter lives in a palace."

And when the bitch heard this, she too was happy. Now there were no more clouds. She raced in circles around him, barking frivolously, then slunk towards him with her muzzle on the ground, as if to pounce on him, and the next second had leaped away again and traced another circle.

"Now then," he said soberly, "no fooling here. Do I run in circles and bark? Do I lie down with my nose on the ground and tomfoolery in my eyes and go for folk? No, my independence has cost me dearer than that: eighteen years for the Bailiff at Rauths-myri and the poetess and Ingolfur Arnarson Jonsson, who they say has been sent to Denmark now. Was it maybe just for a picnic that I used to go and comb the mountains in the south there for their strays, with winter well on the way? No; and I've buried myself in snow. And it wasn't their fault, bless them, if I crawled out alive next morning."

At this reminder the dog's joy subsided considerably, and she sat down and took to biting herself.

"And no one will ever be able to say that I counted my foot-steps in their service; and what's more, I paid the first instalment on the farm on Easter morning as had been arranged. And I have twenty-five ewes fleeced and lambed; there's many a one begun with less, and still more who have been other people's slaves all their lives and never owned a stick. Take my father for instance. He lived to be eighty and never managed to pay off the miserable sick-loan the parish advanced him when he was only a youngster."

The bitch contemplated him sceptically for a while, as if she didn't really believe what he was saying. She thought of barking, but decided not to, and opened her jaws in a long yawn only, like a question.

"No, I didn't think you would understand," said Bjartur. "You dogs are pretty poor objects really, though on the whole I think we humans have even less to boast about. Still, things will go worse with us than I think, if my Rosa serves her folk with the bones of an old horse on Christmas Eve after twenty-three years of housekeeping here, as the poetess of Rauthsmyri thought fit to do, and that no longer ago than last year."

The bitch had again begun biting herself passionately.

"Aye, no wonder their herd's dog is lousy and eats the grass, when even their housekeeper hasn't set eyes on the pantry-key for twenty years. And wouldn't the horses he leaves out in winter tell a fine story, if only their tongues were loosened, poor brutes; and his sheep, too. It has been one eternal martyrdom for them all these years, and probably it's just as well for some people that sheep don't have a place on the judgment seat in heaven, poor brutes."

The farm brook ran down from the mountain in a straight line for the fold, then swerved to the west to go its way down into the marshes. There were two knee-high falls in it and two pools, knee-deep. At the bottom there was shingle, pebbles and sand. It ran in many curves. Each curve had its own tone, but not one of them was dull; the brook was merry and music-loving, like youth, but yet with various strings, and it played its music without thought of any audience and did not care though no one heard for a hundred years, like the true poet. The man examined it all closely. He halted by the upper fall and said: "Here she can wash out socks and so on"; by the lower fall and said: "Here salt fish could be put to soak." The dog stretched her head down to the water and lapped at it. The man lay flat on the bank, too, and drank, and some of the water went up his nose. "It's first-rate water," said Bjartur of Summerhouses, looking at the dog as he wiped his mouth on his sleeve. "I could almost believe that it had been consecrated."

Probably it occurred to him that with this observation he was exposing a chink in his armour to the unknown powers of evil that were popularly supposed to infest the valley, for all at once he turned about in the spring breeze, turned in a complete circle, and said in every direction:

"Not that it matters; the water could be unconsecrated for

all I care. Of you I am unafraid, Gunnvor. Hard shall it go with you to oppose my good fortune, old hag, for spectres never daunted me yet." He clenched his fists and with kindling eyes looked up at the mountain cleft, then at the ridge in the west, and then at the lake, still grinding out words of challenge between his teeth in saga style: " — And never shall!"

The bitch leaped up and, rushing madly at the sheep at the bottom of the knoll, started snapping viciously at their hocks, for she thought the man was angry, whereas he was only filled with the modern spirit and determination to be a free man on his own land, with the same independence as the other generations that had settled there before him.

"Kolumkilli!" he cried, laughing scornfully, after he had called the dog to heel. "What a tale; what nonsense these old wives let their heads be stuffed with!"

3.   THE WEDDING

By the time that Term Day comes round, Iceland's splendidly patriotic grass has begun sprouting for the inhabitants with a welcome rapidity; one could almost take a scythe to the growth in the manured fields. The sheep have begun to lift their heavy heads again and hide their ribs in flesh, and the eyeless face of the carcase down in the marsh is buried in grass. Yes, life is sweet at such a time, and now, surely, is the time to marry, for all the nests of the mice in the old ruins have been pulled out and a new croft has been built. It is Bjartur of Summerhouses' croft. Stones have been carried, turf cut, walls built up, framework nailed, rafters hoisted, boards nailed for a clincher roof, range built in, chimney set in place — and there stands the croft-house as if part of nature itself.

Up-country, in pretty much the same sort of dwelling, the marriage was solemnized at Nithurkot, the home of the bride's parents, and it was from the same sort of farmhouses that most of the guests came: crofts standing at the foot of the mountains or sheltering on the southern slope of a ridge, each with a little brook running through the home-field, marshy land beyond, and a river flowing smoothly through the marsh. When one journeys from one homestead to the next, nothing seems more likely than that they all bear the same name and that the same man and the same woman work them all; yet that is not so. Old Thorthur of Nithurkot, for instance, had cherished throughout the years the dream of building himself a mill across his farm brook. There was some strength in its flow, and if he could build a mill and grind Scotch barley for folk he would make quite a decent little profit out of the enterprise. But no sooner had he got the building finished than they stopped importing unground corn; and in any case folk preferred their corn ready-milled. His children played about the mill-cot in the spring days of childhood with no evening; the sky was blue in those days; they never forgot it as long as they lived.

There were seven of them. When they grew up they left home and went away to distant places. Two sons were drowned in a distant ocean, and one son and a daughter had disappeared to a land even more remote, America, which is farther than death. But perhaps no distance is greater than that which separates a poor family in the same country; two daughters had married in fishing villages, and one of them was now a widow with a horde of children, while the other, who had married a consumptive, was on the parish — what is life?

The youngest daughter, Rosa, had spent most of her time at home, until she went into service with the Bailiff at Utirauthsmyri. There was then no one left on the croft but the old couple, an aged crone who stayed with them, and an eighty-year-old pauper assigned them by the parish. And today Rosa was to be married; that's what she had got out of it. Tomorrow she was going for good and all. And the mill stood by the brook. Such is life.

Though Bjartur had from youth upwards spent his life on a large estate, most of his acquaintances were peasants from up-country, sheep-men like himself who toiled like slaves over their flocks, day in, day out, the whole year round, till they died without ever having transacted a business deal involving more than a few dollars at a time. Some of them succeeded in attaining a degree of culture that was expressed in a timber living-room shaped like a box and roofed with corrugated iron, but such houses are damp and draughty; draughts are the source of rheumatism, consumption breeds in the damp. Most of them, however, thought themselves lucky if they could renew a wall or two of their earthen crofts once every five years, and that in spite of dreams of higher things. In every croft, somehow, there lives and persists the dream of something better; for a thousand years they have imagined that they will rise above penury in some mysterious manner and acquire a large estate and the title of landed farmers, the eternal dream. Some consider that it will only be fulfilled in heaven.

They lived for their sheep, and, with the exception of the Bailiff, they all dealt in Fjord with Tulinius Jensen, manager of Bruni's, a firm of Danish merchants. The Bailiff dealt in Vik, and as he himself decided what price he should have for his sheep, it was rumoured that he must have more than a finger in the business there.

People were considered fortunate to get on to Bruni's books, for he usually allowed them a certain amount of credit. They never saw a penny from that day forward, of course, but they would feel reasonably sure of surviving the winter, and of getting enough rye meal, refuse fish, and coffee to rear the kids on, those at least that didn't die (the others were forgotten), always provided that they restricted themselves to the customary one meal a day in the spring. If he approved of them, as the saying went, Bruni might even help them to buy some land, and then they would own the land, in name at least, and would be styled freeholders on the tax bills and church accounts; and when they were dead there they were in the parochial register for the consideration of genealogists.

These men were not servile in temper, nor did they consider themselves part of the common herd. They stood on their own feet; independence was their great capital. They believed in private enterprise and if they had had a drink of brandy would even quote from the sagas and the rhymes. They were men toughened by the grim, unremitting battle for existence, men whom no physical strain, not even that of starving with their families towards the end of winter, could daunt. Yet they were by no means spiritual paupers, gross materialists who looked upon their bellies as their god; they knew a lot of verse, some of it written in the ingenious traditional form that has middle and end rhymes as well as alliteration, and one or two of them could improvise a quatrain about his neighbour, about his poverty, about danger, or nature, or those hopes of tolerable days that are only fulfilled in heaven; or yes, even about love (dirty verse). Of these poets Bjartur was one. They had also an extensive fund of stories dealing with peculiar old men and women, usually idiots, and in addition tales of eccentric clergymen. Their own divine, though neither a fool nor a rogue, had a certain queerness about him for which they had recorded their gratitude in many pleasing tales of the worthy Reverend Gudmundur. This sense of obligation was greatly deepened by the fact that he had brought with him into the parish an admirable breed of sheep, which they had christened the Reverendgudmundur breed. And though the minister never wearied

of denouncing sheep and slandering that animal species, for it
was his opinion that they seduced the hearts of men from God,
yet with his rams he had been a source of greater help to the
peasants than any one man before or since; for these animals were
well-fleshed and firm, if perhaps a trifle undersized. The crofters
therefore held their minister in great respect and were inclined to
forgive him more than they did others.

In the opinion of the minister, however, it was not only the
sheep that troubled the right thinking of his flock, luring their
hearts from God and the Redemption that is to be found through
Him alone. Under the same imputation lay the famous poetess,
the Bailiff of Myri's wife, whom many felt it more appropriate to
call Madam. The story now turns to her.

This lady, the daughter of a boat-owner in Vik, had been educated in the National College of Domestic Science. She had married Bailiff Jon, she said, purely and simply because he was a
farmer and she loved the joys of the country life. Her acquaintance with these joys had begun at home with the reading of
foreign literature, especially Björnstjerne Björnson, and had been
continued in the college. When she was to be confined for the first
time, Ingolfur Arnarson, Iceland's first colonist, had appeared to
her in a dream and, after singing the praises of husbandry, had
asked her to give the child his name.

She had added a hundred hundreds of land to the estate as her
dowry and had stocked this land afterwards on obtaining her
inheritance. She loved the peasants more than anything else in
life, and never missed any opportunity of convincing them of the
value of the country idyll or of the delight implicit in living and
dying on a farm. A spiritual sunshine emanated from her throughout the district; she was founder and president of the Women's
Institute; she published articles and poems in the southern newspapers extolling the country idyll and the spiritual and physical
health to be gained from the possession of a farm. Domestic crafts,
she considered, were the only form of industry legitimate to Iceland, so she spent much time and much art on cross-weaving.
Therefore she was sent as delegate to the conference of the Fed-
eration of Women's Institutes in the capital, to discuss domestic
crafts and those moral qualities which are nurtured by rusticity
and which alone have the power to save our country from the
calamity that threatens her in these hard times. Such a woman
knew how to appreciate the beauty of the changing face of the
seasons and of the blue mountains, as she sat by her window at

Myri. Oh, yes; she knew also how to talk about this beauty at a meeting; she talked about it with as much feeling as a tourist on a summer picnic. Work out of doors in nature's bosom was, she maintained, a form of healthy physical exercise taken in the midst of the country's indescribable beauty. She envied the crofters too because they had so little to worry about. And their expenses were so very small. Whereas her husband had loaded himself with debt because of extensive new buildings, agricultural implements, and improvements to the land, to say nothing of the cost of the work-people's keep in these hard times, all the dalesman had to do to be perfectly happy was to rise an hour earlier in the morning and work an hour later at night. Rich people are never happy, she said, but poor people are happy practically without exception.

Whenever a poor man married and set up as a crofter in the dales, she, too, would marry in the spirit and kiss his footsteps. She therefore lent a large tent for Bjartur's wedding, so that coffee could be drunk in shelter and a speech made.

The crofters were standing about on the paving in front of the door or leaning against the wall, making faces as they took snuff, or talking to the bridegroom. The conversation was the conversation of spring, the themes fixed and immutable, with the emphasis heavily laid on the various ailments of the sheep. For years and years the tapeworm had been a national curse, but with increasing progress in canine hygiene some ascendancy had at last been gained over this ill-omened guest. Of late years, however, a new worm with, if anything, even less patriotism than the old one had begun to make its presence felt in the sheep. This was the lung-worm, and though the tapeworm never lost its absorbing seasonal interest, the lung-worm showed with each fresh spring that it was rapidly ousting the former from pride of place as a subject of conversation.

"Well," said Thorir of Gilteig, "if you were to ask me my opinion I should say that there's nothing to fear as long as you manage to keep them clear of diarrhœa in the wintertime. Even if the maggots are coming out of their nostrils I don't see why you should worry as long as their bellies are clean. And as long as their bellies are clean, surely anyone would expect them to stand the early spring grass. However, I may be wrong in this as in so many other things."

"No," said the bridegroom, "you're quite right. Ragnar of Urtharsel who they say is lying on his death-bed, was of the same opinion, and he was a genius with diarrhœa, I can tell you.

But where it was lambs that were affected he was a great believer in chewing-tobacco. I remember he told me when I stayed with him a year or two ago that there were some winters when he gave his lambs as much as four ounces of the best; and he said he would sooner stint his family of their coffee, not to mention sugar, than see his lambs go short of their chaw."

"Well, no one ever praised me for my husbandry," observed Einar of Undirhlith, the psalmist and commemorative poet of the district, "and I can't say I mind at all, because I've noticed that those who worry most about making both ends meet prosper least in this world; fortune somehow seems to make them her special sport. But if I was to give you my opinion, according to my own understanding, I should say that if the fodder does little to keep the lambs free of maggots, chaw will do even less. Chaw might well be of some help when things are desperate, but when all is said and done, chaw is chaw and fodder fodder."

"True enough, every word of it," cried Olafur of Yztadale, swift of speech and rather shrill of voice. "Fodder is always fodder. But there's fodder and fodder, as I thought anybody could see for himself, considering the number of times the zoologists have said so in the papers. And one thing is quite certain: it's in some of the fodder that the damned bacteria that produce the maggots are hidden. Bacteria are always bacteria surely, and no maggot was ever produced without bacteria. I thought everybody could see that for himself. And where are the bacteria originally, may I ask, if they aren't in the fodder?"

"I don't know, I don't argue about anything these days," replied Thorir of Gilteig. "We try to see that the animals have decent fodder; and we try to see that the children have a good Christian upbringing. It's impossible to say where the worm begins — either in the animal kingdom or in human society."

Meanwhile the womenfolks, sitting inside, were holding a whispered discussion about Steinka of Gilteig, who was supposed to look after her father, Thorir. She had had a baby the week before, you see, and several of the women had been running to volunteer their services in the croft for the occasion, for all are eager to help when somebody has an illegitimate baby, or at least during the first week, while nobody knows who the father is. She had had a pretty bad time of it, poor girl, and the child wasn't any too well, it was still doubtful whether it would pull through. But little by little the women's conversation veered round to their own confinements and maladies, as well as to the ailments of the children: the country never seems to have its health nowadays, and yet there are no signs of any great epidemic like the smallpox and black death of the old days, only those everlasting complaints like toothache, rash, swollen joints, bruises, bad coughs, often with phlegm, continual shooting pains in the chest and soreness of the throat, not to mention that peculiar rumbling of the insides which comes from wind in the stomach; though perhaps no illness is more deadly to mind and body than the nerves.

The Bailiff's wife fled out of the house and swept along the paving to the men. But when she heard what the subject of conversation was, she bade them cease such chatter; in words that carried weight, for hers was a forceful presence, her broad face, spectacles, and imposing mien not unlike photographs of the Pope. She asked them to choose some topic more in harmony with the beauty of the spring day, and indicated the dear blue moors and the bright cloudless sky above them and the meadows, which soon would be fresh and green. "Here we have at least two poets of local repute," she said, "first the bridegroom himself, and then Einar of Undirhlith. And there is our Olafur of Yztadale, who loves scientific doctrines and is a member of the Patriots' Association. Surely some lovely lines have occurred to you out in nature's sweet bosom this spring?"

But these poets were never so reluctant to recite their compositions as in the presence of the Bailiff's wife, for in spite of the warmth of her protestations of regard for them, and the frankness with which she admitted her envy of their circumstances, the smile was so cold that they felt that nothing could bridge the ocean between them. They were both far removed from the Mistress of Myri in their way of thinking. This lady was an enthusiastic admirer of the world's great poets and could not praise sufficiently the beauty of our life on earth. She had great faith in the God who directs it, believing that He existed in all things and that man's role was to stand at His side and help Him through fair and foul; with any other life she was not concerned. Such a way of thinking was condemned by the minister as the most downright paganism. Einar of Undirhlith, on the other hand, despised the world and usually wrote about people only when they were dead. He sought comfort in the Christian religion, which he thought would be of advantage to the peasants more in the next life than in this. The minister, however, forbade the singing of his elegies at funerals, holding it unseemly that a simple crofter, unversed in theology, should compete with the nation's time-honoured psalmists. As for

Bjartur, he was a devotee of the old heroic spirit of the nation as it is revealed in the rhymes and other classics, and he admired only those people who trusted in their own might and main, people such as Bernotus Borneyarkappi, the Jomsvikings, and other ancient geniuses. From the classics, too, he took his verse-technique, refusing to admit that anything less complicated than ring-handed quatrains could possibly be good poetry.

At this moment the minister appeared on his horse. He fetched a deep groan as he dismounted, then stood there, a man of heroic proportions, blue in the face, grey-haired, crabbed and morose in his replies, and never of the same opinion as anyone else. It helped matters little on this occasion that the first person he set eyes on was the poetess.

"I see no reason for dragging me out here," he grumbled. "There are probably people here already who know more about preaching than I do."

"Maybe," said Bjartur with a grin, as he caught hold of the horses, " but we like it better when we've tied some sort of label to our love."

"Love! Huh!" snorted the minister as he hastened across the home-field in the direction of the house. The good man wanted his coffee before the ceremony began, because he was on an express journey; it was Saturday, and there was a child to christen before nightfall and a parish-of-ease north over Sandgilsheath to visit. "Not a word more than what stands in the ritual," he continued; "I think I've just about burnt my fingers often enough with these marriage sermons. People rush baldheaded into this improvidence without an atom of the disposition that Christian wedlock demands, and where does it all end? Of those that I have married, no less than twelve couples have ended up on the parish — and it is for such people that one has to deliver a speech!" And bending his head to avoid the lintel, he disappeared inside.

Shortly afterwards the bride, downcast and with oblique irresolution in one eye, was led out to the tent by the Bailiff's wife. The womenfolk followed, then came the men and the dogs, and the minister in a crumpled cassock, coffee just finished, brought up the rear. Rosa of Nithurkot was twenty-six when she married, chubby-faced, reserved, and with a slight cast in one eye; red-cheeked, well built, but not very tall. She looked down at the apron of her national costume all the way to the tent. Beside the inner tent-pole stood a little table, the altar; the minister halted behind it and began to thumb over the leaves of the prayer book. No one said anything, but the choir whispered among themselves for a few moments before a few rough discordant voices broke into the wedding hymn in various tunes and different tempos. The women wiped the tears from their eyes, the minister delved into an inside pocket and fished out his watch under the noses of the bridal couple. Then he married them from the prayer book. No hymn was sung after the ceremony, but the minister wished the couple happiness in accordance with official requirements and asked the bridegroom whether his hacks were ready; he had no more time to spare for weddings. Bjartur ran off gladly to look for the horses, while the womenfolk hemmed in the bride and proceeded to kiss her. It was then time to think of coffee.

Tables and benches were set in position and the guests pleased to take a seat. Since the minister had gone, the Bailiff's wife sat next to the bridal pair. Dishes were borne in piled with fat doughnuts and with Christmas cake full of expensive raisins, and the men continued snuffing and talking sheep. Soon the coffee arrived.

The party seemed for a while to be lacking in fire, but each faithfully and noisily swilled his four to eight cups of coffee, while here and there could be heard the crunching of raisin seeds.

"Pile into the fodder, lads," cried Bjartur, aglow with hospitality, "and don't be shy of the coffee!"

Finally everyone's desire for coffee had been sated. Outside, the curlew might be heard crying, for this was his honeymoon too.

Then the Mistress of Myri rose to her feet, the poetess, her face shining over the assembly magnanimous in its papal dignity. Fumbling in the pocket of her skirt, she produced a few sheets of paper closely written.

She said she felt she must say a few words on this solemn occasion which saw two hearts here knit together. It was, of course, not her duty, but that of others, to let their light shine on this young couple who were now going out into life to discharge their duty by the fatherland, the fairest duty it was possible to discharge by the fatherland; and by God. But it was as in the old parable: many are called but many fail, so under the circumstances she thought the best way out was that she should make a little speech, just like any other ordinary woman. She really couldn't help it, she must say something, for these two were in a manner of speaking her own children, they had served her household so faithfully, the bridegroom as long as eighteen years, and she could not bear to see them set out on life's hallowed journey without a few words

of encouragement and exhortation. She was sorry to say that it
was an inborn passion with her never to miss any opportunity of
praising the nobility of the farmer's life. She had been, it was
true, bred in a town, but Providence had willed that she should
become a farmer's wife, and she had certainly never regretted it,
for nature was God's loftiest creation and life lived in the bosom
of nature was the perfect life. In comparison with it, any other life
was so much froth and smoke.

"Townsfolk," she said, "have no conception of the peace that
Mother Nature bestows, and as long as that peace is unfound the
spirit must seek to quench its thirst with ephemeral novelties. And
what is more natural than that the townsman's feverish search for
pleasure should mould people of an unstable, hare-brained character, who think only of their personal appearance and their
clothes and find momentary comfort in foolish fashions and other
such worthless innovations? The countryman, on the other hand,
walks out to the verdant meadows, into an atmosphere clear and
pure, and as he breathes it into his lungs some unknown power
streams through his limbs, invigorating body and soul. The peace
that reigns in nature fills his mind with calm and cheer, the bright
green grass under his feet awakens a sense of beauty, almost of
reverence. In the fragrance that is borne so sweetly to his nostrils,
in the quietude that broods so blissfully around him, there is comfort and rest. The hillsides, the dingles, the waterfalls, and the
mountains are all friends of his childhood, and never to be forgotten. They are a grand and inspiring sight, some of our mountains. Few things can have had such a deep and lasting influence
on your hearts as their pure, dignified contours. They give us
shelter in their valleys and bid us give shelter, too, to those who
have neither our size nor our strength. Where," asked the poetess,
"is there bliss so bountiful as in these tranquil, flowery mountain
glades, where the flowers, those angels' eyes, if I may so express
myself, point to heaven and bid us kneel in reverence to the Almighty, to beauty, wisdom, and love?

"Yes, verily all these influences are great in their power and
far-reaching in their scope." Madam considered that it was of no
small value to live one's life subject to such forces.

"It was considered chivalrous in the Middle Ages to protect the
helpless," she continued. "Why should it not be so considered
still?" She would define as helpless all those who are weaker than
ourselves, who need shelter beneath our protecting wing. "And
when I say these words, there accompany them many and sin-

cere thanks to you, Bjartur, from our sheep in Utirauthsmyri. It was a great and lofty role that you played on the estate as shepherd. 'Love the shepherd as thine own blood,' says the old rhyme.

"The shepherd rises early and goes out into the cold to see to the dumb animals in their stalls. But he does not shrink," she said. "The frozen blast hardens him and steels his nerve. He feels a force within him which he knew not before. The heroic temper is roused in the struggle with the storm as the roots of his heart warm to the thought that his exertion is for the sake of the helpless. Such is the beauty of the countryman's life. It is the nation's greatest educational institution. And our rural culture is borne on the shoulders of our peasants. A wise prudence sits enthroned beside them in their seat of honour, a perpetual fount of blessing to the land and its people."

The poetess read her speech with conviction and ardour, to which was added the heat in the tent; the sweat left the broad forehead and coursed down the blooming cheeks in streams. Fishing out a handkerchief, she dried her face. Then she continued:

"I don't know whether you are acquainted with the religious beliefs of the Persians.

"This race believed that the god of light and the god of darkness waged eternal warfare, and that man's part was to assist the god of light in his struggle by the tilling of the fields and the improvement of the land. This is precisely what farmers do. They help God, if one may say so; work with God in the cultivation of plants, the tending of livestock, and the care of their fellow men. There exists no calling of greater nobility here on earth. Therefore I would direct these words to all husbandmen, but first and foremost to our bridegroom of today: You sons of the soil whose labour is unending and leisure scanty, know, I bid you, how exalted is your vocation. Agriculture is work in co-operation with the Creator Himself, and in you is He well pleased.

"And never forget that it is He who gives the fruits.

"And now," said Madam, "I should like to say a few words specially to Rosa, that well-bred, sober-minded girl from Nithurkot here whom we have all learned to love so much and to hold in such esteem during the two years that she has helped us in Utirauthsmyri—our bride of today, the future housewife of Summerhouses.

"It is no easy matter to be a housewife, no easy matter to know that one's lot is to perform the loftiest function that there is.

"I do not doubt that many a woman will think it an impossible task to make her home such that wherever one looks is one radiant smile; to invest everything indoors with such tranquillity and bliss that all hate and bitterness disappear, and everyone feels equal to the greatest of obstacles; to make everyone feel that he is free and pure and courageous, and to make him conscious of his affinity with God and Love. All this is certainly difficult and perplexing. But that is your part, housewife; the part that God Himself has given you to play. And you have the strength for it, though you may not know it yourself. You are capable of it, if only you do not lose faith in the love within you. Not only the woman whose good fortune it is to tread the sunnier paths of life and who has benefited from a good education, but also she who has had little schooling and who lives on the shadowy side of life in a small house with little to choose from; in her too it dwells, this power, for you are all of the same high birth: God's children all of you. The power of a woman whose home glows with the radiance of earthly bliss is such as to make the low-roofed cottage and the high-timbered mansion equal. Equally bright. Equally warm. This power is the true socialism.

"Remember, Rosa, that every day you quicken into motion waves that undulate on to the very confines of existence; you stir up waves that break upon the shores of eternity itself. And it is of much importance whether they are waves of brightness that are radiated, bearing light and fragrance far and wide, or whether they are waves of gloom, carrying misery and misfortune to loosen pent-up glaciers that will create an Ice Age of the national heart.

"Consider love in its perfect form, in its unconditional sacrifice, its affinity with all that is loftiest and most magnanimous in the soul of man. Consider the force it opposes to everything evil and impure. Consider the power of love, how the hovel is transformed into a palace, how chill winter becomes radiant summer, how poverty itself becomes a very bed of roses."

The bridal pair and the guests listened to this oration in silence perfect but for the chirping of summer birds outside, the hum of two blowflies buzzing round the top of the tent-pole and the snoring, obstructed breathing of nostrils occluded by snuff. Not before the poetess had sat down did anyone dare to blow his nose. A few of the womenfolk discussed the speech in admiring whispers. Then there was silence again. The guests sat staring vacantly at the spot opposite them, heavy with the heat and sluggish with much coffee, hypnotized by the canvas walls glaring in the sun and by the droning of the blowflies.

At last the silence was once more broken. It was Hrollaugur of Keldur, an old crofter with a big nose and a grey beard, who, turning to Bjartur, said, for no apparent reason:

"Any sign of the staggers with you folk at Myri this spring, Bjartur?"

This opportune inquiry roused the gathering from torpor and trance, restoring it once more to an interest in life. The menfolk conscientiously retailed every case of staggers that had occurred in the district during the spring, and gave vent to some less than courteous observations regarding tapeworms. All were agreed that the purging of the dogs had been disgracefully muddled during the past two years, a state of affairs for which some were inclined to blame the Fell King and parish clerk, a man who had managed to worm his way into the office of dog-doctor on the minister's recommendation.

"I for one have made up my mind that I'm going to clean my dog at my own expense this autumn," declared the bridegroom.

Opinion was unanimous that a healthy dog was one of the essentials of life, and that it was scandalous how careless people could be with cysts, and that even on good farms.

"If people knew how to look after a cyst properly," said Thorir of Gilteig, whom experience had given wisdom, "then there would be nothing to fear. But it's the same thing whether it's a cyst or a human being, thoughtlessness is the root of most misfortune, and if only people could see that when they're looking after a cyst the main thing is to know how to do it properly, then the dogs would be all right and there would be nothing to fear. A fellow has only himself to blame."

The theme was discussed from every angle possible, various people contributing their opinions. Einar of Undirhlith declared his lack of faith in human measures, in the first place because the world was headed for calamity and destruction, and, as our own times so amply showed, neither medicines nor doctors nor any science could deflect its course one inch; in the second place because dogs were always dogs, cysts cysts, and sheep sheep. Olafur of Yztadale refused to accept this, maintaining that tapeworm in dogs and the consequent staggers in sheep and hydatid disease in human beings only went to prove that the medicine for the dogs was not scientific from the beginning. "Because," said he, "anyone can see that if the medicine was scientific from the beginning the dogs would never get constipated."

4.   DRIFTING CLOUDS

On the following day the bride was brought home on Blesi. The foal, unaccustomed to the burden of a rider, was restive and apt to lash out with its hoofs, so Bjartur had to lead it all the way. In a sack slung over his shoulder he carried his wife's bedding, while two bags tied across the pommel contained a few wedding presents, among them a pan and a ladle that kept up a continual jangling, scaring the foal so that it shied incessantly and would have bolted had not Bjartur been hanging on to the reins like an anchor. Titla padded along in the rear, carelessly nosing this and that as dogs are wont to do in the fragrance of spring, but watchful enough, every time the foal shied, to rush madly at its hoofs and make it and its rider more frightened still. What with cursing the dog and the horse, the man had little breath for anything else, so there was no conversation on the way up the ridge.

When they reached Gunnvor's cairn, however, the bride, Rosa, wished to dismount. She wanted to add a stone to Gunnvor's tomb, because she thought it would keep ill luck away. Gunnvor demands a stone, she keeps account of all those who cross the ridge.

"Nonsense," said Bjartur, "there's nothing lucky about it at all. I will have no truck with superstition. She can lie where she is, the old bitch."

"Let me down to give her a stone, Bjartur."

"What the devil does she want with a stone? No stone from me or mine. We pay our dues to the living, which is more to the point than pandering to people that have fried in hell for centuries."

"Bjartur, let me down, please."

"Enough of your popery."

"Bjartur, I want to give her a stone."

"If I remember correctly I paid the minister his fee on the spot yesterday, and that even though he did us out of the sermon. I don't owe anyone a penny."

"Bjartur, if you don't let me down something is bound to happen."

"I thought it was enough to believe in old Reverend Gudmundur without believing in Old Nick into the bargain. I am a free man. And you are a free woman."

"Darling Bjartur," pleaded the woman with a sob in her throat, "I'm so afraid that something will happen to me if I don't give her a stone. It's an old belief."

"Let her rot, the old trollop. On with you, Blesi. Shut your trap, Titla."

Rosa held on to the foal's mane with both hands, like a child, and her lip quivered and her head hung, like a child's. She did not dare say anything more. They moved off again.

But when they came down to the level stretches of meadow land on the other side of the ridge, it was Bjartur that halted, for Summerhouses could be seen in the distance. Leaning against the foal's neck, he pointed out the new croft-house, how prosperous it looked standing there on the bright green of its low hill, with the mountain above it and the marshes in front; and the lake; and the river flowing smoothly through the marshes. The house was still brown, the newly cut slices of turf still bare of grass.

He had looked forward to showing her the croft from a distance, and it was on this very spot, actually, among the watercourses on the heath, that he had expected to hear her exclamations of delight. But there was somehow no sparkle in the listless eyes gazing down the valley; the shadows of the pain that his uncompromising behaviour at the cairn had caused her were still darkening her features. He thought she was discontented because the croft was not green yet — "but you can't expect the turf to sprout in five minutes," he said. "Just wait till next summer, and I'll bet there won't be much difference between the roof and the home-field." She said nothing.

"It's a fine house that," he said.

Then she asked:

"Why didn't you let me down at the cairn?"

"Surely you aren't sulking because you couldn't throw stones at that old ghoul, are you?"

But the woman went on staring with stubborn unresponsiveness at the horse's mane, and a shadow had suddenly fallen over the moorland valley, for it was one of those days of early summer which have living faces — white packs of cloud cross the heavens like thoughts, and the shadows sweep over the land and take away the sun from a whole valley, though the mountains stand all around still bathed in sunshine. And when his wife made no reply, Bjartur let go his hold of the foal's neck, took up the reins again, called the dog, unnecessary though it was, and with the wedding presents still jangling in the saddle-bags, led his bride off once more.

The path had begun to slope downhill along the brink of the ravine which the river cuts through the ridge, and a few drops of rain were beginning to fall from the cloud over the valley before the woman broke the silence by calling to her husband. "Bjartur," she said.

"What's the matter?" he asked, turning on his heel.

"Nothing," she replied. "Let me down here, will you? I'm going home."

He stared at his wife in open-mouthed amazement.

"Have you taken leave of your senses, Rosa?" he asked finally.

"I want to go home."

"Home where?"

"Home."

"I've never known you behave like this before, Rosa," said the man, and turning once more he led her off on his way. The tears started from her eyes; there are few things so comforting as to be able to weep. In this fashion they continued their journey down into the valley. The dog padded along quietly in the rear. And when they arrived at a point opposite the croft, Bjartur led the horse out of the path and homeward across the marshes. There were bogs and deep pools to be avoided. In one place the horse sank right up to the groin; as it floundered out on to firmer ground, the woman was thrown and lay there in water and mud. Bjartur lifted her to her feet, then wiped off the worst of the mud with his handkerchief. "You women are more to be pitied than ordinary mortals, I suppose," he said. This remark made her stop weeping, and she walked by his side the rest of the way. She sat down by the brook to wring out her skirts, while the crofter unsaddled Blesi and hobbled him. The shadows had fled from the valley, there was sunshine over the little home-field.

It was a house and a stable in one. All that was visible of the inner, wooden shell was the door and its frame, the door so small, the threshold so high that one had to stoop on entering. Down in the stable it was cold and dark, the air sour with the smell of earth, the toadstools flabby, but when the trapdoor was lifted a faint gleam shown down from the loft. There were mangers along the sides, and in the farther wall a gap just wide enough to allow access to a hay barn that Bjartur proposed building behind the house. A ladder with seven rungs led up to the living-room above; Bjartur climbed it first to show his wife that it was safe. She followed him up and looked round the room. She thought the window was small.

"Anyone would think you had been born in a palace," snorted Bjartur. "If it's sunshine you're after, there's plenty outside."

"I'm afraid it will be a change after the big windows in Rauthsmyri, all the same."

"I wonder if you'll miss anything or anybody else in Rauthsmyri," he said bitterly.

"What do you mean?" she demanded. "You ought to be ashamed of yourself, saying things like that."

It was a medium-sized room, and so low that Bjartur could just stand upright under the roof-tree. Two bedsteads, made from the same sort of wood as the roof and the floor, were fixed to the wall, while the table was nailed to the window-sill. There was a little range on the left of the trapdoor, and above it, set in the slope of the roof, another window with a pane not much bigger than the palm of a hand; a few stalks of grass growing outside the window were swaying in the wind. But the thickness of the turf walls outside was too great to admit much light, no sunbeam could enter unless the sun shone directly on the window.

The bed nearer the table was already provided with a mattress of dry turf, the marriage bed. At the foot of this bed were boxes of provisions, for Bjartur had got his supplies in—ryemeal and sugar, best quality from Bruni, and maybe a handful of wheaten flour for pancakes, if we feel that way, and who knows if there isn't a bag or two of raisins hiding about somewhere or other? Downstairs there was a fine sackful of refuse fish. Then Krusi of Gil had made them a wedding present of a load of dry sheep's dung for fuel, because of a young foal that Bjartur had rescued from drowning in a pit the year before last, but that would have to be used sparingly and mixed with ling and moss at first, and besides, there's plenty of peat, you know, lying only four spade depths down in the marshes east of the house here.

Rosa, her eyes red and elbows muddy, was sitting on the turf mattress on the bed, gazing at the large, irresolute hands in her lap.

"Well, doesn't it suit you?" asked Bjartur of Summerhouses.

"You don't think I expected anything better, do you?"

"Well, there's always one good thing about it: no one that lives here need slave all day long at housework," he said, "and I always thought you had sense enough to appreciate your independence. Independence is the most important thing of all in life. I say for my part that a man lives in vain until he is independent. People who aren't independent aren't people. A man who isn't his own master is as bad as a man without a dog."

"A dog?" she asked indifferently, and sniffed.

He gazed out of the window for a while, without accounting for the trend of his thought, staring in silence towards the mountain.

"This land will not betray its flocks," he said at length.

His wife wiped a drop from the end of her nose with the back of her hand.

"Where the sheep lives, there lives man," continued the bridegroom. "It's just as my father used to say: in a way sheep and men are one."

"I've had such bad dreams," said his wife.

Turning his head to throw her a scornful glance, he said:

"Why pay any heed to suchlike things? Dreams are caused by the blood streaming upwards; you have them when you are lying in a cramped position, or if there's a lump beneath you, that's all. This spring, for instance, when I was busy pulling the stones out of the ruins here, I dreamed that a woman came out of the mountain, a damned fine-looking woman, too, let me tell you."

"Yes," said his wife, "it would be a woman, wouldn't it?"

"Without actually believing in dreams," continued Bjartur, "I bet that means I'm to have some fine lambs for sale in my very first autumn."

"Everybody says that Gunnvor is fit to take the place here. It's only two years since a horse bolted here at midday."

"I don't want to hear anything more about any damned Gunnvor."

"She's driven many a one out of the moors here all the same."

"Some duffer or other who didn't know a rake from a spade," snorted Bjartur. "They can always find something to blame if they have to sell up."

"You seem to think that nothing evil exists."

"No, I don't say that," he replied. "There is danger on land and danger on the sea, but what of it? If you get into danger, either you perish or you escape. But to say that devils and fiends and all that sort of stuff exists is to say that your blood is out of order, that's all."

"Dogs see a lot, all the same," said his wife.

"A dog is a dog."

"Fancy that! I always thought you believed that dogs were all-knowing."

"No," he countered, "that's a thing I've never said. All I say is that a dog is the only animal that understands a man. But a dog is a dog and a man is a man for all that, as Einar of Undirhlith would say."

"Everybody with second sight says this place is haunted."

"I don't care a damn for people with second sight," he snorted. "Give me a man who has some control over his own senses. There they go seeing things and hearing the devil only knows what, like that half-wit of a tramp that everybody made so much fuss about in Fjord a year or two ago. There he was, supposed to be falling into trances, and gabbling off all sorts of drivel from the hereafter about Jesus Christ, Egill Skallagrimsson, and King Christian IX. Then he ended up in prison for forging the Sheriff's signature."

"I'm sure you don't believe in God even, Bjartur."

"I'm saying nothing about that," he replied, "but there's one thing I'll never deny: that the Reverend Gudmundur's is a grand breed of sheep, the best that's ever been known hereabouts."

"You don't mean to tell me you don't even say your prayers at night, Bjartur?"

"Oh, I don't know. If they rhyme I sometimes run through a prayer or two while I'm falling off to sleep, just to fill the time in," he said, "or used to when I had less to think about. But never the Lord's Prayer, because I don't call that poetry. And anyway, since I don't believe in the Devil, I see no point in praying, so we'll say nothing more about it. What do you say to a drop of coffee to freshen us up?"

"What awful talk, Gudbjartur!" said Rosa. "I'm sure it must frighten away the angels of God, the way you talk. You deny everything except what you want to believe; that's the sort of man you are."

"I have my five senses," he replied, "and don't see what need there is for more."

"I know of people who stand much higher in society than you do, and who nevertheless believe in both good and evil."

"Maybe," said Bjartur, "and I think I can guess what they're like. I shouldn't be surprised if one of them wasn't the chap who was hanging around you women at Myri this spring, that fellow who used to frighten you into his arms with ghost stories."

"Us who?" she demanded, looking up, and for the first time a gleam showed in the eye with a cast. "What do you think you mean?"

But he was busy humming an old verse and looking for the kettle to fetch water, for he was determined to have his coffee. On the ladder he turned and left behind him this observation:

"Oh, maybe somebody got as near to somebody as he wanted to. I shouldn't be at all surprised, shouldn't be surprised a bit."

5.   SECRETS

THIS parting observation seemed on superficial consideration neither particularly definite nor particularly significant, and yet few things exercised so profound an influence on the early domestic life of Summerhouses as the imputation it bore, or rather that fact which immediately the first evening proved to be the foundation for it.

"No," she said, "it's a lie."

She turned her face defiantly to the wall, miserable, disappointed.

"Who was it?" he demanded.

"It's a lie," she cried again.

"If I were you I should tell."

"You don't tell me about yours."

"No?" he said. "I've no need to conceal anything."

"I don't want to hear about them!"

"You're all modest enough and shy enough on your wedding day, but for all your blushes no one knows where you may have bedded. You pass on to us men the lifeless corpse of love when the vultures have picked the eyes out of it."

"You're an angel, I suppose," she said.

"Was it that fellow at Tindstathir?"

"Ask him."

"Or that half-wit from the coast who did the ploughing?"

"Maybe."

"Surely you weren't mad enough to go with that whoremonger of a teacher who gave Steinka of Gilteig hers?"

"Why don't you count up all the whoremongers in the country?"

"And find you'd had them all? The cat that creeps is craftier than the one that leaps."

Then she rose in her wrath and cried passionately:

"God knows, and Jesus Christ, that if there's anything I regret it's not having had them all instead of marrying a man that worships dogs and sets more store on sheep than he does on the human soul. I only wish I had had sense enough to turn back today and go home to Father and Mother."

"Oh, I knew all right it wasn't the old ghoul you were afraid of," he said. "I can see a bit farther than the end of my nose, you know. And there's no need to question you; it doesn't take much to see through a woman. This is how you work it usually: you love those who are fine enough gentlemen to kick you out when they're sick of you, then you go off and marry someone you despise."

"You're a liar," cried the woman.

"So this was the reason you were always so sleepy in the day-time when he came back from the Agricultural College last spring. So this was your love of independence. This was your love of freedom. You thought of course that his pedigree was finer than mine because his father was too miserly to eat a decent meal when he was at the fishing, but eked out his dripping with tar and swindled his mates with watered brandy, and bought broken-down horses with his summer's wages when he was in the south, and then came home and put mustard under their tails so that they jumped about as if they had never been broken in. You can be a big man and hop into bed with the skivvies at night and sleep all day after it if you're lucky enough to have a father who's both a thief and a swindler."

"You're lying, lying," raged the woman.

"And it is for this swine that I have slaved for eighteen years — eighteen years of my life gone to pay for his blood-horses, his travels, and his schooling; and for this swine that you stood the Bailiff's sarcasms when he thought you didn't water the home-field proudly enough with the pots from under their beds. And now they even ask me to rear his bastards in my own house."

Here Bjartur of Summerhouses had worked himself up to such a pitch of fury that he leaped out of bed and dragged the clothes off his half-naked wife as if his intention was to flay her. Scrambling to her knees in terror, she flung her arms round his neck and swore by all that was holy that no man had ever known her, and least of all and least of all and least of all — "God Almighty help me if I lie," she cried, "I know there's a curse on this fold; the croft has been destroyed seven times by ghosts and devils, and what good will it be though you call it Summerhouses if you go and kill your wife on her bridal night and give Kolumkilli my bones." And thus she continued to plead for mercy in incoherent prayers watered with tears, until at last he took pity on her. For he knew that women are even more to be pitied than ordinary mortals. He took a pinch of snuff, lay down again, and went to sleep. Their wedding night, one summer night.

Of such a kind was their married life.

6.   DREAMS

BUT in the mornings, when he rose before the first birds, he never had the heart to wake her, she slept so naturally. He would look round at her as he was dressing and say to himself: "She is young, like a flower"; and he would forgive her for many things. Yet he always wondered that she, who lay there sleeping so innocently, should have loved other men, and should have been unwilling to confess, she who had always been so reserved and so unlikely to respond to any advances. He had often said: "There is a girl who keeps herself to herself, and the men at a distance; I will marry that girl and buy myself a farm." And now that he had married her and bought his farm, it turned out that she had loved other men, and no one had known anything about it. When she was asleep she was happy, but when she woke up he saw the disenchantment in her eyes, and therefore he let her sleep on. They spoke little and hardly dared look at each other; it was as if they had been married for twenty-five years, they did not know each other. He would go round the corner of the croft and cross himself to the east through force of habit, unthinkingly. And Titla would come leaping down from the wall, where she slept on the turf sill of the western window. Every morning she fawned upon him with protestations of friendship as fervid as if they were meeting after a fortnight's parting. She would trace great circles in the grass around him and, barking all the time, would race off to the outskirts of the home-field and sneeze and rub her muzzle in the grass. Then she would follow him out to the mowing.

Dawn was very near, the breeze fresh with morning, the lake clear as a mirror. There, on an islet, a pair of swans were nesting, and crested duck and golden-eyes swam there in little companies, but the mallards and the harlequins preferred the deeper pools of the river and built on its banks; sometimes the crofter could not help stopping for a moment to appraise the royal plumage of the drakes. A few redshanks would fly over from the east when they sighted him, bearing him their elaborate morning greeting. There were also some terns nesting by the lake; in their eyes life is a worm. Here and there on the grassy stretches round the lake bean-geese could be seen moving two and two, their long necks showing against the sky. Birds are happier than men, it is their wings that make all the difference; "grey-goose mother, lend me thy wings." The only plaintive cry was the loon's, a dismal song-bird. Bjartur of Summerhouses gripped the handle of the scythe and started mowing.

For the first few whettings he felt rather stiff, not so lively of a morning now as he had been ten or twelve years ago, when he had enjoyed adding night to day. In those days he had not needed sleep, he had not needed rest, but used to eat his morning curds standing in the meadow, leaning against the handle of his scythe. It was only five years since he had discovered what it meant to be tired, and now sometimes the day would begin with a flutter-ing of stinging pains throughout his limbs. But for all that he was a property-owner now, and registered as such with the State. In twelve years' time he would have paid the last penny off the holding, total thirty years. He was a king in his own kingdom, the birds his guests with their rich plumage and their various song. His wife was asleep in the croft and was his legally wedded spouse even though someone might have had her before and might have the first option on her still. As he worked he wove these thoughts into verse, but it was verse that he recited to no one. The dog would be racing about chasing birds over the marshes. Sometimes she might catch a rail or a snipe. She would eat it, then sit down in the field, biting herself and licking herself. Afterwards she might take a thoughtful turn, staring up the valley in an unwinking trance, then last of all she would trace herself a couch on a tussock and curl up. The sun rose in the heavens and the shadows short-ened, but about breakfast-time the sun was often obscured by clouds and a cold wind would blow down the valley; the most beautiful part of day was over. The mornings were never common-place, each morning was a new morning, but as day advanced, the birds would sing less and the Blue Mountains would gradually lose the beauty of their colours. The days were like grown-up people, the mornings always young.

He thought his wife might welcome him gladly now when he returned for his morning drink of coffee, and might perhaps like to hear a new poem about nature; but it seemed that she wasn't feeling well, or at least not well enough to enjoy a poem. In any case she didn't see much point in poetry. He had bought her a rose-figured dress, the very thing for wearing when the weather was dry, but she seemed always to prefer the old canvas apron she had worn for milking at Rauthsmyri, or a threadbare woollen skirt and an old patched coat. And she never felt well somehow; sometimes she was faint and had to sit down, very often she had to retire behind a hillock. In the mornings they had rye bread and coffee without milk. At one time she had been a good hand with the hay and a brisk worker, but now she often hung listlessly over her rake. "You're so grey and lifeless-looking somehow," he remarked. No answer. "That rake could do with a bit more life behind it," he complained. She made no reply, bit her lip. She would go drooping off home just before nine to boil the fish, but very often she could not get the fire to draw. She brought him his fish, rye bread, and coffee out to the meadow. "There's no need to be stingy with that muck," he said of the sugar, for he always spoke slightingly of sweet things. Afterwards he would go and sprawl on the river bank, resting, but never for longer than four minutes. Meanwhile his wife would be sitting in the meadow, rooting up moss with her fingers, preoccupied.

On Sundays he climbed the mountain slopes gathering ling, or walked up to the high moors and amused himself by spying out sheep and seeing if he could tell where they came from, for he knew the various breeds of many parishes. He also had a strange liking for rolling big stones over the edge of a precipice. His wife would be washing out their things in the brook, beside the lower waterfall. One Sunday he was away for a longer time than usual, and when he came home he was very pleased with himself and asked her could she guess what he had seen. It proved to be Mjoinhyrna; he had seen her south in Lindir with a marvellous lamb. "I dare bet anyone she won't be a pound under thirty in the autumn, that lamb of Mjoinhyrna's." But his wife showed no signs of gratification.

"That's a tough breed of the Reverend Gudmundur's," he remarked. "They aren't a rambling breed, there's no straying off into the blue with them. They know what they're looking for, then go no farther; they're intelligent sheep. If there's one thing I've made up my mind on, it's to rear a ram of the Reverend Gudmundur's breed."

"Dear me," said Rosa. "Fancy that, now."

She took no part in any happiness of his, and was indifferent to his ambitions. Whatever her thoughts, she kept them to herself.

"Bjartur," she said after a short silence, "I'd love some meat."

"Meat?" he asked, astonished. "Meat in the height of summer?"

"My mouth waters every time I look at a sheep."

"Waters?" he repeated, "Why, it must be water-brash."

"That salt catfish of yours isn't fit to offer to a dog."

"Are you sure you're feeling quite well, lass?"

"At Rauthsmyri we had meat regularly twice a week," she said.

"Horse-flesh. Never mention that damned muck of theirs again."

"Never a Sunday passed but we had mutton, even in summer," she said. "And anyway horse-flesh is excellent eating."

"They never killed anything for their folk but spent ewes and skinny old nags. Their meat was only fit for slaves."

"Where is your meat, then?"

"A free man can live on fish. Independence is better than meat," he replied.

"I dream of sausages every night. I think I'm cutting up tripe by the handful; they come reeking out of the pot with the suet dripping from them. Sometimes it's liver sausage, sometimes blood sausage. God in heaven help me."

"That means rain and storm," he interpreted. "Suet — that's for cloud with some sunshine. It looks as if we're going to have the same weather all through the dog-days."

"I dream of milk, too," she went on.

"Milk? Snow? In the height of summer?"

This seemed a most peculiar dream to Bjartur.

"Last night I dreamed I was back at Rauthsmyri. I thought I was separating in the dairy and from one pipe ran skimmed milk and from the other ran cream, just like when you work a separator. And I dreamed I put my mouth to the cream pipe."

"Why you should bother your head about such damned nonsense is more than I can grasp, it's meaningless to me," said Bjartur, and in despair gave her dreams up altogether.

"In the daytime too I'm always thinking about milk. When I'm busy in the meadows raking, I think about milk. And meat."

Bjartur sat frowning over the matter seriously for a while, then said at length:

"Listen, Rosa dear, I hope there's nothing wrong with your nerves."

"Can we possibly buy a cow, Bjartur?"

"A cow?" he repeated in gaping astonishment. "A cow?"

"Yes," persisted his wife stubbornly, "a cow."

"There goes the last shred of doubt, woman. It's your nerves. That's how my poor old mother's nerves began. It started with her always being full of some weird notion, then she began hearing voices. First of all we saw a herb woman about it, but when that was no good we had to see the doctor. If this continues you had better let me know so that I can go across to old Finsen's and get something with a bit of a kick in it for you."

"I don't want medicine. I want a cow."

"Where's your field, then? I thought you could see for yourself how little grass there is on this blasted hillock that the croft's built on. And the far meadows are even worse, as you ought to know from your own experience. Where are you going to get the hay for your cow?"

"There's sedge along by the river."

"Who is there to mow it? And who is there to lift it on to the bank? And what are we to ride it home on? Do you think we can afford to indulge in luxuries, crofters in our first year? You aren't in your right senses."

"I thought you were a free king," she said derisively.

"Haven't we plenty of decent fish, maybe? We are our own masters, we are finding our feet on our own land. We don't have to eat the filthy refuse offered to the farmhands at Rauthsmyri, we eat excellent dried catfish, and up to a while ago had foreign potatoes to it. There's plenty of rye bread, tons of sugar. And it isn't my fault if you've let the biscuits grow mouldy. You should have eaten the biscuits if you felt like a change, instead of letting them grow mouldy. Rye biscuits are always confectionery. What's more, lass, rye biscuits are Continental confectionery."

"I'm sure Father would lend us those three draught-horses of his to carry the sedge home."

"I won't take the begging road to anyone for anything, unless life depends on it and I can pay to the last penny," said Bjartur. "And now enough of this. It's vanity and nothing else for crofters on an isolated farm to talk about a cow; this is a sheep farm, we have to build up on sheep, I won't listen to any more nonsense."

"And what if I have a baby?"

"My child shall live on its mother's milk. I had boiled fish and tallow and cod-liver oil in my sucking-bag long before I was a year old, and throve well on it."

She stared at him with anguish-stricken eyes, and everything personal seemed suddenly to have been wiped out of her face. He was touched, and said in apologetic tones: "You can see it for yourself: the most pressing need must come first, and that is to get some of the land paid off. The majority of the lambs will

have to go to reduce accounts with the Bailiff, and it would be
madness to dive head over heels into debt and then have to cut
our sheep down, all for the sake of a cow. But in a year or so
we'll try to get a bit of a vegetable garden going for you, lass."
He clapped her on the shoulder as he would have clapped a horse.

7.   NERVES

BUT in spite of the potent medicines that Bjartur had offered to
procure her from Dr. Finsen's, what happened was that his wife's
nerves, instead of improving, grew steadily worse and worse. At
night she would give him his bread and cold fish, but would boil
some thick oatmeal porridge for herself, standing bent over the
range, stirring away with the ladle while the smoke from the half-
dried brushwood filled the whole room. Bjartur would pick the
bones out of the fish, then, after laying the two halves together
so that each thick part covered each thin part in compensation,
would bite into it as if it were a slice of bread, and all the while
continue eying his wife from beneath his brows. Twelve months
ago she had been a girl with a fresh complexion who used to change
into her best frock in the evenings and wash herself, a girl who
could laugh in her own way at whatever she considered amusing.
Suddenly this girl had become a middle-aged woman, a slattern
in an old sackcloth apron that she had worn for milking at Myri.
She had grown grey and flabby in the face, the light had gone from
her eyes, the colour from her cheeks, the grace from her carriage.
Thus quickly was this flower of his fading in spite of plenty of
fish, bread, and porridge, potatoes up to a week or two ago — and
rye biscuits, which were actually Continental confectionery. "It
looks to me as if she's grieving for some damned sweetheart," he
said to himself — she could hear if she liked. One thing was certain: she shrank away from him so much that she took good care
never to go to bed before he was asleep, and if her movements as
she climbed in woke him up, she would be quick to turn her back
upon him; and if he whispered in her ears, she would lie like a
corpse, and all desire would leave him. He wasn't so damned
frisky himself, either — always that tired, done-up feeling, somehow. He cursed it silently; the best years of his life, eighteen of
them, gone to the Bailiff and his crew, and now a fellow couldn't
get some enjoyment out of marriage when at last he had become
his own master. When he fell asleep he would see cows cropping

his grass. The cows were bad-tempered and made a rush at him, frightening him in dreams as much now as in childhood. He would start up with a jump and, still dazed, mutter: "Sooner a coffin than a cow." And in the mornings when he went outside and round the corner to relieve himself, he would cross himself to the east and mutter: "In the name of Father, Son, and Holy Ghost: sooner a coffin than a cow. For ever and ever, amen."

And there she was standing over her porridge, sticking more and more brushwood under the pan; it crackled and crackled, and steadily the smoke grew thicker and thicker.

"Careful with the firing, lass," he said. But she did not hear and added still more.

"Oh well, it's your own look-out, lass, as it's your job to pull it usually."

At last the porridge was ready and she took a basin and filled it, good God, right up to the brim; how much was the woman going to eat? Dipping her hand into the box she broke off a great lump of sugar-candy to eat with her porridge. He watched all this from under his brows, half scandalized that anyone should even think of such a thing, sugar-candy with porridge, the idea of it! Not that he grudged her it. Far from it; he was proud in his heart to know that his own wife was eating his own oatmeal, even if she did have sugar-candy with it — but when she returned to the pan and filled the basin a second time and broke off more sugar to eat with it, he began to feel a certain misgiving. Two basins full to the brim — one woman? More sugar? Yes, more sugar. He could make neither head nor tail of her nerves and their unfathomable vagaries. Yesterday it had been meat and milk, tonight two basinfuls of porridge and a hell of a lot of sugar, tomorrow it might just as likely be an elephant. He said not a word, but began to recite a few verses to himself, those with the complicated rhyme-scheme that he used whenever he was in a dilemma, murmuring them through with the main accent on the middle rhyme, spiritual soliloquy. After the porridge she took a few muddy stockings to wash in the brook and he went to bed alone.

When he woke up next morning she was not by his side. This had never happened before and he huddled into his clothes, downstairs and out.

"Rosa!" he bawled like an idiot from the paving. He went behind the croft also and shouted up at the mountain: "Rosa!"

But the melodious name raised not even an echo in the landscape. The sun had risen with its long shadows that made of the croft a palace. But it was dark away in the west. Summer was passing and the birds had sung all their sweetest songs; now their cry was short and hurried, as if they had discovered time.

"Titla," he shouted. No dog jumped down from the wall as she had always done. She too had played him false. For the man this was disaster. But he did not give up; he shook his clenched fist at the mountain in the intervals of shouting for the woman and the dog. "Pull me to pieces limb by limb, but I'll never give in, Rosa, Titla, limb by limb, limb by limb," he bawled.

At last he heard a yelping from the west, from the marshes. It was the dog. She came speeding along from the direction of the right, yelping without intermission, vee-vee-vee-vee. The man ran to meet her. "Where is she?" he asked. The dog was muddy and panting from the run, her tongue hanging out of her mouth, but she leaped up at him and thrust her open jaws into his face. Then she turned and raced off again, straight as an arrow, over pools and bogs, the man after her. Now and again she stopped and waited for him to catch up with her, but when he was a few yards away she would race off once more; wise brute. Clouds drifted over the sun, the air grew cool, rain almost certain. And on went this strange journey with a cur as leader and a man on the lead. Nor did it end before they reached the top of the ridge and the cairn of the long-buried woman, and the dog was right after all: Bjartur's wife too had lain down here to sleep. She was lying in the grass that grew up round the cairn, in her old sackcloth pinafore, a cloth tied round her head, her stockings round her ankles, mud up to the knees, like a tramp lost on the ridge at night in an old story, her bundle under her head. He woke her and she looked about her with troubled eyes, her teeth chattering in her head. He spoke to her, but she did not answer. She tried repeatedly to rise to her feet, but failed each time. Had some ghost carried her here in her sleep?

"What are you doing here, woman? Where were you going?"

"Go away."

"Were you walking in your sleep?" he asked.

"Leave me alone."

"You weren't drawn here, surely, were you?" he asked, for strange as it may seem of a person so sceptical, he was not altogether averse from ascribing some share at least in this occurrence to the work of spectres. He lifted her to her feet and pulled up her stockings. She was still shivering and still had difficulty

in speaking. He led her off down to the path; again and again
her legs gave way beneath her.

"Try and stand up, love," he said.

Then she said:

"I had such a craving for milk."

"Yes," he replied, "it's your illness."

So she had been going to Rauthsmyri for milk and had taken
the opportunity to pay her debt to Gunnvor. It was, after all,
no spectre that had lured her here, except the one spectre that
had wormed its way into her heart. But that the wife of the freeholder of Summerhouses should propose to beg from others was
a humiliation too deep for Bjartur to hear even mentioned.

"I wasn't going to beg for anything," she protested.

"What have you got in the bundle?"

But she thrust it apprehensively under her arm, gripping it
tightly, as if afraid he would take it from her.

"It's my own property," she said.

But when he pressed for further details, it came to light that
the package contained wool, her own wool, part of Kolla's fleece,
and Kolla was her own property, her sole contribution to the farm,
her sole possession after twenty-six years of a life of hard work
with long hours and little sleep. She had intended offering the
Mistress of Myri these tufts in exchange for a bottle of milk, but
by the time she reached the top of the ridge she had been exhausted, her legs had always been so very feeble; she had laid
a stone on Gunnvor's cairn and gone to sleep.

"We'll separate six or seven ewes from their lambs and keep
them back for milking next summer," promised Bjartur.

The woman, cold and faint, now began to feel desperately
sick. She retched violently, and Bjartur had to hold her up while
she vomited on the path. Then it started raining; the big drops
fell, first one, then two, and when she had been sick she was
utterly spent and the rain had become a steady downpour. The
man supported his wife down into the valley, then carried her
over the bogs and pools home to Summerhouses while this summer
continued with its showers.

"Doesn't it ever intend to clear up?" asked Bjartur.

The game was won if it cleared, but if it hung mainly fair with
a sea wind and sudden showers, there would be the same uncertainty, the same war; sometimes it spoiled the labour of days.
The vagaries of the sky were incalculable. It was their world

war, and in this world war of theirs Bjartur issued commands like a generalissimo, and the regiment obeyed, that little regiment, the smallest regiment in the records of any war, without meat or milk, without fresh food; and still they did not manage to gather the hay into ricks before it started in good earnest.

She was working near the lake on one of these wet days, raking together the new-mown hay between the marshy streams, and it was in one of these streams, which are full of weeds and slime and the grass that grows down below the edge, that she saw something moving, snaking its way upstream in many sinuous curves. She took the handle of her rake, thrust it beneath it, and swung it out of the stream. Over her head it flew, a big eel, three feet at least, and landed far behind her, sprawling among the hay like an earthworm of troll-like proportions and writhing there in eighteen coils. Her hunting instinct was aroused; it was a fish, and therefore restless on dry land. She had some misgivings certainly, for she knew that Bjartur would chide her if he learned of these doings, but she was determined to make good her catch and eat it, all of it, so she took out her knife and tried to grip the eel, and though it slipped repeatedly from her grasp, coiling even round her arm, she did at last manage to cut it in two. Then there were two fishes, and both these new fishes were just as elusive, endeavouring to make off in different directions, so that it took her all her time to herd them together. Taking off her kerchief, she wrapped them both inside, then placed them on top of a little mound, and there the kerchief kept on heaving until the evening, when she went home to make the supper, it had rolled down into a furrow.

"I'd look twice at my kindling before I'd use it for that filth, lass," said Bjartur, gazing nonplussed at this woman with the nerves busy skinning an eel. The eel writhed in the pot in many coils till it was boiled and ready. Rosa lifted it out and said:

"Would you like some fish for your supper?"

"Good God, no. Not that sort anyway. Do you think I'd eat a worm? It's a water-worm, that's what it is."

"All the more for me, then," she replied, and started eating, while her husband watched her, disgusted that she could eat such a thing, and she ate the whole eel.

"Ten to one it's an electric eel," he said. "It's as bad as eating a sea-monster."

"Really," said his wife, drinking up the gravy.

"I never thought a wife of mine would put filth like that to her mouth while there's plenty in the pantry."

"It's a lot less filthy than that mouldy catfish you've been making me eat all summer," retorted his wife, up in arms in defence of her eel.

But Bjartur did not care to begin any wrangling with a woman with the nerves at that time of night; he began instead to undo his clothes, clawing himself here and there the while and murmuring a verse or two from the Rhymes of Gongu-Hrolfur, of Grimur's oceanic origin, then lay down and went to sleep.

8.   DRY WEATHER

Just what it would do. The rain had cleared at last, but the drought was truly a mixed blessing. A raging land wind tore the dry-meadow hay from their hands and sent it flying anywhere and everywhere, some into the uncut grass, some — at least a third of the fruits of three weeks' strife — out into the lake. Three days they spent on the banks gathering it together and heaping it into ricks. Then the gale subsided once more, and once more claw-like streaks of cloud stretched across the sky, threatening rain; the glory was at an end. The hay must be trussed and carried home immediately before the weather broke again; this was no time to think of messing about indoors, cooking food, and pampering one's belly; this was no time to think of sleeping, even; now was the time to put their backs into it and outwit the elements, for this was Bjartur of Summerhouses' war of independence. As soon as they had finished the ricking, Bjartur attacked the binding in good earnest. It was late in the evening, the light fading, summer well on the wane. At the darkest hour he ran off to look for the foal to carry the hay home, leaving his wife to snatch a little sleep behind a rick. He found the foal at length among a stud of Rauths-myri horses, and before he had put on the pack-saddle and returned, it was growing light again. He woke his wife and they started trussing again where they had left off; ate cold fish and drank water from a bog. The streaks of cloud had stretched and widened over the whole sky, the downpour might start at any moment now, the hay would have to be got in immediately. Rosa was to lead the horse home and ride it back at top speed. She picked her way over the marshes leading the horse with its burden, and then, riding astride the saddle-peg, hurried back to the meadow for the next load. The rain was still holding off. With the approach of night the clouds even thinned here and there and a new moon peeped through. It was refreshing to see such a polished moon, its light so romantic, so fabulous after the unremitting toil of day that one could almost see the elves come out of their crags to gaze on it; elves are much happier than men. But with the passing of the hours the moon lost its power of stimulation, its seductive incitement to indulge in day-dreams; the sense of charmed peace retreated before hunger and fatigue. To and fro over the marshes she stumbled with the horse. There was no longer any feeling in her legs, she fell and fell again. When she rode the horse back on the return journey her head would drop forward on her breast and she would wake up to find the horse grazing.

"Dozing don't do much good when our livelihood's at stake," grumbled the crofter.

She could make no reply, for her tongue refused to move. She saw the moon gleaming on the water of a little ditch, and in the ditch swam three or four phalaropes, their heads rhythmically ducking in leisured grace. Dear little birds, so happy in the moonlight with nothing to do, how lovely they would look on a plate! Presently it began to grow brighter. The horse's steps grew slower and slower, its struggles more and more laborious; the moon disappeared, colourless behind darkening clouds, and the hay seemed somehow to have lost the scent it had had yesterday. She no longer knew whether she was wet or dry; it was as if the face of the world had been wiped out, both nose and eyes, and there was no feeling left but an ungovernable nausea, a bitter taste in her mouth and a stench in her nostrils. Time and again she had to halt and hang on to the foal while she retched and vomited bile. She wiped the cold sweat from her brow and tried to swallow the stinging bitterness in her throat. Such was this world war; yes; and gradually it was growing lighter, and the clouds were growing darker and darker, and once again she led the foal home. Bjartur was busy with the last rick now; soon the victory would be won, but she was not glad; no one that wins a victory in a world war is ever glad; she was utterly exhausted. Kneeling on the moss-grown bank of the brook that flowed past the croft, she leaned forward with cupped hand to drink, and felt, leaning forward, as if tender arms enfolded her and drew her gently to a bosom of rest; and in a moment she passed deeper and deeper into this embrace for ever and ever, like her grandmother, who died hap-

pily and left one mattress to her grand-daughter; deeper and
deeper, and she saw her reflection washed away in the flow of the
stream, and the earth floated off with her into space like the angel
that glides away with us when we die, and once more the good
autumnal scent of the earth filled her senses, and finally the earth
laid its cheek to hers like a mother, while the waters of the world
rippled on in her ears, telling of their love; then there was nothing
more.

9.   A DAY IN THE WOODS

THAT was on a Sunday.

It had been raining for some time before Bjartur found her,
still sleeping by the brook. She was lying there wet to the skin,
with her cheek on the bank and one arm under her. One truss of
hay lay crosswise in the stream, the pack-saddle, girths snapped,
lay broken to pieces on the gravel, and the horse was grazing in
the home-field. The woman looked about her with anguish-
stricken eyes, like one whom some buffoon has waked up from
death, and listened with aching spine to the sarcasms of her husband. Then, while he was busy covering the hay with turf as a
temporary protection from the rain, she dragged herself into the
house and, too dazed to heat up some coffee, went off to sleep
once more.

Shortly before noon it brightened up, and Bjartur hurried
panting into the croft to wake his wife and tell her to make some
coffee; a crowd of people were riding in over the meadows, and
some, at a canter ahead of the others, had reached the flats a
short distance from the croft. "They've no pack-horses; it's some
damned fools on a jaunt from up-country, or something," he said.
"They would choose a time like this."

"I can't let anyone see me like this," objected Rosa.

"They'll have to have their cup of coffee if they drop in on us,
woman," he said. "You're good enough for the like of them, aren't
you?"

He leaned over the table to watch them through the window
and recognized both the people and the horses as they drew
nearer. Some of them were the sons and daughters of well-to-do
farmers up-country, others were summer workers from Utirauthsmyri; then there were the minister's daughters and also
Ingolfur Arnarson Jonsson, the agriculturalist, riding his grey.

But when Bjartur looked round again his wife was nowhere to be seen.

The young men were trying out their saddle-horses, while the girls had come to pick the bilberries that were now ripe on the moors. They called this outing a day in the woods, and they had brought some food along with them in leather bags, intending to picnic in the "woods." Ingolfur Arnarson did not come as far as the croft, but sent to ask if Bjartur minded if he did some shooting over the marshes and tried a cast or two in the lake. And could the ladies take a walk along by the mountain and see if they could find any berries?

Bjartur was proud of his rights as a landowner and it always pleased him to be asked permission. He did, of course, hint that the girls knew best themselves what they were sniffing after, once they started sniffing at all, and he didn't mind if they picked a mouldy berry or two, but he would be surprised if it was only berries they were after, see. And if the Bailiff's son wanted to defile himself with pulling the guts out of the lousy fish in the lake there, and wanted to martyr on a Sunday the innocent birds that flew about the marshes without doing anyone any harm, well, it would probably keep him out of worse mischief. "But," he added, "I would have thought more of him if he'd ridden up to my door and looked me in the face, for it's not so long since I used to help him button up his breeches, and as far as I know I've always paid my way with his father, so I dare look any of his gang in the face, whether they dare look me in the face or not. But I wonder what the hell's become of Rosa. They're so particular about their appearance, these women — never come to the door dressed as they are, only the Sunday best is good enough. But come in all the same, she'll turn up sooner or later, I hope, and welcome to Summerhouses. There ought to be coffee by the pailful, and maybe a lousy lump of sugar lying about somewhere, if we can only find it."

The coffee, of course, was declined with thanks, but most of them wanted to take a look round inside, for, coming as they did from the better-class farms, they thought it quite an experience to crawl doubled-up through the door of Summerhouses and feel the earthy smell breathed in a heavy wave from the darkness as they entered. Some of them climbed the ladder, and it creaked; others contented themselves with peeping in through the window from horseback; you didn't have to stretch far, it wasn't much more than a man's height from the ground. Some of the girls persisted in their inquiries about Rosa, for they wanted her to go

berrying with them, so every nook and cranny was searched and
shouts and shrieks resounded inside the croft and out, while Rosa
tried to press herself closer to the earth wall under the horse's
manger, where, with a prayer to the Redeemer, she had sought
refuge. But Bjartur soon grew tired of this fooling and dragged
his wife from under the manger with a heavy hand, and asked
her where her manners were and what she had to be ashamed
of, a legally married woman. "And I want coffee for my guests,
if it's the last drop we have in the house. And what sort of her-
mit's behaviour is this, that you have to run off and hide from
your own kind? Go and welcome your guests, woman." He hauled
her up the ladder dressed as she was in a canvas skirt and a rag
of a shawl round her shoulders, turf-soiled and dusty, with toadstools entangled in the flock of her shawl. "Look, here she is!" And
they were all suddenly serious and held out their hands in greeting.

No, thanks, they did not feel like coffee, but the girls took
Rosa by the hand and led her out of the croft, led her down to
the brook and sat down beside her, and said it must be lovely
to have such a little brook so close to the house, such a friendly
little brook, too. They asked her how she was, and she said she
was all right; so they asked her why her face was swollen so, and
it was with toothache; then they asked her how she liked living
on the moors, and she sniffed and kept her eyes on the ground and
said she supposed there was plenty of freedom, anyway. They
asked if she had seen the ghost and she said there weren't any
ghosts. Then they all rode away.

The young people roamed about the countryside till the light
began to fail. At home in the croft their merry voices could be
heard from the mountain slopes — their peals of laughter and
their songs. But there were also heard shots from the marshes.
The crofter was resting today, had been working night and day
lately, and was lying on the bed asleep. His wife was sitting by
the window, listening for the shots, staring out over the marshes
and waiting in anguish for each fresh shot. It was as if she knew
that every shot he fired would hit her, and her alone; that it would
hit her in the heart, and in the heart only. But it so happened
that the crofter had not been very fast asleep, and as he woke
from his doze he looked at her from beneath his brows and saw
that with every shot she gave a violent start.

"I don't suppose you know those shots, do you?" he inquired.

"Me?" said his wife, jumping to her feet in confusion. "No."

"That blasted family could never look at a living thing without wanting to make a profit out of it, preferably by killing it," he said. Then he dozed off again.

In the twilight the holiday-makers returned to the croft, where they were going to wait for the sportsman, who intended to keep on shooting as long as there was light. The girls, returning from the mountain slopes with berry-cans filled to the brim, contributed each to a bowlful for Rosa. "Berries from your own mountain, girl," they said when she made as if to decline the offer of such a gift. They gathered into little groups and played various games out in the home-field beside Bjartur; the mountain echoed their laughter. The evening was calm, the surface of the lake unruffled, a few midges about, a new moon in the sky, the valley peaceful and free. Bjartur was in an uncertain temper, and gave it to be understood that haymaking didn't seem to have taken much out of anybody from up-country. "I think I can see you trampling on the Bailiff's manured grass like that," he grumbled, "and I'm looking forward to seeing your people dance like that next spring, when I come without a straw left to beg for a load of hay."

The minister's daughters and the girls who were working at Myri didn't want anyone to be in a sour temper and tried to coax him out of it. They drew him willy-nilly into the ring where they were playing tag, and then they tagged him, and he wished them to hell, but finally he started chasing them, and said he had chased skittish little ewes many a time, and spat on his hands before he tagged them back. They even took him aside and asked him to recite from the rhymes, and then he was in his element and did not stop before he had given them all the smutty ones from Gongu-Hrolfur: from old Olver's accusing Hrolfur of an unnatural passion for Vilhjalmur, when the girls fell on one another's bosoms and tried to stifle their giggles, to Ingibjorg pouring her pot over Mondull, when they could no longer restrain their shrieks of laughter. They ended by asking him to make up something about themselves. The crofter replied that a few lines, in various metres, had indeed occurred to him while they were busy picking bilberries up on the courting slopes, but that he hadn't really had time to polish them up yet, though the first quatrain had double rhyme and double alliteration.

> *Gala and Gunna rioting run*
> *Far from their Sunday's sermons;*
> *Nonchalant nuns in frivolous fun,*
> *Sprightly and sun-warmed wantons.*

Their fingers fleet the bushes strip,
Their merry mouths with care-free quip
From berries sweet the juices sip,
And laughing laud their truant trip.

Dainty dryads, nut-brown, neat,
Gathering berries is no treat,
So winsome wantons, comely, clamorous,
Admit you hope for joys more amorous.

The sport was at its height when the Bailiff's son, Ingolfur Arnarson Jonsson, appeared upon the scene. A cold smile played about his lips, the self-satisfied, overweening smile of his mother, the smile that made the literary efforts of the Mistress of Myri less appreciated than otherwise they might have been. His catch was slung over his shoulders on two strings, on one duck and goose, on the other trout, both brown trout and char, of from one to three pounds. After telling the shepherd to tie them across the pommel of his saddle, he greeted Bjartur with the cold smile and the irritating air of patronage that characterized the whole family.

"The old man must have been dreaming when he as good as gave you Winterhouses and made you lord of this land of plenty. What do I owe you in sports rent?"

"Oh, it would be going too far to expect you to pay a rent on this gift of yours," replied Bjartur. "Besides, as you yourself say, this croft, which, by the way, I permit myself to call Summerhouses, if you hadn't heard it before — Summerhouses is a land of such plenty that I need begrudge you none of the carrion that you carry off with you on your expeditions here, Ingi my lad. My sheep have more faith in the short hay from the Lambey banks there. So you're welcome to all the duck and the trout you can get, Ingi lad. They should make a welcome change of diet for you folk at Myri, because if you have fish and fowl on your table this winter, it will be for the first time that I ever heard of."

"My, what a temper the man's in!" said Ingolfur Arnarson with his cold smile, pulling off a few golden-eyes and one or two char and throwing them at Bjartur's feet.

"I'll ask you to clear this off my property," said Bjartur. "I would far rather that you yourself bore the responsibility for the creatures you murder on a Sunday."

But here the girls intervened and asked him for heaven's sake not to refuse such nice food, for Rosa's sake if not his own, and added: "These birds will make lovely eating."

"In my time," replied Bjartur, "it was the custom at Myri for Madam to throw away the hens so that she wouldn't have any horse-flesh left on her hands, but if fowl is on the menu there now, then the best thing you can do with this carrion is to cart it off with you to the Bailiff's, where it will be more at home."

"I'm sure they would make an enjoyable meal for Rosa. She doesn't look as if she's had too much fresh food this summer."

"For us lone workers," retorted Bjartur, "the main consideration is the fodder for the stock. Man's diet in summer is of less consequence than the welfare of the sheep in winter."

They laughed at this answer, amused rather than impressed by the chant of the lone worker. But many of them were members of the local branch of the Young Icelanders' Association, and Ingolfur Arnarson Jonsson was their chairman, and they had faith in their country; all for Iceland, "Iceland for the Icelanders," was their slogan, and now they were standing face to face with a man who had broken new soil, a man who also had faith in his country, and what was more, who showed it in his deeds. At close quarters his way of thinking might seem not without an element of the ludicrous, but he did not fail to move them as he stood on his own soil in the calm of the Sunday evening, with his little croft behind him, ready and eager to wage his war of independence with hostile powers, natural and supernatural, and undaunted, set the world at naught. They hung about for a little longer, while their herds were bringing in their horses, and no one took exception to Bjartur if he showed that he knew he was on his own ground. Ingolfur Arnarson called for a song. "Bjartur and I are old friends and the same as foster-brothers," he said. "Together we've done a few things in our time that are maybe best forgotten, and I know that really we understand each other. I at any rate know the stuff that Bjartur's made of, and Rosa as well. They have shown that the heroic spirit of the first settlers is not yet extinct in the Icelanders of today, and long may it reign!"

He called on the others to sing, and they sang:

> *Stern the strugge, but as brothers*
> *Shout the slogan, unaffrighted:*
> *"Live for Iceland! Work for Iceland!*
> *Stand we in the strife united!"*

"Hurrah for the pioneer in his moorland dale!" they cried. "Hurrah for this fearless son of Iceland! Hurrah for Bjartur of Summerhouses and his wife!" One patriotic song followed another, echoing from the mountain in the hush of the early autumn evening, till the loon ceased crying from the lake, greatly wondering. At last the lads had brought in all the horses; a hearty farewell was given Bjautur, and some of the girls went inside to say good-bye to Rosa, but she had disappeared. Ingolfur Arnarson bade the singers continue when everyone had got on horseback, and the last song, in praise of the country life, resounded from the marshes as a farewell to the people of Summerhouses.

For a little while longer the happy voices were still heard, then they mingled with the clopping of hoofs as the visitors quickened their pace over the firmer ground of the river bank, and finally faded from the ear; the twilight of early autumn had fallen over valley and heath. And the dalesman stood alone in his home-field. Presently he went inside to go to bed. Rosa had reappeared; she said not a word.

"There's a present for you lying by the brook," said Bjartur.

"For me?"

"Yes, both fish and fowl."

"From whom?" she inquired.

"Go down and see if you don't know his mark on them."

Sneaking out of the house while Bjartur was undressing, she went down to the brook, and, true enough, there lay the fish he had caught and the ducks he had shot. She felt that in the valley there still sounded the voices of those who had sung around him; the songs that had been sung still dwelled fresh in her mind, lingering in the air over the marshes.

A flock of golden-eyes flew low over the home-field with a whistling of wings, still in apprehension.

"You needn't be afraid any longer," whispered the young woman. "He is gone now."

For a long time she stood by the brook in the dusk, listening to the songs that were silent in the valley, to the shots that long since had been fired, and thinking of the harmless birds he had killed. Soon it would be autumn.

10. SHEPHERDS' MEET

THE DAY before the round-up Bjartur decided to shave off his summer beard. That he despised this formality was evident, and while the operation lasted he swore most cruelly, but there was no escaping it, the festival of the sheep was at hand. There was another task, too, equally disagreeable, awaiting him that day. It was, apparently, one of the symptoms of his wife's nerves that she was afraid to remain alone at home if Bjartur was away. There lay before him now three days' search of the mountain pastures, then, following immediately upon the distribution in the pens, the drive to town in company with the other farmers. Rosa had declared that she would not even hear of being left alone in the croft during this absence of her husband's. First she had asked him to leave her the dog behind, but when he had shown her that he would be as much use in a round-up without his right foot as without his dog, she refused to listen any longer to reason and said: "Very well, there's nothing else for it but to go over to Utirauthsmyri, rather than stay in this ghost-ridden hole." Now, nothing was more distasteful to Bjartur than the thought of having to ask any boon of the people of Utirauthsmyri, and the result was that he offered to try to search out a yearling ewe of his, one of a little flock that he had seen grazing in the neighbourhood a few days beforehand. So he set off with the dog when he had finished shaving, found the lamb, caught it with the dog's help, and returning with it towards evening, tethered it on the outskirts of the home-field. The lamb was called Gullbra. The woman slept badly that night, for the animal bleated impatiently in the home-field, unable to understand the whims of mankind.

The shepherds cantered into the home-field with their dogs long before it was light. Bjartur, who was standing on the paving with his stockings pulled over his trouser bottoms, shook hands, his shoulders wriggling with pleasure, and paraded up and down in front of them, or in a circle about them while he asked them all in for coffee. Most of them wanted to inspect the building; some of the lads clumped up the ladder into the billowing smoke to see Rosa, and the dogs tried to follow, but the ladder was too steep for them and they fell back yelping.

"This is my palace, then," said Bjartur, "not a penny behind so far."

"Many a one has begun with less and finished up as a farmer of substance," declared the Fell King approvingly. He himself had begun with little, but by now, with the offices of Fell King, parish clerk, and dog-doctor to his credit, he had attained a position of some note and was reputed to be not averse to a seat on the parish council, should the occasion ever arise.

"Jon from Husavik started off with a lump of peat from the devil," burst out one young man who was used to better surroundings, imprudently.

"Now then, you kids, out with you," said the Fell King, who wanted to get the lads off on their journey immediately, for they had been amusing themselves by riding on his heels over the ridge in an attempt to make his horse bolt with him, and later, when crossing the marshes, they had ridden just in front of him so that they could spatter him with mud. Nor was he of a mind to sit down to coffee in Summerhouses with just anyone; he preferred a few well-chosen men who would warm to a drop of brandy, especially some of the crofters, who, not having hired men, had to attend the round-up in person. One of these lone workers was Thorthur of Nithurkot, father-in-law to Bjartur of Summerhouses. This veteran had lost most of his children in rather unnoteworthy fashion and had met with disappointment in the only enterprise that he had ever hallowed with any serious thought, his corn-mill, but he had not grown jaundiced in outlook or abusive of fortune; no, he took everything as it came with a serenity of mind that approached the philosophic, a cheerful resignation that bordered on piety. Already on the stairway he was heard to express his admiration for the rare smell that his darling's smoke had, and she helped him up through the hatchway and hid her face against his grimy cheek and the straggling hairs of his beard.

"Mother sent her love to her little darling, and she asked me to give you these few scraps," he said, handing her a little parcel wrapped in a handkerchief. It contained sugar and coffee, half a pound of each.

She could not tear herself away from the old man. She clung to him and wiped her eyes on her apron, her manner suddenly so childlike in its intimacy and candour, so affectionate, that Bjartur felt that never in his life had he seen this woman before.

In a moment she seemed to have cast off all the stubborn gloom of the woman of the moors, to have changed into a little girl capable of showing her feelings. "Father, Father," she wept, "how I've looked forward to seeing you!"

This she said. Without Bjartur ever having realized it, she had cherished this hope in her heart, had waited long for her father. And when he saw her clinging to him so childishly free in her embrace, he was gripped as on his wedding night by the unhealthy suspicion that his kingdom on the moors was not as undivided as he himself would most wish it.

The men sat down, produced their snuff-horns, and proceeded to discuss the weather with the deep gravity, the scientific restraint, and the ponderous firmness of style with which this topic was always hallowed. A general review of the weather during the past winter was succeeded by a more minute analysis of the varying conditions of spring, with a comprehensive survey of the lambing season and the condition of the sheep and the wool, followed in turn by an examination, week by week, of the summer. One corrected another, so that there was no lack of accuracy; they remembered every dry wind of consequence, produced complete records of the atmospheric conditions during every period of rain and storm, and recalled what this one had prophesied, and what the other, but how in the end everything had taken its own course in spite of prophecies. Each of them had waged alone his world war against the ruthless elements; each had managed somehow to get his crop of hay, spoiled or unspoiled, home on his own horse. Several of them still had hay lying out in the meadows; one had had his blown away by the wind; another's crops had been flooded.

With the exception of the Fell King they were all lone workers and had not the means to hire capable help, but had often to manage with what little assistance they could get from their half-grown children, old people, imbeciles, or other encumbrances.

"For fifteen years I farmed without a hired man," said the Fell King, who had now risen into the ranks of the middle-class farmers, "and when I look back on them now, it often seems to me that those were my best years. When you start paying wages you can say good-bye to prosperity. Wages are what keep a man down for good and all."

"Your landed farmers can say what they like as far as I'm concerned," declared Einar of Undirhlith, "but it's a dog's life without some lusty lout or other to lend you a hand. And always will be. It's starvation, physical and spiritual. And always will be."

"Well, you shouldn't have much to complain about, Einar, as long as your son Steini sticks at home," observed Krusi of Gil.

"Oh, they all want their wages, sons and strangers alike," retorted Einar. "And it's a short-lived blessing in any case; the land can't hope to compete with the sea these days, and I expect Steini will take the same road as the others before he's much older. The mother's milk is hardly dry on their lips before they're off; the land is the land; the sea is the sea. Take Ragnar of Urtharsel, for instance, how did he fare? He had three sons, all as strong as horses; their beards had hardly begun sprouting before they were off to sea. One was drowned and the other two finished up in America. And did they drop their mother a line in spring, when their father died? No, not a word; not even a couple of dollars to keep her mind off her sorrow. And now the old woman and her daughter have made the croft over to the minister and are staying with him." Einar prophesied that the same sort of thing would happen to him, since two of his sons had already left him and the third was out of hand.

But Krusi of Gil considered that children were no trouble at all compared with old folk. No one would credit their appetite; his father had died a year ago at the age of eighty-five. "And now, as you all know," he added, "they knock me a dollar or two off the taxes and give me my mother-in-law to maintain. She's eighty-two, and so far gone, poor old body, that we've had to keep a continual eye on the tools all summer, because she's determined to hide them all." ("Aye, and a rare worker, too, in her day," mumbled Thorthur of Nithurkot.)

"Personally, I can't see what you chaps have to worry about," said Thorir of Gilteig, whose daughter Steinka, though unmarried, had made him a grandfather a few months before. "The sons can usually look after themselves, wherever they happen to land, and though the old folk hang on with one foot in the grave for a long, long time, the other usually follows in the end. But the girls, lads; the girls are a source of such worry and trouble to their parents that I envy no man who has a daughter in these hard times. Would you say, for instance, that woollen stockings, worked at home from the softest of yarn, were good enough for them nowadays? No, vanity and mischief is all they're after, and all they want from one year's end to another."

The Fell King: "Oh, I don't know. Many a man has had comfort of his daughters. It's always nice to have something with a smile and a song running about the house, surely."

"Running about, yes; and if you don't give them a purseful of money to throw about in town, they worry the life out of you to go into service, preferably in Reykjavik. And if they can't have either, they have their fling at home. They begin by demanding stockings made of pure cotton, which are nothing but a bloody swindle, and there they go flinging money away on that trash, which wouldn't keep a flea warm, though there's no lack of length in them, damn them, and they're not considered to be worth the money unless they reach right up to the crotch; but, if a stitch goes, where are they then? In my time a women was content if her stockings reached as far as her breeches, and she was considered a good wife for all that. There was less flightiness, too, among the women in those days, let me tell you, and maybe it wasn't the custom to lift the skirts as high as nowadays."

"Yes," agreed the Fell King, "that may well be so. And talking of skirts, I don't think anyone will deny that they seem to be a lot shorter these days than they used to be."

Thorir: "And where does it all end? I have it from a reliable source that cotton isn't considered good enough now. I hear that one girl has bought herself neither more nor less than silk stockings."

"Silk stockings???"

"Yes, silk stockings, neither more nor less than stockings of pure silk thread. I can even tell you her name: it's the minister's middle daughter, the one that was in the south last year." ("Oh somebody must have made that story up," muttered Thorthur of Nithurkot indulgently.)

"Our Steinka may have her faults, but she's no bigger liar than most folk, and she's ready to swear to it on oath that she's seen her with them on. First of all, the women stop wearing petticoats, out of nothing but vanity and corruption; then come cotton stockings right up to the crotch — they and the rest of their finery aren't long in equalling the price of a lamb — then they shorten their skirts, and when shamelessness reaches such a degree, it's naturally a small step to silk stockings, and in the end, I suppose, to no skirts at all." (Thorthur of Nithurkot: "I haven't managed a new pair of trousers for seven years.") "And what do they get out of all this? Consumption is nothing. But when decent principles and virtuous womanhood is lost to the nation, where does it stand then?

Many a poor old father's back is breaking with the burden of all this immorality."

Here somebody observed that the minister's three daughters looked healthy enough.

Thorir: "Of course. So would you if your father began the year with fifteen hundred crowns from the national purse for doing nothing, not a single solitary thing, but playing the blasted half-wit. Such people aren't the general public, you know."

(Thorthur of Nithurkot: "I hardly think it can be true that they pay him fifteen hundred crowns. Maybe they only promise it.")

Some of them doubted whether such a large sum of money existed in the lump.

Thorir: "It's the truth, and I refuse to take a word of it back."

"Oh, the old freak has his good points, you know," protested Bjartur then, for he never liked to hear anyone run down the minister, for whom he had at bottom an immense respect because of his breed of sheep. "His rams are right enough, educated though he is. Personally, I'd rather one of his rams any day than all three of his daughters and fifteen hundred crowns into the bargain. But, by the way, have you heard what the mutton's bringing in this autumn?"

The Fell King retailed all the reports that he had heard, but these, as is usual with information on prices, varied considerably. Hrollaugur of Keldur, a tenant of the Bailiff's, said that he would let Jon of Myri have his lambs as usual, as it was to him that he had to pay his rent in any case, and if there was one thing to be said for the old crook, it was that he let you have what was over in ready money, and though his prices were low, well, a bird in the hand is worth two in the bush, and down-country they never see a cent whatever they do, there's nothing but debt there.

Bjartur would not deny that it might be instructive to see coinage occasionally, but when it was a question of whom you had to be in debt to, well, Bruni was the lesser of the two evils — the fellow that usually saw the money in dealings with the Bailiff was the Bailiff himself. The Bailiff was a past master in the art of dealing with those whom Bruni did not care to give credit to; and he gave them only two thirds of what Bruni offered down in Fjord. But how much did he get for the sheep he'd bought when he'd driven them south to Vik? At least half as much again as what Bruni offered. He sold sheep by the hundred where others sold them by the half-score, and what was more, he dictated his own prices to the merchant in Vik.

("Oh, that can hardly be true," said Thorthur of Nithurkot, who could not believe in anything that was on a large scale. "And look at the risks. And it costs a lot of money to hire men to herd the sheep all that way south. And there are often quite a few lost on the way.")

The Fell King maintained, however, that lots of people had had reason to bless the day that Bruni took them on his books. Bruni never allowed a man of his to starve. Had anyone ever heard of Bruni refusing anyone credit, once he had accepted their assurances? "True, he doesn't care about paying out in hard cash in these critical times, and there's been many a year when not a cent has been seen up in the country districts, and as everybody well knows he's tight with the luxuries; but it's very seldom that he has allowed any of his men to suffer real want, unless, of course, it's unavoidable, as, for instance, in the springtime. In any case," continued the Fell King, "it's very far from the truth to think that everything depends on money. There's many a man got on in life and never handled the metal that matters. And by the way," he added as proof of this, "the Sheriff was asking me at the Thing in spring whether I couldn't suggest some dependable fellow to help with the doctoring of the dogs."

"Quite right," said Bjartur. "It never pays to neglect a dog, and as you've maybe heard, I swore on my wedding day in spring that I'd attend to my dog myself if that pissy concoction of yours doesn't clean them out."

"Surely no one would care to suggest that there is anything false or inaccurate about preparations I receive straight from the hands of the District Medical Officer himself," said the Fell King, assuming a look of injured officialdom. "I admit, of course, that no one with all that swarm of dogs to attend to would be prepared to swear on his hopes of salvation that the medicine had been perfectly administered in every single case, which is the reason why the Sheriff is of the opinion that another reliable person should be appointed as my assistant."

The crofters were all agreed that the situation called for desperate measures, since even in Utirauthsmyri there had been signs of the staggers during the previous spring.

"Yes, I shall have to give the matter serious thought," continued the Fell King in the tones of one fully alive to his responsibilities. "It is important work, though of course no more pleasant than any other medical work. And it takes an able man for the job. I should think that with a little persuasion I could get the Sheriff to agree to a pretty fair wage for this proposed assistant of mine. But at the moment I have no authority to promise anything."

"I say, what about the Bailiff?" said Bjartur, who found it difficult to root this Bailiff out of his mind. "I don't see why he shouldn't make quite a suitable assistant dog-doctor."

This suggestion, made partly in jest, partly in earnest, evoked no real response in either mood from Bjartur's guests; they merely sniffed or wrinkled their noses slightly in melancholy derision.

At this juncture Rosa brought the coffee, but as there were very few cups, they had to drink in two sittings.

"Drink up, lads," exhorted Bjartur. "You needn't be afraid of getting stomach-ache from the cream in Summerhouses' coffee, but we aren't niggardly with the beans."

"What about a shot of Danish cream?" said the Fell King, drawing a small flask from his breast pocket. As he took out the stopper, the formless, rigid faces of the lone workers about him broke into the most beatific of smiles.

"I always like to be able to do something for my friends when we're out on the mountains," went on the Fell King. "Who knows, my friends may be able to do something for me when we're all at home again?" — adding, as he poured a little into each cup: "Heavy taxes have kept the smallholder down these last few years, as you all know, but it may well happen that those who have little to come and go on will have someone to speak for them on the council before long. And there we'll let the matter rest."

"Wade into the doughnuts, lads," cried Bjartur, "and don't spare that lousy sugar. Pour the Fell King another cup, Rosa."

"Well, lads," said the Fell King when the brandy had gone the round, "surely someone has strung together a few lines over the hay this summer, unsettled though it was."

"Yes, now's the time for a nice crafty one," said the others.

"Well, you needn't expect it from me," said Einar. "My views on poetry, as you all know, are such that I don't bother with this crafty verse, as it's called. In the few things I set together when occasion allows, I try to pay more attention to the truth of the sense than to the elaboration of the metre."

It was no secret that Bjartur had a poor opinion of Einar's

poetry, for Bjartur had been brought up on the old measures of the eighteenth-century ballads and had always despised the writing of hymns and new-fangled lyrics as much as he despised any other form of empty-headed fantasy. "My father," said he, "was a great man for poetry and was gifted with the tongue; and I owe it to him that I learned the rules of metre when I was still a youngster and have kept them since in spite of all the new-fangled theories of the great poets, Madam of Myri, for instance. I inherited my copies of the rhymes from my father, seven of them belonging to the days when there were men of genius in Iceland, men who knew too well what they were about to trip over their feet; men who only needed four lines to the verse, and yet you could read it in forty-eight ways and always it made sense. Not for them this lyric style that's full of grief and nerves and soggy soulfulness; and no hymns either, they left those to the priests. They were men who didn't believe in tearing their hair and beating their breasts. Take Ulfar's Rhymes, for instance, with their mighty battles each more valiantly contested than the last; those were heroes who didn't crawl round licking a woman's feet, like these love-poets do nowadays. But mind you, if they heard tell of a famous woman they didn't stop to count the cost even if she lived in another hemisphere; no, they were off after her with the light of battle in their eyes, to conquer kings and kingdoms and heap the slain higher than the hills."

They wrangled on without coming to any agreement, the one swearing by the classical form and the heroic spirit of the old ballads, the other unshaken in his faith in the human and the divine. As a result of this difference in orientation neither could be persuaded to recite any of his verse as long as the other was present. "People who like to display complicated technique in their verse are more given to pride themselves on their work than are those who write for their own solace," said Einar. Bjartur retorted that he had never thought himself much of a poet, but to have to listen to anything less capable than internally rhymed quatrains was more than he could stomach, "and were I a poet," he said, "I should see that nothing of mine was ever made public unless it was a crafty verse reading the same backwards or forwards."

Olafur of Yztadale, who was of a scientific turn of mind and interested especially in the obscurities of science, was always out of his element when the discussion was confined to poetry. So far he had been unable to get a word in, but now he could no longer restrain himself from propounding some question, however small, that would ensure for him his share of the limelight in this day-break assembly, he whose inquiring mind was constantly busy wrestling with perplexing problems.

"Yes, the world's a funny place, right enough," he said, stealing into the conversation like a thief in the night. "They say that Easter falls on a Saturday next year."

The company sat for a while stricken to silence at this startling news.

"Saturday?" repeated the Fell King at length, thoughtfully. "That can't be right, Olafur, Easter always falls on a Sunday."

"Aye, that's what I'd always thought," cried Olafur triumphantly. "But I've read it twice in the *Patriots' Almanac*. And it says there that Easter falls on a Saturday."

"It must be a misprint," suggested the Fell King.

"A misprint in the *Almanac*? No, out of the question; they wouldn't dare. But I think I have the right explanation. I believe it was in an old book of the Reverend Gudmundur's that I read it, when I stayed the night there some years ago. It said that the sun occasionally slowed up for a certain period. If that's correct, then it's naturally impossible for time to do anything but go backwards in the meantime. At least a little bit."

"My dear Olafur," said Bjartur indulgently, "for goodness' sake don't let anyone think that you take all that sort of thing seriously. You should beware of believing things you see in books. I never regard books as the truth, and least of all the Bible, because there's no check on what they can write in them. They can spin lies as big as they like, and you never know, if you haven't been on the spot. If it was right, for instance, that time went backwards, even a little bit at a time, then it would end up with Easter falling on Christmas Day."

"Well," said the Fell King, "all I have to say is that the story tells you that Jesus rose again on the Sunday morning, and I'm sticking to that. Therefore Easter must always fall on the Sunday, whether time goes backward or not."

"The story can say what it likes for me," said Bjartur sceptically, "but what I'd like to know is this: Who saw Jesus rise on a Sunday? A bunch of women, I expect, and how much can you rely on women and their nerves? There was a woman from the south in service at Utirauthsmyri a year or two ago, for instance, who came in yelling that she had stumbled over an exposed baby on the landslides there, one late summer evening it was, and she swore it let out a wail. But what do you think it was? Nothing but a blessed wild cat in heat, of course."

"By the way," said the Fell King, who preferred not to encourage the intricacies of a discussion so irrelevant, "I was wondering, seeing that Bjartur mentioned wild cats there, what plans you had for our friend the fox this autumn."

"Plans are one thing," they replied, "and deeds another. What about seeing the Bailiff about it?"

"Oh, the Bailiff's hardly likely to be in any difficulties with the dodger," asserted Bjartur. "Last year he had twenty skins to sell in the south. And got a damned good price for them, too."

The others were of the opinion that the smallholders' sheep would suffer just the same, and cursed Reynard roundly for some time in a variety of tones — he had killed last autumn, he was sure to kill this autumn. The Fell King declared magisterially that foxes were undoubtedly among the nation's worst enemies. And the old man from Nithurkot ended this part of the conversation with the assertion: "He killed last year. He killed in spring. And he will kill again this autumn."

When all had finished their coffee, the Fell King replaced the stopper and pushed the flask back into his pocket; it was light enough to proceed.

"Well, men," he said as he stood up, "I've travelled over the moors here often enough, but never like this. What a difference! A difference that many a one on a rough winter's day will be glad of. We've been entertained like royalty. If you don't feel fit enough to foot it round your sheep now, you never will."

But Bjartur wanted it to appear that his hospitality was a very minor issue. "The chief point," he said, "and the point towards which I have always directed my course, is independence. And a man is always independent if the hut he lives in is his own. Whether he lives or dies is his concern, and his only. Otherwise, I maintain, one cannot be independent. This desire for freedom runs in a man's blood, as anybody who has been servant to another understands."

"Yes," agreed the Fell King, "I for one understand. The love of freedom and independence has always been a characteristic of the Icelandic people. Iceland was originally colonized by freeborn chieftains who would rather live and die in isolation than serve a foreign king. They were the same sort of men as Bjartur. Bjartur and men like him are the free-born Icelanders on whom Icelandic independence and Icelandic nationality have always rested, rest now, and always will rest. And Rosa thrives well, too, here in the valley; I've never seen her looking so plump before. How do you like the life on the moors, Rosa?"

"Oh, it's very free, of course," she replied, and sniffed.

"Yes," said the Fell King, who had now become like a landed farmer in outlook after his drop of brandy. "If the spirit that animates this young couple were to permeate the whole of the younger generation, men and women alike, the country would need to have no fear of the future either."

"Well," said old Thorthur of Nithurkot, "I think the best thing for me would be to crawl along the way a bit on that poor old nag of mine."

He stood there by the trapdoor so worn and decrepit after his long life and few ideas that it was difficult not to say something to him too. So the Fell King clapped a hand consolingly on his shoulder and said:

"Yes, my dear Thorthur, life for all of us is a sort of lottery."

"Eh?" said the old man vacantly, failing to understand the comparison, as he had only taken part in one lottery, and that was a few years ago when Madam of Myri had given a filly to be raffled for the Cemetery Fund. And the result of that lottery was that the Bailiff drew the filly himself.

"Father," said Rosa, when she had taken him out to his horse, "do try to cover yourself well in the hut tonight."

"Why I should be chasing over the mountains after wild sheep at my age," he said, laying the reins over his horse, "is more than I can understand; a man nearly eighty and hardly able to lift my old bones out of bed in the morning — "

The men parted their dogs, which were rolling about, fighting, on the slope in front of the house, and the ewe, still tethered on the outskirts of the enclosure, stood and bleated as it watched them. The old man embraced his daughter, then began painfully to mount his horse, while she steadied the stirrup for him; he had a black sheepskin over his saddle for comfort and protection. She stroked his horse's nose; old Glaesir, dear creature that she could remember as a little foal, and how glorious everything had been at home in those days, eighteen years ago, when all the brothers and sisters had been at home in Nithurkot, the brothers and sisters who were now scattered far and wide! And all at once there was Samur, his tongue hanging out of his mouth after the fray; but he knew her, forgot immediately the recent dispute, and jumped up at her, barking with such joy at the reunion that she could not help running inside to find a scrap of fish to give her father's dog.

"I would ask you to lend me Samur for company tonight, Father, if I didn't know that the sheep have to come first. I seem to have so little trust in that ewe he is going to leave with me."

At this moment Bjartur appeared on the scene, leading Blesi by the reins. He kissed his wife hastily and told her what had to be done in his absence, then swung himself into the saddle and called Titla. And the round-up men rode out of the home-field. She watched them crossing the marshes, her father behind the others, drooping in the saddle and swinging his legs to thump the horse's flanks; old Glaesir was so heavy in the mud.

11.　　SEPTEMBER NIGHT

SHORTLY afterwards it started raining, very innocently at first, but the sky was packed tight with cloud and gradually the drops grew bigger and heavier, until it was autumn's dismal rain that was falling — rain that seemed to fill the entire world with its leaden beat, rain suggestive in its dreariness of everlasting waterfalls between the planets, rain that thatched the heavens with drabness and brooded oppressively over the whole countryside, like a disease, strong in the power of its flat, unvarying monotony, its smothering heaviness, its cold, unrelenting cruelty. Smoothly, smoothly it fell, over the whole shire, over the fallen marsh grass, over the troubled lake, the iron-grey gravel flats, the sombre mountain above the croft, smudging out every prospect. And the heavy, hopeless, interminable beat wormed its way into every crevice in the house, lay like a pad of cotton wool over the ears, and embraced everything, both near and far, in its compass, like an unromantic story from life itself that has no rhythm and no crescendo, no climax, but which is nevertheless overwhelming in its scope, terrifying in its significance. And at the bottom of this unfathomed ocean of teeming rain sat the little house and its one neurotic woman.

She had taken up her mending, but too listless to begin, sat motionless by the window, hypnotized by the pattering hiss of the rain. She gazed in a mindless lethargy at the grey darkness outside, or stared with childish eyes at the pools that formed on the window-sill as the water seeped through. But as the day wore on a gale began to spring up, and the wind chased the rain in howling white squalls, beating them on as if they were so many flocks of sheep. These rain-flocks rushed spuming over the marshes, and taking on the form of waves about to break, they rose still farther, then either subsided or broke.

The ewe had stopped bleating in the home-field and was now standing as far from the peg as the tether allowed, with its head drooping and its horns in the weather. At first the woman pitied it in its misfortune, the only sheep on all the fells to be dragged off and held in captivity, so she decided to bring it into shelter. The sheep tried to run away when it saw her approaching, but the tether limited its flight. She took the rope in her hands, and following it up until she could catch hold of its horns, she gripped the animal between her legs, struggled home with it into the croft, let it loose in the dark stalls below, and closed the door. The sheep soon showed its dislike of the house; when it had shaken most of the rain out of its fleece, it began to range up and down the stalls and, finding that there was no way out, started bleating so loudly that the croft rang to the echo. The woman tried to show it some hospitality and took it down some water, but the sheep refused it; then she offered it hay, but it would not touch that either, and scurried away from her, panic-stricken, and stood at bay in a corner looking at her with suspicious eyes, green in the dark. It beat the floor with its forefoot as if in menace. Finally she offered it bread and fish, but when this too was refused, she gave up, and the animal continued its sharp, apprehensive bleat.

Dusk came and still it went on bleating. The woman heated up some porridge and ate it, and by this time it was dark, but she could not bring herself to let the fire die out, the air was so raw and there was water dripping from two of the rafters, and besides, there were no matches in the croft, and man's security lives in the light of a fire, and after that in the ember that must be kept aglow. She sat by the range for a good while with the door half-open so that she could see into the fire. Thinking to comfort herself with indulgence, she made some coffee from her mother's present. With it she ate sugar, also the gift of her mother, five lumps instead of one because it was her own sugar. Slowly she drank the coffee, cup after cup, staring steadfastly into the embers to keep off the fear of night that waited its chance to creep over her flesh and shiver down her spine. She set herself deliberately to think of pleasant things, and by calling up old memories managed at odd moments to feel almost comfortable. The sheep was silent at last, it had lain down. But the wind had grown wilder still; gradually the beat of the rain took on the rising note of a gale that pounded the window-panes and shook the croft in its eddies. It was so late now that the woman scarcely dared move from the range, so charged with evil did she feel the darkness round her. She sat with her feet drawn up under her and her arms folded tightly across her breast, with the eerie feeling that someone might reach for them if she stretched them out. For comfort she tried to keep her mind engrossed on her memories. She had been sitting like this for some time, and had even succeeded in forgetting her fears, when the sheep, tired of lying down, rose to its feet and with rested vigour gave vent to a louder bleat, shrill and cutting, from the darkness below. It was as if it had taken sudden fright; as if someone had suddenly kicked it to its feet; for a while, as if pursued, it dashed in fright from corner to corner; twice it stopped and beat the floor with its foot, blew into someone's face. Whose? Maybe no one's.

At last she stole forward to the trapdoor and called down: "Little lamb, don't be afraid."

But her heart jumped when she heard her voice in the emptiness of the dark croft. She did not know her own voice; she knew no voice that was so fantastic. And there she stood motionless by the trapdoor, and in an instant all her forebodings of the dark and inevitable calamity that waited in the night had become a frightful certainty. Down the length of her spine there struck a paralysing shudder, like a furious, excruciating pain: there was someone downstairs, someone who was attacking the sheep, seizing it evilly by the throat, someone who throttled its bleat and threw it against the wall — someone, something — till it gave vent to another bleat, more terror-stricken, more despairing than ever before.

No, she did not faint; she fumbled instinctively for more brushwood to add to the fire. The brushwood was her one hope, its blue crackling flame, its glowing embers; the fire in the range must not die out. "No, perhaps it was nothing," she said, sticking the twigs in with numb fingers.

Someone, something; perhaps nothing. She was determined to calm herself by gazing into the little glow, the fire of her own home, the fire that burns for the idea of independence, the idea of freedom. No one walked after death, Kolumkilli least of all; there was only the good God of freedom on the moors, the God who exalts man above the dog (perhaps). Who knew but that she herself might be Bailiff's wife, like the Mistress of Myri in twenty-three years' time? Life is a sort of lottery, as the Fell King had said to her father — poor old man, what if he should catch pneumonia in this lottery, lying out in a mountain hut tonight, and seventy years old. No, she would not think about it, she must not think of anything evil, only of the good and the beautiful.

"Meh-eh-eh."

Into the bleating of the ewe there had crept a note as of madness, a hoarse, almost expiring rattle. Rosa even began to wonder whether it could really be the sheep. It was a bleat no longer, it was an agonized wail. Was the evil presence throttling the life out of it? The plunging and scrambling continued with occasional pauses, something collided with the ladder and bumped into the door, the croft trembled in every timber, then there was a respite and silence except for the squalls beating on the window and the pounding of her heart — she was hoping that the turmoil was over, that the sheep would be quiet, but no sooner had the heaving of her breast subsided than a sudden blow buffeted the door, re-echoing throughout the house, and the attack had started again with a rushing and a trampling, a rumbling and a clatter as if everything was falling down. At first the woman thought the drumming and the rumbling came from the mountain, or that the front of the house had caved in; then there rang out a screaming bellow and she knew that the sheep was being strangled. Shaking with terror, she clung to the bedpost and called upon God and Jesus, repeating the names unwillingly like someone praying on his death-bed. At long last, and with infinite caution, she started to undo her outer garments, slipping them off and standing in her under-clothes, but these she did not dare to remove, for with every movement she risked calling up the furtive powers of the darkness. Inch by inch she slipped under the bedclothes and, drawing them above her head, felt some relief only when she had gathered them so closely to her that no air could get inside. She lay like this for a long time, still quivering and still with a pain in her heart; no memories could comfort her any longer, terror is stronger than the total sum of anyone's happiness. She tried to think with hope of the far-off dawn, for human beings always seek some source of consolation; it is this search for consolation, even when every retreat is obviously cut off, that proves that one is still alive.

Long, long she lay trembling in terror before she sank into a dazed confusion, a tense stupor that was neither sleep nor waking rest, but a difficult, reluctant journey through a world landless and without time, where she lived over again the most incredible events of the past and met people she had once known, in visions most unnatural in their clarity, most horrible in the minuteness of their detail. She heard anew the drawl in a long-forgotten voice, a voice that had never mattered, saw again the long-forgotten wrinkle in a face that had never concerned her. Every face that materialized before her distraught fancy sought like a canker to eat its way into her brain. She saw, for example, the faces of her visitors of the morning before with a detail that was almost nauseating. These visions, which terrified her in proportion to their clarity and their detail, sought stubbornly to burn themselves into her brain, so that they could never be effaced; they sat there in the sleepy greyness of the dawn with their rigid faces, like dead men we know in dreams — they come to us and pretend to be alive, and yet we know in the dream that they are dead because once upon a time we went to their funerals. Their melancholy grin was the grin of dead men. Their conversation, fantastically dreary, was the conversation of dead men; the faces they showed each other were masks, films half-frozen over the horror of the ruin that had engulfed them — no one in his right mind believed that they would ever be landed farmers. Bjartur had once reckoned up that he would be bailiff in twenty-three years' time, "but where will I be then?" wondered Rosa. Her father had dreamed of being a landed farmer too, perhaps bailiff. He had built a corn-mill over the brook, but where was he lying tonight? Tonight he lay in the desert, seventy years old, rheumatic and weak-chested, and the mill stood moss-grown in the brook. Where were the shank-bones and the jaw-bones, the playthings of the children of Nithurkot? In childhood her hopes had been imaginary flocks, dewlapped cows with heavy udders, frisky mares at stud with graceful stallions, all on her own mountain pastures; and she had dreamed, too, of being as clever and as poetical as the Bailiff's wife and of living in a famous mansion. Where was she living now? Where were her flocks, where her genius? She owned one sheep and could hardly write. As a child by her father's mill-cot she had been rich; in those days her hopes had been cows, her dreams the horses of poetry. The brook at home had had its own song. The mill-cot that had never been a mill had had its own soul, a soul such that nothing in life had compared with it since. She saw still the jaw-bones and the leg-bones lying on the bank beside the cot, saw the mussel-shell her father had found by the sea. She had been so fond of her mussel-shell, it had been a treasure beyond earthly price, not one of her brothers or sisters had been allowed to play with her mussel-shell — "what can have happened to my mussel-shell?"

"Ma — a — a — a."

The shrill cry startled her immediately from her coma. In her dozing ears it took on an incredible note: the sheep had been killed, but had risen now after three hours by the aid of the Devil. That hoarse, subterranean cry could not come from any animal born; it was the scream of the tortured souls spoken of in the Scriptures; all the devils and ghouls of the moor had congregated to bellow in this one sheep: the spectres of those who cannot rest in their graves, of children left under a rock in the boulder-wastes to die, peasants with throats cut for the marrow in their bones, popish people who hate God and Jesus, whose one desire is to drag everyone else down into their own eternal hell. In such a fashion did this night drag on.

At long last she summoned sufficient courage to peep from under the blankets, and lo, a faint gleam was lighting the room. To her inexpressible relief she discovered that night was almost over; however long, however grievous the night, dawn always comes in the end. The wind had dropped, but the rain continued, encompassing everything near and far in its heavy interminable beat. And the ewe was still bleating. Slowly the light in the room strengthened and slowly the woman's temper changed; the disordered exhaustion of night was gradually overcome by the courage of rising day. At last it was so light that she no longer felt any fear of the animal. She hated it. It was an enemy. Every fresh bleat was like oil that is poured on flames. Whatever it cost, she would stop its evil mouth — she waited only for more light, more courage, then nothing would stop her from attacking the animal and destroying it somehow, anyhow. At length she could resist no longer and sprang out of bed. She did not even bother to put on her clothes, but ranged the room with bare arms and half-naked breasts, her face pale and sleepless, eyes glittering, wild. She fumbled about under the roof-tree in the grey light of dawn and drew out Bjartur's scythe-blade, unwound its covering of sacking, looked at the edge and tested it on her hair. Then she went down the stairs. The sheep began racing from wall to wall in terror, and she gave chase, stumbling over hay-rakes and tangled ropes that had fallen in the turmoil of the night. But she was no longer afraid, no fanciful fears could prevent her carrying out her intention, and after some pursuit she succeeded in capturing the sheep. Then she uncoiled a rope's end and dragged the sheep out over the doorstep. The sheep resisted stubbornly, blowing through distended nostrils. She dragged it down the home-field to where the brook ran out into the marsh. There she threw it on its back with its head towards the stream. She wound the rope round its feet. It was now light enough to see what one was doing.

Very deliberately she set about the task. Like an experienced slaughterer she parted the wool about the sheep's throat, but now the creature had sensed its death and quivered convulsively under the woman's hand, gaping with open mouth and gaping nostrils, and writhing frantically in its bonds. But any sentimental qualm of compassion was far from the woman at this moment. Sitting down astride of the sheep, she gripped the leaping body between her legs until she had steadied it sufficiently to apply the blade to its throat. The scythe-blade was not much good as a slaughterer's knife, for although it was reasonably sharp, it was so unwieldy that great care was needed not to cut oneself. She had to take both hands to it and lose all control over the sheep's head in its death-throes. But she did not allow this difficulty to impede her and hacked and sawed away at the throat while hot jets of blood played on her hands and spurted into her face. Gradually, as the loss of blood affected it, the creature's struggles grew feebler, and finally it even ceased lifting its head and lay still with gurgling mouth. At last she found the vertebræ of the neck. Deeper and deeper she thrust the blade; a voluptuous spasm shook the animal where it lay gripped between her legs, and nothing moved now but the tail. The vertebræ gaped, showing the whiteness of the spinal cord. She cut straight across it, there was one slight tremor, and the sheep was dead. She severed the head and left the carcass to bleed into the stream; there was a little blood on the grass. The woman sat down by the stream, and after washing her hands and face, carefully wiped the scythe-blade with moss. A shiver struck through her and she was exhausted, almost comatose, and thought no more of what she had done, but reeled home to the croft and put on her clothes. She sat down on the bed. Her passion was spent, her impulse satisfied, and with the fulfilment a comfortable drowsiness flowed through her limbs in the drab light of the dawn. Letting herself sink back, she pulled the coverlet over her bare shoulders and was asleep.

It was bright day when she woke again. What had she been dreaming of? She passed a hand over her eyes and forehead to break the threads between sleeping and waking, to separate dream from reality. She had been dreaming of the Mistress of Myri, it seemed she had done something that would affect the whole parish, she had cut the Mistress of Myri's throat. But when she looked out of the window she remembered that it was only a sheep that she had killed, a sheep guilty of nothing more than having been at least as frightened as she herself in the loneliness of the night. Yet she felt no prick of conscience for what she had done. All she felt was surprise. She could not understand the woman who had risen that morning from her bed, sleepless, armed like Death with a scythe. She put on her clothes, pinned a shawl round her head and shoulders, and was the same woman as yesterday; but the sheep had stopped bleating. She realized immediately that everything depended on hiding from Bjartur the traces of this deed. She went down to the brook, to where the sheep lay headless on the bank, and kicked it with her toe, a butchered sheep. A butchered sheep? Every fibre in her body woke thrilling to the fact in anticipation, in greedy exultation — it was not only a sheep's carcass, it was meat. Fresh meat. Now at last she understood what she had done: she had killed a sheep for fresh meat. The summer-long dream, summer's loftiest and most hallowed dream, was at last to be fulfilled.

Her mouth filled with water, her body with blissful hunger, her soul with the rapturous prescience of satiety. All that she had to do was to prepare the sheep and put the pot on the fire. She found her clasp-knife and sharpened it on two whetstones, then she began to cut the sheep up. Though she had never taken an active part in the autumn slaughter, she had often watched and therefore knew the process in outline, so she took out the entrails to the best of her ability, scraped off the suet, taking care not to pierce the gall, then washed the stomach in the brook. When she had finished most of the work, she wasted no time in running home and putting the pan on. She stuffed the gullet with suet, made the pouch into sausage-skins, and put them all into the pan along with the heart and the kidneys. Soon the croft was filled with the fragrance of boiling offals. And while they were simmering she finished cutting up the sheep and hid the signs of slaughter so that not even the ravens would find anything. She tied the larger bowel to the door and scraped it, then chopped up the carcass with an old axe and salted it in a case.

Presently the meal was ready.

Perhaps there was never served on the high table of any manor house a meal as appetizing as that to which the woman of the

moors now sat down in her own croft. It is at least certain that
never since the days of Gudmundur the Rich and the old chieftains has any delicacy called forth such ineffably wholehearted
joy in the body and soul of the eater as that which was produced
in this woman by the fat-salty tang of sueted gullet, the luscious
meaty heart of the young animal, the tender, delicately fibred
flesh of the kidneys with their peculiar flavour, and the thick slices
of liver sausage dripping with fat from the pot. She drank the
gravy along with it, thick and wholesome. She ate and ate as if
she would never be sated. This was the first happy day of her
married life. Afterwards she made some coffee from her mother's
gift and ate much sugar. After the meal she lapsed again into a
comfortable drowsiness. She sat at first by the range with her
hands in her lap, her head nodding forward, but finding at length
that she could no longer hold herself up, she lay down and went
to sleep. And slept for hours.

12.   MEDICAL OPINION

BJARTUR brought his sheep home late on the fourth day and was
off again next morning in the company of a number of crofters
from up-country on the drive to town. The results of the round-up
had been satisfactory, and he was able to take with him a flock
of twenty lambs. Of these, twelve went in part payment of his debt
to the Bailiff for the land, while for the remainder the dealer
allowed him a sack of rye flour, some salted codfish, a few pounds
each of wheat, coffee, sugar, and oatmeal, and also a little snuff.
Besides these provisions he brought home the lambs' offals, and
after this had to make three more journeys to town for the horse's
fodder. He slept little, travelling night and day, preferring to make
three journeys to the prosperous farmer's one rather than incur
any debt for transport. When he came home, worn out with travel
by night, soaked to the skin in the downpour of autumn, muddy
up to the knees from the slippery paths, he could hardly help
admiring his wife's appearance, so fresh and healthy did she look;
she was like the turnip, which thrives best in autumn, and she
must have forgotten all about her ghosts, for she had freed the ewe
he had left her for company.

But Bjartur was aware that "the nerves" is a stubborn disease
that can flare up in a variety of forms, and he was also aware that
a stitch in time saves nine, so he did not forget her at the doctor's.

He took from his pocket a little phial of pills that he had obtained from Dr. Finsen and handed it to his wife.

"There's supposed to be some real strength in these," he said. "They haven't spared their science on these, I reckon, like they have on the medicine for the dogs. These pills are supposed to keep everything inside you in such good condition that you needn't be afraid of any disease. There's a sort of liquid in them that destroys all humours, they prevent griping pains in your insides, and they give your blood tremendous power."

His wife took his gift and weighed it in her hand.

"And what do you think I gave for them?" he asked.

That his wife did not know.

"What do you think old Finsen said when I was going to pay him? 'We won't bother about a trifle like this, my dear Bjartur; one isn't particular to a penny or two with the members of one's own party,' says the old fellow. 'Why,' said I, 'never have I been set so high before as to be counted among the members of the same party as the doctor, me a crofter in his first year,' says I. 'By the way, my dear Bjartur,' says he then, 'where did we stand at the last election?' 'Where did we stand?' I asked. 'Oughtn't the Althingi member to know best himself where he stood? And as for me, I stood then where I stand now, in that I consider it the height of vanity for farm labourers and smallholders to bother themselves about the government, when anyone with half an eye can see that the government is and always will be on the side of the great and not on the side of the small, and that the small will not make themselves a whit bigger by meddling with the affairs of the great.'

"'Now, you haven't got that quite right, my friend,' says he, talking to me just like man to man. 'The government,' he says, 'is first and foremost for the people; and if the people don't use their votes, and use them with judgment, it ends up with irresponsible folk being elected to the government; and that is something we must all bear in mind, all of us, those who haven't a great deal to come and go on included.' 'Yes,' I said, for I couldn't be bothered to argue with the old fellow, 'it must be grand to be as learned as you are, doctor, and that's why I've always maintained that we in this part of the country are so lucky, with a scientist like you to represent us in Parliament.' — Give him his due, he's learned right enough, the old cock, what with those fine doctor's hands of his, and all that gold on his spectacles. 'But it happens to be a custom of mine,' I said, 'to pay for everything

I buy, it being my opinion that freedom and independence is a question of not being in anyone's debt, and of being one's own master. And that's why I ask you, doctor, not to hesitate to name your price for the damned old pills of yours, because I know that they're good and wholesome pills if they come from you.'

"But it was all the same what I said to him, he wouldn't hear money mentioned. 'We'll just bear each other in mind in the autumn and appear at the right time and place to vote,' he says, 'because these are difficult times,' says he, 'these are terribly difficult times, and Parliament faces many serious problems, and men of judgment are needed to find a way out of all this, and to protect working people from intolerable burdens and fight for the independence of the country.' Then he stands up, a grand old man if ever there was one, and worthy of anyone's respect, and he claps me on the shoulder and says: 'Give your wife my kindest regards and tell her I'm sending her these pills to try. Tell her that they're some of the best pills made as far as humours are concerned, and that they're particularly good for strengthening the nerves.'"

13.   THE POETESS

FREQUENT visits were paid to Summerhouses that autumn, for the road to town from up-country lay through the valley. Daily, long processions of pack-horses plodded along the river banks, heading for the uplands on their way to Fjord, while the landed farmers who owned them rode there and back at their ease, leaving their farmhands in charge of the train. Sometimes these farmers, returning from town in a drunken condition, would wake up Bjartur and his wife in the middle of the night and, noisy and garrulous, would talk of poetry and wenching. They chanted lampoons in full-throated tones, sang patriotic songs, bawdy rhymes, and comic hymns, keeping up the merriment all night long till they spewed on the floor and went to sleep in the couple's own bed. Some of the farmers' wives would also leave the main road to pay a visit, threading their way carefully over the marshes on their gentle-paced amblers just to kiss their darling little Rosa of Summerhouses. One of these ladies was Madam Myri herself. She also was on her way to town, riding her horse Soti, and clad in a habit with a skirt that seemed wide enough to accommodate half the parish. She had an embroidered covering under her saddle, and a riding hat, and a veil; she lifted her veil half-way up her nose and kissed her little darling. Madam did Rosa the honor of drinking four cups of her coffee, and on being allowed to examine her provisions declared that the salt codfish would last till Christmas, and the rye meal till the New Year if economically used. She said that the settling of new land, a movement now popular in the country, was a charming movement. It was the spirit of the colonists. She said that on this movement depended the prosperity of the country in the future no less than it had done in the past. This movement was called private enterprise and it alone could overcome various unwholesome political tendencies, now unfortunately growing more popular in the coastal towns, which aimed at dragging man down to the level of the dogs, both physically and spiritually. She said she considered those who forsook the land for the towns as lost souls; nothing but corruption awaited them. "How can anyone of healthy mind think of forsaking the dear flowers or the blue mountains that lift the heart of man to heaven?" she asked. "They, on the other hand, that take themselves a holding are true ministers of God; they foster and further life itself, the good and the beautiful. On the farmer in his valley rests the increase and the advancement of the Icelandic nation in the past, the present, and the future."

"Yes," said Rosa, "it is good to be independent. Freedom comes before everything."

Such sentiments the poetess was pleased, very pleased, to hear expressed; that was the right way of thinking; neither the pomp of town life nor its show could compare with such a way of thinking. Here was a woman whose soul's gaze was calmly directed on the lofty peaks of idealism, whom the uncanny could not daunt, for well she knew that the stories of spectral visitations on the moors here were only uncouth folk-tales invented by uneducated, craven-hearted wretches who lived hundreds of years ago. She said that the daleswoman's coffee was really marvellous, but if there was anything she envied her more it was this little room where all her housework lay under her eye; what a difference it must be to trailing about these big houses, no one knew the sleepless nights that accompanied a big house. She had neither more nor less than twenty-three rooms in her own house, as Rosa could testify from the days when she was in service in the same, and she had over twenty people to look after, people of every age and temper, as is the way of the world, and every minute, said the poetess, had to be spent in running after other people, seeing to

untrustworthy servants, maintaining peaceful and harmonious relations, and trying to diffuse light and fragrance over the life of
her little community. "The true country idyll," she said, "is not
inherent in owning a large house, but in owning a little house,
small acres, a little home. And why? That, dear, is what I propose
to tell you. It is as the famous poet has it: 'Marriage bliss a haven
doth create, Protection meet from all the storms of fate.' Then the
darling children begin to come, not to lessen, but to add to the
joy. When might you be expecting yours, dear, if I might inquire?"

The unexpected question threw the woman of the moors into
sudden confusion. Her fugitive eyes looked everywhere but at
the poetess, and found no answer; and when the Bailiff's wife
made as if to touch her, she jumped to her feet as if she thought
that such a touch would be something akin to obscenity, and withdrew from reach to glare at her with wild, extravagant eyes, full
of a savagery entirely unwarranted by the sweetness of the late
conversation. It was difficult to say what lay behind this enigma;
was it fear, or hate, or only passionless perplexity, or all this at
once? One thing, however, was unmistakable in her stare, and it
was this: "Do not touch me." And there was also in those strange
eyes a look that spoke of pride rising in exultation against the
Bailiff's wife, a look that might have been interpreted thus: "Have
no fear, I shall never seek help from you."

Whatever the interpretation laid upon it by Ingolfur Arnarson's
mother, it certainly had a disturbing effect upon her. She let the
matter drop and was in difficulties about what to turn to next.
She was careful not to look the young woman in the eyes again.
Instead, she looked out of the window, but unfortunately there
was a haze over the Blue Mountains, so she could not point out
how the mountains lifted their summits towards heaven. She was
disconcerted to the point even of forgetting for the moment to
offer the crofter's wife her support in the present and the future.
The result was that she felt herself constrained to declare that
in life everything depended upon one's finding oneself. One
apothegm and she was once more on an even keel. For her there
was no doubt that husband and wife had found themselves on the
moors — "I have noticed that poor people are always happier than
these so-called rich people, of whom, actually, there are none in
existence. For what are rich people? They are people who have
much business, and own, if everything were reckoned up, nothing
but anxiety; who go to the grave as destitute as anyone else, except that they have had more worry about their means of liveli-

hood and less real happiness. I say for my part that every cent
we manage to scrape together goes in wages to the work-people.
For three years now and more I've been dreaming of a new costume, but I see not the slightest possibility of it yet."

"Dear, dear," said Rosa indifferently.

"There are many whom one would like to help," said Madam,
"but one needs must stay the hand more often than one would
wish in these critical times."

"We have plenty of everything here," said Rosa.

This reply the Bailiff's wife found pleasing, very pleasing; on
such a spirit rested the independence of the country. "I am not
sure, dear," she said confidentially, "whether you are aware that
there was for many years considerable opposition in the parish
council to my husband's selling your Bjartur this land. As you
may know, he had been angling after it year after year. But they
maintained on the parish council that Bjartur would never be
able to support a wife and family, and that probably they would
soon have a flock of children from a deserted croft on their hands,
for they've become so used in these days to whole families coming
for maintenance on to the parish. And the tax-paying ability of
the few who have anything is less than nothing; the taxes on us,
the so-called prosperous people, grow year after year more intolerable. Then towards the end of last winter they began to
whisper about you and Bjartur at home in Myri, and not long
afterwards a meeting of the council was held there, and it was
then that I took the bull by the horns and said: 'Have no fear
of Bjartur. If the daughter of dear old Thorthur of Nithurkot isn't
woman enough to find herself on the moors, and help Bjartur to
find himself too, then there's only one thing that I know for certain, which is that it's time for me in person to seek parish relief,
and that immediately and on the spot. For if there's a trustworthy
and industrious man in the whole of the parish, it's our good
Thorthur of Nithurkot, that worthy old soul who's always running
to be first to pay his taxes — I seem to see him before me now, as
he has been all these years when he comes looking for my husband,
with his money in his pocket. He lays his hat under the chair and
unfastens the safety-pins on his breast pocket and draws out his
purse, wrapped in two handkerchiefs, one red and the other white
— such people do not seek help of others. And Bjartur — I know
him as I know myself; he may not be a money-grubber, greedy
of gain, and no lickspittle, but he is most certainly a thoroughly

upright, trustworthy person, one who could never bear the thought of being in anyone's debt. Such people are not found on the parish. It is such people that are the core of national life.'"

Rosa made no reply. All this had happened some little time after the poetess had found this former servant-girl of hers in a part of the house where she had least expected to see her, and that at an hour that must occasion most comment; but all the same it was obvious to Rosa that the Bailiff's wife was somewhat disappointed at the indifference she showed towards the news of the part, the so important part, that she had played in persuading the council to allow Bjartur to buy the holding. Shortly afterwards the visitor stood up and, after kissing her darling for the coffee, drew the veil beneath her chin and got on Soti's back.

14.　FAREWELLS

AFTER the second round-up Bjartur killed an old ewe for the house and salted it in a keg. This meat, he decided, should be reserved as a change of diet for the celebration of Sundays and other red-letter days during the winter; but there were occasional Sundays when he was served with a surprisingly tender portion, and then he would be heard to remark how unusually tasty it was for a spent old ewe. Now when the year-old ewe Gullbra did not appear in the second round-up he began to feel rather worried about her, hazarding various conjectures, based on various hypotheses, as to her fate. He thought it most probable that she had taken fright because of her captivity and strayed off south towards the Blue Mountains, beyond the limits of any search. He often asked his wife what was the last she had seen of the ewe, but the only reply was that she had wandered away over the marshes out of sight.

Then came the third round-up, and Bjartur of Summerhouses had recovered all his sheep with the exception of this one ewe. He began to feel that there was something strange behind it all, and it weighed heavily on his mind. It was the old story of the lost sheep.

"That most excellent of creatures," he said, "that pearl among animals. Think of that dignified, spiral-horned, broad-backed stock, that firm-fleshed, wary, Reverendgudmundur breed, and the hard, suspicious gaze completely independent of man. Such sheep are like the daughters of kings on the mountains, so distinguished is their appearance. Yet theirs is not the pride or the wariness that leads them into stray paths, but the pride that makes them search for the best and find it."

And when he was undressing at night he would say: "Oh, I wish I could dream of my little Gullbra tonight."

"But you don't believe in dreams, Bjartur," remarked his wife.

"I believe in what I like," he retorted sharply, bridling up. "I believe in anything that has a sensible sort of a meaning in it; but I don't believe in dreams that betray you into nerves and hysterical nonsense" — he turned his back peevishly on his wife.

One morning when he woke, his wish had been fulfilled.

"I have the feeling that she still lives, and in the best of health," he said. "I thought I saw her in a nice little gully where the grass is still green. Damn it, if only I could recall where it was, for I felt sure in my dream that I knew it and that I'd been there before. But however hard I tried, somehow I couldn't get up the hill above to take my bearings, though I'm pretty certain it was somewhere near the hot springs south of the Blue Mountains. But I did know the sheep. It was my Gullbra and no other."

"Dear me," said his wife; and dished him up with his bread a rib, left over from Sunday's dinner, of the sheep he had been dreaming about.

Autumn was well advanced and sleet had taken the place of the early autumn rains. The hills were almost mantled with snow, the moors speckled, the home mountain white down to the middle of the landslides. The weather, however, was still fairly good. There was pasture near by and the lambs were still out; Bjartur's flock and the Rauthsmyri sheep fed together a mile or two away to the west. Some days the sun would shine and melt the snow on the home mountain, but the rime remained on the northern slopes of the gullies.

"It's clearing up nicely for my little Gullbra today," the crofter would observe.

Then it began to freeze in earnest. One morning the level stretches of the marshes were white with a thin film of ice; rime lay on the fallen grass. On the home brook, too, there had appeared little slivers of ice, and under them little bubbles restlessly played. Oh, how clear it was, their little home brook, as it bubbled on between the crystal wafers! She stood on the bank gazing at her cold little brook and listening to its flow; her child would grow up by this brook, as she by the brook at home.

"Now then, lass," said Bjartur, "wrap me up a bite to eat, enough for three days. I'm thinking of taking a little walk to myself over the moors to the south there."

It was a fortnight after Winter Day.

"Don't be such a fool," said Rosa. "I'm sure the sheep has fallen in somewhere or other."

"Fallen in?" repeated Bjartur, greatly offended. "My little Gullbra? The Reverendgudmundur breed? As if she were an underfed yearling! You must be out of your head, woman."

"Maybe she's taken the pest, then," said Rosa.

"No, she hasn't taken the pest. No more of your nonsense."

"But look what month it is, man. You never know what weather to expect now."

"Oh, it won't be the first time I've taken a stroll over the moors at this time of the year, or even later, and that for other people's sheep. No one felt sorry for me then, nor was there any reason why they should."

"You don't consider me, of course," complained his wife.

"Oh, the weather's always fine enough in bed."

"You ought to be ashamed of yourself, saying things like that."

"Now, it's no good you talking," he said uncompromisingly. "There is, as it says in the Bible, less joy in heaven over a hundred sheep that improve their lot than over one lost sheep that is found."

"But what if she's dead of the pest?"

"My conscience will be none the clearer for that," he replied, "unless I've done all I can to find out whether she's dead or alive first. But perhaps you'd like to see the conscience in me die of the pest?"

"But what if I'm taken ill while you're away?"

"Oh, you can hardly be taken so very ill. Not just yet, anyway."

"What if you're lost in a snowstorm?"

"Now that's enough," he said. "I'm sick of listening to this hysterical babble of yours. Whatever happens, you can always comfort yourself with the thought that the sheep are in the home pastures. Now then, stuff the dog with as much as she can hold. And wrap me a rag around a few black puddings and a pluck sausage. Some cold coffee in a bottle wouldn't be a bad idea either, and it can be as strong as it likes."

The woman sat thinking for a while, and though she had it in her power with one word to settle the issue, she was too proud to use this power of hers and instead employed threats, which were unlikely to make him stay at home.

"If you leave me here by myself, Bjartur, I'll go and stay with somebody else."

"Somebody else? Surely you would never lower yourself to that, an independent woman?"

"I'll go all the same."

"I don't doubt it, once you take one of your mulish turns. A sheep's stubbornness is as nothing compared with a woman's."

"You know the condition I'm in and that I'm expecting a child."

"I know only one thing: that my child isn't due till after the New Year. Other people's children are no concern of mine."

"I've felt it kicking for a long time, all the same."

"Maybe, but that doesn't concern me."

However much she argued, nothing could make Bjartur budge an inch. He put on two pairs of socks and both his woollen jerseys, and when his wife showed no signs of packing his food, he did it himself, while she sat by the range with her back turned on him. Yet it never occurred to her to confess that she had eaten the ewe. He hung about for a while, fiddling with this and that, as if waiting for her to come to her senses, and mumbled a line or two of poetry, but she did not come to her senses and sat without moving.

"Well," he said at length, "I can't afford to hang around like this much longer. It's getting on."

She sat with drooping head, still motionless.

Once more he tested the thong of his shoes, swore a little, pushed at the roof and the rafters with his knuckles, as if there might be some danger of the house collapsing, once more quoted a line or two.

"Well," he said, "this won't do."

No answer, no movement.

"Perhaps I'd better leave the bitch with you, then. I don't suppose there'll be much to herd in any case."

Silence.

"So I'll leave you the bitch, and you won't even think of going off and making yourself a burden on other people. Don't forget you're the wife of a landowner."

Continued silence.

"God Almighty, why in the name of hell do you have to behave like a lump of dead mutton?" he cried, losing all patience. "Just as if there wasn't time enough to keep your mouth shut in the grave."

In an uncertain temper he went down the stairs and called the dog, but she saw immediately that he was going somewhere and was greatly cheered by the prospect of accompanying him. When he called her inside, however, she began to feel suspicious and did not wish to obey, as nothing appealed to her less than to be shut up inside while her master was on a journey.

"Here, inside with you," he said. "You women had better stick together."

But as he advanced she kept on evading him with a variety of cringing antics; she let her tail droop half-way but still wagged it, looked round at him, laid her ears back, yelped. At length she sat down on the frozen grass and whimpered like a baby, then, surrendering entirely, lay on her belly with her muzzle along the ground, blinking her eyes as she watched him approach. When he was almost within reach she rolled over on her back and stretched up her paws, quivering. He took her under his arm, carried her home, and slung her by the skin of the neck up through the hatchway. She lay there on the floor, no longer showing any wilfulness, but quivering still.

"There you are, Rosa," he said, "there's your dog. You had better keep her shut up or she's sure to smell out my tracks. Good-bye, then, darling. And promise me not to disgrace me with the damned parish council by running off to other people."

He took his package of food and his stick, and he kissed his wife before leaving. "Good-bye," he said — "my rose."

When she felt the warmth of his farewell her heart melted so quickly that the tears started from her eyes before she had time to stand up and kiss him. "Good-bye," she whispered, raising her hand to her eyes and wiping them on her sleeve. Titla still lay by the trapdoor with outstretched paws.

He went down the stairs and they creaked, closed the trapdoor after him, closed the outer door. Half-running he set off over the marshes, white with rime, southward towards the moors.

15.   SEARCH

BJARTUR of Summerhouses knew better than most people all those nooks and crannies of the far mountain pastures where sheep are still to be found after the last of the round-ups. It was on the eastern slopes of this extensive moorland plateau that he had spent his childhood, on its western border that he had worked as a shepherd all the years of his youth, and in one of its valleys that he now lived as a freeholder, so he knew it from spring to the

end of winter, in fragrance and the song of birds, in frost and
silence, through innumerable journeys in search of the sheep that
bound him so closely to it. But the high heath had also a value
for this man other than the practical and the economic. It was his
spiritual mother, his church, his better world, as the ocean must
inevitably be to the seafarer. When he walked along over the
moors on the clear, frosty days of late autumn, when he ran his eyes
over the desert's pathless range and felt the cold clean breeze of
the mountains on his face, then he too would prove the substance
of patriotic song. He would feel himself exalted above the trivial,
commonplace existence of the settlements and live in that wonderful consciousness of freedom that can be likened to nothing
except perhaps the love of native land shown by sheep themselves,
for they would die on their own mountains were they not driven
back to the farmsteads by dogs. On such autumn journeys, when
he walked from watercourse to watercourse, from crest to crest
of the undulating tableland, as if his path lay through infinity
itself, there was nothing to trouble the proud eye of the poet.
Nothing nurtures the poet's gift so much as solitude on long mountain journeys. He could chew over the same words for hours on
end till he had succeeded in beating them into verse. Here there
was nothing to distract the mind from poetry. Today when he
once more greeted his old friend the moorland breeze, he allowed
no sentimental twinges about his parting from Rosa to delay him
longer from enjoying the true freedom of the wastes. Nothing is
so alluring in the autumn as to make off into the wilderness, away,
away, for then the Blue Mountains gleam with a greater fascina-
tion than at any other time. The winged summer visitors of the
moors have most of them flown, but the grouse has not yet left
for the farms and remains to skim the frozen peat in low flight,
gurgling much, blinking an inquisitive eye. Most of the ducks have
flown down to the seashore, or to the warmer lakes near the coast,
for the moorland tarns are frozen over and the rivers edged with
ice. Occasional ravens may be seen flapping round, croaking horribly, and this may often be an ominous sign that a sheep, dying
or dead, lies somewhere in the neighbourhood. On this occasion
there was still very little snow, but where the ground was bare
of turf it was covered with little flat cakes of ice. In one place a
fox darted behind a hummock, and an hour or two later he crossed
the spoor of a number of reindeer in the snow.

Bjartur that day explored two valleys, in one of which he
remembered sheltered slopes with ling on them, and in the other,

evergreen swamps round a spring which kept the same tempera-
ture all the year round. But in neither place was there living
creature to be seen, except a family of mallards in an open pool
in the river flowing through the more southerly of the two valleys,
just below the swamps. Evening was now falling and there was
scarcely light enough left to search for sheep, so Bjartur headed
for a place in the Blue Mountains where he knew of hospitable
night quarters, intending also to search the mountains on the
morrow, especially those to the south, where there are valleys in
which the ground is warm and sheep have been known to live
all through the winter without harm. Early in the evening the
moon peeped over the horizon and swept first the moorland bluffs,
then the valleys, with its blue light, making the dusty ice-flats
shine like gold. The silence of the moors was perfect. In this silence,
this light, this landscape, the man also was perfect in his harmony
with the soul within him.

Late in the evening he reached his lodging, a cave under
Strutfell formed of projecting rocks, and sitting down in the entrance, he ate facing the moon. When he had eaten he went into
the cave, where a great flat block of stone, lying on some large
pebbles, had served from time immemorial as a resting-place for
travellers. On this Bjartur lay down to sleep, using his bundle as
a pillow. He was practically the only traveller who paid a regular
yearly visit to the cave at this season, and as he had acquired the
art of sleeping on the block without ill effect in any weather, he
was very fond of the place. When he had slept for a good while,
he woke up shivering. This shiver was a characteristic of the lodging, but it was unnecessary to lose one's temper over it if one only
knew the trick of getting rid of it. This trick consisted in getting
up, gripping the block with both arms, and turning it round till
one was warm again. According to ancient custom it had to be
turned around eighteen times, thrice a night. It would have been
considered a most formidable task in any other lodging, for the
block weighed not less than a quarter of a ton, but Bjartur thought
nothing more natural than to revolve it fifty-four times a night,
for he enjoyed trying his strength on large stones. Each time that
he had given the block eighteen turns, he felt warm enough to lie
down again and go to sleep with his bundle under his head. But
when he woke up the fourth time, he was well rested, and, indeed,
dawn was in the sky. He set out at once up the mountain slopes
and looked in several gullies. When he had warmed himself with
walking, he sat down on a stone and ate some black pudding. After

threading a pass in the mountains, he came about midday into the district of Reykjadalir. In the valleys here there are many places where the soil is warm and steam rises from the sands, but there are no open hot springs here; farther down are great tracts of ground stained red with iron-water, and descending towards them from the mountain slopes, strips of grass and ling where stray sheep are often to be found. On this occasion, however, there was nothing to be seen except a bird that Bjartur did not know; it rose from one of the warm spots and flew off, probably a hot-spring bird.

He decided now to make his way eastwards in order to search some gullies running down into Glacier River, then spend the night in a shepherds' hut near the river and on the eastern boundary of the moors, a far cry. There was not much frost, but the sky was overcast, and as day wore on, it began to snow quite heavily. His way lay along the western bank of Glacier River, for on the other side began the far pastures of another county, and as this was a major river, flowing deep and swift all the way from its source in Glacier, sheep had seldom been known to cross from one bank to the other. But on many of the curves of the river flats had been formed, with a fair growth of ling on them, and sheep often hid themselves there until well on into the winter. The river thundered past, dark and heavy in the drizzling snow, with a roar that could be heard for miles around. The nights had long been creeping in, but today the period of light was shortened further the thicker the drizzle grew; the snow fell to the earth in heavy flakes and in a short while it lay so deep underfoot that the going rapidly worsened. In the snow the ice-free Glacier River seemed to stream through its wilderness in redoubled coldness.

Bjartur now realized that there would be little point in trying to find any animal in this light, the snow growing heavier and heavier, the face of the desert wearing a sullen look. He was beginning also to feel anxious about his lambs, which were still out in the open at home, and in danger if it came to a blizzard. But in the circumstances the idea of making his way home now right over the plateau was not very tempting, since night was almost upon him, the weather was rapidly deteriorating, and he was not altogether fresh after the day's tramp; so he decided to make the best of it and hold to his original intention of heading eastward along Glacier River towards the shepherds' hut, there to spend the night.

But it is one of the peculiarities of life that the most unlikely accident, rather than the best-laid plan, may on occasion determine the place of a man's lodging; and thus it fared for Bjartur of Summerhouses now. Just as he was about to cross one of the many gullies that cleave the sides of the valley all the way down to the river, he saw some animals leap lightly down a watercourse not far ahead of him and come to a halt well out on the river bank. He saw immediately that they were reindeer, one bull and three cows. They tripped about on the bank for a little while, the bull next the river and the cows seeking shelter in his lee, all with their antlers in the weather and their hindquarters facing the man, for the wind was blowing from across the river.

Halting in the gulley, Bjartur eyed the animals for some moments. They kept up a continual shifting about, but always so that they were turned away from him. They were fine beasts, probably just in their prime, so it was no wonder that it occurred to Bjartur that he was in luck's way tonight, for it would be no mean catch if he could trap only one of them even. The bull especially looked as if it would make an excellent carcass, judging by its size, and and he had not forgotten that reindeer venison is one of the tastiest dishes that ever graced a nobleman's table. Bjartur felt that even if he did not find the ewe, the trip would have proved well worth while if he managed now to capture a reindeer. But supposing that he caught the bull, how was he to kill it so that its blood did not run to waste? — for from reindeer blood may be made really first-class sandwich meat. The best plan, if he could only manage it, would be to take it back home alive, and with this intention in his mind he searched his pockets for those two articles which are most indispensable to a man on a journey, a knife and some string, and found both, a nice hank of string and his pocket-knife. He thought: "I'll make a rush at him now and get him down. Then I'll stick the point of my knife through his nose, thread the string through the hole, and make a lead of it. In that way I ought to be able to lead him most of the way over the moors, or at least till I come to some easily remembered spot where I can tether him and keep him till I go down to the farms and fetch men and materials." Summerhouses was, of course, easily a day's journey for a man travelling on foot. When Bjartur had completed his plan of attack he stole half-bent down the gully till he was opposite the reindeer, where they stood with their horns in the wind on the strip between the gully and the river. He stole cautiously over the runnels, crept silently up the bank, and, peeping over the edge, saw that he was no more than twelve feet from the buck. His

muscles began to taughten with the thrill of the hunt and he felt
a certain amount of palpitation. Inch by inch he pulled himself
higher over the brink, until he was standing on the bank; slowly,
very slowly he stole up to the bull, half a pace alongside — and
the next instant had leaped at him and gripped him by one of the
antlers, low down near the head. At the man's unexpected attack,
the animals gave a sudden bound, flung up their heads, and
pricked their ears, and the cows were off immediately, running
lightly down the river through the drizzling snow. At first the bull
had intended making off with Bjartur holding on to its head as
if he made no difference at all, but Bjartur hung on and the bull
could not get free, and though it tossed its head repeatedly, it
was none the freer for it. But Bjartur soon found that his hold
on the antler was uncertain, there being something on it like
smooth bark that kept on slipping in his grip, and the creature
too lively to allow a secure purchase anywhere else. He saw too,
when it came to the point, that he would have to abandon his hope
of getting under the animal's neck and gripping it with a wrestling
hold, for its horns were of the sharpest and the prospect of having
them plunged into his bowels not particularly attractive. For a
while they continued their tug of war, the reindeer gradually gain-
ing ground, till it had reached a tolerable speed and had dragged
Bjartur quite a distance down the river. Then involuntarily there
flashed across Bjartur's mind the trick he had been taught from
childhood to use with wild horses: try to get alongside them, then
jump on their backs. It succeeded. Next instant he was sitting
astride the reindeer's back holding on to its antlers — and said
later that though this animal species seemed light enough on its
feet, a bull reindeer was as rough a ride as he had ever come
across, and, indeed, it took him all his time to hang on. But the
jaunt was not to be a long one. For when the bull had hopped a
few lengths with this undesirable burden on his back without
managing to shake it off, he saw quickly that desperate measures
would have to be taken and, making a sudden leap at right angles
to his previous course, shot straight into Glacier River and was
immediately churning the water out of his depth.

Well, well. Bjartur had set out on a trip after sheep right
enough, but this was becoming something more in the nature of
a voyage. Here he was sitting neither more nor less than up to
the waist in Glacier River, and that on no ordinary steed, but on
the only steed that is considered suitable for the most renowned

of adventures. But was Bjartur really proud of this romantic progress? No, far from it. He had at the moment no leisure to study either the distinctive features of his exploit or the rarity of its occurrence, for he had as much as he could do to hold his balance on the reindeer's back. Desperately he hung on to its horns, his legs glued to its flanks, gasping for breath, a black mist before his eyes. The rush of the water swept the animal downstream for a while, and for a long time it seemed as if it intended making no effort to land. Across the river the banks, which rose high and steep out of the water, showed intermittently through the snow, but in spite of the nearness of land Bjartur felt himself as unhappily situated as a man out in mid-ocean in an oarless boat. Sometimes the cross-currents caught the bull, forcing it under, and then the water, so unbearably cold that it made his head reel, came up to the man's neck and he was not sure which would happen first, whether he would lose consciousness or the deer would take a dive that would be the end of him. In this fashion they were carried down Glacier River for some time.

16. BALLAD POETRY

AT long last it began to look as if the bull was thinking of landing. Bjartur suddenly realized that they had neared the eastern bank of the river and were now not more than a yard or two from the jagged fringe of ice that formed the only shore. They were carried downstream along by the ice for a while longer, but as the banks rose everywhere with equal steepness from the ice edge, the matter of effecting a landing remained a most unattractive project. Bjartur nevertheless felt that his best course, if the bull neared the land sufficiently, would be to seize the opportunity and throw himself overboard, then try to haul himself up on the ice, for this stay in cold water was becoming more than he could stand. He realized, of course, that it would be a death-jump that could only end in one of two ways. Finally there came a time when the bull swam for a few yards not more than half an arm's length from the ice, and the man watched his chance, let go of the antlers, heaved himself out of the water, and swung the upper part of his body on to the ice; and there Bjartur parted from the bull, never to set eyes on it again, and with a permanent dislike for the whole of that animal species.

There occurred moments, both then and later, when it struck Bjartur that the bull reindeer was no other than the devil Kolumkilli in person.

The ice was thin and broke immediately under the man's weight, so that he was near to being carried away with the fragments; but as his days were not yet numbered he managed somehow to hang on to the unbroken ice, and succeeded finally in wriggling his lower limbs also out of the water. He was shaking from head to foot with the cold, his teeth chattering, not a single dry stitch in all his clothes. But he did not feel particularly safe on this narrow fringe of ice and began now to tackle the ascent of the river bank. This in itself was a sufficiently hazardous undertaking, for the bank was not only precipitous, but also covered with icicles formed by the rising of the river, and there could only be one end to a fall if hand or foot should lose its grip. As he was fatigued after his exploit in the water, it took him longer to work his way up to the top than it would otherwise have done, but finally the moment arrived when he was standing safe and sound on the eastern bank of Glacier River — on the far pastures of another county. He took off his jacket and wrung it out, then rolled about in the snow to dry himself, and considered the snow warm in comparison with the glacier water. At intervals he stood up and swung his arms vigorously to rid himself of his shivering. It was, of course, not long before he realized to the full what a trick the bull had played on him by ferrying him over Glacier River. In the first place he had cheated him of the quarters he had proposed to use for the night, the shepherds' hut on the western side of the river. But that actually was only a trifle. Altogether more serious was to find himself suddenly switched to the eastern bank of Glacier River, for the river flowed north-east, whereas Bjartur's direction home lay a trifle west of north-west. To cross the river he would therefore be forced to make a detour in an opposite direction to Summerhouses, all the way down to the aerial ferry in the farming districts, and this was not less than a twenty hours' walk, even at a good speed, for the nearest farm in Glacierdale was at least fifteen hours away. Though he were to travel day and night this adventure of his would thus delay him almost forty-eight hours — and that in weather like this, and his lambs still out.

He was pretty well worn out, though loath to admit it to himself, and his wet clothes would be a poor protection if he decided to bury himself in the snow in this hardening frost. The snowflakes grew smaller and keener; no sooner had they fallen than the wind lifted them again and chased them along the ground in a spuming, knee-deep smother. His underclothes remained unaffected by the frost as long as he was on the move, but his outer clothes were frozen hard and his eyelashes and beard stiff with ice. In his knapsack there remained one whole blood pudding, frozen hard as a stone, and half of another; he had lost his stick. The night was as black as pitch, and the darkness seemed solid enough to be cut with a knife. The wind blew from the east, sweeping the blizzard straight into the man's face. Time and time again he tumbled from another and yet another brink into another and yet another hollow where the powdery snow took him up to the groin and flew about him like ash. One consolation only there was: happen what might, he could not lose his way, for on his left he had Glacier River with its heavy, sullen roar.

He swore repeatedly, ever the more violently the unsteadier his legs became, but to steel his senses he kept his mind fixed persistently on the world-famous battles of the rhymes. He recited the most powerful passages one after another over and over again, dwelling especially on the description of the devilish heroes, Grimur Ægir and Andri. It was Grimur he was fighting now, he thought; Grimur, that least attractive of all fiends, that foulmouthed demon in the form of a troll, who had been his antagonist all along; but now an end would be put to the deadly feud, for now the stage was set for the final struggle. In mental vision he pursued Grimur the length of his monstrous career, right from the moment when Groa the Sibyl found him on the foreshore, yellow and stuffed with treachery; and again and again he depicted the monster in the poet's words, bellowing, wading in the earth up to the thighs, filled with devilish hate and sorcery, fire spouting from his grinning mouth, by human strength more than invincible:

> *The monster lived on moor or fen;*
> *The sea was in his power.*
> *He'd shamelessly drink the blood of men,*
> *The steaming flesh devour.*

> *The crags before him split apart,*
> *The rivers ran in spate;*
> *He cleft the rocks by magic art,*
> *His cunning was so great.*

For this fiend there was not a shred of mercy in Bjartur. No matter how often he sprawled headlong down the gullies, he was up again undaunted and with redoubled fury making yet another attack, grinding his teeth and hurling curses at the demon's gnashing jaws, determined not to call a halt before Grimur's evil spirit had been hounded to the remotest corners of hell and the naked brand had pierced him through and his death-throes had begun in a ring-dance of land and sea.

Again and again he imagined that he had made an end of Grimur and sent him howling to hell in the poet's immortal words, but still the blizzard assailed him with undiminished fury when he reached the top of the next ridge, clawed at his eyes and the roots of his beard, howled vindictively in his ears, and tried to hurl him to the ground — the struggle was by no means over, he was still fighting at close quarters with the poison-spewing thanes of hell, who came storming over the earth in raging malice till the vault of heaven shook to the echo of their rush.

> *His loathsome head aloft he reared,*
> *With hellish hate he roared.*
> *His slavering lips with froth were smeared,*
> *Vilely his curses poured.*

And so on, over and over again.

Never, never did these thanes of hell escape their just deserts. No one ever heard of Harekur or Gongu-Hrolfur or Bernotus being worsted in the final struggle. In the same way no one will be able to say that Bjartur of Summerhouses ever got the worst of it in his world war with the country's spectres, no matter how often he might tumble over a precipice or roll head over heels down a gully— "while there's a breath left in my nostrils, it will never keep me down, however hard it blows." Finally he stood still, leaning against the blizzard as against a wall; and neither could push the other back. He then resolved to house himself in the snow and began looking for a sheltered spot in a deep gully. With his hands he scooped out a cave in a snowdrift, trying to arrange it so that he could sit inside on his haunches to pile up the snow at the mouth, but the snow, loose and airy, refused to stick together, and as the man was without implements, the cave simply fell in again. He had not rested long in the snowdrift before the cold began to penetrate him; a stiffness and a torpor crept up his limbs, all the way to his groin, but what was worse was the drowsiness that was threatening him, the seductive sleep of the snow, which makes it so pleasant to die in a blizzard; nothing is so important as to be able to strike aside this tempting hand which beckons so voluptuously into realms of warmth and rest. To keep the oblivion of the snow at bay it was his custom to recite or, preferably, sing at the top of his voice all the obscene verse he had picked up since childhood, but such surroundings were never very conducive to song and on this occasion his voice persisted in breaking; and the drowsiness continued to envelop his consciousness in its mists, till now there swam before his inner eye pictures of men and events, both from life and from the Ballads — horse-meat steaming on a great platter, flocks of sheep bleating in the fold, Bernotus Borneyarkappi in disguise, clergymen's wanton daughters wearing real silk stockings; and finally, by unsensed degrees, he assumed another personality and discovered himself in the character of Grimur the Noble, brother of Ulfar the Strong, when the visit was paid to his bedchamber. Matters stood thus, that the King, father of the brothers, had taken in marriage a young woman, who, since the King was well advanced in years, found a sad lack of entertainment in the marriage bed and became a prey to melancholy. But eventually her eyes fell on the King's son, Grimur the Noble, who far outshone all other men in that kingdom, and the young Queen fell so deeply in love with this princely figure that she could neither eat nor sleep and resolved finally to go to him at night in his chamber. Of the aged King, his father, she spoke in the most derisive of terms:

> *Of what use to red-blood maid*
> *Sap of such a withered blade?*
> *Or to one so sore in need,*
> *Spine of such a broken reed?*

Grimur, however, found this visit displeasing and relished even less such shameless talk, but for some time he retreated in courtly evasion of the issue. But

> *No refusals ought availed,*
> *Words of reason here had failed.*
> *All intent on lustful play*
> *Softly on the bed she lay.*

And before Grimur the Noble had time to marshal his defences, there occurred the following:

In her arms she clasped him tight,
Warm with promise of delight;
Honey-seeming was her kiss,
All her movements soft with bliss.

But at this moment there dawned upon Grimur the Noble the
full iniquity of what was taking place, and springing to his feet in
a fury, he turned upon the shameless wanton:

Up the hero rose apace,
Smote her sharply on the face;
Scornful of such shameful deed,
Thrust her to the floor with speed.

Angrily the hero cried,
Whilst she lay, bereft of pride:
"Lustful art thou as a swine,
Little honour can be thine."

"To hell with me, then," cried Bjartur, who was now standing
in the snow after repulsing the seductive bed-blandishments of
the lecherous Queen. Did the heroes of the rhymes ever allow
themselves to be beguiled into a life of adultery, debauchery, and
that cowardice in battle which characterizes those who are the
greatest heroes in a woman's embrace? Never should it be said
of Bjartur of Summerhouses that on the field of battle he turned
his back on his foes to go and lie with a trollopy slut of a queen.
He was in a passion now. He floundered madly about in the snow,
thumping himself with all his might, and did not sit down again
till he had overcome all those feelings of the body that cry for rest
and comfort, everything that argues for surrender and hearkens
to the persuasion of faint-hearted gods. When he had fought thus
for some time, he stuck the frozen sausages inside his trousers and
warmed them on his flesh, then gnawed them from his fist in the
darkness of this relentless winter night and ate the driving snow
as savoury.

This was rather a long night. Seldom had he recited so much
poetry in any one night; he had recited all his father's poetry,
all the ballads he could remember, all his own palindromes backwards and forwards in forty-eight different ways, whole processions of dirty poems, one hymn that he had learned from his mother,
and all the lampoons that had been known in the Fourthing from

time immemorial about bailiffs, merchants, and sheriffs. At intervals he struggled up out of the snow and thumped himself from top to toe till he was out of breath.

Finally his fear of frost-bite became so great that he felt it would be courting disaster to remain quietly in this spot any longer, and as it must also be wearing on towards morning and he did not relish the idea of spending a whole day without food in a snowdrift miles from any habitation, he now decided to forsake his shelter and leave the consequences to take care of themselves. He forced his way at first with lowered head against the storm, but when he reached the ridge above the gully, he could no longer make any headway in this fashion, so he slumped forward on to his hands and knees and made his way through the blizzard on all fours, crawling over stony slopes and ridges like an animal, rolling down the gullies like a peg; barehanded, without feeling.

On the following night, long after the people of Brun, the nearest farm of Glacierdale, had retired to bed — the storm had raged relentlessly now for a full twenty-four hours — it came to pass that the housewife was wakened from her sleep by a hubbub at the window, a groaning, even a hammering. She woke her husband, and they came to the conclusion that some creature gifted with the power of reasoning must surely be afoot and about the house, though on this lonely croft visitors were the last thing to be expected in such a storm — was it man or devil? They huddled on their most necessary garments and went to the door with a light. And when they had opened the door, there toppled in through the drift outside a creature resembling only in some ways a human being; he rolled in through the doorway armoured from head to foot in ice, nose and mouth encrusted, and came to rest in a squatting position with his back against the wall and his head sunk on his chest, as if the monstrous spectre, despairing of maltreating him further, had finally slung him through the door and up against the wall; the light of the house shone on this visitor. He panted heavily, his chest heaving and groaning, and made an effort to clear his throat and spit, and when the crofter asked him who he was and where he came from, he tried to get to his feet, like an animal trying to stand up on its hind legs, and gave his name — "Bjartur of Summerhouses."

The crofter's son had now risen also, and together he and his father made an attempt to help their visitor into the room, but he refused any such assistance. "I'll walk by myself," he said, "I'll follow the woman with the lamp." He laid himself across the son's bed and for a while made no answer to their questions, but mumbled like a drunkard, rumbled like a bull about to bellow. At last he said:

"I am thirsty."

The woman brought him a three-pint basin of milk, and he set it to his mouth and drank it off, and said as he passed her the basin: "Thanks for the drink, mother." With her warm hands she helped to thaw the clots of ice in his beard and eyebrows, then drew off his frozen clothes and felt with experienced fingers for frost-bite. Fingers and toes were without feeling, his skin smarting with frost, but otherwise he appeared to have taken no hurt. When the crust of ice had been thawed off, he stretched himself out naked in the son's warm bed and had seldom felt so comfortable in all his life. After the housewife had gone to prepare him some food, father and son sat down beside him, their eyes bewildered, as if they did not really believe this phenomenon and did not know quite what to say. In the end it was he who spoke, as he asked in a hoarse voice from under the coverlet:

"Were your lambs in?"

They replied that they were, and asked in turn how it had come about that he had landed here, on the eastern bank of Glacier River, in murderous weather that would kill any man.

"Any man?" he repeated querulously. "What do the men matter? I always thought it was the animals that came first."

They continued to question him.

"Oh, as a matter of fact I was just taking a little walk by myself," he vouchsafed. "I missed a ewe, you see, and took a stroll along the heights there just to soothe my mind."

For a while he was silent, then he added:

"It's been a trifle rough today."

"It wasn't any pleasanter last night either," they said, "a regular hurricane."

"Yes," agreed Bjartur, "it was just a trifle rough last night, too."

They wanted to know where he had put in the night, and he replied: "In the snow." They were particularly curious about how he had managed to cross Glacier River, but he would give no details. "It's a nice thing to have one's lambs out in this," he said mournfully.

They said that in his shoes they wouldn't trouble themselves about lambs tonight, but think themselves lucky to be where they were.

"It's easy to see," he replied, "that you people have found your feet. But I am fighting for my independence. I have worked eighteen years for the little livestock I have, and if they're under snow, it would be better for me to be under snow too."

But when the woman had brought him a meal in bed and he had eaten his fill, he lay down without further discourse and was asleep and snoring loudly.

17.   HOMECOMING

ON the afternoon of the fifth day Bjartur ploughed his way home across the marshes, knee-deep in snow. He was feeling anything but pleased with himself, ashamed of what he felt had been a most ignominious journey, and alternating between hope and fear as to the fate of his sheep in the home pastures; and now, to cap it all, there wasn't even a flicker of light in the window to welcome him home when at last he did return, for the croft was buried in snow and no attempt had been made to clear the door or the window; nowhere was there a passage cut through the drift, not a wisp of smoke rose from the chimney. He crawled up on to the roof, scraped the snow from the window and shouted: "Rosa, see if you can't get me a shovel out through the door."

The dog gave a pitiful howl inside in the living-room, the only answer; and when the crofter started shouting to his wife again, the dog leaped up at the window from inside and scratched at it with her paws. He began then to wonder whether his wife might not have been taken ill, and feeling rather apprehensive about it, he started on the drift like one in a frenzy. He had to scrape the snow aside with his hands, slow work, but eventually he managed to clear sufficient space about the door to worm his way inside.

When he got to the top of the stairway the dog jumped up at him madly, howling bitterly, as if someone were steadily tramping on her tail. The winter darkness had fallen early, and it was as black as pitch inside, the windows snowed up; he had to feel his way about. But he had not taken a full step across the floor before he struck his foot against some unwonted obstacle. He swore, as was his habit whenever he lost his footing — what the devil had he fallen over?

It took him a long time to find the matches, and when he had

found them the lamp proved to be empty, the wick burned down,
the glass black with smoke. But when he had filled the lamp and
the wick had begun drawing again, it was possible even in this
feeble light to make out some indication of what had happened
in Summerhouses in his absence. It was his wife. She was lying
dead there in her congealed blood. It looked as if she had got
out of bed for something, and, too weak to climb in again, had
collapsed by the bedside; in her hand a wet towel, blood-stained.
The condition of the body showed plainly what had happened.
And when he looked into the bed, whither the dog had suddenly
leaped, he saw peeping from under the dog's belly a small, yellow-
brown face, wrinkled, with closed eyes, like a new-born old man,
and over this face slight quivers were playing, feeble and spas-
modic, and from this unfortunate there came, if he heard aright,
an occasional very faint whimper.

The dog strove to spread herself as closely as possible over the
little body that she had taken to foster and given the only thing
she possessed: the warmth of her lousy body, hungry and emaciated; when Bjartur came nearer to look more closely, she showed
her teeth, as if wishing him to understand that it was not he
who owned this child. The mother had wrapped the poor creature
in a woollen rag as soon as she had cut the cord, and had probably
risen from her bed to heat some water to bathe it with, for on the
range stood a pan full of water, long since cold above the dead
fire. But the infant was still hanging on to life in the warmth from
the animal's body.

Bjartur lifted the body of his wife from the floor, and after
laying it in the empty bedstead opposite their own bed, wiped
off as much of the blood as he could. It cost him a good deal of
effort to straighten the corpse out, for the limbs had stiffened
in the position in which the body had lain; the arms obstinately
refused to lie in a cross over her breast, the dull eyes would not
close, the right eye especially, the one with a cast — her stubbornness again. But Bjartur trusted himself even less for what was
now of greater importance, and that was to quicken the spark
of life still left in the new-born infant. This put him in no mean
quandary, the independent man, for experienced hands were
needed, probably female hands; he himself dared not have anything to do with it. Must he then ask help of other people? The
last thing that he had impressed upon his wife was not to ask
help of other people — an independent man who resorts to other

people for help gives himself over into the power of the arch-
fiend; and now this same humiliation was to be pronounced on
him; on Bjartur of Summerhouses; but he was determined to
pay whatever was asked of him.

18.   RAUTHSMYRI

"WELL, at least you're getting about a bit these days, my lad,"
said Bjartur to himself as on the evening of the same day he
knocked at the kitchen door at Rauthsmyri.

"So it's you at last, is it?" said the workman who came to the
door. He was in his stocking feet and had in his hand some steaming cloth that he was fulling — the domestic crafts were in full
swing. "We thought you were dead."

"Far from it," replied Bjartur. "I've been over the mountains
for sheep."

"Are you sure you're right in the head?" asked the other.

"I lost a ewe."

"It's like you to leave all your other sheep in danger to go
chasing over the mountains after one ewe."

"Well, I may be wrong, mate, but as far as I know it says in
the Bible that one sheep on the mountains is worth more than
a hundred at home," said Bjartur, who had his own fondness for
those passages in the Scriptures which mention sheep. "And besides, one doesn't live next door to the local potentate for nothing
if the weather happens to break."

Such, indeed, proved to have been the case: the Rauthsmyri
herds had taken Bjartur's sheep in with their own the evening that
the storm broke, but had not been ordered by the Bailiff to drive
them back home tomorrow morning and to find out at the same
time whether their owner was dead or not. "Did you find the ewe?"

"No, there wasn't a damned thing to be seen, except a hot-
spring bird in the springs south of the Blue Mountains," replied
Bjartur. "But by the way, have the lambs taken to hay yet?"

Oh yes, they'd had a sniff or two at the hay, said the workman,
and gave Bjartur to understand that these valiant lambs of his
would soon learn the art of eating. But while they were discussing
the matter, the housekeeper, Gudny, came to the door, for she
had recognized Bjartur's voice; she bade him now come into the
kitchen, and would he like a bowl of porridge and a rib of horse?

He scraped the snow from his clothes with his knife and dusted his hat against the doorpost.

It was a big kitchen, used partly as a living-room; the workmen were fulling or busy with horsehair, the servant-girls with their wool, and the dogs were lying full-length on the floor, all old friends of Bjartur's, dogs included. Bjartur was very hungry. They were all discussing the unexpected blizzard and its effect on the livestock; "we can look for a dirty January," said the womenfolk, "when it's started already and Advent not here yet. How is Rosa keeping?"

"Um," said Bjartur with his mouth full, "it was a trifle rough on the other side of Glacier River, but I've seen it worse many a time."

"On the other side of Glacier River?" asked the workmen in surprise. "You aren't trying to make us believe that you crossed Glacier River, are you?"

"Why not? Many a brook can be waded, even if it is up on the moors," replied the crofter, "and maybe we aren't all such hearth-hounds as the lot of you."

"Do you mean to tell us that you've been fooling about up on the moors, and poor Rosa in the condition they say she is?" cried the housekeeper compassionately.

"I please myself what I do, Gunsa lass," retorted Bjartur with a scornful grin. "I'm my own boss these days, you know, and need give account to no one, you least of all." And throwing the horse-meat he had been given to one of the dogs as he spoke, he added: "But by the way, do you think our good Madam has gone off to bed yet?"

The Bailiff's wife came sailing in, high of head and full of bosom, looked inquiringly at Bjartur through spectacles that ploughed creases in the fat, red cheeks, and switched on the cold, cultured, aristocratic smile that in spite of ideals and poetic talent built such a high, wide wall between her and those whose well-being was less dependent on romanticism. Bjartur thanked her heartily for the horse-meat and the porridge.

"Surely you haven't sent for me to thank me for a ladle of porridge," she said, without referring to the horse-meat.

"No, oh no, not exactly," replied Bjartur. "It was something else I was wanting actually." He was ashamed to ask of course, but he was wondering whether she wouldn't be able to give him a little help with something, if he could have a few words with her in private — "and besides, I have to thank you and your husband for my sheep, which your lads got in all ready for me while I was away on the round-up."

The poetess intimated that Bjartur ought to be sufficiently well acquainted with the household here to know that she never concerned herself with the lifestock, but left it to more suitable people.

"Well I know it," said Bjartur, "and actually I'm fully determined to fetch them tomorrow — I only hope they don't eat the poor Bailiff out of house and home tonight. But if he's short in spring, bless him, he can always come along to me for a pack-load of lamb's hay later on."

"I'd rather you told me how dear Rosa is getting on," said the poetess.

"Yes, I was coming to that," said Bjartur. "In fact I only asked to see you because I had something to tell you. Nothing important, of course."

The Bailiff's wife looked at him as if half expecting that he was about to ask her for something, whereupon the soul within her receded like a star, far out into the frozen wastes of infinity, and only the cold smile remained on earth.

"I hope for your sake it's nothing my husband may not hear," said she with much determination.

"Oh, no," replied Bjartur, "it takes more than a trifle to upset the Bailiff, bless him."

Madam showed Bjartur into Bailiff Jon of Myri's sanctum, one of the smallest rooms in this great house. The pair had long since given up the habit of sleeping together; Madam slept in a separate room with her little daughter Audur. This little room of the Bailiff's would have resembled nothing so much as the miserable garret where a pauper allotted by the parish is left with little honour to his own devices, had it not been for one of the walls, which was completely hidden by book-shelves carrying volumes of parliamentary transactions bound in black, with the year on a white label. The bed, nailed to the wall, was fashioned like a peasant's of unplaned boards and covered with a ragged self-coloured blanket. On the floor stood a blue-glazed spittoon shaped like an hour-glass; above the bed a crudely made shelf on which stood a flowered porridge-basin, a heavy china cup, and a bottle of liniment for rheumatism; by one wall a rude table bearing writing materials of indifferent quality, and beneath the window a huge chest; in front of the table a wretched old armchair without a cover, tied up with string where the joints had sprung. On the wall there hung a bright-coloured picture of the Redeemer on the

Cross, another, equally bright, of the Czar Nicholas, and a calendar bearing the name of the merchant in Vik.

Bailiff Jon was lying on his bed with his hands under his head and his spectacles on the tip of his nose; had just laid aside the latest batch of newspapers. He greeted his visitor with a vague snort, careful not to lose any of the precious tobacco juice that had been accumulating in his mouth for some time now. It was his custom not to spit too quickly, but to derive as much real benefit as possible from the juice he managed to suck from every quid. He was dressed much the same as a beggar, in a shapeless old jacket, patched out of recognition and fastened at the neck with a safety-pin. Besides the various forms of dirt that had stained it for some time past there were some fresh patches of earth and some tufts of wool on it which indicated that he had just come in from the sheep-cotes. His trousers were so worn that the original cloth no longer held the patches and was giving way at the stitches. Turned up over the bottoms was a pair of yellowish socks, undyed, and the down-at-heel horsehide shoes on his feet lent support to the theory that he was newly returned from a thoroughgoing inspection of the stables, stronger testimony being provided by the smell. In clothing and general appearance Bjartur of Summerhouses was far superior to this tramp-like Bailiff.

Was there then nothing individual about the man, nothing to distinguish him from the crofter's half-wrought appearance? There was. In spite of the tramp's equipment, no one could doubt even at first sight, that this must be a man who ruled over others and held their fate in his hands; his lips wrinkled about the quid of tobacco as an unconscious symbol that he released nothing before he had sucked everything of value out of it. The peculiarly clear eyes, hard and cold grey; the regular features; the breadth of the brow beneath the strong, dark hair, grey as yet only at the temples; the shapely lineament of jaw and chin; the pale complexion that spoke of a sedentary life; and last but not least the small, shapely hands, strangely white and soft in spite of the obvious lack of care — all these were outward manifestations of a definite personality, a nature more forceful and more complex than is usually found among those who have to depend on their own toil to win their meagre living.

Bjartur offered his hand in greeting to his former employer, and the Bailiff gave him as usual his thumb and first finger, carefully reserving the other three clenched in his palm, without say-

ing a word. During his twenty years' practice Bjartur had evolved
a technique of dealing with the Bailiff that was entirely his own.
This technique was based on the defensive attitude of an insignificant youth towards a suspicious despot, an attitude that, as
the years go by, develops into the conscientious man's passionate desire to assert himself against the superior power, then passes
finally into persecution, into unremitting tension, always militant,
which eyes only its own cause and refuses to meet the stronger
personality on impartial ground.

The poetess offered her visitor a seat on the chest under the
window with the remark that no one knew the knack of sitting in
the armchair but the Bailiff himself.

"Pshaw," exclaimed Bjartur indignantly, "what good did
sitting down ever do anybody? There's time enough for sitting
when senile decay sets in. I was just telling Madam, Jon, that if
you happen to run short of hay towards the end of winter through
your lads' housing my sheep for a couple of nights, well, just send
along to me for a load in the spring."

Raising his head slowly and cautiously from the pillow, so that
his chew retained a level permitting it to spill neither down his
gullet nor over his lower lip, the Bailiff opened his mouth a fraction of an inch and, gazing at him with tolerant contempt, replied:

"Look after your own self, my lad."

This complacent, commiserating tone, though never definitely
insulting, unconditionally relegated other people to the category
of pitiable rubbish and always reacted upon Bjartur as if some
criminal tendency were imputed. It had fostered the aggressive
in his nature all these years, his passion for freedom and independence.

"Look after myself? Yes, you can bet your life on that. I'll look
after myself all right. I've never owed you anything so far, my
friend — except what was agreed upon."

The Bailiff's wife drew the crofter's attention to the fact that
she had understood him to say that he had something to tell the
pair of them; would he please be so kind as to tell them immediately, it was getting on.

Bjartur sat down on the chest, as he had been asked to do at
first, said: "Hm," clawed his head a little, and grimaced.

"The idea was this," he said, looking at her out of the corner
of his eye, as was his custom when he had to feel his way. "I was
a ewe short, you see."

A long silence followed, during which she watched him

through her spectacles with severe eyes. When she had given up all hope of his proceeding, she asked: "Well?"

Taking out his horn, he tapped a long train of snuff on to the back of his hand.

"Gullbra she was called," he said. "She was a year old last spring, poor beast, and a first-rate sheep. She was sired by your Gelli, you know, one of the Reverendgudmundur breed that I've always had so much faith in; they're such grand animals. I left her at home during the first round-up to keep the wife company, and then, how it happened I'm damned if I know, but she must have been missed in the second round-up and the third as well. So I said to myself a few days ago: the best thing you can do, my lad, is to take yourself a walk over the moors and have a look for this Gullbra of yours, for many's the lamb you've sought south on the mountains long after the last of the round-ups, and that for other people, as I think you should both be able to testify, it being no longer ago than last autumn."

The Bailiff's wife still stared inquiringly at the crofter, still uncertain as to where all this was leading.

"So I went southward over the moors," he continued, "I went south to the Blue Montains, and I even popped across Glacier River."

"Across Glacier River?" asked Madam in surprise.

"Yes," he said, "and crossing Glacier River would have been nothing if only I'd seen any sign of living creature, but there wasn't a damned thing to be found except a bird in the warm springs south of the mountains, a hot-spring bird I expect. But as for anything with four feet to it, not a sign, with the exception of one buck reindeer (which I don't class as an animal), and into this trip of mine went, you may say, five days and four nights. Well, and what sort of welcome home do you think I had tonight?"

The others were either unable to solve this riddle or disinclined to begin cudgelling their brains too much, for the Bailiff's wife recommended that Bjartur should tell them the answer immediately if he attached any importance to their hearing it.

"Well, my dear lady, it's because you're so fond of poetry that I thought I'd let you hear this little quatrain, a poor thing that happened to occur to me when I looked round me by the trap-door at home an hour or two ago."

Then Bjartur recited this verse:

Fearful for his flock,
Little light he knows;
Frozen the fells mock,
Fallen the one rose.

The Bailiff slowly rolled his head to look at Bjartur and raised his brows as if in question, but he was very careful not to part his lips lest he unwittingly ask anything by word of mouth. It was his wife who was left to make this observation:

"I hope we aren't being given to understand that something has happened to Rosa."

"Hm, whether anything's happened to her is more than I can tell you," said Bjartur. "It all depends on how you look at it. But she lives no longer on my earth, whatever follows it."

"Our Rosa?" asked Madam in great agitation. "Are you telling us that Rosa is dead — only a young woman?"

Bjartur inhaled his snuff with great precision, then looked up with staring eyes wet with tobacco tears, answered proudly: "Yes. And she died alone."

At this news the Bailiff rose up in his bed and, swivelling his feet over and on to the floor, sat on the edge-board, continuing for yet a while to ruminate on his chew, and still considering the moment premature to rid his mouth of the notable juice.

"But that isn't the worst," pronounced Bjartur philosophically. "Death, after all, is only the debt we all have to pay, you people out here as well, whether you like it or not. It's this so-called life that many a man finds more difficult to bring into line with his purse. It's always springing up, as you know, and actually it's silly to go making a fuss about who the father is, though in certain cases it may be instructive as far as paying for it is concerned. So to tell you the truth, it wasn't because of the wife that I popped over here tonight, for I don't suppose there's much point in trying to quicken the life in her now, the way she is; it was rather about that poor little wretch that was just hanging on to life by a thread, under the dog's belly there, that I thought I might ask you for a little information, my dear lady."

"What do you think you're hinting at, my man?" was Madam's immediate question; and the cold smile was now one in iciness with the eyes behind the spectacles. The Bailiff bent over the spittoon and discharged all his juice in one stream, then rolling the quid all the way from under his tongue to the back of his jaws, pushed his glasses on to the bridge of his nose and sharpened his gaze on the visitor.

"May I ask what information you think you're asking for here?" continued the poetess. "If you are saying that your wife died in childbed and that the child is still alive, then try to say so plainly, without so many circumlocutions. Probably we'll try to help you as we've helped many another before you, with no thought of repayment. But one thing we do demand, and that is that neither you nor anyone else should come here with veiled insinuations about me or my household."

When the Bailiff saw that his wife had assumed the leadership in this affair, he settled down quietly again and started yawning, a habit of his if, when listening to a conversation, his mouth was not full of tobacco juice; in such circumstances he was always sleepy and let his eyes wander all over the place in obvious boredom. His wife on the other hand was not completely mollified until Bjartur had fully and explicitly removed all suspicion that he had come with the intention of inquiring into the paternity of the child at home in Summerhouses. "My tongue, you see, is more used to talking about lambs than human beings," he said apologetically, "and the idea was simply to ask you whether you didn't think it would be worth while pouring a few drops of warm milk down its throat to see if it can't be kept going till morning. I'll pay you whatever you ask, of course."

When all this unfortunate misunderstanding had been cleared away, Madam declared, and meant it, that for her indeed the supreme joy in life was to offer the weak her helping hand even in these difficult times; to sustain the feeble, to foster the awakening life.

Her heart was all his, not only in joy, but also in sorrow.

19.   LIFE

THE BAILIFF'S wife was as good as her word.

That same evening she sent her housekeeper down to Summerhouses on horseback with some bottles of milk, a portable oilstove, and various clothing for a new-born babe; Bjartur trod the snow in front of her horse in ballad mood after the adventures of the last few days.

The first thing that this midwife mentioned on entering Summerhouses was the smell; the stalls beneath were offensive with the damp of earthen walls and fish refuse, while the room upstairs stank of death and a reeking lamp, the wick dry again, the last flame guttering, ready to die. The housekeeper demanded fresh air. She spread a coverlet over the corpse in the empty bedstead. Then she turned her attention to the child. But the dog refused to leave it, nursing it still; a mother, thirsty and famished, and yet no one thinks of rewarding an animal for its virtues. The housekeeper tried to drive her away, but she made as if to snap at her, so Bjartur had to take her by the scruff of the neck and throw her down the ladder. But when the child was now examined, it showed no signs of life whatever. The woman tried turning it upside down and swinging it in various directions, even taking it to the outer door and turning its face into the wind, but all to no purpose; this wrinkled, sorrowful being that so uninvited, so undesired, had been sent into the world appeared to have lost all desire to claim its rights therein.

But this housekeeper, who had been widowed when young, refused to believe that the child could possibly be dead; she herself knew what it meant to be confined when blizzards were raging in the dales. She heated some water on her oil-stove, the second time that preparations were made to bathe this infant, and soon the water was hot, and the woman bathed the child and even let it lie for a good while in water that was much more than hot, with the tip of its nose sticking up. Bjartur inquired whether she intended boiling the thing, but apparently she did not hear what he said, and as the child still showed no signs of life, she took it out and, holding it by one leg, swung it about in the air with its head downward. Bjartur began to feel rather worried; he had followed everything with great interest so far, but this was more than he could stand, and he felt he had better ask mercy for the unfortunate creature. "Are you trying to put the kid's hips out of joint, damn you?" he inquired.

Whereupon Gudny, as if she had not been aware of his presence before, retorted sharply: "That's enough. Be off with you and don't show your face up here again before you're asked."

That was the first time that Bjartur was ever driven out of his own house, and had the circumstances been otherwise he would most certainly have had something to say in protest against such an enormity and would have tried to drive into Gunsa's head the fact that he owed her not a cent; but as it was, nothing seemed more likely than that he had been provided with a tail to trail between his legs as in utter ignominy he took the same path as the dog and crept down the stairs. But for the life of him he did not know what to turn his hand to down there in the dark; a completely exhausted man who had never felt less independent in his heart than that night; who felt that he was almost superfluous in the world, felt even that the living were in reality superfluous compared with the dead. He pulled out a truss of hay and, spreading it on the floor, lay down like a dog. In spite of everything one had at least got home.

The crying of a child woke him next morning.

When he went upstairs Gudny was sitting on the bed with the babe in her arms, and, what was more, had unfastened the clothes about her bosom to share her warmth with the infant, while his wife, its mother, lay lifeless in the bedstead opposite. She had tied a few tufts of wool round a bottle-neck and was teaching it to suck. Bjartur stood watching in some embarrassment, his modesty offended, and then the smile stole over his bearded, frost-bitten face, and into his eyes, bloodshot after the blizzard.

"Here you see your daughter sound in wind and limb," said Gudny, proud of having recalled this object to life.

"It sounds like it," said he, "poor little mite." And marvelled that it could be so small and delicate. "You can't really expect it to be much of a thing," he added apologetically, "the way mankind is such a sorry affair when you come to look at it as it actually is."

"Little sweetheart," cooed the woman, fondling the babe. "What would daddy be thinking of christening us?"

"Mm, I'll be her father as far as that's concerned, anyway," he said. "She'll have a pretty name and no other."

Gudny said nothing, cooing away to the child and persuading the bottle into its mouth.

Bjartur stood gazing at them for a while in obvious commune with his soul, then declared with great conviction:

"Yes, it's all settled," and touched the babe's face with his strong, grimy hand, which had battled with the spectral monsters of the country. "She shall be called Asta Sollilja."

He was proud that this helpless little thing should have no one in the world but himself, and was determined to share with her one and the same fate — "and that's all I want to hear about it."

There was much to be done: the sheep were still over at Rauths-myri; then there was the funeral to be attended to, the coffin, the minister, the bearers, the journey to town, the burial feast. "I was thinking, Gunsa lass, that maybe you'd like to mix a batch of

Christmas cake for the feast. You'd be welcome to spice, raisins, and if you like even those big black things that look like horse's dottles, prunes I think you call them. Don't consider the expense; I'll pay. And, of course, as many pancakes as everybody can hold. And strong coffee, woman; coffee strong enough to tar a tup with; I won't stand for people drinking any old dish-wash at the funeral of a wife of mine."

20.   ERRANDS

EVERYONE took it for granted that the ghost was active again in Summerhouses, so Gudny had a servant-girl sent from home to keep her company, and round the death of Rosa were spun strange stories, the stranger the greater the distance of their origin, but all in agreement as to its cause and all, indeed, of a pattern with the tales that had been told of this lonely croft from time out of memory. Great concern was therefore felt for the moor-crofter's future, especially as events had taken such a course in his very first year, and a few days later, when the Sheriff's Officer ran across Bjartur up-country, he intimated that he might have a workman's job vacant any time now and hinted that the difficulties in which it was expected Bjartur would shortly find himself might sooner or later become the concern of the whole parish; here he was, a widower left with an infant child on his hands, what was he going to do? He said he had heard that the Rauthsmyri people might be persuaded to take the child to foster, without the usual fee even, though with the stipulation that the land be returned to them free, "and in your shoes I would say I was well rid of it on such liberal terms."

Bjartur, however, thought that if the Rauthsmyri people were offering him liberal terms for anything it was certainly not before time, even though the offer did reach him by a circuitous route. "It may be possible that you parish-council potentates call it good riddance to pack your kids off to be fostered at Rauthsmyri," he declared. "But I don't call it a good riddance. For it so happens that I was fostered by this same Rauthsmyri crew myself for eighteen years. And as long as I can call myself an independent subject of this country and can pay my way with God and men, I intend to see that it is I that brings up my children and not the Rauthsmyrians."

"There may come a time," said the other, "when legal causes

will prevent you from continuing to pay your way, especially if you have to farm those mountains of yours with hired female help; all of which might have its effects on this so-called independence of yours."

"It took me eighteen years to scrape that stock of mine together and pay the deposit on Summerhouses," replied Bjartur, "and though I may not have built myself a king's palace of marble and sapphire, I've built myself at any rate a palace that stands on a foundation of eighteen years. And as long as I owe neither the parish nor the dealer, and can pay the Bailiff his instalments on the land, it is at least a palace that is as good as any palace that either you or the Bailiff ever built. And now let me tell you this, my friend: I have never concerned myself with the Bailiff's children or made a fuss about whom they're called after, and never will; but I demand in return that the Bailiff keep his nose out of my business and leave my children, and whatever names I happen to christen them, entirely to me. And tell him I was asking about him."

Bjartur that day was on his way to Stathur to see the Reverend Gudmundur, the man for whom he had such a great respect, greater indeed than for almost anyone else, because of the excellent breed of sheep he had introduced into the parish. He was ushered into the eddying smoke of the room where, busy with his sermons and his farm accounts, the minister was as usual parading the floor. He had seldom been known to stand still, had no time for it, rarely sat down, was a master of the querulous, peremptory technique of the busy man. He was well on in years, rather corpulent, his cheeks and nose blue-tinted. Scion of an old family of rank in the west, he had held a living in the south in his younger days, but had spent most of his life here and was now in a very comfortable position. Though a very able farmer, he always reviled earthly matters when speaking to his parishioners and never aired his knowledge of agriculture in any discussion. Like most very busy people he was usually very curt in his conversation, and he always thought that anything anyone else said was nonsense. He was severe in his judgment and had bigoted opinions on every subject, but changed them immediately if anyone agreed with him. He had very little faith in human nature and was incredulous of good in anyone but the Danish royal family, whom he held in high esteem because of their intelligence and moral virtues. His special favourite was the Princess Augusta, of whom, although she had been dead for many years, there still hung a portrait in his study. He had no great opinion of his parishioners' morals and would frequently touch upon the subject in dark innuendo, implying always that a multitude of hidden crimes had been committed in the parish during the years of his ministry; and yet it was always said of him that he never refused anyone who came to him in distress. It was equally painful to him to hear anyone spoken ill of as to hear them praised. When in the company of people who had little faith, he would discuss religious matters with tremendous fervour, but among the devout his attitude was one rather of irreverence and derision. His parishioners found his sermons scrappy and disconnected, at times even completely unintelligible, and few people made any effort to live according to the precepts they contained.

"On the tramp again," he grunted in his peevish way, offering Bjartur a lightning touch of the hand as he rushed past him on his circuit of the room. He puffed furiously at his pipe on the way, the clouds rising above his head like puffs of dust from a horse's hoofs.

"I'm not so sure that it's usual for me to be on the tramp," replied Bjartur, "but one thing I can't deny is that I've just met the Sheriff's Officer."

"Tcha, the Sheriff's Officer!" snorted the minister, spitting disdainfully into the coal-bucket as he sped past the stove.

"So I thought I'd give the minister a look-in too," continued Bjartur, "just to see which of the two had the greater thirst for freedom."

"Freedom?" repeated the minister, and actually pulled up, sharpening his gaze on his visitor as if demanding an explanation.

"Yes — I mean for the poor."

"I lay no claim to freedom either for the poor or the rich," hastily intimated the minister, and was off again.

"What I mean," said Bjartur, "is that the difference between the parish council and me is that I have always made some demands in the way of freedom. They want to keep everyone down."

"There is no freedom but the freedom of the one true Redemption of Our Lord Jesus Christ," intoned the minister in the colourless gabble of an impatient clerk explaining to some insignificant customer that the only material for sale here is the canvas named after the master Hessian. "It is as it says in the old one," and he produced a quotation in a foreign language, then asked: "What is freedom? Yes, just as I expected, you haven't even the faintest notion yourself. Not that I've any objection to your living up among

the glaciers; you're welcome to them. As it says in the old one" —
another quotation in a most unintelligible language.

"Oh, I'm not going to argue with you about Hebrew, your
reverence. But I don't care what anybody says, I think I know as
much about sheep as the next one and I say that your rams have
done a power of good in these parts."

"Yes, curse them," said the minister, accelerating, "a power of
good for those whose belly is their god and who pride themselves
on the wretched beasts."

"Hm, as far as I remember, the sheep is called the lamb of the
Lord in the Bible."

"I deny that the sheep was ever called the lamb of the Lord
in the Bible," replied the minister with some heat. "I don't say
that sheep weren't created by God, but I do absolutely deny that
God favours them any more than He does any other quadruped."
A moment's silence, then in a voice full of bitter reproach: "Chasing sheep over mountains and deserts, what's the point of it anyway? As if there was any sense in that!"

"Well, to tell you the truth just as it strikes me, your reverence,
I expect that at bottom, if we spoke as man to man, from the heart
like brothers, you know, we would maybe find that our opinion
of sheep didn't differ nearly half as much as you'd have an ignorant
man like me believe. And I'd like to tell you, your reverence, that
my main business here tonight, which I've been thinking of and
dreaming of for long enough, was to see whether you couldn't be
persuaded to sell me a nice young ram in the autumn. Maybe, if
God grants it, I'll be able to pay for it in ready money, but in any
case, with the help of the Almighty, by a conveyance to my account
with the dealer if things are bad."

Bjartur was trying to tread with all possible care the middle
course between the fear of God and the worship of Mammon,
so as to give the minister no loophole for attack. But it was no use.
The Reverend Gudmundur refused to be hoodwinked into agreement with anyone.

"Conveyance!" he repeated crossly. "I will have no conveyance
between God and the Devil. You can go to the steward and haggle
it out with him."

"Yes, but I'd rather not talk to underlings before the matter is
settled with you."

"If you're wanting any coffee," said the minister, "you'd better
say so now. But there's not a single drop of brandy in the house, so
help me God!"

"Oh, I've never spat my coffee out yet because there was no brandy in it. Many a poor soul has had to go short of his brandy before today, you know."

The minister then went out into the kitchen to see how the coffee situation was, and returning after a few moments, resumed his perambulation at the same excessive speed, his head still hidden in the clouds of smoke puffed from his pipe.

"You'll get nothing but the grounds here, my man," said he, "for I've never noticed that you've ever had a thought to spare for your spiritual salvation. You follow your own unheeding ways up on the mountain peaks there, not only in perfect improvidence, but also in obvious hardness of heart, and then you think you can come and tell a man what's what."

One of the minister's elegant daughters brought in fragrant coffee in a bronze pot, porcelain cups and saucers painted with Japanese figures, two plates covered with a variety of cakes, all delicious, sugar and cream. She reminded Bjartur of their last meeting and still remembered the verses he had composed in the summer, and recited them in his honour while the minister, listening with sour disapproval, mumbled away to himself.

"Tcha," he said, "anything that can't be translated into Latin on the spot is unadulterated doggerel. Go away, Gunna, you've nothing in common with this fellow."

No sooner had the door closed on the young lady than he bent down and opened one of the drawers in his desk and, coughing in the clouds of smoke pouring from his pipe, drew out a brandy-flask full to the neck. In high dudgeon he poured half a pint or so of the brandy into the coffee-pot, then filled both cups with the mixture. Bjartur said nothing, out of reverence for the minister and admiration for the brandy. They began to drink the coffee. After three cups Bjartur was sweating.

"Drink up, man," exhorted the minister. "What do you think the womenfolk give you coffee for in this weather?"

"I've stabled three already, you know," said Bjartur politely.

"That can be as it likes, but I never drink less than thirty a day," rejoined the minister, and kept on refilling the cups and urging the crofter to drink, till each had had six cups and the coffee-pot was empty. By this time the sweat was pouring from Bjartur's brow and down his temple. He gazed at the pictures on the cups and saucers thoughtfully for a while, then made the following observation:

"There's nothing dowdy about those damsels there and all their finery," referring to the Japanese ladies on the cups, "and it will be a while, I know, before the lasses on Summerhouses cups smile as sweetly. And that reminds me, your reverence," he added, wiping the sweat from his face with his sleeve, "that I'm in a nice mess just now: my wife, as I suppose you would call her since you blessed our marriage in the spring, died a day or two ago."

"How was that?" inquired the minister suspiciously. "I can't help it if she's dead, surely."

"No, heavens above, I know that. And it wasn't meant that way either," said Bjartur, absolving the minister of all guilt in the matter. "She just died, in a natural way, probably through loss of blood, and I know well enough how it happened. But what's happened to Gullbra, a fine year-old ewe of your breed that I had tethered at the bottom of the home-field this autumn, during the first round-up? I left her behind with my late wife, you see, to keep her company, well, that's something I really can't fathom at all."

"I know nothing about it," said the minister coldly. "I'm no sheep-stealer. I deny any participation in these affairs."

"What I mean," said Bjartur reasonably, "is that some arrangements will have to be made, at least as far as the wife is concerned."

"I can furnish you with another woman while you wait, a fine woman, docile as a nun, and very obedient. But an old woman accompanies her, a decrepit old vixen, so you know what you're in for — she knows the whole of the Videy Psalms off by heart."

"Quite; but I'd thought of asking you to bury this one first," said Bjartur politely.

"Oh, Lord, I simply loathe the thought of burying folk."

"Yes, but what you don't realize is that I can't keep anybody on the croft as long as she's lying there. You've no idea how foolish people are nowadays. And superstitious."

"You'd better dump her in a temporary grave till the spring, then," said the minister. "I'm certainly not going wading over mountains at my age, an old man worn out years ago, chesty by nature, and probably with a cancer on the liver. Then again, nothing is known about how this woman of yours came to die. You wretched mountaineers can always get out of it by saying you were away in the deserts looking for strays when your wives pass out. But women, as far as I know, need looking after the same as cattle. And it wouldn't be so very difficult for me to prove a thing or two about the death of many people, men and women alike, in this district, since I wandered here in my misery and doubt thirty years ago — and certainly would prove too, did I not love my parishioners and were I not grown too old and feeble to importune a corrupt administration that neither pillage, arson, nor murder can stir to action."

"Oh, I expect you've sprinkled a few that died a stranger death than my Rosa."

"Yes," sighed the minister mournfully, "I'm just a helpless old wretch, I suppose, and sick unto death."

"All I ask is that you take a trip out to Rauthsmyri on Saturday first if the weather's decent."

"The spade in the church there is broken, God help me," said the minister, raising all the difficulties possible. "I can vouch for nothing with regard to the death, judgment, and future life of anyone whose last obsequies are performed with the help of such a ghastly old implement. Then again, you're sure to demand a sermon of me, but I intend telling you once and for all that I don't see the point of making a speech over a corpse in this sort of weather. One gets nothing out of it in any case."

"It needn't be a long speech, you know," said Bjartur.

"Can't the old wife at Rauthsmyri make a speech over her? She made a speech over her last spring. Why can't she make a speech over her this autumn?"

"Now, honestly, I don't mind telling anybody," said Bjartur, "that I have very little faith in any speech that the Rauthsmyri crew may make. And I could easily be persuaded that things might have turned out better had it been you instead of her that did the sermonizing at the wedding, though, to be perfectly frank, I have in general no great faith in any speech, whether for one purpose or another, and least of all long speeches."

"If I make a speech at all," snapped the minister, "it's going to be a long speech. Because once you get started, there's no end at all to what has to be said, the way that people conduct themselves nowadays towards one another and to the parish."

"It all depends on how you look at it actually," said Bjartur. "Some think the least said soonest mended. But one thing we needn't argue about is the contents of the speech; it's all the same to me as long as there's nothing objectionable in it. The main thing is to have a speech for the right person made in the right place by the right authority, otherwise they hold it against you and hint that perhaps you can't afford a speech, but that is a slur that I'll never have cast in my teeth as long as I can call myself an independent man. My wife was an independent woman."

"And how much do you think you can give for a speech?"

"Well, that was really one of the things I wanted to arrange. Actually I consider that you owe me a speech from last spring and I think I might as well have it now. It won't improve with keeping."

"No," said the minister decisively. "I will hold no sermon over a woman who lives in marriage for one summer only, then dies. You can think yourself lucky that I don't have the matter inquired into. There might be ways and means of letting you have your next marriage sermon for nothing, but to trade a funeral sermon for a wedding sermon is a type of jobbery that I'll have nothing to do with."

"I imagine, your reverence," said the crofter, "that fuller investigation might prove that I had a legal right to the sermon. Even if she never saw thirty, she was my wife, a good wife, a Christian wife."

"So she was a Christian, was she?" said the minister angrily, for he could never bear to hear anyone praised.

"Well," replied Bjartur, preparing to concede a point or two in the interests of harmony, "perhaps I ought to say that she was a Christian in her own way. But everything in moderation, you know."

"It's news to me, let me tell you, if the people in these parts have suddenly become Christians," cried the minister furiously. "In Rangarvellir you did have Christian people, I agree. There you had a holy person and a prophet on every other farm, but I've lived in exile here for thirty years and never yet come across living Christianity or true repentance before God in any shape or form, only monstrous crimes, monstrous crimes, fourteen murders and exposures of children, besides all the abortions."

"Those are things I know nothing about," said Bjartur, "but I do know that my wife was a good woman who must in her heart have believed in God and mankind even though she didn't proclaim it from the housetops. And if you say anything, I would like you to speak well rather than ill of her, for I had a great admiration for the woman."

The minister's tact forbade him to dispute this eulogy of a simple, undistinguished woman who had lived for one summer only and then had died; but he pointed to the portrait of the Princess Augusta with an air of admonition that was all the more expressive, and said: "If you would see the likeness of a woman who was an example to others as a princess, a wife, and a human being, then there it hangs. It would do you no harm to remember it, you scurvy little runts who have always thought yourselves too proud to bow your lousy heads before the grace of the Holy Ghost, even though you stand lower in the community than the very sheep you kill with famine and tapeworm every spring that God grants us. But King Christian's children were wakened up there every morning at six, to be one with their Saviour in every kind of weather, and there they went on praying till the court chaplain himself spewed with hunger. What do you think of that?"

Bjartur could no longer restrain his laughter. "Hahaha, hahaha," he guffawed, "it was very like that business with the dog at Rauthsmyri, then, the one that couldn't keep away from the horse-meat, a year or two ago."

"Eh?" said the Reverend Gudmundur very seriously, pulling up in mid-floor, his mouth gaping in perplexity and his eyebrows raised in astonishment.

"Why, it was like this," said Bjartur. "There was a lad at Myri who came from the town, a daft fellow and rather a vicious customer, and he took it into his head to make friends with all the dogs and lure them from their rightful masters, my dog among them. I've always been great on dogs, she was a grand little bitch, trusty and clever. Hahaha, hahaha."

"I don't understand," snapped the minister, still not moving.

"I didn't think you would," said Bjartur laughing. "I didn't understand it either until she began to vomit up gobbets of horse-meat as big as your fist, man. If the young devil hadn't been up to the same trick all winter; stealing horse-meat from the kitchen to entice the dogs."

"Here, I can't stick any more of this," said the minister. "For heaven's sake get on your way."

"Yes, your reverence," said Bjartur soberly. "No one can control his own thoughts. I hope it harms nobody. And thank you kindly for the coffee. It's some of the very best coffee I've tasted for many a day. And we can rely on each other about the young ram in the autumn and the other business."

"It is to be hoped that I am dead before the spring," said the minister piously, "dead, dead to this monstrous rabble. Good-bye."

But Bjartur was by no means disposed to leave at this stage. He continued hanging about the minister, fiddling with this and that, till finally he plucked up courage and said:

"By the way, Reverend Gudmundur, did I hear you say something about a woman, or rather two women, just now?"

"Now then, what are you after?" demanded the minister testily. "Do you want them? You needn't think I'm keen on getting rid of them."

"Who are they, anyway?"

"God in His mercy alone provides for them. I brought them from Sandgilsheath on my own pack-horse, they belong to my own parish-of-ease. The father of the house died of internal trouble, and all they had were seventeen miserable-looking sheep, a few broken implements, and a couple of twenty-five-year-old mares, which they gave me as contribution to their keep when they came here in the autumn, so help me God. They are, of course, quite prostrate with grief. The old man farmed for forty years and never saved a penny, it was such a ghastly holding."

"Oh?" said Bjartur. "So they do own a bit of land."

"Certainly they own land," said the minister; then rushing to the door, opened it and bawled: "Fetch me Finna and old Hallbera immediately. There's a man here wants to take them away."

A few minutes elapsed, then in through the opening there edged a couple of women, the mother knitting, a brown skull-cap on her head and hairs sprouting from a wart on her chin, sour-faced as anyone that has been shut up within herself for three score years and more, not looking up, but peering with blinking eyes down her nose at her knitting, her head on the slant; the daughter a woman in the late thirties, clumsily built, especially below, but making up in mildly smiling anticipation for what the mother lacked in tenderness. They halted shoulder to shoulder not more than a span from the threshold, making it impossible for anyone to close the door behind them. The old woman kept on knitting, the daughter looked at the men with big eyes that hoped for everything. She had the purple mark of an old chilblain on her cheek, and obvious palpitation.

"Here stands a gentleman who is going to lighten us all of a heavy burden," said the minister. "He intends to take us home with him. His wife lies on her bier, God help me, and he is absolutely prostrate with grief."

"Yes, I know, poor man," mumbled the old woman into her needles without looking up. Her daughter gazed with eyes full of heartfelt sympathy at the unhappy gentleman.

"Well, if it isn't the womenfolk of Urtharsel, Ragnar's widow and his daughter," exclaimed Bjartur, offering them his hand in greeting and thanking them from the bottom of his heart for their old hospitality; he had stayed a night with them one autumn four or five years ago when he was out tracking down some stray or other for the Bailiff, and not the first time either. Yes, he remembered Ragnar all right, a genius: nobody could handle an infected sheep like him — he would sooner see his family short of sugar and coffee than his lambs without their chaw. "Hadn't he the right ear tipped and the left pierced and double-snicked? Yes? Bull's-eye for Bjartur. Hadn't he a sandy-haired dog as well, a marvellous animal that could see better in the dark than most other dogs in daylight? Damn me if it wasn't second-sighted; not everybody's fortunate enough to fall in with an animal like that, I can tell you."

All this proved to be correct. Finna beamed with gratitude at the genial condescension implicit in her erstwhile guest's tenacity of memory. She herself remembered as if it were yesterday the occasion when he had spent the night at Urtharsel, neither more nor less than the shepherd of Utirauthsmyri in person; it wasn't so often that people came to stay the night, and very seldom anyone from the bigger farms. Mother and daughter, indeed, whispering together, had concluded that it wasn't so easy to entertain a man that came from the Big House itself, a man who was accustomed surely to nothing but the best, what was to be done? Hallbera had suggested baking ember scones, but her daughter had said: "No, he'd never even dream of allowing stuff that's baked on the bare peat to pass his lips, a man from Utirauthsmyri — you haven't forgotten that surely, have you, Mother?"

But the old woman said that she had long since forgotten everything; she no longer remembered anything from the past or the present except her young days and a few sacred verses, she had grown such a terrible old wreck, and if it hadn't been for the good minister, who had taken pity on them when the hand of the Almighty had seen fit to take poor Ragnar —

"Aren't I telling you that the man wants to take you away?" interrupted the minister impatiently. "You'll be all right with him. He started a farm on that wonderful estate of his last spring, and he's a sort of new-fangled progressive with decided views about this desert shall blossom like a rose movement that they are always voting through Parliament and writing about in the papers in Reykjavik."

"Oh, I don't bother my head too much about what they write in the papers in Reykjavik," said Bjartur. "But I maintain all the same that there's a great future in Summerhouses for those that value their freedom at all and want to be men of independence."

Then the old woman said in her strained, quavering voice:

"They wouldn't have thought your wife's death so natural in my time, Bjartur my good man. And that lambing fold of yours has a funny reputation according to all that I've heard."

"Pshaw," snorted the minister in angry disagreement. "Urtharsel was swarming with all sorts of ghosts as well. Twice I've lost my way over the fell there, both times in broad daylight and the height of summer, so help me God."

"One or two people from the homesteads did have a pixy to announce them sometimes," agreed the old woman, "but our neighbours on the moors were good neighbours all the forty years that I lived there, as God and men may witness."

"Mother means that we were never haunted except when certain people were coming," said the daughter in explanation. "But we had good friends there on the moors, and they were often very useful to us."

"I refuse to discuss anybody whose name isn't in the parish register," said the minister.

"We had many a nice cup of coffee from them in dreams all the same," said the daughter. "And they were never anything but liberal with the sugar."

"Um, we'd many a tasty bite and sup from them," confirmed the old woman reverently.

The minister paraded the floor, snorting his disapproval, but Bjartur declared that he had never denied that there was much that was strange in nature. "I consider that there's nothing wrong in believing in elves even though their names aren't on the parish register," he said. "It hurts no one, yes and even does you good rather than harm; but to believe in ghosts and ghouls — that I contend is nothing but the remnants of popery and hardly fit for a Christian to give even a moment's consideration." He did his utmost to persuade the women to accept his views on these matters.

21.   BEARERS

ON Saturday morning the bearers came trudging over the marshes with their dogs. There were four of them, all old acquaintances: the Fell King, Einar, the poet of Undirhlith, then Olafur of Yztadale, friend of the incredible, and lastly the father of the deceased, old Thorthur of Nithurkot. They were walking not in a group, but at a great distance from one another, like men who have set out on journeys of their own to destinations that do not concern the others. The Fell King arrived first, and the others trailed in one by one after him, Thorthur of Nithurkot last. They were all in their Sunday clothes, with their socks turned up over their trouser bottoms.

Bjartur was not the one to harbour his grief; he welcomed his guests in royal style. "Step into the palace, lads," he cried; "it's biting sharp today, but comfort yourselves, the womenfolk have the kettle on." They took out their knives and began scraping the snow from their clothes. It had been terrible going, they said, hard on top, soft beneath, slippery. The old man, groaning and reluctant in his movements, cautiously took a seat on the doorstep, his joints creaking as if he were about to break in pieces. He seemed all shrunk in upon himself, blue in the face, rime in the tatters of his beard, the lids and corners of his eyes inflamed and the iris colourless with old age. On freshly cut turf between the sheep's mangers stood the coffin, decorated by tufts of wool that had stuck by chance to the tarred planks when the sheep crowded out for their midday drink from a hole broken in the surface of the ice-bound brook. The old man pressed his gnarled blue hands here and there on the coffin, as if to test its strength — or were these his caresses? Carefully and with an innate sense of tidiness he plucked some of the tufts from the wood. This outer part of the stable was reserved for the ewes, the inner part being divided into a pen for the lambs and a stall for the horse. The smell of the horse's urine overpowered all the other smells in the stable, for the drain was out of order.

The two women on loan from Rauthsmyri were busy upstairs with the baby and the fire. They had scrubbed the roof and the floor clean. The men left their dogs outside as a token of their respect for the dead, but otherwise their behaviour was much the same as usual, no impediment being allowed to interfere with their wholehearted discussion of the weather, no fastidiousness to temper the special frame of mind sacred to that topic. The snuff-horns went the rounds. Einar of Undirhlith handed Bjartur the usual elegy, written on a tattered piece of paper, and Bjartur gazed at the superscription with a wry face, mistrustful in advance of the tenor of his friend's poetry, then stuck it indifferently up under a rafter. The old man from Nithurkot wiped the moisture from his eyes with his snuffed-stained handkerchief. When the company had decided that the wind looked like settling in the southwest, Thorthur gave it as his opinion that it would stay there for the winter. This was his only contribution to the discussion, for he had reached an age when one begins to lose all faith in the weather, and there was really so little left to him in the world, except the mill-cot by the brook at home. It was not that he felt bitter against anyone, it was only that he found it difficult to speak. Whenever he opened his mouth to say anything, it was as if something suddenly gripped him by the throat; he looked as if he might burst out giggling on the spot. Something idiotic would appear in his features, some dissolution, as if his face were cracking from inside and would fall in pieces at the slightest exertion — even that of making a trivial little remark about the weather.

Olafur of Yztadale declared that a frosty winter was easy enough to understand after a showery summer: the wet and the dry must balance in nature.

The Fell King considered that since the hard weather had begun so early, surely it would thaw before Christmas and then give them a long period of mild weather, like, for instance, the winter six years ago. He was, on the whole, of the opinion that it would prove to be no worse than a fairly good winter and said that there was certainly no need to despair even though it did show its claws early.

Einar of Undirhlith said that in general his prophecies were based on intuition and dreams, and that he had a feeling, in spite of what the Fell King had just said, that it would be a severe winter and that they had better not be too generous with the hay. But he felt sure they would have a fine spring, for in a dream he had seen, at a great distance from him, a beautiful young girl from the south-country.

"Well, personally I never had much faith in these dreams of women," said Bjartur, refusing to be infected with such ill-founded optimism. "They're little enough to be relied on when you're awake, bless them, but still less when you're asleep."

"But surely if you could only interpret dreams, you'd find the sort in which women appear just as reliable as any other kind," protested Einar.

"You're quite right," interrupted the housekeeper with great heat. "Certainly they're reliable; and he ought to be ashamed of himself, the way he talks, and his wife lying there."

"Let's forget about dreams for the moment, then," suggested the Fell King, who was always prepared to act as mediator between these two noteworthy poets. "Well, to turn the conversation to what we were discussing earlier in the autumn, I want

everybody, while I remember, to know that I have now received
a new physic from Dr. Finsen. I referred to him the complaints
made by several of our local worthies, yours among them, Bjartur,
and he wrote for an absolutely special preparation for us. And
according to what he said himself, the makers give an out-and-out
guarantee that it will cleanse the dogs thoroughly, not only as
regards tapeworm, but as regards the blood and the nerves of
the whole body as well."

They said that it wasn't before time; a fox was a curse and tapeworm a damn sight worse. All of them had the same story to tell
of their dogs, every single one infected. Men and beasts were in
danger. They demanded that the Fell King strike a decisive blow.

"Of course," said he, "and you'll receive from me as soon as
possible the annual circular dealing with the subject. My idea was
to administer the treatment about the same date as the parliamentary elections, so that you could bring your dogs along with
you on your way to vote and get everything over on one journey.
It's a help to the smaller farmer, with no one to do his bidding, to
have to make only the one trip."

"What happened about the assistant dog-doctor?" inquired
Olafur of Yztadale, who perhaps, like many another, had dreamed
of a morsel of food and honour in this connection. "Didn't you
say in the autumn that the Sheriff was half-thinking of appointing
an assistant for the district?"

"Yes, but there are one or two things to be taken into consideration first," replied the Fell King with some gravity. "These
are difficult times, you know, and the county is hardly in a position to increase its expenditure to any great extent. And then
again, well, I've always been of the opinion that to appoint an
assistant in the parish here, when I am supposed to fulfil these
duties, would be to pass a sort of vote of no confidence not only in
me and Dr. Finsen, but in the government as well, for it is the government that supplies the physic. I would be only too pleased, on
the other hand, to resign at any time. And that was what I told
the Sheriff; that either I handed in my resignation or I did the
work on my own responsibility."

"Well, it's the same as I've always said," declared Olafur, whose
disappointment had not been so very great. "If the physic was
scientific from the beginning, then the dogs wouldn't be constipated."

"As I said before," rejoined the Fell King, "it is the authorities
that provide the medicine."

("Oh, the authorities will never cheat you," interposed the old man from Nithurkot, full of gratuitous trustfulness.)

"Quite right," agreed the Fell King. "I personally consider that the government we have had in the country for the past few years has served the people well. And in the person of the doctor we have had a most public-spirited gentleman to represent our constituency in Parliament, a man who has ever been willing to do everything possible for us, both as a doctor, a man, and a member of the Althingi."

There was silence for a while, and the crofters, feeling that the conversation was verging on the political, thoughtfully studied the broad, calloused palms of their hands.

"I shouldn't be surprised if some people didn't look at the doctor with rather different eyes," remarked Einar of Undirhlith at last. "And one thing is certain: those who don't deal with the merchant in Fjord won't vote for the candidate put up in Fjord."

"Yes, I think we all know our good Bailiff," said Bjartur. "If the government was for sale he would buy it up, stick on a percentage, and peddle it round to see if anybody would be fool enough to buy it."

(The housekeeper muttering to herself in front of the range: "It's shameful to hear the way he talks about his benefactor, almost, you might say, his foster-father. No wonder misfortune dogs such a person.")

It was obvious that Einar's political opinions were not of the healthiest, so the Fell King proceeded in a helpful spirit to show him where he erred. "I don't suppose, for instance, Einar," he said, "that you ever had a bill from Finsen for all the medicine your poor mother had a few years ago."

Einar could not deny that it was still owing the doctor — there were about two hundred bottles of it.

"Yes, it doesn't take much medicine to add up to the price of a cow," observed the Fell King.

This silenced Einar of Undirhlith for the moment, because he knew that the others must all be acquainted with the fact that he had mortgaged his cow and half his stock to pay off a debt owing to the Bailiff in Utirauthsmyri; but he added finally that a cow was a cow, medicine medicine, a government a government, and actually he was thinking of sitting at home during the next elections.

But whenever the conversation turned to politics, Olafur of Yztadale was apt to let his attention wander, for his interests lay in other directions. The baby had waked up and was now crying, so the housekeeper left what she was doing to attend to it. Olafur was of the disposition that marvels at these little human creatures, if creatures they can be called, which come thus into the world to replace those that disappear. "It's marvellous, you know, when you come to think of it: there you have a new body and a new soul suddenly making their appearance, and where do they come from and why are they always coming? Yes, I've asked myself that same question many a time, both night and day. As if it wouldn't have been more natural to let the same folk live in the world continually; then there would have been at least some likelihood of ordinary people like you and me working their way up into a comfortable position eventually."

But even the housekeeper was unable, or unwilling, to solve this problem. So Olafur of Yztadale continued:

"To me the strangest thing about these little whippersnappers is this, though: that they say it has been proved that new-born children can swim absolutely of their own accord, if you put them in water. Have you ever tried it, Gudny?"

No, the housekeeper had never tried it, and advised Olafur dryly not to advertise it too widely if he ever thought of trying it on his own children — such an experiment might be variously interpreted.

Olafur said there wasn't much danger of that, he was the type that wasn't much given to messing about with new-born babies. "But," he added, "I've sometimes had occasion to do away with new-born pups, and I can tell you something that's extremely interesting about them. I've lopped off their heads on the river bank at home there, with the clasp-knife, you know, and then flung the bodies out into the river, and now there's one question I'd like to lay before you: what do you think the bodies do; do you think they float, or do you think they sink?"

This question switched the minds of the assembly away from all consideration of politics and the dilemma that these two candidates, the one from Fjord, the other from Vik, imposed upon the troubled electors. The women thought that naturally the pups' bodies would sink, Einar was of the opinion that they might conceivably float on top, while the Fell King favoured the theory that they would float under water.

"No-ho," cried Olafur triumphantly, proud of having diverted everyone's interest into scientific channels. "They swim; they neither more nor less than swim exactly the same as any grown-up dog complete with head and everything, and that's as true as I'm sitting here."

But at that moment the beloved coffee arrived, to put an end to this instructive discussion of the stranger phenomena of nature. It was good coffee; no one need have been ashamed of such coffee, however high he stood in the social scale. Such coffee made you sweat like a horse. Drink up, lads, drink. And there were also lovely cakes with the coffee, thick slices of Christmas cake with big raisins, fat doughnuts, and pancakes loaded with sugar. Eat up, lads, eat up. Happily they fell upon these luxuries; to the devil with personal opinions and interests. Cupful after cupful they swilled, without making a sound other than guzzling and crunching and the snuffling of nostrils charged with tobacco.

"It may be a while before I invite you to another feast," said Bjartur of Summerhouses.

Finally each had had his fill and had wiped his mouth on his sleeve and the back of his hand. Then there was silence. It was the silence of the occasion, the silence that sooner or later must impose itself on all funerals, broken occasionally by a churchlike clearing of the throat and accompanied by a vacant staring of the eyes.

"Had you thought of any ceremony here in the house?"

"No," was Bjartur's reply. "I couldn't persuade that mule of a parson of ours to drag himself up into the valley here, all because of his blasted whimsies. Not that it makes any difference."

"Her mother would maybe like it better if we sang something nice while she is being taken out," said the old man apologetically, " — so I brought the *Passion Hymns* with me."

"Why man, what difference do you think that will make?" asked Bjartur.

"She was our own Christian child," said the old man dejectedly.

When Bjartur saw how determined he was, he allowed him to have his own way.

Blesi was standing ready-saddled, tethered to the doorpost, a heavy horse, long in the head, twitching his nether lip a little now and again as if he were talking to himself, moving his ears in turn, the events of the house mirrored in his receptive, introspective eye. The dog whined, shivering behind the stairway with its tail between its legs and fawning on no one.

Most of the sheep had returned from the brook home to the croft. A few wiggled their way past the horse into the house and after sniffing at the mangers gave a disappointed bleat because they had not been replenished. More and more trickled into the house to meet with the same disappointment. Others thronged about the doorway or faced defiantly up to the visitors' dogs. They helped to give the funeral the appearance of a good following, much sympathy, and the increased warmth that is so much appreciated on such a day in the midst of the marsh's frozen snow, the high moor's glacier-covered reaches. The folk had all arranged themselves round the coffin. Old Thorthur of Nithurkot unfolded the handkerchief from his wife's volume of Hallgrimur Pjetursson's *Passion Hymns* and started looking for the place he had marked with a dog's-ear.

"Wouldn't somebody with a good voice like to begin?"

The book was passed round from one to another, but it seemed that no one knew the tune: it was so seldom that anyone went to church, and they had forgotten all the hymn tunes long ago. So the old man took the book himself and began trying to reach the note. A ewe looked at him and gave vent to a full-throated bleat.

Then the old man began to sing over his darling. He sang of when the Redeemer is led out, hymn twenty-five: "So many wounds that I may rest in peace." He knew it all by heart, without looking at the book, but his voice was toneless and husky and could not keep to any definite tune. Even the men around him felt that he did not sing well.

> And so the angels of the Lord will say:
> Look upon this man.

The horse pricked its ears and snorted. Again and again the dog gave a pitiful howl, as if someone were torturing it, and the ewes bleated on, like a long funeral procession, both outside and in, because they had not been given their fodder. He sang the last verse in a tuneless screech: "Truly art thou Son of God," and the tears streamed unending from the inflamed lids down into the scraggy beard. His pronunciation too was difficult and lisping, because of his missing teeth; sometimes his song was nothing more than a feeble tremor of the throat and jaws. He was like any speechless child that has long wept. Then there was silence.

"Wouldn't it be better to say the Lord's Prayer?"

The Fell King took the old man by the arm so that he should not fall, and whispered: "Gudny here wants to know whether it wouldn't be better to say the Lord's Prayer."

So the old man wept the Lord's Prayer, without ceasing to tremble, without lifting his head, without taking the handkerchief from his eyes. More than half the words were drowned in the heaving of his sobs; it was not so easy to make out what he said: "Our Father, which art in Heaven, yes, so infinitely far away that no one knows where You are, almost nowhere, give us this day just a few crumbs to eat in the name of Thy Glory, and forgive us if we can't pay the dealer and our creditors and let us not, above all, be tempted to be happy, for Thine is the Kingdom" — perhaps it was difficult to imagine a place equally well chosen for this engaging prayer; it was as if the Redeemer had written it for the occasion. They stood with bowed heads, all except Bjartur, who would never dream of bowing his head for an unrhymed prayer. They they lifted the coffin out. They lifted it on to the horse and tied it across the saddle, then laid a hand on each end to steady it.

"Has the horse been spoken to?" asked the old man; and as it had not yet been done, he took an ear in each hand and whispered to it, according to ancient custom, for horses understand these things:

"You carry a coffin today. You carry a coffin today."

Then the funeral procession moved off.

The Fell King walked in the van, keeping as far as possible to the patches that were bare of snow, so that there would be less danger of mishap. Einar of Undirhlith led the horse, Olafur and Bjartur walked at each end of the coffin, and the old man limped along in the rear with his stick and the huge mittens with the flapping thumbs.

The women stood at the door with tear-swollen faces, watching the procession disappear in the whirling snow.

22.   DRIFTING SNOW

THE GOING was slow over the ridge, for it was often impossible to find a clear path however far they deviated from their route. They sank repeatedly into deep snowdrifts on the hillsides and had to be on the watch all the time lest the coffin roll off the saddle. The body did not arrive at Rauthsmyri till late in the afternoon. Dusk was beginning to fall. The minister had arrived some time beforehand; though his face was completely inscrutable, he was obviously pressed for time. A few other visitors were also waiting for this funeral and the coffee that would follow it. The coffin was carried straight into the church in compliance with the minister's request and the bells were rung. Feeble was the sound

they made, feeble their intrusion on frozen nature's winter om-
nipotence, their peal reminiscent of nothing so much as the jingle
of a child's toy. And the folk came trailing out of the drifting snow
and into the church, timid in the face of death, which never seems
so irrevocable as when bells of such a kind tinkle so helplessly in
the cold, white spaces of declining day. The Bailiff's wife had not
come to the funeral, not even as a mere spectator. On such a
winter day not even she felt very well; she had caught a chill
apparently and was sitting at home in her room snuffing hot water
and salt up her nose, guaranteed to kill any cold. The Bailiff himself, however, had turned up, and if he was wearing his old
trousers that were giving way round the patches, he had at least
thrown on another jacket in recognition of the occasion, and took
his seat in the chancel as usual and was careful not to open his
mouth throughout the service. Blesi had been tied to the gate,
and as the dog was not allowed inside because of the rites, it
waited outside on the threshold, shivering.

The minister entered, wearing his crumpled parish-of-ease
cassock and a pair of white bands round his neck because the
occasion was not important enough for a ruff. Some of the crofters
began singing: "I live and know," each to a tune of his own. The old
man was sitting at the back, no longer weeping, as if his emotions
had dried up. During the music the minister pulled his watch out
twice in front of the coffin, as if he had no time for this sort of
thing. When the music was over, he put on his spectacles and
read the prayer from his tattered old book. It was an old prayer,
as was only to be expected in such weather, and besides, the man
was hoarse. Then, instead of the long one he had threatened, he
delivered a short sermon, in which, after declaring that evil spirits
lay in ambush for mankind, he proceeded to discuss unbelief in
terms that were none too complimentary. He said that many people had neglected their Creator while they were chasing stupid
sheep over the mountains. "What are sheep?" he asked. He said
that sheep had been a greater curse to the Icelandic nation than
foxes and tapeworms put together. "Sheep's clothing disguises a
ferocious wolf that has sometimes been referred to in this district
as the Albogastathir Fiend, whom others name Kolumkilli. People
run after sheep all their lives long and never find them. Such is the
lesson we may learn from the parting that oppresses us today."

The sermon over, he spared a few words for the dead woman's
career; no career, really, but a proof of how insignificant the
individual is as he appears in the parish register. What was the

individual considered as a separate unit? "Nothing — a name, at most a date. Me today, you tomorrow. Let us unite in prayer to the God who stands above the individual, while our names rot in the registers." No weeping or wailing or gnashing of teeth, no emotion, no flirting with the heart-strings — a sleepy Lord's Prayer and a clipped amen. In his contradictions he was as much an enigma as the country itself: a religious devotee out of spite at the soullessness of men who thought of nothing but dogs and sheep, a scientific breeder of sheep because of his contempt for sheep, the Icelandic pastor of a thousand years' folk-stories, his presence alone was a comfortable reassurance that all was as it should be.

The coffin was now borne out.

It was lowered into the grave by means of two ropes, and the mourners hung about near the edge for a while longer. Three crofters with bared heads sang "As the one blossom" in the drifting snow; it was a sort of commemoration day for Hallgrimur Pjetursson, a cold day. The dog stood whining near Bjartur, its tail between its legs as if it had been whipped, and still shivering. The minister threw a few handfuls of earth on the coffin in silence, then with noisy gusto sniffed up a couple of good pinches of snuff from the box offered him by the Fell King, his parish clerk. The bearers eagerly grabbed their spades and set to work with a will. One by one others trailed off.

23.   FIRE OF FROST

BJARTUR did not make the journey back to Summerhouses till the following day. The dog padded along beside him in blissful anticipation. It is lovely to be going home. And whenever she was a few yards ahead of her master, she would halt and look back at him with eyes full of an unwavering faith, then return to him on a big curve. Her reverence for her master was so great that she did not presume even to walk ahead of him. A dog finds in a man the things it looks for. He leaned into the gusts of driven snow, leading Blesi by the reins and casting an occasional glance at his dog — poor little thing, lousy and wormy, but where is fidelity to be found if not in those brown eyes — where the loyalty that nothing can subvert? Misfortune, dishonour, the pricks of conscience, nothing can quench this fire — poor little bitch, in her eyes Bjartur of Summerhouses must always be highest, greatest, best; the incomparable. Man finds in the eyes of a dog the things he looks for.

Hell, but Blesi is heavy on the lead today. And yet there is a living creature on his back. A living creature? Who? It is the old woman from Urtharsel, riding sideways on the saddle and muffled up to the eyes in sacks and shawls. Her belongings and those of her daughter dangle from the saddle. Finna follows in their tracks, her face weatherbeaten, her gait clumsy, her skirts kilted above her knees.

Nothing was said. And on crawled the little procession in the direction of Summerhouses, men and animals, men-animals, five souls. The pale red sun grazed the surface of the moorland bluffs on this northern winter's morning which was really only an evening. And yet it was midday. The light gilded the clouds of snow flying over the moors so that they seemed one unbroken ocean of fire, one radiant fire of gold with streaming flames and glimmering smoke from east to west over the whole frozen expanse. Through this golden fire of frost, comparable in its magic to nothing but the most powerful and elaborate witchcraft of the Ballads, lay their homeward way.

The women from Myri greeted the new arrivals with dumb courtesy, but were none the less importunate in their demands for the milk which Bjartur had promised to bring back with him; they had had to give the baby thin gruel in its sucking bag. When they had made coffee for the newcomers their task was over, so they gathered their belongings together and made ready to go. Bjartur offered to accompany them over the ridge, but they declined with thanks and took leave of both him and the newcomers with the same kind of politeness as that with which they had welcomed them. Finna was left with the baby in her lap, to give it its bottle for the first time. And the old crone began fussing about in the house.

Though it was still early in the evening, Bjartur went to bed as soon as he had seen to the livestock. He felt really that he had had no rest since the last night he had spent at home with Rosa. He was glad that he had at least said good-bye before he left. It had been an adventurous round-up, and it was only this evening that he felt he had really returned. Every time that he had gone to bed since his return from the deserts he had felt, just as he was dozing off, a sudden storm of snow beating in his face and a voluptuous torpor stealing up his legs, up his thighs, all the way up to his stomach. And he had jumped up in a panic, certain that if he let himself fall asleep he would die in the blizzard. It was for this reason that he always slept so badly afterwards. In the middle of the night he would start up with a bawdy verse on his lips, or some scurrilous old lampoon ridiculing bailiffs or merchants, and would be on the point of jumping out of bed to thump himself warm before he recollected himself.

But tonight he felt he was no longer in any danger.

The light in the wall lamp had been quenched for economy's sake, but there was a glimmer from the little dip flickering on the shelf above the old woman's bed. Mother and daughter sat for a long time together, murmuring in the gleam from the little dip. From down below, a sheep could be heard belching occasionally, or Blesi in his narrow stall would shift his feet and give a little snort into the manger. The dog, lying against the wall under the range, would rise now and then to scratch itself, its hind leg thumping the wall in the process, yawn, curl up again. From the bed on the other side was heard the child's shallow breathing, and an occasional whimper as if it were going to cry. However, it did not start crying, but fell asleep again.

At last the whispering was over and Finna came to take off her clothes. He heard her unbutton her coat and step out of her skirt. She drew a tightly fitting underskirt over her head with some difficulty. Then she got into bed beside the baby and removed the rest of her clothes beneath the coverlet. He heard her unfasten two or three buttons more, then wriggle out of her underclothes. She stretched herself out and scratched herself here and there, yawning sleepily and noisily.

The old woman still remained sitting on the edge of her bed in the glimmer from the dip, with her elbows in her lap now and a finger between her toothless gums. She was gazing down the hatchway, muttering something occasionally. Twice she went forward to the hatchway, cried shame on something and spat. On the second occasion she stood rocking herself backwards and forwards for a while, staring down and mumbling:

> *"Fie upon thee, false fox,*
> *Fare from my dwelling;*
> *At this door Jesu knocks,*
> *Flee hence at His telling.*
> *Out Kurkur,*
> *In Jesus,*
> *Out Kolumkel,*
> *In God's angel,*
> *Out Ragerist,*

In Jesukrist,
Out Valedictus,
In Benedictus — "

When she had recited this holy old prayer she crossed herself and said: "We give ourselves all into God's hands and good night."

Then she closed the trapdoor and went to bed.

And with that they all composed themselves for sleep.

PART II

Free of Debt

---

24. WINTER MORNING

SLOWLY, slowly winter day opens his arctic eye.

From the moment when he gives his first drowsy blink to the
time when his leaden lids have finally opened wide, there passes
not merely hour after hour; no, age follows age through the immeasurable expanses of the morning, world follows world, as in
the visions of a blind man; reality follows reality and is no more
— the light grows brighter. So distant is winter day on his own
morning. Even his morning is distant from itself. The first faint
gleam on the horizon and the full brightness on the window at
breakfast-time are like two different beginnings, two starting-
points. And since at dawn even his morning is distant, what must
his evening be? Forenoon, noon, and afternoon are as far off as
the countries we hope to see when we grow up; evening as remote and unreal as death, which the youngest son was told about
yesterday, death which takes little children away from their
mothers and makes the minister bury them in the Bailiff's garden,
death from which no one returns, as in grandmother's stories,
death which will call for you, too, when you have grown so old
that you have become a child again.

"Is it only little babies that die, then?" he had asked.

Why had he asked?

It was because yesterday his father had gone across to the
homesteads with the little baby that had died. He had carried
it away in a box on his back to have it buried by the minister and
the Bailiff. The minister would dig a hole in the Bailiff's churchyard and sing a song.

"Shall I ever be a little baby again?" asked the seven-year-
old boy.

And his mother, who had sung him remarkable songs and told

him all about foreign countries, answered weakly from the sick-
bed on which she was lying:

"When anyone grows very old he becomes like a little baby
again."

"And dies?" asked the boy.

It was a string in his breast that snapped, one of those delicate
childhood strings which break before one has had time to realize
that they are capable of sounding; and these strings sound no
more; henceforth they are only a memory of incredible days.

"We all die."

Later in the day he had broached the subject again, this time
with his grandmother:

"I know somebody who'll never die," he said.

"Really, my pet?" she inquired, peering at him down her nose
with her head tilted to one side, as was her fashion when she was
looking at anyone. "And who might he be?"

"My father," replied the boy resolutely. Yet he was not absolutely certain whether he might not be making a mistake, for he
kept on gazing at his grandmother with questioning eyes.

"Oh, he'll die, he'll die all right," snorted the old woman re-
morselessly, almost gloatingly, and blew sharply down her nose.

This answer only roused the boy's stubbornness, and he asked:
"Granny, will the pot-stick ever die?"

"That'll do," snapped the old woman, as if she thought he was
making fun of her.

"But, Granny, what about the black pan? Will that ever die?"

"Nonsense, child," she retorted. "How can anything die when
it's dead already."

"But the pot-stick and the pan aren't dead," said the little boy.
"I know they aren't dead. When I wake up in the morning I often
hear them talking together."

How foolish of him: there he had gone and blurted out a
secret known only to himself, for he alone had discovered that,
during what was perhaps the most remarkable of all the morning's
expanses of time, the pots and pans and other kitchen utensils
changed their shapes and became men and women. Early in the
morning, when he lay awake long before the others, he could
hear them talking away to one another with the grave composure
and the weighty vocabulary that is proper to cooking utensils
alone. Nor was it merely by chance that he had referred to the
pot-stick first, for the pot-stick, after all, is a sort of aristocrat
among utensils; rarely used, and then as a rule for meat soup,

that most appetizing of dishes, it spends most of its time hanging on the wall in spotless cleanliness and decorative idleness. Once it is taken down, however, the part it plays in the pot is most noteworthy. The boy therefore regarded the pot-stick with particular respect, and felt there was no one he could liken it to but the Bailiff's wife. The black pot, which was so often full to the brim and sometimes had a burnt crust at the bottom and a lot of soot underneath, the black pot was no other than the Bailiff of Myri, whose mouth was always crammed with tobacco. He could easily be seen simmering at times, and it was quite certain that there was a fire in his inside and that he had a Bailiff's wife to stir him up so that he didn't boil over on official occasions. The other cooking things were all the same: in the dark they changed into men and women, some rich and important, others poor and of little account. The knives were ugly peasants whom he loathed and feared, the cups dumpy young women with roses on their aprons who made the boy feel shy with their roses; and at meals in the bright light of day he avoided touching these people, avoided giving them so much as a side-long glance even, lest they read in his face all that he knew of their adventures. By night they were complacent and full of self-assertion, by day slatternly and soiled, abject as sheepish visitors who sit and sniff and dare not move — he who knew so much about them in the liberty of their night felt sorry for them in the bondage of their day.

But one there was among them independent of night and day, of the freedom of the dark, of the bondage of the light; one that eclipsed the others with its splendour and made them look like so much trash. Such was the value attached to it that it was kept stored away at the bottom of the clothes-chest. The children saw it only if important visitors came at Christmas or on Summer Day, and even then they were never allowed to touch it, so precious was it. It was mother's cake-dish — a gift from the Bailiff of Myri's wife. It was the most beautiful dish in the whole world. On it there was a picture of a marvellous house half-hidden by flowering bushes. Leading up to the house lay a smooth winding path with green grass and smiling bushes on either side. And who was that standing on the path in a blue dress and a white hat, with flowers in her hand and the sun in her heart? He knew very well who it was, but he had never told a soul. It was the Bailiff's daughter, Audur, who had gone abroad in the autumn and who would

return in the spring like a bird. And the house half-hidden
by flowers was Audur's house in far-off countries. Some day little
Nonni would no longer be a little boy who slept in his grandmother's bed.

For a while he was silent as he sat beside her on the bed, busy
with his knitting. But presently he could contain himself no longer.

"I know something," he said, letting the needles droop as he
gazed at his grandmother. "I bet you I know something that can
never, never die."

"Oh?"

"Never," he repeated.

"Well, tell me what it is then, child. Out with it."

"No," he said with great resolution. "I'm never going to tell
a soul."

Taking the wool with his right index finger, he looped it ready
for the next stitch. It might be that now and then he did let out
a secret or two, but one thing was above life and death, above the
freedom of the dark, the humiliation of the day. What it was not
a soul would ever get to know. The secret of mother's cake-dish.

There are few things that fill the soul of man with greater disappointment than to wake up when everybody else is asleep,
especially if it happens to be very early in the morning. Not before one is awake does one realize how far one's dreams have
transcended reality. Often the youngest son would dream of a
dime, a quarter, even two quarters, but he would lose it all as
soon as he woke up. He would drink meat soup, not from a bowl,
but from a tub, and eat meat so fat that the grease trickled down
to his elbows. He would eat huge slices of Christmas cake from
a cake-dish without horizon, slices so thick that he could pick
raisins out of them easily as big as a man's eye. Such is the benefit that the human soul has from its dreams. But however hard
he tried he could never fall asleep again to these delicacies, nor
to the coins he had had in his hands, which were always of silver,
like the money his father paid the Bailiff on the land, and which
in his dream he had been going to spend on raisins and biscuits,
as well as a pocket-knife and some string.

He was usually very hungry when he woke up, and would lie
yearning for his dream like a dog for a bone it had lost, but he
had been strictly forbidden to wake anyone up and ask for bread;
otherwise his father would tie him up in the outhouse with the
Reverend Gudmundur and his brother ram, who sometimes fought

the whole night through. This was a most unpleasant prospect, for no animal scared him half as much as the Reverend Gudmundur. This ram, which hated the sight of human beings, had a nasty trick of chasing the boy all the way into his dreams and through his dreams, and the boy would run as hard as he could, from one dream into another, fleeing in terror from this monster, which in spite of his father's faith in its pedigree was as preternatural in its hideousness as the Christmas cake and the meat soup in their splendour. Thus there may also be an element of danger in a person's dreams.

To forget how hungry he was he would often settle down to listen to the pots and pans holding their nightly meeting in the cupboard and on the shelves. What did they talk about, then? It is not so very easy for a little boy to follow the thread of adult conversation — they talked like the people of the district round about, everyone competing with everyone else to get a word in somehow, so as to attract at least a little attention, and everyone grumbling about parish paupers and the burdens of old folk, who never seemed to die off at a respectable age. And the taxes these days, man alive! They complained bitterly of the extravagant habits of young women, the migration of youth to the towns, the difficult times, the high price of corn, the new worm that was attacking the sheep in place of the tapeworm. The pot-stick held that all these evils were due to the lack of music. It was strange how grown-up these kitchen things could be in the expressions they used. What impressed the boy most was not the powers of logical thought they showed in their conversation, but the knowledge, the experience, and the richness of vocabulary it revealed — names of distant places, marriages in other parts of the country, crafty verse, swear words, news from town. Sometimes they even fell out with one another. Someone would say that the harmonium in the church was not good enough, or that the merchant in Vik was better to deal with than the merchant in Fjord; some of them would have illegitimate children, others did not believe in national independence, while there were even those who went so far as to say that the best thing to do was to fill the pot with horse droppings. Some of them wanted to write poetry like this:

> *If strife be strong oh lake my lad,*
> *A mongrel to my say;*
> *If fought no favourer is sad*
> *To end his moilsome may.*

Others like this:

> *Sirry rimsy pomsy prams,*
> *Pirry limsy firry,*
> *Kirry simsy romsy rams,*
> *Rirry dimsy nirry.*

Oh dear, wasn't it getting any lighter yet?

Very cautiously, so as not to disturb the spectres in the dark, he would raise his head and peep over the foot of the bed.

The further it wore on towards morning, the more obvious did it become that the kitchen things were gradually exhausting their night's supply of wisdom. And as soon as their conversation dwindled, the boy's ears were free for other voices. The sheep below would scramble to their feet and, grunting a little, would ease themselves after the night. Some of them would rear on their hind legs to sniff the leavings of last night's hay, stick their horns into the mangers, or push each other about. As soon as the boy heard them get to their feet, hope would wake in his breast.

But of all the morning's time-signals the most reliable were his father's snores.

At dawn when the boy awoke, he would still be snoring with long, long, deep, deep snores. This kind really belonged not to morning but to the night itself. These snores bore no relation to the world we live and wake in; they were an alien excursion over tilted space, immeasurable time, extravagant existences; yes, the horses of this cavalcade had little in common with the horses of our world, and still less was the landscape of the snoring life akin to the landscape of day.

But as morning came nearer, his father's snores gradually lost their resonance, the resounding chest-notes dissolved on a slowly ascending scale, moved by degrees into the throat, from the throat into the nose and mouth, on to the lips with a whistle, sometimes only with a restless puff — the destination was near, the horses prancing with the joy of traversing scatheless the sounding wastes of infinity. The homeland lay spread before the eyes.

The breathing of the others lacked altogether the range and the magnificence of his father's snores, and was, moreover, heedless of time. Take Grandmother's breathing for instance. Who would ever imagine from her breathing that it was a living being that was sleeping beside the boy? She breathed so low and stirred so seldom that for hours on end nothing seemed more likely than that she had stopped altogether. But if he leaned over her and listened intently, he might occasionally hear signs of life, for her lips sometimes emitted a very faint puff. She had another trick too. After having lain for hours as if dead, life would rise to the surface in her like the slow little bubbles rising at long intervals from the bottom of the stagnant pools down in the marshes — life revealed in strange mutterings, whisperings, and grumblings, in odious psalms from another world. For she, too, had a world of her own which was unintelligible to others, a world of prayers and hymns, those long tiresome verses which his father detested so much, the world of the merciful and compassionate God, the forbearing Father and the terrors of hell. Of this world she never gave any description, unless, indeed, it was to mumble another prayer even more incomprehensible. No one who sang so many hymns and knew so much about the joys of the eternal life and so on could be more devoid of missionary fervour that was his grandmother. True, she had taught him to lie down to sleep with its language on his lips, but her world of prayer remained as bewilderingly isolated from human reality as his father's world of snores; he discerned nothing of its landscape through the words, and still less of its unsubstantial inhabitants. The alien life of the hymns, as it rose to his grandmother's unconscious lips, aroused in him the same dread as the pools in the marshes with their muddy, acrid water, their slime, and their shaggy, loathsome plants, their water-beetles.

Opposite their parents' bed slept the three older children, Helgi and Gvendur at the head, Asta Sollilja at the foot. To what world did Helgi's sleep-language belong, to what world the weeping of Asta Sollilja, the grating of her teeth? — a language without words or meaning, lacking all save imbecile fury; a weeping that had no tears to accompany it, no sob, only a sudden tearing pain that came without warning and vanished without trace, as if some frightful summons had been flashed through her limbs from world to world. None of these worlds, none of these voices, observed the laws of day or the feelings of this world.

Where was his mother on these mornings of winter when no one was at home and all were far away, each in his own sleep, while the shadows of other worlds pregnant with wonders brooded over the little living-room in Summerhouses? Was she asleep or awake? Were they her waking groans that were drowned again and again in his father's snores, or was the soothing hand of oblivion forbidden even in her world of sleep? Great was his longing for day as he lay there alone, surrounded by alien, cold-hearted worlds which did not even know that he existed — but greater still for his mother's arms.

There was one terrible night that he would always remember, no matter how long he lived. It must have been very early when it happened, yes, long before winter day made his first effort to open his weary eye, for the boy himself was still asleep, still abroad in the drifting landlessness of his own dream-worlds. So pleasant was his absence, so sweet and heavy the drowsiness of midnight pervading all his limbs, that he was reluctant to leave, but presently there came a moment when he felt he must cast off his lethargy and return — there was someone calling.

Who could it be? At first the cry was so distant that he did not seek to inquire, paying it as little attention as if it had been news from another shire. But gradually the noise came nearer; groans and wails, coming nearer and ever nearer. For a while it was as if they had even reached the mansion at Rauthsmyri, but they did not stop there, they came nearer and nearer still, until finally he found that they had come all the way into the room in which he was lying. They came from his mother. He was wide awake now. He was lying alone in his grandmother's bed. There was a candle burning in the room. His grandmother, mumbling, bent, and shaky-handed, was wrestling away with something over by the parents' bedside, while sitting on the edge was his father, holding his mother's hand. The children in the other bed had covered up their heads, but now and then staring, terrified eyes peeped out from under the blankets. But they did not dare to look at one another, they pretended to be asleep. Mother was dreadfully ill tonight. The groans became sharper and sharper, more and more painful to hear; it was the suffering of the world; the boy had been thinking of rising to ask about it, but now he thought no more of asking, he huddled down under the clothes. Then after a while his mother stopped groaning. His grandmother began to struggle with the fire in the little range, her endless struggle; for many generations now she had been struggling to kindle fires and heat water. A few moments passed. The boy's understanding ebbed away, the whispering voices of his father and his grandmother dwindled away up-country, vanished into another county. His father went creaking noisily down the staircase of a distant building, most probably the church at Rauthsmyri, or some church even more distant, and, closing the trapdoor after him, hurried away out into the night. But no sooner had he closed the door than his mother started screaming again, more painfully than ever; and again it was as if a cold paw with sharpened talons gripped the boy's heart. Why should those of whom one is fondest have to suffer the most, and why is it that one can never do anything for them?

Across the boy's mind, involuntarily, there flashed the idea that his father was to blame for all his mother's troubles. It was he who always slept with her, he who imagined he was her owner and her master. There must have been something on his conscience to make him so attentive to her tonight: he had held her hand, a thing he had never been seen to do before, and then he had rushed off somewhere in the middle of the night, as if he were afraid.

Few things are so inconstant, so unstable, as a loving heart, and yet it is the only place in the world where one can find sympathy. Sleep is stronger than the noblest instinct of a loving heart. In the middle of his mother's agony the light began to grow dim. The kettle's gurgling receded; the crackling of the fire, the bustling of his grandmother, her muttering and grumbling, her snatches of forgotten hymns, everything dissolved into fleeting half-wakeful dreams that no longer had beaks or claws, dreams empty of passion and suffering, blithe and desirable as the lives of the elves in the crags. The drowsiness of midnight, so sweet, so heavy, began again to flow through his limbs; and little by little, like a hundred grains of sand, his consciousness filtered down into the abyss of his sleep-world until oblivion had once more filled it full.

Yesterday his father had taken the little baby away over to Rauthsmyri to bury it.

Was his mother happy again, then? Was she again, like the children, reconciled to the monotony of horizonless winter days? Or were her groans still drowned in the pitilessness of depths that do not know the individual heart? Pain came to the children and was gone after a short while, but the mother's suffering was eternal. Never had the boy known the family to sleep so long as on this morning. The sheep had long since scrambled to their feet; he could hear them butting one another every few moments. His father had covered mile upon mile of chest-snores, the crockery was silent at the approach of morning, and winter day's eye was opening in bluish pallor on the window. Were they afraid to wake up, or what? He began tapping quietly with his fingernails on the sloping roof, a thing he could never, in spite of threats, restrain himself from doing when he felt that the morning was being prolonged too far. When this had no effect he began to squeak, first

like a little mouse, then sharper and higher, like the squeal of the dog when you tread on its tail, and finally higher still, like a land wind shrieking through the open door.

"Now then, that's enough of your nonsense."

It was his grandmother. The boy had succeeded, then. Mumbling away to herself, the old woman gathered her strength and, after one or two fruitless efforts to rise, managed finally to scramble out of bed with all the gasps and groans which always accompanied that task. She put on her sackcloth skirt and her short coat. Then the search for the matches began. It always ended with the matches being found. In the uncertain light of the wall-lamp he saw her bending bareheaded over the range, saw her mahogany rune-carved skin and her protruding cheek-bones, her sunken mouth and scraggy neck, her thin wisps of grey hair — and was afraid of her, and felt that morning would not come until she had tied her woollen shawl round her head. Presently she tied her woollen shawl round her head. In these tottering movements and twitching eyes he greeted each new day, greeted afresh the return of concrete reality in this age-old, closed-up face which peeped mumbling and grumbling from its hood as, toiling, straining, and wrestling, she once more set about her endless task of lighting the fire. Then, without warning, his father started scratching himself, clearing his throat, spitting, and taking snuff. He put on his trousers. It was time to think of feeding the sheep.

That part of morning which belonged to reality had at last come round. It was comforting to reflect that one thing at least never varied from day to day: his grandmother's desperate wrestling with the fire. The brushwood was always equally damp; and although she broke the peat up into little pieces and laid the bits with the most wood in them nearest the kindling, the only result for long enough would be a dreary crackling and a damp, offensive reek that filled every cranny and stung one's nose and eyes with a smarting pain. And even if the boy put his head under the clothes, the smoke would have got there too. The flame in the wall-lamp would gutter low on the wick. But his grandmother's ritual grumbling was never so protracted that it did not carry with it the promise of coffee. Never was the smoke so thick or so blue, never did it penetrate the eyes, the nose, the throat, the lungs so deeply that it could be forgotten as the precursor of that fragrance which fills the soul with optimism and faith, the fragrance of the crushed beans beneath the jet of boiling water curving from the kettle, the smell of coffee.

The longer the kindling took and the more acrid the smoke that eddied about the room, the longer the anticipation, the stronger the anticipation. To pass the time away he always made an examination of the roof. True, it was the same examination every morning, and it was, moreover, an examination the result of which he knew to a nicety beforehand, but all the same it was an inevitable examination every morning, provided his eyes were open. There were two knots especially that always drew his attention; when the smoke grew thin enough and the light bright enough for him to make out the features of these knots, it was a sign that the fire was drawing as it should and the water heating. What were those two knots, then? They were two men, two brothers. Each of them had one eye in the middle of his forehead and was plump in the face, like his mother. How was it that they were like his mother? It was because they were his mother's brothers, who had sailed away to far-off countries and found everything they wanted, long before he was born.

"What things the child sees!" his mother once said when, alone with her, he had told her of this in confidence. They were whispering together of various things that no one else might know about; of song; of far-off countries.

"If you go far, far away," he said, holding her hand as he sat there on the edge of her bed, "can you get everything you want?"

"Yes, my darling," she said wearily.

"And be whatever you'd like to be?"

"Yes," she answered, abstractedly.

"When the spring comes," he said, "I think I'll climb to the top of our mountain and see if I can see the other countries."

Silence.

"Mamma. Once last summer I saw the waterfall in the gully flowing backwards in the wind. The water was being blown back over the edge."

"Listen, my dear," she said then, "I dreamed something about you the other night."

"Me?"

"I dreamed that the elf-lady took me into the big rock and gave me a bowl of milk and told me to drink it, and when I had drunk it the elf-lady said: 'Be good to little Nonni, because when he grows older he will sing for the whole world.'"

"How?" he asked.

"I don't know," said his mother.

Then he rested on his mother's breast for a while and was conscious of nothing in all the world but the beating of his mother's heart. At length he rose up and asked:

"Mamma, why shall I sing for the whole world?"

"It's a dream," she replied.

"Shall I sing for the heath?"

"Yes."

"For the marshes?"

"Yes."

"And shall I sing for the mountain, too?"

"The elf-lady says so," replied his mother.

"I shall have to sing for the folk in Rauthsmyri church too, then, I suppose," he said thoughtfully.

"I suppose so."

He nestled up to his mother again, turning it over in his mind, wrapped in the glamour of this prophecy, the winged words.

"Mamma," he said at length, "will you teach me to sing for the whole world?"

"Yes," she whispered. "When the spring comes."

And closed her eyes wearily.

And so, if he let his eyes wander from the knots in the roof to the dishes in the cupboard and on the shelves, or to the potstick hanging on the wall and the pan standing on the floor, all of them with the strangely guileless expression that cooking utensils alone can assume in the helplessness of day; or if he caught the glitter of the flowery, extravagant cup-women, fragile and afraid of being laughed at; then he would always feel so noble that he would promise never to tell tales of any of them and, closing one eye out of politeness, would gaze at them with the other one only. "I too am altogether different from what I seem," he would say; and meant the unsung songs and the great countries, distant as the courses of day, which awaited him.

And so at last would be heard from the kettle the far-famed gurgle which proclaims that the water is on the point of boiling. By this time the boy was usually famished enough to feel that he could eat anything he could get his teeth into, not only hay, but peat and dung as well. So it was no wonder that he waited longingly to see what his slice of bread would be like: whether his grandmother had cut it right across the loaf, or whether she had given him only half a slice and that perhaps with one edge thin as paper. And how would she spread it? Would she just dab a lump of tallow and cod-liver oil in the middle so that the crust was as dry as it had been yesterday? Of this delicious mixture the boy could never have enough, it left such a pungent flavour in the mouth; and if there was one thing to his grandmother's credit, it was that she was rarely stingy with it, but smeared on liberal quantities with her right thumb. She was inclined to be sparing with the sugar, however, and had an unfortunate habit of breaking different-sized pieces from the lump, in which case he might easily be the one to get the smallest. The consideration of these matters was never without its elements of anxiety and suspense.

Presently the smell of coffee began to fill the room. This was morning's hallowed moment. In such a fragrance the perversity of the world is forgotten and the soul is inspired with faith in the future; when all was said and done, it was probably true that there really were far-off places, even foreign countries. Some day, incredible though it might seem, spring would come with its birds, its buttercups in the home-field. And very likely Mother would get up too when the days began to lengthen, just as she had done last year and the year before.

As the steaming jet curved down into the coffee-pot, the first words of the day were heard in the croft: the prelude employed by his grandmother to conjure Asta Sollilja from her depths of sleep. This ceremony was repeated morning after morning in accordance with an unvarying rule, and though to Asta herself it seemed every morning equally strange, the boy knew it well enough to remember it his whole life through.

"Merciful heavens, what an awful sight! Just look at her lying there, a half-grown woman, fast asleep at this time of day! When in the name of heaven will they ever begin to show some sense?"

Was his grandmother really so silly as to believe she could wake anyone with a feeble, quavering rigmarole like that? It was for all the world as if she were just gabbling away to herself in between her morning hymns. Anyway, Asta Sollilja slept on, her head in the corner, mouth open, chin up, and head back, with one hand under her ear and the other half-open on the coverlet as if she thought in her sleep that someone would come and lay happiness in her palm. Her shift was patched at the neck. After a few moments the prelude was resumed:

"It's plain enough to see that these poor wretches haven't a thought in their heads. How anyone is ever going to make anything out of them" — she often used the plural of Asta Sollilja —

"and hardly a shirt to their backs!" (Higher) "Sollilja, your needles are waiting, woman! It's nearly nine o'clock and soon midday."

His grandmother's idea of time was for the boy an endless source of wonder.

The water followed its fascinating curve from the kettle into the bag, making a heavy, hollow sound and sending up a cloud of rich, aromatic vapour. And Asta Sollilja slept on. But as the coffee filtered through the bag, the old woman went on with her task of waking her:

"You'll be a lazy good-for-nothing all your life long, Asta Sollilja."

But Asta Sollilja slept on.

"You needn't think you're going to get your coffee in bed like somebody grand, a twelve-year-old girl, nearly thirteen and soon confirmed. I'll have your father take the whip to your back before that, my lady."

But these matins had no visible effect on Asta Sollilja.

Only when old Hallbera went over to the bed and shook her did the girl open her eyes. She opened them with difficulty, her lids fluttering in terror as she stared wildly round her. At last she realized where she was, and hiding her forehead in the crook of her elbow, she started snivelling.

She was a dark-haired maiden, pale, with a long jaw and strong chin and a slight cast in one eye. Her eyebrows and lashes were dark, but the pupils were the grey of broken iron. Hers was the only face in the croft that had color and form; and it was because of that that the boy used often to stare at his sister as though wondering where she came from. She was very pale; the long, mature face was stamped with concern, almost with experience of life. For as long as the boy could remember, Asta Sollilja had been his big sister. But though breast and shoulders lacked the budding form of childhood, had outgrown it by now, or had never attained it, she lacked no less the rounded softness of maturity; child she was not, but she was equally far from being a woman.

"There's your coffee for you, Sollilja," said the grandmother as she placed her cup in the farthest corner of the room. "That's as near as I care to carry it for you."

The girl scratched her head for a while, yawning and tasting her mouth; then she pulled her petticoat from under the pillow and put it on in the warmth between the blankets. Slipping her long, slim legs from under the clothes, she thrust her unwashed feet into thick woollen stockings and crossed one ankle over her knee, without shame, and in such a manner that when the boy considered her immature limbs, it was as always only to arrive once more at the conclusion that though she was his big sister, she was nevertheless, as far as form was concerned, a much inferior being to the brothers.

But now the period of speculation was at an end, for at that moment, the grandmother brought him his coffee and woke his elder brothers. At last the boy would know from what part of the loaf his slice had been cut, whether the dripping reached all the way to the crusts, whether his lump of sugar was a big one or a little one. By this time there was light on the window. Once more winter morning had succeeded in opening his heavy eyelids.

Now day began.

25.   DAY

MEALS in this family were eaten as a rule in silence and in an atmosphere of almost furtive solemnity, as though some dark impressive rite were being performed. Each and every one huddled intently over the plate on his knees and picked the bones from his fish with a precision worthy of a watchmaker, or, holding the bowl up under his chin, swallowed his porridge with undivided attention. It was marvellous how much porridge the boy's father could guzzle in a very short time. The old woman, her back turned on the others, would eat, without a knife, near the fire. For the morning meal there was always hot oatmeal porridge, black pudding, a slice of bread, the cold leavings of yesterday's salt fish, and coffee warmed up and served with a piece of sugar. The sugar was the object of most anticipation. The mother, who had not the appetite of a small bird, would raise herself with difficulty to a half-sitting position in bed and get herself some medicine from one of the eighty bottles supplied her by her Member of Parliament. Her face was grey and flaccid, her eyes large and fevered; she could not chew because of an affection of her mouth. Sometimes the youngest son felt that it was unkind of his father to sit right in front of her there and slop so much porridge into himself when she was nibbling at her bite of fish with such obvious distaste and swallowing the food with a pitiful shudder. Never did the children long so much for a nice juicy piece of meat or a

thick slice of rye bread and dripping as when they had finished eating.

After the morning meal Bjartur would lie down on the bed,
a childish habit, snore cruelly for a moment or two, then spring
up with the eyes of a man dogged by incredible peril and disappear to look to his sheep. A hut, now full to capacity, had been
built at one end of the croft for the ewes, but the lambs and the
two-year-olds were still housed under the same roof as the family.
The elder brothers swept the mangers, raked out the muck on the
floor, and cleared pathways round the house, which the stubbornly falling snow filled up again. The sheep had to negotiate
eighteen steps cut in the snow to climb out of the drift in front of
the door, the folk after them, and a cleft had also to be cut in the
drift over the window to admit daylight.

And after the morning meal, when father and the elder brothers
had gone to see to the sheep, then first was day begun in the
croft, begun in all earnest, begun in its length, its breadth, day
with its evening that no one could foresee. The light was scanty
because of the small window and the thickness of the snow. Two
of the beds had been made; in the third lay the mother, motionless, her confinement coincident as usual with the illness, lasting
rarely less than three months, which laid her up every winter with
such dutiful regularity. She had had a baby for the Bailiff and the
minister the year before last also, and on that occasion had been
bedfast for four months. She would turn over to a fresh position
occasionally, suppressing her groans and moving slowly and cautiously because of her bedsores. On the edge of her bed, by the
window, Asta Sollilja was sitting, knitting herself a vest. She was
sitting so far back on her bed that her feet were dangling out
of reach of the floor, but in this position of course she could rest
her head against the wall occasionally. Now and then she would
let herself slump against the wall and fall asleep.

Grandma took her wheel and spun.

And the wheel-whir of the long days filled the croft; and this
one wheel spinning was like the wheel of time, which carries our
souls away to its own land.

Little Nonni might now play for a short while. So he herded
his sheep-horns into pasture up on all the beds, sticking some
of them under the rafters, which represented mountain peaks,
though actually the sheep were climbing the inside of the mountain peaks, and tethering the jaw-bones, his cows, to the feet of
the range, for that was where he and Bjartur of Summerhouses

differed: little Nonni had ten cows. Then he set off on long journeys on the leg-bones, taking his bearings in unknown places behind the moors and the mountains and riding his horses to the
fjords, long journeys and stiff, for in this room there were distances past all reckoning, if a journey followed the laws that only
he could understand. Even the bed-ends were dangerous mountain
paths, complete with ravines, snowdrifts, and ghosts. He had to
stay overnight at one place on the way (under the table near the
window). It was not before spring, when the distances of reality
reappeared with thawing snow and an improvement in his mother's
health, that the room's distances began to dissolve. And so obscure were these distances that, in spite of the length of the journey, the destination by the hatchway was not more than a hand's
breadth from his own cow-shed.

Arriving in town, he had a chat with the doctor and the merchant. He bought an enormous load of raisins, for in his household they lived exclusively on such things, raisins in cases, raisins
in sacks, likewise loaf-sugar. In his dispensary the doctor had about
as many bottles of medicine as the Bailiff had ewes, five hundred
or thereabouts, but, strange as it may seem, the boy bought not a
single drop. He therefore refused to promise the doctor his vote in
return for medicine as his father had done. He had never
come across anything so rank-smelling or so bitter as this medicine
of the doctor's. He suspected at bottom that it prevented his mother
from getting better, even that his father bought it to make sure
that his mother would not get up, and that the doctor was party
to the conspiracy. For this reason he did not like the doctor and
refused to vote such a man into Parliament. He voted for the merchant instead, out of respect for his raisins. And now the doctor
grew angry and threatened to call in the Sheriff. But the boy was
not at all afraid; he promised to pay his debt by giving the doctor
an old dog, a sheep's ankle-bone, and this started a mighty quarrel
in Fjord.

"What in the name of goodness is all the row about there?" exclaimed his grandmother; but the boy made no reply for the
moment, because Grandma belonged to another plane, other dimensions. Should she say anything further, it would be at most a
light flurry of snow from the north.

"If you can't live in peace with yourself, I'll have to give you a
taste of the belt."

"Grandma," said the boy then, "you don't exist. You're only a
storm in the air. I'm on a trip to town."

"Don't be so silly," answered his grandmother. "You ought to be ashamed of yourself, a big boy like you with such foolish fancies in the middle of the day; and can't knit yet."

The boy broke off all discussion with the gentry of Fjord and said:

"There, what did I tell you, she's blowing up for a gale," and scattering hurried farewells, he set off homeward at full speed, urging on along the winding paths that lay up and down the floor. But half-way there his grandmother overtook him like a storm springing up without warning on the moors, so he died in the snow and was placed on his grandmother's bed and given his needles.

Looping the yarn languidly round his finger, he started knitting. It was the same stocking foot that he had been struggling with for a full week now, and yet it was still far from half finished. It was as if nothing wanted to make any progress these days, as if everything was determined to drag itself along as slowly as possible. One saw no end to anything, no end to the foot, no end to day, no end to life at home. The consideration of this endless protraction made him very sleepy. Then suddenly he remembered that he had perished in a storm on the heath.

"Grandma, I'm a ghost," he said, yawning.

"Poor little wretch, you haven't heard anything good today yet, have you?"

No, quite true now that he came to think of it: he hadn't heard anything good yet, and worse things could happen than hearing something good. Often his grandmother grew so absorbed in the something good she was busy reciting that she forgot to scold him for his knitting, especially if it was something really good:

> *In dulsi jubilo*
> *Lies our heart's desire,*
> *Impre sepio*
> *The heavenly choir,*
> *Alfa hesido,*
> *Alfa hesido.*

> *O Jesu parvuli*
> *My soul rest with thee,*
> *O pura optimi*
> *In thy kingdom free,*
> *O prince of glorii*
> *Drag on postea,*
> *Drag on postea.*

O Peter's Karitas,
O holy Penitas,
From his side riven
Per nostra krimina,
And all sins forgiven,
Selorum gaudia,
Oh that we were there,
Oh that we were there.

On and on, on and on it went. Never do hymns seem so long as in the days of childhood, never is their world and their language so alien to the soul. In old age the opposite is true, the hours are then too short for the hymns. In these pious old verses, age-hallowed and Latin-sprinkled, which the old woman had learned from her grandmother, in these lay hidden her other world; their rhythm in time with the regular pressure of the treadle was her music, to which she surrendered herself till the walls of the narrow room had floated out to the horizons of eternity and she was sitting with her hands fallen in her lap, the thread snapped, the wheel silent. With the echo of the verse in her soul and on her lips she began looking for the thread on the spindle, and when at last she had found it, she would suck the end through the pipe and wake the boy up.

"Heavens, what a lamentable sight!" she said. "Today it's like a salmon net, yesterday you couldn't have driven a nail through it. Double-loop the wool round your finger, you silly, or I'll undo it all for you."

Now to find some method of escaping this invariable daily criticism, though without openly calling its purpose in question. It could be managed in various ways. Sometimes the old woman could be cajoled into another hymn, sometimes a story, but it was safest when her attention could be directed to some scandal even more flagrant than a couple of loose stitches. Today he was lucky. Asta Sollilja was lying back against the slope of the roof, her head lolling forward, the needles motionless in her lap, fast asleep.

"Grandma," exclaimed the boy, highly offended, "our Asta's sleeping, look."

Thus had the boy succeeded in diverting his grandmother's attention from himself to Asta Sollilja, that sleepy being who had a queer shape and who was, if the truth be told, only half a human being. Merciful heavens, what a lamentable sight! But when Asta Sollilja had been waked up with all the appropriate ritual, everything simply began all over again; day seemed not to have moved onward one inch, his mother was groaning as painfully as ever, o pura optimi, drag on postea.

Drag on postea.

The wheel had begun to revolve again before the boy remembered that he had been a ghost for some time now.

"Ghosts," he remarked, " — don't they get everything they want?"

"Oh, rubbish."

"They can do anything they like, can't they?"

"Get on with your knitting, you little silly."

"Grandma, will you tell me a story about a ghost?"

"How have I any time for stories?"

"Just one ghost."

"What stories would I know about ghosts, a bedridden old woman who can't remember a thing?"

After a few moments, however, she could be heard muttering away to herself; it was like the first sighing of a gale that would soon be raging in full blast. Her stories were cast all in the same mould. In the famine after the Eruption folk ate scraps of leather, they were so thin that the lice ate their way into them, her grandmother could remember the time. There was once a French cutter, this happened when I was in the south, they were wrecked on the sands in a terrible gale, the crew all perished on a sandbank, a rich farmer stole everything that drifted ashore, including a cask full of money and a barrel of claret. The captain walked again and the cook as well, they followed the thief to the ninth generation, they aren't free of them yet, many stories about it. Two brothers went to market, one set off home again in the morning, the other wanted to stay a day longer. It was a long way, over the mountains. A terrible storm came on, but the brother managed to reach a hut. The hut was haunted a lot. During the night the ghost started pounding on the walls and the door, but the brother pulled some stones up from the floor and piled them up against the door. Outside, the ghost was screaming horribly. The brother piled more stones against the door and bade him never thrive. In the morning there was a keen frost, but the snow had stopped. The brother clears the stones away and opens the door. But as he opens it, in tumbles his brother, frozen to death. He waked again and haunted his brother. Endless space with bottomless drifts of snow, precipices over which men stepped blindly to their death, frozen rivers where people fell into holes and were carried under the ice and out to sea, walked again, knocked at windows, and chanted poetry. Sea-monsters attacking people at the foot of cliffs, destroying the houses of women who were alone at home. The fiend Kolumkilli, they say, is immortal and the witch Gunnvor lived on this croft and made a pact with him and murdered folk, there are many stories about it, endless stories, at last she was broken at the lich-gate at Myri Church on Trinity Sunday and her limbs cut off, guest of Gunnvor was no man with God or good grace, she has broken my rib-bone, my leg-bone, my hip-bone; and if Kolumkilli call me should, this is what he'd say, bones and red blood, bones and red blood and dododo —

All at once Bjartur stuck his head up through the hatchway and cried:

"Stick the kettle on, Hallbera, there are visitors coming."

Pushing her spinning-wheel aside in the middle of a story, the old woman grudgingly answered: "Oh, there's no need to tell me. They're never off the roads, some of them. And there was quite a crowd of bogles here this morning to announce them, too."

"Sola will give you a hand to mix some pancakes, and you can make the coffee as strong as you like in honour of a man who never came here yet but he was after something or other. And no dawdling."

A few moments later the sharply chiselled features of the Bailiff in their frame of strong, grey-streaked hair rose above the hatch-way. He was wearing a thick riding-jacket and muffler, sealskin boots, and long snow-stockings pulled over his trousers and up to his thighs. His whip was adorned with three resplendent silver bands. He was on his way to town, and had one of his farm labour-ers with him for company; he stretched out two or three fingers in greeting and mumbled something into his beard. Asta Sollilja cleared a seat for him on the children's bed, while Bjartur sat down beside his wife. The smell of the first pancake reached them.

"Well, well, old lad," said Bjartur as though he rather pitied the Bailiff, "so you're seeing what your horses think of the roads in this weather, are you?"

"Oh, the roads are right enough," replied the Bailiff sleepily, caressing his chin and yawning as his eyes wandered about the room.

"Oh? That's funny. I seem to remember a time when you would have said the moors were too dangerous for horses in this depth of snow," said Bjartur, who was always in the right in his dealings

with the Bailiff, " — particularly if it was me that wanted to use
the horses. But naturally a man knows best himself how far to
tax his own horses."

"Oh, it isn't so very often that I fool around the moors for no
reason," said the Bailiff significantly. "And they're my horses."

Bjartur countered this insinuation by remarking that both rich
and poor alike always had some purpose in mind, whether at home
or in the deserts, and the Bailiff could say what he liked, but there
had been no shortage of snow up on the moors here lately, whatever it was like across at Myri.

The Bailiff replied that it was no worse than was to be expected
in the middle of winter. Producing his silver tobacco-box, he
measured off a nice length of chew with his finger, then bit the
piece off and, after carefully replacing the remainder in the box,
closed it with great caution. Then he lay back on the bed, unafraid
of lice.

"Well, well, old cock," said Bjartur affably, "just so, yes. And
what's fresh up your way these days?"

The Bailiff said that everything was as usual with him. How
other people were faring he didn't know.

"No sign of worms or diarrhœa?"

"With me?" asked the Bailiff.

"Oh, you usually speak for yourself first, if I know you at
all well."

"It's all one whether they have worms or not, the price that
folk get for them nowadays," said the Bailiff. "The wretched animals are simply a burden on folks these days."

Ejartur doubted whether the gentry really meant it when they
spoke disparagingly of their sheep.

"You can doubt what you like for me," retorted the Bailiff.

"Are you clearing the snow from the home-field?"

"No. I haven't been short of hay yet," replied the Bailiff.

"Nor me either," said Bjartur.

The Bailiff, now lying at his ease well up on the bed, was sucking away with all his might, and had already accumulated so much
saliva that he had begun to avoid long sentences. The half-closed
eyes flitted from one thing to another until finally they settled on
Asta Sollilja, busy with her cooking.

"There have been occasions," observed the Bailiff, "when you've
had to ask other people for what you needed most."

"Well, it's your own wife's fault if she refused to take anything

for the few drops of milk I fetched to put in the kids' gruel when
they were little; and I don't owe you a penny on the land, as everybody knows, my lad, though it did take twelve years."

"It strikes me you're still using other folk's land the same as
ever."

"Eh?"

"Wasn't there something on your back when you came to see
me yesterday? This is the fourth time, if I'm not mistaken. What
I can't fathom at all is why you bought land from me up in the
valley here if you intend taking over my churchyard as well."

"Maybe you folk at Rauthsmyri have managed to get the better
of death," said the crofter, but to this sarcasm the Bailiff made no
reply.

"What am I to say if I meet the Sheriff in town?" he asked.

"That the black-face I pulled out of a bog for him last Midsummer Day was rotten with disease," retorted Bjartur.

The Bailiff's only reply was to mouth his chew a moment or
two longer, then squirt it all in one stream at Bjartur's feet. "How
old is that girl of yours now?" he asked without taking his eyes off
Asta Sollilja.

"She's getting on for fourteen, poor kid. I shouldn't be surprised
if she wasn't born about the same time as I made the first payment
on the land."

"It just shows you what you're made of: farming for fourteen
years and not a cow on the place yet."

"If it hadn't been for this scrap of land on my conscience all
those twelve years, I would certainly have bought a cow and have
had hired help as well. But it so happens that all my life I've held
the opinion that freedom and independence are worth more than
all the cattle that any crofter ever got himself into debt for."

The Bailiff gave a faint snort.

"What did you say she was called, again?" he asked.

"Oh, Asta Sollilja is her name."

"What's that supposed to mean?"

"It's supposed to mean, my friend, that she'll never need to be
dependent on others, either in body or soul, for as long as I live
in this hut. And now we'll talk no more about it, mate."

But the Bailiff's contempt of Bjartur's independence knew no
bounds, and he said:

"You can send her along to me with the turn of the year; my
wife is rather fond of teaching kids to read and so on. We'll give
her her food for a month or so."

"There's plenty of food in Summerhouses," said Bjartur. "And the soulful drivel you people of Myri call learning is probably healthiest for the children you acknowledge as your own."

The Bailiff, leaning forward, landed an immense stream at Bjartur's foot, then sleepily passed a hand over his brow and cheek and suppressed a yawn.

"I'm for my folk, you're for your folk," added Bjartur without looking at the spit.

"Your wife's much the same as ever, I see," observed the Bailiff. "How much have you paid for medicine for her this year?"

"That's another matter altogether. It would never occur to me to deny that I'd had the misfortune to marry women both of whom were troubled with their hearts, which, being nothing but God's will and malignant fortune, concerns no one, you least of all."

The Bailiff, who never took offence over a snappish answer, but liked this sort of tone best, clawed himself here and there, for they had started crawling, and said to no one in particular:

"Oh, it's all right, it doesn't worry me. But the wife thinks the girl should have some teaching, and a law has been passed about compulsory examinations. Not that anybody need be in any doubt about my opinion: I consider that all this education business will be the ruination of the lower classes."

"In that case I think it's best that those who belong to the lower classes should educate their lower classes, and that those who belong to the upper classes should educate their upper classes; and give Madam my best wishes."

"I don't gain anything by people being educated," said the Bailiff. "But it's what the government wants. And, by the way, the womenfolk up there are all raving and saying you should get yourself a cow."

"I am a free man."

"Um. What shall I tell the Sheriff if he decides to inquire into it?"

"Tell him that we people on the moors stand on our own feet."

"Yes; and up to the neck in your own graves," snorted the Bailiff. Before Bjartur had had time to think of a suitable rejoinder, a voice, long-drawn and wavering, broke in from the region of the range:

"It is just as his honour says: this is no sort of life for a human being. I lived at Urtharsel for forty years and we always had a cow of one kind or another. I never needed to ask God for anything special in all those forty years."

"Listen," said the Bailiff, as if something has just occurred to him. "I can sell you one that's due to calve in the summer, a fine beast, doesn't give too much milk, but keeps going a long time."

Is he at it again? thought Bjartur, who knew his Bailiff from of old; this wasn't the first of their discussions, it was like beating one's head against a stone wall. He had the habit of beginning again where he had left off before, the old mule. To try to turn his mind from anything was hopeless. It was difficult to say whether this trait in his character irritated Bjartur more than it excited his admiration. Then something happened to delay Bjartur's answer for the moment: all at once Finna made an attempt to lift herself up and, looking at the two of them with fevered eyes, whispered blithely:

"I only wish the good God would grant it." And she lay down again.

Only when this sigh had passed away did Bjartur find an opportunity of answering the Bailiff: "You wouldn't have been so keen on offering me a cow last year or the year before, mate, when it was still uncertain whether I would make the last payment on the land."

"I could provide you with hay for her, too," offered the Bailiff.

"God's blessing on the man," sighed the woman again from her sick-bed.

"Oh, you get your medicine from Finsen, lass," said Bjartur. "You've never been short of medicine."

The Bailiff, who had some local repute as a homœopath, asked if he might see some of the medicine that Bjartur obtained for his wife from the District Medical Officer and Member of Parliament, Dr. Finsen. Finna drew aside the curtain from the corner cupboard by her bed, revealing a large and imposing collection of medicine bottles of all sizes and colours, three shelves full. Most of them were empty. The Bailiff took one or two of them, removed the corks, and sniffed. They had all the same inscription, written in the doctor's scholarly black-letter: "Gudfinna Ragnarsdottir. To be taken thrice daily at equal intervals. For internal use." When the Bailiff had taken a disdainful sniff at the contents of a few of the bottles, he replaced them with the remark that he'd brewed his poison too long, the blasted old rogue.

But coffee had now been served and Bjartur generously exhorted the Bailiff and his attendant to fall tooth and nail upon those pancake things or whatever you call them. The old woman, still mumbling to herself, kept on fussing about around the range, but Asta Sollilja, who had followed everything that had been said, about cows and schooling alike, stood sucking her finger and gazing full of respect at the way in which the Bailiff was disposing of the pancakes she herself had cooked. The boys' eyes widened and widened as the sugar-sprinkled mound grew smaller on the the dish, their faces longer and longer as its roses, its romance, and its damsel reappeared. Weren't they going to leave a single one?

"By the way," said the Bailiff, "my son Ingolfur may be up this way on some business or other in the spring."

"Really," said the crofter. "I won't forbid him the road. I hear he's become quite a big bug down in the south nowadays."

"Co-operative Secretary," corrected the Bailiff.

"Oh, so there is a difference, then?"

"I don't know whether you're aware that the wool last year reached three times the price that Bruni was giving for it. And the profits he made on the mutton this autumn don't seem to have been any smaller."

"As far as I'm concerned," said Bjartur, "as long as I can pay you and the dealer what I legally owe you, well, it's much the same to me what you gentry think fit to accuse one another of; embezzlement or burglary, it's all the same to me."

"Yes, you're all cravens, the lot of you," observed the Bailiff. "You live and die in complete trust of the one that fleeces you most."

"I don't know, but according to what I've heard, you don't give so very much more for what you buy alive, mate. The dealer was telling me only this autumn that you make a profit of five to eight crowns on every lamb you sell in Vik. And that wasn't the biggest estimate."

Now, the Bailiff's nature was such that had he been accused of theft or even of murder he would have preserved an unruffled exterior and have seemed, indeed, to be quite gratified. But with one crime he would not have his name connected: if anyone insinuated that he was making money, the ice was broken and his tongue was loosened; such a slander was more than he could stand. Leaning forward, he opened his mouth on a flood of words, the muscles of his face twitching passionately, fire in his eyes, his reasoning full of extravagant assertions and discordant similes. In a moment all his sleepiness had disappeared:

"Fortunately enough, I happen to be better acquainted with my affairs than the dealer in Fjord is. And I can provide documentary proof at any time that my dealings in sheep have done more harm to me than all the foxes have to all the farmers in this district and for miles farther afield for the last two or three generations. You let the merchant down there delude you into believing that I buy sheep in the autumn for the fun of the thing. But the truth of the matter is that when I've bought sheep from people in these parts, it's always been out of charity. And what is charity? A fellow goes and gets himself mixed up in the mess that ought first and last to be the individual's private concern, a fellow lets himself be fooled into saving irredeemable folk from starvation, or debt, or imminent bankruptcy, all for the sake of the taxes, instead of letting them go on to the parish, and the parish on to the county, and the county on to the country. And the whole damned lot to hell. Have I perhaps asked them up for the pleasure of their company? No, I ask no one up, but they come all the same, and there I am. One comes asking for grain, another for sugar, a third for hay, a fourth for money, a fifth for snuff, when I maybe haven't a chew for myself even. The sixth comes asking for all this at once, the seventh even demands mixed snuff, as if it was my job to start mixing snuff for people, and does Bruni imagine that I'm some sort of gift dispensary, where everybody can come and ask for what he wants and never think of payment? Then why doesn't Bruni turn his business into an everlasting gift establishment, may I ask? No, mate, you can tell Bruni from me that all the year round there's a constant stream of penniless men coming to me, men he has fleeced to the skin, then forbidden like murder to charge even as much as a single mouthful for their starving and emaciated tribes of youngsters. And what do you get out of these people in the autumn? A few pitiful rattle-bones that you could lift with your little finger, hardly worth poisoning for fox-bait."

After this outburst the Bailiff fumbled through his pockets in a furious search for his tobacco-box, but he rarely resumed his chewing before he had either won over his opponent or given him up as hopeless.

"The time has come," he said, instead of biting off a plug, "and come long ago, when the farmers with any guts in them at all must lay their heads together here the same as in other places and find out where their bread would be best buttered, so that feeble individuals like myself, with small incomes and heavy responsibilities, should not have to look after people that the merchant is bent on starving to death — and then be called a thief for their pains."

"At one time folk would have said there was something the matter with you if you had considered other people's interests before your own," remarked Bjartur.

"Anyway, one thing you can be certain of is that I could mix a better bottle for your Finna than those blasted camphor-slops you get from old Finsen. He and Tulinius Jensen are a couple of birds out of the same nest. To the best of my knowledge he's never done anything in the Althingi but have quays built for the merchant. They've already stung the Treasury for subsidies for two piers that were reduced to sand by the breakers as fast as they were built, of course, so now they've decided to milk them for another hundred thousand crowns to build a breakwater stretching out to somewhere near the horizon as a bulwark for the ruined piers. And who pays for all this building and construction that's thrown to the waves as if it were refuse? We farmers, of course; plucked to the bone in direct and indirect taxes to the Treasury. No; if the Icelandic farming community is not to become the miserable doormat of merchant power, then we farmers must unite in defence of our interests the same as they started doing in Thingey over thirty years ago."

He stood up, stretched, and began winding his muffler round his neck.

"Well, well, little girl," he said, halting in front of Asta Sollilja; and his eyes were so warm and his hewn features so strong that the child blushed all over and her heart began hammering against her ribs, "I think I'll give you a couple of crowns; young ladies sometimes like to have some money for hankies." He took a real silver coin out of his purse and gave it to her. She had long been afraid of the Bailiff, but never so much as now. The boys he did not even look at. Then he buttoned up his jacket.

"A hundred and fifty for the cow and never a cent more," he said. "And hay according to agreement."

26.   EVENING

Soon the dusk falls. The boy no longer feels sure of himself after the day's song and story, no longer dare leave his legs dangling over the edge of the bed, but huddling up because of the world's hidden powers, knits without venturing on the slightest movement. His grandmother and his sister stand with their backs to him, piously attentive to the ritual of their cooking. The brushwood is spitting sullenly, filling the room with a dense smoke that makes his throat smart; it is in this smoke that there dwells the poetry of day, with all its furious gales, its ravines and its spectres per nostra krimina. Though the quarrelsome voices of the elder brothers may occasionally be heard from the outskirts, they afford him no relief, and in these oppressive surroundings the stitches become more and more netlike; his left index finger has long been dead from sticking straight up in the air. In the dusk the room's dimensions seem to increase still further; no earthly power can bridge them now. Remotest of all is his mother. Even her heart seems to have disappeared irrevocably in the plumbless depths of this fog which is instinct with the poetry of life, the poetry of death.

Supper was tense with exertion and a frozen silence. One or two of them stole a glance at Bjartur, then at each other. Asta Sollilja scarcely touched her food. Presently they had all had their fill of salt coalfish, the potatoes were finished, no one wanted any more of this morning's porridge. Asta Sollilja began to clear the table; she had an amazing squint. The elder brothers said something nasty in a whisper, and the mother said: "Darlings," also in a whisper. The old woman took her needles down from the shelf, and from the middle of her story spoke these words aloud: "Moo now, moo now, my Bukolla, if you are alive at all."

"Eh?" demanded Bjartur crossly from his bed.

"Pluck a hair from my tail and lay it on the ground," mumbled the old woman into her knitting without explanation. In the silence it was like the crackle of frost. The boys had started knocking one another about near the hatchway. Halting suddenly in front of her father with a plate in her hand, Asta Sollilja looked at him with the straight eye and said:

"Father, I want to learn."

The ice had been broken.

"I didn't do any learning before the winter that I went to the minister's and read Orvar-Odds Saga while I was being taught my catechism," replied Bjartur.

"Father, I want to learn," insisted the girl, lowering her head and drooping her eyelids, her throat and mouth twitching slightly, and the fragile plate in her hand.

"All right, lass, I'll spell through the Bernotus Rhymes with you."

The girl bit her lip a little and said:

"I don't want to learn the Bernotus Rhymes."

"That's strange," said Bjartur. "What do you want to learn, then?"

"I want to learn Christianity."

"You can learn that from old Hallbera."

"No," said the girl, "I want to go over to Rauthsmyri, like the Bailiff said."

"And what for, do you think?"

"To learn to know God."

"None of your nonsense," said Bjartur of Summerhouses.

"I want to go to Rauthsmyri all the same."

"Oh, indeed, my lass," he said. "But it so happens that I'd sooner bring Rauthsmyri children up myself than allow the Rauthsmyri folk to bring up mine."

"I want to go to Rauthsmyri."

"Yes, when I'm dead."

"To Rauthsmyri."

"Your mother wanted to go to Rauthsmyri, too. But she would rather die than give in to herself, and she died; there was a woman for you. Rauthsmyri is Rauthsmyri. I went there when I was eighteen, thirty years ago, and I've never straightened my back since; and they haven't finished with me yet. Now they're threatening to force a cow on me. But your mother died in this room here, without letting anybody offer her anything. She was an independent woman."

Bjartur was very proud of this wife of his, thirteen years after her death. He was in love with her memory and had forgotten her faults. But when he saw by her daughter's quivering shoulders that she was weeping over her washing-up, he remembered once more that women are more to be pitied than ordinary mortals and need daylong consolation. Then again, if he had a tender spot at all in him, it was for this crosseyed slip of a girl with the lovely name, whom sometimes he gazed at on Sundays and sometimes protected from the rain in summer, both without remark. So he promised to teach her to read tomorrow, so that they wouldn't have anything to complain about at Rauthsmyri. "And we might be able to buy ourselves Orvar-Odds Saga this spring. And even a hanky."

Silence.

"You ought to hand that money over to me, girlie. It's Judas money."

No answer.

"Who knows, perhaps I have a rig-out for you, wrapped up in my Sunday coat down in the chest. But you'll have to get a move on and grow up for the spring coming."

"Moo now, moo-cow," muttered the old grandmother to the spindle as she kissed the pipe.

"I won't have this nonsense in front of the youngsters, Hallbera," said Bjartur sharply.

"Pluck a hair from my tail and lay it on the ground."

Asta Sollilja's tears continued to fall on the dishes.

"I've been thinking," said Bjartur, "that since you're as old as you are, it's about time I gave you a lamb to call your own. There's one yellow-brown ewe with a tufted nose that isn't unlike my little girl."

For some moments he stood looking half in embarrassment at that slender body which had its own longing in a valley so thick with snow, and which wept and would not be comforted; then he went over to her and stroked her for a few moments as if she were an animal — this little flower.

"When the spring comes," he said, "I'll let you go down to town with me. That's much better than going over to Myri; you can see the sea and the world in one and the same journey." And when he touched her like that, she was sorrowful no longer, and forgot her sorrow, it was so seldom that he touched her. She nestled up against him and felt that he was the greatest power in the world. There was one happy place on his neck between his shirt and the roots of his beard; when her mouth was quivering hot with tears, she would yearn for this place, and find it. Thus would life's animosity disappear, perhaps all at once; only a moment in the dusk and it was gone.

Presently the lamp was lit.

The little world of humans that eked out its existence there in the oblivion of the frozen wastes was once more its normal self. Bjartur whittled away at a crosspiece for a hay-box, testing it repeatedly for size, with moss and chips of wood in his beard and half a line of poetry on his lips at long intervals. The older boys were teasing wool. They were examples of two diverse temperaments; the elder frizzy-haired and long of limb, a tortuous, inexplicable soul; the younger thickset and, as is usual with self-willed people, enthusiastic and quick-tempered. The elder used to make faces behind his father's back. In the middle of the day he would sneak into the house and scratch the table with a nail, looking foolishly and obstinately at his mother between whiles

and knocking his knees together as he sat. The middle brother
would hold his eyes open with match-sticks of his own accord and
would keep on working till he fell over unconscious. They teased
and teased and kept on digging one another in the ribs; it would
probably end in blows. And Asta Sollilja added another round
to her shift, pooh, she was only half a human being, there was this
and that wanting on her, and the slightest thing set her off howling, no one would dream of howling the way she did. At last she
had finished howling. Mother, on the other hand, was no better
today, everything the same as yesterday and the day before. Perhaps the Bailiff could mix the medicine that would cure her?

And the wheel went on spinning through time's expanse.

Little Nonni was no longer thinking of evening, and though
it had come, he did not regard it. Family and cooking utensils
alike glided gradually out of the range of his senses; the dimensions of the room expanded into improbability itself, where nothing
was any longer possible; how could anything be sillier than an
expanding room? Even the sound of Grandmother's wheel had
lost the qualities of proximity; it was like some far, far wind whistling among unknown crags; her cheek fringed by the hood dis-
solving into irrelevant fog. Was our Sola sent over to Utirauthsmyri to learn to know God? Or did she get a cow? No, it was only
the dog by the hatchway, yawning and scratching itself and striking the wall before it curled up. His mother was only a mute
recollection of some indistinct world-song, some goal or other that
one had been longing for all day long but had now forgotten. Oh
that we were there, oh that we were there! The hour that held
the goal of all desires was approaching, though none in particular
had been fulfilled.

In such a fashion would evening come, before one had realized
that the long day was over. It came in disguise, in images that
dissolved and faded away. And the boy faded out of time along
with the other images that were fading away.

His grandmother unlaced his shoes.

27.   LITERATURE

Once I loved a maiden shining
    (Mine so long ago),
Round her forehead fair locks twining,
    Sweet her voice and low.

Warm her eyes, so brightly gleaming
  (Tender were her vows),
As the radiant sun were beaming
  Underneath her brows.

In her cheeks the red blood beckoned
  (Red blood in the snow).
Naught of doom in love I reckoned;
  Doom fell long ago.

In the earth they laid my dearest
  (In the earth laid low).
All my life is labour drearest,
  Lonely now I go.

WITH this maid-song from the Jomsviking Rhymes, Asta Sollilja
began her education. When she had spelled her way through one
stanza, Bjartur leaned back in his chair with half-closed eyes and
chanted. Every verse that she read she learned by heart, the chant
as well, humming them away to herself whenever she was alone.
All the love-songs in this group of ballads were addressed to the
same girl; she was called Rosa. Asta Sollilja never inquired who
the girl commended so highly by these songs might be, but
she saw her together with her father, and loved her with him
in the primitive, rugged language of the Rhymes, reminiscent
of nothing so much as the pious but despairing cuts in the carving
of her grandmother's spindle-holder. Her notions about how
poetry is composed and circulated were vague: she could not distinguish between the voice of her father chanting and the love
that lived in the heart of a poet who died in a distant century,
but looked at her reflection in the water-bucket in a childish desire
to make herself resemble the maiden shining, who in the earth
was laid low.

But once they left the maid-songs for the ballads themselves
the going became much heavier. Here Bjartur's explanations did
little to dispel the obscurity and knit the few intelligible passages
together; the inexperienced reader wandered lost and despairing
in an unlit fog of unpronounceable words and difficult kennings
that seemed to lack any sort of connection — the Jomsviking heroes,
their voyages and battles, were far beyond her meagre imagination. And when the story turned to the lives of the Jomsvikings, her
father read it to himself only and laughed, my God, what wenching, then closed the book and said it did young people harm to

hear about such things, it's smut. Finally the wenching of the
Jomsvikings developed to such a pitch that they had to give the
book up altogether. Her father produced the Bernotus Rhymes,
they are much nicer for youngsters.

"Why can't I hear anything about wenching?" asked the girl.

"Eh?"

"I want so much to hear about wenching."

"Hussy," he said, and slapped her face; did not talk to her for
the rest of the day. After that she never dared refer to such things
openly. And when she had reached the passage in the Bernotus
Rhymes where the disguised hero visits the bedroom of the Princess
Fastina, who has been honoured with the name "Rosary-thwart,"
she blushed. Bernotus said:

> *Since I saw you, noble lady,*
> *Never can my heart find rest;*
> *So to love you, that is best.*

> *Slow she answered: Hear my promise:*
> *Love to me is but a name,*
> *Till your touch awakes the flame.*

And there they sat all night, the Princess and the knight, till
the sun rose. Asta Sollilja said nothing, not a word, and was careful not to look up. But in the evenings when she went to bed she
would draw the blanket over her head, and the little living-room
in Summerhouses no longer existed; rather was Fastina, fair-
fingered Rosary-thwart, sitting in her bedroom thinking of the
knight who conquered all and waiting for his return.

Long, long was the wait she had at home, after Bernotus had
had to flee the wrath of the King and had wandered to Borney,
where the worst villains in all the world were sent to destroy him.
And she sat at home in her bedchamber, alone, while he struggled
alone on a distant strand against innumerable foes, one against all.

> *Stout in arms the strand he trod,*
> *Dauntless swapt his dooméd foes;*
> *Swung his brand with single hand,*
> *Clave the knaves from neck to toes*

> *The gory spear at Thorleif aimed*
> *Through the air a vengeance bore;*
> *The braggart's spirit soon it tamed,*
> *Pinned him howling to the shore.*

Grim he waded seas of blood,
Dealing death with baleful blows;
Hewed off heads till none withstood,
Round him piles of corses rose.

It was her father chanting.

She peeped out from under the blanket, and there he was, still sitting on the edge of his bed, when all the others had gone to sleep, mending some implement or other. No one stirred any longer, the living-room fast asleep; he alone was awake, alone was chanting, sitting there in his shirt, thickset and high-shouldered, with strong arms and tangled hair. His eyebrows were shaggy, steep and beetling like the crags in the mountain, but on his thick throat there was a soft place under the roots of his beard. She watched him awhile without his knowing: the strongest man in the world and the greatest poet, knew the answer to everything, understood all ballads, was afraid of nothing and nobody, fought all of them on a distant strand, independent and free, one against all.

"Father," she whispered from under the blanket, for she was convinced that Bernotus Borneyarkappi was he and no other and that she simply must tell him. But he did not hear.

"Father," she whispered again, and did not know her own voice. But when it came to the point, she dared not say it; when he looked at her, a tremor passed through her, all of her, and she retreated beneath the blanket with loudly thumping heart. Maybe he would have slapped her face as he did in the Jomsviking Rhymes. She was lucky not to have told him.

He went downstairs to see to the lambs before retiring. She counted his footsteps on the ladder, he hummed to the lambs, she followed everything attentively, he came humming up the stairs again, her heart was still thumping.

Though words alone can never sway
Your heart, my lady bright,
Know that my songs shall be alway
Of you and your delight.

When she peeped out again he had put out the lamp.
Night.

28.   THE SEA-COW

It was in the snow-lit brightness of one tranquil day early in
March that there befell great events, never afterwards to be forgotten. Those who have experienced such a thing will know what
it means. There was movement in the west, on the ridge, extensive, mysterious. The boys, who by now had also made the
acquaintance of the Rhymes, maintained that it was a troop of
berserks on their way to join battle. Here was no small relief in
the monotony of mid-winter, when even a man with a stick is a
phenomenon. Slowly the troop wound its way down into the
valley. Both little Nonni and Asta Sollilja had climbed to the top
of the snowdrift at the door. Even Grandma scrabbled her way
up the eighteen snow-steps to the top and shaded her eyes with
her hand. It was a cow.

"Yes, it's a cow all right," cried the boys.

Last to join the group was Bjartur himself, grey with hay-mould
and foul of temper, there was no room for cattle here, he wasn't
going to have the hay taken from his sheep like this and thrown
to cattle, nor had he any desire to take the stall away from his
horse, to which he owed more than to any animal alive except the
bitch, and hand it over to a strange cow — whereupon he disappeared and did not show himself again before a formal demand
was made for his presence.

And on crawled the expedition home across the marshes, the
cow followed by its fodder on a horse-drawn sledge. It was a
sea-cow.

"Yes, it's a sea-cow all right," cried the boys.

She was not very big. Over her back and flanks was bound a
cloth from which there stuck a dapple-grey head, wondering and
suspicious, and under her udder was tied a woollen rag to prevent
her teats from trailing in the snow; housekeeper Gudny of Rauthsmyri had crossed the ridge herself on a winter's day, unaccustomed
to travelling and ill prepared. The breath hung in steaming clouds
about the cow's nostrils in the still, frosty air; there was rime on her
whiskers. The smoke from the chimney and the smell of home
roused her curiosity still further; she sniffed and snorted and tried
again and again to fetch a moo, as if in greeting, but the halter
muzzled her too tightly.

The old woman hobbled forward on her stick to meet her.

"Thrice-blessed creature," she mumbled, "welcome, and a blessing on her."

And the cow sniffed at the old woman and, as if she recognized such a woman immediately, tried repeatedly to moo in greeting to her.

"Thrice-blessed creature," mumbled the old woman again. It was the only remark that occurred to her, she who never addressed anyone else in so kindly a manner. She stroked the cow's rimy cheek, and the cow rumbled deep down in her throat. They understood each other immediately. The strangeness of this halting-place continued nevertheless to fascinate the new arrival; her movements were still a little panicky, her hoofs restless; she was trembling slightly, breathing uneasily, snorting, complaining.

Bjartur asked the visitors what they wanted. Wanted? They had been told to bring him a cow. From whom? From the Bailiff, of course.

"May he be of all men the most cursed for his gifts!" declaimed Bjartur in saga style and was already threatening to whet his knife.

"Please yourself," replied the others.

"For thirty years the Bailiff has been trying to cut the feet from under me, and if he thinks one cow will do the trick now, you can tell him he's mistaken," said Bjartur; and the outcome of it all was that the cow was housed in old Blesi's stall and dry turf brought to lay under her, while the horse was stabled next door to her in what had formerly been a pen for the weakliest of the lambs. Bjartur carefully plugged up all the crevices through which there was any danger of light and air penetrating; he had handled cows before today and knew from experience, the nation's thousand years' experience, that beasts of such a kind must have no communion with those prime elements if they are to give milk.

But when the messengers were on the point of taking their leave, Bjartur bade them hang on a moment, and after rooting about in the bed for a while, produced finally an old glove that was kept in his wife's mattress.

"You will inform the Bailiff," he told them, "that hitherto I have owed him nothing beyond what was agreed upon. If he expects to distrain upon my lambs next autumn, then he had better think again. And I call you to witness that if he considers this amount insufficient, he must remove the animal not later than tomorrow; otherwise I reserve full powers to decide whether or not I kill it tomorrow night."

Well, this was proud behaviour, if you like; here was a man who, in ready money if necessary, could flaunt his freedom and independence in the face of the Bailiff or anybody else up-country. But the messengers shrank from accepting the money, they had no authority to accept it, didn't even know whether it was Bjartur whom the Bailiff expected to pay for this so-called animal, maybe it's paid for. Paid for? Yes, from elsewhere. From elsewhere?

Were they mad, was there some conspiracy behind it all, then? Was he, then, dependent on somebody or other elsewhere? Perhaps they thought up-country that it was poverty that had prevented him from buying a cow? No, mates, he was short of neither dung nor doughnuts here, and what was more, he had plenty of money. It was, of course, against his principles to keep cows at the expense of his sheep, but he could, if necessary, buy as many cows as anybody, and pay for them on the spot. Ever since he began he had had a distant goal in view in his running of the farm. He knew quite well what he was going to do with his money. What was he going to do with it? What? If your orders were to inquire about that, you can say that I'm maybe going to build myself a palace with it. And dig an orchard all the way round it. Good-bye.

But it was not long before this same sea-cow had became the bosom-friend of everybody in Summerhouses except Bjartur, the dog, and old Blesi. When the grandmother came scrambling up the stairs that evening with a little milk in the bottom of her pail and proceeded to give each of the children a cupful of the heart-warming luxury and Finna a good measure in a can, a new era might be said to have dawned over this moorland valley. From the beginning of March life seemed to quicken in everything; there was spring in these narrow souls that lived here encompassed by the frozen deserts. The brothers stopped their eternal bickering and dropped all unseemly nicknames and threats of retaliation. Asta Sollilja finished her vest and began without untimely drowsiness on a new pair of knickers with all the industry, forethought, and optimism that such garments demand. From Grandma's memory there even thawed better hymns, easier to understand, less sprinkled with Latin. The ghosts in her stories suddenly became less baneful than before; all at once she even recollected a famous ghost in the south who would do as he was told if he was given his daily cupful the same as other people. Her descriptions of the fate of travellers lost in the snow were no longer so harrow-

ing; there were occasions even when men who had fallen over
precipices would be rescued after two days, incredible as it sounds,
and would live to a ripe and honourable old age though both
thighs had been broken. But a greater marvel still was that not a
full week had elapsed before the mistress of the house was rising
from her bed and trying out her shaky limbs around the room with
assistance from the others. She found her voice again and began
inquiring about the firewood three weeks earlier than she had
risen from her winter sick-bed the year before. She even asked
about the clothes, and everything was in holes, so she found her
darning-needle and sat up in bed to mend them. One morning she
was neither more nor less than out of bed before anyone else,
kindling the fire with those skilful hands of hers. There was much
less smoke in the room that morning, the brushwood started crackling earlier, the coffee warmed up more quickly. And another
morning, when Bjartur went downstairs he found his wife beside
the cow; she had been giving her her fodder and making her comfortable and was now standing beside her in the stall, scratching
her and talking to her.

"I never knew that that blasted cow had to be served before
the others," he grumbled, and began feeding his sheep.

But from that day forward it became a regular habit with
Finna to rise every morning and feed the cow. She brought water
for her too, and saw to it that the floor of her stall was always dry
and comfortable; cows are grateful for such attentions. She milked
her with supple fingers, they had long conversations together.
Finna had intuition that set at naught the nation's thousand years'
experience, and therefore she occasionally left the door ajar for
a few minutes and took the turf plug out of the vent in the roof
if the day was a fine one. Old Blesi was very dissatisfied about
being so close to this tiresome sea-cow; his temper had grown
uncertain and he did not relish such company in his declining
years; it was bad enough having the Reverend Gudmundur and
his brother in the pen on the other side of the drain, fighting and
cursing the whole night through. He would stand sometimes for
hours on end with his ears laid back in token of contempt and
would watch his chance to stretch over the partition and snatch a
mouthful of the fine Rauthsmyri hay from the cow's manger. If
he could not sleep at night, he would bite her whenever he got
the opportunity. So Finna herself nailed up an extra crossbar between them.

"She has deserved well of all of us," she said, full of love and reverence.

"Then I only hope you're prepared to pay a hired man wages to mow hay for her in the autumn," retorted Bjartur, "because I'm certainly not killing off any of my sheep for the sake of that gutsy old parasite."

"I know that God will provide for our dear Bukolla," said his wife with tears in her eyes. She began stroking the cow even more tenderly than before, for this woman knew God in her own way and found Him in a cow, as they do in the East, where the Almighty reveals Himself in cows and the people worship the holy creatures.

They were having quite a decent spring this year; the ground would soon be clear of snow. Bjartur started driving his sheep out into the marshes, where they sought out the spring grass, the famous first-shoots, which cure everything if only the sheep can stand them. The ewes of course were never very lively even in the mildest spring, and though this year they were in rather better condition than usual, it was a lazy, scraggy-necked, feeble-voiced flock that trailed wearily about the marshes. In their dirty fleeces they looked the very picture of melancholy. Bjartur wandered about ready to pull them out if they got stuck, but this year comparatively few of them showed any desire to remain inactive in the bogs, even if they had sunk as far as the hocks. Soon the snow in the hollows had melted.

The sun shone on the pale, withered grass of winter, on the swollen brook, on the thawing marshes redolent of growth and decay. Somewhere in the warm breeze the golden plover was piping its shy vernal notes, for the first friends of the heath had flown home from the south. The garrulous redshank would follow the shepherd home almost to the door, feeling that it simply must tell him this amusing story, of which it never grew tired: he, he, he, he, he, he, he. Little Nonni took the leg-bones, the jaw-bones, and the horns outside on to the slope; the brook was nearly as big as the sea, so big that one could imagine that the world was on the other side. After a day or two the brook had grown little again and all the snow had melted from the mountain. Had the brook lost its charm, then? No, far from it. Clear and joyful it flowed over the shining sand and pebbles, between its banks white with withered grass, its joy eternally new every spring for a thousand years; and it told little stories, in its own little tongue, its own little inflections, while the boy sat on the bank and listened for a thousand years. The boy and eternity, two friends, the sky cloudless and unending.

Yes.

29.   GENTRY

THE BAILIFF came riding into the enclosure on his way home from the coast. He was travelling, as on his last visit, with an escort, but on this occasion his attendants were much more in keeping with his dignity: his son and daughter, both of whom had just returned from the south — Ingolfur Arnarson, the co-operative secretary, and the beautiful, twenty-year-old, newly educated Audur. The folk had been spreading manure on the home-field, but now they stopped spreading manure and, leaning forward on their rakes, stared with marvelling eyes at this portent. Bjartur came home to the croft, leaving his sheep and the helpless lambs they were giving birth to. The daughter refused to step down into the mud and remained sitting on horseback, but the Bailiff dismounted, though obviously bored by whatever was afoot, and the big-booted secretary also dismounted. The Bailiff gave his usual greeting, offering at most two fingers. But for Ingolfur Arnarson a handshake was a very different matter. A representative of the world, of the life of power, privilege, and infinite possibility that those who live in close contact with the government may enjoy, Ingolfur Arnarson was not the man to be shy with the lower orders. He made no bones about wringing Bjartur of Summerhouses' paw; he even went as far as to clap him on the shoulder; for a moment, in fact, it looked as if he was about to fall on his neck, kiss him, and who knows what else. It was his mother coming out in him of course. Nor was he by any means the old irresponsible student whose idea of a good time was to murder the helpless and inoffensive birds that flew over a fellow's marshes on the Sabbath; no, with the passing of the years he had acquired a sober, public-spirited deportment, and he had also developed the corpulence that is so necessary to anyone who wishes his words to carry conviction in an assembly. He had learned to imbue his gestures with authority, to puff out his chest, to hold his head high. But Bjartur of Summerhouses was the man he was in Asta Sollilja's eyes: he had scant regard for his superiors, however public-spirited they might be, and in his shadow they seemed all at once to suffer some incongruous loss of dignity, some deformity even, as if they had suddenly acquired six fingers or even three eyes.

"May I help the young lady down in case she goes bow-legged sticking in the saddle there?" inquired Bjartur politely; but no sooner had he spoken than she hopped down without assistance and made her way on to the paving by herself. She was in breeches and glittering knee-boots, healthy and strong as a plant that grows on sheltered slopes facing the south. Elegant, southern-travelled and blooming she stood before the low door, on the paving that it had taken Gudbjartur Jonsson and his children, both living and dead, twelve years to buy — and eighteen years before that; she who had her home on the smooth pathway leading up to one immortal house half-hidden in flowers.

"Thanks, thanks very much," she said, "but we won't bother coming in. I want to get home as soon as I can."

But the Bailiff would like just to pop upstairs with the master of the house for a few minutes, he and Ingolfur wanted a word with him; worse luck, there's always something. But when they had got safely upstairs after negotiating the mud and the filth in the entrance, she tried all the devices she could think of to prevent their taking a seat on the beds, because of the lice, but the Bailiff would not hear of any fastidiousness, he had been reared on lice. He sat carefully but solidly down on the bed he was accustomed to using whenever he paid a visit to Summerhouses. Ingolfur Arnarson Jonsson found a seat on the clothes-chest, then looked around the room with cocked head and face radiant as the sun, but with his mother's cold smile. The young lady perched herself on the table. The Bailiff, who was sunk in deliberation so profound that he made no answer to Bjartur's inquiries about the condition of the sheep and the state of the weather, sat fumbling in his pockets with limp and tremulous fingers. Over his face there stole a look of solemn devotion, an expression almost fanatical in its pious gravity, and his hand, never very steady, especially when it held money, trembled visibly as he produced his purse. He opened it and looked down into it, yet in such a fashion that by a slight backward tilt of his head and an upward protrusion of his lower lip he contrived to retain all his chew as he spoke.

"This is the first chance I've had of repaying the money you sent for the cow last winter. It's been paid from elsewhere."

"Really? Who is this person who thinks he can boast of having made me, Bjartur of Summerhouses, a gift of something? Paid from elsewhere? I've never asked anyone to pay my debts, either here or elsewhere. To hell with anyone who thinks he has the right to pay my debts."

"Quite so; but it's paid all the same," said the Bailiff.

"I take alms from no one, either in heaven or on earth. Were it the Redeemer Himself he would not be privileged to pay my debts and I would forbid Him to do so."

"Well, it isn't the Redeemer actually; it's the Women's Institute," said the Bailiff.

"I might have known," said Bjartur, and proceed to heap this Institute with all the vituperation he could lay his tongue to. They were, he said, nothing but a gang of insolent slanderers whose one aim was to force their lousy patronage on honourable men and make them their debtors and lickspittles so that they could brag about it later both on earth and in heaven. "But you can lay your life on it," he continued, "that I'll slaughter that bloody old cow and chop her into mincemeat just as soon as I think fit, for she does nothing but take the youngsters' appetites away so that they go slouching about without even the strength to quarrel with one another — apart from the fact that she makes the womenfolk fractious and fosters their stubbornness."

"Yes, but everybody up-country says that your family is looking much better since the cow arrived."

But this observation had no very soothing effect on the moor-crofter's temper. Never were his suspicions so easily aroused as when the dalesmen up-country showed any regard for his welfare, and is there any reason why you or the Women's Institute should concern yourselves with me and my wife, may I ask? Or my children? As long as I owe neither you nor the Women's Institute I shall demand in return that neither you nor the Women's Institute meddle with my wife or my children. My wife and my children are mine in life and death. And it is my business, mine alone, and neither yours nor that pack of blasted old scandalmongers' whether my children look well or not. Sooner shall all the hummocks on Summerhouses land hop up to heaven and all the bogs sink down to bottomless bloody hell than I shall renounce my independence and my rights as a man.

The Bailiff had no reply for this squall, but his expression remained quite unruffled — he himself was the independent man on a large scale, and in consequence had at bottom probably even less faith in loving-kindness and the Christian disposition than Bjartur had. He put the bundle of notes back in his purse with the same gravity and the same obvious solicitude, intimating, as he did so, that the best thing in that case would be to return this trifle to where it came from, I'm certainly not going to force it on

anybody. And there ended an act of charity that might otherwise
have been so beautiful. One would have thought that the country's
aristocrats would now have given up the attempt to work miracles
up this independent moor-crofter, but such was not the case. The
secretary, passing him his silver snuff-box with its finely ground,
aromatic contents, now began to do his share towards helping the
nation's lone worker.

"Well, well, old lad," he said. "You've life in you yet, I see."

Snuff was then taken. When they had finished, the secretary
hinted that Bjartur of Summerhouses might possibly have been
expecting him on business of some slight importance.

"Have I forbidden you the road?" inquired Bjartur.

"There was once," began the secretary, "a certain movement
that began among the weavers of cashmir, in England. This movement is of great assistance to impoverished farmers who seek
redress against the depredation of the merchants. It won its way
into Iceland during the last century, when the poverty-stricken
peasants of Thingey, whose sufferings were due to the rapacity
of their merchant, formed themselves into an association for the
direct purchase of supplies. This buying organization was the
origin of the co-operative movement in Iceland, and now consumers' co-operatives have gradually spread through the length
and breadth of the land, to insure for the farmer fair returns for
his produce and a reasonable price for the goods he needs. These
co-operatives are in a fair way to becoming the most powerful
business enterprises in the whole country, and with time they will
eradicate the whole of the merchant class. The destitute Thingey
crofters who followed the example of the British weavers have
become a guiding light for the young Icelandic community.

"Now, the position in this part of the country is that the merchant in Fjord, having only his own interests at heart, gives you
smallholders as little as he thinks fit for your produce, then sells
you your necessities at an exorbitantly high price that fleeces you
annually of huge sums of money; so huge, in fact, that after careful
calculation I estimate that the embezzlement thus practised on
the impoverished farmers of the district must amount annually
to the cost of a well-built concrete house, in some years two, or at
least the cost of an expensive plant for the production of electricity
in addition to the single dwelling." ("Oh, I shouldn't be surprised
if most of this electricity you talk about isn't in your own backside," interposed Bjartur.) "The firm sticks all this money into its
own pocket, though of course the better part of it goes as spend-

ing-money to the manager himself, whose family, though continually tripping off to Denmark for the sake of their health and
amusement, still doesn't manage to squander all the plunder
looted by the firm from men destitute and reduced to starvation
level." ("Oh, you've been to Denmark, too, Ingi, lad," said Bjartur.) "As everyone knows, the manager has gone and built himself a magnificent palace down in Fjord, with some sort of a tower
on the top, and he's spent thousands on improving the store's buildings." (Bjartur: "Well why shouldn't the poor old devil have a
tower if he wants one?") "Now then, in addition to all this, and
equally a matter of common knowledge, the doctor speaks for the
firm in Parliament and has persuaded the Treasury to pour out
thousand upon thousand to the firm in subsidies for the building
of piers and breakwaters, the reason being that the doctor himself
owns a substantial share in the fishing carried on by the firm down
in Fjord.

"Though we live in a district that has from time immemorial
been renowned for its natural advantages, it cannot be denied
that in social matters we have long lagged behind less fortunate
districts. But now there has come a time," said the secretary, "when
public-spirited men in the south, aware of the pass to which the
farmers in isolated districts have been brought, realize that a
serious effort must be made to persuade them to follow the example set by the Thingey crofters. They must be persuaded to
take organized action against this gang of conspirators who fleece
the individual and the State of every cent they can lay their claws
on for the maintenance of their extravagant undertakings. Night
and day you poor crofters slave over your little holdings without
a decent rag to your backs or food enough to stave off the famine
that preys upon you at this time every year. Money you never see
for years on end, except for a few random cents that come your
way from the hand of uncertainty itself" — (Bjartur: "Plenty of
money in Summerhouses") — "Perhaps a crown or two a year.
You know yourself that it's true, Bjartur, and there's no point in
trying to gild this destitution with glowing colours. Now I ask you
as an honourable man: what have you to say of all this highway
robbery of a whole community?"

Bjartur: "Well, to be quite candid with you, I've never been
in the habit of looking on when you so-called gentry start slinging
mud at one another; it's never a very pleasant sight. I don't interfere with the merchant; whatever his way of life, it's no business
of mine as long as I have no complaints to make against him. All

I know, and care to know, is that my sheep are doing well after
the winter and that I owe nothing to God or man either. I have
plenty of money and my family are, comparatively speaking, just
as healthy as you Utirauthsmyri folk, who I don't suppose are
more than mortal, and apparently much healthier than the merchant's family, who you say are sent abroad every year to distant
continents in search of doctors. We people on the moors here
would not care to exchange with anyone."

"But, my dear Bjartur — "

"I am no dear Bjartur of yours. My name is Gudbjartur Jonsson,
farmer of Summerhouses."

"Very well, then, Gudbjartur Jonsson," said the secretary with
his cold smile and his head cocked in arrogant indifference. "And
my name is Ingolfur Arnarson. And as my name implies, I am a
colonist." (Bjartur: "Yes, you've tried your hand at most things
in your time.") "I want to colonize this country, and persuade
others to colonize it. People have starved themselves and their
animals to death in it for a thousand years, but it has still to be
colonized. Let me tell you this: there are two parties in the land
who from now on will never be at peace, but will fight on till a
conclusion is reached. On one side are the conservatives and the
reactionaries who do all they can to keep the farmers down, and
to this party belong the merchants, the boat-owners, and officials
like the doctor. The other party consists of those who want to do
everything to help the farmers. We want to give the farmers a
fair price for their produce and sell them their necessities without
profit by founding co-operative societies; then we want to provide
them with cheap labour. That can be done by destroying capitalism in the coastal towns so that the workers are forced to return
to the land. Last but not least we must provide the farmers with
money, and that we will do by establishing agricultural banks
through which the State will lend the farmers working capital at
a low rate of interest so that they can extend their buildings, in-
stall electric plant, and buy implements suitable for farming on a
large scale. That is our program, the program of the new Icelandic
colonists. A new age of colonization is beginning in which the
Icelandic farmer will be a free man in a free land. We will exalt
the Icelandic farmer to a position of honour and repute appropriate
to the class that is born to the august destiny of assisting the Creator Himself in His struggle with the powers of darkness."

"Yes, I think I've heard that last bit before somewhere," said
Bjartur, scratching himself.

"But heavens above, man, surely you can understand that we're showing you a way of making money?"

No, that was just the point that Bjartur of Summerhouses couldn't understand. However hard he tried, he simply couldn't get it into his skull that big farmers and the sons of big farmers were wanting to help him make money. They could found as many Women's Institutes and co-operative societies for themselves as the spirit moved them to, but until I ask the great for charity, the great will have to wait for me to run their errands. You big people generally make money whether banded together or not, but if you happen to lose, you lose thousands, and you'll never wheedle me into any society for paying your losses. This is the first year in thirty that I've been free of your old man there; who knows but that, given time, I might not build a fine outhouse for the ewes and separate quarters for the lambs? My livestock has increased, not diminished. As far as I am aware, I have seventy well-fleeced ewes in lamb and twenty gimmers, and that I owe to never burdening myself with a cow, though of course there's no reason why I shouldn't own as many cows as you people of Rauthsmyri eventually, and even knock up a house for the family, just for the fun of the thing, though there's no real need, most of the beams here are still pretty sound, though maybe it leaks a bit here and there under the roof-tree. But to go surety for a crowd of big bugs in competition with the merchant, who has always treated me fairly since the day when I first had anything to sell him, more than twenty years ago —

"Yes, but, man alive, can't you see you'll end up on the parish?"

Then Bjartur fired up, raved incoherently, swore he was a freeborn Icelander and and and it's all the bloody same to me, and and I'd sooner be chopped up alive into little pieces like old Gunnvor at the lich-gate at Myri, and she never gave in but cursed them for all she was worth as she died and it all came true. Women's Institute or Co-operative Society, I shall never give in —

"For heaven's sake, Ingi, come away home now. Can't you see you're just wasting your breath on the man? I'm setting off by myself if you're going on with this damned nonsense."

The Bailiff's daughter had had her fill of this entertainment. Lacking the mulishness of her father and her brother, she saw no reason why they, these men of position, should go to such lengths to convince one peasant of the moors and save him — as if the man hadn't full permission to be as mad as he pleased. No one knows how long they might have sat there had she not interrupted.

"This little girl is called Asta Sollilja," observed the Bailiff to his son, and pointed to the crofter's daughter, who was standing in the home-field with her rake, gazing at them with wondering eyes as they rode out. "She's thirteen."

"Why, of course," said the secretary, reining in his horse to look at her. "I'd quite forgotten. How do you do, Asta Sollilja? You've grown quite a big girl, I see."

"Have you bought that handkerchief yet with the money I gave you in the winter?" asked the Bailiff.

"The money you're talking about," shouted Bjartur from the paving, "it happened to drop into a bog in the marshes there. Quite by accident, of course. But we didn't mind. It was that sort of money."

"Yes, you always were a pig-headed mule," replied the Bailiff.

"Oh, do hurry up," called the Bailiff's daughter from the road. "Let's get off home."

"Well, well, Asta Sollilja," said the secretary, "you've grown into a really fine girl. Good-bye to you. And good-bye to all of you." Good-bye.

30.   OF SONG

WISELY *the whimbrel tunes her lay,*
Plaintive the plover calling her love;
From southern seas wheeling his way,
Glides the grey gull crying above,

— all the singers from the south flown home to marsh and heath, the snow-white grass of winter one with the green of the sward, green, all green in the dingles and everywhere along the streams, and yes, so many days of spring gone by that surely it must be time to let out the cow. They talked about it for a few days, but Finna wanted to choose a day that was bright and warm for the ceremony. Soon there came a day that was warm and bright. The cow-shed was opened and the cow unfastened. Unsteady on her legs, hesitant, puffing and snorting through distended nostrils, she stuck her head out of the door with a rumble of anticipation; out of the darkness and stench of winter into the light and fragrance of spring. The change was sudden, she needed time to adjust herself. On the paving she gave a great low at the sun, then, after cautiously picking her way forward for a step or two, she halted once more to drink in the fragrance of fine weather. She tried to low again, but it seemed as if she could say nothing more for amazement; was she dreaming? There had been so many times when she had dreamed of sunshine and green pasture in the darkness and smell of her shed that she could hardly believe that at last her dream was coming true. She made off down the slope at a sober trot, but after a few moments she could confine her joy no longer, this was really freedom at last. She broke into a gallop, clumsy and stiff after the confinement of winter, and, waving her tail in the air, raced away down into the marshes at full speed. Insensible of all dimensions, she galloped aimlessly in great haphazard curves and circles, lowing and bellowing her song for the spring; and the children ran after her laughing and shrieking till at last she halted in a bog, up to the hocks in mud and panting heavily. Day was far spent before she had calmed down sufficiently to think of grazing.

For the first few days she was graciously allowed to stay in the home-field, though Bjartur grudged her every mouthful that she cropped, for the manured grass, though the total yield would do no more than lace the cow's fodder, was indispensable to the ewes towards the end of winter. He continued to talk disparagingly of the animal which had broken in upon his household and upset all proportions. And the bitch followed her master's example. She was an old and conservative bitch now, and in any case had never had the sagacity of her mother, who was wont to take new-born children to foster and give them life. She often lay on the paving, sleepy-eyed and dejected, but always wakeful enough to follow the cow's every movement with sour eyes. When least expected, she would slink out over the home-field and, stealing up from behind, would watch her chance to sink her teeth in the cow's shanks. The cow would try to defend herself and would lash out with her hoofs or turn with lowered head and try to chase her off, but she would give up; the bitch was too elusive. Then they would stand facing each other, the bitch with ugly sideward glance and teeth bared in a snarl, yelping now and then, the cow tossing her head and sputtering.

"Why can't that blasted cow leave the poor bitch alone?" said Bjartur, who always took the bitch's part against the cow.

Bjartur was rather worried about the children. Day after day they showed ever less liking for the so-called refuse fish, salt catfish, coalfish, codfish, and the sour sausage from last autumn, so he felt that it was unseemly of his wife to bless the creature that deprived the children of their natural appetite for the food that he bought at such exorbitant prices down in Fjord.

Then one day the cow was driven out to Krok, which is a place along by the mountain, heath with grassy hollows. The spring shoots had grown through the withered grass; the marshes were green, the whole valley green. But the cow did not feel happy alone in her pasture and tried to run away over the ridge. Next day the elder boys were sent to look after her, but such company did not console her; she wanted her stall-sisters in Utirauthsmyri and stood for hours lowing up the valley in their direction. Eventually she lost all her respect for the boys and ran off. It was a great chase. They caught up with her in a trench half-way over the ridge, bridled her with cord, and led her home. She stood on the paving exhausted and forlorn, the veins in her neck swollen, her ears twitching in despair, nor did she stop complaining till Finna came out to her and stroked her and talked to her about life. When life is a weariness and escape impossible, it is wonderful to have a friend who can bring us peace with the touch of a hand. After this Finna decided to tend the cow herself. She took little Nonni along with her. Those were good days. They were serene days and quite undemonstrative, like the best days in one's life; the boy never forgot them. Nothing happens; one simply lives and breathes and wishes for nothing more, and nothing more.

Those were the days when the willow twigs were budding on the heath, when the bilberry opened its fragrant flowers in red and white and the wild bee flew humming loudly in and out of the young brushwood. The birds of the moor had laid their first eggs, yet they had not lost the love in their song. Through the heath there ran limpid little streams and round them there were green hollows for the cow, and then there were the rocks where the elves lived, and then there was the mountain itself with the green climbing its slopes. There was sunshine for a whole day. Mist came and there was no sunshine for a whole day, for two days. The heather-clad hummocks rose up in the mist, but the mountains were no more. The moss grew brighter in colour, the fragrance stronger and stronger; there was dew in the grass, precious webs of pearls in the heather and on the soil where the ground was bare of turf. The mist was white and airy, overhead one could almost glimpse the sky, but the horizon was only a few yards away, there at the top of the dingle. The heath grew into the sky with its fragrance, its verdure, and its song; it was like living in the clouds. The cow curved her tongue round the grass and

cropped away steadily; she even stretched out for the willow twigs
that hung over the brook. And the boy sat with his mother knitting
on the edge of the hollow, and they listened to the cow and the
grass and the brook and everything.

"There was once a man. He was on his way home. It was a dark
autumn night. He was very tired. He had been in such trouble
with the bailiff and the merchant, probably there would be nothing but the parish for him now. He had not been able to pay his
debts, the dealer would not give him any more credit, and the
bailiff had threatened to sell him out. Perhaps the council would
make him flit; then the children would be sent here, there, and
everywhere, to be starved on week-days and thrashed on Sundays.
They were waiting for him at home now, and he was returning
empty-handed from the town; he was so proud that he could not
bring himself to ask others to buy him anything. Yes, his footsteps
were heavy. Many a heavy footstep has this country felt above it
and no one has known. What was he to do?

"Then all at once he sees a light among the rocks.

"He had passed this way scores of times, both in daylight and
darkness, and he did not know what to make of it, a light shining
there among the rocks. So he made his way towards the light,
and there stood a little house. A man was standing at the door, a
pleasant-featured young man; it was the fairy farmer. He did not
say very much, but all his words were kindly. He had the pleasant,
thoughtful air of the elves, the elves have no worries, they look
for what is good and find it. In the rocks he was given coffee with
plenty of sugar and cream, and before he was aware of it he was
telling this kindly young man all about his troubles. When they
parted, the elf farmer said to him: 'When you wake up tomorrow,'
he said, 'you must look in the passageway at home.'

"So the crofter set off home and he and all his family went to
bed. He had not dared to tell them of his troubles. In the morning
when he came down into the passageway, what do you think he
saw? The whole place was stacked up with provisions. There were
sacks full of flour, cases full of sugar, and some lovely fish in a
bag. The people on the croft there had never tasted such lovely
fish before. There was even a little jar of syrup.

"And there was once a little boy. He was a foster-child with
some people who lived in a valley up on the moors, and he was
not allowed to go to church, though all the others went to church.
He had no brother and no little sister either, because they had
been taken away from him. It was one Sunday in the summertime.

They had all set off for church in their Sunday clothes, each of them on his horse, and he was standing on the paving watching them draw farther away, and how the puffs of dust rose from the horses' hoofs on the paths along by the river! Don't you think he must have taken it to heart?

"He wandered, weeping, away from the farm and up to the rocks at the foot of the mountain, quite overpowered by the evil that seems so often to prevail in life and even to rule it. But what do you think he heard from the rocks at the foot of the mountain? Why, he heard the most delightful singing! Who could it be that was singing so beautifully? It wasn't a solo or a duet, and it wasn't a trio either; it was a whole congregation singing. A service was being held; never had the boy heard such a lovely hymn before. And where was all the singing coming from? Then the boy saw that the fairy rock was no longer a rock, but a church, and the church was standing open in the sunshine, and the elves were all sitting in the church, and the priest was standing in front of the altar in vestments of green. And the boy went into the elves' church. He had never seen such people before, so noble and happy. Such is life when it is lived in peace and in song. When the hymn was over, the priest mounted the pulpit and preached a sermon. Never had the boy heard a sermon so beautiful or so touching. And never afterwards did he hear a sermon like it. All his life through he remembered it, meditating upon it in secret and trying always to live up to it; but the theme of the sermon he told to no one. Some people think that it must have been about how in the end good will be triumphant in the life of man. Then the priest went to the altar and intoned in a warm, gentle voice; quite differently from our priests here on earth. It was as if a good hand was laid over his heart. Then when the last hymn had been sung, all the people stood up and went out. And the boy stood up too and went out. But when he looked around, the people had all disappeared and the church had gone too. There was nothing to be seen but Fairy Rock, as bare and steep as it had always been, and all he could hear was the twitter of some birds flying in and out of the clefts, probably they were white-tails. He never saw Fairy Rock open again. But he kept the memory of this Sunday ever afterwards in his mind and it consoled him when he had to do without the happiness that others enjoy in life; and he grew up into a man pleased with what he had and contented with his lot."

From the white heaven of mist where the sun was hidden like a delightful promise there dropped into her hair a thousand

precious glittering pearls as she told her stories. She pursed her
lips at the end of each with solemnity, almost with adoration, as
if they were sacred chronicles. Gently she smoothed the loops
on her needles; the landscape was shrouded and holy, breathe
quietly. Her best friend had been an elf-woman and she had known
an elf-man, too, the elf-woman's brother; but all that had been
long, long ago, when she was at home in Urtharsel. "Have I
dropped a stitch?" she asked, and sighed. "Ah well, it doesn't
matter. What is gone is gone. And will never return."

But the boy felt that it mattered. He proposed that they should
go to her friends and become elves with them, when Father and
Asta Sollilja were down in Fjord. "And we'll take our Bukolla
along with us," he said.

"No," said his mother pensively. "It's too late now. Who would
there be to look after Grandmother?"

That was more than the boy could answer; he simply kept on
gazing into his mother's face, which was the noblest and most
exalted of all things that lived in the world, unequalled in its goodness, its beauty, and its sorrow. And when later in life he thought
of those days and of the face that reigned over them, then he
felt that he too, no less than the blue mountains, had been fortunate enough to experience the holiness of religious contemplation.
His being had rested full of adoration for the glory which uni-
fies all distances in such beauty and sorrow that one no longer
wishes for anything — in unconquerable adversity, in unquenchable longing, he felt that life had nevertheless been worth while
living.

> When the fiddle's song is still,
>   And the bird in shelter shivers,
> When the snow hides every hill,
>   Blinds the eye to dales and rivers,
>
> Often in the halls of dreams,
>   Or afar, by distant woodland,
> I behold the one who seems
>   First of all men in our Iceland.
>
> Like a note upon the string
>   Once he dwelt with me in gladness.
> Ever shall my wishes bring
>   Peace to calm his distant sadness.

> *Still the string whispers his song;*
> *That may break, a love-gift only;*
> *But my wish shall make him strong,*
> *Never shall he travel lonely.*

His mother taught him to sing. And when he had grown up
and had listened to the world's song, he felt that there could be
no greater happiness than to return to her song. In her song dwelt
the most precious and the most incomprehensible dreams of mankind. The heath grew into the heavens in those days. The song-
birds of the air listened in wonder to this song, the most beautiful
song of life.

31.   OF THE WORLD

ST. JOHN'S EVE; those who bathe in the dew may wish a wish.

Young and slender she walked down by the brook, down to
the marshes, and waded barefoot in the lukewarm mud of the bogs.
Tomorrow she was to go to town and see the world for herself.

For weeks the prospect had filled her day-dreams with pleasur-
able anticipation; every night since the Bailiff came she had gone
to sleep in the middle of a dozing reverie crowded with fancies
of the promised journey. In daylight or in dreams she had seen
herself set off a hundred times, and lately she had been so reluctant to waste time in sleeping that she had lain awake till early
morning, savouring the delight to come. The hours today had
passed like a distant breeze, her fingertips had been numb, her
cheeks hot, she had heard nothing that was said. She had knitted
herself underclothes of soft blue-grey yarn and had laid them
aside for this excursion, looking at them only on Sundays. And
she had knitted herself a brown petticoat with two stripes round it,
one blue, the other red. And a few hours ago her father had opened
the clothes-chest, which was the only receptacle in the house that
had a lock to it, and had taken out a flowered frock wrapped in
his Sunday jacket. "Though you're maybe a shade too thin to fill
it," he said, "it's time you began wearing your mother's best frock.
My daughter shall lack nothing outside or in, the day she goes
out into the world."

She had blushed with pleasure, her eyes sparkling. It was a
solemn moment. The dress was crumpled of course, the material
crisp and thin with old age, but neither moths nor damp had ever
touched it. It was printed with the fertile vegetation of foreign

countries and had numerous flounces on the bosom. But though Asta Sollilja had grown at an incredible rate these last few months, her figure beginning to round to life's youthful curves, she was still a leggy stripling and far too slight to fill such a garment. It hung loosely from her thin shoulders and billowed widely about her waist. "She's like a scarecrow in the meadow at Utirauthsmyri," said Helgi, and his father pushed him away downstairs. Apart from its size the dress suited her admirably.

She threw her arms round her father's neck in gratitude and found the place on his throat and hid her face there. Her lips had grown thicker. When one looked at her profile against the window, one saw that she had a heavy lower lip, rather like a charming curl; her mouth was beginning to look so mature, poor girl — and his beard tickled her eyelids.

The lukewarm mud spurted up between her bare toes and sucked noisily when she lifted her heel. Tonight she was going to bathe in the dew, as if she had never had a body before. On every pool of the river there was a phalarope to make her a bow; no bird in all the marshes is so courtly in its demeanour on Midsummer Eve. It was after midnight, wearing slowly on for one o'clock. The spring night reigned over the valley like a young girl. Should she come or should she not come? She hesitated, stole forward on her toes — and it was day. The feathery mists over the marshes rose twining up the slopes and lay, like a veil, in innocent modesty about the mountain's waist. Against the white sheen of the lake loomed the shape of some animal, like a kelpie in the pellucid night.

A grassy hollow on the margin of the river, and leading up to it through the dew the wandering trail left by two inexperienced feet. The birds were silent for a while. She sat on the bank and listened. Then she stripped herself of her torn everyday rags under a sky that could wipe even the sunless winters of a whole lifetime from the memory, the sky of this Midsummer Eve. Young goddess of the sunlit night, perfect in her half-mature nakedness. Nothing in life is so beautiful as the night before what is yet to be, the night and its dew. She wished her wish, slender and half-grown in the half-grown grass and its dew. Body and soul were one, and the unity was perfectly pure in the wish. Then she washed her hair in the river and combed it out carefully, sitting with her feet in the water and her toes buried in the sand at the bottom. Those strange waterfowl still swam round her in strange curves, turning about courteously when least expected and making her a bow for no reason at all. Nor was there anyone else in the whole of the world who could make so fine a bow.

She began to feel cold, and she ran to and fro on the river bank, her trail criss-crossing like the streets in the cities of the world. She was light and impersonal, new-risen from the dew like the mist itself, wonderful in the moist green landscape of the sunlit night. She grew warm again after running about for a little while, and the birds woke up and the sky was radiant with the flickering of gorgeous colours; in an hour's time the sun would glint in the dew of the lady's-mantle, and the dew would disappear in the sun, St. John's holy dew.

With the first morning rays, long before the snores of night had risen as far as the throat, Bjartur sprang out of bed, took a hasty pinch of snuff, and started dressing. Did Asta Sollilja over- sleep this morning, the morning of the great day on which she was to see the world? No, let no one say it; she rose up too, and rubbed the sleeplessness from her eyes as she watched him putting his clothes on. Then he went out for the horse. And when he had gone she took out her new underclothes and drew them over the clean body that she had bathed for the first time last night, the body that she had just discovered for the first time, the body she had actually just been given. She put on her petticoat, her new woollen stock- ings, and her new sheepskin shoes, and last of all she donned the lovely dress, memory of her mother. She tripped up and down the floor, her heart beating high with eagerness and the joy of de- parture, while her stepmother warmed up the coffee. The grand- mother too was awake, sitting up in bed with her index finger be- tween her gums.

"Don't forget your coat, maiden. You're badly dressed for a shower of rain."

That was just like Grandmother. As if Asta Sollilja would even dream of showing herself down-country in such a filthy old rag.

"Oh, it can come on at any moment," replied her grandmother.

"But there's not a sign of cloud in the sky," said Asta Sollilja.

"Fine weather fools fine wits," said the grandmother. "And heedlessness has its own reward."

But nothing fills the soul with such perfect confidence as a cloudless morning of this kind; the sun was beaming over the green valley and the Bluefells lay resting on the blue of the sky in dreamy security, like the children in a rich house, their faces exalted and happy, as if nothing, nothing would ever cast another shadow on the tranquil sunshine under this deep eternal sky. To drag out a torn old coat was like an evil thought on such a morning, and Asta Sollilja said good-bye to her grumbling old grandmother.

Then she set off into the world with her father. The cart old Blesi was pulling was heaped with sacks of wool, and when they had reached the road, her father said she might ride on top while he walked in front leading the horse. It was a lovely morning. Never had Asta Sollilja felt the day to be so spacious, never had she been so free. After a short time new vistas were unfolded and she began to feel that she had left the meagreness of all her past existence behind her. The winds that blew over the moors had never smelled so fresh in her nostrils, never had the song of moorland birds sped off to such outer distance. The echos had changed, the voices were altogether different. They no longer heard the old familiar valley-birds, they heard new birds, birds that sang to other landscapes, the birds of the world. The hummocks alongside the road took on a different shape and different vegetation, the mountains changed their positions and new forms peeped out, while old ridges and promontories retreated upon themselves or resolved themselves into independent hills. The streams ran in a different direction, the stones had a different appearance; from the dingles the scent of unknown flowers was wafted towards the inexperienced traveller. So bad was the road that she was shaken and jolted unmercifully in the cart, but her senses were alive to the smallest detail of day and route, the world new as on the first morning of the Lord's creation.

The road wound backward and forward among the watercourses, ascending gradually to the moors above, and the travellers were met on the crest of every rise by fresh families of moorland birds, which followed them with passionate song to the next escarpment and the next escort. The morning was half spent before they reached the plateau. Here the vegetation was thinner, the breeze colder. The heath spread itself out before the young traveller's eyes, lonely and grey, with fewer and fewer birds, no brooks. Far, far away sparkled the white surface of a lake. One undulation succeeded another with its windswept, naked crest, its desolate gravel plains, and its tracts of thin soil, stripped of vegetation. Here and there were flats sparsely covered with moss, where mountain ewes and their lambs lay ruminating in the morning sunshine and took to their heels when they approached. The girl jumped down from the cart and walked along by her father's side in the wide flowered dress, in an effort to warm herself up. The chill isolation of the moorland plateau reigned over these two wayfarers and they were silent. The dreary monotony of the landscape dulled their senses; she began to feel hungry and no longer looked for or delighted in the things that were strange to her.

Again and again the girl waited for the next hilltop to refresh the eye with some variation, some new prospect, but always it was the same endless repetition except that the gleaming waters of the lake had long since been left in the rear. She had lost all her anticipation and had long grown tired of expecting anything in particular when the road, turning suddenly, dipped downward along the side of a deep ravine with a river at the bottom. And when she looked eastward along the gap, expecting to see another hill in front of her, lo and behold, there was nothing to see; it was as if the world came to a sudden stop before her eyes and the depth of the skies took its place, though with a different shade of blue. Or was it that the sky was supported out on the horizon there by a gleaming wall of blue-green glass? This strange blue colour seemed to embrace all the mysteries of distance, and she stood for a moment overwhelmed by the prospect of such infinity. It was as if she had come to the edge of the world.

"Father," she said in a perplexed and hesitating voice, "where are we?"

"We've crossed the heath," he replied. "That's the ocean."

"The ocean," she repeated in an awe-stricken whisper. She went on staring out to the east, and a cold shiver of joy passed through her at the thought of being fortunate enough to stand on the eastern margin of the moors and see where the land ends and the ocean begins, the sea of the world.

"Isn't there anything on the other side, then?" she asked finally.

"The foreign countries are on the other side," replied her father, proud of being able to explain such a vista. "The countries that they talk about in books," he went on, "the kingdoms."

"Yes," she breathed in an enchanted whisper.

It was not for some time that she realized how foolish had been her question, and that she might well have known that this was the very ocean over which young heroes sailed to win fame in the Rhymes; far, far across this mighty sea lay the lands of adventure. To her had been given the good fortune of looking upon the sea that swirls about the lands of romance; the road to the incredible. And when they halted at the top of the first slope on their way downhill, she had forgotten her hunger and was still staring out to sea in speechless wonder. Even in her wildest fancies the ocean had never been so huge.

The eastern sides of the heath were steeper even than at home. Soon they were looking down upon the roofs of the market town and the coffee-brown vegetable gardens with their arrow-straight paths between the beds. Asta Sollilja had conjured up remarkable pictures of Fjord, but she would never have dreamed that so many houses, every one of them as impressive as the mansion at Utirauthsmyri, could have stood in a row along such a short stretch of road. And the smoke that was wafted up the hillsides from these houses smelled almost sweet in her nostrils, far different from the troublesome reek that poured out of the poor turf at home in Summerhouses. Soon they were passing the first houses on the hillside and beginning to meet all sorts of wayfarers, some walking, some riding, and some driving carts. They even met some finely dressed young men, wearing collars and ties on a week-day and with cigarettes between their lips, and these young men were so pleased with life that they looked at her and burst out laughing and had forgotten her with the next step they took.

"Who were those young men?" she asked.

But her father, it seemed, was not so deeply impressed by these elegant youths as she had been. "A crowd of cigarette-sucking louts," he replied. And now they were walking on a paved road and there were houses on either side, and curtains and flowers in the windows; isn't it wonderful the things that grow out in the world? And there, walking towards them arm in arm, came two girls, both wearing laced shoes and coats, one with a red hat, the other with a blue one, and they were both so smart that at a distance she thought that one of them at least must be Audur of Myri, but when they came nearer she thought the other must be Audur too, and could make neither head nor tail of it, but it turned out that they were only two town girls, and they shrieked with helpless laughter as they passed her. The people of Fjord seemed to be extraordinarily generous with their laughter and their happiness.

But her father hadn't even noticed them. "Who are they?" he repeated when she asked. "A couple of brazen-faced young sluts, of course, fit for nothing but parading the streets and living on their parents like parasites."

The houses crowded closer and closer together, till finally there was no longer any room for a home-field between them, let alone a decent bit of pasture; all they had was a tiny garden. Townsfolk and travellers, pack-horses and carts crowded along the street, boats on the sea. So many things caught her eye at one and the

same moment that soon she grew tired with asking questions. Her
mind was in a whirl, she flitted through it all as if in a dream, and
strangers sped off in various directions without a handshake or a
word of greeting. Before she realized what was happening, she
was standing beside her father in front of the counter in Bruni's
shop itself, gazing at all the goods that the world and its civilization have to offer — snow-white stockings, fifty raincoats, cups with
roses embossed on them, an oil-stove, chewing-tobacco. Behind
the counter beautifully dressed men of imposing appearance were
standing writing things in books or showing people gold watch-
chains and biscuits. She stood there bewildered, her dress flapping
loosely about her, her stockings round her ankles and mud on her
shoes, staring blindly in front of her, her wits scattered by the
spectacle of such magnificence. Then the warehouseman came,
brisk and impressive. He weighed the wool for Bjartur out in the
so-called porch, and looked at Asta Sollilja twice. He said he had
never suspected that Bjartur had a daughter who would soon be
old enough to get married. "Give her a while longer and she'll do
nicely for our Magnus," he said. But Bjartur said there was plenty
of time to think about that; "she won't be confirmed till next spring
and she's all length so far, poor lass." The dale-girl blushed furiously at this unexpected suggestion of marriage and was very
grateful to her father for not coming to any arrangement without
further inquiry, and also for excusing her on the plea that she was
not fat enough for such things. She did not allow for the fact
that townspeople often come out with things that in the country
would be thought lacking in deliberation.

Afterwards Asta Sollilja was allowed to accompany her father
into the merchant's office. She had always imagined that the merchant was called Bruni, but it now appeared that his was a name
even more remarkable, Tulinius Jensen. She felt as she might have
done had she been invited up to the altar in Rauthsmyri Church
in the middle of the service, but on her father this signal honour
had no effect at all. Nothing on earth could surprise him. Not even
when Tulinius Jensen clasped him to his bosom and held him there
in loverlike embrace did he show any trace of astonishment. No,
the embraces of the great ones of the world were obviously no
novelty to her father.

"It is a pleasure to see such a trusty old friend," said this fine,
heavy-built gentleman, "especially in these difficult times when
no one seems to value friendship any longer. You have heard about
the meeting, of course?"

"This and that," replied Bjartur. "I won't say that I haven't heard rumors of that society business of theirs. And visitors came to Summerhouses in the spring on the same sort of errand. But so far I've made it a rule to do what suits myself rather than other people, even when it happens to be the Rauthsmyri pair."

"Quite right. Ingolfur Arnarson has become temporary manager of this so-called Co-operative Society. Their first sorry consignment arrived by steamer a few days ago, and immediately all the farmers that could free themselves deserted me and rushed off to join the society; but I wonder if there'll be as much enthusiasm among them in two or three years' time, when they start levelling the rich men's debts out on the poor and begin distraining on their crofts as they did in the Hrappsvik Society last year?"

"I don't know," said Bjartur. "But as long as I don't hanker after other people's profits, I certainly don't want to pay other people's losses."

The merchant asserted that co-operative societies could never lead to anything but national disaster; like any other form of monopoly, their one aim was to destroy private enterprise, the liberty and the independence of the individual. "Our warehouses, on the other hand, stand open to you, my dear Bjartur, with all that in them is. But, by the way, that daughter of yours has grown into a big, fine-looking girl, and no mistake."

"Oh, she's only a nestling yet," said Bjartur, "she hasn't been confirmed even. But she has it in her. And she can read. And knows a thing or two about the classics. What does 'shield-tree' mean, Sola? Let the merchant see how much you know."

"That's what I call well done," said the merchant when she had explained the kenning. "Very few people know their Edda these days, I can tell you. I must tell our little Svanhvita about this; she never reads anything but Danish."

"Oh, Danish," said Bjartur, refusing to be impressed. "It may be all right for the big countries, but we folk up in the dales have more faith in the geniuses of the past, like Magnus Magnusson of Magnuswoods. Iceland will never see the like of him again. Let the merchant hear one of his maid-songs, Sola, lass."

Asta began immediately and without complaint to recite the prologue to the twelfth canto in Bernotus. With hanging head and red to the roots of her hair she reeled it off, gasping for breath and running one word into the next at such tremendous speed that it was impossible to distinguish them. But half-way through she got into a muddle with the lines and stood panting for breath and growing more and more terrified until finally she lost her tongue altogether and felt like sinking through the floor.

"Marvellous," said the dealer. "A masterpiece. That's what I call genius" — and saved her by taking both her hands in his in consolation. He felt sure that she had the makings of an exceptionally gifted young lady, and proposed therefore to make her a gift of a bright new penny so that she could buy herself a pretty handkerchief, for the disposition to present everybody with a handkerchief is a characteristic of all great men. Then he opened the door for them and pushed them courteously out into the shop, which, actually, he had just given them with all that in it was.

The rest of the day went in purchasing supplies and in odd errands. Asta Sollilja was allowed to buy her handkerchief, and it was her first handkerchief and had flowers round the border. She was also allowed to buy a string of sky-blue beads, which she hung straightway round her neck in order to be in harmony with this great town. She carried her handkerchief in her hand, since she had no pocket. But that was not all. "I seem to recollect that I made you a promise of Orvar-Odds Saga awhile ago," said her father, so they made their way to the bookseller's.

The bookseller was an old man who was no longer able to stand without assistance and had to shuffle about indoors with the aid of a walking-stick. In spite of this he was reputed to keep remarkably well abreast of the times. His shop was at the top of a tumbledown old house hidden behind other buildings, a little room partitioned off from the rest of the garret. The way lay up a dark, creaking staircase that seemed as if it would never end. The bookseller was busy boiling some fresh fish on an oil-stove; the steam from the pan filled the room, and the many shelves sagging beneath the weight of literature were lost like belts of crags in fog. He stood up from his pan, took his stick, and shook his visitors' hands in greeting.

"Can we get books here?" inquired Bjartur.

"Books and books," replied the bookseller; "it all depends."

"Well, it was just something for our Sola here," said Bjartur. "The little wretch has begun sniffing about between the covers, and it seems I must have promised her Orvar-Odds Saga at some time or another. I pay on the nail."

"Pray God for guidance, man. It's thirty-odd years since I sold the last copy of Orvar-Odds Saga. The country stands on an entirely different cultural footing nowadays. I can recommend the story of *King Solomon's Mines* there, all about the hero of Umslopogaas, in his own way a great man, and in my opinion no whit inferior to Orvar-Oddur."

"That's rather more than I'm prepared to believe. Some more of that damned modern rubbish, I suppose. And no one is going to tell me that that fellow you mentioned just now could ever have stood up to Orvar-Oddur, and him fully twelve Danish ells in height."

"Maybe, but the country happens to have reached a stage in its development when it wants to keep abreast of the times, and we booksellers have to take that into account. Surely you, Miss Sola, will agree that one must adapt oneself to the times? Come here, love, and take a look at my up-to-date books. Here we have a world-famous novel about a man who was murdered in a cart, and here a scientific account of the depravity of the Papacy, all about how those bad people abroad, monks and nuns, led immoral lives in the Middle Ages. And here I can show you a book that's practically new and absolutely the height of fashion nowadays; just look at it, little miss, don't you think we'd like to read it?"

Though the man was old and decrepit, Asta Sollilja could not help blushing to the roots of her hair at the title he used in addressing her; even in her most extravagant dreams she had never imagined that one day she would be called Miss Sola or that she would ever have literary interests in common with such a man. And when she looked at the title-page of the topmost volume, she was struck with such amazement that her heart almost stopped its beating. That strange, significant business which she had never heard mentioned by its name, but of which both the animals at home and her reading of the Jomsviking Ballads had given her an inkling — whole books had been written about it, then: *The Secrets of Love, Wholesome Advice Regarding the Union of Man and Woman.*

Union? thought the girl, trembling with fright, as if she thought her father was about to slap her face — how can there be union of a man and a woman? She hoped and prayed that her father would not catch sight of this book. Seldom has a book awakened a young girl's curiosity in such measure, seldom has a young girl been so shy of a book. Even if there had been no one with her, she would never have dared to ask for such a book. But though she looked hurriedly aside and pretended not to have noticed anything, the title continued to fascinate her with such power that she could see no other book in the whole of these remarkable premises.

Her father, of course, must choose this very moment to notice it too, and naturally he lost his temper, as he always did when this subject cropped up. "This looks like some of the damnable filth brewed by those misbegotten swine in Reykjavik to rot the hearts of the women," he growled.

"It's what the women want, all the same," replied the book-seller. "I've sold thirty copies of it in the last five years and it's still in demand. Murder and science are by no means enough. There has to be a certain amount of love in our literature also. Orvar-Oddur was a long man in his time, but who would care to measure the length of love?"

The result was inevitable; Bjartur and the bookseller started wrangling about the spirit of modern literature and the superior skill of the classics, while Asta Sollilja stood looking on in utter bewilderment till the water in the bookseller's pan boiled over. The visit ended with Bjartur buying his daughter the story of *Snow White and the Seven Dwarfs.*

"He has seven or eight bastards, as anyone would expect after seeing the sort of stuff he deals in," said Bjartur when they stood safe and sound at the foot of the dark and creaking stairs that led to the Secrets of Love.

He trudged along with stooping shoulders and long, clumsy strides that showed how unaccustomed he was to walking on a level surface. Thin and hesitant in her billowy dress, the string of beads round her neck, the handkerchief grasped in her sweaty palm, Asta hurried along in the rear, trying to imitate his gait, for she did not know how to walk on her own responsibility. Every-one watched them as they passed.

In the evening they went to a lodging-house to spend the night. It was a big building, floor upon floor of it, clad in unpainted cor-rugated iron, and with steps up to the door. And what a house! Asta Sollilja had never dreamed that such hubbub could exist, such shouting, howling, singing, scuffling, such banging of doors, rattling of plates, screeching of girls, and barking of dogs, such jesusing. This must be the famous revelry of the world. Heavens, how much must happen in such a house in only one day even! The varied life implicit in all this noise affected the bewildered child with a sad sense of her own isolation, her own insignificance; she stood outside the boundaries of life; this great house was to her comparable in its way with the book about the secrets of love, full of seductive charm, but closed. Happy were they who lived here in life's enchanting tumult and could share in the noisy merriment of

the kitchen. She sat like some crudely finished object on a bench
out in a corner of the dining-room, making no complaint whatso-
ever, while her father mingled with the other men, mostly dalesmen like himself, discussing trade, worms, and this year's grass.
One thing only comforted her: the country folk did not give her
such queer looks as the fine people of the town; hardly a soul
looked at her at all.

She was tired and hungry, her mind slow-moving after all the
multitude of impressions that had met on her consciousness during the whole of that long day. She did not even have the energy
to adjust the inner sole that had worked half-way out of one of
her shoes and up her instep; she sat staring in front of her with
the handkerchief in her hand, and the handkerchief was dirty
and crumpled already. Then there entered a big girl with glowing
complexion and blue eyes and broad bosom, thrice as broad and
full as Asta Sollilja's; such a girl should be able to fill a dress out
all right. She came sailing enviably in out of the uproar of the
kitchen, carrying steaming fish on a colossal plate and bidding
everyone sit down to table. Asta Sollilja was so thin that she dared
not look at her with more than one eye. With a vigour in keeping
with her beauty she asked who Asta Sollilja was with, then put her
next to her father and saw to it that no one went without his share;
and the valiant wrangling of the argumentative guests subsided
in the face of such thick slices of fish.

Only when they were preparing for bed were their tongues
loosened again. Trade and worms began once more. To make matters worse, there now entered the dormitory a number of queer-
looking men who sang for no obvious reason and seemed to find
great difficulty in keeping their feet on the smooth floor. They
were red-eyed and muddy, and smelled of something yeasty. Asta
Sollilja took fright immediately, for she felt that they looked at
her so strangely, and besides they began pawing at her, but her
father said she mustn't be frightened, they were only drunk. But
they persisted in spite of that, asking even who it was that had
a wife so young and beautiful, and Bjartur told them angrily to
leave the child alone, she was only thirteen and not even confirmed yet. The men said they could have sworn that she was old
enough for a man, and one of them spewed on the floor. No one
showed the slightest resentment against the newcomers, and the
controversy about business matters continued as if nothing had
happened. Opinion divided the disputants into the usual two
groups, one warm in its praises of those who wanted to do every-

thing to help the farmers, the other siding with those who did everything to damn them. It was contended that the whole country ought to set up consumers' co-operatives the same as the Thingey crofters had done more than thirty years before. Asta Sollilja felt nevertheless that it was going too far to say that the merchants were all bloodsuckers and thieves, since her father stood up for the merchant. But one thing she would never be able to understand was why her father should say so many nasty things about Ingolfur Arnarson, that handsome, kind-hearted man who had greeted her so warmly once in the spring. Then again, the secretary's father had twice given her two quarters for doing absolutely nothing at all; and though the merchant had given her a shiny penny for reciting ballads, she still could not help wishing that her father would stop being so bitter towards the Bailiff's noble-looking son, who wanted to do everything for the farmers.

The dispute grew more and more heated, and finally the girl hardly knew which she could afford to love less, the merchant or the co-operative secretary. She tried only to keep as close to her father as possible. One of the crofters said that the merchants were not only thieves but murderers as well; he knew lots of folk who had had to go hungry simply because Bruni had refused them credit, and he could give them a list of people in his own locality who had actually starved to death for the selfsame reason, and that in the last few years. The co-operative societies, on the other hand, were the farmers' own stores; in them even the meanest peasant could feel safe against being first swindled, then finally starved to death. Another one said that it wasn't the small farmers who controlled the co-ops nowadays, as they had done in Thingey originally; the landed men had taken the societies into their service now, or why was the Bailiff of Myri fighting for a society? Was anybody so simple as to believe that it was out of concern for the smallholders? No, it was because his own business in Vik was on its beam-ends. The Vik Co-op had ruined it, and now he was wanting to recoup his losses in Fjord here. No, the small man would be no better off with the co-operative society than with the merchant; there would be the same old pile of debts heaping up again, only there would be a monopoly adding to them as well; don't you even read the papers, damn you? "I'm in no debt," retorted Bjartur of Summerhouses. But the protagonists were both in debt, for each of them owned a cow, as was only to be expected, and they had no time to waste on an independent and unencumbered man like Bjartur. The question was not whether

one ought to be in debt or not, but whom one ought to be in
debt to, and on this issue tempers mounted higher and higher till
one of them said you couldn't expect common sense from the
other anyway, a man who couldn't even do his duty by his wife.
The other immediately called on all present to witness this insult,
adding that it was public knowledge that his opponent's wife had
fooled him for twelve years with a farm labourer, and that he
couldn't call the children his own. "No, you're going a bit too far
now," interrupted Bjartur; "remember there's a youngster here
when you talk such filth" — though Asta Sollilja had noticed nothing filthy about it and had not concerned herself in the slightest
about whose the children were. They asked him what he thought
the place was, a kindergarten or something, and what the hell
was he doing here anyway with a half-grown girl among grown-up
men when serious matters were being discussed? One word led
to another; they knew to the hour and minute when they had
been together, what's more she was wearing red pants that particular day, and then of course words were not enough, the only
solution was a smack across the chops — red pants, did you say?
Well, I say a red nose. Yes, and a black eye. Asta Sollilja now
began to realize that serious matters were being discussed. Warriors slain in the ballads and heaped to the hilltops were as nothing compared with the sight of a man struck in a lodging-house
all because of red pants; so there did exist evil men after all. The
others tried to separate them, even Bjartur giving a hand, but they
landed all in a struggling mass in the middle of the floor. Asta
thought that everyone was fighting everyone else and that they
would kill her father. She screamed and started crying as if her
heart would break. Slowly the cluster moved towards the door,
more and more flinging themselves on top, and at last the enemies were slung out into the open air, where one or two of the
crowd took it upon themselves to effect a reconciliation and give
them snuff. Bjartur and several others came in again, and the
girl trembled and kept on weeping in spite of her father's efforts
to console her.

"Father," she sobbed, "I want to go home. Father, Father,
let me go home."

But he told his little love to stop her whimpering. "The silly
lads are only amusing themselves; they've had a drop too much
to drink, and in a minute or two they'll be weeping down one
another's necks; so take your clothes off now, we save a dime by
using the same bunk."

The bedsteads were ranged along the walls of the room and had each an upper and a lower bunk. The child crept into one of the lower bunks and slipped off the flowered dress, but did not dare take off her petticoat.

The peacemakers talked on, still discussing the fight and its causes, over and over again in various forms and from various points of view. Finally they began whispering in confidence out in the middle of the floor, the amount of adultery that was going on was really something terrible. Though she heard little of their whispering, Asta Sollilja could neither sleep nor rest and was still shivering under the coverlet, so strong was her emotion after having lived the Rhymes in this unrhymed, commonplace fashion.

She was thankful when the company, showing signs of sleepiness at last, proceeded to blow their noses, unfasten their shoes, and pull off their trousers. Her father, too, sat down on the edge of the bed, blew his nose, unfastened his shoes, and pulled off his trousers. She listened expectantly to his movements, feeling that he took an age to rid himself of every garment. Not before he was lying beside her did she think herself safe; never had she felt such an impatient or so irresistible a desire to nestle close up to him as after this brawl. She could not yet control the trembling of her limbs; her teeth were still chattering in her head. The men bade one another good-night in Christian fashion, and their beds creaked as they lay down.

"Move over a bit, lass," said her father, "there's no room at all in these damned things," and she tried to squeeze herself as close to the wall as possible. "There we are, chicken, turn your face to the wall now and go to sleep."

But she simply could not get to sleep. There seemed to be so much cold coming from the partition, probably that was why she was shivering so much. The coverlet was far too thin and her father had pulled it nearly all away from her, and the warmth from him only warmed her back; her shivering fits continued with little pause. The men around had fallen asleep immediately and were now snoring loudly, but there was no sleep for her in the cold from the wall.

The hours passed and she was still lying awake. At last she opened her eyes. The curtains had been drawn over the windows and the room was dim; it must have been well after midnight and both her knees were sticking from under the coverlet and there seemed to be a draught from the wall above her; her father had not even said good-night to her, though he knew how much she

was afraid. All around her strangers were sleeping in this great,
mysterious house of the world, the world that she had looked
forward to with such anticipation that she had thought sleep a
waste of time. And now, when at last she had got out into this
world of hers, she found herself suddenly so terrified of it that
no matter how she tried she could not sleep for fear; she was
surrounded on all sides by evil men whose wives wore red pants.
How could she possibly sleep here alone, in an ominous, un-
recognizable world? Alone? No, no, no, she was not alone. As long
as her father was with her, she could never, never be alone even
though he forgot to say good-night; only to have him lying beside
her was enough, dear Father, darling Father, your little Asta
Sollilja is near you. And then before she realized it she was thinking of the soft white place on his neck, the place that would relieve
all apprehension if only she could rest her mouth on it. And because they were all snoring; and because she could not get to
sleep; and because she was so cold; because she was so lonely;
so sad and apprehensive out in the world — and yet so happy at
having him by her side, security itself, he who could do anything
he liked and owed not a soul; whom nothing could surprise; who
had an answer to everything; the king of Summerhouses; and a
poet — because of all this she began very slowly to turn over, so
slowly that there was not a single creak; so slowly that no one
would be able to tell that she was moving; only a very, very little
at a time; and then a very little once more; and the house silent
except for the snores of night as if from another world and the
birds crying high over the great town; and finally she had turned
right over, turned towards her father; no, she was not alone out
in the world, she was awake beside her father's strong breast.
She edged her head nearer on the pillow, till her lips found rest
on his throat and her closed eyes in his beard — the man who had
fought the country's spectres barehanded on the very night that
she was born.

At first she thought he was asleep and had not noticed anything. The moments passed. She heard his breathing and listened
also to the strong, heavy beating of his heart. But gradually she
realized from his movements, which were far too small and wary,
that he could not be sleeping; he was awake. And she was ashamed
of herself — would he rise and strike her, angry because she had
dared to turn round after he had ordered her to face the wall?
In her despair she nestled even closer to him, and for a while

they lay thus with their hearts beating quickly one against the other. She was lying motionless now, with her face against his neck, pretending to be asleep. Little by little, almost without her being conscious of it, his hand had come nearer, involuntarily of course; all that he had done was to make a very slight change of position. One of the two buttons of her knickers had by some chance become unfastened, and in the next moment she felt his hand, warm and strong, on her flesh.

She had never known anything like it. All her fear was suddenly gone. The shiver that now passed through body and soul was of a kind altogether different from the cold shivering that had kept her awake all night, and in her mouth there was suddenly something that resembled a ravenous appetite, except that it was not the sight of food but his movements that had roused her hunger. Nothing, nothing must ever separate them again; and she gripped his body fiercely and passionately with both hands in the intoxication of this impersonal, importunate selfishness that in a moment of time had wiped everything from her memory. Was this the delight of the world come at last —

And then — then there occurred the event that she never afterwards forgot; that was to cast an indelible shadow over her waking youth and fill to overflowing the cup of harshness and cruelty that was already her lot; at this very moment when she had forgotten everything but him — he pushed her away from him and jumped out of bed. Hastily he pulled on his socks and his trousers, tied his shoes, slipped on his jacket, and was out of the room. He closed the door behind him, she heard his step in the passage, he opened the outer door and was gone. She was left there alone among the snoring men. She lay for a while exhausted, every thought wiped from her mind, but he did not return. Little by little the reproaches began to steal into her mind. What had she done? What had happened? She had not the remotest idea, felt only that it must be something terrible, something a hundred times worse than when he had slapped her face because of an unreadable passage in a ballad; something that he would never afterwards be able to forgive her, however long she lived. What had she done to him? And why did she have to go and do just that? How could she possibly have suspected that such dreadful, incomprehensible things lurked behind something so good and innocent as nestling up to his throat? What had happened to her? "Father, father, what have I done to you? Am I so terribly bad, then?" The tears began to flow and, sobbing bitterly, she pressed her face into the pillow for fear of waking the snoring men. Her father had gone home and would chase her away if she followed.

At length she could weep no more and sat up in bed and looked about her despairingly. Yes, he must certainly have left her; she was alone and helpless out in an evil world. Who would give her anything to eat now when she was hungry? It occurred to her that possibly she might be allowed to stay with Magnus's father, the warehouseman who had weighed the wool yesterday. Or should she try to pluck up sufficient courage to approach the merchant himself? Perhaps the secretary, Jon of Myri's son, who had spoken so nicely to her once, would be willing to shelter her. She arrived at no conclusion and got out of bed in her utter despair. She slipped on her dress and pulled on her shoes, and then she noticed that her necklace had snapped, the beads were lying scattered all over the bed. But it was all the same to her, she had lost all interest in these beads of hers now that her father had forsaken her; her life was ruined and she was left alone in the world.

She stole quietly to the door, sneaked out into the dark passage, and in a few moments was standing outside in the light of the spring night, in the deserted streets of the town. A fine rain was falling; there was mist down to the middle of the hillsides. She did not know what time it was, but it must still be very early; no one about, the screaming of gulls out on the fjord unlike the song of any other bird. She wandered mindlessly away up the street.

She could never have imagined a world so soulless, a town so desolate. Not a single living soul to be seen; the chill mist and its fine rain hanging over gravel and houses. Many of the houses were out of the perpendicular. There were broken windows everywhere. The paint had scaled off the corrugated iron, and here and there whole sheets had been blown away and not fixed up again. The rain had washed the mortar off the tarred paper, which in many places hung in great shreds from the walls. Smelly fish-heads and fish-bones on fences and palings. Dejected cows chewing the cud on the open slopes. No elegant men, no fine girls. Desolation.

Aimlessly she trailed away up the main street in the direction of the mountain, her legs uncertain, her mind void of thought. The rain wet her hair, and her dress was soon soaking, but it did not matter. Then through the mist there loomed up before her a man leading a horse. As he approached she saw that it was her father. He had been fetching the horse from the pasture.

"What's the matter? Why aren't you in bed?" he asked. She

stood motionless, with downcast eyes, then turned away from him without replying.

"Wait here," he said. "I'll go and get the cart."

She sat down on a stone by the roadside, and the rain continued to wet her hair and her neck; soon her fingers were numb with cold. But she remained where she was, cold, sleepy, hungry, dazed. At last she heard the rattle of the cart in the quiet night air and saw her father approaching once more with the horse yoked in.

"You can sit in the cart if you like," he said.

But she preferred to walk.

He led the horse along the steep winding path up the mountainside, the girl stumbling along behind. The higher they ascended, the heavier grew the rain; by the time they reached the top of the gap it had become a steady downpour, which had long since soaked the girl to the skin. The water streamed from her hair down her back and over her chest. Then all at once she remembered the handkerchief that she had looked forward to for such a long time, the handkerchief that the great ones of the world had been so eager to help her buy. Where was little Asta Sollilja's handkerchief? It was lost. But it did not matter. It was all the same to her. Nothing mattered. She slipped in the muddy road, and when she got to her feet again, her dress was dirty and torn.

"I'm going to rest the horse at the top here," said her father. "And we'd better finish what we have to eat."

Yesterday's great ocean had disappeared completely in the sullen cloud of mist and rain below, and of the foothills and the plain with its great town there was nothing to be seen. In front of them the moorland hills rose in the rain and were lost to view. The road home and the distance yet to be covered seemed cold and unending and the girl thought cheerlessly of all the monotonous eternity that lay before them.

They sat down on a wet stone on the brink. Her father sat with his back to her, the bag of food on his knees. He passed over his shoulder a slice of dry bread and a piece of fish, the remains of the food that had been packed yesterday morning. But though she had been hungry a few minutes ago, she found that she had no appetite at all now and that the rain made these hard scraps even less tempting than otherwise, so it was with difficulty and disgust that she swallowed each bite. Her father was silent. They sat with their backs turned upon each other, while the rain splashed drearily on the stones all around. The food was so nau-

seating that after a few bites she had to stand up; she walked
forward a few paces and was sick. She spewed up the few mouth-
fuls that she had managed to swallow and continued retching till
finally she vomited a little gall.

Then the moors began.

32.   THE TYRANNY OF MANKIND

THE SUMMER that followed was in one respect without precedent:
it was the first time that Bjartur of Summerhouses ever employed
hired labour. This major event soon became a date of reference in
the history of Summerhouses, anything that had happened previously being so-and-so long before the summer that I had that
old bitch of a Fritha, and anything that happened subsequently
so-and-so long after old Fritha was here, damn her.

Who was Fritha?

The reason for her was this: now that there was a cow on the
croft the number of hands would have to be increased to mow
the additional hay. And just as it had been the perseverance of
the Rauthsmyri folk that had forced the cow on Bjartur, so was
it perseverance from the same quarter that now dumped an extra
worker on the farmer of Summerhouses — though of course only
after the latter had made the usual reflections on the former's
characters. And the workwoman came.

The Bailiff, who had sense enough for a whole parish, could
of course be relied upon to choose someone who would suit Bjartur's purse, so it was a stunted old wretch that turned up, a woman
who had been living on the parish for years and years and who
was, moreover, cursed with such a scurrilous tongue that very
few could put up with her for any length of time. She had never
been known to live on peaceful terms with her superiors and always reserved her most venomous abuse for her employers of
the moment. As they were usually peasants, she had ample reason
for criticism; she thought aloud. She had her own sort of delicate
health, and unless supplied regularly with quantities of medicine
to keep her up to the mark would take to her bed and stay there,
medicine being her luxury, her particular form of self-indulgence.
At first this medicine had been supplied by Dr. Finsen and put
on the parish account, but there arrived a time when the Bailiff
felt that he must put his foot down; these eternal bills were doing
their share in ruining the taxpayers; so, being an expert in the art

of medicine, especially where paupers were concerned, he started
brewing the medicine for her himself. These preparations, though
poisonously strong, never appeared on any bill, and though he
rarely handed them over without some grudging comment, he
was always very liberal with the measure once he got started, never
less than a three-gill bottle at a time, sometimes two. It was not
usual to pay her any wage except in the height of summer, but
this summer the Bailiff arranged that Bjartur should have an option
on her services and should pay her a few crowns a week, of which
half was to be in wool. She believed in Jesuspeter and invoked him
endlessly.

To this croft, the inmates of which seemed to have so little
to say to each other, especially in public, old Fritha came like a
new element. It was Bjartur's habit to address his wife from the
paving outside, calling in to her through the door or speaking out
into the blue as if he were addressing the universe, and it was
always a matter of uncertainty whether she heard him at all up in
the loft. For the most part they were observations regarding the
weather or reflections about the work of the farm and indirect
commands regarding the same. Their subject-matter was perfectly impersonal and it made no difference if she answered or
not. The elder brothers punched one another on the sly, but if their
father saw them he would hit them, sometimes with the implement he was lucky enough to be holding. "Helgi you brat, leave
the boy alone," for it was always Helgi that was to blame, Gvendur
was the boy. Grandmother sat rocking backward and forward,
mumbling away to herself. And Asta Sollilja's mature, questioning
eyes gazed through the wall; or through the heavens. She who
lived with a wish must think in private, like Bjartur, who composed
verses without anyone knowing and surprised everyone when he
recited them to visitors.

Suddenly the pauper's irresistible flood of talk engulfed the
great independent household where everybody stood on his own
feet. Talking she came across the marshes with her bundle on
her back, and she talked ceaselessly all that day long till naked
she climbed talking into bed beside the grandmother and little
Nonni. Her talk dripped through the days like a leak that nothing
can stop. She talked to herself as she raked the hay together in
the meadow, and the boys closed slyly in upon her and listened:
she discussed parish affairs, agriculture, and private matters, inquired into paternities and adulteries, flayed even the landed
farmers for starving their sheep, branded respectable parishioners

as thieves, and attacked the Bailiff, the minister, and even the
Sheriff, reviling the authorities where others could see nothing
but the wet marshes, and always getting the better of the issue
because her opponents were many miles away. She poured out
a continual stream of curses, complaining most of all over what
she called the scandalous tyranny of mankind. This tyranny of
mankind was such a thorn in her flesh that, regardless of whether
she was talking to herself, to the others, to the bitch, to the sheep
that chanced to cross the mowing, or to the ignorant song-birds
of the air, all her discourse, waking and sleeping, revolved about
this one hub. She lived in continual and altogether hopeless revolt
against this loathsome oppression, and for that reason there was
something rash, insolent, and vindictive in her eyes, something
reminiscent of the eyes of an evil but indeterminate animal that
one had seen in dreams; formless, but terrifying in its proximity.
The grandmother turned her bowed back to the incessant storm
and withdrew even deeper into the age-old heath-silence of her
secret self. The mother found suitable places to interject a meaningless monosyllable in a sympathetic voice. Helgi would narrow
his eyes in a malicious grin, and sometimes he hid her petticoat
at night or slipped a pebble into her porridge. Bjartur, himself
the recipient of many a gabbled gibe, would never lower himself
to answer a bloody old cackler like her, so his face was all contempt whenever he passed her, and Gvendur followed his father's
example in this as in other things. But little Nonni listened large-
eyed to everything that she said, trying to find some coherence in
it all. He often stood right in front of her, the better to examine the
working of her organs of speech, and not without admiration for
her volubility and the wealth of her vocabulary. When talking to
him she drew no distinction between him and any adult, modify-
ing neither language nor subject-matter to suit him; her conversation ranked him as a man.

And once upon a time in a great snowstorm in mid-winter a
certain Queen was sitting by the window in her palace and was
busy sewing — it was one night just before the hay-harvest, and
Asta was sitting on the paving watching over the home-field and
reading her book. She read it all through out of doors and, having
finished it a little after midnight, turned straightway back to the
beginning. When she had read it a second time, the sun was rising.
For a long time she sat staring southward over the moors, running
over the story once more in her mind. Again and again she trod
in Snow White's footsteps over the seven mountains and found

refuge in the dwarfs' house after being spared by a cook. Finally, after she had been exposed to all the wickedness of the world, the handsome Prince came and took her home to his realm in a glass coffin. So deep was her sympathy with little Snow White in joy and sorrow, in happiness and tribulation, that her breast heaved and her eyes were filled with tears; but it was not the bitter, crushed feeling of one who suffers because of the evil men have done him, rather the emotion of one who would willingly live and die for the good that there is in life. So lifelike was the fairy tale that she saw the Prince through her tears in living flesh and blood. She saw herself lying in the glass coffin, and the King's men carrying her off, and the stumble, and the apple starting from her throat; and she rose up and they looked at each other, and greeted each other, and it was as if they had known each other from all eternity, and he made her his Queen — after all that she had suffered since the day of her birth. This was the first time that her soul was charmed by the power of poetry, which shows us the lot of man so truthfully and so sympathetically and with so much love for that which is good that we ourselves become better persons and understand life more fully than before, and hope and trust that good may always prevail in the life of man.

Bjartur did not abandon the methods of the lone worker, but still rose just before daybreak, as he had done in his first summer. Close on his heels came his adult workers, Finna and Fritha, who worked till well on in the morning on empty stomachs. The old woman did what she could with the fire, then woke the children, who were allowed to sleep until the coffee had been warmed up. The grandmother found the task of rousing them as difficult in summer as in winter; she had never known the like of them. When they made no answer to her preludes, she would try to drag them out by main force, but it was like pulling at a length of elastic; when she released her feeble grip they were farther off than ever, their eyelids heavy as sorrow. Even after they had managed to crawl out and were busy pulling on their stockings, their eyelids would droop afresh and then they would lose their balance and fall back across the bed. Often the old woman had to slap their faces with a wet dishcloth before they could open those curious eyelids. Every morning she decided afresh that nothing would ever come of them.

And when at last they were on their feet, they often felt so sick that they could swallow neither the coffee nor the slice of bread: delicacies had no charm for them before they had been working an hour or so. They would trail away down the marshes with some coffee in a bottle for the grown-ups, as unsteady on their legs as the much-discussed giddy sheep, their feet still asleep, a tickle in their knee-joints, something in the nature of pins and needles, their bodies thirsting voluptuously for more rest. It was lovely falling between the hummocks. No one could forbid them to fall, and it did not matter if they got wet or had immediately to gather their strength for the effort to rise, the fall was so lovely, a moment in the blissful embrace of rest. So sick did they feel that cold beads of sweat would start from their brows, and sometimes they stood doubled up in the marshes and retched, while the sweat grew colder and colder, icy water on their brows and temples in midsummer. The coffee that came up was no longer sweet, but bitter, and finally some unknown fluid would fill their mouths. Often they had toothache in the morning and until well on in the day, sometimes all day long, and it was incredible the number of different kinds of disagreeable tastes they could feel in their mouths.

The elder boys had each been provided with a scythe, but little Nonni had to help with the raking so that the women could keep up with the mowers. It was a sixteen-hour working day for the children, interrupted twice for a meal and once for a drink of coffee, with a few minutes' sleep beneath the open sky at midday. When the sky was unclouded, the mind, flitting off to distant goals, would find relief in the hope that somehow the years to come would grant a freer life and better surroundings, sun-fostered dreams that have always been the thrall's title of nobility; but this summer, unfortunately, the occasions were few indeed when day-dreamers by rake and scythe could visit the lands of desire, for this happened to be a wet summer, and no one who is working soaked to the skin in marshy ground is apt to forget immediate realities. These children had as little to wear for rain as they had for Sundays, owning at most a ragged jersey of scrim and thin nankeen; it doesn't pay in these hard times to weave your wool or knit it unless it's for the most necessary underclothes. Bjartur had a jerkin that he used on the more ceremonial occasions such as the shepherds' meet and the autumn drive; it was the only rain-proof garment on the croft that was worthy of such an honourable name, and though he never donned it for his work, as it was only a symbol of his independence, there were occasions when he would hand it to Asta Sollilja if it looked like raining all day. And Asta

Sollilja would take it and look at him without lifting her head, and nothing more. Old Fritha, strangely enough, owned an old cloak of thick homespun in spite of being on the parish, and she was also the possessor of an immense sail-cloth skirt. And the ceaseless rain of this inclement summer poured down upon the three little unprotected workmen of the moors and on the woman who every winter spent sixteen weeks in bed, soaking every thread in their rags, turning their headgear into a shapeless, sodden mass and running down their necks and faces in rivulets stained with the colour from their hats. It oozed down their backs, and down their chests. Thus they stood in bogs and in pools, in water and in mud, the close-packed clouds above them interminable, the wet grass whistling drearily under the scythe. The scythe grew heavier and heavier, the hours refused to pass, the moments seemed to stick to them as soggily as their sodden garments; midsummer; the birds silent but for the redshank gliding busily about, reciting a fragment of his marvellous, unending story, he, he, he, he; these lucky birds are so made that the water does not stick to their soft, thick plumage. The sound of old Fritha's talk was lost in such heavy rain, and for hours on end the children heard no sign of life other than the rumbling in their own stomachs, for not only were they soaking wet and infinitely tired, they were also famished, and with no comforting hopes of the possibility of communion with the elves.

Great is the tyranny of mankind.

"It doesn't matter so much if he kills me, the devil, for as God and anyone can tell you, I'm doomed in advance — slaved to death a hundred times and on the parish. But never was I so badly off that I didn't have something to keep out the wet in spite of fraud, tyranny, and murder. And you mark my words, my lad, and see if he hasn't racked the life out of your poor mother before God gives her another summer, the bloody slave-driver."

That was her text. Nor was it to be denied that even in the height of summer their mother was often away from work because of illness, and as for the children, the green issue of their nostrils mingled with the rivulets that coursed down their faces.

"But I've only myself to blame for agreeing to let that flaming Bailiff throw me summer after summer to these lousy peasants. A stingier crowd you never met in all your born days; devil a bit of colour do you ever see in all your coffee, and day in, day out, living or dead, it's rotten salt fish down your gullet, when it isn't that mouldy old sausage of theirs that burns like flaming fire and tastes as sour as hell. As for a bite of meat on a Sunday, Jesuspeter, it's like mentioning murder itself."

The tyranny of mankind; it was like the obstinate drip of water falling on a stone and hollowing it little by little; and this drip continued, falling obstinately, falling without pause on the souls of the children.

"As if I didn't know these accursed smallholding scum after being their slave and their doormat for a couple of generations! It isn't the first time by a long way that I've watched them sacrifice what little wits they have to their worm-eaten sheep. You can always tell the Devil by his cloven hoof. And they all want to be rich men, too; there's no lack of ambition among them. They aren't on the parish, not they, it's free men they are. Independence, and plenty of it. But where is their independence, may I ask? Isn't most of it in their sheep's guts when they're starving to death in the spring of the year? Is their freedom worth as much as the worms that feed from eternity to eternity on the bags of skin and bones they call their sheep? And let me see their kingdom, my lad, in the colourless coffee and stinking fish of this world or the next. No wonder Kolumkilli sucks the marrow out of the pitiful little devils they are supposed to provide for."

The children had long listened to this endless gabble as to some funny rigmarole that with time and constant repetition can become an unbearable nuisance; and as their father said: empty vessels and paupers make the most sound. It was like a new case of nerves on the croft, a new kind of psalm, though without any claim on their respect; one could pull a face at her on Sundays. The children had been conditioned from birth to the absolute authority of the father. He was at one and the same time supreme authority over the croft and source of everything that happened in it. In this little world he was immutable fate, a source of adversity that they could neither control nor accuse of responsibility, for his dictatorship outlawed all criticism and made organized resistance to his measures inconceivable. Nevertheless the boys had long nourished vague emotions, a wordless antipathy against the father, not least because of their mother's long winter illnesses and the still-born children that, subconsciously and without any spark of revolt, they had always associated with him. But when the last week in August had seen no end to the rain, there came a time when Fritha's gabble could no longer be regarded as the detestable blather of a nerve-ridden old pauper, for, after all,

there was something in it that sided with them against the cold
showers, against the ceaseless beating of the rain that glued the
coarse old rags to the young skin and drowned every glad feeling
of the soul; against the desperate, destroying labour of a sixteen-
hour day. It was something new for them to hear their misery and
their thraldom traced to a perceptible source. In this wretched
old woman's irresponsible babble there lurked argument against
life's crushing yoke; it was the voice of emancipation itself, which
in this strange guise had joined forces with their own subcon-
scious minds, and finally a stage was reached when Helgi no longer
saw the fun of teasing her or pulling a face at her on Sundays,
but showed less haste than ever in obeying his father's commands
and started grimacing into his face as often as he had previously
grimaced behind his back. Little Nonni declared in the meadow
that Mamma was lying ill in bed today because our father won't
give her a coat.

Then was there no oasis in the desert of the days? Yes, the days
had their oases: mealtimes, the salt fish, the porridge, and the
sour black pudding. In these lay the only joy in life, for the cow
had not calved yet. The day's first ray of hope was the moment
when their father called to Asta Sollilja and gave her the long-
desired command to go home and boil the fish. At first it had always
seemed that no matter how long they waited, this moment would
never arrive, but eventually the boys discovered that the more
often they looked at their father in reminder and expectation, the
longer did he delay in calling to Asta Sollilja.

At last Asta Sollilja would set off home to boil the fish. Never
were her steps so light, for she, too, had long been waiting for the
moment when her father should think fit to indicate that she might
lay aside her rake in the cruel thick of the daily strife and go home
and busy herself with the fire. The fire; as soon as it began to burn
up she would take off her wet things and dry them by the stove.
Sometimes she might break off a little piece of sugar to sweeten
her mouth, and when the fish had been put in the pan, she would
sit down in front of the fire and warm herself.

Her grandmother, busy with her needles, would be mumbling
away at her hymns without an upward look. But the girl knew
not God nor His psychology, rather savoured to the full these
moments under the roof of the hut, their security and the mellow
calm that is characteristic of midsummer — fatigue, heavy grass,
miry puddles, all was forgotten for the moment. Slowly the por-

ridge began to bubble and boil, the smell of salt fish to fill the room; in front of her burned the home fire. But the boys in the meadow were no longer mowing, they had long since lost all the power of their muscles; they were simply beating the wet grass with their scythes in some endless imbecility and raising only a spurt of water, a slice of sod, or at most a few broken straws; Asta Sollilja has fallen asleep of course and forgotten all about us. It was a joyful sight when at last they caught sight of her with the meal-tub on the outskirts of the home-field.

Dinner in the meadow was like all true joy, sweetest in anticipation. The salt codfish and the rye bread, the thin porridge and the sour blood pudding, the interminable rain that streamed down into these dishes while they were busy eating — a more rigid menu could not have been found anywhere. The fish gave off a vigorous odour in the rain, and the smell hung in the nostrils for hours afterwards, in the clothes, on the hands. Never did the children long so much for food as when they stood up from their meal under the hay-rick.

Whatever the weather, Bjartur always left the others when the meal was over. He would lie down on a truss of hay with his hat over his face and fall asleep at once. As soon as he moved in his sleep he would roll off the truss, sometimes into a pool, and would be awake immediately, which pleased him greatly. He considered that it was proper for a man to sleep for four minutes during the daytime, and he was always in a bad temper if he slept longer. The womenfolk wormed in under the hay-rick when they had finished eating. Then the shivering would begin, for they were sitting on wet grass, and they would rise with hands benumbed and pins and needles in their legs and go to look for their rakes. And if Bjartur heard them complaining about the damp, he would reply that it was pretty miserable wretches that minded at all whether they were wet or dry. He could not understand why such people had been born. "It's nothing but damned eccentricity to want to be dry," he would say. "I've been wet more than half my life and never been a whit the worse for it."

33.   GREAT EVENTS

ONE evening when the meadow mowing was almost over, when dusk was already falling, for the days were rapidly drawing in, what should they see but a man with a pack-horse picking a track-

less way down from the top of the heath to the flats on the other side
of the lake? Here was a peculiar, sort of expedition — obviously a
stranger to the district, maybe not quite right in the head. Or
was it an outlaw? What did the fellow think he was doing, running
around on other folk's land? Perhaps it was an elf-man. At any
rate it wasn't any normal sort of person. Even Bjartur stopped
work and leaned forward on the handle of his scythe to watch this
person who scorned so much the beaten track. What was the
fellow looking for? He explored the flats near the lake, surveyed
the lake itself, likewise the air. Was it a foreign scientist? Or a
land speculator from the south? Was he speculating? On other
people's land? Finally he took the baggage from his horse's back
and let it loose in the marshes on the other side of the lake, what the
devil. Then he walked round the lake and made his way towards
them. They stood watching him, work forgotten. Riddle. Mystery.
Is there anything more enthralling than a stranger in the landscape?
The children forgot even the cruel fatigue of the fifteenth hour.

He did not seem to bear much resemblance to other people.
He was bareheaded and wearing a brown shirt and armless pull-
over; sunburnt, slim, newly shaved, slight stoop, fine features and
judicious eyes like a foreigner, good evening.

"Good evening," replied the others warily.

"Summerhouses people?" inquired the visitor as he came up.

"It all depends on how you look at it," replied Bjartur rather
testily, advancing a pace or two on the visitor with his scythe at
the ready. "I've always understood it was my land anyway, whoever you may be. And I can't say that I see what the idea is of
prospecting on other people's land."

The visitor did not offer his hand in the customary greeting, but
halted a few paces away and looked about him in the dusk, then
thoughtfully produced a pipe and tobacco. "A pretty valley," he
remarked. "As pretty as any I've ever seen."

"Pretty," said Bjartur; "hm, that depends on whether the hay
goes to hogwash or not. You don't happen to have been sent here
by anyone, do you?"

Sent? No, the visitor hadn't been sent by anyone, he had just
felt that since the place was so nice, he might ask leave to pitch
a tent there, on the other side of the lake.

"This land," said Bjartur, "this land reaches south to the heath
there and up to the mountain peaks in the north, west to the middle
of the ridge, and east as far as Moldbrekkur. All the lowland
belongs to me."

The visitor made some rather incomprehensible observation about all this lowland making one park.

"Whether it would make one park or not," replied Bjartur, "it's still my property, and I can't say that I care to see strangers nosing about on it. It's thirteen years and more since I raised this farm from the ruins, and as for the Rauthsmyri crew, I owe them not a penny. I was told when I started that there was a ghost here, but I fear neither ghosts nor men. I own good sheep."

The visitor understood and nodded his head: "Private enterprise."

"I don't know," said Bjartur, "and I'm not praising myself up either. I only know that I'm no worse off than most private individuals hereabouts, and, if anything, maybe a trifle better for never having made it a habit of mine to get into debt, which I've managed quite easily by always endeavouring to keep parasites away from my hay, until last winter, when I had cattle forced on me from a certain quarter. But naturally I never consider myself the equal of the big men, except that I feel I'm a big enough man for myself, and therefore I refuse to allow any meddling with my affairs and have no desire to be in partnership with anyone."

But the visitor was quick to explain that by private enterprise, naturally, he hadn't meant that they should all become landed farmers or rich men; and in any case he wasn't too fond of dealing with the big farmers, he preferred to see his coppers passed on to the smallholders —

Bjartur, leaping at once to the conclusion that it must be somebody with some new business methods in his head, declared that he had determined to deal with no one but his own merchant; "the old fellow has kept body and soul together for more than a few in his time, and though Jon of Myri founds his co-operative societies and promises a bonus when times are good, I expect the bonus he talks about will be thickest where he bites it off, with his three hundred and fifty lambs every autumn, and thinner for us men with only thirty or forty for sale. And what about the bad years? If the whole thing crashes, it will be we who will have to pay the losses, I expect; and not only ours, but theirs as well, damn them. So, as far as business deals are concerned, my friend —"

The visitor hastened to assure Bjartur that he had never even dreamed of trying to undermine the good relations that existed between the crofter and his dealer; he was just a chap that liked to try a gun or a hook and line when he was out in the country in the summertime, "and as I had heard that you didn't bother much about your game, I wondered whether you wouldn't allow me to try a line — for a consideration, of course."

"There's nothing worth fishing for," said Bjartur. "Sensible people haven't the time to waste on the rubbish you'll find in the lake, and in any case whatever was caught in the marshes here, fish or fowl, wouldn't do my sheep much good. It may possibly do the big proprietors' sheep some good, or the big proprietors' sons even; there's that son of the Bailiff at Utirauthsmyri, for instance, the one they call the secretary now, who's bred on the Persian religion and has been made manager of that society he and his father started — he could never see anything draw the breath of life without wanting to blow the brains out of it, blast him."

Old Fritha, imprudent and spiteful as ever, bawled out from the meadow: "Listen to them running down their betters, these flaming bog-trotters that grind everybody down, relations and strangers, dead and alive; and everything but the lice that crawl over their own mouldy hides."

The visitor exhaled smoke in her direction without being quite clear what attitude he ought to take in this affair.

"Oh, don't bother your head about what spews up out of that over there. It's only one of those bloody old paupers, and it's not the first time her tongue's run away with her," said Bjartur in order to prevent any misunderstanding, and in such a fashion that the stranger now considered himself free to renew his petition.

"Well," replied the crofter at length, "if you aren't speculating and you aren't sent by any company either, I don't see why you shouldn't pitch a tent for a night or two, provided you don't trample the grass down too much for me. But I won't tolerate speculators on my land. And no members of any company or society either, because I consider societies the ruination of the individual. And my land isn't for sale, anyway, and least of all for money. I and my folk live here for our sheep in peace and quiet, and we have enough of everything as long as our sheep have enough of everything. If only this damned rain would piss itself dry some time."

The ground was cleared for negotiation when the stranger had at last managed to convinced Bjartur that he was neither a speculator nor a member of any sociey. He was only an ordinary southerner, the sort of fellow you often see in the summer, a holiday-maker, in innocent exile. Someone had told him that there was good sport here, the name of his informant he had forgotten. He

would like to hang around for a few days, lacked nothing, was
provided with everything. As proof of this he produced a note-
case bulging with banknotes, real money in a bundle; they and
the banks see eye to eye, these southerners; some folk say they use
this stuff in the backhouse. In spite of Bjarur's disdain for money,
the sight of it did not now fail to produce a certain impression.
He offered even to help the man with his tent, but the visitor declined with thanks, he could manage everything himself. He took
leave of them with a farewell as perfunctory as his greeting, leaving behind him a cloud of blue smoke that dissolved over the
meadow in the calm of the evening, and a fabulous fragrance. He
had said so little, been so offhanded in his greeting, and displayed
so much money that there was no end to what the imagination
could spin around such a man, a great man, an elegant man, distance itself in one man, the prince of the fairy tale; and now he had
become neighbour to the Summerhouses people. His proximity
was like the flavour of Sunday in mid-week, like an interval in
the downpour, colour in drabness, material for thought in apathy,
stimulation in the midst of life's cheerlessness. That night Asta
Sollilja dreamed repeatedly that the apple started from her throat.

Then on the following day the cow calved, and thus inside
twenty-four hours there befell two great events on the moors.

She had been terribly heavy, poor thing, these last few weeks,
and Finna, who knew what it was like, would trust no one but
herself to bring her out in the morning or home at night. No one
else was slow enough with her, no one had the patience to wait
while she persuaded herself out of the narrow cow-shed door with
her flanks grazing the doorpost on either side. To Finna it would
never have occurred to beat this creature as she laboured up to
the hocks through the mud in front of the croft. Bukolla would halt
after every step, snorting and grumbling, but looking round occasionally at the woman, twitching her ears, and mooing. They
parted company usually up in the hollow by the brook, and the
woman would stroke her dewlap, and soon we'll be having a little
calf with a round forehead and feeble legs, long and clumsy, and
I hope everything will go all right for us, and you'll see me tonight;
and we'll take things easy and think of each other. Then Finna
would go off home and the cow would begin cropping noisily at
the grass, her nostrils wrinkling with the pleasure of luxury, for
the grass along the brooks was strong and juicy.

But that evening Finna did not find the cow in her usual pastures, and she thought it rather strange, for the cow had shown

little desire to wander of late now that she was expecting, and
had long given up her attempts to run away. She wandered along
from hillock to hillock, farther and farther along by the mountain's
side, calling: "Bukolla, Bukolla dear." At last the cow answered
her from a grassy little hollow by a ravine; she lowed once only
in reply and was found. She had calved. The woman understood
at once.

Finna found her unusually difficult to handle; she would not
behave and had to be driven along, circling continually about
the calf, sniffing at it and licking it and mooing softly at every
step, not a thought to spare for anything else. But Finna understood. When one has had a calf, the calf comes between the mother
and the object she had been fondest of before. The busy aggres-
siveness of happy motherhood had mastered her behaviour and
wiped out its more civilized features. It was as if this creature's
dreams had all come true in one day, and as if she needed nothing
more; the sympathy of others had become a superstition. It was
a long, long time before the woman managed to coax her home to
the croft.

Everyone except Bjartur was waiting outside to welcome the
cow and her new-born calf. The children left the home-field to
meet them and examine the grey-spotted calf. The sea-cow
breed was obvious. It was a little bull, and Asta Sollilja greeted
him with a kiss, and the cow watched the kiss, mooing low in
her throat. The dog did not try to snap at the cow's hocks
tonight; she didn't even bark at the cow that night, silly as she
was, but with her tail between her legs retreated politely to a
distance whenever the cow showed any signs of attacking her, and
regarded the new relations with great respect from some yards
away. The old grandmother dragged herself along by the wall with
the aid of a broken rake-shaft to fondle the calf and the cow. Even
old Fritha was warmer-hearted than usual. "God bless the poor
creature," she said, "Jesuspeter."

Then Bjartur came out of the house.

"So-ho," he said. "We'd better get the knife ready."

"Just what I thought, the bloody murderer," cried old Fritha.

But Bjartur's wife only looked at him appealingly and said half
in a whisper as she passed him on the paving: "Bjartur dear." So
the cow was tied up in her stall with the calf by her side.

It was later in the evening, when they were all going to bed
and the womenfolk were with blissful unction discussing the birth
and the calf, when everyone was so happy because of this new

personality on the farm and thankful that everything had gone so
well with the cow, when everyone was sharing so intimately in
the cow's happiness, that Bjartur continued from where he had
left off before: "The worst of it is that I haven't time to take the
carcass down to Fjord before the end of the week."

The next day there were curds of the cow's first milk since
calving.

The days that followed, they were great days. One had only
to look at the creature that once had been so lonely and see how
light was her step now as she trotted away out of the home-field
with the calf prancing giddily at her side — she had no longer
any need of consolation or caresses. She would try to leave the
children behind as soon as she could, for they had fallen in love
with the little bull and were never done fondling him. Care-free
in her new life, she would wander off with her son far along the
mountain and would almost lose herself, so independent of mankind did she consider herself, she who before had had her refuge
in the woman's protection; no more dealings with mankind! When
Finna came to bring her home in the evenings she would look
at her as if wondering what concern it was of hers, but Finna was
not at all hurt by such behaviour, for she understood the joy of
motherhood and how it exalts one proudly above mankind and
makes everything else seem of such little value. Yes, so well did
she understand her joy that though the cow gave far too little milk
in the evenings, she did not dare tell anyone about it for fear that
Bjartur would order the calf to be shut up in the daytime; she
could not bear to think of the cow losing the joy of having her son
with her in the pasture these days, she who had been lonely for
so long.

Sunday morning; they usually stayed late in bed on the Sunday, sometimes even as late as nine, all except Bjartur, for whom
all days were alike and who was usually to be heard pottering
about with something or other on a Sunday morning, mending
implements and suchlike, poor soul. On this particular morning
he stuck his head up through the trapdoor and asked if everybody
was dead here, or what? "Is the tyranny to be spread over on to
the Sunday as well now?" asked Fritha sourly.

"The calf's tripes are lying on the paving," he announced. "I
leave you to decide whether you're going to let them be washed
into the muck in this damned rain. I'm off down to Fjord with the
carcass."

That day the wife of Summerhouses did not trust herself to

leave her bed; she lay there facing the wall, she was not feeling very well. Old Hallbera got up, and old Fritha, and the children. The calf's steaming entrails were lying in a trough on the paving when they got downstairs, but Bjartur was well on his way, riding over the marshes on old Blesi with veal for the merchant's oven.

"In this way he'll kill you all," said Fritha, then gave vent to a stream of horrible abuse as she took charge of the offals; and the children stood on the paving with their fingers in their mouths and watched; and listened.

Bukolla's little calf, they all remembered the look in his eyes; for he too had had a look in his eyes the same as other babies. He had looked at Nonni, he had looked at Helgi, he had looked at them all. Only yesterday he had been hopping about in the home-field, here, lifting his front feet in the air both at once, then his hind feet both at once, in a little game all of his own. And the crown of his head was as round as a ball; little calves are like that always. Asta Sollilja had said that he was very near being three-coloured. He had roamed about the slopes along by the mountain, too, and had sniffed at the wild thyme of the world; when it rained he had sheltered behind his mother. That was a dark Sunday. The cow bellowed unceasingly from her shed, and when they tried to drive her to pasture she was back again at once, bellowing in the home-field; she stood on the doorstep and bellowed in. The mountain echoed her cries, from her great eyes there ran great tears, cows weep.

For a whole week Finna dared not look at the cow, old Fritha had to milk her. There is nothing so merciless as mankind. How can we justify ourselves, especially to the dumb animals around us? But the first days are always the worst, and there is much comfort in the thought that time effaces everything, crime and sorrow no less than love.

34.   THE VISITOR

CONTINUAL rain.

Asta Sollilja, busy cooking, had taken off her wet things and laid them to dry on the hot range. The steam was rising from them, and she was cutting the fish ready for the pan, barefooted, in a tattered old slip, and the bubbles were just beginning to rise when suddenly she heard something on the move down below: the door opened, a footstep sounded in the stalls, the ladder creaked, the hatch was lifted, and a man stepped up on to the floor and looked about him. He was wearing a sou'wester. His coat was long and strong, fitted with collars, flaps, tabs, and buttons; the rain that could penetrate such a garment was non-existent. He wore high waterproof boots, his blue eyes were clear and kind. He said good-morning. She did not dare to say good-morning; she said nothing. She usually gave her hand in silence when any-one greeted her, but this man did not offer to shake hands. She had thought that he had looked so very slim and youthful the first time that she had seen him, but in this tiny room he and his huge coat assumed such bulky proportions that she was afraid that he would bump his head on the roof. The old woman did not reply to his greeting either, but she stopped knitting and tried to focus her peering eyes on him. With him he had a string of trout and string of barnacle geese.

"Fresh meat," he said. "A change."

The white teeth gleamed like trinkets in the brown manly face; there was an unfamiliar ring in his voice.

"Sola," said the grandmother in her dim, hoarse voice, "aren't you going to offer the man a seat?"

But Asta Sollilja hadn't the courage to offer the man a seat, her slip was so terrible, her arms so long, her hands so big; there was mud on her feet. She didn't dare look at him, not even at the pleasing colour of the trout he was carrying. The rags she wore for underwear were lying there on the range staring him in the face and steaming with damp. He thought of course that they hadn't enough to eat. What ought she to say? What would Father have said?

"Let's sling a few trout into the pan," said the visitor, picking up the knife. He had slim brown hands free of dirt, free of calluses and scratches, hands that played deftly with the knife. Quickly he gutted the fish, placing the offals in a dish and the fish itself in the pan. "First-rate fish," he said, holding them aloft for the grand-mother's inspection, "three-pounders at least, fine fish."

"Uhuh," said Hallbera, "very nice for anyone that can take them, maybe. But one man's meat is another man's poison. And fresh fish, especially fresh-water fish, is more than I can stand. I've never been able to take much fresh stuff somehow. I come out in a rash with it. It's too strong."

That, he considered, could hardly be right; fresh food was good for you.

"Where might the gentleman hail from?" she inquired.

He said: "From the south."

"Yes, of course, poor man," she said with all the sympathy that old folk usually show for anyone who lives in a distant part of the country.

And Asta Sollilja just stood and gazed at him preparing the fish. His hands were so skilful, the movements so few and so sure, the work seemed to be doing itself, and yet at such a marvellous speed. And there was a smile on his lips though he was not smiling, he was so good to look upon; and such a good man. He filled the pan to the brim; he was a great man, no one must discover what she had dreamed since this man came to the valley; he asked for the salt.

The fragrance of fresh trout on the boil filled the room. He took out his pipe and pressed the tobacco down before lighting it. The smoke had a smell like meadow-sweet, only much more delicious; there is another world in a sweet smell, and the fragrance remained to live and talk when the visitor himself had gone. "Good day to both of you," he said, and went.

And was gone. He closed the door behind him. Hurrying to the window, she gazed after him as he ran into the driving rain in his huge coat, and his sou'wester. Rain could do little harm to such a man — how light was his step! The girl felt her head swimming slightly, her heart knocking against her ribs. She stayed by the window till the palpitation wore off and the rain had entranced her. Then the old woman suddenly remembered that she had wanted to ask him something, seeing that it was the south he hailed from, but her wits were so gummed up nowadays that she could never remember anything, shame on you, Sola, why couldn't you have offered the poor man some coffee? But Asta Sollilja did not hear what she said, for she felt so ridiculous somehow with her bare arms and bare feet, her old slip, her thin legs; ugly.

"Geese," said Bjartur that evening, glancing disdainfully at the birds the visitor had left. "No one ever grew fat on fowling. May he be of all men the most cursed for his gifts!"

"We might try to boil them," suggested his wife.

"I've heard that the gentry are supposed to eat bird-flesh," said old Hallbera.

"Yes, and Frenchmen are supposed to eat frogs," snorted Bjartur, and never tasted the geese. Nevertheless he forgave the visitor for both fish and fowl, and after breakfast on the following Sunday morning he was heard to say:

"It's just like the lot of you to snatch the gift from a stranger's

hand and say thank-you like a bunch of tramps. But that it should
ever occur to you to send the fellow a drop of milk on a Sunday
morning is of course far above the flight of your imagination."

The upshot was that Asta Sollilja and little Nonni were sent off
round the lake with some milk in a little tub. She washed her face
and hands and combed her hair. Her eyes, one straight, the other
crossed, her eyes were very large, very dark. She donned the sheepskin shoes and her dead mother's gown. It had been washed after
her journey to town and mended where it had been torn, but it
was very faded and not a bit pretty now; actually rather a miserable rag. But fortunately the soul's joy had blossomed considerably
in these ten days since the cow calved, as was obvious from her
complexion.

They walked across the marshes with the tub between them.
Asta Sollilja was so nervous that she was silent all the way. For
three days now there had been intervals of reasonably fine
weather, which, though too short to be really useful, had sufficed
to rush most of the hay home. There was sunshine today also, but
the marsh grass had begun to grow yellow, and the delicate blue
that characterizes the spring had long since disappeared from the
sunshine. The plovers had begun to gather into flocks, but the
snipe crouched low in the grass in moping solitude, as if they rued
all that had happened. They flew up from beneath one's feet with
a sudden flutter of wings that startled one; no song now, only the
song of the heart.

There was no movement to be seen about the tent, and as they
had no idea how to knock at a dwelling that had neither door nor
doorpost, they halted in perplexity a few yards away. Finally they
mustered sufficient courage to peep in under the edge. The man
then crawled out of a fur-lined bag, pushed his head through the
flap of the tent, and blinked at them with sleepy eyes.

"Were you looking for me?"

"No," said Asta Sollilja, and setting the tub down in front of
the tent, gripped her brother's hand and took to her heels.

"Hi, there!" he shouted after them. "What do you want me to
do with this?"

"It's milk," shouted little Nonni in full flight.

"Stop!" he bawled, and as they didn't dare do otherwise, they
halted and looked over their shoulders at him as if ready to make
off again at the slightest suspicious movement, like young deer.

"Come on," he said encouragingly, but they didn't dare for their
lives and simply stood still and watched him. He lifted the lid off

the tub, cautiously took a little drink, wiped his mouth with the back of his hand, spat.

"I'll give you a fry," said he.

They gazed at him for a while longer, then they sat down, both on the same tiny hummock, ignorant of what a fry meant, but willing to wait for whatever might appear. The visitor began to set some things out in front of the tent, barefooted, in trousers and shirt, while they followed his every movement with marvelling eyes.

"It won't hurt you to come a bit nearer," he called to them, without looking up.

After waiting awhile longer, they seized the opportunity when his back was turned on them and sneaked a few yards nearer. He said they could come into the tent if they liked, so they followed him into the tent, first the boy, then the girl, and stood with their backs against the pole. They had never landed in such an adventure before; the whole tent was redolent of tobacco, fruit, and hair-oil. She gazed at his arms, brown as coffee with cream in it, and watched him light the oil-stove and melt some butter in the pan. He had three ducks all ready for cooking, and soon the smell of frying was added to the other smells.

"Don't you know any games?" he inquired without looking up.

"No," they answered.

"No?" he said. "Why not?"

"We have to keep on doing something," said little Nonni, without explaining the process of his thought.

"What for?" asked the man.

They didn't know.

"It's great fun playing games," he said, but they didn't know whom he was referring to — whether he referred to them, to himself, or to the people of the district. The young girl's cheeks were burning for fear he should look at her or address any remark to her in particular.

"Why don't you shoot some of the birds?" he asked.

"Father doesn't want to," said the boy, without remembering that his father had published his considered opinion on the subject.

"What did you do with the geese I gave you the other day?"

"We boiled them."

"Boiled them? You ought to have fried them in butter."

"We haven't any butter."

"Why not?"

"Father doesn't want to buy a churn."

"Does your father want anything?" inquired the man.

"Sheep," replied the boy.

Then at last the visitor looked at the children, and it was as if he realized for the first time that this was a conversation, and that there was, moreover, some real substance in this conversation. He was rather surprised. "So he wants sheep," he said, with a heavy stress on the "sheep," as if unable to understand the word in this context. Presently he turned the birds over, and then it came to light that the side that had been below had turned brown; the butter spat and crackled as he turned them, and a dense smoke filled the tent. "So he wants sheep," said the man to himself. He shook his head, still to himself, and though they did not really fathom his disapproval, they felt nevertheless that there must be something not quite right in wanting to have sheep. Nonni decided to tell his brother Helgi that it was questionable whether this great man was in complete agreement with all their father's opinions.

She looked at him all, and at his belt, and at his toes, and his shirt was made of brown cloth, open at the neck, and she had never known the like of him; he could no doubt do anything he wanted. His house — in her mind's eye she saw the house, lovely as a dream, on her mother's cake-dish; but that was impossible. And why was it impossible? Because there was a girl standing in front of it. This man's house stood by itself in a wood, like the house on the lovely calendar that the sheep had trodden into the muck when it fell downstairs two years ago — by itself in a wood. He lived there alone. In his house the rooms were more numerous and more beautiful even than those in the mansion of Rauthsmyri; he had a sofa that was more beautiful even than the Rauthsmyri sofa; this was he of whom it is written in *Snow White*.

"What do they call you?" he asked, and her heart stood still.

"Asta Sollilja," she blurted out in an anguish-stricken voice.

"Asta what?" he asked, but she didn't dare own up to it again.

"Sollilja," said little Nonni.

"Amazing," said he, gazing at her as if to make sure whether it could be true, while she thought how dreadful it was to be saddled with such an absurdity. But he smiled at her and forgave her and comforted her and there was something so good and so good in his eyes; so mild; it is in this that the soul longs to rest; from eternity to eternity. And she saw it for the first time in his eyes, and perhaps never afterwards, and faced it and understood. And that was that.

"Now I know why the valley is so lovely," said the visitor.

She hadn't the faintest idea what to say — the valley lovely? For weeks afterwards she racked her brains. What had he meant? She had often heard people talk about lovely wool and lovely yarn and, most of all, lovely sheep — but the valley? Why, the valley was nothing but a marsh, a sodden marsh where one stood over the ankles in puddles between the hummocks and deeper still in the bogs, a stagnant lake where some people said that a kelpie lived, a little croft on a low hillock, a mountain with belts of crags above, very seldom sunshine. She looked about her in the valley, looked at the marsh, the evil marsh where all summer long she had lifted the sodden hay, soaking and unhappy; the days seemed to have had no mornings, no evenings to look forward to — and now the valley was lovely. Now I know why the valley is so lovely. Why, then? No, it wasn't because she was called Asta Sollilja. If it was lovely it was because a wonderful man had come into the valley.

The ducks went on sizzling.

"Let's go outside," he suggested. They sat down on the bank by the lake. It was nearly three o'clock, a summer breeze in the valley, warm. He lay flat in the grass looking up at the sky, and they gazed at him, and at his toes.

"Do you know anything?" he asked up at the sky.

"No," was their reply.

"Have you ever seen a ghost?"

"No."

"Is there anything you can do?" asked the man.

At this point the children felt that perhaps it was scarcely polite to answer all his questions in the negative, so they did not absolutely deny that they could do something. What could Asta Sollilja do? She racked her brains for a few moments, but found when it came to the point that she had forgotten everything she could do.

"Nonni here can sing," she said.

"Let's hear you sing, then," said the man.

But apparently the boy had suddenly forgotten how to set about singing.

"How many toes have I?" asked the man.

"Ten," answered little Nonni at once, and immediately regretted his hasty answer, for he had not troubled to count them, and who dare guarantee that such a great man did not have eleven? Asta Sollilja turned her head aside; she had never in all her life heard anyone ask such a funny question, and however hard she

tried she simply couldn't keep back her smile. And when she
looked around again, the man was giving her such a funny look
that she laughed out loud. She was very much ashamed of herself. But she couldn't help it.

"I knew it," said the man triumphantly, rising from the grass
to watch her laughing. She came all to life with the laughter, ro-
guery in her eyes; she gave up, and it was a girl's face.

Then he had to see to the ducks again. The odour of frying
spread out all around the tent, and the children's mouths watered
as they thought with delight of eating food with such a lovely
smell. The man brought some tins full of sweet fruit and turned
them out into a basin and was so occupied with his fragrant delicacies that he had little time for the children, and Asta Sollilja
was suddenly angry with her little brother Nonni for being so
stupid and so tiresome. "Why couldn't you have sung for the man,
you fool, when I let you come with me?" she said. But that evening when she was sitting outside on the paving alone, she re-
proached herself bitterly for not having shown what she herself
could do — why, for instance, hadn't she told him the story of
Snow White, which she knew practically off by heart? Once upon
a time in a great snowstorm — she had been on the very point of
beginning. But the truth was that she had felt that he might possibly misunderstand such a story. Yet, whatever the result might
have been, she could not help thinking of what she had left undone and regretting the story that had gone untold. She did not
tell anyone, only sat gazing towards the tent gleaming in the dusk
on the bank of the lake. And then she saw what, to the best of her
vision, was a man walking away westwards over the marshes, as
if he were making for Rauthsmyri. It was he.

When bedtime is near in Summerhouses he walks away westward over the ridge. Where could he be going so late at night? She
had never noticed it before, but perhaps he went there every night
without her knowing. But hadn't he said that the valley was lovely?
What had he meant? Nothing? Had he said it just for fun, and she
so sure that he meant it? For, if the valley was lovely, why did he
go away over the ridge — and night fallen. It had grown cold.

They did not see him for two days, but she heard him shooting. Then he came. It was at nightfall again, and they were getting
ready for bed. Fortunately she had not taken her slip off yet. There
was a light in his pipe as he stuck his head up through the hatchway in the dark and said good-evening. From his pocket he took

a box that gave out a light and the women were standing in their under-petticoats. He was puffing vigorously at his pipe; the clouds of fragrant smoke filled the room immediately.

"I'm leaving," he said.

"What's all your hurry?" asked Bjartur. "I always thought a week or two extra made no difference to you southerners. And the marsh is as good a place as any for you, mate."

"Yes, quite so."

"You were giving the youngsters some duck to eat the other day," said Bjartur.

"Oh, it was nothing," said the guest.

"Quite right," agreed Bjartur. "It's famine food, no pith in it; the stuff they ate after the Eruption. I suppose you've been half-starved in the marshes there, poor chap, as was only to be expected?"

"No, I've put on weight."

"Well, we prefer our food with a bit of strength in it," said Bjartur, "we like it sour and salt. By the way, you know all about building, I expect. I was thinking of starting to build myself a house, you see."

Here old Fritha could restrain herself no longer. "You building?" she interjected. "Huh, it's about time you were thinking of building some sense into your thick skull. And painting it as well. Both inside and out."

Yes, he had decided to build, but it would perhaps be wiser not to say too much in case these half-wits heard, spiteful old paupers, parasites battening on the community, but whatever happens, you're welcome here on my property at any time, be it night or day.

The visitor thanked Bjartur for his royal hospitality and said that he would most certainly return to such a pretty valley. And Bjartur answered, as in their first conversation, that pretty, well, it all depends on the hay.

Then the visitor began to shake hands in farewell.

The old woman seemed to have some difficulty in withdrawing her feeble hand from his farewell grip. She who so rarely needed to say anything to anyone seemed, strangely enough, to be trying to produce something from a recess in her mind; there was a little question she had been wanting to ask him. What was it?

"Did I hear aright the other day, does the gentleman hail from the south?"

"Yes," answered Bjartur loudly, relieving his guest of the inconvenience. "Of course the man's from the south. We've all heard it a hundred times."

But the old woman said that she had thought she might have misheard, she was such an old wreck these days.

"Yes," agreed Bjartur, "you're getting the worse for wear. The fellow can see that."

"I was wanting to ask the gentleman before he went away, seeing that I was brought up in the south, whether you might happen to know anything of my sister or perhaps have seen anything of her down there lately."

"No, no," cried Bjartur, "don't be so silly, he's never seen her."

"How the devil do you know?" asked old Fritha.

But the visitor wanted to make further inquiries into the matter, and said that there was always a chance that he might have seen this old woman's sister, what's her name?

He shone his pocket lamp on her and she tried to look at him with her dull, blinking eyes. Her sister's name was Oddrun.

"Oddrun? Is her home in Reykjavik?"

No, her home wasn't in Reykjavik. She hadn't a home anywhere, had never had a home. "She was a housemaid in Methalland for a long time — that's where we come from."

"Tcha," interrupted Bjartur. "How do you expect him to know folk like that, common folk?"

"The last I heard of her, she was in service with some people near Vik in Myrdal and was in bed with a broken hip. She asked someone to write me a letter. I got it from the postman. More than thirty years have passed since then. We were two sisters."

"Tcha, she must be dead long ago," cried Bjartur.

"For shame!" bawled old Fritha, taking up the cudgels. "You don't rule over God and men, thank goodness."

The visitor excused his ignorance of Oddrun by informing them that he had never been in Methalland.

"Oh, she left Methalland years ago," said the old woman. "But she's in the south all the same."

"Well, well," said the visitor. "Just so."

"News takes a long time to travel so far," remarked the old woman.

"Yes," agreed the visitor.

"So I was wanting to ask you to give her my greetings if you should ever run across her, and please tell her that I am well, praise the Lord, but failing fast and not much good in soul or body, as you can see. And tell her that I lost Ragnar thirteen years ago; and that the boys have all been in America for years now. I am living here with my daughter now. She is married."

"He knows that," cried Bjartur.

The visitor shook the old woman's hand once more in farewell and promised to convey these tidings to Oddrun in the south. He then said good-bye to the others. And he said good-bye to Asta Sollilja.

"Asta Sollilja," he said. And passed his hand over her cheek as if she were a little child. "Lovely name in a lovely valley. I'm sure I shall never forget it."

She lay awake praying to God without knowing God, endlessly revolving his promise in her mind, never forget it. Never. She looked forward to next summer, when he would come back again. Then came the doubt. If he were never going to forget it, why had he gone off across the ridge the night before last?

When they rose next morning he had packed up his tent and was gone from the valley. The rain was raw, summer far-waned, and in the rain there was the dreary beat that reminds one of ever-lasting waterfalls between the planets; it brooded oppressively over the whole countryside, smooth, smooth, over the whole shire, without rhythm or crescendo, overwhelming in its scope, terrifying. But the fragrance of his tobacco remained for a while in the house, she smelled it when she came home to do the cooking. But with the passing of time it faded. And finally there was no fragrance left.

35.   BUILDING

THIS Bailiff Jon of Utirauthsmyri was a person who had long been renowned for his ability to sell sheep wherever he pleased and at whatever price suited him best, while lesser farmers had to content themselves with revolving on Bruni's tether of debt. He was the one man in the district who could afford to hate Tulinius Jensen in public. He bought people's sheep and drove them north over the high heath and sold them for huge sums of money in Vik, because he had a share in the business there. But as time went on this co-operative society epidemic began spreading farther and farther afield till eventually a society was established in Vik, and this society grew so rapidly that the Vik business died of a wasting disease, and that in spite of the Bailiff's support, which goes to show

how dangerous societies can be for the individual in these hard times, however strong that individual may happen to be. One would naturally have imagined that Jon of Myri would now turn tooth and nail upon such unions of the crofters as the one that had just destroyed his business in Vik. But what happened? He sent away to the south country for his son, the secretary. He started a society in Fjord along with Ingolfur Arnarson Jonsson. And into this society he not only raked all the solvent farmers from the surrounding districts, including everyone down to the most abject peasant, but started lending people money on whatever terms they liked so that they could throw off Bruni's yoke and join his co-operative society. "We must stand together, we farmers," he said. He who so far had always stood alone was now of a sudden standing together. Such people know the tricks of flattering and fawning all right. "If the Icelandic farming community is ever to become anything but the miserable doormat of merchant power, we must take concerted action and rally round the standard of our own financial interests. The co-operative societies give full value for the farmers' produce and sell them their necessities at practically cost-price; they are actually not business enterprises, but charitable institutions owned and used by the farmers themselves for their own benefit. A man who sells us thirty lambs receives something like sixty crowns in dividend if world markets are favourable. A man paying in three to four hundred lambs would receive a dividend of say a thousand crowns. Anyone can see how essential these societies are to rich and poor alike. No one steals from anyone."

But with the autumn a letter arrived from Bruni informing all and sundry that he had just returned from a trip abroad. On this trip he had been fortunate enough to secure goods at particularly advantageous prices and had concluded negotiations with the Continent that insured his customers quite exceptional terms in the future; price-list enclosed. He was undercutting Ingolfur Arnarson's society on all shop goods, outbidding it on all forms of produce. Never had marketing been so profitable in Fjord as it was that autumn. If Ingolfur Arnarson clapped them on the back, Tulinius Jensen patted them on the cheek. When Ingolfur Arnarson addressed them as my dear friend, Tulinius Jensen called them my love. If it was Ingolfur Arnarson that fell on their necks, it was Tulinius Jensen that kissed them. The Christian frame of mind had, in business, overstepped all the bounds of propriety. No one ever mentioned the word "debt." Costly luxuries were slung at you as if they were so much rubbish. Everybody was to be a landed farmer in two years. Bjartur made use of the opportunity and bought some timber and some iron.

"Gladly, even if it was for a two-storey house of concrete," cried Tulinius Jensen as he fell on his neck. "And if you want to borrow some money, help yourself."

Building, said the Summerhouses children in an ecstasy of anticipation. They would sit there planning it out, debating whether it should have two floors like the mansion at Rauthsmyri or one floor like the Fell King's, but with a drawing-room as well as a kitchen. The building material lent wings to their imagination, but if they made so bold as to ask Bjartur any question, the reply was always short-spoken: keep on doing something. Asta Sollilja pictured a great kitchen, a range with numerous compartments, and shelves and racks for the china just as at Rauthsmyri; for of course there had all at once appeared china in plenty. She looked forward to coming home and cooking in the summertime. The kitchen door opens suddenly, and into this lovely kitchen steps a visitor in a huge coat, with ten toes and a string each of birds and fish; he offers her his kindly hand, some people have such good hands, you remember them on your death-bed. "But," she reflected, "if Father were to build a drawing-room, where would we get the pictures? And the sofa?"

They were busy taking the last loads of wet hay home from the marshes. She had been carrying the hay for him with great industry while he did the binding. She liked working near her father when no one else was about, nothing could compare with a word of his praise. Finally the last truss was bound. They sat down on a haycock, wet and muddy. He took out his snuff. She rested her big, work-weary hands in her wet lap, staring down at her feet, which were over the shoe-tops in water. She had a high forehead; no, they were not of his kin, those high foreheads; his forehead was low and broad. Her eyebrows, arched and dark, indicated a different stock, as did the fine slender lines of the lower face with its sculptured chin, strong of form and curved in artistic continuity of the cheek. And that full, ripe lower lip with the exotic grace of its curve. Then she looked at him and he saw her eyes. The right eye was strangely clear; it was young, almost happy, and quite free. But her left eye, which saw nothing straight, her left eye was a different soul, a different nation pursuing a different course; it held things undreamed of, fragile, delicate longings circumscribed by anguish itself, the longing of a man bound in the hands of his enemies; it was the cross-eye of her mother, who had died without achieving speech, who had lived in dread and disappeared, whom he had married but never owned. She had been young as a flower. It was as if he saw down through the years to far-off days. And was suddenly tired; autumn swept over his face in a moment, or rather his face dissolved into the paths of autumn without colour or form; one stands and faces one's life, a stranger —

"Father," she said. "It will be lovely when you start building."

And then she noticed his face, the face that he never showed in the light of day, which no one knew or had ever been allowed to see, which never realized expression even in his most expert verse, the face of the man within. His poetry was technically so complex that it could never attain any noteworthy content; and thus it was with his life itself. Once more she longed to throw her arms round his neck and bury her face in a certain spot. He stood up and stroked his daughter's head with his muddy palm.

"Some day Father will build a big house for the flower of his life," he said. "But it won't be this year."

Nor was it.

He contented himself that autumn with building a ewe-house with a corrugated iron roof to replace the old hut he had thrown up ten years ago on the bank of the brook. The cow-shed was made into a lamb-house and the ground floor of the croft adapted for the cow and the horse. The floor was paved and a door made in one of the sidewalls so that a muck-heap could be started behind the croft and the dung would not have to be shovelled out of the same door as the folk used.

In spite of all their disappointment this was still a sufficiently great event. New men on the croft, famous master builders who turfed the ewe-house walls in such a fashion that the courses took on a herring-bone pattern; a journeyman carpenter with foot-rule, pencil, and saw, mental arithmetic in his eye; the fresh scent of shavings blending with the smell of autumn's mud and rain; boisterous conversation at meal-times, fragrant snuff, poetry, merchants and co-operative societies, sheep, sheep again, interesting information from irrelevant quarters, unknown phrases, brawls, sweet coffee.

"From time immemorial the dealers have been swine enough to oppress the peasantry by buying cheap, selling dear, and sticking the difference in their own pockets. Anyone can see that the dealer is one of the farmer's arch-enemies."

"They've saved the lives of a few in hard years all the same."

"Maybe, but how far did this love of theirs ever reach? How high had the debt to be before they would refuse to add a pound of rye meal to your bill? A man may well hang his head in shame if he has to ask for a handful of rye meal to be put on somebody else's account."

"And now the co-op has introduced percentages. They pay you a percentage now on top of what you get for your produce, provided the market is good. When did it ever occur to the merchants to pay percentages, may I ask?"

"Oh, it's just like the Rauthsmyri gang to invent percentages. I shouldn't be surprised if these percentages of theirs are nothing but a lot of guff."

"They're thinking of starting a savings bank in Fjord, too, so that folk's money can give off interest."

"Interest?"

"Yes, it's a sort of offspring that money spawns if it's put in a savings bank. Some reliable man or other borrows it from the savings bank and pays it back at an even higher rate of interest."

"Yes, the Rauthsmyri crew wouldn't give a damn if they lost what they had had lent to them as long as there was money in it for themselves."

Bjartur was true to his merchant in spite of all opposition, steadfast in his conviction that it would pay him better to deal with Tulinius Jensen than with the Bailiff, positive that all the Rauthsmyri societies and inventions had one aim only, to gain percentages and interest alike for themselves.

But higher than all dealers and societies stand the dreams of the heart, especially in the autumn when dusk is falling and the clouds of the world are full of marvellous pictures. Asta Sollilja sits by the window watching them. Her mother is downstairs talking to the cow, feeding it and stroking it and waiting for it to be thirsty, while her grandmother sits drooping on her bed in the dusk with her finger in her mouth and scarcely a single line of a hymn on her lips — incomprehensible being who in spite of everything has a sister in the south. And then from the heavens there gleam remote continents with varicoloured oceans and protean seaboards; faerie lands, cities. Up from the glass-green sea rise purple-red palaces which submerge once more with their towers, and the ocean dissolves and transforms itself into a fruitful orchard encircled by fantastic mountains with living peaks that curtsy low and fall into an embrace before they finally disappear. She had never sat by the window like that before. And now into the fugitive apparitions of the air she interwove her thoughts of him. Him. Those strange countries with oceans and flitting sails, cities and orchards that lived and swirled in the skies in exotic brilliance, were all one wordless thought of him, one long recollection of occasions that had never been, one dream of the future without world, without days. Him; him; him. She heard the cow slunking up her water down below, and far, far away her mother telling the cow about the life of man, and the girl listened to the murmur of their remote irrelevant talk from the distance of the clouds above, where she had her home; where she had her kingdom with him as in the words of the folk-dance:

> *My love he lives under a far, far roof,*
> *By a hearth that knows no sorrow,*
> *No tears, of bitter grief no sound;*
> *To my love is my joy for ever bound.*

> *My love I have met in the green, green wood,*
> *In the orchard of wondrous beauty*
> *His house of gladness I have found;*
> *To my love will my joy be ever bound.*

Oh, that it might never end; that it might live on to eternity in the restless splendour of its colour. And thus night after night she sat watching the silent music of the clouds.

36.   ONE FLOWER

THE FLOOR space in the newly built ewe-house was inviting, and Bjartur, though well aware that he now had a cow to feed, boldly yielded to the temptation to retain a greater number of sheep than usual that autumn. He was thankful for every opportunity of sending them out to graze; the boys watched over them in the marshes. But though Bjartur was very fond of sheep, was continually thinking about sheep, and even had a reputation for handling sheep rather well, it was always touch-and-go whether these much discussed animals survived the winter, let alone the spring. They tell the same story everywhere, it takes next to nothing to finish a sheep off in the springtime, and such has been the case for a thousand years. From the time of the colonization this guileless creature has always had a quite remarkable propensity for death in the spring.

The family, on the other hand, were thriving famously this winter, and for the first time in many years Finna was not brought to her usual mid-winter bed; it was the beginning of March before she showed any signs of pregnancy. She had always some trouble with her chest, of course, as had her mother too, that dreadful range with its eternal smoke, they coughed from the time of kindling till well on in the day, then started another fit in the evenings. To make matters worse, there was the strong stench of cow-dung and horse's urine in the croft, and this, coupled with the reek, caught Finna in the chest and gave her all sorts of sickly feelings. She kept on looking after the cow herself, but was no longer allowed to give her her hay, as she was far too prodigal with the small supply of home-field hay, which Bjartur preferred to reserve for the lambs and such of the ewes as were off their fodder. But she fed her and swept out for her, watered her and raked out the muck, striving always to keep her stall as clean as possible, for cows are grateful for such things. She would scratch her and stay with her in the stall talking to her as long as she could. She gave her many a fish-bone that she had managed to filch from the dog unnoticed by Bjartur, even lumps of dough when the bread was being made. The cow often fell into fits of depression nowadays, moaning querulously in long-drawn despair as if there would never be another spring. On these occasions the woman knew that her heart was beating in anguish, that she felt her life empty and pointless. At such a time Finna would go down to her in the middle of the day, this woman who had so little comfort herself, and stroking her dewlap and her head, would say that the forces of good would triumph finally in the life of man; and the cow would be quiet again and begin chewing the cud. Old Blesi, who despaired of ever escaping this inane and ruminating fellowship, snorted coldly over the crossbar. The children, however, had learned from their mother to love the cow and respect her because of the milk that augments the soul's joy and induces more harmonious relationships in the household. But Bjartur would not touch the swill that deprives one of one's appetite and makes one costive; he only gave the lambs that had diarrhœa some chewing-tobacco boiled in milk.

Why, they even acquired a rosy colour in their cheeks and the sparkle of healthy youth in their eyes, these children who had hitherto been nothing but snivelling colds and slothfulness. All intentional laziness had disappeared; they no longer experienced

their old unhappy listlessness or the joyless emptiness that felt
as if their stomachs were blown out with wind and water. Asta
Sollilja improved in her understanding of the more obscure passages in her father's ballads, learned to shape letters on a smoked
glass, and made rapid progress in mental arithmetic. And so
quickly did she sprout in this one winter that she could hardly get
her old things on without splitting them, so they cut pieces out of
the arm-holes and sewed gussets in the arms and sides; she was
a lanky fourteen-year-old now, with a complexion, a bosom, peculiar feelings, and healthy occasional indispositions. They even
had to add a broad strip to the bottom of her skirt because of her
knees, which showed under the hem and had grown strong and
plump since the preceding summer.

The minister came during the winter and asked her to read for
him, and admired her skill in reading; she had taught her eldest
brother to read as well; but how much religious knowledge had
she learned? It turned out that she hadn't learned any religious
knowledge at all, only prayed to God once or twice without knowing Him. "We can't have this," said the minister. "It's illegal. The
girl is old enough to be confirmed."

"I can't say that I have much faith in this modern religion,"
said Bjartur. "But we had a grand pastor here once; those were
the days. Those who were fortunate enough to know old Reverend
Gudmundur will remember him as a great man to their dying day.
His breed will perpetuate his name in this district. For ever and
ever."

This new minister, tut, he was no minister at all, a baldheaded youngster, what did he know about sheep? It wasn't that
he didn't do his best, for he was always eager to talk sheep and
pretending that he had a natural flair for the animals. He was
continually dishing up some theory or other from the *Agricultural
Journal,* and just now he was trying to persuade everybody to
keep a ewe-book, and mark the lambs and write each lamb's number in the book so that they would know the pedigree of every
lamb in the autumn — it was a deadly sin against one's stock, one's
self, and one's family to retain the smallest lambs in the autumn
just because their carcasses wouldn't bring much in, and thus
allow the worst dregs to shape the coming generation — and so on.

"The Reverend Gudmundur never talked sheep with anyone,"
said Bjartur. "And he never kept a ewe-book, nor any other book
except his Hebrew book. But he was a great man with sheep, for
all that. His men used to swear that he knew his own hoof-marks

from anyone else's. We shall never see the like of him again in this parish."

They agreed finally that Asta Sollilja should be allowed to wait a year after Helgi. But the minister insisted that they must both go over to the homesteads next winter, before they were confirmed, to learn the rudiments of religious knowledge and the other subjects that were prescribed by law for such confirmation: geography, zoology, Icelandic history. "By the way, did you say geography?" They knew every inch of the valley, every crag, every hummock, every curve of the brook; whatever the weather, they couldn't get lost if they tried. And as for zoology, they knew every single sheep on the place; they had been brought up with animals and knew as much about them as anyone. And Icelandic history — "Who was Grimur Ægir, Asta?" Asta Sollilja, shyly: "Gongu-Hrolfur's enemy." Bjartur: "Right first time. And where did he go when he was killed?" Asta Sollilja, shamefacedly down into her bosom: "To hell."

"There you see what happened to him anyway," said Bjartur with a loud guffaw; and a little later: "Good-bye, then, Reverend Teodor, and see and look after yourself."

It was early in March and Bjartur was making one of his frequent journeys down to the marshes to herd the sheep home. The weather had been very unsettled most of the day — showers of wet snow with fair intervals and even sunshine. The boys had been taking turns watching over the sheep. As he was rounding them up, the crofter suddenly noticed that one of his ewes, Hetja by name, was bleeding copiously from the head. At first he thought that she had cracked a horn, but on closer examination he found that the sheep had been, of all things, double ear-marked in his own pastures. The discovery astonished him greatly, as was only natural. Cautiously he fingered the bloody ears, trying to discover what sort of mark it was and what trickery was afoot, but the ears had been clumsily and even viciously cut, and though he detected resemblances to one or two of the conventional markings, he could not be certain which had been intended. There was more of the phenomenal than of the accidental in such an occurrence, and it gave him much food for thought. On arriving home he inquired closely whether anyone had been seen in the valley that day, but the answer was in every case definite: no one.

"If it is true that there has been no one about, then it's the first time in all these years that anything has happened in the valley here," and he told the news of the marking.

Helgi remarked gratuitously:

"I thought I saw someone riding into the lake in one of the showers."

"Into the lake? Are you mad, boy? What colour of horse was he riding?"

"I couldn't make that out clearly," replied the boy. "It didn't seem to be a horse at all."

"Who would you say the man was like, then, you little idiot?"

"I couldn't make him out; it was in that heavy shower, you see. He didn't look like a man at all."

"What was he like, then?"

But the boy couldn't say, it was just some sort of a bundle, that sort of rolled along through the shower and made off out into the lake.

Bjartur sat heavy in thought. They all sat heavy in thought. The old woman muttered this and that to her needles, a bad sign, better look out with the spring. We've all noticed a thing or two on this croft, and folk know more or less that the ghost isn't dead yet, but to take a sheep from the flock and mark it in broad daylight —

The days that followed, mild days of warm breezes, springlike rain, and snow melting on the lowlands, did much to dispel the gloom cast by this phenomenon. The valley emerged yellow-brown with its withered grass, the hollows grew rapidly green, and colour spread over the home-field. The river was free, the ice broken on the lake; Finna stood in the doorway to feel the lightness of the breeze. The farm ravens had flown.

Little Nonni took his sheep-bones out on the hill to play. It was he who one day came in with the news that there was a dandelion in bloom on the wall of the croft. Rare occurrence in an isolated valley at that time of year. The children and their mother went round to inspect the little dandelion, which spread its petals so bravely and so happily in the winter sun, those tender young petals. One small eternal flower. Long, long they gazed in pious admiration on this new friend, this harbinger of summer in the very depths of winter, so gay and adorable. In silent devotion, like a company of the faithful touching the bones of some saint, they felt it with their fingertips. It was as if they wished to say: "You are not alone, we also live, we also are striving to live." There was a brightness over that day. The apprehensions of winter disappeared all in one day. The cloudless brightness of that day lay infinite over the soul as over the vault of heaven; it was one of life's happy days, and they remembered it as long as they lived. Then the plover was heard, and the plover's first cry has a marvellous ring. It is at once shy and grateful, as breathless as the first greeting after grave danger, and yet bursting with quiet joy.

And the young girl who knew nothing of Christianity, winter had passed in her soul too. Had she, then, felt no anxiety in the foul weather and long darkness of winter? Yes, she had often been anxious. They had all been anxious. The nights were very long. And the days were no days at all. One lives for the spring, and yet one does not seem to believe in the spring before it has come. One dandelion, one plover, and it was as if everything was coming, everything that one lives for till one dies. Soon the marshes would be green and humming with life the same as they were last year, with the phalarope preening itself in courtesy on the surface of the deep pools. And the little waterfall up in the mountain would be flowing backward in the sunny breeze. And he, he who came from afar —

Good Friday arrived, the longest day of the year. They suspected that someone had been crucified on that day, God or Jesuspeter, but otherwise had very vague ideas about how people were crucified, for they had never seen a cross, let alone crucified people, and didn't care very much whether they saw them or not and asked no questions; the countryside was seething with old rumours. But on that day of all days of course the weather would have to break; it started freezing and by evening a high wind was blowing and the sky was thick with cloud. By bedtime snowflakes had begun to drift. Bjartur of Summerhouses was also gloomy of appearance that evening, and about midnight, after slipping on his trousers and shoes, he went down to look at the weather. It was blowing hard and the snow lay almost an inch deep. By morning it had grown to a howling blizzard with a biting frost.

It was Bjartur who had found least material for rejoicing in the period of fine weather that had just passed, the tokens of spring had left him unmoved, he was not the man to place much faith in the blooming of a flower or the piping of a bird. The truth was that in spite of the exceptionally fine weather so far, his sheep were not in good condition, the hay was of very poor quality after last year's wet summer, and the lack of snow had tempted him to graze his sheep in the open more than was good for them. But one fact had disturbed him more than any other: time and time again the sheep had shown signs of lung-worm, with all the concomitant symptoms of cough, sluggishness, and foul-smelling diarrhœa. It

was as if the sheep were eating to no purpose; some of the ewes
had grown so lifeless that he was anxious for them and had been
thinking of taking them home and feeding them on home-field
hay, even cooked food. Now it had blown up for an Easter gale,
goodness only knew how long it would last. The sheep had got
used to being in the open and had begun to crop the spring grass
in the marshes; now they would have to be penned in again, a return to misery for an indefinite period.

It was an incredible blizzard. It was one of those peculiar gales
when the mountain sang above the croft as if the trolls that inhabited it had gone demented and taken out their drums; the dog
hung whining about the trapdoor, shivering in every limb. And
Easter morning was one of those comparatively rare mornings
when old Hallbera recited her gale-hymn from beginning to end,
while the children huddled beneath the bedclothes like a stricken
host — the extraordinary hymn of the storm and the maniac, which
lived in their minds as the most unpleasant poetry in all the world:
then there came a madman, of evil spirits tormented, naked, raving, wild, demented. The horrible hero of the gale-hymn continued to haunt their dreams long, long after the storm was over.
Often in later days the sudden thought of him would rob them
of all their joy in the summer weather; when least expected he
would break loose in their memory like a crime, even when in
later years they had at last begun to live in comfort.

> *With fearful strength those rabid hands*
> *   The captors' chains soon rent;*
> *Then raged with glee o'er desert lands*
> *   A madman nowhere pent.*

> *He lay in wait by lonely roads*
> *   At dusk, his murderous glare*
> *Fixed on the traveller as he strode,*
> *   Unwitting, nearer to his lair.*

When the old woman felt constrained to sing this hymn it
was a token that all the evil powers in and on the earth had broken
loose of their bonds. Turning her senses away from the world, she
sat rocking slowly backwards and forwards with her knotted
hands crooked together over her withered bosom, her voice like
the sound of a roughly hacked blade sawing through living flesh.
Never is winter more powerful than on such days of spring. In
wordless fear these anxious hearts beat free of debt in the face

of the grim powers that encircled the little independent farm.
The mother unlaced her shoes and crept under the bedclothes
again, on Easter morning.

37.   THE BATTLE

FIVE days' blizzard — it was simply incredible how far the sheep
could decline in such a short space of time. And since they could
not be persuaded to touch the mouldy hay from the out-fields, the
only alternative was to feed them on the home-field hay, which
hitherto had been reserved for the cow and the lambs. But how
long would the manured hay last if it was to become the sole
fodder for the entire stock? There were only two or three feet of
the stack left. The ewes of course had to be considered first. But
it was equally futile to deprive the cow of her manured hay and
put her on the other; she refused to look at it, grumbled sullenly
over her full manger, yielded less and ever less milk. She would
have lost the use of her legs long before the time that pasture
could be expected for her, perhaps as late as Midsummer Day,
in a capricious future. It was conceivable, however, if only the
weather improved and the ground cleared again, that he might
manage to keep the ewes alive with the handful of home-field hay
that he still had left. The struggle for sustenance lay therefore between the cow and the ewes, and with every additional day it
became more and more evident that only the one or the other
could survive. Such are the serious effects that the blizzards of
spring may have on a little farm in a valley. No wonder that the
soul is cheerless, that hope is small in the people's hearts, that
there is little comfort in lying awake at night. Even the most beautiful memories lose their lustre like a shining silver coin that col-
lects verdigris because it has been lost. The four children watched
their father getting up in the mornings, grim-faced and sleepless;
saw their mother's face swollen with the night's silent weeping.

She still went down to the cow to stroke her and console her.
"It won't be long before it's over now," she would say. "Soon the
sunshine will come again for both of us, and the snow will be
melting away; then the sheep will be going down to the marshes
and we'll both have plenty of nice hay again. The green grass will
start growing and little Nonni will be coming with his mother to
sit beside her Bukolla up by the mountain. And the birds — " The
birds? — no. Words failed her at this point and she went on strok-

ing the cow in silence only, for though the birds might sing in the summertime, the cow was still moaning over the mouldy hay, and the hay lay untouched in the manger. Music, there is no comfort in music for one who stands face to face with death in the spring. She stroked her in terror. Finally the cow started bellowing.

Gradually this Easter storm died away like any other storm. The sun came out. The snow cleared away pretty quickly in the longer daylight. But the raw cold remained in the air, and the frosts were hard at night. Bjartur started driving his flock down to the marshes once more, but the young grass was either withered at the tips or dead altogether; the marshy hollows were black when they emerged from the frozen snow. Many of the ewes were so feeble by now that he had great difficulty in driving them; some of them could not be moved at all. When they were crossing the home brook it took them all their time to climb on to the bank on the other side, though it was hardly knee-high; they managed perhaps to heave the front part up, but the after-part stayed behind and there they would stand swaying, half in, half out. When Bjartur lifted them out, they would slump down on the bank, and once they were down, it was difficult to make them show any desire for further movement. He would take them by the horns and try to lift them on to their feet, and they would rise at most half-way and straddle along on their knees, a mode of progression that ever since the days of the first settlement has been known as stumping. When they had stumped along for a few minutes, they flopped over again. Down in the marshes they stuck fast in the ditches. If they sank over the hocks, they would make no further effort. The ravens had returned to the marshes, waiting their opportunity to rive a hole in their backs, tear the entrails out of them alive, peck their eyes out. One day three of them lay inert at the bottom of the home-field; though the dog was sent barking and snapping around them they made no movement, only blinked their eyes a little. Bjartur took out his clasp-knife. He parted the wool about their necks and cut their throats, buried them.

The majority of the ewes had lung-worm. Bjartur segregated several and fed them inside, but they hardly looked at the hay. In the mornings one or more would be lying unable to move or already dead. He ordered his wife to knead some rye-meal dough; some took it, others refused. The rye meal was running short, and at this rate would not last very long even though the family economized on bread. In the evenings he tried to entice the sheep home by walking backwards with a cake of dough stretched out towards them and allowing them to nibble at it every other step, but it was extremely slow work, and it was only possible to coax them along one at a time by this means, and before he knew, they would be lying sprawling. The children did what they could to help him in this novel method of herding. Yes, there is a great difference between a sheep in the summertime, that haughty creature, pride of the mountain pastures, queen of the moors, as it struts proudly about the hillsides, snorts warily from a hillock, or peeps mockingly from the withies, and the tragic caricature that one sees in the marshes in spring. He cut the throats of more and more.

A fair number of ewes, however, were still keeping their strength remarkably well and feeding with good appetite. For these it behoved him to do everything possible, and not to spare the manured hay while there was a single blade left. And the stack diminished day by day, the cow grew thinner day by day, her yield less and less.

Her supply was by now nowhere near sufficient for the family, though they were making it their custom, by no means unusual in the spring, to eat only one meal a day. Men and animals starved. At length Finna got busy and whittled a piece of wood down to a shape with a knob at one end which she fringed with coarse yarn. The children gazed at this contrivance with wondering eyes. "What's that supposed to be?" they asked. "It's a whisk," explained Finna. "Once there was a woman who was very poor. And Jesus came to her and taught her to make a whisk and whip up the milk to make it go further." Finna put some rennet in the few drops that could still be squeezed out of the cow, then whipped it up in a pan, and in a few moments the milk had increased so much in volume that it filled the pan to the brim; no one knows how much further it might have gone had she kept on stirring. The children had whipped milk to drink and were all very impressed with Jesus.

Then one evening Finna said:

"Bjartur, you'll have to go up-country and see if you can't get some hay from someone."

The crofter rarely opened his mouth at home these days, and when he did speak, it was mostly in abrupt commands like a skipper in deadly peril at sea, but this request made him jump as if pricked by the point of a knife.

"Me? Up-country? I have no debts to collect from anyone up-country."

"But, Bjartur dear, the cow's almost dry and it's terrible to see her hunger. The poor creature is wasting away before my very eyes."

"That's no business of mine," he replied. "I don't intend to be in anyone's debt up-country. We are independent people. I am beholden to no one. I am a free man living on my own land."

"We have so much to thank poor Bukolla for," protested his wife.

"Yes, I know that," he said. "And we'll probably have more to thank her for before she's finished. Especially if she manages to kill off all that's left of my sheep."

"If it was only a truss or so of good manured hay," begged Finna.

"No power between heaven and earth shall make me betray my sheep for the sake of a cow. It took me eighteen years' work to get my stock together. I worked twelve years more to pay off the land. My sheep have made me an independent man, and I will never bow to anyone. To have people say of me that I took the beggar's road for hay in the spring is a disgrace I will never tolerate. And as for the cow, which was foisted on me by the Bailiff and the Women's Institute to deprive the youngsters of their appetite and filch the best of the hay from the sheep, for her I will do only one thing. And that shall be done."

"Bjartur," said Finna in a toneless voice, staring at him in distraction from the impassable distance that separates two human beings, "if you are going to kill Bukolla, kill me first."

38.   DEATH IN THE SPRING

THE SAME weather, no sign of improvement, ugly skies, frequent hail-showers. The whole croft stank with the putrid smell of maggoty dung, the worms were growing more virulent, the rattling cough of the ewes blended with the moaning of the cow. The maggots wriggled out of their nostrils and hung like threads from the matter about their noses; every morning one or more would be lying trodden in the muck, sometimes still faintly breathing, and he killed them, dragged them out to a turf grave, wiped his knife on the moss, swore. Twenty-five gone, all of his own rearing. He had known each one's pedigree, had been able to recognize every one of them from the day of its birth; a picture of each was graven on his mind as sharply as the features of any close friend, both appearance and personality. Beyond his memories of these animals he saw the passing of many seasons; he remembered them healthy and heavy-fleeced as they came down from the mountains on autumn days, proud of their frisky sons; he remembered them in the spring as they licked their lambs, new-born and helpless, in some green dingle. Each of them had had its own characteristics, its own temperament. He remembered minutely how each one's horns had been, tufted on one, grey-spotted on another, yellow-streaked on a third; one was as timid and as shrinking as the shyest maiden, another would spring impudently on to the walls or swim out into impassable rivers, a third liked to slink about in the gullies — and he had had to cut their throats. The worms had writhed out of their bleeding trunks, their lungs had been as riddled as rotten carrion. Hringja, Skella, Skessa, and the others — these creatures had been the mainspring of his existence and its strongest support. Twenty-five. Which will be next?

Heavy snow, not a chance of letting the sheep out to graze today, three ewes doomed to death this morning, Kupa, Laufa, Snura. Not a word spoken in the croft; the last of the hay broached; the cow had refused to stand on her feet. As day advanced, the intervals between showers grew shorter and shorter till once more a blizzard was raging. There was darkness on the little window, and the smoke blew down the chimney to add its discomfort to the stink of polluted dung from below; it was almost impossible to breathe.

And elsewhere in the world there was an orchard and a palace.

Then had the world quite forgotten this little croft in the valley? Had it, then, abandoned it altogether with its anxious hearts, its heroism unchronicled, unrecorded in books? No; oh no. There were visitors at the door, the snorting of horses in the storm, the champing of bits, strange voices — sudden expansion of mind from its mute, congested fear, unexpected pleasure for man and dog.

Through the hatchway there emerged a snow-beaten girl whose generous curves were accentuated by her close-cut riding-breeches; whose grey-blue eyes were complacent, and comely cheek ruddy with the wind. She dusted the snow from her clothes down through the opening, showed her healthy teeth in laughter, and swore here and there, hahaha. Her riding-whip gleamed expensively in these surroundings where not a single article would have fetched more than a dime, Audur Jonsdottir of Myri. Her escort, one of the Bailiff's men, followed her up into the loft. He was taking her down to Fjord to catch the mail-steamer south to-morrow, to Reykjavik and a happier clime.

"Dear little lady, how she spreads amidships!" cried Bjartur, clapping her courteously on the buttocks. "Still fed on the fat of the land, I see. Make her coffee good and strong and don't spare the sugar. She wasn't reared on dish-wash, bless the darling little head that hardly reached my middle when I married the first time."

Lining up shoulder to shoulder on the floor, the children stared at her in admiration, greatly impressed by her size, her self-confidence, the length of the journey she was undertaking, and the expert manner of her swearing; and presently she had finished dusting off the snow and was standing there like some ripe, fertile plant that bows beneath the weight of its newly opened flowers, soon to seed.

No, to set out across the heath in this weather was unthinkable, a blizzard like this would be the end of any woman; she would have to stay here until it cleared up. She looked around for a seat, but the coverlets on all the beds were equally uninviting. Finally she was persuaded to perch on the foot-board of the parents' bed. She didn't want to trouble them at all, hoped the weather would clear before evening, asked politely about the sheep.

"There was somebody or other afoot here at the end of February who ear-marked a sheep for me. But that will be nothing to what you have to report from up your way, I imagine."

Yes, there was gloomy news from up-country, confirmed the escort, gloomy news. Olafur of Yztadale had lost forty or so in spite of all his science, and Einar of Undirhlith over thirty, though possibly they would find greener pastures in the next world. Thorir of Gilteig wouldn't even say how many he had lost now that his youngest daughter also had gone and given birth to a bastard (the Bailiff's daughter: "Why don't they marry the fellows decently?"); but Bjartur said that as you sowed so must you reap, and laughed. "It's all the cows' fault," he said. "They end up by eating a man's soul out of him, the bloody parasites; their bellies are as bottomless as the Mediterranean." Things were not too bad with the Fell King, however, continued the Bailiff's man, and at Myri they were giving them dough, but some of them were very listless, as so often in the spring, and they had had to cut an occasional throat.

Quite, Bjartur knew all about it; it was an old custom at

Myri. One black pudding more or less at slaughter-time never had
made much difference to the Bailiff as long as his saddle-horses
were well fed.

The blizzard refused to abate and the girl grew restless. Again
and again she went downstairs to look outside; the snow blew
straight in through the door, straight into her face; blizzards are
never so biting as in the spring. She cursed for some time, then
stopped cursing and grew thoughtful, then had a fit of hysterics,
which culminated in her losing all control of herself. "My brother
Ingolfur's expecting me tonight," she cried. "He's certain to think
I've been lost in the hills. Heavens, if I miss that ship!"

"Oh, its bound to clear up tonight."

"Merciful heavens, if I miss that ship!"

"It's letting up a bit now."

"God Almighty help me if I miss that ship."

"Oh, there'll be another ship."

"But if I miss this ship!"

"Reykjavik will still be there though you miss one ship and
catch the next."

"Yes, but I must go with this ship," she insisted. "Even if I
do die in the hills. I must get to Reykjavik on Saturday."

What was all the hurry?

No answer; despair. She complained that she was on the point
of suffocating, refused to eat or drink. But she stayed the night in
spite of all the stench; there was nowhere else to go. She did not
undress, but lay down on a couple of boxes after wrapping herself
in one of her own horsecloths. She would not hear of lying in bed.
Through the night she could be heard sighing and groaning; time
and time again she crept down the ladder in the darkness and out.
Did she want a pot? inquired Bjartur. No, she had only been looking at the weather. And being sick. She would have to reach Reykjavik by Saturday.

There was little sleep for anyone on the croft that night. What
was she after in Reykjavik? Who could it be she was going to
meet? Had not Asta Sollilja a high brow and full-curved eyebrows
as well as she? Asta Sollilja was no longer slim either, she also was
a young girl full of longing and despair. His house stood by itself
in a wood, not with a girl in front of it, as on mother's cake-dish,
but by itself in a wood, as on the calendar that fell downstairs the
year before last and was trodden into the muck under the sheep's
hoofs. She had had him first, he had been a guest on their land,
not hers. Dear God, what dreams she had dreamed all winter

through and into the red death of the spring; she too was lying
awake tonight and wishing just as passionately as ever before,
more passionately than ever before. Some are left sitting behind
in the death of spring, when others are on their way south.

Asta Sollilja was awakened early next morning after a short
doze by the sound of clear joyful laughter; the storm was over and
the Bailiff's daughter happy and wolfing down her sandwiches
with plenty of time to catch the ship. Her escort, it was true, maintained that the outlook was none too good, but the Bailiff's daughter laughed and asked what the hell that mattered, and having recovered her powers of swearing, went out to her horses, and
shouted up to her escort at frequent intervals: "Oh, come on there,
isn't it time we were going?" But he happened to be busy upstairs drinking coffee with the family. "What a damnable row she
makes!" he said.

"She's not long of one temper, bless her."

"True," agreed the guide, noisily swilling his coffee. "These
womenfolk are all on edge when they're getting married."

"Am I wrong, or is she fattening in that direction?" asked Bjartur.

"It doesn't take much of an eye to see that."

"Someone or other has passed that way, I suppose?" said
Bjartur.

"Huh, do you think they try their rods out only on your land,
these co-operative heroes from the south?"

"Oh-ho, so he was one of that gang, too, the swine," said the
crofter. "I might have known."

But in spite of that he showed his visitors as far as the road.

The wind was raw, probably more snow in the offing. To hell
with it all. "Isn't it time those lazy little devils were out of bed
yet?" He took down two butcher's knives in a piece of sacking,
unwrapped them and laid them on the bed at his side, took a
whetstone from the shelf, spat; the noise of whetting clawed
through living and dead.

"Helgi, up with you, boy. I want you."

The lad got sullenly out of bed, pulled on his trousers, began
searching for the rest of his things. Bjartur went on whetting.
The other children peeped out from under the bedclothes. He
kept on whetting for a while longer, then, plucking a hair from
his head, tested the edge. Next he took a rusty screwdriver from
the lumber-box, wiped it on his trouser-leg, and sharpened it.

"Haven't you got into your clothes yet, boy?"

"What have I to do?"

"What have you to do? You have to do what I damn well tell you. Down with you."

He drove the boy downstairs before him while Finna stared with frantic eyes at her husband as he stood by the hatchway with a knife in each hand. Did she perhaps think, this worn-out woman who believed in the ultimate victory of good and who had made a whisk according to the teachings of Jesus Christ, that she could do anything to deflect that uncompromising will to conquer on which the nation's freedom and independence have been built for a thousand years? Iceland's thousand years. She threw her arms round her husband's neck as he stood by the hatchway with a knife in either hand. "It's the same as killing me, Gudbjartur," she moaned, "I can't bear to see the children starving any longer," and shook from head to foot with her weeping. One eternal flower with trembling tears. But with a jerk of the shoulders he threw her off, and she watched him with her frantic eyes as he disappeared down the stairs.

For a while there was nothing to be heard but wordless movements. He untied a rope's end and made a halter; then the cow, more dead than alive, was prodded on to her feet, groaning with the exertion. He unfastened her stall-rope; she lowed piteously through the open croft door.

For Finna of Summerhouses, that silent, song-loving woman who had borne many children both for the independence of the country and for death, this moment marked the end of all things. She was good. She had friends among the elves. But her heart had long beaten in terror. Life? It was as if life at this moment once more sought its source. Her knees gave way and in perfect silence she sank into old Hallbera's arms; like insignificant dust she drifted down upon the withered bosom of her mother.

BOOK TWO

PART I

Hard Times

39.   ON THE PAVING

WHEN there is death in the spring, summer passes with a funeral, and the soul — the soul? What thoughts does the soul harbour, in a new autumn, at the onset of winter?

"And if it happened to be a long winter," says the eldest boy as he sits on the paving in front of the croft in the dusk, "if there happened to come the sort of winter that keeps on stretching out and stretching out and spinning round and round in a circle from there on, senselessly, like a dog running in circles because somebody's taken hold of its tail; and then keeps on spinning, round in a circle, on and on, always in the same circle, till at last it can't stop, whatever anyone tries to do — what then?"

And answers his own question: "Nothing could happen any more."

The youngest brother: "There couldn't be such a long winter. Because if there was such a long winter — a hundred years, for instance — I for one would go up the home mountain."

"What for?"

"To see if I could see the countries."

"What countries?"

"The countries my mother told me about, before she died."

"There aren't any countries."

"There are, I tell you. In the springtime I've often seen the waterfall blowing back over the top."

The elder brother naturally did not deign to answer reasoning so inimical to all common sense, so obviously emanating from the world of wishes, but contented himself, after a pause, with continuing from where he had left off.

"But suppose there was a long funeral," he said. "Suppose there was a funeral so long that the minister's sermon kept going of itself, like a leak, for instance, drop after drop, you know, and suppose it never ended. Suppose he said about a hundred and fifty amens one after another. Suppose he kept on saying amen for a hundred and fifty years. What then?"

"There couldn't be such a long funeral. The folk would stand up and walk out."

"But the coffin, you fathead. Would that stand up and walk out?"

"The folk would take the coffin with them," replied the youngest brother.

"Are you daft, man? Do you think anyone would have the nerve to pick the coffin up and take it away with them before the minister had said amen for the last time?"

"When my mother was buried, the minister went on talking and talking, I know; but he did stop in the end. When the minister begins to feel like a cup of coffee, he stops of his own accord. I always knew he would stop some time."

The elder brother moved nearer still to the younger where they sat together on the paving and laid his hand on his shoulder like a protector. "You're so little yet, Nonni lad, you can't be expected to understand."

"But I do understand," objected young Nonni, and would not suffer his brother's protecting hand on his shoulder. "I understand everything you understand, and more."

"All right, then," said the other, "since you're so clever, what is a funeral?"

The youngest brother bethought himself awhile, because he was determined to give the right answer, then he bethought himself a little longer, and still without finding a completely satisfactory answer, and finally he bethought himself so much that he couldn't for the life of him discover any sensible answer to this simple question, and so the elder brother had to answer it himself:

"A funeral is a funeral, you idiot," he said.

And young Nonni was half surprised at himself that it should never have occurred to him, and it so obvious.

Then the elder brother continued: "And it never ends from then on. Though the people go away; though the minister says amen for the very last time; even though the waterfall runs backward over the mountain, as you say it did last spring, which actually isn't true, because no waterfall could ever run backward over a mountain — it never, never ends from then on. And do you know why?"

"Don't be so silly, you great fool."

"It's because the corpse never comes to life again."

"Oh, why must you always be on top of me? Can't you leave me alone?" and the younger brother moved away a little.

"Are you frightened?"

"No."

The dusk over the paving grew heavier and heavier; freezing; dark banks of cloud on the horizon; maybe it was coming on for something, Grandmother was expecting a new moon.

"Listen, Nonni lad, would you like me to tell you something?"

"No," said the little boy, "you needn't bother."

"If we sat here on the paving for a hundred years, maybe a hundred and fifty years, and it was beginning to get dark like it is now, and Father was always feeding the same sheep with the same hay from the same truss, and —"

"If Father was at home he would give you a good beating for sitting there blathering like idiots when you know you have to keep on doing something " — it was the middle brother, Gvendur, who had come stealing into the mystical conversation, like a thief in the night.

But incredible as it may seem, it was the brother who had understood least who took up the cudgels for the one who had talked the most, and demanded sharply of the middle brother: "Was anyone talking to you?" And the eldest added: "No one's so daft as to talk to you." Their brother Gvendur had never understood the soul, whereas they in private endlessly argued about its hopes and its despair. This difference in outlook united both of them against the other, who thought only of keeping on doing something.

"Oh?" replied Gvendur. "You ask Father and he'll tell you that there's more of a man in me than there is in the pair of you put together."

"Who cares? It was us that Mother liked best."

"I like that, when there wasn't a sign of a tear in your eyes when she was buried; neither of you; and old Gunna of Myri said it was a disgrace to see you, your mother being buried and sitting there gaping at the minister like a couple of calves, she said."

"So you think we would do Father the favour of blubbering and crying? No. Not likely. We don't give in either; we are Jomsvikings too. It's you that blubbers. We curse."

Just when the quarrel was warming up nicely, Asta Sollilja

showed her head in the doorway and peered through the dusk towards the road, wiping her long-fingered, water-bled hands on her rag of a skirt. "Boys, don't you see anything of him yet?"

"Who do you mean?"

"Who do you think I mean? Show some sense for once in your lives."

"Do you think he's dead, or something?"

"For shame! I don't know what you're coming to the way you think and speak about your father."

Gvendur: "Yes, there's nothing they'd like better than seeing him dead so that they needn't keep on doing something and could lie like dogs out on the paving here chewing the rag all day."

Young Nonni: "Oh, we'll go away and travel the whole world over when we feel like it, and leave the lot of you behind."

Asta Sollilja: "Oh, for heaven's sake, get away off into your world, then, and the sooner the better. There's no one will envy you" — this she said because she knew the world from personal experience. She turned and went inside again.

So they were left sitting alone on the flags as before.

"She was blubbering too," said Helgi at last, when the silence had grown too long.

Nonni: "Yes, and she still blubbers. She was blubbering the night before last. And she was blubbering again last night. No one would think of blubbering half as much about it as our Asta Sollilja."

"Do you know what, Nonni? She has no right to be crying. She wasn't even a relation of Mother's. And therefore no relation of anybody else's here."

"Yes, no relation of anybody's."

"You can tell best from her eye, too. It's a cockeye."

"Yes, it's a cockeye."

"And though she thinks she's big and can boss everybody about because her chest is beginning to swell on both sides like a woman's, actually she isn't big at all and she can't boss anybody, as I saw again last night when she was getting into bed. But look out that she doesn't hear you; she has a nasty habit of listening and giving you a thump when you're least expecting it."

"I don't care. It was her fault that Mother died. It was her that got a coat when Mother couldn't have a coat, and she was allowed home twice a day while Mother had to keep on working out in the fields though she was ill."

"Nonni, do you remember when Mother fell into Grandma's

arms and couldn't stand up again? Do you remember how her whole body shook?"

Once more the little boy didn't dare to answer.

The elder: "It was the day our Bukolla was killed."

Silence.

"Nonni, have you ever noticed that some people are dead though they are alive? Haven't you ever seen it in some of the folk's eyes that come here? I see it right away; they only have to look at me and I see it; they don't even have to look at me. That day that Mother fell into Grandma's arms, that was the day she died; she was never alive after that. Don't you remember how she looked at us that night?"

"Oh, shut up, Helgi. Why must you always be on top of me?"

"Everything that old Fritha prophesied a couple of years ago has come true, mad as she was. 'The tyranny of man,' she said; 'in this way he'll kill you all.'"

It was the eldest brother who said this. Some people are gifted with a sense of the working of fate. Their perceptions incline all towards what is obscure, even what is most obscure: they sense even those terrifying dimensions that open behind life and behind the world, the sight of which God has otherwise spared mortal eyes. In the face of such powers, such vision, the younger brother stood ignorant and helpless, he who cherished a wish, wishes. "Helgi, I wish I was grown up," he would say, for with his wishes, and the wishes with which his mother had endowed him, he tried to evade the decisions of fate and of that which lies behind fate. Yes, it would be nice to have wings and fly over destiny, like the birds that flew over the big fence at Utirauthsmyri; yes, even over the telephone; but however hard he tried, he was always like a farm animal, four-footed and wingless, and his elder brother was around him like a many-stranded fence, an enormous entanglement of barbed wire; he could spin out the dusk over the paving into an eternal amen, and though one shifted one's seat on the paving and sat on the next flag, it availed nothing, for there came only an amen even more prolonged, an amen still more sepulchral.

"Listen, Helgi," he said at last, for he had just had a brainwave, "why can't we run away? You remember the foster-son at Gil who ran away. He ran away. He ran away all the way to Vik."

"His father and mother lived in Vik," Helgi informed him, "and they took him in when he came down from the hills. But us: who would take us in? And where? Nobody. Nowhere."

The paving in front of the croft again, and the dusk of evening growing heavier and heavier, especially over the younger brother, who was unfortunate enough to cherish rosy dreams; and when he could stand it no longer, he tried another suggestion:

"When Mother was a girl she used to be very friendly with some elf-people; it was when she lived at Urtharsel," he said. "Last year when we used to go out along the hillsides, Mother and I, watching over Bukolla, she told me all about them. And she recited poetry. And once upon a time, when I was little, the elf-people told Mother that when I grew up I should sing — songs" — he did not dare confide in his brother that he was to sing for the whole world, lest his brother pour scorn upon this shy ambition of his, for the soul's fairest wishes are as its deepest sorrow; he said only: "I'm to sing for the people in Rauthsmyri Church."

"Listen, Nonni lad, don't you know yet that they tell you all sorts of things when you're little? And why do they tell you these things? Just because you're little. She told me the same thing. There are fairy-people, she said, they live behind the good weather and behind the storms; behind the sunshine, in another sunshine. Behind the days. And then she had a baby and it died, and she lay ill for weeks and weeks, and every time she breathed I could hear how much it hurt her, and sometimes I lay awake at night and listened to it hurting her. At night I used to go out, sometimes it would be snowing, and though no one knew about it, I went to every rock along the whole mountainside and whispered into them all, and knocked the snow off some of them so that they could hear me better, and I asked every single rock to help her, the same as the rocks had helped the people in her stories. One night I asked ten rocks, I'm sure I must have asked thirty rocks, for I thought to myself that if there weren't any elves in this rock, perhaps there would be elves in the next rock. And I was sure that if they existed at all, they would help her. And maybe all of us. Until she died. Then she died. Tell me why they didn't help her — you who think you know everything! Yes, I know you can't tell me. I know I shall have to tell you myself why they didn't help her. It's because there aren't any. Not in this rock and not in that rock; not in any rock. Mother told us those stories just because we were so little, and because she wasn't bad enough."

"You're a liar," cried Nonni, hurt, almost with a sob in his voice.

"And when I had grown up," continued the other, "I often went up into the loft about dinner-time, and she was lying there ill, and I would think of asking her whether it was true. But I never did ask her. Because if it was true, the elf-people would help her. And all of us. And if it wasn't true, well, I didn't want her to think that I had grown up. Then Father would come along and chase me out."

"You're a liar, a liar, a liar," screamed little Nonni, laying into his brother with clenched fists as a tangible argument for the existence of another and better world.

"Nonni, do you remember the gale-hymn?" asked the big brother, logically unshaken, when the other had stopped thumping him. "Nonni, do you know what?"

"No," said the younger brother, "leave me alone; it's funny you can never leave a fellow in peace."

"Have you noticed that when anything happens Grandma always says yes I know, or she says there's worse to come, there was something unclean about here this morning? She's always the same, whatever happens. Never glad and never sorry. Do you remember what she did when Mother died and Sola had laid out the corpse? She kissed the corpse and said: 'And I don't wonder.' "

"That's because she'll soon be a hundred," said the younger brother tonelessly and as if at random.

But not even in this was he allowed to be right.

"No," said the elder brother, "it's because she understands everything. She knows everything between heaven and earth. Don't you remember the madman in the gale-hymn, and how he entered into the animals? Whoever understands Grandma understands everything."

"Mother never sang any hymns," said little Nonni. "And Father says there aren't any Jesuses."

"Maybe there aren't," said the other, "but the man in the gale-hymn exists all right, and it's Kolumkilli and no other, as I can tell you myself. How do I know? I know because I've seen him with my own eyes. When? Often. Do you remember that evening in March last year, for instance, when Father was bringing the sheep home? You remember he found one of them with its ears all cut to pieces? Well, I saw it done. I watched him with my own eyes as he came out of a squall of rain and went up to one of the sheep and did something to her. I didn't know at the time who or what it was, but it was that. It was him."

"Was it him?" asked the little boy stupidly.

"And the spring before last, when the sheep were dying off, it was because he did something to them first. And afterwards they died. It was Kolumkilli, Kolumkilli, who has been killed seven times, but who has always come to life again and laid waste to the croft. He has laid waste to the croft seven times, as anyone can tell you. I see him every day."

"You're a liar. You never see anyone," cried the younger boy, beginning again to thump his brother, this time half-wailing.

"And do you know why I see him?" continued the other. Gripping little Nonni's wrists, he held them fast as he whispered into his face: "It's because I'm dead too. Nonni, look at me, look at me closely, look into my eyes. You see a dead man."

Two complementary antitheses, the eternal antitheses in human form; in a new autumn, at the onset of winter; dusk; the boundaries of world and unworld obliterated; a new moon behind the clouds.

40.   RATS

ADVENT.

Bjartur had gone out to the ewe-house. The snow was frozen hard and there was no prospect of pasture. Numb-fingered, the grandmother was fighting her eternal fight with winter's stubborn fire, while huddled up in the smoke lay the children, sleeping or waking the same as last year and the year before, and either listening or not listening to the feeble crackle of the brushwood in the range; and before the grandmother had made her first fruitless attempt to rouse Asta Sollilja, little Nonni was making an attempt even more fruitless to apply his mind to something that might happen at least some time; somehow; somewhere; and, it was to be hoped, when someone or other was present. Last year they had all been living here in the shelter of one living agony, one painful breathing that was as silent now as the violin string of the poem; gone is the anguish that loves us all and gives life to the soul, gone the anguish that gives life even to the inanimate objects within the soul; the wooded cake-dish too has long been broken.

Then suddenly, long before the fire had begun to draw, longer still before the water was anywhere near bubbling, their father came raging up the stairs. He rushed across the room and, grabbing his slaughtering-knives, unwound them.

"Huh! It looks as if something else is to be butchered," said the grandmother.

"Out you get, you kids," he cried, hauling the children out of bed with the gleaming steel in his hand. "You had better come with me into the huts and see the signs of what has happened so that you can answer your grandmother."

"Oh, no one need wonder though things happen here," replied the old woman. "It's only what's to be expected."

Thin ranks in the stalls this winter. The fittest survive, the rubbish goes, as Olafur of Yztadale often said, hoping to comfort himself and others with a scientific doctrine that even foreigners have times without number reiterated in the newspapers. And they were fine sheep all right, lovely sheep, that stood at Bjartur of Summerhouses' mangers that winter, and the crofter was, if not fonder of them in their fewness, at least as fond of them as he had been of the entire flock. His was not the custom to lament what he had lost. Some people do so, but Bjartur of Summerhouses thought that a man should console himself with what he had; or rather with what he had left, when he had lost what he had. Worms are not the worst calamity that can befall a moorland crofter; rather the secret powers that cannot be kept in check even with a good crop of hay. The old woman had been right when she had said there was worse to come. These secret powers were now at work.

That morning he had been going down the ladder in the ewe-house for hay, and what should he find there rammed in between the rungs? In this incredible place he had found one of his ewes, dead, trodden into the steps, stuffed like an old rag between the rungs, the spine crumpled, one of the horns twisted round the edge of the ladder. He gave vent to all the profanity that he could lay his tongue to at such short notice, pulled the ewe out of the rungs, laid her outside on a snowdrift, called the children. And now he stood looking down at the dead sheep, and the children stood looking down at it too, all wondering, in the grey light of the morning. It was frosty but dull. Some days seem strangely idiotic when one looks about one; they appear to be incapable of answering anything, whereas other days are intelligent and can provide the answer to everything. Gvendur thought the sheep had been trying to sneak into the hay-barn and had got itself fast. "Fool," said Helgi.

Young Nonni took hold of his eldest brother's hand and released it again. Asta Sollilja's teeth were chattering. "You don't take after your mother," said Bjartur; "she didn't jump at trifles, like an old woman on a pot." But she said she wasn't afraid, for it was naughty to be afraid, she was only cold.

For two days the shadow of this atrocity brooded over the farm. There came visitors from the homesteads, harmless un-named people, but Bjartur was in anything but a pleasant mood and declared that it was with grudging hand that he offered such vermin coffee. Actually it was wrong to encourage such folk about the place with coffee, such folk should be given hogwash. They were almost certainly the descendants of criminals, especially sheep-stealers; never before had such misbegotten scum set foot on Summerhouses land. What had happened? "If you were sent here to ask that, my lads," he replied, "you can say that you didn't find out." So the visitors set off on their return home, as wise as when they had come.

It was on the third morning, when he was going into the lamb-house, that he bumped his head into something hanging from the roof. "Well, damn me," he thought, and had begun swearing immediately. It was one of his finest lambs, with a halter round its neck. He cut it down and examined the cord closely, but could not recognize it as any of his. "No, this can't be the work of man," he thought — he could not imagine any human being so vile as to think of hanging a sheep. On inspecting the snow around the hut, he found it hard, frozen and icy, no tracks — and this had to happen to him, to Bjartur of Summerhouses of all people, a man who didn't even believe in the soul, let alone devils and ghosts. But this time he made light of it in the croft, saying that he had had to kill a lamb that had eaten wool. No one, least of all his own children, should find any chink in the armour of scepticism that from the beginning had endowed him with greater moral fortitude than that possessed by the other men. Yet when he was alone, the events of the past few days continued to prey upon his mind. He would stand staring at the sheep, frowning and muttering to himself; damn and blast it, he thought for the hundredth time. He could not apply himself to anything, either inside or outside the croft. "Find me a pair of clean oversocks," he said at last to Asta Sollilja, "I think I'll just take a walk over to the homesteads." "The homesteads?" "Yes," he replied, "I think there may be rats in the sheep-cotes." This he added by way of explanation, apologetically, like someone with cancer who pleads that it is only a touch of the colic.

"Rats?" asked the parish in wonder. "Whence come these rats? Surely they're only mice?"

He found his neighbours Olafur of Yztadale and Einar of Undirhlith prophesying and taking snuff in the dusk, as is usual in Advent, so Bjartur also took snuff and prophesied. They said it couldn't be a rat. Bjartur replied that in his view there was very little difference between a rat and a mouse. Einar said that his opinion was, naturally enough, of little account, but he had always understood that a rat was considered to be a rat, and a mouse a mouse, "and as long as I remember I'd better hand you these few verses that I wrote in the autumn, when the thick of the hay-making was over. I wrote a memorial for your first wife," he added, "so I thought I might as well write one for the second one too. They were excellent women, inestimable women both; yes, in-scrutable are the ways of the Lord." Olafur, however, affirmed that if it was a mouse, and if it was attacking the sheep, it was an old man's remedy that practical experience had established beyond question, though maybe it hadn't got the length of the papers yet, that if it had eaten its way into the withers, for instance, and you could get your hand on it and rub it into the wound so that its in-sides were squeezed out and mixed with the wound, the wound was supposed to heal.

"You can keep your memorials," was Bjartur's reply to Einar. "I've no time for hymns, either for the living or the dead, and never have had, as I thought you knew years ago. No hymns were written for the Jomsvikings, and yet they fell with good fame; and if memory serves me right, Grettir was avenged all the way south in Miklagard, without any hymns, and yet he was considered the greatest man in Iceland. So I see no reason why, just because a couple of womenfolk have kicked the bucket, people should start writing religion about them. I've never been particularly fond of religion, or on the whole anything spiritual. But if either of you would like to sell me a tom-cat, I would consider it a good turn, and it can be as wild as it likes."

He came home in the evening with a tom-cat in a sack and emptied it out on the floor, and what is that, inquired the children, and it's a cat, said he, and there was joy in the evening, while the story swept the countryside like a change of weather and every-one said: the rat in Summerhouses. There by the hatchway stood the tom, grey-striped and suspicious and casting his eyes warily about, with huge dilated pupils and one paw lifted, mewing in perfect misery, yet showing no signs of losing his courage; cats may make the most mournful noise in all Iceland, but no one has ever heard of a cat giving in, cats don't give in. "Just see that the bitch and he don't get at each other," said Bjartur. Outside under the wall he began to wonder whether he must not have been mad to have brought a cat back with him.

Yes, there was a cat on the croft. Sometimes he sat on the edge
of the hatchway in the daytime, listening with taut attention to
the vehement barking of the bitch from below, for the bitch was
very angry that there should be a cat on the croft. The hair on her
back would stand on end if she knew that he was anywhere near,
and she would start barking immediately. If she came upstairs,
pussy would spring into the window recess above the end of the
grandmother's bed, where he just managed to squeeze on to the
sill; then he would watch the bitch attentively for a while, then
the pupils would contract and the eyes close in philosophy. When
the bitch had gone, the cat would spring down on the old woman's
bed and, after washing himself with meticulous care, would lie
down to sleep with his head across his hind legs. The old woman
never called him anything but that scum of a cat or that brute of
a tom, and yet he liked to be with her best, for he valued not vocabulary but disposition. She had never been known to hurt any
animal. It is strange what a great liking cats have for old people.
They appreciate that lack of inventiveness, rich in security,
which is the chief virtue of old age; or was it that they understood
the grey in each other, that which lies behind Christianity and
behind the soul?

41.   THE LEFT CHEEK

WELL, what luck had this scum of a cat in forestalling further misfortune on the lonely croft in the valley?

Just before bedtime Bjartur took him under his arm and set
off with him out to the ewe-house. His confidence in the cat, however, was not of the fullest, and instead of going straight to bed
he sat up longer than usual, pottering with some small job long
after the old woman and the boys were all asleep. Last to bed was
Asta Sollilja. She messed about, over beside the range, till a very
late hour, first rinsing out a few of her things and mending them,
then giving herself a wash and sprucing herself up a little; she had
reached the hair-combing age. Sometimes she would heat herself
water and wash her feet and her legs up to just above her knees,
and her neck, and a little way down her back; and her chest; and
he couldn't very well forbid it; this water-fury manifests itself in
the female sex at a certain age and lasts for a few years. It is youth,
it is the flower — does not the grass suck the dew to itself while
it is growing? Then after a few years they stop washing them-

selves; when the babies begin to come. He put out the light at his
end of the loft and lay down on the bed, yawning, with his head
pillowed in his hands, but without thought of sleep. She was still
washing and combing away in the glimmer of the candle, standing in her slip with an old piece of mirror propped up in front of
her. She pushed the straps over her shoulders and washed herself
there and in the armpits, poor kid, she's getting a big girl now,
she can't help it. Asta, however, was very much aware that he
was looking at her, and she would have washed herself much
better if he had not been looking at her — if she washed herself
better and he saw, it was naughty. It was strange how passionately
she longed to convince him that she never even thought of anything naughty, anything not right; and why? It was because she
had nestled up to him out in the world when she was little and because she could never forget it. Before her stepmother's death she
had often blushed red when she thought of it, but since then some
fear had struck through her almost every time that the memory
had recurred to her — strange how the bygone errors of childhood's
unwitting days continued to prey on the mind, though actually
nothing at all had happened; she had only been afraid out in the
world because she was so little — and he had pushed her aside and
gone away. And here the fear would flame up in her body, around
her heart, the fear of something she did not understand. This dread
of the incomprehensible lay ever smouldering in her body, and
when she began to think of this thing, it would flare up, though
never so much as when she had determined not to think about it
at all. Sometimes it followed her into her dreams, taking on the
form of monstrous beasts and ghosts or evil men; or a precipice
where she could no longer find any way either up or down; or,
worst of all, quite incomprehensible piles of filth which she had
to carry away, but which grew bigger and bigger the faster she
carried. Why had it been naughty, why had it not been right?
She had not meant anything wrong, it was simply that she hadn't
been able to help herself because she had felt so unhappy — thus
over and over again, and then: no, never would she take off this
slip when anyone was there, and least of all her father.

And he gazed at her cheek in the glimmer of the candle and
had certainly no inkling of the emotions that tormented her soul;
but he saw that it was her left cheek, her left soul, that old, unhappy, afflicted soul which was a thousand years older than the
girl herself, a soul from another century with oblique malicious
vision, fragile desires, and features that reminded one of sworn

oaths and deadly hatred. The full lower lip, whose curve was so
delightful when seen from the right, seemed from this side distorted in a grimace. It was impossible that she could be a fifteen-
year-old child; it was as if her profile, when viewed from this side,
gave evidence of some complete loss, blindness even, blindness
which lived nevertheless in some hateful harmony with its own
world, without demanding another and a better, and which was
endowed with that contempt for death which senses all misfortune and endures it.

"Listen, wench," he said, and thought: "surely I'm not going
wrong in the head or something?" The girl jumped with fright at
the sound of his voice and hastily pulled the straps on to her
shoulder again. She gazed at him terror-stricken, with palpitation
in her eyes, gulping for breath, what had she done? But it seemed
that he only wanted her to turn round on her chair, he preferred
the right side of people, he had said something the same to her
mother when he was running after her, the right side, girlie, you're
so like a changeling somehow on the left cheek and it's always
getting more and more pronounced, just like that, yes. And see
you don't catch cold with all that washing. It's unhealthy to dabble
much in water unless it's absolutely necessary, girlie; I've never
dabbled much in water. And heap up the fire for your grandmother
in the morning, she has such a devil of a job with it these days, she's
such a decrepit old woman grown.

A little later he rose and went out.

He inspected the stalls to see that everything was as it should
be. Everything as it should be. The green eyes of the cat gleamed
now at the far end of the manger, now up in the beams; on the
whole they despised each other, for Bjartur was a dog man. When
he came in again Asta had gone to bed; oh well, poor girl, as long
as she keeps herself warm. In spite of the cat he felt the sheep vul-
nerable enough to get up twice every night, sometimes thrice.
He would go out to the ewe-house and spit in all directions; the
sky bright with stars, the bitch barking up into the air. Otherwise
it seemed that people slept the same as usual and dreamed the
same as usual, sometimes of a silver dollar, sometimes only of a
dime; sometimes of the ocean itself, sometimes only of a distant
glimpse of the little lake.

42.   CONVERSATION WITH HIGHER POWERS

THE WEATHER changed after mid-Advent, thick snow falling quietly, gently, but persistently, day after day; otherwise nothing, not a footprint to be seen. Calm-weather snow is the most incommunicative of all things that fall from the skies; one looked blindly out at the drift of it, it was as if one was cut off from everything, as if one no longer existed. Good, as long as nothing happens, said Bjartur. Some people grumble about monotony, — such complaints are the marks of immaturity, sensible people don't like things happening. Of animals, of course, few have the same capacity for monotony as a tom has. While the snow accumulated in the window, veiling the pane like bluish wool-combings, the cat only closed his eyes in facetious dignity and suave malice. Finally it stopped snowing. The skies brightened, but the frost grew harder; and cold, gusty winds blew the snow into deep drifts. This winter, however, there was no lack of hay; one need fear no natural causes this winter. But what of the supernatural? Was that in evidence? Not at the moment. The sense of insecurity that had sent the farmer up-country in search of a cat seemed to be on the wane again. He stroked the beast from head to tip of tail, though once only and in great haste, and said: "See that the dog and the cat don't flare up at each other." Yet when he came to think the matter over in cold reason, he could not understand how it could ever have occurred to him that a cat should have any power over the supernatural. All the same, he was no longer rising in the night to keep watch on the ewe-house.

But the intangible forces of existence were not yet worsted, in spite of tom-cats. They had only been waiting for a frost, of course, because they dislike leaving their footprints in the snow. It was early one morning and Bjartur was making his usual trip out to the ewe-house. He opened the door, and after lighting the candle, looked about him, to be faced by one of the most horrible scenes that he had ever had the misfortune to set eyes on: ten of his ewes lay dead or in their death-struggles, some on the floor, some in the mangers. They had been butchered in the most monstrous fashion; some of them had had their throats cut half-way across, others had had rusty nails driven into their skulls, and others still

their heads battered in as if with a club. It was a scene of slaughter
that baffled description, which was possibly one of the reasons
why Gudbjartur Jonsson never had much to say about it whenever, in later days, the subject cropped up in discussion. He had
never had such a shock in his life. He tore his hat off and scratched
his head with both hands as hard as he could, then he laid hold of
carcass after carcass, examined their injuries, and made an end
of those that were still breathing. But he could contain himself no
longer. Turning on his heel, he struck his clenched fists together
and swore and spat in every direction. He challenged the devil
Kolumkilli and his trollop Guthvor to come forth and fight. In
language pagan and Christian alike he called upon them to take
the field against him, both together, and chose the slope in front
of the croft as his ground — what could the man do, what could he
say? He demanded that the secret powers of existence show some
sign of manhood and come out into the open. Surely they could no
longer hide behind the skirts of existence if they wished to pre-
serve a last shred of repute. "It's easy enough to murder and
destroy when everybody's asleep," he cried, shaking his fists into
the frozen face of nature and up at the sky. Finally he could find
no words strong enough and squealed; the bitch squealed too.
It was pure blasphemy; and availed nothing, the faint, blue gleam
in the east dull and sluggish. Then he began to wonder whether
by swearing at monsters he was not pursuing the wrong course of
action, for there had occurred to him an old story of goblins that
throve on the like — but what was the man to say? Hymns, thought
he. Ought he perhaps to ask old Hallbera to drag herself out here
and sing a hymn? Or fetch the minister and have him call upon
Jesus in Hebrew? Not, of course, that he, Bjartur of Summerhouses, had any faith in religion; independent people have no
need of religion, he was a match for any spectre. On the other
hand, he had heard old stories which said that ghosts believed in
theology and yielded to the power of Jesus' names pronounced in
famous old tongues, though of course there was little hope that
the Reverend Teodor, that baldheaded youngster, would be able
to do much in the way of disciplining fiends whom the stalwart
old priests of yore, with all their hard-mouthed exorcisms, had
repeatedly consigned to hell without result.

The children stood out on the pile of snow that had drifted
up against the ewe-house, gazing at him in silence as he laid the
heads of the butchered sheep on the wall. It was little Nonni who
at last found something to say.

"Father," he said, "our Helgi often sees something around the house."

Bjartur straightened his back and with the bloody knife in his hand asked: "What?"

"Nothing," replied Helgi. "He's telling lies."

"Oh, am I? Don't you remember what you told me one night awhile ago, when father was down-country and we were sitting on the flags there talking about the waterfall?"

Bjartur strode over to his eldest son with the knife in his hand and in no uncertain terms demanded more explicit details of what he had seen. But the boy maintained that he had never seen anything. Then Bjartur took him by the shoulder and shook him and said it would be the worse for him, whereupon the boy grew frightened and confessed that he had occasionally seen some lad or other, or an oldish sort of chap, though sometimes he had grey pigtails like an old woman.

"Where do you see him about?"

"I've seen him running from the ewe-house towards the croft sometimes. I've often tried to catch him."

"Why didn't you tell me about him before?"

"I knew that no one would believe me."

"Where did he go to?"

"He was running."

Bjartur grew more insistent and demanded a detailed description of this mysterious athlete, but the boy's answers grew wilder and wilder; sometimes the man had a beard, sometimes pigtails, finally he had got into a skirt —

"A skirt?" inquired Bjartur. "What sort of a skirt?"

"It was a red one. And he had something round his neck."

"Round his neck? What had he got round his neck?"

"I don't really know what it's like. I think it's like a clergyman's ruff."

"A clergyman's ruff, you bloody little fool!" cried Bjartur, losing his temper and giving his son a smack on the jaw that almost knocked him over. "There's the penny for your story."

Supernatural phenomena are most unpleasant for this reason: that having reduced to chaos all that ordered knowledge of the world about him which is the foundation a man stands on, they leave the soul floating in mid-air, where it does not rightly belong. One dare no longer draw any conclusion, even from the soundest of common sense, for all boundaries, even those between antitheses, are in a state of perpetual flux. Death is no longer death, nor life life, as Einar of Undirhlith maintains — he who sorts every-thing out into its appropriate group, as one does when one sorts out the cards in one's hand — for the hidden powers of existence have burst without warning upon this human sense-world and set everything afloat, as if it were September hay in the autumn rains. Some people are of the opinion that supernatural phenomena result from the Lord's desire to remind mere mortals that He is much wiser than they. What was Bjartur of Summerhouses' opinion? Was he to allow the uncanny to drive him into a corner? Or was he to go to others and ask advice? Or curse in private and wait till the misbegotten spawn of another world had butchered all his stock, and laid waste the croft as in 1750?

The evening was calm, so he was in no hurrry to bring the sheep in. Absent-mindedly he wandered away from the croft, talking to himself, bandying vituperation with higher powers, and perhaps not noticing where his feet were leading him. Then suddenly the going began to stiffen. He had come much farther than he realized and was now ascending the ridge; perhaps he had been going to see Einar and the others. A golden new moon mirrored itself ostentatiously in the hard-frozen snow, the dusk was taking on a deeper and a deeper shade of blue; many people say the nicest time of day is when dusk begins to fall. And there in the calm winter landscape, at the highest point of the ridge, near the brink of the ravine, stood the spectre's stony burial mound with one side in shadow and the other in the pale light of the moon between day and evening, in an innocence almost charming, a serenity almost dignified. But Bjartur was feeling far from charmed as, increasing his speed, he rushed up the slope like a mad bull charging some unfortunate whom it has decided to gore to death. Yet he did not attack the cairn immediately; rather loosened a stone from the gravel and stood for a while holding it behind his back. "So there you lie, the pair of you," he said, glar-ing with frozen hatred at the place of their burial. He stamped his foot in their faces. But they made no reply.

Nevertheless he addressed them for some considerable time. He said he was no longer under any delusion about their inten-tions. In unequivocal terms he accused them of having murdered wives and children for him, and now, apparently, it had come to the sheep. "Go on," he said, "just go on if you dare. But I allow no one to act the tyrant over me. Tumble the mountain over the croft, if you dare, but here I shall stand while I have breath to draw. No one, you least of all, will ever subdue me."

No answer, except that the small stars of heaven smiled with their strange golden eyes upon this mortal man and his enemies.

Then he said: "Here I have a stone," and under their noses he waved the little stone he had loosened from the gravel —"Here I have a stone. You think I'm going to give you this stone. You say, he must be afraid now that he's standing there with a stone. You say, he has brought us a stone at last because he's afraid of losing his Asta Sollilja the same as he lost both his wives. But I say, here stand I, Bjartur of Summerhouses, a free man in the land, an independent Icelander from the day of the colonization till this hour and moment. You may throw the mountain on top of me. But I shall never give you a stone."

As proof of this lack of respect he threw the stone into the ravine, and the stone could be heard raising the echoes as it fell on the pinnacles at the bottom, and from below there rose the sound of old apprehensive voices, as if the troll and his family had waked from the sleep of centuries in sudden and startled inquiry. Never had Bjartur been further from seeking anyone's assistance than at this moment when he had rendered his account. Never had he been more determined to stand alone and unsupported against the monsters of the country and, single-handed, continue the struggle to the bitter end.

Turning on his heel he strode off, homeward to his valley.

43. TO WALK

But country people on their way home from town had called at Summerhouses and learned the news from the children. They bore the tidings up-country to the homesteads, where the story of the ghost was not long in taking legs to itself. By young and old alike it was welcomed warmly in the lack of emotional titillation that is so far-famed a characteristic of mid-winter's short days; and everyone was the more willing to be convinced of the prowling of ghosts the more sceptically they had queried the scampering of rats, for the soul of man has a liking for the incredible, but doubts the credible.

Before long the number of visitors had begun to increase. Strange though it may seem, people rarely show such enthusiasm as when they are seeking the proof of a ghost story — the soul gathers all this sort of thing to its hungry bosom. Bjartur, of course, declared that it was just like the dalesmen to froth at the mouth with excitement, then rush scampering after a ghost, but that they had full leave to wear out their shoe leather in whatever way pleased them best. He personally hadn't the time to answer any of their rubbish about ghosts, but one thing he could tell them was that that blasted tom-cat of his had gone and frightened the sheep through the night so that they had gone mad with terror and, running into the walls and the mangers, had either broken their necks or impaled themselves on rusty nails.

The children, on the other hand, were eager to entertain the visitors and stood outside against the wall blethering incessantly about ghosts. For the first time in their lives they were persons of importance with a willing audience; Madam of Myri even sent Asta Sollilja some coffee and sugar behind Bjartur's back, likewise a book called *The Simple Life* by a famous foreigner of talent and literary genius. It transpired moreover that the boys had actually seen the ghost and talked to him. The eldest and the youngest, particularly, needed only to pop out into the ewe-house and shut the door behind them and the ghost would appear. They could see his eyes shining in the dark, but they could never rightly understand what he said, because he talked with an awful lisp and snuffled a good deal. This much he had nevertheless managed to convey: having long since grown tired of silence and neglect, he was determined to make his presence felt again and wouldn't behave unless he was treated with proper respect, preferably with songs and sermons, likewise prayers, preferably burial prayers. Several of the visitors went out to the ewe-house to hum a line or two of a hymn or mumble a bit of the Lord's Prayer. Asta Sollilja had her hands more than full pouring coffee. More visitors, said the ghost, send more visitors tomorrow. He was obviously no false god, but a real god who prayed to men and said: Give us this day our daily prayer. Then he felt much better for it.

The parish was seething with the most outrageous rumours of this fiend who rode the roofs in the moorland valley and could be seen scurrying up to the top of the thatch and down again in broad daylight, what time he uttered the direst threats of what would befall if he didn't get his prayer. The little croft that no one had taken any notice of until today had suddenly become the sole topic of conversation in a whole district, even other districts. Men and dogs that had never been heard of before drifted along to the paving and even invaded the living-room. The stories of this ghost, the heated discussions, the various points of view, the theological and the philosophical explanations — it would have been no joke for anyone to have had to write them all up; the result would have been almost as long as the Bible.

In this, as in other religions, there were various sects. Some folk were convinced that it was a manifestation; others asked: what is a manifestation? A third group maintained, in face of all the facts, that the sheep must have killed themselves. Some people said that the ghost was the size of a troll, some that he was only of average size, while others contended that he was little and thickset. There were various people who advanced historical evidence that he was masculine, others who had equally valid proof that she was feminine, and lastly there were those who had evolved an instructive and highly noteworthy theory that it was neuter.

Finally someone who was friendly towards the Summerhouses folk went to see the minister about it, for there was a rumour afoot that the ghost intended to destroy the croft at Christmas, someone had had it from the boys, who were in constant communication with the ghost — would the minister be so kind as to visit Summerhouses and hold some sort of small ceremony to see whether this fiend would not yield to the bidding of the Lord? It cheered the minister greatly that there should at last have arisen a situation that reminded his lukewarm flock of the existence of the Lord, for he himself had not dared mention His name out of the pulpit or of his own free will since he accepted the living, as anything spiritual either annoyed them or simply made them laugh.

Thus it was that one evening the croft was so crowded that anyone would have thought a feast was to be held in the home-field. The weather was peaceful and the stars bright, the moon near the full, frost. A great crowd of young people had arrived and were standing like dolts on the snowdrift, savouring the tense horror that the night brooded over with its stiff blue light. Entertainment was being provided by a jaunty young man from Fjord who worked as a winter help on one of the farms up-country. He knew all these new-fangled tunes that people dance to nowadays in Fjord, and the others tried to join in with him to drive away their apprehension. But there were others besides mere thrill-seekers in the company; there were men of maturity and experience, trusty old acquaintances, among whom was our Fell King, who had secured election to the local board two years ago and was therefore often heavy with the responsibility that burdens the parochial administration in these hard times. And the minister, that baldheaded young man with eczema on his hands, had been persuaded to turn up, and was now observing that the time had come to hold ram-shows in the district and to procure an expert from the south to supervise the arrangements. He quoted the latest words of wisdom on this subject from the *Agricultural Journal*. Several people drew the boys aside to ask them about the ghost, his appearance and speech, but Bjartur was in a surly mood and scarcely acknowledged his visitors' greetings. He asked no one up, but stood muttering snatches from the Rhymes into his beard.

For a while the visitors lounged about from one group to another in idleness, out on the drift or in the doorway, in company with the shadow of the night, many of them with the knowledge that they were only more or less welcome, till finally old Hrollaugur of Keldur, an open, industrious fellow who could never stand the sight of anyone dawdling, called out: "Well, lads, isn't it about time we were thinking of walking?"

So it was to be one of those so-called prayer walks round the farm buildings which had now with the passage of time evolved into a definite ritual and had given the language the term "to walk." Yes, the others agreed solemnly, it must be about time to walk. The boys were sent for and the young people called back, for some of them had begun to walk in their own way along by the mountain, as the night with its floating blue shadows was very alluring, not only for a ghost, but also for love. The boys arrived with eyes dilated, and the minister, who had been trying to forget occult powers in feverish discussion of the *Agricultural Journal's* theories, gasped for breath and answered Hrollaugur's summons with "Yes, in God's name." The Fell King, Einar of Undirhlith, and Olafur of Yztadale came in single file with their hands behind their backs, each with his own peculiar expression, each with hay in his beard, dogs before and behind, excitedly and importantly conscious of the solemnity of the occasion. Various people offered the girls their support, and the girls were red in the face with ghosts, though Bjartur considered that it was something else they were nosing after, see.

"Now, then, you kids, just pop into the huts and ask which way we have to walk," repeated Hrollaugur of Keldur — It was safer to make inquiries first, as sometimes the ghost made them go sunwise round the huts, sometimes contrariwise. Helgi took his brother's hand and they tiptoed up to the door; no one had permission to interview the ghost but them. After sliding the bar along, they peeped in cautiously. "Shh," whispered the elder boy, waving the more inquisitive visitors away, "not too near!" The sheep rushed to the far end of the half-empty stalls in unnatural fright. The boys disappeared inside and shut the door after them. A middle-aged woman from the homesteads began singing "Praise the Lord." Many of the others joined in. But Hrollaugur of Keldur said it would be time enough to sing when they had begun to walk — he managed this affair as he would have managed any other sensible job of work that demanded its own set routine. Suddenly all of them jumped, for the boys shot backward out of the hut and rolled head over heels on the ice as if they had been slung. "The hymn books, the hymn books," they yelled, still rolling. The ghost required that they should walk nine times round the hut and sing nine stanzas.

"I suppose he means verses," said Einar of Undirhlith stiffly. Whatever his meaning may have been, the procession now began. The older people hummed the hymn to the best of their ability, the dogs howled too, but the young people did not know the hymn and were thinking of other hymns, and there were small surreptitious squeezes while the moon's blue shadows floated one into another. Bjartur stood on one side, calling to his dog in case it landed in a fight.

After a while, however, it became evident that the younger people could not be bothered to do all those circles; a little group detached itself and wandered off along the foot of the mountain to hear once more from the mouth of the singer the newest dance tune from Fjord: "Supple in reels, supple in reels, supple in lancers and reels." Two brave men popped into the ewe-house without permission, to see the ghost. But they did not stay long there. Hardly had they crossed the threshold before they saw two evil flaming eyes glaring at them from the nook by the hay-barn door, at the far end of the manger. It was as horrible a sight as the dead thrall's eyes in Grettis Saga; when these men have grown old they will tell a new generation of that night long ago when as young men they looked into the eyes of Icelandic legend. Nor was it a silent regard, for a hellish noise accompanied it, more frightful than the voice of any Icelandic creature and reminiscent of nothing so much as the insane screech of a devilish old door. According to the minister, who himself took a lightning peep into the stalls, it was the voice of a being condemned to eternal despair outside the gates of Heaven, and the greeny-yellow glare was the glare of eyes that had never seen the light of heaven and never would; so he seized the opportunity to offer up a prayer that to us might be

opened heaven's gate, that we might see the light thereof. And at
that moment the moon floated angrily behind a bank of clouds,
and the pallid blue snow-world passed simultaneously into an
obscurity more ghostly even than before. The features of the
countryside dissolved; even the people themselves seemed unreal
one in the other's eyes as they stood in the shadows of this unusual night-watch that passed the bounds of all reason. They
groped involuntarily for one another's hand, fearful that they
might be alone; what more was it really possible to do? Thus they
stood, holding hands and shivering as the moon disappeared into
a deeper and deeper gloom; they were wanting coffee, they were
cold.

44.   OF THE SOUL

Yes, somebody had proposed coffee, and, everybody being in
agreement, the religious ceremony was now breaking up of its
own accord. More and more people drifted uninvited up the
stairs; the whole countryside seemed to be billeting itself on
Bjartur. Soon the floor started creaking dangerously, so someone
told the younger people to be off, what the devil were they doing
here anyway, this was neither the time nor the place for the
screeching of hoydens, or, for that matter, for any other form of
music; if they wanted coffee they could wait for it downstairs in
the stable. The trapdoor was closed after them. The men arranged
themselves in rows on the beds, squeezing in as best they could,
while the women helped to quicken the fire.

"That's that, then, I suppose," said one.

"Yes, that's that," agreed another.

"Um," said a third.

The visitors were still under the influence of occult phenomena and were therefore experiencing some difficulty in switching
their minds immediately to the consideration of material affairs.
Hrollaugur of Keldur, however, was an exception. This stalwart
did not classify phenomena according to their origin, but took
everything, natural or supernatural, just as it came, and then accorded it the attention he considered it deserved.

"Well, Mr. Minister," he began, "I have, as everybody knows,
a couple of fine young he-lambs that I couldn't bring myself to geld
in the autumn. Perhaps it's suicide to rear such expensive animals
just on spec, but what I was thinking was that maybe I could get

a decent price for them if somebody from the *Agricultural Journal*
could be persuaded to take a look at them and write an article
about them in higher places in the south."

"Quite so," agreed the minister, happy to have succeeded in
convincing at least one soul of his knowledge of sheep and his
desire to promote a good breed. He began at once to expound for
his audience the results, as reported in the *Agricultural Journal*,
of the ram-shows held in the west, especially with regard to
mutton-sheep.

And the Fell King, who, though he had managed to sneak
into the parish council, had not yet become a big farmer, but
only a middle-class farmer who for more than a year had lived in
great distress of mind because of the competition between dealer
and co-operative society, for when two powerful rivals are at
grips with each other it is essential to have the patience to wait
and see — he too considered that it was of paramount importance
in these hard times for the public to be made to realize the necessity of improving the stock. "But," he added, "I should like to
make it clear that I have never been a wholehearted believer in
fat stock in and for itself alone, as our good friend the minister
would appear to be. In my opinion, it has been shown repeatedly
that in a hard year, like last year, for instance, your fat sheep have
not that power of resistance in the hour of trial that various worthy
men would have us believe. Your tough, hardy, outdoor sheep, on
the other hand, the Rauthsmyri sheep for instance, and no one has
ever dared to maintain that they were lacking in flesh — such
sheep have always seemed in my eyes the acme of breeding, the
model of what good sheep should be. In my eyes they are a breed
that one can trust to the uttermost through good years and bad
alike, at least as long as there does not appear another and a
better breed."

Now, it was only a few days since the assessments had been
made, and since the Fell King had entered the conversation, it
occurred to Olafur of Yztadale that it might be a good idea to
inquire of him what luck the smaller fry would be having with
the taxes that winter; for Olafur had voted for the Fell King in
his time, trusting his rich sense of responsibility and believing that
he would fulfil promises half-made to the smallholders, just as
in his time he had nourished the hope of a little extra to eat as
assistant dog-officer, trusting the Fell King in that matter also.

"Yes, the taxes," replied the Fell King soberly. "I'm sorry to
say it, Olafur, my friend, but the parish council is no entertain-

ment committee these days. Bailiff Jon of Myri, the county council, and the government will all testify that it's no game assessing
parish taxes in times as grave as these, when traffic and competition rage in every sphere of life within the district and without
and no one really knows which side is going to gain the upper
hand. It is difficult to forecast whether it will be Bruni that takes
men bankrupt and worse than bankrupt under his wing, or
whether the co-operative society will take smallholders oppressed
by a terrific burden of debt into its arms. Or whether Jon of Myri,
that most public-spirited gentleman, that magnanimous pillar of
the State, will be the community's last resort and salvation. Or
thirdly, or even fourthly, whether the parish itself, though long
since bogged in bottomless insolvency, will be forced to come to
the relief of the public."

"Oh well, it's just the same as I've always said," replied Olafur,
without showing too much disappointment in the parish councillor
he himself had voted for, "the life of man is so short that ordinary
people simply can't afford to be born. But I still maintain that if
society was scientific from the beginning, and there was therefore
some sensible relation between the amount of a man's labour and
the amount of supplies the merchant will give him for its product
when he goes down to town, and if a fellow could put up a decent
roof over his head before his children were rotten with consumption, then — damn it, what was it I was going to try and say? I see
no possibility of ever paying my debts, though I keep on scratching and scraping along like this for another three thousand years."

But at this point Einar of Undirhlith intervened to say that
he hoped they would forgive him if he felt that talk of this kind
was rather unspiritual at such a solemn moment, when mysterious
powers had just trespassed upon their lives in unique fashion.
"Are we then completely incapable," he went on to ask, "however
much the Lord admonishes us, of forgetting our lives of hunger,
debt, and consumption even at such a serious moment?"

"I didn't begin it, so you needn't blame me," retorted Olafur.
"Anybody will tell you that I'm the sort of chap who is prepared
at any time to dismiss all frivolity and concentrate on serious
matters; but it isn't so very easy to talk with authority, or even
knowledge, when you're so poor that you're completely cut off
from all cultural communication with the outside world, and when
in addition you have to suffer the same home conditions as I have,
the children consumptive as everybody knows, and the wife prac-

tically on her last legs, not that she has anything to do with the
question. It's just ten years since I was forced to resign from the
Patriots' Association, the only society that I ever managed to be
connected with. And that so-called reading club that we used to
have here at one time has long since gone completely to rack and
ruin. Some folk say the rats have got into it. Whether that's true I
don't know, but it's an undisputed fact that no one has dared to
open the cupboards for the past five years, so personally I don't
see how anyone in this part of the country can possibly have anything to say with very much sense in it, the way things are now."

Einar of Undirhlith felt that we ought in that case to make
good use of the present moment, for we were now in the company
of educated men, the minister for instance, "and the minister, if I
know him at all well, is the sort of gentleman who I am sure will
readily excuse my lack of learning, despite the fact that the
Reverend Gudmundur of blessed memory went to his grave without ever forgiving me for my ignorance. But the question I was
wanting to ask was this: How does it come about that certain souls
can never find peace, either on the heights, on the surface of the
earth, or in the depths of the ocean?"

"Why, I expect it's because there's a devil in them," replied
Krusi of Gil briskly, long before the minister had managed to
decide on a suitable answer. Several of the others countered with
their opinions, though without shedding much light on the problem, and Olafur of Yztadale even referred to a book, several pages
of which a friend of his had once obtained as wrapping-paper
around some cups, in which it was flatly denied, according to evidence furnished by foreign scientists, that evil so much as existed.

"Now, really, Olafur, really," said the Fell King, "that's an
assertion I would never dream of making, at least in the present
circumstances. I for one have always believed that both good and
evil exist, and, as the Mistress of Myri, a highly educated woman
as everyone knows, has constantly emphasized in speeches both
private and public, a belief in the existence of good and evil is said
to be part of the Persian religion also. On the other hand, I consider that the world's invisible powers are not nearly so good in
their main points as they are usually reputed to be, and probably
not nearly so evil either. Don't you think they're more likely to be
somewhere more or less half-way between, Olafur?"

The minister, who had now had time to think things over, suggested that it was more in conformity with modern thought to

suppose, as he had already pointed out during the procession, that they were here dealing with unhappy souls that were driven from one world to another like outlaws.

But now it was Einar of Undirhlith who had had more than he could stand.

"No, your reverence," cried he, "this is where I am not afraid to tell you, on my own conscience and responsibility, that you have gone too far. It may be true that the late Reverend Gudmundur was never very friendly towards me and that he paid little or no attention to the poor religious verses that I wrote, not for praise or fame, but for my own spiritual solace; but though he was very severe on uneducated men, no one needed to be in any doubt as to his creed: he wasn't the man to lend an ear to any sort of balderdash simply because it was supposed to be modern, and he would certainly have been the last person on earth ever to soil his lips with the statement that Satan and his missionaries were nothing worse than unhappy souls. Though he had good rams and fat sheep, he never got muddled up between unrelated objects; he knew who it was he believed in, which is maybe more than can be said for some of you young clergymen who believe in anything as long as it's new-fangled."

The Reverend Teodor then had to try to convince Einar that the modern theologians also knew whom they believed in, though possibly they worded their ideas rather differently from the old theologians.

"May I ask the minister one question, then?" said Einar, gradually growing bolder. "Do you believe everything it says in the Bible, Old and New Testaments alike?"

The minister: "You may rest assured, Einar, that I believe everything in both Testaments. I believe in the New Testament. And I believe also in the Old Testament."

Einar of Undirhlith: "Might I then ask you another question? Do you believe for instance that Jesus, God's Son, raised Lazarus from the dead after he had begun to rot in the grave?"

The Reverend Teodor bethought himself for a moment, wiped the sweat from his brow, and finally said with great conviction:

"Yes, I believe that Jesus, God's Son, raised Lazarus from the dead after he had lain at least three days in the grave. But naturally I am of the opinion that in that time he hadn't really rotted very much."

"Oh, what's it matter whether the poor old devil had begun to rot or not," cried Olafur in his piping gabble. "I should have thought the main thing was that he came back to life again. Anyway, since the minister is one of the company and we're waiting for a drop of coffee and I don't suppose I'll get to bed much before daylight in any case, I'd like to profit from the opportunity the same as Einar and ask the minister a little question. What exactly are your views about the soul, Reverend Teodor?"

The minister shook his head with a tortured smile, then said that on the whole he had no special views about the soul, only the good old views, the soul yes the soul, the soul naturally was in a way immortal, and if it wasn't immortal, well, it wouldn't be a soul.

"Oh, I know that already," said Olafur, quite unimpressed by this answer. "That's exactly what they told Jon Arason just before they chopped his head off. But now I'm going to tell you something that I have on the authority of a reliable southern newspaper which a friend of mine lent me last year; and that is that they reckon it's nothing unusual nowadays for dead souls to enter into the furniture in the houses of highly placed men in Reykjavik."

Good old Olafur, always the same, no end to the claptrap he would believe as long as he saw it in print. Some of the crofters shook their heads and laughed.

"Yes, laugh," he cried, "laugh if you want to. But can you point to one single instance where I've made any assertion without having the best possible authority for it? Of course they enter into famous people's furniture in Reykjavik, and that's as true as I'm sitting here. The funny thing about you folk hereabouts is that you refuse to believe anything that happens more than a hundred yards from your own cow-shed door; you credit not a single solitary thing, physical or spiritual, except what you either see or don't see in your own wretched cow-barns."

The minister was inclined to back Olafur up. In apologetic tones he said that, much as it was to be regretted, eminent men in the south had undoubtedly noticed some rather strange things about their furniture lately, but whether it was correct to say that souls were the cause of it was another question altogether. Some authorities suggested that they might possibly be vagrant spirits who had not been allowed to see the light of heaven.

Olafur, passionately: "Now I'd like to ask the minister one thing. What is a soul? If you cut the head off an animal does its soul rush out of the top of its spine and wing its way up to heaven like a fly? Or is the soul like a pancake which you can roll up and swallow again like Bjarni the Liar is supposed to have done? How many souls has any one man? Did Lazarus die a second time?

And how does it come about that souls, or whatever they ought to be called, behave politely to important officials in Reykjavik while they do nothing but molest poor peasants in the valleys?"

But at this very moment, when the soul was beginning firmly to take root in the conversation, the master of the house stuck his head through the hatchway and looked around the crowded room. It was a scene from which he appeared to derive little pleasure. With one blow he cut the scientific knot that his old friend Olafur of Yztadale had just placed before the assembly:

"I am off to bed now," he said, "and so are my family. We haven't the patience to listen to any more of your rubbish about the soul this Christmas. And if in future you need to bawl any more hymns, then may I ask you to go and bawl them elsewhere. I have sent for the authorities. It is they who will find the guilty person and punish him. And when you have gone from here to-night, I hope you will look upon this visit as if it had never been made. Off with the kettle, Sola lass. I don't know these people, nor did they come to see me."

He did not acknowledge his best friends that night; he drove them to the door. And they did not recognize their old friend either, or rather the deadly, frozen hatred in the eyes of the man who had entered at the moment when they had lost sight of natural reasoning; and it was he, this man, who seemed suddenly to have understood everything and who now asked for nothing more except the authorities. Shamefaced and fumbling, like pantry-thieves caught red-handed, mumbling, forgetting even their farewells, old friends and new friends alike crept one after another down the stairs and, disbanding on the snowdrift outside, went their different ways. The moon had disappeared; there was no enchantment left, no coffee, no anything.

And, strange though it may seem, this night was rarely heard mentioned in the district afterwards. It fell straightway out of history in the same fashion as the bull reindeer that Gudbjartur Jonsson rode once upon a time over Glacier River on the moors. In the days that followed, when bearded, moss-covered men met by chance at home or out in the open, they cast one another a quick, embarrassed glance, like a boy and a girl who went too far last night but are resolved that it will never happen again. Even many years later this night still lay on the parish like an unhappy stain; it lived on at the bottom of their consciousness like a morbid fancy, heavy with shame and guilt — the livid, flickering shadows, the eyes of legend, the blasphemous singing of hymns, coffee that never came, the soul; and Bjartur of Summerhouses, who denied his friends when they had forgathered to attack his enemy, Kolumkilli.

45.   JUSTICE

WITH this victory of Gudbjartur Jonsson's there was an end, for the time being at least, of all spectral activity on the moors. As a man cuts down worm-diseased sheep in the spring, so did he cut down both religion and philosophy on the night when he drove the parish to the door and ordered his children to bed. Some folk say that he also hanged the cat. If the ghost thought that Bjartur would lose heart, sell out and seek a new home because of this second disaster to his sheep, then he was due for a disappointment. The devil had had all his trouble for nothing, Bjartur stood firm as a rock. And though he suffered a great loss in the engagement, the crofter learned never to yield an inch of ground. What followed now was merely the aftermath of events that had already taken place.

It was the shortest day. The sky grew overcast during the morning, with low clouds, snow-charged and threatening, hanging half-way up the mountain slopes. No wondrous gleam lit soul or landscape; there was only a little midday no sooner come than gone, yet how much darkness was needed to wrap it round! And the Sheriff was expected soon. The crofter gave no one his orders for today's work; it was as if he wished to await the decision of the authorities as to who was master here, he or Kolumkilli; but all the same little Gvendur followed him out with the bitch when he went to feed his few remaining sheep. The eldest boy sat by the window, knocking his knees together and staring in silence at an old drawing scratched on the table. He did not speak even when spoken to, let alone think of doing a hand's turn at the yarn on the spindle, and little Nonni, who sat knitting beside his grandmother, looked at him and, understanding him in the subtle, inexplicable way that reaches farther than words or images, went over to him consolingly.

"Helgi," he said, "don't fret about it. The Sheriff can't do anything with a ghost."

And when the eldest brother made no reply, little Nonni sat down again beside his grandmother. No story; no hymn; only a trivial mumble that no one understood.

Presently the Bailiff arrived from up-country to meet the

Sheriff from down-country, for a judicial inquiry was to be held.
But so far there was no Sheriff to be seen, rather had it begun to
snow, and the Bailiff was sullen and abusive and had no time for
this sort of nonsense, and it was very doubtful whether that blasted
old Sheriff would risk his precious carcass on the moors in this
weather, university men crawl back to bed as soon as they see a
sprinkling of snow. The Bailiff lay down on the parents' bed; he
was in long snow-stockings and called to Asta Sollilja to pull them
off for him. Neither was in a pleasant mood, visitor or crofter —
you're always in some damned mess, said the former to his host as
he fished about for his tobacco-box; if it isn't dying wives and
starving sheep, it's rampant fiends and raging devils; and the
crofter replied that as far as death and devils are concerned, mate,
I have never asked anyone to come along here and bawl their
guts out with prayers and spiritual balderdash in the middle of the
night, to the ridicule of God and men and the eternal disgrace of
the whole parish. All I ask for is the justice that every free man is
entitled to in a free country. Every year the authorities apply to
me for taxes, but this is the first time that I apply to the authorities
for anything, so I consider that I owe them nothing, and don't have
to put up with any of your lip.

"Look here," said the Bailiff, adjusting the quid in his mouth
with his tongue, "you ought to sell this lousy hole back to me and
swindle me a second time."

But after the emotional turbulence of the past few days Bjartur
was determined to meet everything with equanimity. The Bailiff
was not to be allowed to nettle him. "Yes, old boy," he replied
compassionately, "you always would have your little joke, wouldn't
you?"

The Bailiff: "I don't see why you should bother keeping such
a paltry venture going any longer now. Your two wives are dead,
your sheep dead, your youngsters dead and worse than dead.
What the hell's the sense of it all? And there stands poor Solbjort
or whatever you call her, almost a grown woman, heathen, illit-
erate, and no move made to have her confirmed yet."

"It's something fresh," commented Bjartur, "this desire of yours
to have people Christianized. Maybe you feel you've arrived at
an age when you'd better be prepared for anything."

"You needn't worry yourself about that," replied the Bailiff.
"I've always kept my Christianity before me, and I demand that
others also should have the Christianity necessary to bring them
within the rule of the law. I've always had a picture of Christ

hanging in my room, a picture that was left me by my mother"
("Yes, and one of the Russian Czar, too," interposed Bjartur) —
"yes, one of the Russian Czar, and I'll have you know that the
Russian Czar is a highly respected sovereign who has always ruled
his subjects well, and that they at least aren't a gang of stubborn
heathen who call ghosts and monsters down upon their heads in
the way you do."

"Huh," snorted Bjartur. "Grettir Asmundarson was never considered much of a religious hero in his day, and yet he was avenged
all the way south in Miklagard, and acclaimed as the greatest man
Iceland ever had for that very reason."

But far from deigning to answer such irrelevant nonsense, the
Bailiff took the quid out of his mouth and signified his intention
of lying down for a while, I'll have more to say to you when I
wake up, swung his legs on to the bed, turned his face to the wall.

"Mix up a few dung cakes for the authorities, Sola lass," said
Bjartur as he went out to see to his work; and the snow grew
gradually heavier, and day went on passing somehow, anyhow,
or nohow, with deepening snow and sleeping Bailiff and Sheriff
expected soon.

The most unpleasant feature of mid-winter is not its darkness.
More unpleasant still, perhaps, is that it should never grow dark
enough for one to forget the endlessness of which it is a symbol;
the endlessness that in reality is akin to nothing but justice itself;
which fills the world, like justice, and, like justice, is inexorable.
Mid-winter and justice are two sisters; one realizes best of all in
the spring, when the sun shines, that they were both evil. Today is
the shortest day. Perhaps those who manage to survive this day
will be safe, let us hope so. Today is also the day of justice, and the
little people in the little croft are awaiting the justice that fills the
world and is void of understanding. It is the father who has sent
for justice. He who makes hay for his sheep has justice on his
side, the sheep are the sheep of justice; and though a mother be
coffined and children be planted in the churchyard, yet justice is
in the sheep and in the sheep alone. Whether it be he who loves
dreams and the soul, or he whose hopes are centred on revolt,
justice is inimical to both of them, because they had not the wit to
conquer; and because justice is stupid in its nature; and evil; nothing so evil; one need only listen to the Bailiff sleeping to realize
that, one need only smell the cakes that are being baked for justice
and its officers. And the eldest son of Summerhouses closes the
door after him.

The Bailiff was still asleep, snoring loudly; one would think this elderly man with the strong, chiselled face had not had a decent sleep for a whole lifetime. Sola girl, haven't you a bit of brisket for the Bailiff's guts when he wakes up? — For there was no need to be sparing with the meat in Summerhouses this winter, every keg and every case was bursting with this delicacy, which no one would buy because it was dead meat. Dead meat be damned, of course it wasn't dead meat, there was nothing the matter with the meat, except for the mark that stupidity and superstition had stamped upon it. Anyway, we'll stuff the authorities and let them decide. Where's Helgi?

Yes, where was Helgi? Wasn't he here a few minutes ago? Oh, he won't be long, it's his turn to muck out the horse today. No sign of the Bailiff waking; oh well, it's none of our business, I suppose he can sleep as long as he likes, the old owl. This has finished it good and proper, the Sheriff won't have laid foot on the heath in this weather, the snow's coming down thick as soup now and you can't see your hand in front of your face. If you look out from the drift at the door, you would think the world had disappeared, no vestige of line or colour, no world left, one might be blind or falling into a deep sleep.

Where can the boy have got to? Gvendur, pop down and have a look, sonny. He can hardly have gone out to the stalls. Presently they had all had their fill and Bjartur himself went out to look for the boy. The Bailiff woke up and rose yawning and dishevelled.

"Eh?" said the Bailiff.

"Our Helgi," said Asta Sollilja. "We don't know what's become of him."

"Helgi?" asked the Bailiff, who knew no one of this name on the croft.

"Yes," she replied. "My brother Helgi."

"Oh," said the Bailiff, bemused with sleep and the search for his tobacco, "my brother Helgi. Listen, pet," he added, "you should tell Bjartur he ought to sell the croft. You can come along to us whenever you like, you needn't ask anyone's permission. You have my mother's mouth."

"What?" said the girl.

"You must be fifteen or so by now."

Yes, she was fifteen just over a month ago.

"Yes, it's a shame, but what can a fellow do? We ought to have taken you right away. But what was I going to say again, did I see you with a bite of fish there, girlie?"

"No, meat."

"Yes, of course, meat's the thing in Summerhouses this Christmas."

"I've made you some pancakes," she said.

"Oh, to blazes with pancakes. My stomach won't stand that sort of thing any longer now; I'll champ a bit of meat instead. It's just like the Sheriff to fool me into coming down here, and lie snoring in bed himself, damn him. I don't see how I'm going to get very far from here tonight."

But Asta Sollilja's ears were far away from the conversation, for she did not understand what could have happened to Helgi. Gripped suddenly by a misgiving that verged almost on terror, she neglected even the Bailiff's needs and fled down the stairs and outside on to the snowdrift. So the Bailiff was left sitting alone upstairs with the old woman and the youngest brother, to consider his tobacco and stroke himself and scratch himself and yawn. Time passed, and he felt no doubt that he ought to say something.

"Well, well, Bera," he began, "what have you to say to all this accursed nonsense?"

"What?" she asked.

"Don't you think that everything's gone completely crazy in heaven and earth, Bera old girl?"

Though he addressed the old woman in a voice that was very far from being unfriendly, he did not seem to be awaiting her answer with any great interest, for he followed up his question with a succession of tremendous yawns.

"Oh, I don't suppose I've much to think or say at all, except that I always knew this was bound to happen some time. Or worse still. It isn't by any means God's angels that swarm around this hut, let me tell you. Never has been. And never will be."

"No, never has been and won't ever be," endorsed the Bailiff, "and have you any objections to having a chimney corner found for you on a nice farm up-country if the Sheriff should ever bestir himself sufficiently to clear Bjartur out of here by order of the law?"

"Oh, I don't suppose I'll have much to say against the authorities, whatever they decide to do, and in any case it doesn't matter very much what happens to me. As the Bailiff knows, poor Ragnar and I lived for forty years in Urtharsel, and nothing happened in all that time. Our neighbours on the moors there were good neighbours. But here it seems as if something always has to be happening all the time. Not that I mean that anything has ever happened except what Providence has willed; for instance, that I should be allowed to live on, if you can call it life, while my poor daughter is called away from house and home in the first sunshine of the haymaking; not to mention the loss of sheep last spring, and now this latest outbreak of devilry."

"Devilry, yes," agreed the Bailiff, "a hell of a damned outbreak."

The old woman went on muttering to herself for a while.

"What?" asked the Bailiff.

"What?" asked the old woman.

"Yes, I mean what do you think about it," said the Bailiff " — this so-called devilry?"

"Well, since the Bailiff condescends to ask me," she replied, "may I tell you this, Jon my good man, that in my time it was the custom, and often stood people in good stead, to sprinkle these restless beings with stale urine, and many a fiend was glad to flee from a soaking when every other means had failed, but the master of the house here won't hear of anything that has to do with the Christian religion, he's a very queer person, this Bjartur, and anything sacred is spurned and flouted and trampled on the same as everything else nowadays."

"Quite," agreed the Bailiff. "He can neither be pulled nor pushed, the pigheaded lout. And never could be. The children ought to be taken away and settled on some nice farm, by order of the law if necessary. And as for us, grannie, I'm sure Markus Jonsson of Gil would take pity on us, the state we're in, he's looked after old folks for me for more than twenty years now. He's a harmless soul, I've never known him lift a hand to old folk yet."

"I would be the last to complain about anything," mumbled the old woman, "and anyway I know that my Maker will do with me as suits Him best. I'm more or less nothing at all, as anyone can see, and though I don't seem able to die, I can hardly say I'm alive. Sometimes it takes me all my time to know which I am. But I would like it much better if I knew that little Nonni here was somewhere near me, because he's a promising boy in word and deed and doesn't deserve to wander among strangers; he's slept in the corner here beside me ever since he was in diapers."

"Yes, I'll mention it to the Sheriff, should steps ever be taken to sell out the place."

"The Bailiff will naturally tell the Sheriff whatever he thinks fit, as he has doubtless always done. But if I might only choose, it would naturally be Urtharsel rather than anywhere else. But it's never been a habit of mine to expect anything special, not even when I was younger. Nor have I ever been afraid of anything, either man or fiend. And if it is the Maker's will to lay waste this farm for good and all, well, it's nothing but what everybody has been expecting; everybody knows what sort of place this is. And as for what becomes of me, Bailiff, I just don't bother about it at all, blind and deaf as I am; as I most certainly am; and I can't say I've any fingers left, they're all dead, look. And my chest gone. But they were very nice, the sunsets in Urtharsel."

The Bailiff stared at her for a while as if rather at a loss. What could be done with a being like this, who was actually a being no longer and, according to her own story, neither dead nor alive? How was he to keep this conversation going any longer? So he stroked his jaws, yawned, and bit off a nice quid. "Won't you have a chew, old lass?" he asked charitably.

For long enough she neither heard nor understood what he was referring to, but finally it dawned upon her that it must be tobacco. "To freshen you up," he added. But she declined the offer courteously. "No, dear dear no," she said, "I've never needed to-bacco. And the reason is that I know the Lord arranges everything as pleases Him best."

46.   THE RIGHT CHEEK

ONE boy's footprints are not long in being lost in the snow, in the steadily falling snow of the shortest day, the longest night; they are lost as soon as they are made. And once again the heath is clothed in drifting white. And there is no ghost, save the one ghost that lives in the heart of a motherless boy till his footprints disappear.

What news of the soul's welfare on the day after the longest night?

This was by no means the first time that there had closed down upon heart and heath that gnawing weight of fear which makes happiness a phenomenon so noteworthy in the eyes of the nation. But, on the other hand, there was plenty of meat, more meat than anyone could remember, meat both in round tubs and square cases, dead meat no doubt in the opinion of the parish, but, damn it, it wasn't dead meat at all, though no one could be found to buy it and the folk were forced to eat it themselves; it was just the same as any other Christmas meat from a nice fat sheep, and such a

thing was a novelty on this croft, where tough old ewes had been
eaten to mark a festival. Everyone was now red in the cheeks,
heavy in the head, and limp with stomach-ache; meat with breakfast, meat between meals, soup more often than porridge, gravy
more often than water; and when even the dog is helpless with
overeating, what more can the soul of man desire?

And now Christmas began with all its ritual.

That evening, when the old woman laid aside her needles
long before bedtime and said to Asta Sollilja: "Now then, girl,
you'll be able to give yourself a wash" — then, and then only, did
Christmas begin. She believed of course that Asta Sollilja never
washed except on that one particular evening, and that she would
not wash even then were she not ordered to do so. She herself had
given up washing long ago, and besides, people no longer believed
in stale urine, either for one purpose or for another.

But was this the whole of Christmas? No, the old grandmother
also took out her kerchief that night. She unfastened her ragged
old shawl and bound the kerchief about her head. It was a relic
of the Monopoly, the middle part still whole, a black silken cloth
handed down from grandmother to grandmother, smoothed
through the centuries by the caress of stringy old hands, like a
fragment of a fragment of the world's riches, or at least a proof
of their actual existence.

But that was not everything. When the old woman had donned
her kerchief, she proceeded to take out her ear-pick. The ear-
pick was the symbol of world civilization on the moors. Like the
kerchief it was an heirloom many centuries old, fashioned of expensive silver, turned, black with age in the grooves, polished
with wear on the curved ridges between. Presently she began to
pick her ears. And when she had begun to pick her ears, with all
the mumbles and grimaces that were reserved for that task,
Christmas might enter in all earnest, for then only was the con-
secration over.

On this occasion Bjartur had ordered a whole ewe's leg to be
boiled. Soon the ewe's leg was boiled. The crofter, surveying it as
it lay, fat and fragrant, in the trough before him, felt it impossible not to give some vent to his admiration in spite of everything that had happened of late. "God, this is a hell of a Christmas all right," he remarked enthusiastically.

Never before had the children heard him refer to Christmas
as anything special, yet now he was saying that it wasn't everybody's ewes that could show so fine a leg at Christmas-time. They

chewed away in silence, with sullen, listless faces; there were only three of them left now, and those that were left could not help thinking of their eldest brother's disappearance and of how the parish had searched for him in vain these last two days. But Bjartur of Summerhouses never thought of anything he had lost once he was certain he had lost it, and he wasn't very pleased with the children for not showing any signs of cheerfulness at Christmas of all times; and in such a fashion did bedtime draw nearer and Christmas Night take over with its stomach-ache and its restless sleep; or its silent tears.

Though it was after bedtime, Asta Sollilja went on combing her hair and heating water and messing about in the glimmer of the candle. From his bed he lay watching her long after the others had laid themselves to rest; her water heated little by little in the quiet of this Christmas Night. She was careful not to look in his direction. Was it because she was a bad girl — oh, why must she begin thinking of it again? And yet it had risen repeatedly to the surface of her mind this winter, and always she had associated it with the death of her mother, as if she felt that she had been an accomplice and that it was her blame that Father had not bought enough medicine, that he had not given Mother a coat — and yet, yet there had been no evil in her heart that night out in the world when she was little, it was just that she had not been able to help it. Even when, as on this Christmas Night, everything was quiet and blissful in the midst of the world's mid-winter, she would suddenly be gripped by the fear of it; the fear of the fear of that which had really been nothing; the fear that she had not been forgiven yet; the fear that something had not forgiven her for something; and that that something would remain always so horribly unspoken between her and him; between her and it. Possibly they were both fighting the same thing, without understanding it, each with his own soul, he strong, she weak. Yes, there was quite certainly an utterly impassable ocean between them. His life was poetry too complex to rhyme with her mute, unmetrical existence, his strength with her sensitiveness. Even when her brother had been lost, he who had lived here and breathed only a few nights ago, even then he had ordered them all to shut up; and she had wept all night long while he slept, perhaps not so much because she grieved for her brother as because the darkness was so big in which he had disappeared; and because she felt so profoundly stirred at the thought of having forgiven him his frequent ill-treatment of her when they had been brother and sister — but her father, how were they ever to understand each other, he and she; he who slept while she wept? And what was more important, how were they ever to be guiltless of each other if they did not understand each other? Though she were to take off every single single stitch and wash herself and wash herself and wash, time and time again without end, she would never manage to wash away the shadow of the vague, incomprehensible guilt that lay between them, the shadow that brooded over body and soul. And while she was thinking he was resting the back of his head against the bedpost, gazing in wonder at the steam and the shadows, how restlessly they played about this youthful figure.

She had the sort of right cheek that was never the same at any hour of the day. Its thoughts were determined between dread and anticipation, like the summer skies of the land with their living weathers, their fugitive patches of sunlight, and their shadows which pass away. Such a cheek is in reality like a living being, helpless in its over-susceptibility to what lies without and what lies within. It is almost as if its life-nerve were exposed, as if its body were all one continuous soul that cannot endure evil, and encounters perhaps nothing else; anticipation it is that saves such a soul, never happiness itself. Where would this girl be if she did not have her evil left cheek to help her?

He called to her and bade her listen. No, she had not misheard. She stood up and went across the room to him. He wanted her to sit down a moment. Yes, he was going to have a little talk with her, seeing that she had arrived at years of discretion. She said nothing. Then, without further warning:

"I am going away after Christmas and leaving you behind. I will not be back before about Easter-time."

She looked at him with great questioning eyes, and there was something that fell in her face.

"I have lost many sheep," he went on. "It is as Odin said: Sheep die."

"Yes," she said, and was thinking of saying a great deal more; that she hoped she and her brothers could help him to get more sheep; but he was going away, and she found she could say nothing.

"I'm not grumbling at all," he continued. "I'm not by any means the first to suffer loss in this country. I say as the proverb says: There's room in bed, the goodwife's dead. What matters, girlie, is that I'm not dead myself yet, not yet. Not that it isn't the same to me if I die myself. But I'll stand as long as there's anything to stand on."

She looked at him with palpitating heart and knew that he was talking of serious matters though she could not understand him; two human beings have such difficulty in understanding each other, there is nothing so tragical as two human beings.

"I told you last year, lassie, or was it the year before, that with time I would build a house. What I have said, I have said."

"A house?" she asked vacantly, for she had forgotten all about it.

"Yes," he said, "a house. I'll show them," and added in a milder voice as he touched her shoulder with his paw: "When a man has a flower in his life, he builds a house."

She had thick chestnut hair which fell naturally in waves, eyebrows curved in a questioning bow, and eyelashes that fostered great tears. He looked once more at her cheek and saw into the sensitive mobility of its life; then she breathed low into her bosom: "Are you going away?"

"I'm thinking of putting you in charge of everything, indoors and out," he replied, "and tomorrow I'll explain all about the sheep's feeding to you and little Gvendur."

Then she began to cry, for the dread in her heart was swelling to mountainous proportions. She was in utter despair and surrendered herself to the power of that strange voluptuousness which in perfect despair penetrates body and soul. She did not know what she was saying, for it was despair that was talking in her heart, despair that said it didn't matter if she fell ill and died like her mother in mid-winter and glaciers over the heath, and oh, I wish to God they had never revived me never to live a happy moment and it's my fault my foster-mother died, because I didn't love her enough, but my poor little brother Helgi, he was so fond of her that he thought of her night and day, and I heard him say on the paving that he was dead, and it should have been I that was lost in the dark and died in the snow on the heath, oh I am sure it must be so good to be dead, because if you leave me, Father, there will be no one to help me — and thus she continued for a while, nestling up to him as she wept, her head shaking on his chest in despair.

For once the crofter was rather at a loss for words, for to him nothing had ever been more completely unintelligible than the reasoning that is bred of tears. He disliked tears, had always disliked tears, had never understood them, and had sometimes lost his temper over them; but he felt that he could not now rebuke this flower of his life, this innocent form, water and youth are inseparable companions, and besides it was Christmas Night. So he merely hinted that she must have forgotten again that he had promised to build her a house; it was the autumn after old Fritha was here, damn her.

But it seemed that she didn't care at all for living in a house; yes, maybe once, years and years ago, but not now, this croft was quite good enough for her, if only you'll stay with your Sola, if only you won't leave your little Asta Sollilja. If I am to be alone, Father, everything that threatens here, everything that might happen —

But he assured her that nothing would happen and that there was nothing threatening; yes, he was quite sure of it. He knew what she meant, she meant a ghost, but it was as he had often told the dog: a man finds what he looks for, and he who believes in a ghost will surely find a ghost. He had decided to go away and work for money to buy more sheep in the autumn. This would be the first time in his life that he worked at all for money; he would get some sort of a job with Bruni provided Tulinius Jensen hadn't gone bankrupt. Now then; there was just a chance that the children needn't be left on their own, for there was a fellow down in Fjord he might think about — but here he stopped, in case he was tempted to promise too much, there there lass, cheer up a bit, your mother was a hundred times more alone when she died in the loft here in the old days, and I don't see why anyone should regret having run his nose up against life, lassie, for at least he's had a cheap opportunity of trying himself out, and there's plenty of time for grumbling in the grave, so dry your face now, chicken, and see about getting to bed.

Here the discussion ended. He was first in getting to bed. With drooping head she wandered back to the fire. Her throat was constricted with weeping, but it made no difference; though she had been a famous orator with a tongue of gold, all further prattle would have been in vain; he had lain down and pulled the clothes over him, the snow on the window blue. But there were no frost roses, it was warm in the room, the water boiling in the pan, steam, huge shadows, little light, Christmas. The power did not exist, either of strength or of endearment, that could shake his decisions. It was no child's-play having such a father, and yet she would never, never wish for any father other than him. She was in that limp, soulless condition which grips the body after heartfelt weeping, as when water evaporates after much boiling and remains in the air. She sniffed and sniffed; slowly the tears dried in her eyes. Even her agony of soul had evaporated. She took off her stockings, then her slip, laying garment after garment vacantly on the bench before her and looking neither to the right nor to the left; everything that she did henceforth was justified. She stood over the steaming water long and drooping like a plant, her high, cupped breasts in soft silhouette against the faint gleam of the candle on Christmas Night, against the steam's fluttering shadows; her lips swollen with weeping, her lashes heavy with salt.

47.   O PURE OPTIMI

IN its own way misery no less than revelry is varied in form and worthy of note wherever there lurks a spark of life in the world, and these children who for some mysterious reason were still alive on the moors had experienced many of its noteworthy phenomena, not only during festivals, but between festivals as well. It is always very instructive to lose one's mother in the first sunshine of the haymaking; and when one's father goes away after one's eldest brother's disappearance, then that too is a special kind of experience, a new type of misery, quite the same as in revelry, where people are said to draw an enormous distinction between song and dance. A little loss borrows its power from the greater loss, and so, after their father's departure, their motherlessness comes like a creditor clamouring its demand upon memory; few like father, none like mother; and in the depths of winter the children see once more in imagination that summer day when their mother was laid on a bier out in the lamb-house, among the toadstools at noon, and still the sun went on shining. Yes and the blowfly had gone on buzzing in its sunbeam, in the shelter of the window-frame, unmoved by the fact that the loving agony of life was no more on the croft and that it was the silence of death that reigned upstairs, unrelated to the silence of the heart — that song-loving insect which restricts itself to one single note. Today this song returns, this other world, which is one immutable note, loveless and remote — today it sings once more in their minds, when the window is deep in snow. They consider it separately, without looking at one another, sky and glacier-mountains in flames on the horizon at midday, the Bluefell peaks white-glowing in the burning frost. And their life, which was already without sheltering walls, is now all at once without a ridge-beam, like a roof that is broken down. The sheep standing in sanctity by the hole in the brook stares bleating over its frozen hills, unable to impart to the children of men the virtues of its mentality. So when they have given the stock their last feed of the day, the two boys sit down on the snowdrift, without understanding one another, and gaze with little energy over the same hills. It is hard never to be allowed a moment's rest, but harder still to be alive when there is no longer anybody to tell one what to do — for how in such a case is one to be able to keep on doing something? Then the younger brother suddenly remembers his grandmother, she who knows everything if one can only fathom what she says, and he tells his elder brother that whenever anything happens she knows it all beforehand and keeps on knitting.

"Yes," said Gvendur, "it's easy enough if you're nearly a hundred years old and needn't do anything but knit. But what about us? How are we going to manage things?"

Little Nonni thought and thought, and at last he replied:

"It's tobacco we want."

"Tobacco?" asked Gudmundur, far from following this line of reasoning.

"Yes, tobacco. He who knows not his Maker needs tobacco. I heard Grandmother say so when she was talking to the Bailiff."

"Maker?" asked Gvendur. "What maker? Are you sure you know what you're talking about?"

"What I mean," explained little Nonni, "is that if you chew tobacco you needn't worry if your Maker doesn't arrange everything as pleases Him best."

Gvendur: "You've started talking like our Helgi used to talk. You ought instead to be thinking of how we'll grow up some day, and how we'll help Father to treble the stock and start farming on a big scale like the Rauthsmyri people, and how we'll keep cows, and build houses. And lots of other things."

"Yes, I've often thought about all that," replied little Nonni, "but it's such a long time to wait. And sometimes I've thought of going away, for instance if nothing happens for a hundred years. Because it must be possible to get away, even though Helgi said it wasn't. But if nothing happens, and it isn't possible to get away for years and years and years, for surely something is possible some time or other, then it's possible not to let it worry you if you don't grow up immediately, or if the stock doesn't get any bigger at all, or if you don't start keeping cows. You just chew some tobacco."

Unwilling to listen any longer to such rubbish, Gudmundur Gudbjartsson walked away in silence, and another day dragged its length over the mighty snow and the small apprehensive hearts of the nation, till the boys stood once more on the same snowdrift the day after, viewing a landscape in which there was not a speck of bare ground to be seen. Then it was that Gudmundur Gudbjartsson said, without preamble:

"Listen, Nonni, have you stolen the lambs' tobacco that was left over from last year? It ought to be in the lumber-box in the entrance."

Nonni: "You said you didn't want tobacco yesterday. What makes you want it today?"

Gvendur: "Hand it over immediately or I'll give you a good hiding."

There followed some slight scuffling on the snowdrift, till the elder brother drew from the younger's trousers a twist of mouldy chewing-tobacco. "Do you think I'm going to let you eat all that yourself, you little glutton?"

Peace was finally restored, and after smelling at the tobacco, licking it, and tasting it on their tongues, they agreed to share it in brotherly fashion and eat not more than one plug per day as long as it lasted. But later in the day they began to feel terribly ill. They crawled upstairs with pains in the stomach, dizziness, and vomiting, and Asta Sollilja had to undress them and put them to bed; but however much she pestered them with questions, they could not be persuaded to reveal anything of the sedative that should be taken if one fears that the Lord is not arranging everything as pleases Him best.

And Asta Sollilja, who sat teasing her wool, how was she to forget all those tomorrow evenings which make tonight so long? She tried to think of how the stairs had creaked yesterday morning when Father went down for the last time, how the bits had jingled in old Blesi's mouth when he threw the reins over, put his foot in the stirrup, and sat down astride his luggage, how the frozen snow had squeaked beneath the horse's hoofs as they moved off. She forced her mind to dwell on this departure for as long as possible, as if on the first part of a story, so as to be able to cheer herself the more with the thought of his return at Easter; and possibly there would be a green Easter since there had been

a white Christmas; and then, after an incalculable number of evenings, she hears the jingle of harness outside, for now he is taking
the bridle off, and once more the stairs creak, and she sees his
face and his strong shoulders rising above the hatchway, and it is
he, he has come at last. She hopped towards this vision of the
future over innumerable endless evenings. But when it came to
the point, she found she couldn't do it; she couldn't lift herself
high enough into the air. She stood alone facing the many evenings that had yet to come like crowds of dead men trooping
through one living soul; the soul of man needs every day a little
consolation if it is to live, but there was nowhere any consolation
to be found.

"When this festival is over, Grandmother, what comes after
that?"

"Eh?" asked the grandmother. "What do you expect to come?
I shouldn't think there would be very much coming; nothing very
much, I should say indeed. And a good job, too."

"But surely something is bound to come next, Grandmother,
after the New Year is over, I mean some festival or other" — something nearing Easter, she added to herself, but did not dare say
aloud.

"Oh, I don't know that there's anything in the way of a big
festival, except that after the New Year you have Twelfth Night,
but that's no very great festival. No, I don't think there's anything much in the way of big festivals."

Yes, it was Twelfth Night and no other that Asta Sollilja had
been fishing after, for anticipation prefers to forget the interminable weekday evenings and to use festivals only as its step-
ping-stones into the future. "Yes, Twelfth Night, and what then?"

"Then it will be getting on towards Thorri."

Thorri, thought the girl drearily, for it reminded her only of
great snowstorms and sudden thaws, which came in turns and
were therefore without a purpose, a thaw that turned into a frost,
a frost that turned into a thaw, eternity after eternity. "No, Grandmother, not Thorri, not it; I meant festivals. Festivals —"

"In my time we took note of the weather both on St. Paul's Day
and at Candlemas, but in those days of course there were more
of the old customs left."

But Asta Sollilja had been hoping for Ash Wednesday, as she
seemed to remember that Ash Wednesday was a summit from
which Easter might be descried, but now it appeared that there
was all the month of Thorri and all the month of Goa to fill in

first, and then would come — the Fast of the Nine Weeks. Fast of the Nine Weeks? Nine weeks? Who would ever manage to survive that? Nevertheless she took fresh heart and expressed the hope that when the Fast of the Nine Weeks was at last ended, surely Ash Wednesday couldn't be so very far away.

"Oh, I always understood that Shrove Tuesday came first."

"But surely Ash Wednesday is bound to come some time, Grandmother, and then it can't be long till Easter."

"It will be something fresh, then," replied the old woman, leaning her head back and looking askant down at her needles. "In my time Ash Wednesday was always followed by the Fast."

"What fast?"

"Why, the Long Fast, woman — Lent. Did you ever hear of such ignorance! Nearly sixteen years old and thinks Easter comes straight after Ash Wednesday! In my time you would have been counted a simpleton indeed not to know Lent and all the most important festivals in it, the Ember Days, for instance, and Lady Day."

"I know Good Friday, though," said the girl with sudden inspiration. "That will be coming some time, won't it?"

"Oh, I should think St. Magnus will come first," replied the grandmother. "And Maundy Thursday."

This finished the young girl's attempt to bring Easter into focus; she gave up. She had gone completely astray in the deserts of the calendar, had lost all sense of direction, the wool suddenly clammy between her fingers, every tuft a tangled mass that she would never be able to comb. Why couldn't these young folk comfort themselves with the thought that everything passes somehow or other, just as pleases the Maker best?

"Oh, your fortune isn't made with big festivals only, my girl," said the grandmother in a sudden access of compassion. "I remember one Whit Sunday, for instance, years ago, when my poor father led the cow out so that she could take a bite at a few blades of withered grass that were sticking up through the ice. And it was by no means uncommon in my time for a blizzard to start on Midsummer Day itself."

48.   BETTER TIMES

HARNESS jingling? Hoofs clattering on the ice? Isn't that old Blesi snorting in the darkness out on the drift? Yes, of course it is. They were not long in streaming down the stairs, out through the snow corridor, up on to the surface — is there anyone there?

"God be praised!" was heard whispered in the darkness just beside them. "So the blessed creature has found its way home after all. I am here. Come nearer."

And when the children went nearer, they found a man standing on the snowdrift. They took his cold hand in greeting. Each party was equally delighted to know of the other's presence.

"Isn't there a door into the house?" inquired the visitor.

"No," they replied, "but there's a hole down through the drift."

"Will you kindly show me the way into the hole at once, then?" said the visitor. "I am afraid I am ill. I still don't understand how I wasn't frozen to death on the heath. This has been a terrible storm for me."

While Gvendur took old Blesi along to the stalls, the other children led the newcomer into the drift and showed him how to crawl over the doorstep. "Not too fast," he complained, "I have to use a stick to walk with, you see." Then he scrambled up the stairs, greeted the old woman, and stood shivering and far from erect on the floor near the hatchway. He was badly equipped for mountain travel, a townsman obviously. He said he thought he had frost-bite, with possibly a touch of pneumonia. Later the children often thought how funny it was that he should have seemed quite an old man the first time they saw him in the croft, he who afterwards grew so youthful in appearance. No movement of his, no button in all his clothes, escaped their greedy senses, which so passionately had hungered for some incident in this world of desolation where there was not a speck of bare ground to be seen — yes, he was even wearing patent-leather boots, a very fine gentleman indeed. The grandmother was the first to collect her wits sufficiently to inquire where the gentleman hailed from; and he hailed from the coast.

"Yes, I thought as much, poor man," was her reply. "Sola girl, see and give him a hand with his boots and stockings if he wants to take his outer things off, and hurry up and heat something warm for him. May we ask whether you would care to stay the night?"

Yes, he was going no farther, and a good job too, he whispered. Yes, he whispered, everything in confidence, one felt that it simply must not be allowed to go any farther. Asta Sollilja hoped and prayed that he would not get pneumonia, she was so afraid that she would not know how to look after him; she felt that hers was such a great responsibility, for she had been put in charge of everything inside the croft and out, and this was the first time she had had a visitor. Oh, if only she knew what to do for him, what to offer him, how to nurse him, what to say to him. But in the end it was he who broke the silence and whispered, no, thus far and no farther: "I was sent here by one Gudbjartur Jonsson, who, though he forgot to mention it explicitly, must certainly have sent his best wishes to all of you. I am the teacher who has to stay with you till spring. I don't believe it myself, but it's true nevertheless."

He took off his threadbare town overcoat and he took off one of his boots, but the other boot he did not take off; the other boot was inanimate, expressionless, and quite devoid of any living nature, for all the world as if it had been frozen through and through, and she was on the very point of asking him whether she ought not to pull this boot of his off for him and then examine his foot, when it occurred to her that perhaps it was not altogether proper for a young girl to concern herself with a man's foot, even though there seemed ample reason to suspect that it had been frozen. He then lay down on the parents' bed and bade Asta Sollilja cover him up, and she had never covered a man up before, and her heart began to pound, but she tucked the man in all the same, just as she had tucked the boys in when they were little, right up to the chin, but not over the boot on his right foot, which he did not even draw beneath the clothes. It stuck out from the bottom of the bed, motionless, and it grew gradually more and more difficult to know exactly what attitude one ought to adopt towards it. He had a high brow and thick hair which swept up from his brow perhaps rather in tangles than in curls; a regular face, deeply lined, which grew more and more pleasing as the skin recovered from its exposure to the cold. And when she was covering him up, she noticed that he was wearing a brown shirt, yes, once again a visitor had come to stay on their land, and he had come in confidence and was making the loft here his dwelling-place. No one would ever find out, she would invite no one in all winter through so that the news should not spread, so that there should be no danger of his being taken away from her like the other visitor long ago when she was little.

"And how is everything down-country?" asked the grandmother. But instead of retailing the news, he began to speak of

the incomprehensible labyrinth of fate that had sent a man of
his health on so hazardous an expedition in the depths of winter,
after he had dwelt for tens of years in the genial warmth of the
world's clamorous, stove-heated cities.

"Oh yes," said the old woman, "but I've heard that these so-
called stoves are by no means all that they're supposed to be. I
never saw a stove in my day, and yet I never ailed a thing, at
least as long as I could really be called alive, except for nettle
rash one night when I was in my fifteenth year, though it wasn't
so bad that I couldn't get up next morning and see to my work.
It was caused by some fresh fish that the boys used to catch in
the lakes thereabouts. This was in the south where I was brought
up."

The man did not answer for a while, but lay pondering in
silence the medical history of this incredible old creature who,
without ever having set eyes on a stove, had suffered no ailment
for the past sixty-five years. At length he replied that when all
was said and done, the stove flames of world civilization were
probably the very flames that fed the heart's inextinguishable
distress, and it is also an open question, old woman, whether
the body itself is not better off in an environment colder than that
engendered by the flickering flames of civilization's stoves. True,
the world has great superficial beauty when it is at its best, in the
murmuring groves of California, for instance, or in the sun-gilded
palm-avenues of the Mediterranean, but the heart's inner glow
grows so much the more ashen the more brilliantly the diamonds
of creation shine upon it. But for all that, old woman, I have
always loved creation, and always tried to squeeze out of it all
that I possibly could.

"Yes," replied the grandmother, who had misunderstood what
little she had heard of the teacher's words of wisdom, "and that's
why I simply can't see what Bjartur means by sending decent
folk here in this sort of weather, and making off himself."

"Have no fears for me, old woman; the time has come that
I must rest awhile from the Elmo's fire of civilized life," whispered
the visitor meekly. "I have dwelt out in the great world for many
years and have long gazed out over the ocean of human life.
When a man has suffered what I have suffered, he begins to yearn
for a tiny world behind the mountains, a simple and blissful life
such as may be found in this loft; but unfortunately it is not
everyone who can escape thither, for the world is unwilling to

release its prey. I thought I would perish out on the mountains, like those men, spoken of in books, who fled from their enemies into the hands of enemies worse still; that is to say, out of the frying-pan into the fire; and I felt that the least I could expect would be a fatal illness. But now that this slender maiden steps forth like a flowering plant of human life with coffee, I feel that I have yet a little longer to live. No, old woman, a man is never so wholly destitute but that good fortune will not favour him with one more smile before he dies."

He sat up gratefully to welcome the coffee and the slender flowering plant of human life, but the booted foot still protruded as stolidly as ever from the bottom of the bed. The boys went on staring spellbound at this distinguished extremity, which, together with the walking-stick, was to remain for them the surest token of the man's unquestioned nobility. Yes and she had sugared the dripping that she gave him on his rye bread, a thing that she never did for anyone, except for herself sometimes on the sly, which was the highest she ever attained in luxury, this marvel of beauty and talent. And he had never tasted anything half so delicious, and God be praised, he added, that there are still girls who blush, for she blushed every time that he thanked her. How could he really be thankful to a thin girl in a colourless frock, out at one elbow, he who had gazed far out over the ocean of human life? How humble great men always are! With every word of thanks she grew the more determined to do everything to please him, this man who had travelled over snow-clad mountains all the way from the murmuring groves of California and the sun-gilded palm-avenues of the Mediterranean in order to teach them many good things. She who for so long had dreaded the thought of waking was now of a sudden looking forward to rising first thing in the morning to make him pancakes for his breakfast. True, he had not the sort of face that smiles of itself without smiling, which was hardly to be expected, as he was a winter visitor rather than a summer visitor, but he had wise, serious eyes, full of good-natured fun, which gazed in blithe understanding deep into her body and her soul, eyes such as seem capable of solving all the body's problems and all the soul's problems, eyes that one thinks about perhaps when one is unhappy, knowing that they can help one; no, she wasn't really shy of him any longer even though she did blush a little; she even found the courage to ask about Father.

"Yes, my dear," said he, "he's a real viking, that man; but that he should prove to have such a pale little daughter with chestnut hair was more than I would ever have dreamed of."

"I hope Bruni has been able to give him something to do," said the old woman.

"No, far from it," was the visitor's answer; "those days are over. The days of autocracy and monopoly are no more in this district. At last we are mature enough to enjoy the blessings that democracy brings in its train."

"Fancy!" said the old woman.

"Now it is Ingolfur Arnarson Jonsson who counts, old woman," said the visitor. "Those who batten on widows and orphans have as last received their just deserts. For lo, a better age is here our woes to assuage and boldly challenges the ancient wrong; cries justice for the poor and those oppressed of yore, and feels itself unfettered, great and strong, as it says in our 'Ode to the New Century.' Power has passed into the hands of those who carry on trade on a healthy foundation. Tulinius Jensen departed with the last ship before Christmas. We have fought for the commercial ideals of Ingolfur Arnarson and we have won. This young aristocrat who returned to Iceland inspired by the commercial ideals of the world's humanitarian economists, and who proceeded to break the shackles of debt forged by merchant power, offering credit even to those who for years on end had been denied an ounce of rye meal on their own account — we have placed him in an unassailable position. I know a poverty-stricken father, with a large family, who couldn't afford a thing because all his inclinations lay towards literature and foreign learning; Ingolfur Arnarson sent him half a firkin of salt mutton in the fall of the year, as well as a large box of colonial goods. What do you think of that? Furthermore, he gave him a fortnight's employment in the slaughter-house, while many local heroes were out of work and had nothing else to do but hang about on the street corners playing mouth-organs, all because they believed in autocracy and oppression, and thought their salvation lay in the leech that had sucked their own blood. Yes, old woman, Ingolfur Arnarson is a great man, a genius who could twist the whole world round his finger, a philanthropist who gave up his position, which was in close contact with the government, that he might risk his life and his reputation for the sake of the scorned and the neglected. Because they aren't very particular what they write in the newspapers about anyone who enlists himself on the side of the down-

trodden. But in spite of that we have now managed to instal him
in Bruni's abode. And when I last saw him, Gudbjartur Jonsson
of Summerhouses was moving Ingolfur Arnarson's furniture into
the Tower House. I understand that when that was over he was
to be given some sort of a warehouseman's job with the co-
operative society."

"Yes, I know," said the old woman. "One comes when another
goes, as has long been the case. Many people speak ill of the
merchants, and it is true that coveted wealth is hard to keep
safe. The new one is always thought to be the best, and the last
one is always the worst, I have outlived many merchants, bless
you."

The teacher, realizing that there would be little point in going
into greater detail with a woman so ancient, closed this part of
the conversation with the remark that tardy though it be, the
sun of justice would rise in the end. There's a better time coming
for all of us now.

Yes, there's a better time coming for all of us. This refrain of
his, this new motive, rose singing with sudden joy through winter's
sombre music, to warm winter's chilly hearts, crushed beneath
the laws of an inflexible calendar, and lo, festivals were no longer
in great demand, and tobacco ceased to be the only conceivable
remedy for a Maker whom no one understood. Presently he began to unpack his traps. He allowed the children to stand some
distance away in a semicircle.

Up from the mouth of the sack he drew first of all his own
belongings, his own luggage, those possessions which bind a man
to life with the strongest ties, or at least make life tolerable for
him. And what were those possessions? They were a patched
shirt and one solitary sock, heavily darned. He fondled these
treasures with mysterious gravity as if they possessed some
cabbalistic virtue, then stuck them both under his future pillow
without saying a word. The children watched these two articles
disappear under the pillow as a proof of how great men reveal
themselves in small things. Next he produced those articles which
were directly concerned with the children themselves — the educational apparatus that he brought them in the power of his
office. And he stroked these rectangular parcels affectionately and
said: "Now then, children, here we are: in these parcels lies the
wisdom of the world." And such, indeed, appeared to be the case.
From the packages there emerged new, fragrant books, each
wrapped in glossy, colourful paper and tied round with white

twine; books in all the colours of the rainbow with pictures inside
and outside, full of the most incredible reading, one about unknown animal species, another about dead kings and irrelevant
peoples, a third about foreign countries, a fourth about the
peculiar magic of number, a fifth about Iceland's long-desired
Christianity — everything, everything that the soul thirsts for,
regiment after regiment of marvelous tidings to lift the soul to
higher planes and banish desolation's manifold gloom from the
lives of men. Yes, there's a better time coming for all of us.

They were allowed a little touch at each of the books, but only
with their fingertips tonight, literature cannot bear dirty hands;
first we'll have to back each volume with paper, the covers must
not get dirty, nor the spines slit, books are the nation's most
precious possession, books have preserved the nation's life through
monopoly, pestilence, and volcanic eruption, not to mention the
tons of snow that have lain over the country's widely scattered
homesteads for the major part of every one of its thousand years.
And that's what your father knows full well, hard as his shell
may be. And that's why he's sent you a special man with these
books, and now we'll have to learn to handle them nicely; and
the children thought of their father with a gratitude which almost
made them swallow, he who had left them but had not forgotten.
So theirs was such a father after all, and Asta Sollilja could not
suppress herself and said to the boys there you are, now you see
that nobody else has a father like ours, who sends us a special
man to teach us about everything.

"Do the books tell you about the countries, then?" inquired
little Nonni.

"Yes, my boy, of new countries and old; of new lands that
rise from the ocean like young maidens and bathe their precious
shells and thousand-coloured corals in the summer's first light,
and of old lands with fragrant forests and peacefully rustling
leaves; of castles a thousand years old that tower up from the
blue mountains in the Roman moonlight, and of sun-white cities
that open their arms on green waveless oceans lapping in one
perpetual dancing sunlight. Yes, as your sister says, it isn't everyone who has the good fortune to learn of the great countries of
the world from one who has actually been on the spot."

For a while longer they continued to play with the books,
but they mustn't look at all the pictures at one go, only one from
each book tonight — the picture of Rome for instance, which is
nearly as big as the mountain above the croft here, and the giraffe,

which is so long in the neck that if it was standing down in the
doorway there, its head would stick up through the chimney, for
it's to be hoped there's at least a chimney on the place. And what
do you think, the evening was over already; never in the mind of
man had an evening passed with such speed. The books were
carefully wrapped up in their papers again; no, no more tonight,
when they had been thinking of asking him a hundred questions.
He was tired and wanted to go to sleep, and they did not dare to
be prodigal in the expenditure of his wisdom.

The boys stood reverently over him while he undressed,
watching his manner of undressing, but Asta Sollilja turned her
back and went along the loft to her grandmother. He laid his
stick beside him in bed and covered it up with the clothes, maybe
the stick had a soul. Finally he began to unlace the boot on his
right foot. Every movement seemed to cost him considerable
exertion. Sometimes he reminded one of the Bailiff; sometimes,
much more rarely, of the bookseller; oh, what nonsense, he often
coughed very loudly into his handkerchief, everything bore witness to the fact that he was a very special kind of person. And
what ultimately emerged from this inanimate right boot? A foot.
But it was no ordinary foot, no work of creation, like ours, with
a white or at least a light-coloured skin and little hairs on it;
rather was it a special foot, a dark-brown, highly polished product
of the workshop, without flesh or blood, carpentry. And now it
was little Nonni who could no longer suppress his feelings and
cried: "Ooh, come and look at the man's foot, Sola!" But Asta
Sollilja, of course, did not wish to look at a man's foot, such an
idea offended her sense of modesty, as was only natural. "You
ought to think shame of yourself, the way you behave," she replied
without turning round. But out in the huts next morning she
could not help asking the brothers what sort of foot it had been,
and whether there had been anything queer about the foot. They
discussed this foot from every possible angle, over and over
again, after they had finished feeding the sheep, and then they
discussed the whole man: what a marvellous person he was, and
what rapture it would be to have him teaching them, and what
a lot they would know in the spring, when he had finished teaching them. He was an inexhaustible theme of debate for them
when they were alone; everything about him was individual and
veiled in mystery, everything from his whispering voice down
to his carpentered foot, not excepting the stick which was allowed
to sleep with him, as if it had a soul. The Summerhouses children

were lucky indeed to get such a man. And then they somehow had the idea that it was he who had taken the Tower House away from Bruni and handed it over to Ingolfur Arnarson Jonsson so that poor people might be allowed an ounce of rye meal on their own account. And isn't it strange that men of handsome, dignified appearance who come from large indeterminate places should all be wearing light-brown shirts?

Now he was lying here in their little room, he who had seen new countries and old bathing themselves in the morning's first sunshine and in the moonlight of abroad; yes, and such a lot and such a lot. If only one could remember what he said and could repeat it afterwards; no one had such a golden tongue. Yes, and he was lying there with that look of wise seriousness in his eyes, and he had pulled the coverlet up to his neck and was resting beside them, under their roof, after a hazardous journey over the heath, all for their sake, he who had been reared in rustling groves; oh, if only we could repay him and could show how much we appreciate him! When the children went to bed that night, they · felt they could easily live to be a hundred, without tobacco, like Grandmother, and without ever growing tired of undressing the same body night after night and dressing it again next morning. And to be able to look forward to the morrow in joyful expectation is good fortune indeed.

"Yes," he whispered, "this is the kingdom of innocent hearts. Strange that I should still have had this in store for me, especially when one had seen the world's gaudy show in great places, as I have." Then he sighed and added: "Yes, yes, yes, my foot has travelled distant lands and clambered up steep slopes of dissension in a densely populated world of self-love where the fluttering wings of the human spirit find little rest; where the glacier cold of solitude hovers over the moss-grown tracts of the everyday life, without innocence or rest; without love. Asta Sollilja, darling, I wonder if you would be so sweet as to leave a drop of coffee standing beside me here, in case my heart should affect me tonight. But I feel that tonight my heart will not affect me."

And now the boys had gone to bed and the wall-lamp had been extinguished. The only light was the glimmer from the little candle burning on the grandmother's shelf. Yes, and then the girl remembered that she had not washed herself since her father went away, so she gave herself a little wash and combed her hair a little, on the sly, before taking her clothes off. Then she came down the room again to her bed, she was little Gvendur's only bed-mate now, and her frock squeaked complainingly as she persuaded it over her head. It was really nothing but a rag now and far too tight for her. She did not dare take off her slip for fear the teacher saw; rather slipped stealthily in beside her brother in the bed opposite. At the same moment the grandmother put out the candle.

"Good night," whispered the teacher in the dark, but Asta Sollilja did not know how to answer such courtesy, and her heart began to hammer, but after a little cogitation she whispered in reply: "Yes."

Long after the guest had started snoring, the children lay awake, the fragrance of the books still in their nostrils, savouring the glory of this new era which they knew had dawned upon their lives. But gradually their perceptions dissolved into a blissful confusion and glided imperceptibly into an elastic world, which may well be the most authentic of all worlds, though nothing seems half so irrational; especially when the animals' necks stick out of the chimney-top and the mountain has become a beautiful Christian church with dark, creaking stairs leading all the way up to the tower. Her name was Asta Sollilja and now she proposed to go all the way up to the tower. At first she was terribly cautious and very much afraid, but since she had started climbing she would have to go on and on, higher and higher. The stairs kept on creaking and creaking. It was because she knew that her father was somewhere behind her that she was so very much afraid. Faster and faster she hurried; she must get to the top first. Finally she was terribly out of breath and terribly frightened, but it was so nice running up dark stairs all alone and climbing all the way up to the tower, all, all, all the way, no, no one would ever get to know. Then the stairway began to narrow and she bumped into the walls and they creaked louder and louder still, and then her fear grew stronger than her joy; oh, why had she had to come into this Christian church in the first place, instead of staying quietly outside where no one need fear anything, and now Father would soon catch her and would slap her face if he caught her. At last she glimpsed a chink of light above her, a door left ajar, the clock-tower, and a face was standing there, watching her approach. What face? The face of joy? No, no, no, it was another face altogether, it was the ugly old evil bookseller who had all the ugly old evil bastards; and it was

he who was coming hobbling towards her on his stick in a brown
shirt; where had this ugly old man got his brown shirt? So it was
he who had been waiting for her with his book in his hand:

"Here I can show you a book that is practically new and quite
the latest fashion nowadays. Just take a look, little miss, don't you
think we'd like to read it?"

She started up, bathed in sweat, her hands dripping, shaking
in the grip of that uncontrollable shudder which is a characteristic feature of bad dreams and which, after spoiling a whole
night's sleep, can saturate every moment of the coming day with
an apprehensive weariness of life. She heard the tail-end of her
own terrified scream as she opened her eyes, jumped up in bed,
gasped for breath. She heard her heart pounding like a sledge-
hammer falling on glowing iron. She passed a wet hand over her
brow. No, no, no. There was no danger, only a bad dream. Not
more than two yards away lay the guest who had come to bear
them better times and to raise their lives to a higher plane; and
she was going to make him pancakes in the morning so that he
would feel better. Gradually her terror evaporated as she listened
to him sleeping and wished him well. Yes, there's a better time
coming for all of us. And she lay down again.

49.   POETRY

AND the light of learning began to shine.

The distinctive features of the world's civilization are not
simply and solely the giraffe and the city of Rome, as the children
may perhaps have been led to imagine on the first evening, but
also the elephant and the country of Denmark, besides many
other things. Yes, every day brought its new animal and its new
country, its new kings and its new gods, its quota of those tough
little figures which seem to have no significance, but are nevertheless endowed with a life and a value of their own and may be
added together or subtracted one from another at will. And
finally poetry, which is greater than any country; poetry with
its bright palaces. Over all flies the soul, viewing the heavenly
light, like an eagle in the vestibule of the winds.

Out in the ewe-house in the mornings they often tried to find
some answer to the riddle of why, after all the thoughtlessness that
seemed to rule the world, there should come men who not only
were acquainted with the contents of books, but had actually

een with their own eyes the world that is described in print, and
ıad, moreover, travelled it with their own foot. Not only had he
een cities and zoological gardens, he had also wandered in the
voods where one finds happiness, or at least peace, and he knew
he words that fit the locked compartments of the soul, like keys,
ınd open them.

While little Gvendur was content to meditate upon those
ınimals which stand higher in the scale of honour than sheep,
ır to make an attempt to multiply the lambs by the ewes and
ıubtract the boards in the roof from the planks in the floor, little
Nonni thought endlessly of his countries, feeling that at last he
ıad obtained valid proof of their actual existence and that he
ould therefore dismiss the theory that they were nothing but the
dle chatter of kind-hearted people who wanted to comfort little
hildren. And Asta Sollilja, it was she who swept on wings of
ıoetry into those spheres which she had sensed as if in distant
ıurmur one spring night last year when she was reading about
he little girl who journeyed over the seven mountains; and the
listant murmur had suddenly swelled to a song in her ears, and
ıer soul found here for the first time its origin and its descent;
appiness, fate, sorrow, she understood them all; and many other
hings. When a man looks at a flowering plant growing slender
ınd helpless up in the wilderness among a hundred thousand
tones, and he has found this plant only by chance, then he asks:
Vhy is it that life is always trying to burst forth? Should one pull up
his plant and use it to clean one's pipe? No, for this plant also
roods over the limitation and the unlimitation of all life, and lives
ı love of the good beyond these hundred thousand stones, like
ou and me; water it with care, but do not uproot it, maybe it is
ttle Asta Sollilja.

She had early had some instruction in the understanding of
he complex language of the ballad poets, and this preliminary
raining stood her now in good stead. But there was this differ-
nce: the ballads were suggestive of barren lands, poor in vegeta-
on, but rich in stones, whereas the new poetry was full of the
lissful flowers of the spirit and a melancholy fragrance. The
eacher read poetry in a manner altogether different from her
ather's; instead of laying the main stress on the rhyme, and
specially the internal rhyme, this man whispered his poems with
honeyed, fascinating eloquence, for he understood the secrets
f the poets themselves, so that every inanimate object in the
oom acquired a secret, and if you passed your hand along the

cold bed-boards, the wood would feel soft and warm, as if a living heart were beating within. He knew the words that she had tried to read in the clouds when she fell in love for the first time, but she had only been a little girl then, as she realized now, and it was only natural that she should not have understood the clouds, she who had looked there for something that did not even exist. — He who had come to shoot on their land in those days, he knew no poems, he wouldn't have understood poetry, the most precious thing in the life of man. The thought that even though Audur Jonsdottir had married him she would never hear a poem from his lips filled her with proud exultation. True, he had smiled, and smiled without smiling, but his eyes had lacked the twinkling brilliance of colour, his voice the confidential wiles of the man who knew poems and could whisper them in such a fashion that a tearful shiver would pass through her listening body; and dead objects would acquire souls.

One would have thought that a young girl on a lonely croft would have been stirred most at hearing a poem that tells of virtue, or at least of sacrifice — of great souls who lived in self-denial or undertook some incredibly heroic task for the sake of some worthy object, the fatherland for instance, such as she herself had felt capable of that night on the paving last spring. But such was not the case, not altogether. The poems that touched her heart most, suffusing her with exalted emotion, so that she felt she could gather everything to her, were those which tell of the sorrow that wakes in the heart whose dreams have not been fulfilled, and of the beauty of that sorrow. The ship that in autumn lies deserted on the shore, rudderless, mastless, used no more; the bird that cowers low in shelter, likewise in the autumn featherless and forlorn, driven before the storm; the harp that hangs trembling on the wall, silently mourning its owner's fall — all this was her poetry, all this she understood. And despite the fact that Colma's song on the heath was nowhere rhymed, she had it by heart before she knew. Whereas one might have imagined that her favourite poetry would have dealt with love meeting love on the heath, she was no sooner in bed in the evenings than there sang in her heart lines telling of when the heath and love meet in the night, love and the heath, and the tears would soon be trickling down her cheeks, and she would feel that she was weeping not for Colma alone, and not for herself alone, but weeping with all the world in an ecstasy of love:

Rise, O moon,
From behind thy clouds!
Stars of the night arise!
Guiding light,
Lead me to my love
Where he rests in sleep alone.

Soft awhile,
Ye roaring winds!
Soft, ye rushing streams!
Let my song
Resound on the hill of storms,
Let my loved one hearken to me.

And she would bury her face in the pillow to stifle the sound of her sobbing, for no one might discover that she was weeping because of Ossian, no one would ever think of blubbering as much as our Asta Sollilja. But why was she weeping over this poem? It was because she understood both love and the heath, like Ossian, for he who understands the heath understands love, and he who understands love understands the heath.

And the hunter by the Mississippi. There was once a man. He was a hunter and must surely have travelled over all the world. It says in the poem that he was born in the lovely field of France — "There lived my noble parents." Everything that is good and everything that is delightful vied in their effort to please him. In childhood he read flowers in the meadows by the Seine. Paris with its fascinating hubbub — there stood his cradle. He lived among loving brothers, and he had playmates, and the girls among them were so pretty, a thousand times prettier than Asta Sollilja:

A dark-eyed maiden I remember
And the love-born smile on lips so warm.

And yet he did not find the happiness he had dreamed of, nor the peace he had so much desired, and she understood him, and loved him for that very reason, that he had found neither happiness nor peace; deep, deep inside her she loved him because he had fled. And now he sat on the wooded shores where the Mississippi rushed along:

Where pads the wolf in forest shade
And weary hart from hunter flees;
Where slinking forth on murderous raid
The dreaded panther threads the trees.

She had always understood both poetry and other things in
a way of her own. For example, she had gone to bed one night.
And she was pretending to be asleep, as she always did as soon
as she was in bed, but she was not asleep. She was waiting for
the old grandmother to put out her candle. The moments passed.
And then out of the corner of her eye she saw a man sitting up
in bed, resting his chin on his hand. She surveyed the sharply
hewn cheek-bone, the shaggy brow above the dark, searching
gaze which held at other moments the whole of poetry's bewitching play of light and colour, and she saw also his throat bare down
to the open neckband of his shirt; and he went on staring and he
went on thinking, as in the poem:

O'er hill and dale and cold, cold sea
I wandered far from childhood scene,
But always peace eluded me
Till in these lonely woods serene

—for over his head the rotten boards of the clincher roof had
become a rustling forest where deer and panthers roamed, and
the Goa storm that was sweeping the snow into deeper and deeper
drifts was the roar of the Mississippi in flood, and he who had
fled from the lovely cities of the world was sitting here, running
his eyes over his former life.

The flower of ardent youth is faded now,
And life grows sere, like leaves in wintry frost;
The sable curl is flecked with age's rime,
The hard-won fame of former days is lost.

No. It was neither heroes nor sacrifice nor yet virtues that she
loved most; rather the poetry which spoke to her of dreams that
were either fulfilled to no purpose or never fulfilled at all; of
happiness that came as a visitor or did not come, of how it came
and went, or of how it never came. She saw and understood this
man, not in an objective way, but in her own way: in the lambent

colours of poetry, with woods in the background, and penetrating everything, the roar of the world's deepest and mightiest river.

50.   GOD

AND now to tell of God.

For two years or more she and the others had longed to make the acquaintance of God, to know where He was and what He was thinking and whether He ruled the world in actual fact.

And now there were available on the croft two books, the Bible stories and the Catechism, which dealt exclusively with God, and there was likewise a teacher whom one would have expected to know all the principal features at least of this peculiar being who lives in exaltation far above all other beings. The story of how He created the world aroused their interest immediately, even though they received no answer to the question of why He had had to do it; but they found it difficult to understand sin, or the manner of its entry into the world, for it was a complete mystery to them why the woman should have had such a passionate desire for an apple when they had no idea of the seductive properties of apples and thought they were some sort of potatoes. But less intelligible still was the flood that was caused by forty days' rain, and forty nights'. For here on the moors there were some years when it rained for two hundred days and two hundred nights, almost without fairing; but there was never any Flood. When they began to question their teacher more closely about this riddle, he replied, perhaps not without a trace of irritation: "Well, I don't vouch for it in any case." It said in the Bible that God once came, attended by two angels, to visit a famous man abroad, but the narrative was in other respects extremely vague; what did God look like? "Oh, I expect He would have a beard," replied the teacher without much conviction; he had been lying motionless on the bed for some time now, with his head pillowed in his hands, staring up at the roof in obvious preoccupation. Then it occurred to little Nonni to ask whether God had had any clothes on — or was He naked? "You ought to be ashamed of yourself," cried Asta Sollilja. Later He sent us His only begotten Son, that good man who told stories and performed miracles, but somehow or other the children associated it all with Olafur of Yztadale, whose interest in the incomprehensible had never earned him much respect, and both parables and

miracles alike left the children as utterly unmoved as if they had
been news from a country so remote that one had never even
heard of it. Even little Nonni, whose love for countries was un-
deniable, did not wish to go there. And since, whenever they
began to discuss this matter, the teacher always tried to change
the subject, the children conceived involuntarily the idea that
it was something rather improper. The crucifixion acted upon
them as something unnaturally horrible, even though they had no
idea of a cross; they associated it involuntarily with what had
happened last Christmas, something that might not be mentioned,
something that belongs only to the most frightful of dreams,
something that makes one wake in a sweat at night, when one
lies in an awkward position, or with a lump beneath one; and one
looks at the window and hopes that some light will soon be showing there. Asta Sollilja closed the book with a shudder; she felt
that it was all so horrible, and she hoped that her brother Nonni
would not read about it until he was older, he was so sensitive.
She laid the book on the shelf. They did not learn about the
Resurrection or the Ascension of Jesus. God was never farther
away from them than when they had read this book. Asta Sollilja
had been greatly disappointed in God. Yet He did not entirely
vanish from her sight until she began to read the Catechism.
She was very sad and very pensive about the whole affair. Again
and again she sought to wake Him up from death and to stammer
forth some clumsy question addressed to her teacher. But it
ended always in one more defeat for God.

"Have you ever tried to pray to God?" she asked one day.

For a good while he was reluctant to answer, but at long
length it emerged that he had prayed to God. What for? Without looking up, and obviously much against his will, he told her
in confidence that he had prayed to God that he might be allowed
to keep his foot; he had lain in an infirmary. And then the foot
was taken off.

Asta Sollilja: "I think a man looks very nice with a foot like
yours."

And God was finished for that day.

The second time:

"It says that God is infinitely good. Is He infinitely good too
when someone is in trouble?"

The teacher: "Surely."

Asta Sollilja: "Then He can't very well be infinitely happy."

He: "I know that, my dear" — and suddenly losing his patience: "There's not a word of it true. It's utter rubbish. It's meant for soft, neurotic people."

Asta Sollilja: "My father is hard."

"Yes," said the teacher. "He's a tough proposition."

And once more God had evaporated from the conversation.

Third day: "I woke up early this morning, and as I opened my eyes I began to think about God, and I realized suddenly that He must exist. For how could anything exist if God didn't exist?"

After lengthy deliberation the teacher whispered: "Yes, it's probable that something may exist. But we don't know what it is."

Full stop.

Fourth day: "Then why did God allow sin to enter the world?"

At first the teacher seemed not to have heard this question; he lay for a good while staring blindly in front of him, as if in a trance, a thing that occurred more and more frequently every day now; then suddenly he sprang up with a startling abruptness, gazed intently at the girl with huge eyes, and repeated questioningly: "Sin?" Then he burst into a long fit of coughing, a deep, toneless, rattling cough; his face grew red and finally almost blue, the veins swelled in his neck, his eyes filled with tears. And when at last the fit was over, he dried his eyes and whispered breathlessly:

"Sin — sin is God's most precious gift."

Asta Sollilja went on gazing at her teacher, both with the straight eye and with the squint eye, but she did not dare ask any further question, because she was afraid of the unpredictable conclusions arrived at in theology, and besides, the teacher was quite exceptionally breathless today. She stood up and, as unobtrusively as possible, laid the Catechism on the shelf beside the Bible stories.

"Yes," whispered the teacher, "it's quite inevitable"; but she did not even dare ask him what was inevitable, for it is better, she thought, not to know the inevitable before it happens, and possibly one thing is more inevitable than anything else: the two standpoints that struggle for superiority over the soul of man till one or the other is vanquished, like the hart and the panther which lurk in the forest around the hunter. Early in the evening he wrote a letter in an elegant hand, almost a masterpiece of ornate calligraphy, put it in an enevelope, addressed it to Dr. Finsen, sealed it.

"Gvendur my boy," he said when the brothers had come in,

"if you should see anyone making for Fjord tomorrow, just ask them if they'll take this letter for me. It's to old Finsen about my cough."

That evening she heard him sighing heavily, yawning, and muttering occasionally a long-drawn "yes" or "oh dear me," or "oh"; or simply "a." Sometimes in the middle of it all he whispered despairingly to himself:

"It's no good at all." Or: "What difference does it make anyway?"

And when she heard this she was gripped by the fear that he was tired of this little low-roofed croft and had discovered that this was not the kingdom of happiness, perhaps not even the kingdom of innocence, which he had first imagined. She was more afraid of his soliloquy than of his cough, for she had been reared on coughing, her foster-mother had coughed, her grandmother coughed night and morning. What really cut her to the heart was that he should be no longer happy with them, that possibly he wanted to leave them and to go out into the world.

And she asked him, as she had often asked her foster-mother: "Wouldn't you like a drink of water?" She had grown used to offering people a drink of water if they were not feeling very well, cold water always helps a little.

But he replied with a long-drawn no. She kept on gazing at him on the sly, so distressed at the thought of not being able to do something for him that she could not turn her hand to anything, oh dear, if he should go away and leave them. She had tried to do all that she could for him, always served him with the best piece of meat at dinner-time, given him coffee six and as many as eight times a day, with the result that she would soon have no coffee left, and nothing seemed to have been of any use, what was she to do? Every new day saw a further increase in his despondency; he recited fewer and fewer poems, grew less and less inclined to enlarge upon the world's civilization, found it more and more difficult to rid himself of his melancholy thoughts. She longed so much to say something comforting, for though young, she knew from personal experience what the soul may sometimes have to contend with in private, and how one kindly word can disperse the clouds that gather there; but she had not the courage to say anything, rather turned her head aside as her eyes filled with tears.

Grandmother dragged herself along to his bed next day and said: "Your health doesn't seem to be up to much, my man," for in all her long experience she had never heard of a man lying in bed with his hands under his head, staring up at the roof all day, unless he was very ill indeed. For a moment he stared panic-stricken at that old face, which held no hope but endured everything. "Maybe the poor man hasn't any tobacco," she said. But he didn't want any tobacco, he shook his head and waved her away with his hand. "Sit yourself down again, old woman," he whispered.

On the very first day after the dispatch of the letter he began asking: "Can't you see anyone coming up from town? If you see anyone coming up from town, run and meet them and ask if they haven't anything from old Finsen for my cough."

And as the days dragged by, he asked more and more often, sometimes five or six times a day, like a little child. Asta Sollilja took part in his expectation and went out on the drift many times a day, shading her eyes with her hands and scanning the flats to see if she could descry anyone on his way from town. Again and again she sent her brothers to stop people, but no one had anything with them for the teacher.

And finally there came the day that she had dreaded ever since she had been aware of his dejection. She had brought him his coffee, and now he asked her to sit down on the bed beside him. He drank. Then he gave her the empty cup. She sat with the cup in her lap, uncertain whether to go or stay, for this was the first time that he had asked her to sit down beside him and she did not dare go unless he told her to, he was her teacher. Then he said: "If there's nothing for me from Finsen tomorrow, I shall have to go myself."

Had it been someone else she would have had the right to look up, and she would have looked at him with large, questioning eyes, and something would have fallen in her face. Now she did not even look up, she had not the right. Instead of lifting her eyelids she dropped her lashes, gazing down at the cup in her lap in shamefaced silence. And the man looked at her all, at how the youthful lines and the freshness of her body lay concealed beneath the torn, colourless clothing; and her form spoke to his senses all the more eloquently for its covering of rags, in much the same way as the slender plant that God has created behind many glaciers, then left forgotten, owes its charm to a hundred thousand stones, an endless wilderness. And finally he touched her, as a man is bound to touch a little flower growing by itself behind many glaciers among a hundred thousand stones. His hand passed gently over her shoulders and her back, and finally the palm rested on her buttocks; but for a fraction of a second only. And when he had taken his hand away, then, and not before, did she look up. Her eyes questioned timidly and helplessly, like those of a child who has been smacked and given a piece of candy, all in the same moment. But she said nothing. She shook her head abruptly, closed her eyes fast, and opened them. He laid his damp palm on the back of her hand and tried to see into her eyes — strange how her left eye can look at one without the pupil touching the lower lid; one looks into her eyes until one no longer understands one's own soul. Something moved in her throat, as if she was trying to swallow. She rose hurriedly, in an effort to escape the palm that rested on the back of her hand.

Just as if she mightn't have known from the very beginning that there was nothing here for him. This low-roofed croft in the snow — oh, why had he had to come, he too? Why had he needed to stay here and call on her care every day, like a child on its mother, so that her last thought at night had always been what she could do for him next morning — and then go away? What was she to think of when he had gone?

51.   WISHING–TIME

WHEN little Nonni came rushing jubilantly up the stairs with the teacher's medicine in a bottle, Asta Sollilja could hardly control her delight, as may well be imagined. She looked at him with glad participation and clapped her hands together quite involuntarily. But only once. For when she looked at him, it was after all not delight that showed in his face, but a savage, staring greed as he tore the bottle from the boy's hand, scanned the label intently, and sprang out of bed with a greater burst of energy than she had ever seen him use before. Then he stuck the bottle under his pillow and asked whether supper wouldn't be ready soon. Asta Sollilja put more wood under the pan.

At length she asked him shyly whether they had sent him the right medicine, for she felt that thereon depended their whole future. If perhaps he had got the wrong medicine, then — it would be the same as no medicine at all. But he replied that they wouldn't bother with books that evening, we'll go early to bed. We will go early to bed so that the teacher's medicine will do him good, said Asta Sollilja.

So they retired much earlier than usual, except that the old woman sat up knitting in the glimmer of the candle, with an occasional insignificant mumble, until her time had come. At last she also put out her light and lay down. By that time Asta Sollilja was asleep and dreaming. Her dreams had regained the qualities that make of sleep a welcome friend; and now once more, in the peerless splendour of the glossy painting, she saw the elegant wooded landscape of the old calendar, which so long ago had been trodden to pieces under the sheep's hoofs; unnaturally green, yes, it was still the landscape of her best dreams. And in her nostrils was the heavy scent of wild thyme, such as was wafted from the mountain sometimes in summer, especially early on Sunday mornings, when the night's dew was disappearing fast before the sun that shines on the day of rest. Lazily she drifted over this landscape, like a bird sailing on motionless pinions past the mountain's embattled crags; in this dream there was nothing that anyone need fear, no one laboured under any affliction, she was happy. And what was more, there was not even anyone chasing her; so healthy are the dreams that may occasionally be dreamed in youth. Then it seemed in her ears as she glided along that the earth had begun whispering beneath her feet, or beneath her wings, as if the mountain with its belts of crags were preparing to whisper one irresistible poem beneath her wings; and she woke up. She did not know how long she had been asleep, but the dream had been lovely and at first her heart-beats were free from fear, though she opened her eyes on pitch-darkness. And there really was a whisper from somewhere, it had not been merely a dream. Yes, it was poetry. And it was here in the room. It was he. He was reciting poetry. Why was he lying awake in the middle of the night reciting poetry? She raised her head and gave a little cough, in question, and he whispered a whole verse more.

"It's only me," he said.

"Couldn't you get to sleep?" she asked.

But he replied:

> *Dainty*
> *Dew-begotten flower,*
> *Delicate and fine,*
> *Wildly*
> *Grows desire in power,*
> *Fevered now with wine,*
> *To make thee,*

Mountain maiden, mine,
Now that Adam's inner
Nature gives new sign.

"What's that you're reciting?" she asked.

"It's only an old poem."

"Oughtn't we to get up, then?" she inquired, thinking that perhaps he wanted them to begin their lessons.

"The time is nigh," he answered, and went on with the poem, whispering, and she felt that he was whispering it over to her, as if he were addressing it to her in particular, and it seemed such an odd sort of poem, she had never heard anything like it before; and he was whispering it as if it had something to do with her, as if it concerned her directly and intimately. She blushed furiously in the darkness and had not the remotest idea what to do or say, especially as it was after midnight; for poetry was meant to be read aloud in the daytime, but understood in silence during the night. But how was a young girl to understand poetry that is whispered for her ears only, in the middle of the night? Could she take it impersonally, like the poetry of day?

Scarcely
My clamorous thoughts I know.
Errant, feverish, bold,
Madly
In wanton strength they grow
When that I behold
Thy lovely
Grace, thou sweetest beauty's mould;
For I count thee e'en more comely
Than Aaron's calf of gold.

No, surely he was only saying it to himself. Surely he realized that she was much too young to understand such strange verses; that though she often gave him coffee, and sometimes pancakes, it was because she was only a little girl, and there was therefore no point in addressing such stuff directly to her; and though she might feel at times perhaps that she was really a big girl now, she had never let anyone know about it; and besides she would never have thought it possible that anyone could have spoken of a calf in connection with love, even a golden calf. No, it couldn't really be a serious poem, and obviously it couldn't be her he was referring to. What ought she to say?

> *Fairest*
> *Of the lovely company*
> *Of maidens sweet and wise;*
> *Rarest*
> *Thy tongue's sweet symphony,*
> *The glance of thy dewy eyes.*

No, heaven be praised that such odd poetry could not possibly refer to her. It would have been nonsense to suggest that she was dewy-eyed, and sillier still to describe her as the fairest of maidens. It must have been written a hundred years ago by some other poet, for some other girl. She had never been in the company of other girls; she was like a lonely plant growing in the midst of a wilderness of stones; but she had always, always been quite certain that the other girls of the world surpassed her by far. And anyway she wasn't really a girl yet, she was only a child — or had it got about somehow that she was grown up, even though she had been so careful to keep it secret? Heavens, what would Father say if he knew? — she who wasn't even confirmed yet. With every verse her heart grew more and more uneasy; soon she would be able to stand no more of it.

> *To sing*
> *This maiden's praises*
> *My muse lacks words and skill*
> *That bring*
> *To life in coloured phrases*
> *The charms that melt my will.*

Why was he laying on all this the emphasis that one lays only on words whispered in confidence, which no one else may hear? Didn't he know that there were limits to what a little girl, who no one knew was grown up, could listen to in the middle of the night without losing control over herself, and falling in a faint, and possibly dying? He who could have anything he wished of her, who knew the world's poetry and story from personal experience — wasn't he going to have mercy on her in her helplessness?

> *Thou piercest*
> *The soul that in me sighs*
> *For thy budding, fragrant beauty,*
> *For thy charms unseen, a choicer prize.*

With her wits in complete turmoil she leaped out of bed, fumbled for the matches, and lit the lamp. Then she saw that she had forgotten even her slip, so terrified had she been, so distraught. Wildly she pulled it over her head and smoothed it down over her hips; and there was a light in the room, and, heavens above, if he should have seen!

Finally she brushed her hair away from her face with a jerk of her head and looked at him, panic-stricken.

Yes, he was better. He was feeling so well that, far from being asleep, he had actually got out of bed in the middle of the night. Now he was sitting on the edge-board with a red face and glowing eyes; and the lines that had marked his face so deeply in the past seemed suddenly to have been smoothed away, so that he looked no more than a lad in his teens. The joy that shone in his face was almost childlike; he sat there with the medicine on his knees, smiling contentedly at the girl and at the light she had lit. The light woke the boys too, and they sat up to inspect this new happiness.

Was he then — quite well? Yes, he was quite well. And more than well. He was happy. He was all-happy. And added: "And good as well; all-good. And why?" He flourished his medicine in the face of the universe. "Because tonight there is no suffering for anyone. I have crossed it all out. In future there will be no more hardship, no more illness. Tonight it is I who rule. No more sorrows for the trembling heart, no half-naked children in dark huts on a spit where the brook runs out into the sand, no more worms in the peacefully ruminating sheep of the valleys, no more cruel loads on the backs of the independent man's noble pack-horses; rather rustling groves over the Equator's sandy deserts and heartfelt birthday wishes between hunter, hart, and panther on the banks of the Mississippi. All that the heart desires I give you; come unto me, ye children, and choose your countries. This is wishing-time for all of you."

For a good while the children, still half-asleep, were unable to draw any distinction between this new happiness of his and the poetry that he had taught them. But their brains cleared as he went on talking. The boys got out of bed and came forward to participate in the redemption of the universe. He took them to him and, setting them down on the bed beside him, laid his arms over their shoulders and hugged them to his breast with incredible quotations from the poets.

Wishing-time had arrived so much like a bolt from the blue that at first the children hardly knew what to make of it. It is by no means the first time that people have stood tongue-tied in the presence of wishing-time; it is, moreover, very rare for people to understand wishing-time when it comes, though it may be the only moment that they have always longed for; and even, perhaps, expected. Even little Nonni, he who had always believed in wishes, he who was their child — even he hesitated when the hour arrived. And Asta Sollilja thought it was all poetry, only in a new form. Strange as it may seem, it was little Gvendur, the materialist, who was first to pick up his bearings, first to grasp the fact that the sacred moment had arrived. His was the reasoning, in common with that of Hrollaugur of Keldur, that takes things strictly in the order in which they come, without inquiring into their origin or their nature. He was the first to wish a wish.

"My wish," he said, "is that Father's sheep should have a good winter. And that he should earn a lot of money before Easter. And buy more sheep next autumn."

"My friend," replied the teacher, and kissed him, "your wish shall be fulfilled. The peacefully ruminating, twin-bearing ewes shall return to the fold with the finest lambs in the district. The stock at home and the assets in Fjord shall increase in equal proportions. A mirror-smooth, macadamized road shall be led here all the way from the world's civilization, and along it shall trundle large silver coins like carriages in endless procession. And here on the hillock there shall rise, like a palace in a fairy tale, a two-storeyed house of stone, illuminated with the most powerful electric light that modern science can provide."

Such was the first wish, and such the manner in which it was approved and expedited. And little Nonni realized that though this moment might be nothing more than a dream, it would be prudent not to let the opportunity slip through his fingers just in case it wasn't a dream, in much the same way as people acknowledge the existence of God on their death-beds in case there should actually prove to be a God after all. And what did it please him to decide upon at this moment when the fates had seemed to lay their entire will at his feet? In the blood of some people there is bred only one wish, and they are the children of happiness, for life is exactly big enough for one wish, not for two. In her suffering his mother had planted in his bosom this one wish: he wished for other countries.

"What countries?" asked the teacher.

"A country with woods in it," he said. "A country something like the one where the Mississippi rolls along, as it says in the poem. Where the hart and the panther live in the woods. That's the sort of country I want."

"Bring me pen, ink, and paper," said the teacher.

He leaned over the table and wrote in a large flowing hand, and the pen spluttered. And the boy watched him writing with marvelling eyes and was still uncertain whether it wasn't all a dream or whether he was really awake; whether it was all fun and poetry or whether there actually are moments that determine all the other moments in life and give them purpose.

"There you are," said the teacher as he handed him the letter with a dignified flourish. "Send that letter down to Fjord at the earliest opportunity. It is your letter of hope. And your wish shall be fulfilled."

The boy stared inanely at the address; it was to a lady with a foreign name, care of the Sheriff on arrival, no further explanation. Before he went back to bed he laid the mysterious letter of hope on the shelf above his grandmother, then pinched the lobe of his ear — surely it was all a dream; perhaps there would be no sign of a letter in the morning. And when he woke in the morning, the first thing he did was to grope about on the shelf, and what do you think? — there lay a letter addressed in huge handwriting to a foreign lady care of the Sheriff. And he watched out for people making for Fjord and asked them to deliver it for him.

And now that the second wish was fulfilled, it was time for the third. He told the boys that they could go back to bed now. And the boys went back to bed. As soon as they had lain down and closed their eyes again, he reached for the lamp, blew it out, and took Asta Sollilja.

52.   THE INEVITABLE

IT was really terrible.

Never, never might anything so terrible happen again.

> *Ave Lord God, dark sins oppress*
> *Thy shameful daughter poor,*
> *Abandoned now to wickedness*
> *And snared by Satan's lure.*
>
> *The pains of hell my weak soul rack,*
> *O'erwhelmed in depths of woe.*
> *From shame and guilt I see no track,*
> *No path where I may go.*

Asta Sollilja was standing by the fireplace early in the morning listening to this hymn behind her. Her hands were girl's hands, with a coarse bluish skin, broad palms, fine bones, and strong joints. The knuckles were big but the fingers long; the thumb-sinew prominent, the wrist bony and mature-looking. She laid the black twigs of heather on the grate, for she had cleared out the ashes. The slender, sappy dwarf-birch twigs from the heath crackled sullenly when she put a light to them, and she covered them hastily with dry slabs of dung; a gust of wind blew down the chimney, the room filled with smoke. Yes, she was a big girl now, it was she who lit the fire these days, and no road back.

It was early in March, a grey light beginning to show on the windows in the mornings. But it was very cold. It was particularly cold after the night that had just passed. A shiver struck through her and again and again she had to clench her teeth. Her hair was all in disorder, one of her plaits had come undone, and it had not been touched with a comb yet. The tight rag of a frock, which she had forgotten to smooth down her sides, hung in baggy rumples above her hips, so that every time she bent down she showed the hams of her knees, coarsely fashioned in comparison with the slender, undeveloped, childish knees; almost gross, with the strong curve of the thighs above and of the fully grown calves below. — She had forgotten to put on her slip, what could have happened to her slip? — and she hadn't pulled her stockings up either, they were hanging in thick folds round her ankles — but it didn't matter. She seemed to have grown suddenly so unnaturally broad, she who had always been so unnaturally slim — she felt rather like a fish that has been cut up the middle and split open; yes, with a knife, with a whetted knife. From top to toe she was one living ache, and every movement cost her a twinge somewhere; yes, not only as if she had simply been cut open, but as if she had been pulled to pieces and pounded as well. There was nothing she would have liked half so well as to creep deep under the bed-clothes and lie utterly motionless for days on end, without anyone ever disturbing her, just sleeping, sleeping, even dying — all the sleep she had had was one short restless doze, just before dawn, from which she had started up in terror — no, never never might anything so dreadful happen again, no, nor anything like it.

Her only care was to avoid looking round at her grandmother; and yet she saw her as through the back of her head, where she sat rocking slightly to and fro with the knitting in her lap, her head dithering, her face a rune-carved enigma, her eyes blinking weakly under the heavy blue lids; yet seeing everything and knowing everything, and symbolizing that reality with God and the Devil which rises when the night that came with dreams and forests has run its course. From the elysium of wishing-time she had waked to the grandmother's age-old hymns, even before day had dawned over the blood; and long before the neutral, soothing fire of everyday life had started blazing, there was recited a hymn in which ebbing delight was multiplied by flooding torment, as when a thousand is multiplied by a million; it was as if the whole of life had happened in one night. She felt as if she had been butchered. Her body was like meat that has been chopped up and bled. Never never —

With dark and gloom the day is filled
That brings no help from Thee;
No cleansing of my tenfold guilt,
No sign of mercy free.

For Death's grim hand I therefore pray,
Though thought of death I fear.
Then end, Lord God, my joyless day,
And bring me to my bier.

She tried to muffle the cough that seized her in the thickening smoke, so as not to waken anyone. If only none of them would ever wake up, if only they would all just go on sleeping, never noticing her, never speaking to her. If only day would never break and the water remain standing thus for ever and ever, half-cold, over a half-burning fire; for she was certain that she had changed, that everyone who saw her would be frightened and, not recognizing her, would drive her away. Her brothers were her brothers no more, or rather she was no longer their sister. She had long known that hers was a different nature from theirs; she had envied them ever since they were little and from the very first had understood their mysterious superiority; and now in the end it had come to this, that she had had to pay for what she had not been given. Nothing like this could ever happen to them. And the difficulties they would experience in understanding her fate separated her from them to all eternity; no, no one in the world would ever be able to understand what had happened to her; she stood alone, outside the whole world; it was eternally impossible ever to rectify it, in this isolation she would die. All communication with kindred beings was destroyed, she belonged to another life. Everything was the same as before, except that she was otherwise; and nothing had happened to anyone except to her. Henceforward day would be foreign to her, every day, all days; and more than foreign: an insoluble problem, a labyrinth, chaos. If only she might be allowed to stand thus over this unheated water to the end of all time, without ever running the risk of waking the community from which she had been isolated, the bonds that she had severed, the unity she had broken; living, or rather not living, on the boundaries between existence and non-existence, beside the half-cold fire and its crackling birch twigs, in a grey indeterminate dawn, without seeking any explanation of the night's experience, as if in vague memory of a nameless, repulsive bird with a greedy beak that they had once seen flapping its way over the marshes, and had never set eyes on since.

And then in the next moment she had begun to demand of herself an explanation of that which had taken place. — What had taken place? And, above everything else, what had she done? No, she hadn't done anything. She had rejoiced in his joy, a current had passed through her and she had leaned up against him quite involuntarily because a current had passed through her in the middle of the night when he put the light out; and could she help it if a current passed through her? Why did a current pass through anyone? Life itself, one couldn't help life, one was living. Was it forbidden, or what? Yes, but why was one born, then? Why did a flicker of life have to keep going in her when she was lying under the bitch's belly? One warm bitch that was certainly lousy, perhaps wormy — why hadn't her father taken the bitch with him when he went off to search the mountains? No, she had done nothing, nothing — from the time that she had lain under the bitch's belly until this very morning. All that had happened was that some unknown current had passed through her —

And yet. She had let him — why had she let him? Why hadn't she thought of her father instead of letting him? Father — it was like a bitter pain cutting straight through her heart. No, no, he must never find out, he who had entrusted her with everything, inside the croft and out, had he not entrusted her first and foremost with herself? He who for one abrupt second had pressed her to his bosom in the loft here — she was the flower of his life. He was going away that he might build her a house, and he had gone down the stairs, and she had sworn that she would never have a

father other than him. He had closed the door after him, and it
was the same as if he had closed her heart after him when he went
away, and she had cried when he went away, and no one might
come in, and no one knew that she had cried, and now he was
coming back at Easter-time, and how was she ever to look him in
the face? And now an ungovernable spasm of weeping struck
through her breast. Try as she might she could not control herself;
the tears flowed through her fingers to mingle with the water in
the pan, and she pressed her elbows against her sides to stay the
heaving of her breast, but weeping too is an independent element
in the breast of man, another current, and weeping also is controlled from another world, and man is defenceless against his
own tears and cannot get away and cannot get away and cannot
get away; and it was the same last night, when he put his arms
round her and they were each beside the other, and there was
nothing that separated them, and she thought it was joy itself,
and she had forgotten her father and everything, and still something had told her to try to get away, away — but she could not
get away, she could not get away, she could not get away. One
cannot get away, such is life. And stands weeping here over the
lifeless fire that one has lit.

> *Wearily, wearily lags the dawn*
> *That holds no hope from Thee;*
> *And drearily, drearily drags the morn*
> *Unlit by clemency.*

This droning procession of sacred philosophy shambled along
behind her back like a file of penitent ghosts, while the arch-fiend
attacked her on the open flank, the inimical over-self which con-
demns human nature on Christian grounds. Finally she could
stand no more of it. She was driven to utter desperation, for after
all there are limits to the amount of Christian ethics that human
nature can bear. She fled in a panic away from her grandmother
and halted by the teacher's bed, as if his arms were certain sanc-
tuary. In mortal fear she touched his cheek, then laid her cold
palm under the open neck of his shirt. But instead of saving her,
he gave a pitiful groan in his sleep and turned over so that he
was facing the wall; and the coverlet fell away from him, and
he was naked, and there lay her slip all crumpled up beside him.
She snatched it away, then threw the coverlet over him, all in
the same fit of panic; she had never seen a naked man, and luckily

she didn't see one now, because the light was still so grey on the window, and what had she done? Who was this man?

It was almost full daylight when she returned from the ewe-house with her brothers. It had done her good to get out into the fresh winter wind; her exertions with the sheep and the hay had brought momentary relief, but she had not dared to look at her brothers and had kept her face averted in case they did not recognize her. He was still lying in bed, still facing the wall; she listened, but could not hear him breathing. She was filled with immediate foreboding, for she thought that perhaps he might be dead. "Wouldn't you like something to drink," she whispered. "The coffee is hot." But he wasn't dead after all. He woke up and opened his eyes, and even though he replied only with bitter groans she was overjoyed that he should have waked; she hoped he would soon feel better. She brought him his coffee and helped him to sit up. His face was grey and sick, unshaven, long stubble, his hair in disorder, he did not look at her. She sat on his bed, uninvited, and passed her stump of a comb through his hair — "Here's your coffee," she whispered, as if in confidence. Then she went on combing his hair; yes, combing his hair, it was quite incomprehensible and yet she did it naturally and without thinking. She even moved closer and held him while she adjusted the pillows to support his back; all as a matter of course, shyness completely gone. She asked him whether he felt any pain, and where he felt it — was there anything special he would like? What did it matter what happened to her as long as nothing happened to him?

"I'm as good as dead," he whispered from the middle of his coffee. Then later: "Let me be. I don't deserve it."

He did not thank her for combing his hair, he did not thank her for taking the empty cup; he lay down again, sighing bitterly, and she tucked him in with great care, her throat dry, her heart pounding as if it would never stop; and still he did not look at her, much less give her a pleasant word, whisper. But when he had lain thus for some time, while she sat over him, gazing at him fondly and faithfully, she saw his lips moving and heard him whisper: "God Almighty help me. God Almighty forgive me."

Unable to tear herself away from his torment, she remained sitting on the edge of the bed, listening to his sighs and lamentations. The medicine was finished, the bottle empty; when all was said and done, there was nothing left but God —

God that day had suddenly assumed a position of prime importance on the croft. Everyone seemed to understand Him, each in his own way. So this was what He was like. As day advanced, the teacher rapidly overhauled the grandmother in divine service; his prayers were the unrhymed prayers of the heart and they soon gained the ascendancy over the grandmother's stereotyped recitations. Again and again he sat up in bed and, staring blindly in front of him with wide, despairing eyes, wiped the sweat from his brow and sighed: "Oh my God, I'm lost. Oh my God, what have I done?" Or: "If you intend to trample on me, O Lord, then trample me to pieces immediately."

The young girl offered him water to drink, she still had some unreasoning idea that cold water had the power of curing body and soul. He sipped a little cold water, then lay down again with a groan. She hoped he would fall asleep. But suddenly he sat up again and cried: "What have I done?" This time she did not offer him more water, but, leaning up against him, whispered:

"You haven't done anything." And added, still more softly, right in his ear: "I didn't mind you doing it. If it was wrong, then it was I that was to blame. But it wasn't wrong at all. And you didn't hurt me a bit. And you can do it again whenever you like; I will never let Father know. God isn't nearly as bad as you think."

Laying her arms round his neck, she pressed her cheek against his face, the more determined to follow him to the ends of the earth the greater the depths of his unhappiness; and to forget herself. He did not release her hand when he lay down again; sweet is a hand that soothes. He went on gazing with half-shut eyes at the redeeming face above him; little by little he grew more peaceful.

53.   WHEN ONE HAS A FLOWER

He had walked all night.

He had set off at midnight, and by daybreak was nearing the western verge of the high heath. This was on a frosty morning of Holy Week. Slowly it was growing brighter; slowly night was disappearing behind him with a thousand steps, a thousand thoughts in wild confusion, like sleeplessness from the depths of night to the break of day. Soon dawn would throw its cold, shadowy light over the heath's frozen expanse, over the stony ridges that jutted above the snow, over the glittering ice of the hard-trodden bridle-path, and would gild them. And now once more his gaze travelled over the solvent world that he had bought so long

ago, as he greeted it in the dim, grey-blue light preceding sunrise two weeks before the first day of summer, two weeks after
the spring equinox. The marshes were still bound in ice, no sign
of thaw on the lake, the moors in the south white-coated; and soaring up from them rose the Bluefells in mystic guise that had nowhere any kinship with the substance of the earth; or with the
spirit of the earth. And there stood the man's little farmstead still
under the rift in the mountain, with trodden snow all around and
flood-water mark delineated by two filaments of ice in the gully
above. From where he stood the outline of the roof could be made
out quite plainly beneath its covering of snow. He set down his
burden on the brow of the heath and, leaning against a cairn
marking the road, gazed at his own land, the land that held his
little nation; and that flower which inadvertently he had mentioned
during the winter to — a total stranger. He stood there like an
army that, having marched into other countries to wage desperate
war, was returning now with victory in its soul; provisions from
town; and — most remarkable of all — money in the co-operative
society.

Incredible things happen in this world between important
festivals. And upon the dale-farmer the effect of these events is
always equally devastating, for this helpmate of God's is so indifferently endowed with the power of divination that he forgets to
allow for the fact that the land may turn completely over and
deposit itself upside down on the surface of the sea without warning him and without asking his permission, at any time between
Christmas and Easter. No one had been more faithful to his merchant than Bjartur of Summerhouses; few had ever been less disposed to envy the light that shines in a house with a tower on it.
Had he not always been accustomed to say it makes no damned
odds to me whether he happens to live in a tower that he's supposed to have sucked out of the bones of the poor as long as he
deals fairly by me, the old rapscallion? This was his creed, and
neither logic, threats, nor promises could alter it one jot. And then?
In spite of all Gudbjartur Jonsson's faith, it had come to this: that
the merchant no longer existed. Finished, gone up in smoke, the
shop empty, the account-books lost, the Tower House sold for the
benefit of creditors. In such a fashion, one fine day, were the foundations upon which the crofter had built his life swept aside; those
almighty giants of commerce who stood with one foot in Iceland
and the other on the Continent itself — one fine day saw them
wiped away like so much spit. The credit that stood to Bjartur of

Summerhouses' name was lost, and there was no one left to answer
for it. Such was the state of affairs that winter, when Bjartur came
down to Fjord in search of work: Bruni had gone bankrupt with
the fellow's money in his pocket. After calamity among the sheep
and havoc wrought by spectres, he stood penniless on the street-
corner, like an idiot. Surely God and men could go no farther in
fleecing this independent individual of his property; and what
made it worse was that there was no one he could give a drubbing,
no one to play the devil with, or at least no one who would take it
very much to heart if he told them frankly what he thought of
them.

Nevertheless he went along to the Sheriff's. "Where the devil is
this marvellous justice of yours," he snarled, "if you're going to allow folk to amuse themselves by the same as robbing a man of his
soul while he has other things to think about and is maybe doing
his damnedest with a ghost? What the hell are the authorities
for if they can't get hold of my money and return it? You funked
coming up at Christmas because there was a little drizzle, and it
was your fault I lost my eldest boy; he took fright and wandered
into the storm while you were busy warming your backside at
home here. The Bailiff turned up, lousy as he is, so what about
showing some sign of guts now, damn you, and getting hold of my
money if it takes every law in your blasted old book?"

The Sheriff, however, stood up for Tulinius Jensen. "The business has failed, man, there's not the remotest chance of anyone
ever seeing a penny, at least for years and years to come yet. I
have nothing at all to do with it. The King has appointed somebody to make an inquiry into the whole affair. It's impossible to
do anything when a business has gone bankrupt. You'll just have
to try to understand all the circumstances: Bruni has been losing
money for years, and in the end the co-operative had filched all
his customers away from him. There you have the whole story in a
nutshell. Men like you had plenty of opportunities of clearing out
in good time, so you've only yourselves to blame if you stuck it out
till the whole affair had sunk to perdition instead of joining the co-
operative society in time."

"In time? The annoying thing," said Bjartur, "is that one
shouldn't have had the sense to cut these bastards' throats in time."

"You have only yourselves to blame," repeated the Sheriff.

"Yes. And the fact that we're too good-natured to strangle all
these thieving swine at birth."

"Who's a thieving swine?"

"Who? He and they whom you're so keen on sticking up for. Not that I consider that you're very much better, you mealy-mouthed gang of damned officials who hang on to their coat-tails through thick and thin, but daren't stir a foot across the ridge there in a bit of a drizzle though somebody's life is at stake."

"Look here, Bjartur, won't you take a seat so that we can discuss matters calmly and sensibly?"

"I'll sit when it suits me."

"May I offer you a pinch of snuff, then?"

"You may please yourself what you offer. I please myself what I accept."

At the doctor's:

"Tulinius Jensen has always had a reputation for the greatest honesty, Bjartur. I knew him well myself. And he never swindled anyone to my knowledge. It was he that was swindled, rather than he that swindled. His troubles started when the farmers started lending their ears to the ranting demagogy of the co-operative chiefs. No one can protect himself against that sort of thing, you know. It was the farmers that swindled Bruni."

"Yes and I want my money for all that," insisted Bjartur. "You were Bruni's member of Parliament, and it was you that I always voted for ever since I first had the right to vote. And why the hell do you think I voted for you? Do you think it was because of your spectacles, blast you? If I don't get my money back, the Devil himself can vote for you instead of me. And if you as a member of Parliament propose to stand there and tell me that it is legal for a man to be robbed of his property, then I am against the government. I am against the government."

"Listen, Bjartur my friend, I'm an old man now, and it's time I went into retirement as far as politics are concerned. But because we've always been good friends and staunch supporters of the same party, may I offer you a glass of real corn brandy?"

"You may offer me nothing but my own property."

"These are difficult times, my dear Bjartur. All the countries abroad are labouring under a severe crisis. Our losses in Iceland are nothing compared with what they are losing in America."

"It takes a long time to find some people out, but I see now that you're another of the same damned type as the authorities, a hanger-on of thieves and robbers."

"Oh, I think I've always tried to do my bit for the people, Bjartur, both as a member of Parliament and in my capacity of medical officer. My bills, as you may remember, were never very hard on my own supporters. Year after year I've lost hundreds and hundreds on medicine that I've let people have. And no one's conscience seems to trouble them though they forget to pay me. But I never complain."

"If my memory isn't at fault, Bruni paid you out of my account for the poison that you made me brew for my own wives. And they both passed on without further ceremony. I shouldn't be surprised if you had killed them both."

"Oh, come, come, Bjartur; that's not a very nice thing to say to anyone. Maybe you'll have better luck with these new fellows, these co-operative people who are so busy sweeping everything before them just now."

"The Rauthsmyri gang could never be worse than you Bruni people. I thought so once, but I don't think so now."

They talked to him as if he was a refractory child, and again he stood like an idiot on the street. There was no one left but the Rauthsmyrians now; all sanctuaries were closed except the gracious embrace of Ingolfur Arnarson Jonsson.

Hitherto this man had sought to express his convictions by nailing wings on Tulinius Jensen's shoulder-blades and painting Ingolfur Arnarson black. For thirty years he had worn himself out for the Rauthsmyrians, first as a workman, then as the purchaser of a farm, and he had always eyed his freedom in the far-off change implicit in not wearing himself out eternally for the same robber. He had thought there was some difference in robbers. Then Bruni had gone and disappeared with his money, leaving him drifting about in ignorance and uncertainty. There was no difference in robbers after all; whether they lived on the coast or up in the country, they were all tarred with the same brush. But there was one point in the Rauthsmyrians' favour: they had never fled to a distant part of the country with his credit in their pockets. The freedom and independence of mankind were not founded on Tulinius Jensen after all. And Ingolfur Arnarson could never be worse than Bruni. It was not to be denied, of course, that it would be a severe blow to the soul to have to resort at last to the co-operative society, after being disappointed in the freedom that was built on Tulinius Jensen. Or would he find, when all was said and done, that freedom was really founded on the Rauthsmyrians — the true freedom, the freedom that makes of the lone worker in his valley an independent man?

"Ah, the independent man. It's high time you came and looked us up in the society here."

"Oh, it wasn't out of politeness," said Bjartur apologetically.

"No, my friend, I know that. You wouldn't take my advice, but perisisted in sticking to Bruni to the bitter end, so now you're having to pay the penalty, I suppose. But what of it; there's no ill will on my side at least. How are you all keeping in Summerhouses?"

"How are we keeping? I don't answer that sort of question. I can't see that our welfare concerns anyone. I lost a lot of sheep, but that, of course, is only what the country has had to contend with ever since it was first settled. You Rauthsmyri people have also lost sheep, you lose sheep every spring. My sheep stand the winter better than yours."

"Yes, but I was referring actually to those mysterious goings-on at your place the other day. You lost a boy — "

"Yes. My own boy."

"Somebody was saying that Kolumkilli had been showing his claws again."

"Kolumkilli? Oh, of course, hasn't he something to do with the Persian religion?"

"All right, forget it. What can we do for you?"

"Nothing," replied Bjartur. "I have been robbed. I want work. I'm not asking anyone to do anything for me. But I am prepared to work for others, for a wage."

"Yes, Bjartur, old friend, everything that I told you last year has come to pass. But I can't help it if you wouldn't believe me. There are two parties in the country, those who seek to prey on the farmers and those who seek to promote their economic welfare and raise them to a position of honour and esteem. You believed in the former, and where do you stand now? We, who wish to govern the country for the people — we alone remain."

"Yes, go on, Ingi boy, go on. But I believe in nothing, and in words least of all. And that's why I ask for no gifts. I'm not complaining about anything either. Perhaps I ought to have stayed where I was with all that's left of my sheep, and there are those who would argue that there was nothing I really lacked: it's only a couple of years since I built fresh accommodation for my stock. And if you think it's a house with a tower on that I'm after, I can tell you now that you're wrong, Ingi lad, for I have never envied those who dwell in tower-houses. But," he added, "when a man has a flower in his life — "

Then he seemed to feel that he had said too much, and he did
not finish the sentence.

54.   SPRING DAYS

Soon the lowlands were free of snow, and the ewes were beginning to feed to some purpose on the grass in the marshes. At
meal-times, when Father and the boys came in from work, there
was their food laid all ready for them on the table. But where was
Asta Sollilja? She was down at the brook washing stockings and
suchlike, or seeing to the clothes hanging out on the line, or
kneading bread down in the entrance; she was very seldom
seen in the loft when anyone else was in the loft, and at night she
went to bed after all the others had gone to bed; if she washed
herself at all these days, no one ever saw her doing it. Once she
was in bed, she would draw the coverlet over her head and lie as
still as a mouse. She had developed suddenly a habit of hanging
her head, as if she wished to hide her face. Long lashes drooped
over eyes that looked at no one in particular. If her father addressed her she would answer with a monosyllable, then slip away
as soon as possible. He had grown used to seeing her look at him
questioningly, with wide, guileless eyes, and he had replied with
silence; now it was he that looked at her questioningly, she who
replied with silence.

It was possibly no great novelty though no one on the croft
knew quite what anyone else was thinking, and it is possible that
such a mode is all for the best. One might be inclined to believe
that on a croft everyone's soul would be cast in the same mould,
but this is far from the truth, for nowhere are there souls more
varied in nature than on a little croft. The two brothers, for example — when had they ever understood one another? — Gvendur,
who longed for the fulfilment of reality in a definite place, Nonni,
who longed for the solution of dreams in some remote indeterminate distance. Sunshine and thawing snow, the ice in the gully
melting, the waterfall in flood — the little boy gazed enchanted
out into the spring, and a breeze came away from the south and
blew the waterfall back over the mountain, get on with your work
and stop glowering into space, said the elder brother. They were
busy in the enclosure spreading manure. This waterfall in the gully
and its wind from the south, a whole human soul could find its
symbol in one small peculiarity of nature and could mould itself

upon it; he had discussed it with his mother and she had understood and told him a dream. Now there was no one to understand, but he lived on this dream; and on her wishes. He walked alone whenever he could. In his breast there dwelt a lyrical sadness, a strange sorrowful longing; when he was tending the sheep he sang part-songs that he had never heard. Yes, there was such a wonderful instrument in his breast; and though he could not yet play upon it himself, he toyed with its strings and listened to this note or that note early in the spring, sometimes trembling, often with tears in his eyes, and his eyes were deep and sorrowful and pure as a rill, and like silver deep, deep at the bottom of a rill, silver in a rill.

In spite of the mild weather there was little show of green on the hills yet, and as the possibility of sudden storms could not be excluded, the crofter had little desire to allow his sheep to wander away up to the high moors. He searched the moorland watercourses in the south and the east at regular intervals, chasing all the sheep he could find down to the lowlands. The more oppressive the silence at home, the more did he appreciate the freshness of spring with its bewitching intensity, its odour of thawing snow and snow that had thawed, of sunlit space and the promise of eternity; for the moors stand in indissoluble communion with eternity. Little by little the snow retreated before the sun, and soon there was in the air the scent of heather and withered grass and the first fresh shoots as they emerged from the drifts on the slopes. The ewes loitered among the hollows and the gullies, cropping at whatever they could find above the snow. But when least expected they would take to their heels and, rushing to the top of the gully or the hollow, would race off into the wind at full speed, into unlimited space, into eternity; for sheep also love eternity and have faith in it.

For some days a raven had been seen flapping about over the gully. He took a walk along the bottom to see whether it was some prey the bird was so intent upon. The river was in spate, but not so high as it had been previously. All at once the dog came to a halt and stood barking over something that the river had washed on to the gravel. The raven hovered croaking over the gully. Now, the last thing that Bjartur had expected was to find anything dead here, for he had lost no sheep that spring, and anyway, as good luck would have it, it wasn't a carcass, it was a corpse. It was a boy's slender body. It had tumbled over the rocks at some time during the winter and, after lying in a drift until the snow had

thawed, had been floated off by the river when in flood, then left
stranded on the gravel here when the level of the waters sank. No,
it bore no likeness to any human being. The bone of the nose was
bare and the mouth laughed without lips at the sky, the eyes torn
out, the rags that stuck to the body so rotten that the decay had
eaten its way into the bones; and then of course beasts of prey had
been busy on it, so that all together it was rather a gruesome sight.
The man touched it once or twice with his stick, told the dog to
shut up, and mumbled: "As one sows, so does one reap." He took
a good pinch of snuff. The bitch went on barking.

"Yes, you can cut out the cackle for all the good it will do," he
said. "You don't understand these things. Some folks want to lay
the blame on Kolumkilli, but it's more likely that each of us bears
his destination in his own heart."

Nevertheless he found it difficult to absolve Kolumkilli of all
intervention in human fate, for it often happens that though one
is quite certain that the story of Kolumkilli is not true, or even
that it is a downright lie, there are times when this same story
seems to hold more truth than any truth. There is some devil or
other on the moors who eats people. Ah well, he would have to do
something for the body, seeing that he had found it, and that as
quickly as possible, for the ewes had taken to their heels and were
out of the gully by now. He was wearing a pair of thick, heavy
gloves that were practically new, and he took the glove from his
right hand and threw it to the corpse, for it is considered discour-
teous to leave a corpse that one has found without first doing it
some small service. A few seconds later he was standing on the
brink of the gully: it was as he had thought, the ewes were in full
flight. The leaders showed against the sky as they raced across the
top of a distant roll in the moors; they were heading for the Bluefells. He ran off in pursuit, happy to own such ewes as these,
which yearned like ascetics for the solitude of the endless wilderness early in the spring.

"Hallbera," he said that evening, throwing her a glove, "knit
me a glove to match that odd one."

"Hullo, where's the other?" asked the old woman, for she had
never known the crofter to lose a glove.

"Oh, we won't bother our heads about that, old girl."

"No?" she said, tilting her dithering head up and away from
him, as was her custom when she looked at anyone; and had no
need to ask any further questions, had no need to ask.

55. THE BIG SISTER

THEN there came great rainstorms that seemed to fill the whole world, and a hundred seasonal rills, rushing down the sides of the mountain, washed winter's snow away to the sea. When next the sun was seen, there was no snow in the valley, the hills green, buttercups in the home-field, blissful breezes. The brook in the home-field had swelled to full spate and dwindled again without the crofter's youngest son having noticed it. Only one year had passed, and he was standing no longer by the home brook. He was standing in the enclosure with his rake, spreading manure in perfect aimlessness, like an idiot, he to whom the elves had promised better lands in a dream. The lands that his winter's books had brought so near to him had drifted away with the spring and vanished over horizons even more remote than before. He had only to look at Asta Sollilja to realize how inaccessible were the countries that once had mirrored themselves in the skies because of the white landlessness of winter. Yet the soul refuses to give up the struggle. Spring, its birds from beyond the blue mountains, its breezes, its sky — spring called and called. Each time that he came out of the low door and halted on the paving it called to him. And went on calling. He listened. The melancholy longing, the sad sympathy with life, awoke in his breast. He had listened to her silence all through the spring, ever since the teacher left at Easter-time. But he had not known that she wept, until one day. It was a Sunday. From where he was standing in the home-field he saw her lying in a green hollow. He went to her. She did not move, for she did not hear his approach. But when he came up to her he saw that her shoulders were shaking. She was weeping, her face buried in the grass. He was well aware that though she was their big sister she was really a more insignificant being than he and his brother, and he was struck with immediate pity. He himself wept more and more seldom now, he had hardly wept at all since last summer, he would soon be a big boy. Finally he spoke her name. She gave a start and, sitting up, wiped her tears away with the hem of her dress. But the only result was that the tears flowed faster and faster.

"What are you crying for?" he asked.

"Nothing," she replied with a sniff.

"Have you lost anything?" he said.

"Yes," she said.

"What?"

"Nothing."

"You mustn't cry," he said.

"I'm not crying," she replied, and went on crying.

"Has Father been nasty to you?"

"Yes."

"What did he say?"

"Nothing."

"Did he hit you?"

"Yes, once. A long time ago. But it's such a long time ago. It didn't matter. I've forgotten all about it. No, he didn't hit me at all."

"Is it something you want badly?" he asked.

And she replied almost greedily, gasping for breath: "Yes" — and burst into a storm of weeping.

"What?" he asked.

"I don't know," she wept in despair.

"You needn't be afraid of telling me, Sola dear. Maybe I can get it for you when I grow up."

"You wouldn't understand. You're so little. No one understands. I don't even understand it myself — day and night."

"Is it because of the way you're made?" he asked, full of sympathy and conscious that the discussion was verging now upon the most intimate secrets of the human body, which it is otherwise customary never to mention — possibly it was wrong of him, but the words had slipped his tongue before he realized.

"Yes," she sighed after a little reflection, disconsolately.

"It doesn't matter, Sola dear," he whispered then, and patted her cheek, determined to console her. "There's no one need find out. I won't tell anyone. I shall ask Gvendur not to tell anyone."

"So you know, then?" she asked, taking the cloth away from her eyes and looking him straight in the eyes " — you know?"

"No, Sola dear, I know nothing. I've never had a look; it doesn't matter. And anyway nobody can help it. And when I'm a big man, maybe I'll build a house in another country and then you can come and live with me and eat potatoes — "

"Potatoes? What do I want with potatoes?"

"Like it says in the Bible stories," he explained.

"There aren't any potatoes in the Bible stories."

"I mean what the woman ate in the Bible stories," he said.

"I don't want anything in the Bible stories," she said, gazing into space with tear-swollen eyes. "God is an enemy of the soul."

Then suddenly he asked: "What did you wish for in the winter, Sola, when the teacher gave us all a wish?"

First she looked at him searchingly, and the squint in her eyes seemed more pronounced than ever, because of her weeping; then her lids fell and she began uprooting grass from the sward. "You mustn't tell anyone," she said.

"No, I shall never tell anyone. What was it, then?"

"It was love," she said, and then once more her weeping burst its bonds, and again and again she repeated from the midst of her sobbing: "Love, love, love."

"How do you mean?" he asked.

She threw herself in a heap on the ground again, her shoulders shaking with sobs as they had done when he came up to her a few moments ago, and she wailed:

"I wish I could die. Die. Die."

He did not know what to say in the face of such sorrow. He sat in silence by his sister's side in the spring verdure, which was too young; and the hidden strings in his breast began to quiver, and to sound.

This was the first time that he had ever looked into the labyrinth of the human soul. He was very far from understanding what he saw. But what was of more value, he felt and suffered with her. In years that were yet to come he relived this memory in song, in the most beautiful song the world has known. For the understanding of the soul's defencelessness, of the conflict between the two poles, is not the source of the greatest song. The source of the greatest song is sympathy. Sympathy with Asta Sollilja on earth.

56. THE BOY AND THE COUNTRIES

THE MOST remarkable thing about man's dreams is that they all come true; this has always been the case, though no one would care to admit it. And a peculiarity of man's behaviour is that he is not in the least surprised when his dreams do come true; it is as if he had always expected nothing else. The goal to be reached and the determination to reach it are brother and sister, and slumber both in the same heart.

It happened on the day before Ascension Day. At this part
of the year a good number of people wend their way through the
valley, though very few ever leave the main road and pay a visit
to the croft. But on this day a man left the main road and paid
a visit to the croft. In no respect was he a noteworthy person.
There was nothing at all individual about his appearance, and
probably nothing very indispensable about the function he performed in life; at least there was nothing that one could point to
definitely and say: "This is his function"; unless it was to deliver
this one letter. In later years, when Jon Gudbjartsson tried to
call him back to memory, he always refused to show himself.
He was, in other words, just like a hundred other natural objects
that one does not notice because they are so natural. He simply
handed Bjartur of Summerhouses this one small letter, said good-
bye, and left.

Now, it was something rare and almost unique for Bjartur of
Summerhouses to receive a letter, with the exception of tax-
bills, for independent men do not receive letters; such things
are for those who rely on others rather than on themselves. He
read the address twice aloud, turned the letter in various directions, studied it back and front. Both the boys stole nearer to
their father as he opened it. He held it a short distance away
from him, slightly to one side, knitted his brows, tilted his head
back. It was impossible to read in his face what the contents
might be. Then he read it again. He scratched his head carefully and it grew even more difficut to guess what the letter was
about. Finally he read it a third time, stuck it in his pocket, went
his way. No one knew what news it might contain.

A bright evening with feathery clouds over the green marshes;
and the song-birds of life so happy that there was no lull in their
song after sunset; yes, how spring was welling up in everything
and flooding farther and farther afield with every day, every
evening! And once again Bjartur was going down the valley, to
look for a sheep that was due today, and though it was bedtime
he called to his youngest son.

Gvendur: "I'll come with you, Father, so that little Nonni can
go to bed."

The father: "I said that little Jon was to come with me. You
go to bed. I shall remember to wake you so much the sooner in
the morning."

The father set off over the marshes with long strides, the boy

skipping along behind him, jumping from tussock to tussock.
They went down to the flats along by the river; the slender mouse-
vetch had grown to a good length, the butterwort had pushed
its way up with its blue bells, and there were water-avens as well.
The ducks resting peacefully on the river's grey, unruffled pools
had finished building their nests. The garrulous redshank followed the crofter, cheerfully prattling his long and marvellous
story; though when one listens to it one feels sometimes that there
is too little matter in a story so long, only hee, hee, hee, for a
thousand years. But one fine day, perhaps in a far-off continent,
this story returns to one's mind and one discovers that it was more
beautiful and more charming than most other stories, and possibly
the most interesting story in the world; and one hopes that one
may be allowed to hear it after one's death also, that one may wander about the marshes of a night, the night before Ascension Day
after one's death, and listen to this incredible story; yes, this story
and no other. They found the sheep on the flats and she had
lambed. Splendid. Bjartur caught the lamb and marked it. The
ewe came nearer and he took hold of her and felt at her udders
to see if she was giving milk, and she was giving milk. Yes, tomorrow is Ascension Day and little Sola is going over to the
homesteads to attend at the minister's for a week; she is to be
confirmed on Whit Sunday. "Probably there will be a shower
about sunrise, do the grass a lot of good." Seating himself on a
clump of heather near the river, he gazed at the smoothness of
its flow as it ran past him; at two ducks under the opposite bank;
at two phalaropes swimming to and fro, bobbing curtsies. The
boy too sat down and gazed at them; everything was so mild, so
unassuming; it was as if the marshes wanted to make amends
for everything. This moorland valley could change its face and
show itself in any mood. Thus did the moors take leave of their
darling, who was greater than all other Icelanders; they were
taking leave of him for the last time.

"Well, Jon," said the father. He had suddenly started calling
him Jon. He did not look at him, rather at the river flowing past.
"I believe there was something I was wanting to say to you before
we went back home."

Silence.

"There's a woman down in Fjord," he continued. "I don't
know her at all, but now that I come to think of it I've heard
her mentioned once or twice. They say she's some relation of

the Sheriff's, but that's no concern of mine. Anyway, she doesn't live here, she lives in the Western World, which some people call America; it's another continent."

"I know that," said the boy.

"Oh, you know that, do you?" said the father.

"I've learned about it," replied the boy.

"Yes, of course," said the father. "But don't for heaven's sake get it into your head that you should believe all you learn. It may be true, as most people say, that there are better pastures there than in this country, but when they come along and tell you that the sheep there can be left out to graze all through the winter, then you know of course that it's nothing but a lie, like, for instance, so much they tell you about the feeding of cattle in America. But there's supposed to be a lot of trades carried on there, and some of them seem very suitable for youngsters who would like to be independent people."

"Yes," said the boy. "And there's a river there."

"A river? Yes, there are rivers in lots of places."

"And cities."

"Pshaw! These cities; you mustn't believe all that they tell you about cities. However, this woman has been asked to take you with her to America. I understand that your uncle's sent the money and that he wants you to stay with him so that you can learn some suitable trade. She sails on Saturday morning. Your mother had always thought of making something of you, so maybe you had better go."

The boy said nothing.

"I'll take you down to Fjord tomorrow evening, then," went on his father, "though only if you yourself want to go."

Silence.

"Do you want to go?"

"Yes," said the boy, and burst into tears.

"Right," said his father, preparing to rise. "It's all settled, then. I asked you simply because I consider that a man should make up his mind himself and follow none but his own behests."

Then he stood up, adding as he did so:

"It's a useful habit never to believe more than half of what people tell you, and not to concern yourself with the rest. Rather keep your mind free and your path your own."

When father and son came home, everyone was in bed and asleep. Little Nonni undressed in silence and lay down beside his grandmother. In the air there still floated the sound of birds singing down in the marshes. Or was it perhaps the echo of the marsh's bird-song lingering in his soul and unwilling to be silent for the brief space of this tranquil spring night? It was a sound that was never afterwards to forsake his soul, however far he travelled and however resplendent the halls in which he was later received — the marsh with its Icelandic birds, one short spring night.

Yes, thus gently, thus demurely, did spring dawn over its moors after their winter. And before him there lay new lands which rise from the ocean like young maidens and bathe their precious shells and thousand-coloured corals in the summer's first light; or old lands with fragrant forests, sun-white cities that open their arms on green waveless oceans; the rustling groves of California, the sun-gilded palm-avenues of the Mediterranean; the Mississippi and its banks where the hart and the panther lay hid in the shelter of the woods. And he himself, he was to sing for the whole world.

Then surely he was happy, surely he was filled with great bliss as he lay under the tiny window at the foot of his grandmother's bed, with all the boundless expanse of the world open before him? — The boundless expanse to which he had been born. No, there was calm in his soul, the calm of the spring night and its tranquillity. Except that he could not sleep. He felt that never more would he wish to sleep, felt as if the whole of life would henceforth be one lingering spring night — after all the incredible storms that, young as he was, lay behind him. Gone were the days when he had been told that there were no countries behind the mountain, gone the nights when pots and pans had made speeches on the shelves and in the cupboards in order to banish the boredom of life and the horror of emptiness; and the snores, those alien journeys over tilted planes, immeasurable time — what journeys? It was he, he himself who was about to make a journey.

No, he could not bear the thought of closing his eyes, rather lay staring up at the roof, at the knot in the wood which he had once dubbed a man, even though he had only one eye. He had gone further and made this knot into his kinsman, and now this kinsman of his had sent him some money — in such a fashion did everything come true. Everything that one has ever created achieves reality. And soon the day dawns when one finds oneself at the mercy of the reality that one has created; and mourns the days when one's life was almost void of reality, almost a nullity; idle, inoffensive fancies spun round a knot in a roof. His eye had

already, this first night, become a mourning eye. Mother, he
thought, and recalled her who was nobler than the world; recalled
the sighs that had planted sorrow in his breast, that sorrow which
henceforth was to follow him all his life, colouring his every song.
No, though in the woods of better lands, the hour would never
come when he would forget her, or those days when the heath
and the heavens were one. And it never did come. He felt he was
looking back over an incredible life, back over oceans and
countries, over years and seasons, and seeing once more before
him this little room where he had listened to her groans in the
darkness of the night and had asked: Is she asleep or awake? In
the woods of better lands it would be this little room —

"Well, child," said his grandmother the following day as she
sat with idle hands, a rare thing for her, and gazed at him with
eyes almost closed, her head half-turned away from him, and a
finger between her gums, "it's marvellous the things one lives
to see."

The afternoon sun shone in through the window and the ray
fell vibrant with motes on the floor. Asta Sollilja was sitting by
the window mending Nonni's clothes before she left for Rauthsmyri; he had no Sunday clothes. But he had a new pair of stockings and a new pair of gloves that his grandmother had knitted,
and Sola had made him some new sheepskin shoes to go to
America with. Then suddenly he remembered that he had once
intended, as a pastime, to count the wrinkles in his grandmother's
face. But now he found that he no longer desired to count them.
He was going away without having counted them; but they
remained in close keeping somewhere in his soul, all of them,
each and every one. He stood by her bed for the last time, gazing
mutely round him. He looked at the clinker-roof that had sagged
between the rafters and was growing rotten at the joints; at the
two knives wrapped in linen; the beds with their torn blankets
of natural colour, their woodwork that glistened with fifteen
years' human friction; at the floor, indifferently clean, that gave
under the weight of one's foot; the front window with one pane
broken and the other whole; the straws on the ledge outside
unnnaturally long, a corner of the marsh, a glittering loop of the
river; at the family's little range, where during all these years the
fire of home had burned, and standing on it an ill-washed pan
containing the cold remains of some porridge — the pan that he
knew so well. — And Asta Sollilja. He had talked with her up in
a grassy hollow, but he dared not talk with her again. Poor big

sister, she had made the acquaintance of love and therefore she longed to die. Yes, love; love was dreadful, and he shuddered at the thought of leaving her solitary, solitary in love, but there was nothing he could do to help her. He had had a letter as to his destiny, but there had been no letter for her. Her mother had died before she could give her a wish, the only cradle-gifts she had ever received were the wishes of one wormy bitch; and during the winter, at wishing-time, she had asked for love, which was surely the most dreadful of all things in existence; Asta Sollilja, I must go, in love no one can help anyone else; no one but oneself alone; now you are going to Rauthsmyri to attend at the minister's and be confirmed, but I have been sent a letter.

Then the old woman dug her hand under her pillow and withdrew a little bundle. It was made up of useless old rags, both woven and knitted, which were wrapped tightly one round another. Numb-fingered and with trembling hands she proceeded to unwind them.

"Are you there still, urchin?" she asked finally when she had reached the heart of this mystery.

"Yes, Grandmother," said the boy.

And what should it turn out to be but those two treasures of hers, the only things of value that she possessed: the kerchief and the ear-pick. She was going to give him these treasures at parting, he who had slept in the corner there beside her ever since he was in diapers. She could do no more.

"Oh, it's not much of a gift to offer anybody," she said. "But you could wrap this cloth round your neck on festival days when the weather's good. And this ear-pick, they say it's been in the family a long time."

She did not recite any hymns, did not mention Jesus or Kuria, did not warn him against sin. Neither did she ask to be remembered to her sons in America — she had never been able to sense ties of kinship that stretched farther than Methalland in the south. Nor did she ever on any occasion ask about little Nonni when he had gone.

"There are two things I want to ask you to remember when you've gone," she said, the wrinkled old face trembling much more than usual. "I want to ask you never to be insolent to those who hold a lowly position in the world. And never to ill-treat any animal."

"Say thank-you to your grandmother, Nonni," said Asta Sollilja. "She's given you the only thing she has."

And he put his hand in hers and thanked her in silence, for he knew no words that could express his gratitude for such a gift; she was giving him the nation's poorest Christmas to cheer him on his way when he went out into the world, and he knew that henceforth she would no longer celebrate Christmas.

57.   MADAM OF MYRI SUFFERS DEFEAT

On the Saturday before Whitsun Asta Sollilja returned from Rauthsmyri; let us hope she had learned her Christianity, for she was to be confirmed on the morrow. But why had she come home today? Had not Bjartur arranged for a woman up-country to make her a dress and had he not paid for it in advance? Surely it had been decided that the girl was to return only when the confirmation ceremony was over, on Whit Sunday evening? What of it: she came home on the Saturday before Whitsun, late in the afternoon. It happened in this way:

Through the marshes, in a skirt that could have held half the parish, there came a woman riding a smart roan that picked its way daintily between the patches of bog. No, it was no lumbering old draught-horse, it was Rauthsmyri-Sorli with his spirited hoofs and his arched neck. Jumping from tussock to tussock behind them came Asta Sollilja, with downcast head and eyes looking neither to right nor to left, only one step at a time. She was crying.

Bjartur, lavish as ever in his hospitality, marched down the enclosure and out into the marshes, where he gave them a royal welcome. He grasped the reins near to the horse's head and threaded the driest path home to the enclosure, turning every now and then to throw some waggish remark at Madam, a white raven is a rare sight in these parts and so forth, then lifted her down when they reached the paving. "She gets more and more like herself every day, bless her," he said, for she was fat and dignified and just like the Pope. "Gvendur my boy, allow Madam's roan to graze at the bottom of my home-field while she is waiting for coffee. And upstairs immediately, Sola dear, and see if there's a spark of life left in the fire, though I'm afraid we haven't troubled it much since you left, we boiled a bit of fish on Sunday to last us the whole week. But what's all this, child? You look frightfully sad and dreary to say that you're in the company of Iceland's poetess."

She gave her father no answer, but stooping to avoid the lintel of home, disappeared inside, heart-broken. On the pavement there remained Bjartur and the Bailiff's wife, to expatiate on the poetry and the economics of the Icelandic spring which they both saw in the valley, each in his own fashion.

"The old man will be pretty well on with his lambing by now, I suppose?" asked Bjartur. "Yes, I thought so. And the sheep in fairly good condition for a bungler like him? Yes, quite so; it's nothing fresh for him to lose more than a few, poor chap; but fortunately he's got plenty to go at. And the grass fair to middling? Yes, it has a habit of growing here too. And very few foxes and suchlike vermin about this spring? Fine. Same here. Nothing for them to batten on here, no dead sheep at this address. Can't even say I've seen a black-backed gull, let alone a fox; though come to think of it I did hear a raven one day up in the gully there. And worms less rampant than usual with the old man? Tut, tut, what a pity. Why, there's not a sign of a worm here, not even an ordinary belly-worm, and the lambing has gone beautifully and ought to be finished with today if old Kapa is as punctual as ever. She's an old ewe of mine that I'm particularly fond of. She's due today, bless her, and as she's on the heavier side I was thinking of going down to the moors in the south there to see how she's getting on with it. A few words with me? Eh? What the devil do you think we're doing now if we aren't having a few words with each other? Behind the house? In towards the mountain? This is something fresh all right. It's not the first time her ladyship offered to dodge behind a bush with me, even though one's technique may have been growing a little rusty of late."

But Madam was in no mood for joking, and gathering up a handful of her skirt so as not to tread on the hem, she led the way round the corner and along the brook towards the mountain. She proposed that they should each sit on one of the little mounds by the brook.

"Listen, my high-born heroine, I always understood it was my privilege, and not yours, to offer people a seat on my own property," he said with continued facetiousness; but this pleasantry was received just as stiffly as the others. They sat down. Soulfully and artistically she stroked the grass on the mound, smoothing it backward and forward with her eloquent, ladylike hand, small and fat, and dimpled in the knuckles — but what little plot was the old hen hatching out now; surely she wasn't going to try and swindle the croft out of him? and surely the question of breaking up the home was no longer on the agenda now? Who could figure out their little manœuvres? So he took some snuff. "May I offer her ladyship a pinch of snuff while she's getting her breath back?" he asked. But Madam did not like snuff; or jokes either.

"Bjartur," she said at length, "I don't know whether you noticed that your daughter's expression was scarcely radiant with girlish happiness when she came home a few minutes ago."

"Maybe she thought it funny that you didn't stick an old mare under her backside for the journey," suggested Bjartur. "But perhaps they were all at work carrying peat, except for the saddle-horses. Not that it matters. I and my people have always walked on our own feet."

"Well, as a matter of fact, a horse had been brought in for her, but she declined it. The poor child has a mind of her own. She inherits her stubbornness from you."

"Maybe they couldn't drive their Christianity into her," said Bjartur. "It would be like that fool of a minister to go and say something to her. She isn't used to having people say much to her. At home here there's always peace and quiet, you see. And as for religion itself, I can't say that I've ever done much to encourage her in suchlike studies, as, if the truth be told, I've always felt that all this Christianity was really rather a nuisance in the community, though the late Reverend Gudmundur was of course a great expert with sheep. But I dare bet that though she may not have a particularly good head for religion, our Sola is just as quick on the uptake as any youngster who was ever confirmed at the proper time. And I'd like to see the youngster of her age who is as strong as she is in the classics. And though most of these little chits dissolve in tears as soon as you find fault with them, that's no reason why it should have any really serious after-effects."

"No," said the poetess. "It isn't her religious knowledge that's at fault. More's the pity, as I almost feel like saying."

She went on stroking the grass on the man's mound with those artistic movements of hers, full of deep thought. Then Bjartur said:

"I don't know whether I told you that it's an old ewe that's pegged along with me through thick and thin; she was sired by one of the late Reverend Gudmundur's rams. She seems to be so remarkably heavy in the rear this time, and yet there's no fat on her ribs. I'm half afraid that if it's twins she's carrying, it will

take her all her time to bear them, so I was thinking of taking a
walk down the valley before nightfall, because her time is almost
upon her."

"Yes, Bjartur," said the woman. "I won't delay you much
longer now."

Then came the story. "It all began when Gudny, who, for
reasons of her own, has always considered that she has some
small share in little Asta Sollilja, decided that she would like to
have her sleeping with her for the few nights that she was staying
at Rauthsmyri with us. Well, she noticed on the very first evening
that there was some gloom darkening the child's spirits. Something seemed to be preying on her mind; in fact, she was so worried
that it took her all her time to give a sensible answer when anyone
addressed her. And when they were in bed Gudny began to notice
that she wept into her pillow. Sometimes she wept far into the
night."

Here the Bailiff's wife paused for a moment, but went on
blessing the grass with her artistic fingers. She was nevertheless
much affected; but she had to breathe. She had the sort of breathing that is characteristic of fat people.

"Well?" said Bjartur at length, for he did not know how to
appreciate artistic silences. "Is it any novelty if the tears are
always on tap with these young people, particularly if they happen
to be of the female sort? — it's just as I've said time and time
again to the bitch and my wives: the female sex is even more
pitiable than the human sex."

"For the first two or three nights the girl refused to tell what
was weighing on her mind."

"Yes," said Bjartur, "why should people who've been reared
on independence describe what goes on in their minds? The mind
is just like a weathercock. And just as apt to box the compass
every five minutes.

"She was so lost during the daytime that we thought at first
that she was unhappy in her new surroundings and could not
stand the company of other people. She couldn't be persuaded
to join in games with the other children." (Bjartur: "Yes, she
probably had more sense than to wear her shoes out with all
this fat-headed hopping and skipping.") "Then in the mornings
Gudny began to notice that the girl was by no means well. She
was miserable and listless; and sick while she was dressing."
(Bjartur: "The horse-meat can't have agreed with her.") "If we
offer our guests horse-meat to eat, Bjartur, it's the first I've heard

of it. The children actually had had a lovely ragout the evening before, and the housekeeper thought that perhaps she had over-eaten, for at times she had seemed strangely ravenous with her food. But when this was repeated morning after morning, Gudny could not help thinking it rather suspicious, and she began to pay more attention to the shape of the girl's figure when they were going to bed nights. It had struck her at once that the girl was pretty well-developed for her age, her figure is almost that of a grown woman; and then in addition, as we had all noticed immediately, though without giving it much thought, she has grown quite unnaturally big round the waist for a girl who is otherwise so very slim. So last night Gudny asked her whether she could examine her a little, saying that she thought she might have something wrong with her stomach. And then of course the housekeeper soon saw what was the matter; and she accused her of it. At first the child would admit nothing. It was then that the housekeeper called me up. And naturally I saw immediately what was wrong. I told the girl that it was quite useless to try to hide it from us. Finally she owned up. She is pregnant. She is about four months on."

Bjartur looked at the woman with eyes like those of a horse that, hearing some unpleasant clatter behind it, pricks its ears, rears its head, and is on the very point of shying; then he jumped to his feet and took one step backward, incapable at first of finding any suitable form in which to take this news. At length he gave a foolish laugh, out into space, and said: "Pregnant? My Sola? No, you don't pull my leg this time, my dear lady."

"Very well, then; in that case it's the first time I've run round to my neighbours with lies and gossip, Bjartur," said the woman. "And I thought I deserved more of you than to be accused of falsehood. I have always wished you well. All of you. My heart and my home have always stood open to you country folk. I have been the spokeswoman of all that is most noble in rural life. I have looked upon the farmer's work as holy work. And at the same time I have looked upon the farmer's sorrows as my own sorrows, his defeats as my defeats. Never have I lost sight of the fact that the dale-farmer's dogged perseverance is a lever with which to lift the nation to higher things." ("Yes, the Rauthsmyri nation," interrupted Bjartur angrily, "but the Rauthsmyri nation has never been my nation, though I have been crushed under you for thirty years and have been forced to join your co-operative society at last.") "All right, Bjartur, your opinions are your own,

but I can tell you this: that every time the parish council has been
on the point of breaking up your home I have invariably taken
up the cudgels on your behalf and said: 'It is the Icelandic peasant
who has been the life-blood of the nation for a thousand years,
leave my Bjartur alone.' But now it has finally reached a point
where I have to confess that I am beaten. For fifteen years I
have tried to stand up in your defence while the parish sat with
its heart in its mouth; first of all poor Rosa dies in that awful
fashion, then your children die year after year, either at birth or
in their swaddling clothes, and year after year you come with
them on your back to have them buried in our little churchyard;
then your second wife dies last year, and everyone knows what it
was that finished her off, and finally come these strange happenings here during the winter and the loss of your oldest boy. And
yet I never completely withdrew my protecting hand. But now
I can do no more. To run away from all the enormities of the
past winter and send an infamous wretch in your place, a notorious
drunkard and jailbird who is not only a parish pauper with a
horde of children but also rotten with consumption, and this
blackguard is to look after your children, to look after Asta Sollilja,
a full-grown young woman —"

"Now listen here, damn you, that's enough from you, yes, go
to hell, you aren't on your own land here, you're on my land. And
if you've come along here today because of Asta Sollilja, let me
tell you that you've come just fifteen years too bloody late. You
palmed her off on me while she lay in her mother's womb, damn
you, and if she is my child, then it's only because you as good as
abandoned her to die and sold me some ground so that she could
die on any property but your own. Do you think I didn't know
from the very first that it was you Rauthsmyrians who begot the
child that was born in the hut here in the days when I rode the
Devil over Glacier River and could not be killed? And if you
propose to sit there and tell me that you've never lied, I say you
lied at my wedding, when you stood up in the tent at Nithurkot
with a lot of new-fangled fantasy and foreign religion on your
lips after dumping your son's bastard on me to save the Rauthsmyri reputation. And if you've come here to take me to task
because Asta Sollilja is pregnant, then I say that that is something
which has nothing at all to do with me, in the first place because
I haven't made her pregnant, and in the second place because I
am in no way related to her and am therefore not responsible for
her. It is you who are related to her and therefore responsible

for her. You people in Rauthsmyri begot her and then abandoned
her. She has nothing to do with me. And now let me tell you once
and for all that in future you can go to hell with your own
bastards, and can christen them with your own names; and
whether they are pregnant or not pregnant is your business
entirely; henceforward they no longer exist for me."

"Bjartur my friend," said the woman mildly, as she sat uprooting the grass on the man's mound, "we must try to control
our tempers and discuss what has happened like rational human
beings. Actually it had occurred to me while she is expecting she
would be more than welcome to find shelter with us — "

"It's no damned business of mine any longer whether you give
your own children shelter or expose them to die. I know no better
than that I did my duty when you wriggled out of doing yours.
When your own child lay lifeless under the bitch's belly, and you
had abandoned it to die, I took your own child and gave it
shelter, and made it the flower of my life for fifteen years, but
now I say that I have had enough; and if you come along and
threaten to sell me out and drive me from house and home, then
do it if you dare and if you think you have the legal authority for
it. But I order you to go to hell with your children in future, and
leave me in peace with my children, and that's all we have to
say to each other and I'm off down the valley to see whether my
ewe has lambed or not."

With these words the dale-farmer shouldered his skins and
lumbered away, down the brook, southward over the marshes;
and no further word of farewell was spoken. The bitch joined
him. He did not look around. The poetess was left sitting where
she was, disconcerted and at a loss, with the man's ground under
her hand. She stared after him in perplexity: he was like an invincible army. It was she who had suffered defeat.

58.   IT IS I

THE EVENING was far spent when he came home. The return was
a very dengthy business, as he was driving two ewes before him,
a ewe that had lambed and another that was still carrying. The
mother-ewe had had one lamb and her udders were swollen with
milk; the other was old Kapa. She was suspiciously heavy for a
skinny old ewe, and since her udders were practically dry, there
was no prospect of her being able to suckle two. It was a devil

of a job herding them along, damned if they would keep going in
the right direction. The bitch was very impatient and the man
had to keep calling her off, one must not set dogs on them, never
set dogs on ewes in the spring. The mother-ewe bolted off with
her lamb in the opposite direction. When at last he had headed
her off, old Kapa had turned also. So he had to go and fetch Kapa.
The other was not long in seizing the opportunity, and raced off
at full speed, with head in the air, in another direction altogether.
This went on and on, and it was for this reason that the crofter
was so long in returning home. But he got his own way in the
end, for he happened to be more stubborn than both ewes put
together; he had learned too much from sheep in his day to give
in to sheep. The ewes stood at last at the foot of the home-field;
now he would have to get the mother in and milk her. There was
no sign of life in the house, probably they were all in bed, but he
was averse to waking them up and asking for help, and went on
running round the ewe. The ewe ran in endless circles; the man
ran in endless circles also; for a while each party's obstinacy
seemed quite indomitable, but finally the ewe submitted and
suffered herself to be driven into the stalls. The lamb hopped
light-footed about the pavement and the vegetable garden; it
hopped on to the roof and bleated. It sprang down from the roof
and jumped on to the garden wall and bleated. It ran away in
towards the mountain and down along the brook. Gripping the
ewe with her head between his legs, he milked her into a bowl,
and though she floundered about as if in a frenzy, he managed to
get three gills or more from her. When he had released her she
bleated her way to her answering lamb. Old Kapa was grazing
away at the bottom of the home-field, quite contented now. The
night was bright, but by no means mild; showers on the moors,
mists on the mountains. The birds were silent for the space of an
hour except for a loon complaining at long intervals down by the
lake.

When he went inside, he saw something sitting huddled up
on a box in the entry. It did not move. It was a human being
nevertheless. She had changed into her old dress with the holes
in the elbows and was sitting with her hands in her lap, those
mature, woman's hands with their long bones and their peculiar
thumb-knuckles. Her calves were too heavy, her hips too full for
a girl of her age; it was easy to see that she was a grown woman.
She was Madam of Myri's grand-daughter. She did not look up
when he crawled in through the door, did not move the hands in

her lap. Was she sleeping in a heap there with her face in her bosom? Or was she afraid to look up and meet his eyes?

He struck her across the face. She cowered back and thrust one hand against the wall to prevent herself falling, shut her eyes and raised her hand to ward off a further blow, hid her face in the crook of her elbow. But he did not strike her again.

"Take that," he said, "for the shame you have brought upon my land, the land that I have bought. But fortunately there is no drop of my blood in your veins, and therefore I will ask you to rear your bastards in the houses of those who are more nearly related to them than I am."

"Yes, Father," she said, gasping for breath; and standing up with her elbow in front of her face, she shrank away from him towards the door, " -- I'm going."

He went along the entry, climbed the ladder, stepped into the loft, and closed the trapdoor after him.

Yes, it was well that he had struck her and driven her away; his blow had been better than the thought of what was to come; now she knew what lay ahead of her, and what lay behind her. This blow of his had lifted a leaden weight from her heart, it had been a sort of confirmation. She stood on the paving surveying the spring night of life before her, like someone who is about to jump over a perilous ravine to save his life; with pounding heart, to be sure, but without weeping. No, it was not warm, it was very cold. There were showers on the heath, like dark walls that are built here and there and moved about. She looked to the east, but not to the west. Yes, he had beaten the uncertainty and the fear out of her body and her soul, and now she knew how she stood with him; now they both knew how they stood -- and as if by revelation she realized, and felt that she would not have needed him to tell her, that in her veins there flowed no drop of his blood; the blow that he had given her at parting had been a moment of truth in both their lives. Until that moment the life of each of them had been, in its relation to the other's, a false life, a life of lies. She had lived with him in troll's hands, thinking that she was a troll herself. And now all at once she was standing outside his door and was discovering that she was not of the race of trolls. In one short moment she had been freed of this troll. She was only a human being, possibly a princess like Snow White and the other girls in fairy tales, and now she had nothing more to thank him for. Away.

When she had reached the marshes, she realized that she was

wearing thin, worn shoes that were already soaking; and her old dress with the holes in the elbows; and nothing on her head; could such a bedraggled dale-girl really become a princess, as it says in the stories? No, it did not matter though she was wet. She did not look around at the croft. At least she was free, like the Princess, and had set out to find him whom she loved; this was the fairy tale of the dale-girl who had dreamed so much. She belonged to him alone. She would dwell with him all her days. She would never, never leave him. His bright house stood in a meadow by the sea, and she saw the ships coming and going. They, too, would go away on a ship one day. They would go to the lands that lie beyond the seas, for he owned lands there too, lands with sun-gilded palm-avenues. Yes, yes, yes. She would walk all night until early in the morning, and it would not matter if she walked her shoes off her feet; he would give her new shoes. She would not be long in finding his bright house in the meadow by the sea. She would knock on his door before he had risen from his rest, and he would hear that someone was knocking. "Who is there?" he asks. And she answers: "It is I."

Her heart sang with joy as she crossed the marshes, she would never have believed that her steps could still have been so light; she flew, the heart in her breast flew. It flew to meet happiness, freedom, and love. She was the poor girl who would become a princess; no, she belonged to no one but him. Again and again she heard his whispering voice as he asked: "Who is there?" And again and again she answered: "It is I." Light-footed she followed the path that wound its way up to the brow of the heath. She was no longer the dreaming child, newly bathed in the dew of a vague, unreal St. John's Night; no, now she knew who she was; and where she was going. She was the woman in love who, having burned all bridges behind her, resorts now to her beloved. This was reality. This was love and the heath. Henceforth all that came to pass in her life would be true.

Love and the heath; there were still snowdrifts in the deep hollows, and the earth was muddy under the snow. A raw wind blew in her face. Soon her shoes were quite useless, and her feet grew very sore. She felt thirsty and drank from a pool beside a snowdrift, it had a nasty taste. Then she grew hungry. Then tired. Then sleepy. Suddenly she was in the middle of an ice-cold shower; it was sleet; she could not see a yard in front of her, and in a few seconds she was soaked through. She began to feel afraid. For the heath is also frightening. Perhaps it is life

itself. Across her mind there flashed the thought of her brother
Helgi, he who had been lost on the moors and never found. Many
people perish on the heath. Her father could not perish on the
heath — but suddenly she remembered that he was not her father,
but a troll. That was why he could not be afraid either. It was
she who was afraid, she who might perish. Terror banished
hunger and all desire for sleep, and she began to wonder whether
it might not have been wiser, when all was said and done, to throw
her arms round his neck when he struck her and ask for mercy.
She tried to forget her dread and to think of his bright house by
the sea — what house? Was it not a dark hovel standing on a spit
by the sea that he had mentioned, and many starving children?
No, it was most assuredly a bright house in a meadow by the
sea, it must be; his bright house on heaven and earth. Soon the sun
would rise, and she would stand at his door in the rays of the
morning sun, and there would be ships on the sea, and he would
call out and ask: "Who is there?" But at that very moment she
saw far in the distance the glint of the heath's little tarn. The
shower was passing over, and that must be the lake of unpleasant
dreams; oh, why should one have to dream of such a dismal lake
when one was miserable and unhappy, instead of dreaming of
the ocean itself? So this was all the distance she had covered,
this lonely, sore-footed wanderer of hope, and there were miles
upon miles to cover yet, and she drank more water from a pool and
stood up with difficulty, and then she hears the voice of her beloved as he calls to her from within his bright house and asks.
He asks: "Who is there?" And she answers for the thousandth
time and says: "It is I."

Bjartur of Summerhouses did not take his clothes off that
night, but went out at intervals of an hour to see to the two
ewes that he had left in the home-field the evening before. At
one o'clock old Kapa had lain down and was chewing the cud,
but the other hoyden had made off up the mountainside and was
now right under the crags. She had lain down, however, and her
lamb was lying beside her. There was calm over everything; the
first morning birds had begun their song, but most of them were
still silent.

Yes, it was just as he had thought, old Kapa had been on the
heavier side. Early in the morning she dropped three lambs, and
these poor mites were now struggling to rise to their feet and
get at her udders while she stood and licked them at the bottom
of the home-field. It is pretty good work for an old ewe to have

triplets; she had lived through many things with Bjartur, this old sheep, weathering worms and famine and ghosts, and now she had duly delivered her three lambs into the world as if nothing had ever happened. He thanked his lucky stars that he had allowed her to profit from her qualities as a leader and had not slaughtered her last autumn. Thus did she show her gratitude, poor creature. Triplets made a lot of difference when one's stock was so depleted. But there was very little in her udders, poor brute, she had grown so old. He warmed up the milk that he had kept from the previous evening and carried the lambs under his arm home to the paving. The ewe followed, bleating anxiously, for animals are mistrustful of man, even when he wishes them well. He sat down on the flags with the lambs between his knees and began to spit the milk into them through a quill. Heavens, how tiny their mouths were! Life was not much to boast about, especially when one examined it with a critical eye. The ewe stood on the grass some yards away, watching him suspiciously. She had always been rather a shy creature and had never been dependent on man; she was one of the Reverendgudmundur breed of course. But when she saw what the man was doing she drew nearer and nearer; she fastened upon him her large, intelligent eyes of black and yellow, full of motherly tension. Sympathy has perhaps no alphabet, but it is to be hoped that one day it will be triumphant throughout the whole world. It may be that this was by no means a remarkable heath and by no means a particularly remarkable croft on the heath, but nevertheless incredible things happened occasionally on this heath; the man and the animal understood each other. This was on Whit Sunday morning. The sheep came right up to him where he sat with her lambs in his arms, sniffed affectionately at his hard-featured face, and mewed a little into his beard with her warm breath, as if in gratitude.

PART II

Years of Prosperity

---

59. WHEN FERDINAND WAS
SHOT

THIS so-called World War, perhaps the most bountiful blessing that God has sent our country since the Napoleonic Wars saved the nation from the consequences of the Great Eruption and raised our culture from the ruins with an increased demand for fish and whale-oil, yes, this beautiful war, and may the Almighty grant us another equally beautiful at the earliest possible moment — this war began with the shooting of a scruffy little foreigner, a chap called Ferdinand or something, and the death of this Ferdinand was taken so much to heart by various ill-disposed citizens that they kept on hacking one another to pieces like suet in a trough, for four consecutive years and more. And in the little loft in Summerhouses, where on the occasion of the Shepherd's Meet there had assembled once more all those indomitable warriors who themselves had waged a lifelong unremitting struggle much more serious than any World War, and one that was prosecuted for reasons far weightier than that any Ferdinand should ever have been assassinated, this war was now the theme of debate.

"But don't you think they ought to have been glad to be rid of the bastard?" asked Bjartur.

"I shouldn't care to say," replied Einar of Undirhlith. "They reckon he was the king of some small country or other, whose name I can never remember, but I'm not saying he was any the better man for that. We Icelanders have never had any great respect for kings, except perhaps Fell Kings, for everyone is equal before God; and as long as a farmer can call himself an independent man and no one else's slave, so long can he call himself his own king. But one thing at least is certain about this Ferdinand or whatever you call him: he was always a man, poor fellow. And I don't think it becomes a Christian to use bad language about him. A man is always a man."

"Well, apart from this one fellow and his name, whatever it may have been," said Krusi of Gil, "what I could never understand about this business was why the others had to start squabbling simply because this bastard of a Ferdinand was shot."

"Oh, let them squabble, damn them," said Bjartur. "I only hope they keep it up as long as they can. They aren't half so particular about what they eat now that they're face to face with the realities of life. They'll eat anything now. They'll buy anything from you. Prices are soaring everywhere. Soon they'll be buying the muck from your middens. I only hope they go on blasting one another's brains out as long as other folk can get some good out of it. There ought to be plenty of people abroad. And no one misses them."

"Oh, there are ideals in war too, though they may not be particularly noticeable," said Einar apologetically, for to him Bjartur invariably seemed a thought too forceful in expression, whether in prose or verse. "Bjartur," he added, "you who are an old ballad enthusiast ought to know that there is always an ideal lying behind every war, though that ideal may not loom very large in the eyes of men who have more serious things to think about."

"Ideal?" asked Bjartur, and did not understand the word.

"Well, significance, then," said Einar in explanation.

"Huh, you're the first I've ever heard say that there was any significance behind these wars of theirs nowadays. They're just madmen, pure and simple. It was another matter altogether in the olden days, when your heroes sailed off perhaps to distant quarters of the globe to fight for a peerless woman, or anything else that they considered some sort of flower in their lives. But such is not the case nowadays. Nowadays they fight just from sheer stupidity and obstinacy. But, as I've said before, stupidity is all right as long as other people can turn it to account."

"There may be a good deal in what you say, Bjartur," said the Fell King then, "but I think it behoves us also to examine this war from rather a different point of view. What we have to realize is that such a World War is accompanied not only by great blessings, such as the extra money we farmers now make on all our produce, but also by extensive damage and all sorts of hardship in the countries in which it is being waged, as for instance the other day there when they destroyed that cathedral in France, a magnificent edifice that had stood there for upwards of a hundred years."

"What the hell does it matter to me if they destroy the cathedral in France?" cried Bjartur, spitting contemptuously. "They're more than welcome for me. They could shell Rauthsmyri Church itself and I still wouldn't give a damn."

"Unfortunately it isn't the cathedral alone," said the Fell King. "They say they don't even think twice about blowing whole cities to pieces. Just think, for instance, of the amount of gold and jewels alone that must be destroyed if a large city, London or Paris for instance, is razed to the ground. Think of all those marvellous palaces of theirs. And all the libraries."

"Well, they don't destroy the gold and the jewels for me. And they don't blow up the palaces for me. And as for the libraries, they tell me that both mice and worms have been busy eating up the parish library here for the past ten years. It didn't require a war."

"Then what about all the valuable statues that must be destroyed when a city is shelled?"

"Statues, what the hell are statues? When the devil did you ever see a statue?"

The Fell King was slow to answer, for the truth was that he had never actually seen a real statue; none of them knew precisely what a statue was, save that Madam of Myri had once been heard talking about a statue and Thorir of Gilteig's eldest daughter had bought a little china dog many years before. "Yes, that reminds me, china — "

"Oh, it's all to the good if they start smashing rubbish like china, which is nothing but a rotten fraud and a swindle," said Bjartur, who no longer regretted anything. "I don't see why I should worry if a gang of foreigners have to start drinking out of ordinary bowls or enamelled mugs. I've done it all my life and thrived well on it."

"Now, if I were to give you my opinion," said Thorir of Gilteig, "I should say that this war was being waged principally to give a dissolute rabble the chance to invade other people's countries and rape all the foreign women. I heard from a man who was abroad for some time that these swine of soldiers and generals are the most lecherous beasts that ever crawled on the face of the earth. And some of the stories I have heard about these military whoremongers are such that it would be pointless to repeat them;

no one in Iceland here would believe them. I have three daughters myself, I'm saying no more about it, it isn't my fault the way that things have gone, but I've often thanked my lucky stars lately that at least no Franco-German generals have ever forced their way into the country to practise their abominable manoeuvres on our innocent daughters."

"Oh, they can always get into plenty of trouble without generals," retorted Bjartur. "I should say from my experience of womenfolk that most of them want to be raped, more or less. Maybe they don't like to hear the truth, but I think I'm pretty near the mark, worse luck."

Thorir of Gilteig, however, felt that this was a little too hard on the poor girls, and thought, not without emotion, of the fate of his own three daughters. "If only they could withstand guile as well as they can force," he argued, "many a girl would be in better case."

"Personally I see very little difference between guile and force as long as the object is the same," said Bjartur.

Einar made no contribution to this part of the conversation. His wife and his only daughter were both dead of consumption, so that there had never been any question of guile or force in his household. "But," said he, taking up his own thread again, "I agree with our worthy Fell King in this, that if you look at the war with one eye upon the ideals that lie behind it, and the other on all those thousands of men and women whom it robs of life and limb, then you can't help wondering whether it wouldn't be better to lay more store upon preserving people's lives than upon fulfilling a set of ideals. For if ideals aim not at improving the lot of mankind on earth, but at slaughtering men by the million, one may well ask whether it wouldn't be more praiseworthy to be wholly devoid of ideals, though such a life would naturally be a very empty one. For if ideals are not life, and life is not ideals, what are ideals? And what is life?"

"Well, if they simply must have it that way," said Bjartur, "they've only themselves to blame. Surely anyone who wants war must also be willing to have himself killed. Why can't they have leave to be as idiotic as they please? And since the swine can be bothered to go to the trouble of butchering one another — from imbecility or ideals, it's all the same to me — well, I'll be the last man on earth to grieve for them. To hell with the lot of them. All I say is this: let them continue till doomsday, as long as the meat and the wool keep on rising in price."

"But what happens if there's no one left in the end?" asked Krusi of Gil.

"Why, in that case we simply fit out a boat together, lads, then sail off south to the Continent and see how they are off for pasture-land in those parts; yes, it would be a first-rate chance of discovering whether there are any prospects of good farming down there. It wouldn't half be a joke if Thorir of Gilteig's grandchildren should end up by making dandelion chains on the ruins of London city, after all their damned china rubbish has been smashed to fragments; yes and their statues. And I might even set to and dig myself a vegetable garden on the plain where Paris had been razed to the ground hahaha."

The Fell King: "You may be right in maintaining that the war arose from nothing but sheer stupidity, Bjartur, but personally I'm inclined to agree with Einar when he says that such a statement is an exaggeration of the truth. At least I doubt whether we, both you and I, who enjoy all the blessings of an increasing prosperity because of the war, have the right to call it by such indiscreet names. But, on the other hand, I am convinced that Einar likewise overshoots the mark when he says that the war sprang from some definite ideal. I should like to point out that I am not speaking as a parish councillor in this matter, for the war does not concern the parish council as such. But if I were to give you my own personal private opinion of this war, which in my eyes is only a sort of disagreement, I should say that this disagreement was, like most other disagreements, begotten first and foremost of a misunderstanding. This war, so far as I have been able to discover, is being waged principally between two countries, France and Germany as they are called, though naturally England also plays an important part, especially at sea, where she has a whole host of elegant warships that would be a credit to any country even if they were put to some useful purpose. Now, one day in the summertime, shortly after war broke out, it so happened that I had occasion to visit the District Medical Officer on some small business connected with the animals' physic, and while we were sitting over a cup of coffee he brought out a most interesting foreign book and showed me some pictures of these two countries, France and Germany. I should like to make it clear that I examined the pictures as closely as circumstances allowed. And I came to the conclusion, after minute scrutiny and conscientious comparison of the pictures, that there is no fundamental difference between France and Germany at all, and that they are actually both

the same country, with not even a strait between them, much less
a fjord. Both countries have woods, both countries have mountains, both countries have cornfields, and both countries have
cities. It is at least impossible to see any difference in the landscapes. And as for the inhabitants of these two countries, I am
not afraid to declare that they are neither more stupid nor more
vicious in appearance than any other folk, and certainly no more
stupid-looking in the one country than in the other. To judge
from the pictures, they would appear to be quite ordinary people,
except that whereas the Germans are said to keep their hair close-
cropped, many of the French are supposed to stick to the old
custom of growing beards, much the same as in our own parish
for instance, where some people keep their hair short while others
prefer to grow a beard. The truth, I imagine, is that both the
French and the Germans are just ordinary sort of folk, fellows
of a decent, harmless sort of nature such as we find so many of
around here, for instance. That is why I have arrived privately at
the conviction, and I am fully prepared to maintain it in public if
need be, that the aforesaid disagreement between these men
sprang from a misunderstanding. And that the cause of it is that
each thinks he is better than the other, when as a matter of fact
there is no real difference between them except perhaps some
trifling variation in the manner of wearing the hair. Each maintains that his country is in some way more holy than the other's,
though in strict reality France and Germany are exactly the same
country, and no one in full possession of his faculties can possibly
see any difference between them. But in spite of that, it is always
a serious business to side with one when two are fighting, and the
most sensible course, obviously, is to stay on good terms with
both parties and speak ill of neither. I say for my part that I shall
wait patiently until one or the other wins, and it's no matter to me
which it is, as long as somebody wins, for then there will be a
greater likelihood of the two countries being combined and made
into one country, so that there need rise no future misunderstanding about their being two different countries."

Olafur of Yztadale had never been fond of discussing matters
with the superficial wisdom that merely scratches at the crust
and leaves the kernel undisturbed, for his was the type of mind
that prefers to inquire into a thing's deeper causes, and loves
especially to probe into the utterly incomprehensible and inexplicable aspects of any question. He had been waiting impatiently
for an opening, and when at last the Fell King was silent, he

lifted up his piping voice and crammed on full speed in order to make best use of that short space of time that he knew from past experience was his grudging dole in every conversation.

"When ten million men murder one another in bad will," he said, "I for one don't give a damn whether it's from no reason at all or because of a dirty little cock-sparrow like this chap Ferdinand. It's just as Bjartur says: Why can't they have leave to be as idiotic as they please? Now, one idiot is a curiosity, as everyone knows who has seen an idiot; their jowls stick out beyond their shoulders and they slaver at the mouth. But what is one to say of ten million idiots? Let us imagine that these ten million idiots murder one another, possibly because of a dirty little cock-sparrow, possibly for no reason at all, it's no matter to me. Let us take it mathematically and say that five million of each are killed, for twice five are ten, as everybody knows. Suppose now that all these idiots go to heaven, for even if I believed in hell I would never wish anyone so ill as to send him there. Suppose further that they meet each other in heaven on the same day as they murdered each other on earth — it's no matter to me whether it was out of imbecility, it doesn't affect the question at issue, as I said before, because murder is murder as Einar of Undirhlith says. Now then, here are three questions which I ponder over night and day and which, since this seems a favourable opportunity, I intend to put to you also. In the first place, do they forgive one another in heaven for having murdered one another? it's no matter to me whether it was out of stupidity. In the second place, do they perhaps thank one another in heaven for having murdered one another and thus helped one another on the way to heaven? Or, in the third place, do they go on fighting with undiminished imbecility in heaven, and if so for how long? And if they murder one another afresh, where do they land then? Will there eventually arrive a time when the whole universe will be too small to accommodate people who want to murder one another in stupidity, for no reason and to no purpose to the end of all eternity? I expect I'll be pretty grey at the temples before I get an answer to that, as to so much else."

60.   MATTERS OF FAITH

AND so, to the ever increasing prosperity of the land and its inhabitants, the World War proceeded. For four lucrative years and more it went on, and the longer it lasted, the greater was the gratification it aroused in the hearts of the community. All good men hoped and prayed that it might go on till doomsday. Many, especially those of a nice ingenuous nature, never called it by any other name than the Blessed War, for Icelandic goods were still rising in price abroad, and on the Continent whole nations were fighting, among other things, for the honour of importing them. These gifted but singular belligerents who hitherto had been content to turn a blind eye upon an Iceland racked with famine, slavery, merchants, and every other scourge conceivable, were now of a sudden falling over themselves in the rush to buy our exports and to help us onward and upward along the road to wealth and happiness. Many tenant farmers undertook the task of purchasing from their landlords the land they held, and those who already before the outbreak of hostilities had gone through fire and water to acquire theirs began now to think of renewing their buildings. Those who were in debt were given opportunities of incurring greater debts, while upon those who owed nothing, but who might be likely to require a loan for extensions, the banks smiled with an incredibly seductive sweetness. Folk began to farm on a larger scale, folk increased their livestock, folk even sent their children to be educated. In some houses there were to be seen not one but as many as four china dogs of the larger size, even musical instruments; womenfolk were walking about wearing all sorts of tombac rings, and many persons had acquired overcoats and wellington boots, articles of apparel that had previously been contraband to working people. The government embarked upon a huge program of public works, and those who were fortunate enough to have an energetic idealist like Ingolfur Arnarson as their representative in Parliament were granted roads and bridges throughout their constituency. A highroad was built from Fjord up through Bjartur of Summerhouses' valley all the way to the homesteads around Rauthsmyri, and soon the first automatic carriages were thundering along this road at unbelievable speed, scaring everyone's horses so that they bolted under them.

Now, in this welter of money and joyous prosperity that had burst like a flood upon the country's scattered homesteads, some, it was to be regretted, appeared to have lost their powers of sound judgment, for there was no disguising the fact that holdings were being bought at prices which were ridiculously high, that the passion for building was exceeding the bounds of good sense, and that many children were returning home from school both hurriedly educated and over-educated. There were, however, those

who preserved their sanity, men who took everything with the
greatest calm. Such men made no changes in their mode of living,
neither did they buy china dogs. They spent nothing on the education of their sons, rather increased their stock by steady degrees,
exercised moderation in the improvement of their property, and
kept jogging quietly along towards the higher goals they had set
themselves. One such was Bjartur of Summerhouses. He was no
fonder of needless luxuries now than he had ever been, but with
every year that passed he was spending more and more money on
the hiring of work-people and the buying of sheep. Time was
when he had based his calendar upon the arrival of an old bitch
named Fritha, as grim a misfortune as any that had to do with a
cow, but those days were over now; in less than no time he had
reached two hundred and fifty sheep, two cows, and three horses
and was employing hired labour, male and female, in the summer,
and a housekeeper and a herd in the winter. Furthermore, to house
all these new people he had adapted the old stable under the
living-room, and where once there had been a hole in the wall
as an exit for the dung, there was now a little window with four
panes. Many a little makes a mickle, as the saying goes, and this
was the sure and trusty growth that proceeds without revolution,
without noise, and as if of itself alone, the healthy development.
The man himself remained unaltered. He allowed himself no
greater luxury in his mode of life than that of sprawling on a haycock for four minutes during the daytime, in the hope that he
would soon roll off, preferably into a puddle. Of his work-people
he demanded a suitable degree of exertion in their labours winter
and summer, and he still had the habit of muttering crafty verse
to himself on any occasion when he was alone.

The old woman lived on in her own peculiar fashion, like a
candle the Lord has forgotten to snuff. She mumbled her psalms
and knitted, never noticing the existence of a new era and refusing
to admit that a carriage-way had been laid through the valley,
or that automobiles could reach the fjord in forty-five and Utirauthsmyri in fifteen minutes. The fact was that she did not believe
there was any way at all, except at most the way of the Lord.
And there's a world war on too, cried folk joyfully. But she said
there was no world war; she said that at most it was just the same
old war that had been going on abroad ever since she could remember; world war, what nonsense! This she said because she did
not believe that the world existed. But she still persisted in maintaining that there was a curse over the croft. Sooner or later it

would be fulfilled, and those who lived to see it would know it to their cost; Kolumkilli has rarely allowed anyone who hung on to this hut to escape scot-free. But the sunsets were lovely in Urtharsel, I lived there forty years and nothing ever happened. She was always wanting to get back home.

And now we come to the co-operative society, that flourishing business concern of the farmers' own which renders middlemen superfluous and guarantees the rural producer a fair return for what he has to sell. Before long these societies will have saved the country's peasantry and made all poor farmers into affluent people, as they are said to have done in Denmark. The co-operative society in Fjord flourished, co-operative societies everywhere flourished. The nation's parasites, the merchants, either went completely under or struggled on with heads barely above water; the farmers were taking a firmer and firmer grip on all their own affairs, trade, agriculture, building, even electricity, and the farmers' newspapers in the south said that the foundations were now being laid for large-scale agriculture in Iceland, agriculture of an order fully capable of keeping abreast of the times, agriculture that would be the principal occupation of the people and the cornerstone of the community's freedom. Those who oppose the farmers' interests are the nation's worst enemies. Down with the middlemen. You save twenty-five per cent by dealing with the co-operative societies, the co-operative societies were founded to resist the tyranny of capitalism and to safeguard the interests of the small producer and the common man. But the most important point is still to mention. The co-operative societies aim at a higher ideal than that of mere financial gain. They seek to better mankind itself, to widen man's horizons, educate him, make him kindlier in his dealings with those of inferior status.

In connection with all this, peasant culture had suddenly become the great gospel preached by the newspapers in the south. Everything for the farmers. The peasantry are the life-blood and the backbone of the nation. The mountain valleys are the cradle of all that is most admirable in the race. The countryman walks out to his green meadows in an atmosphere clear and pure, and as he breathes it into his lungs some unknown power streams through his limbs, invigorating body and soul. Townsfolk have no conception of the peace that Mother Nature bestows, and while this peace is yet unfound, the spirit allays its thirst with ephemeral novelties. The shepherd, on the other hand, is filled with the heroic spirit, for the frozen blast hardens him and steels him. Such is the beauty of the rustic life. It is the nation's finest educational institution. And the peasants bear the rural culture on their shoulders. A wise prudence sits enthroned beside them, a perpetual fount of blessing to the land and its people. And nature, yes, the Icelandic scene is beautiful with its hillsides, its dingles, its waterfalls, and its mountains; no wonder that those who dwell in the mountain valleys are the true people, the people of nature, the only true people. Their life is spent in the service of God.

The dignity of the peasant's life and the virtues of his culture had hitherto been only a peculiar sort of gospel that the lady of Rauthsmyri had preached at social gatherings, especially wedding feasts, probably because she so much regretted ever having left the town herself. No one had ever bothered to pay it any particular attention; it had made no more impression and evoked no more response than, for instance, the minister's sermons. But now it was appearing in fine newspapers that were printed in the south and sent to every household in the country, every week it turned up in some form or other. It was as if one met Madam Myri on every page that was published, with a motherly face like the Pope. And people in general began to believe in this gospel, and soon rural culture was in great demand in the country districts; away with the traditional niggardliness, away with the heritage of spectres — Kolumkilli, who can be bothered to listen to such rubbish nowadays? No, the Icelandic crofter had waked from the sleep of centuries. It was even a matter of great doubt whether he had ever slept at all. In less than no time he had formed his own political party in the land, a party whose endeavours were directed against conservatives, egoists, middlemen, and thieves; the party of co-operators, small producers, common people, and progressive reformers, the party of justice and ideals. One of the first who went into Parliament with the express aim of wiping out injustice and fighting for the ideals of the new golden age that was dawning was Ingolfur Arnarson Jonsson; one of those who voted for him was Bjartur of Summerhouses. The credit that stood to his name in the books of the co-operative society was mounting year by year. Then had he begun to believe in Ingolfur Arnarson and the rest of the Rauthsmyrians? Whether he had actually begun to have any real faith in them I cannot say, but this much is certain: that when the State roadmen were building a bridge over the ravine that cuts the ridge, the spring after Ingolfur Arnarson had persuaded the government to build a highroad through the valley and to bridge all the rivers, he took a stroll as far as the ridge one

evening just before the roadmen ceased work, and there entered
into conversation with them. That conversation reflected in some
measure the state of his faith in these times.

The men were driving wedges into the rock and breaking it
off in small blocks, which they then proceeded to dress with their
chisels. The river was being bridged far above the ford, at a place
where it fell into a narrow gully, so that high piers were needed
and a great deal of stone to make them up.

"You're dressing stones, lads," said Bjartur, proud of the benefit
that the State was deriving from the rocks on his property.

"Yes, but we'd rather be undressing the ladies," they replied.

"Now look here, damn you," he said, "do you think I've walked
all this way to swap dirty jokes with you?"

"No, of course not. What's the use of a dirty joke to you, a
weakling who hasn't had the strength to beget a daughter or two
to brighten up the landscape for us?"

"Weakling?" snorted Bjartur. "If you would like to pit your
strength against mine, you'd better practise on something tougher
than that stuff there. It's softer than whey cheese."

"Were you wanting anything?" they inquired.

"It is not yours to ask — on this estate anyway," he said. "It is
mine to ask, yours to answer."

"Hum, quite the little king, isn't he?"

"He who is without debt is as good as any king," replied
Bjartur. "And if I take a man into my employment, I pay him at
rates as good as the government's. But while I remember, I don't
suppose any of you fellows could chisel me a headstone?"

"A headstone?" the men asked gravely, for they had an immense respect for sorrow. "That's really a finer type of work than
we're accustomed to, you know."

"Oh, it needn't be anything particularly fine. All I want is
something more or less in the shape of a headstone, just for the
sake of appearances, something a little thinner at the top than
it is at the bottom, you know."

"That goes without saying," said the men, "but naturally no
one takes on such a job unless it's at overtime rates."

He said he had never had a reputation for cheese-paring, and
least of all in such matters. This they fully understood, the graves
of one's loved ones are holy ground, a man doesn't count his
coppers in such circumstances, they stopped talking filth.

Bargaining then began. Neither party had much experience
of such deals, so progress was slow. For some considerable time

they haggled. There was caution on both sides, even courtesy, especially on the part of the stonemasons; but an agreement was reached eventually. Bjartur emphasized repeatedly that fine work was unnecessary. Did he want an inscription? Yes, an inscription. Ah, that made matters complicated, they were by no means expert in the art of lettering.

"Oh, it needn't be anything very ornamental," said Bjartur. "The initials would do, or the Christian name, together with the name of the person who had the stone raised for her."

"Is it for your wife?" they asked.

"Oh no," replied Bjartur, "not exactly. But it is for a woman, though. A woman whom both I and others have wronged for many a long year — perhaps. A man is often unfair in his judgments, and consequently, perhaps, in his deeds. One is afraid of other men's bread."

"Is she buried in Rauthsmyri?" they asked.

"In Rauthsmyri? Her?" he repeated, greatly offended. And added, proud of his woman: "No, oh no, she was never very fond of the Rauthsmyrians, or their churchyard either. She lies in my land; she lies, let me tell you, a bare stone's throw away along the ridge here, on the brink of the gully."

For a few moments they stared at him in astonishment, uncertain what to make of these tidings, till eventually one of them said: "Surely you don't mean the old ghoul, do you?" and another: "Are you trying to make fun of us, blast you?"

But Bjartur was not making fun of anyone, he had never been particularly fond of fun, he was in sober earnest, and actually it was quite a while since he had conceived the idea of giving poor old Gunnvor a stone. She had lain in his land for centuries, in a dishonoured grave, and she had been the butt of slander and calumny which coupled her name with that of a devil; but now the time had come to make amends and to cleanse her name of all these popish superstitions. He did not, of course, deny the fact that she had been a most luckless woman, but he doubted whether she had been dogged by any worse misfortune than the nation as a whole. He himself had known hard times, but what were they in comparison with the hard times the country had had to suffer in the past, during the Great Famine, for instance, or in the time of the Monopoly, when the devil Kolumkilli had seemed to have a stranglehold on the whole nation? It was quite possible also that the woman had made mistakes, and who hasn't made mistakes? Some people said that she had killed folk, and who hasn't killed folk, if it comes to that? What are folk? Folk are less than the dirt beneath your feet when times are bad. He said he looked upon her as his neighbour on the heath here, and though he had hitherto never espoused her cause, there was a boom in both farming and fishing now, and surely the time had come to make some little amends to a long-misunderstood woman. He had therefore decided to give her a stone and to let bygones be bygones. And what was more, he was willing to lend her his name to bear her company through the centuries, in place of the popish monstrosity that had stuck to her so far; and instructed them to inscribe the stone thus: To Gunnvor from Bjartur.

61.   ADMISSION TICKETS

AND now little Gvendur had grown up.

He was a promising young fellow, not unlike his father in build and carriage, but of a milder disposition, and yet, strangely enough, devoid of any great feeling for poetry or skill in its composition. That, however, was not considered a serious drawback, for by this time poetry had been written about most subjects worthy of a poem, some of it reasonably well, and then again the years of his adolescence had been less noted for poetry than for general prosperity on land and sea and all the manifold blessings of a heaven-sent World War. He was thickset, even a trifle clumsy, had fair hair seldom clipped or combed, and he was ruddy in the face, with eyes that, though good-natured and not over-sharp, were by no means void of resolution; but what is resolution? He was very strong. He was known as the freeholder of Summer-houses' only son, and such a title carried no small dignity in these days, when the price of lambs had risen as high as thirty or forty crowns, or even higher; when there was a cow being kept on the farm, and then another, and their presence was provoking no displays of temper, no sharpening of knives, but was apparently being accepted almost as a natural phenomenon; when, too, the former lone worker had become an employer of labour, of strangers who arrived spring and autumn from near and far and who, though demanding high wages and working only fourteen hours a day, were nevertheless placed much lower in the social scale than the crofter's son. One fine day he would inherit this little kingdom in the valley. From childhood upwards his interests, waking and sleeping, had been centred on the welfare of the farm:

he loved the soil, as people say, though mostly without being conscious of it, and he was ready and willing to fight hardship and adversity, without wanting to overcome them by ideals. He had never asked for any other joy than the joy of knowing that the sheep were breeding with good result in their regular season, and of seeing them weather the winter strong enough to struggle out of the bogs in spring. Possibly that is the true joy. Though the loft might be growing a little distorted in shape, and the floor sagging deeply beneath the foot, he never considered it any special problem. Bjartur thought nothing more natural than that he should have such a son; what did puzzle him was why he shouldn't have had half a dozen of the same type, but why complain? The boy was now seventeen years old and the owner of six sheep, a pair of patent-leather shoes, a blue Sunday suit, and a watch and chain. Very few Icelanders are as rich as that when they are only seventeen. In his case it was the result of keeping on doing something, instead of sitting gabbing a lot of pointless rubbish on the flags outside, or of surrendering oneself to the power of nonsensical dreams, or even ghosts, as his brothers had done. And now of course they were both dead, each in his own fashion, whereas he was alive and the owner of six sheep.

Now, at this time there was a great movement, or dissolution, as some people preferred to call it, making itself felt among the community, and there were not many who could withstand such a movement without being moved, such a dissolution without being dissolved; no, only a few. The principal movement and the main dissolution was taking place in money matters, for human life hangs together with the aid of money, and some people consider that money is the only thing that governs it, either by being none at all or enough, or by being somewhere in between. Men suddenly came to realize that the amount of money that could be owned by any one person at any one time was much greater than had previously been imagined. Those who hitherto had seldom mentioned a higher sum than two crowns in sober earnest were now beginning to talk about crowns by the score, ten-to-twenty-crown men were refusing to discuss anything unless it topped the thousand, and even tearful old invalids who hadn't earned a penny for years were now doing business involving sums reminiscent of nothing so much as the figures in the astronomical poem *Njola*. Thorir of Gilteig managed to buy his croft, and some people said that he paid for it, but all records went by the board when a consumptive philosopher like Olafur of Yztadale could enter upon a contract to purchase his holding, for a sum reported to be in the tens of thousands. Others paid their profits into the savings bank in Fjord. This savings bank was usually linked with the Bailiff of Myri's name, because he had a hundred thousand in it, though this was probably a lie, as no one groaned half so bitterly under the everlasting burden of debt as he did; and in this savings bank the money gave off interest at a phenomenal rate, some people saying that once their deposits were entered in the books, they bred like rats. Among those who had money in this establishment was Bjartur of Summerhouses. His name was a good name in the savings bank and he was allowed interest. In spite of all that had passed, the Rauthsmyrians were now giving him interest. It was as if the whole world had turned upside down.

And now who should be standing on the paving but the Bailiff himself, with a team of three horses as if he thought he had been endowed with a triple backside, and a pair of boots that must surely have been given him in liquidation of a debt; war showers great blessings on high and low alike. He was making some complaint or other about one of his horses having worked a shoe loose. "And by the way," he grumbled, "they've made a hell of a mess of the grazing-marshes with that blasted road of theirs."

"Oh, they're my marshes, you know," replied Bjartur.

The Bailiff: "Your mother-in-law is still living, they tell me."

Bjartur: "Yes, at my cost, not yours. She has never yet eaten other people's bread, though there was a time when you wanted to have her taken away from here and kept at the parish's expense."

"What's happened to her croft?"

"What croft?"

"Her croft. Her own croft. What's happened to it?"

"Oh, I expect it's still sitting on Sandgilsheath the same as ever."

"You're always been a cross-grained swine," said the Bailiff. "The worst I've ever known. Damned if anyone can get a decent word out of you on a lovely day early in the spring."

"One remembers best the things one learned as a child. And I got my education not a hundred miles from someone I know."

"I hear you're thinking of selling this place and flitting away there," said the Bailiff.

"Away where? It's a lie."

"Maybe you're thinking of building yourself a decent house here, then?"

"I'll do as I think fit, in building as in other things."

"I just thought I'd ask you, in case it happened to be true. And even if it didn't, I might possibly have considered making you an offer for these old winter sheep-cotes of mine."

"This place happens to have been called Summerhouses for the last eighteen years, mate," said Bjartur. "But it's not surprising you should have forgotten, it's so long since we had anything to do with each other. And now let me tell you this: it's far more likely that Rauthsmyri will one day be tacked on to Summerhouses' land than that Summerhouses will ever be added to Rauthsmyri."

"Rauthsmyri is yours for the asking," said the Bailiff. "Seventy thousand crowns and you can take it with you."

"I'll buy it when I think fit."

"Then you might just as well sell me back my sheep-cotes while you're thinking the matter over. Ten thousand on the nail."

Bjartur: "Yes, and probably all counterfeit money."

"Fifteen thousand," said the Bailiff.

To this offer Bjartur made no reply other than that of parading slowly round and round the Bailiff while he summed up his ancestry and reputation in a few forceful words, the same as he had done at least a hundred times before. But by this time the horseshoe had been nailed on again and the Bailiff was preparing to mount.

"I said fifteen thousand," said the Bailiff when he had got on horseback. "It isn't certain that I shall repeat such an offer. But if you would rather build, you can please yourself entirely. And if you should need a loan from the savings bank for building-purposes, I certainly shan't stand in your way."

Fifteen thousand crowns — this patch-breeched skinflint who could never part with a penny without turning it three or four times over in his hand, had he said fifteen thousand crowns? Was the man mad? Everyone knew that fifteen thousand in a lump must be counterfeit money, unless one had worked for it oneself, and no one would ever do that — it would serve him right if I rode after him and killed him, like Egill Skallagrimsson, when Skalaglamm left his shield behind at Borg, and sagas were written about him, and the spaces between the writing were all lined with gold and set with precious stones. Why did he have to offer him money, if not for the croft, then on the security of the croft? How was it that the Rauthsmyrians could never leave this dale-farmer in peace? Why were they always making him these bargain offers? No, he was determined to keep his land to the very end, the land that he had

lived on with his sheep, lived for with his sheep, where he had
lived for his sheep. And one fine day, when he was dead, the same
as sheep, his only son would take up the dale-farmer's banner and
would bear the rural culture on his shoulders, and so on and on
into the future for a thousand years to come. And if he built new
buildings, and he was determined to build, all in his own good
time, it would be not at the instigation of the Rauthsmyrians, but
for reasons that concerned himself alone. "Never let them snare
you with money, Gvendur boy, if you live, as I know you will
live, to be the owner of this land. The land — it is on the land that
sheep live; and good sheep, healthy sheep, sheep heavy-fleeced
and in fine condition after the winter, are the foundations of a
man's freedom and repute."

Yes, it was a good man indeed who could stand immovable
as a rock in these times, when everything around him, including
money and views of life, was afloat and swirling in perpetual
change; when the strongest boundary walls between men and
things in time and place were being washed away; when the
impossible was becoming possible and even the wishes of those
who had never dared to make a wish were being fulfilled. Why,
the sheep were being served with bread, just like the Sheriff and
other high officials, and pailfuls of first-class herring were being
stuck in front of uneducated cows — they crunched away at these
delicacies with the most amiable of expressions, laying their ears
back and closing their eyes in dreamy ecstasy. Icelanders were
sailing their ships to America, a thing they had not done for more
than nine hundred years, when Leifur the Lucky found that land
and went and lost it again; yes, verily all this was mighty in power
and far-reaching in scope, and then, right in the midst of this
flood of good fortune that had burst its every sluice and over-
flowed its every channel, at a period when men had got past the
ability to marvel at great events or to be disturbed by sudden
calamities, there arrived for Mr. Gudmundur Gudbjartsson a
letter, which he had to seek and sign for with his own hand at
Rauthsmyri, and he did not dare to open it before he had reached
the top of the ridge again, because the last thing he wanted in all
the world was to let the Rauthsmyrians nose out any secret of his,
and he sat down in a hollow, and the new grass had barely begun
to push its way through the withered grass of winter, for it was
early in May; and he opened the letter. And out of it there fell two
slips of blue paper, with foreign letters on them and a learned
signature with all sorts of ornamental flourishes. On a third slip

were written a few words in a legible hand, signature Nonni, contents thus: "Two hundred dollars, which Uncle is sending you so that you can come to America immediately, the war is over, times are good, you can be anything you like."

Even the most earth-bound man that ever existed was never so earth-bound that he would not go to America. It is said that for the past hundred years the most earth-bound men in the world have gone to America, in large steamships, over a vast ocean. The one thing that hinders the most earth-bound men from forsaking their land is not the land itself, and not man's ties with the land, but the lack of money with which to reach America. Just as Iceland's dalesmen, the core, the flower, the life-blood, and the backbone of the nation, the healthy rural culture in person, had emigrated to America over a period of forty years, inane of expression as the Israelites in the desert, with platters under their arms and coverlets fragrant with puffin down, as if there were neither platters nor bedclothes in America — so, we are told, did the flower of Poland flit to America over a period of from fifty to a hundred years, and still do flit if they get the chance, not with their bedclothes only, but with the wheels from their beloved muck-carts as well, for fear that wheels should still be unknown there. Take for example this lad who was sitting here in the white winter grass of Iceland, Gudmundur Gudbjartsson, seventeen, six sheep, patent-leather shoes, and what not. It would be difficult indeed to imagine anyone whose heart had been so deeply rooted in one little patch of land on the moors, a valley with a home mountain and a lake, a patrimony of limitless descent through the generations, of boundless possibilities in the eyes of his children dreaming in the spring. No one had ever dwelt more happily in the bosom of the Mountain Queen, as they say in poetry. Two slips of blue paper decorated with illegible flourishes, and it was all over and done with. He was quite certain that never again would he hear the singing of Iceland's birds, and already in his mind he had begun to bid farewell to the valley that had created him, the valley that was in reality himself, fully determined to be something else, to be what he wanted in the land where a farmer's stock is measured in cattle, and no one deigns to mention a form of animal life so low as a sheep.

When he returned to the valley, back to Summerhouses, and Heaven above knew that the croft had begun to lean across the landscape at rather a ridiculous angle these days, it was to inform his father that he proposed going to America — two notes, tons of money, the war over, he could be what he liked, a cattle-farmer on a big scale, maybe a joiner like his uncle.

The father stood on the paving, gazing deep in thought over the valley where we will suppose that in spring dreams of the future he had seen his family line grow and flourish. True, he may never have seen any such vision, and may never have had any articulate ideals about his toil or endowed it with any poetical significance, any more than the French and the Germans, who slew a million men for no reason at all or, as some people believe, just for the fun of the thing; but that did not alter this salient fact; which remained certain, and fixed and immutable: one fine day would see him dead and gone to the devil, and who would take over the sheep then? Were two counterfeit pieces of blue paper all that was needed to uproot a healthy young country lad who had a past of a thousand years in the country, and who was, as an individual, in perfect harmony with the land and the people? Did it need nothing more to persuade him, in the few minutes' walk from ridge to croft, to betray the land, the people, and himself in the past, the present, and the future? Yet all he said was this:

"Never trust letters from America, they're always full of swank. And what they say about the feeding of cattle is mostly lies."

"Yes, but I could always be a joiner," said the boy.

The father spat and replied: "I have known many joiners, my lad, but I have yet to meet one who ever got on at all. They go rushing around the countryside from parish to parish, nailing nails for other people. A rolling stone gathers no moss."

The lad maintained a stubborn silence, so after a while his father went on: "I have lost the most of my children now, each in his own way, and never uttered a word. What is gone is gone. But you who knew how to handle sheep — I would have taken a stick to your back had you been a year younger."

"When a fellow has been given as much money as I have," said the lad, "why shouldn't he use it to take a look round in a bigger country?"

"A bigger country? Don't talk such damned nonsense. Summerhouses is as big a country as any, and he who cannot get on in Summerhouses will never get on elsewhere. You will never make good anywhere else. It was another matter altogether with your brother Jon; he was born with the love of travel in his blood, and his heart was set upon other things than sheep. But you, you know sheep as only a few know them, and I will never let you go. It was to you that I had intended leaving the croft. You have always been the most loyal of my children, and though you are only a youngster still, the day may dawn when you will make a good marriage and be able to count yourself among the landed farmers."

The boy answered, word by word, deliberately: "I am seventeen years old. And I am allowed to manage my own affairs. And though I have always been fond of sheep, you know nothing of what I may sometimes have thought to myself, though I may never have thought aloud. I have often thought that if any opportunity ever offered itself, I would seize it, and such, I am sure, is the case with everybody, whether of my age or older. A fellow dare not think anything or hope for anything aloud, so he simply keeps on doing something, and some people just keep on doing something until they are dead. I could hardly believe my eyes when I opened the letter on the ridge, for I have never dared to think anything or hope for anything aloud, though I may perhaps have thought and hoped unconsciously. This may be the only opportunity that will ever come my way in the whole of my life. I am not a fool, but I would be a fool indeed if I did not take this one opportunity of going out into the world and of being something in the world, just the same as those who dared to think aloud."

"Don't talk such utter twaddle," said the father. "What the devil do you think you know about any damned world? What is a world? This is the world, the world is here, Summerhouses, my land, my farm is the world. And though you propose to swallow the sun in a fit of momentary madness because you've seen a couple of blue banknotes from America, which are obviously false the same as any other large sum of money that falls into the hands of the individual unless he has worked for it himself, sooner or later you will find out that Summerhouses is the world and then you will have cause to remember what I have said."

It was with feeling of little warmth that they broke off their conversation.

62.   GRIM ON GUARD

HE made no further attempt to talk his son over; it is a mark of weakness to try to talk anyone over. An independent man thinks only of himself and lets others do as they please. He himself had never allowed anyone to talk him over. But from that day forward his son was gone as far as he was concerned. He no longer spoke to him, not even to give him his orders for the day, but setting to work with the labourer on a deep trench he intended digging in the marshes, he worked like a madman from dawn till dusk. The boy said nothing either, but the impending parting weighed on his mind with a sorrow mingled with apprehension, for the soil ran in his blood, without words, without ideas; and now he felt as if he were about to quit the soil and set off out into the atmosphere, out into the blue. But he could not help it. No one can help it. One is a realist. One has put up with it all ever since childhood; one has had the courage to look it full in the eye, possibly courage enough to look it in the eye all one's life long. Then one day the distances beckon with their floating possibilities, and in one's hands are the admission tickets, two slips of blue paper. One is a realist no longer. One has finished putting up with it all, one no longer has the courage to look it in the eye, one is in the power of beckoning hospitable distances, floating possibilities, perhaps for ever afterwards. Perhaps one's life is over.

"I'm off tomorrow," he said.

No answer.

"Would you like to buy my ewes from me?"

"No, but I'll drown them in a bog for you."

"Very well, in that case I'll make Asta Sollilja a present of them as I pass through Fjord."

"Huh," said the father. "You must have gone mad. You'll be killed."

"There's no war on now, the war's over."

And there the conversation ended.

"Grandma," said the lad, "I'm going tomorrow."

"Oh, not very far, surely," she said.

"I'm going to America."

She laid her needles in her lap and looked at him askant for a little while; then sticking one of her needles under her hood, she scratched herself with the point for a moment or two. "Well, that's shaken all the lice out of my head," she said, then resumed her knitting.

Next morning he rose with all his faculties dull and sluggish, as if he were about to set out into the atmosphere. He took leave of his grandmother with a farewell that had no elements of poetry in it; she did not ask to be remembered to her relations in America. As his father had not offered him a horse, he set off on foot in his blue Sunday suit, with his watch and chain, and his patent-leather shoes wrapped in a handkerchief under his arm, for his luggage had gone on ahead of him. He turned his socks up over his trousers to protect the bottoms. The birds were singing. There were white belts of mist lying here and there on the mountains. Dew in the home-field, the marshes yellowy-brown, green in the drier patches. His father was already at work in the trench and he walked over to say farewell; Bjartur did not go to the trouble of even scrambling out, but said good-bye from the mud down below.

"Father," said the boy shyly as he stood on the bank, "you mustn't think ill of me."

"I'm afraid they'll mishandle you, sonny," he replied. "They kill everyone who has any decency in him. But had you stayed here, you could have been an independent man like me. You are forsaking your own kingdom to be the servant of other men. But it's no use grumbling. I'll just stand here alone, that's all. And I'll stand as long as I stand. You can tell little Nonni that, too. And good luck to you."

Thus did he lose his last child as he stood deep in a ditch at that stage in his career when prosperity and full sovereignty were in sight, after the long struggle for independence that had cost him all his other children. Let those go who wish to go, probably it's all for the best. The strongest man is he who stands alone. A man is born alone. A man dies alone. Then why shouldn't he live alone? Is not the ability to stand alone the perfection of life, the goal? He had taken to his digging again. Then all at once some new thought struck him; throwing down his spade, he swung himself on to the bank; the boy had got a short distance away over the marshes.

"Hey," cried the father, and hurried after him until he caught up with him. "Didn't you say something about Asta Sollilja last night?"

"I was talking about giving her my sheep if you didn't want to buy them."

"Oh, I see," said his father, as if he had not remembered the connection. "Oh well, good-bye then. But remember this: though the war may be over it doesn't alter the fact that they are capable of murdering you out of sheer imbecility. Do you think that men who are mad enough to wage a war for four years will suddenly become models of virtue and intelligence just because they have signed a peace? No, they're madmen all."

His son could think of nothing appropriate with which to answer reasoning so profound.

"By the way," said the father then, still hanging about him, "if you should chance to see Asta Sollilja, you might tell her that I took a trip over the mountains in the south one day early in the spring, and that when I was standing looking at a certain rock, two verses occurred to me. They go like this:

> *Grim on guard where mountains loom*
> *Palely through their hazy shroud,*
> *There rears a rock in frowning gloom,*
> *Black and sullen, scowling, proud.*

> *No lovely blossom in its lee*
> *Seeks that gloom to dissipate.*
> *Its flower is fled. Accursed be*
> *The Norns that rule its fate.*

Do you think you can remember them?"

"I can remember anything I understand," replied the boy. "But what does it all mean? That line about Norns, of instance?"

"That's no concern of yours; they're only a couple of verses about a rock. I don't believe in any Norns and never have. And as proof of that you can say that I've had a headstone erected for old Gunnvor in my name. But that, of course, doesn't prevent me from saying whatever suits me best in poetry."

The boy committed the verses to memory and asked no further questions.

"For the rest," said Bjartur finally, "you can tell her that everything is much the same with me here, except that the loft canted forward a bit a year or two ago, in that winter of hard frost that we had. But that when I build my house, it will be built in such a fashion that it will not cant. And that I shall build it sooner rather than later. But you don't tell her that from me."

And with these words he returned to his work.

63. RE THE LAND OF DREAMS

IN these times it was no longer considered an act of ignominy and shame, comparable to seeking parish relief or being sent to jail and fit only for the scum of society, to go to America; nowadays it bore almost the same dignity as going on a pleasure cruise. Emigrants were no longer referred to as tramps and chronic loafers, or as bad goods gladly exported by the parish councils; no, they were men with money in their pockets and they were going overseas to see their relations and friends, who were high-minded people. Icelanders in America had all at once become high-minded people, as it had been reliably reported that they had lots of money; and it was considered rather praiseworthy to set out in search of these magnanimous plutocrats. Gvendur of Summerhouses, a youth who had never created any stir in Fjord on his previous visits, Gvendur of Summerhouses was in town with money in his pocket, a hundred crowns, a thousand, maybe more, and about to take ship across the Atlantic to see his relations, prosperous gentlefolk. He became immediately a highly respected figure in Fjord, while he waited for the coastal steamer, and the Sheriff gave him coffee when he called about his passport, and even the Sheriff's wife came to take a look at him because he was going to America. A person of great intelligence whom he had never set eyes on before hailed him on the street, invited him in, supplied him with more coffee, and taught him to say yessmonnee-ollright so that he could make a success of life in America. At the offices of the shipping company he was given an hour's lecture on how to comport himself in Reykjavik, whom to meet and what to say and where to pay his passage money, and somebody gave him a cigar to smoke and he was sick down on the beach. Lots of people stopped him on the street and asked him if he was the man. Yes, he was the man. Women appeared at the windows, lifted the curtains, and measured him from top to toe with romantic curiosity because they knew it was he. Children stood behind house corners and yelled after him: "America, America hey!" In this atmosphere of fame two days passed. He bought himself a knife and some cord to take with him to America, for nothing is so essential on a long journey. The ship was due early the following morning, and when he had finished all his preparations he still had the afternoon and evening before him. "I'd better go and see Asta Sollilja now," he thought. He found her at last in service with a boat-owner and his wife; with her was her child of five winters and a summer less, a little girl.

"I christened her Bjort," said Asta Sollilja. "I was so much of a child myself when I had her, it was all I could think of, it wasn't meant to please anybody in particular. She's big for her age and has plenty to eat now, poor kid, and she's cross-eyed like her mammy." She kissed her. She was a tall young woman, long in the leg. She was broad, possibly too broad, over the hips, with shoulders that were slight in comparison, a back that was too round, and a bosom not so high as in the year when she was fifteen. Her eyes were silver-grey under their dark lashes, her complexion pale, and in her mouth the former lines of grace had given way to hardness. One of her front teeth was black with decay, her squint was more pronounced than before, possibly from fatigue, her hands long and heavy-boned, but pleasing in shape, her arms too thin, her neck still white and young, her voice cold and harsh, not bright. She had had her hair cut short and the fringe hung down into her eyes. There was something about her looks and her manner that was at once both strong and weak, attractive and repellent. One could not help taking notice of her; there was not a single feature that was dull in her face, not a moment of muteness in the glance of her eyes, not a movement of her limbs without vital personal expression, and the expression all in contrary sharps and flats, a debasement and a rehabilitation at one and the same time. Her life was one unremitting impassioned torment, so that one could not help wanting to be good to her; and then to push her away; and then to return to her again because one had not understood her — or oneself either, perhaps. Gvendur realized immediately that she was of superior stock, even though she stood there bowed in apprehension over the wet washing, clad in rags, clad perhaps in the shame of a whole nation, of a nation innocent for a thousand years, with a decayed tooth and an illegitimate child, — and marvelled at her in the same way as he and his brothers had always marvelled at her in the old days, when she had been their big sister at home. No, they were not related.

"I'm off to America," he said.

"Poor boy," she said, but without pity, without feeling of any kind.

"I'm certain I can do better for myself over there, even though the prospects are good in Iceland."

She smiled coldly.

"Who sent you to me?" she asked.

"No one," he replied. "I just felt that I had to come along and say good-bye."

"I should have thought you would have been the last of the family to entertain any longings," she said. "I thought you would have been a free man, like Bjartur of Summerhouses."

She said Bjartur of Summerhouses with a cold smile, without hesitation. What she had gained in strength she had lost in sensitiveness.

He stood deep in thought, eyes fixed on the ground for greater

concentration. "There's always someone in the valley there who
rules over you and holds you in his hand," he said at length. "I
don't know who it is. And though Father may be hard, he isn't
free. There's someone even harder than he, someone who stands
over him and holds him in his power."

She looked at him searchingly for a while, as if seeking to
read in his mind how far he was capable of understanding. "You
mean Kolumkilli?" she asked in a tone of cold jocularity. Perhaps
she was just as puzzled by him as he by her.

"No," was his reply. "There is something that never allows
you any peace, something that makes you keep on doing something."

"I should never have known you again for the old Gvendur,"
she said.

"That's because I've got money now," he replied. "You look at
things differently then."

"You'll never be free of him," she said.

"Free of whom?"

"Bjartur of Summerhouses. You can hate him. But he is in
you. You simply hate yourself. He who reviles him reviles himself."

This the boy did not understand. "If a fellow goes abroad," he
said, "and starts a new life in distant countries, surely he ought
to have a good chance of freeing himself?"

She laughed out loud, a mirthless laugh. "I thought that too,"
she said. "It was one night, I left him, he kicked me out, I tramped
all the way over the high heath there, and was barefoot by morning. I too went abroad, to a distant country."

"You — ?"

"Yes," she answered. "I went to my America. Off you go to
yours. And a pleasant journey to you."

"Then do you think, like Father, that I'll never make good out
there?"

"I'm saying nothing about that, Gvendur boy. All I know is
that Bjartur of Summerhouses is in you; as he is in me, even though
we may not be related at all."

"Oh well, it may be quite an advantage, you know," said the
lad then. "Father is the sort of man who never gives in. Only the
other day I heard someone offer him fifteen thousand for the croft,
and he turned it down. Anyone with his hardness in him could
make a great man of himself out in the world — for instance in
America, where a farmer's stock is reckoned in cattle."

"Didn't you say there was somebody harder still than Father, someone who ruled over him and held him in his hand?"

"Well, I did say so in a way, but it wasn't because I believe in Kolumkilli."

"No, and it isn't Kolumkilli either," she said. "It is the power that rules the world, and you can call it what you like, Gvendur boy."

"Is it God?"

"Yes — if it is God that benefits from people slaving like brute beasts all their lives long and never having a chance at all that life has to offer — then it is God all right. And now I am afraid I shall have to leave you, Gvendur, the washing is waiting for me."

"No, listen," he said, without having fathomed this deeper wisdom, "there's something I've got to tell you before I say good-bye, Sola: I was thinking of making you a present of my ewes."

She checked herself in the middle of her first step and looked at him; there was perhaps a trace of unfeigned pity in her eyes, as when people regard an incredibly stupid person who has given himself away in conversation. Then she smiled again.

"Thank you, Gvendur," she said, "but I don't accept gifts, even from Bjartur of Summerhouses' son. You mustn't take it in bad part, it isn't the first time I've refused a gift. Last year when I was starving with my little girl in an unheated cellar along the fjord there, the most influential man in the district came to see me one night in secret and said I was his daughter and offered me a a lot of money; yes, he offered to provide for Bjort and me as long as we lived. 'I would rather see my child die,' said I." Once more she gave her cold laugh, then added: "My little girl and I are independent people also, you see; we also are a sovereign state. Bjort and I love freedom just as much as our namesake does. We would rather be free to die than have to accept anyone's gifts."

It was she who had come down from the high heath early one morning in spring. She had walked all night, a young soul, charged with dreams, with holy dreams, the holiest of dreams; she had been barefoot by morning. She too had had her hopes of America. To leave childhood behind and attain maturity and discretion is to have found America. She crowed over her brother who had not yet reached this world-famous land of helpless dreams; yes, it was one morning, one Whit Sunday morning. New lands rise from the ocean, she thought, and bathe their precious shells and thousand-coloured corals in the summer's first light; and old lands with fragrant orchards and peacefully murmuring leaves. And on

the meadow by the seashore stands his bright house. It was a
black shed, clad in tarred paper that had blown loose in places.
In a little window, which looked out to sea, stood two rusty tin
mugs full of soil. Sticking out of the roof a broken stove-pipe that
was out of the perpendicular. Leading up to the door two broken
steps. And the woods? Withered seaweed that the breakers had
washed up on the beach all around. A little brook, scarcely a yard
in width, ran out into the sand, and kneeling on the bank were two
half-grown boys playing at stirring up the mud at the bottom. She
stepped over it. A half-grown girl of about her own age, only
thinner, was busy near the door with two screaming children, they
had a rash, they were blue in the face. And on the threshold stood
the mother, pregnant like the girl herself, with a baby in her arms
and swearing. It is for Asta Sollilja and her beloved that cheap
poets and misanthropists and liars write books full of sunshine and
dreams and beautiful sun-gilt palm-avenues to fool them and
ridicule them and insult them. All that her loved one possessed
were these dreams. And the ability to drink himself stupid.

Then suddenly Gvendur remembered that he had not finished
his errand yet, and again he asked her to wait but a moment
longer — "Father asked me to tell you that things are still very
much the same at home, except that he's going to start building
his house soon."

She spun round on her heel and cried in astonishment: "Father
asked you? To tell me!"

As soon as he heard her question the boy realized that he had
said too much, and he hastened to correct himself by saying:
"No, he didn't ask me to tell you. But he said it nevertheless. And
he asked me to recite you these verses" — and he recited the two
verses.

She laughed.

"Tell him," she said forgetting that he was bound for America,
"tell him from me that I know the cow-barns he builds. And tell
him that I also know the empty, drivelling doggerel that he
cudgels into shape with hands and feet. But I, I am engaged to
a young man who loves me. He has been to school, and he is a
modern poet, and he and his mother own a sweet little house
on Sandeyri. It's two years since he first asked me to marry him,
and he will never drive me away from him, because he loves me.
Tell Bjartur of Summerhouses that."

This was her last word. Such had she become, the little Midsummer Night girl of bygone days. It was the left cheek in her

life that had gained the ascendancy; or, much more probably, that had saved the helpless right cheek that she had turned to Bjartur of Summerhouses many years ago, one Christmas Eve.

64.   AMERICA

"Is it you?" she asked.

"Yes," he answered, "it is I."

Thus did their acquaintanceship begin.

In a lush green meadow towards evening stood a lofty and distinguished house, with a rectangular tower, bathed in sunshine. The meadow gleamed almost with a tinge of fleeting red in the evening sun, so bright and charming was it.

"You're frightfully lucky going to America," she said. "Aren't you really awfully excited about it?"

She was wearing high boots and breeches that were close-fitting at the knees but full above, and she was leading two spirited young thoroughbreds whose coats glistened with good feeding, glossy as silk. The sunshine and the breeze played in her golden hair, in its waves and its curls; her young bosom rose cupped above her slender waist, her arms were naked to the shoulder, her eyebrows curved in a high care-free bow. Her keen eyes reminded him both of the sky and of its hawks; her skin, radiant with the fresh bloom of youth, colour incomparable, made him think of wholesome new milk in May. She was altogether free. She was beauty itself. He had never seen anyone or anything in any way like her. She had a slight trace of a nasal pronunciation, her voice slipped into low, singing notes at the end of every sentence, and she laughed in fun and earnest. He was completely lost.

"You can go in on the lawn if you would like to," she said.

He opened the gate for her.

"You may hold my horses for me while I go inside," she said, and was gone. He stood there with the horses on the rein while they champed their bits and rubbed themselves against him impatiently. For a long, long time he waited and still she did not return, and just when he was beginning to think she would never return she returned.

"Like some chocolate?" she asked, and gave him some chocolate.

"More?" she asked, and gave him some more.

"I wish I were going with you," she said. "Lord, how I'd love to go to America! I say, how would you like me to come along with you?"

He blushed furiously at the thought of running away with such a girl. The idea seemed somehow a little improper. Nevertheless he gave her permission to accompany him to America. "The ship will be arriving tonight and leaving early in the morning," he told her. She burst out into hearty laughter; it amused her enormously that he should intend taking her with him to America. "You're very kind, I'm sure," she said, laughing in fun and earnest, "I think I shall have to treat you to a trip on the roan instead, though there's only a rope halter on him at the moment. I was thinking, actually, of popping over to Myri to see my grandfather and my grandmother, and if you've no objections to riding barebacked for a mile or two, you can see me as far as the top of the heath."

No, no, he had no objections to riding bareback, even if it were fifty miles, and was astride the horse immediately. No sooner had they mounted than the eager animals were off at breakneck speed, the grey leading at a gallop with the girl, the roan in furious pursuit, shaking his head and tugging viciously at the reins, utterly heedless of his rider's efforts to guide him. She turned the grey on to the road leading up to the heath at full speed, while the roan chased along behind at an erratic gallop, snorting and swerving and bucking as if he had never experienced a bridle before; once or twice she looked around at him and laughed, her hair streaming in the breeze, golden in the sunshine. In spite of his mount Gudmundur Gudbjartsson had never known anything so glorious, so romantic. They dashed up the scarp as if it had been levelled into a race-track, the horses taking the bends in the zigzag road at such speed that he had to hang on to the mane to prevent himself being shot sideways.

Only a few moments had passed and already they were within sight of the summit. At one point near the head of the pass the road skirts the bottom of a grassy hollow, and just as they were passing this hollow the grey gave a sudden swerve, made for the side of the road, jumped clean over the ditch, landed in the hollow, and bump, there on the bank lay the girl with her legs waving in the air. The roan, following hard in the other's tracks, threw his hind legs up with such vigour that his rider catapulted forward, landed on his head, and turned a somersault before he could stop. The horses, tossing their heads and snorting, trotted away farther up the hollow and began grazing. The girl lay giggling in the grass.

"You haven't hurt yourself, I hope?" he asked as he picked himself up.

But all she could do was giggle. "Lord, what a joke!" she cried, writhing with laughter. He went after the horses and pulled the reins over their heads to hamper their movements; they were eating greedily, snorting into the grass and jingling their bits. When he returned she was sitting up tidying her hair. The town lay beneath them in bird's-eye view, with coffee-brown garden plots and newly painted house-roofs as testimony to the bountiful blessings of a prosperous war; and they could see far, far out over the ocean, and the ocean lay spread before them like eternity, smooth and mirror-bright as far as the horizon, so that one felt that surely the world must end there and a new and better world take its place, maybe it's true.

"You're frightfully lucky having the chance to sail over all that sea."

"I was afraid you had hurt yourself," he said chivalrously. "Great horses, those of yours."

"Pooh, they're just a couple of ordinary nags. I would swap them immediately for the chance to sail to America."

"What do they call you?" he asked.

But she only looked at him and showed her even, milk-white teeth in a lilting laugh. "Why should you trouble to ask, you who are going to America?"

"I only wanted to know."

"All right, I'll tell you; but not before you come back from America. Listen, what are you going to do when you get to America?"

"Oh, I don't really know yet," said he, himself retiring, though not without reluctance, behind the same shroud of coy mysteriousness as she.

"You don't want to tell me, that's what's the matter."

"A man can be anything he likes in America," he said. "Take my brother, for instance. He is in America, but no one knows what he is. All we know is that he has an awful lot of money. Money printed on blue paper. He has just sent me a whole bundle of them. There are countries in America with big forests and wild animals in them."

"Wild animals!" she repeated excitedly. "Are you going to hunt wild animals?"

Yes, of course he was, now that he came to think of it; how lucky he was to have mentioned wild animals, he who had every intention of hunting wild animals!

"Listen," she said, "you haven't a photograph of your brother in America, have you?"

No, he hadn't a photograph of him.

"What's he like? Isn't he awfully, you know what I mean, sort of foreign in appearance?"

"He's tall," replied Gvendur, "yes, awfully tall. And he's much stronger than I am. He can sing too. Awfully well. And he's always well-dressed. I should think he must have two or three Sunday suits. And he's clever, too. You can see it in his eyes. He has learned everything; no one knows how much he has learned. He always wanted to travel."

"Has he hunted wild animals, too?" she asked.

"Yes, yes, in a forest," he replied. "Harts and panthers. In a frightfully big forest. He lives in a forest. I will be with him in a month's time."

"Just think of it," she said. "Lord, how I wish I were going to America!"

The speed and felicity with which he answered this lovely girl's questions astonished him greatly; but she was so nice to talk to; he had never met anyone so easy and inspiring to the tongue, it was almost as if a flower sprang from every word, however insignificant, that one addressed to her. But now that he had time for reflection, it struck him that there was something rather odd about her. "I don't quite understand why you should want to go to America when you live in a big house with a tower on it," he said. "And when you can have anything you fancy out of the co-operative stores. And when you have such a fine pair of horses."

After a few moments' introspection she was inclined to agree with him. "Yes, I suppose you're quite right really; yes, I suppose it's all just a lot of nonsense," said she. "I haven't the slightest desire to go to America really, I wouldn't go if I was paid. Though I believe I might have thought about it if Father had been going with me. It's just that I get all excited when somebody else is going to America, because it's such a long, long way and because it's so romantic and because I think the sea is so marvellous, it's so big, and they're such great men when they come back, they're so manly. When I was little, I thought that everyone who went abroad must be a great man, like Father for instance. Maybe it's all nonsense. But there's no reason why it shouldn't be true for all that, is there? Listen, you mustn't forget me while you're in America."

"No," he said, blushing and not daring to look up, because he knew that she was looking at him.

"Do you know what?" she said. "I've taken such a fancy to that brother of yours that you were talking about just now. Tell me more about him. Isn't he ever coming back at all?"

"No," said Gvendur, "I don't suppose he'll ever come back. But I, I may come back some day." Then, plucking up courage, he added: "That is, if you would like me to."

She looked him over a few moments, weighing him up in the present and in the future, in reality and in imagination, and mixing the two together, with one eye on the vast ocean he was about to cross; and he enchanted her so because of the vast ocean he was about to cross, and because he was such a great man on the other side of the ocean, and because there were wild animals in America, and yes, because he would be so very manly when he returned, that she said:

"I'll be awfully glad when you come back."

Yes, she was young, very young, possibly fifteen, possibly no more than fourteen; and possibly it was nothing but sheer pedantry to mention any particular year in connection with her, for she was youth in person, the youth that the Summerhouses children had never known. No, he had never seen the like of her, or she the like of him, for that matter. "When you come back, you'll be taller than you are now, and you'll be just as broad across here," and she passed her hand across his chest and shoulders, "or even broader perhaps, and you'll be wearing a light grey summer suit and brown shoes. Yes, and a hat. And a striped shirt. And a lot of other things, too. And when it rains you'll go about in a big rainproof coat. And you'll have hunted wild animals." She leaned her head back and looked at the sky with dreaming vision, and he saw the under side of her chin; then she leaned forward laughing almost into his arms, and he was looking at the white parting in her thick, fair hair, the golden hair that the sun loved. Yes, she laughed into his arms almost, and his thoughts were in whirling disorder, and he did not really believe that it could be true. Why should this happen to him just when he was leaving? Already he was firmly resolved that some day he would return.

Presently she began to prepare herself for the rest of her trip.

She sat in the grass and tidied her hair and canted her head to one side; the boy watched her and canted his head to one side also, just a little, unconsciously, and presently they had finished canting their heads to one side. "Now we'll have to get hold of the horses," she said. They got hold of the horses. The horses went on snorting and trying to rub the bits out of their mouths. They hung to a rein each, she gazing once more in admiration over the ocean he was about to cross, he no longer able to take his eyes off her.

"I suppose we'll have to say good-bye now," she said very sorrowfully.

She offered him her hand, so warm, so young, stretching her arm so smooth and bright over the horse's neck. He took it in silence and she saw that he wanted to accompany her farther, and thought she was in some ways very, very pleased, in others she was half inclined to be sorry.

"When you come back again, you can come and see me, then," she said, to comfort both herself and him.

He made no reply. She lingered for a while and went on gazing at him; rested her elbows on the grey's withers and went on gazing at him over the horse's neck.

"They're a fine pair of horses," he said, stroking the grey. She laughed then, for men are always the same, always seeking some excuse to spin out the occasion.

"Would you like to sell me them?" he asked.

"Sell you them? When you're leaving for America? What would you want with horses?"

"Oh, I just want them," he replied. "I have so much money, you see."

"No, I won't sell them to you, I'll make you a present of them," she said, "until you come back."

"What do they call you?" he asked.

"I'll tell you when you return."

"I want to know your name while I'm away," he said.

"Why, were you going to write to me?"

"Yes."

"Ride a little farther with me, then," she said, "and we'll talk it over."

They sprang on horseback and set off at the same furious speed as before, the grey leading, the roan following, westward over the moors. The ground was dry and the dust rose behind them in billowing clouds; the wind blew in their laughing faces

as they sped straight into the eye of the westering sun, like
supernatural beings riding the clouds into a burning fire. It was
the loveliest journey in all the world. On and on they sped, without slackening speed, without talking it over. Far over the heath
they glimpsed the sheen of a little white lake, otherwise the moss
was grey and the withered grass white, the rocks black, the
turfless patches of earth red. The mountains far away to the south
were bathed in violet, the glaciers beyond them snowy white,
the ocean lost behind them long ago, night day. Along the side
of the road panic-stricken heath-birds scuttled squawking over
the grass before they rose into the air. Mother ewes and their
lambs took to their heels and were lost to sight.

When at length they reached the lake, she turned her horse
without warning off the road, and the roan followed, first over a
tract of moss-grown stones, then over a marshy patch, and finally
on to the banks, which were covered with dry meadow grass,
green as if it had been cultivated. There were two swans on the
lake. She jumped down from her horse, and he also jumped down.
They were on the higher part of the moors now; the shadows
very long, the sun touching the western brink of the heath, the
air growing rapidly cooler. Strapped to the back of her saddle
she carried a thick coat, and when she had unbuckled it and cast
it over her shoulders, she produced sweets from all pockets and
offered him some. Then she sat down on the bank.

"Sit down," she said, and he sat down.

"Look at the swans," she said, and he looked at the swans.

"Aren't you cold?" she asked.

"No," he replied.

"I can see from your face that you're cold. Come a little closer
and I'll give you a corner of my coat round you."

"It isn't at all necessary," he said, moving closer so that she
could throw a corner of her coat round him.

"Your clothes smell of smoke," she said with a laugh. "And
feathers too."

"Eh?" said he. "Smoke? Feathers?"

"Yes, but your hair is ever so lovely," she said, stroking his
hair with her bright hands, "and you're so broad across here.
And here. And you have such manly eyes."

The swans swam nearer the land, peering at the girl and the
boy curiously, with an occasional low gobble. "Look how nobly
he swims, how gracefully she follows in his wake."

"Yes," he said, looking at the swans and seeing all that she saw. At first they had seemed just ordinary birds, but now he realized that they were a couple, a he and a she, not just any two birds, but two birds with a significance.

"They're in love, you see," she said, her eyes still fixed upon them.

He gripped her hand in silent answer, quite involuntarily; what other answer could he make? He sensed the warmth of her young bosom; it was life itself; and he sat holding her hand and she offered no objections and went on gazing at the swans as they swam to and fro in wary patrol, a yard or two from land, peering at them inquisitively. "Aren't they lovely?" she said, and she shivered and moved nearer still; her hair tickled his face. He pressed his burning lips to her cheek.

"How do you think you're going to get back to Fjord again now?" she asked, with a roguish sidewise glance of her eyes.

"There's no hurry," he said. "I have the night before me." And added, in a whisper: "I'm ever so fond of you. Won't you promise to wait for me?"

"Sh, don't talk like that," she said, and kissed him on the mouth, first once with a laugh, then twice with a little sob, then repeatedly and passionately, as if she owned him; and closed her eyes.

When at long length he threw aside the coat, under which they had been lying, and rose to his feet, the sun was far below the mountains, the air chilly, and the swans — the swans had disappeared. Perhaps there had never been any, all sheer illusion, it was only an ordinary night, a spring night over the heath. She told him to go look for the horses, then turned her back on him and hiding herself under the coat, proceeded to arrange her clothes and tidy her hair beneath its protection. He was completely devoid of thought, a man who had lost every aim in time and place, both point and line. The horses had wandered round to the other side of the lake, far away. The roan had rubbed his bit out, the rope halter was lost. He was very refractory without a bridle, and the lad had great trouble in catching him; he had to wade knee-deep in mud through the bogs. There was very little glory left in his patent-leather shoes by the time he was finished. He enticed him eventually alongside the grey and, catching hold of him, hastily tied the cord he had bought under his lower lip. When he returned at last with the horses, the girl had grown very impatient and asked him why he had been away so long. She threw the reins over the grey's neck without loss of time, mounted, slapped her horse on the groin, and was off at full speed, over all that lay before her.

The roan proved, if anything, even more intractable now that he had only an improvised bit and a single rein. He ran for a while in erratic curves and circles, then followed this up with a variety of other antics, so that soon Gvendur came to realize that he was sitting an unbroken foal whose tricks and whimsies made him an impossible mount. When at last he had got him on to the road again, the girl was far away on the crest of a hill and still maintaining her initial speed over the undulating heath. The roan caught sight of her and, giving vent to a loud neigh, set off in wild pursuit. But gradually it was borne in on Gvendur that his mount was less of a stayer than a sprinter; already he was in a bath of sweat, and when descending a hill, he lost his footing and tumbled, with the result that Gvendur grazed his cheek-bones and his knuckles. He took out his watch to see whether the throw had broken it, but it was unbroken; and two o'clock. The girl continued to increase her lead. Two o'clock — he had come much too far, he would be lucky indeed if he got back to Fjord by rising-time — and what was he to do with the horse? He would have to return the girl her horse, surely, before setting out on his return walk to Fjord. "Hey," he yelled, "hey!" But they were so far apart by now that there was no hope of her hearing him, and besides, she was out of sight beyond a roll in the moors. "There's no two ways about it, I'll have to catch up with her and give her the horse," he thought. He tried to make the cord into a double rein, to see if the roan would answer any better, then mounted and endeavoured to urge it forward. "Hey," he yelled, "hey! Your horse, your horse!" But when he had reached the western brow of the plateau, whence one could see right down to Summerhouses, it was past three o'clock, dawn at his back, and far, far away down the valley puffs of dust from her horse's hoofs told him that her speed had not lessened. There was no longer the remotest likelihood of his catching up with her, especially now that the roan was showing unmistakable signs of fatigue. He dismounted, and curlews, wide awake, bubbled at him from every rock, every mound on the ridges; what the devil was he to do now? If he left her horse here and walked back to Fjord, there was little chance of catching the ship the way that matters stood now, unless of course its departure had been considerably delayed. It was three o'clock. He was tired already, spent with the long bareback ride and the falls he had sustained; and not only tired, but hungry as well; he remembered all at once that he had eaten nothing, except the sweets she had given him, since leaving the lodging-house some time early yesterday morning. Suppose he were to borrow the horse without, but in anticipation of, the owner's consent, as was said to be justifiable in cases of extreme necessity; suppose he were to ride it straight back to Fjord, would it avail at all, would he be in time for the ship? After cudgelling his brains for a while, he decided that he ought at least to make the attempt; this was obviously a case of extreme necessity and no occasion for an over-scrupulous sense of honesty — and having decided to ride back to Fjord, he mounted once again. But the foal now refused to budge, and though the lad thumped it repeatedly with heel and fist, no amount of blows could produce any effect beyond a half-hearted effort to unseat him. It knew that its grey stall-brother was making off to the west, and no human power could persuade it to take the opposite direction. In the end the rider gave up in despair and allowed the horse to take its own road. Off it ambled down the hillside, picking its way cautiously down the road into the valley, with an occasional yawn, because of the cord, and an occasional shake of the head, an occasional snort or a neigh. When they reached the marshes opposite Summer-houses they caught a last distant glimpse of the girl and the grey on the skyline before they disappeared over the top of the ridge in the west. He managed to force his steed up the path leading to the croft. After unfastening the string, he let it loose in the home-field; the corners of its mouth were sore. It rolled about in the grass in front of the croft, stood up and shook itself, shivering a little at groin and shoulder, lathered in sweat. The sun was shining, the shadows cast by the croft long as those of some mighty palace. No part of night or day wears such beauty as the time of the sun's rising, for then there is quiet, loveliness, and splendour over everything. And now over everything there was quiet, loveliness, and splendour. The song of the birds was sweet and happy. The mirror-like lake and the smoothly flowing river gleamed and sparkled with a silvery, entrancing radiance. The Blue Fells lay gazing in rapture up at their heaven, as if they had nothing in common with this world. They had nothing in common with this world. And in the unsubstantiality of its serene beauty and its peaceful dignity the valley, too, seemed to have nothing in common with this world. There are times when the world seems to have nothing in common with the world, times when one can no more understand oneself than if one had been immortal.

No one awake, or anything like awake, on the croft, and yet the lad had never known such a day. He sat down in the grass, with his back to the garden wall, and began thinking. He began thinking of America, the glorious land across the ocean, the America in which he could have been anything he chose. Had he lost it for good and all, then? Oh, well, it mattered little. Love is better; love is more glorious than America. Love is the one true America. Could it be true that she loved him? Yes, there was nothing half so true. There is nothing half so unlike itself as the world, the world is incredible. True, she had ridden away and left him, but then she had been on one of the famous Rauthsmyri thoroughbreds, and possibly it had wanted to get home. She had never looked around, never slackened speed, but in spite of this seeming indifference, he was convinced, on this incomparable morning, that at some future date, say when he had become the freeholder of Summerhouses, he would bring her back home as his wife. Since it had begun in such a fashion, how could it end otherwise? What he had found was happiness, though she had ridden away and left him behind — and again and again he excused her on the ground that she had not been able to manage her horse. He was determined to spend his American money on a good horse, a first-class thoroughbred, so that in future he would be able to ride side by side with his sweetheart. Thus he lay stretched out in the grass of his native croft, looking up into the sky, into the blue, comparing the love he had won with the America he had lost. Leifur the Lucky also had lost America. Yes, love was better — and thus over and over again. He saw her still in his mind's eye as she swept over the undulating heath, flitting through the lucid night like an airy vision, her golden locks streaming in the wind, her coat flapping against the horse's rump. And he saw himself following her still, from crest to crest — till she was lost in the blue. And he himself was lost in the blue.

He slept.

65.   POLITICS

WHEREIN lay the secret of Ingolfur Arnarson's success? To what gifts, what accomplishments, did he owe the speed of the ascent that had carried him so rapidly from obscurity to fame, from nonentity to national eminence? Already, in spite of his youth, he was one of the most important and most influential men in the country, a national figure whose photograph was the daily delight of the newspapers, whose name the euphonic pride of the fattest headlines. Did he perhaps owe his rise, like great men before him, to a constant rooting and grubbing for personal profit? Was he always on the hunt for anything that people in need might have for sale, so as to be able to sell it again to others who could not do without it and who were driven, possibly, by an even greater need? Had he, for example, appropriated a croft here, a croft there in years of depression and sold them again when prosperity returned and prices rose? Had he perhaps lent people hay in a hard spring and demanded the same weight in sheep as security? Or food and money to the starving, at a usurious rate of interest? Or had he achieved greatness by stinting himself of food and drink, like an ill-provisioned criminal in flight through the wilds, or a peasant who, in spite of slaving eighteen hours a day, has been told by his dealer that his debts are still increasing and that he has now reached the limit of his credit? Or by having one solitary chair in his room, and a broken one at that, and shambling about in a filthy assortment of mouldy old rags all day, like a wretched tramp or a farm labourer? Or was the method he employed that of accumulating thousand upon thousand at the bottom of his chest until he was rich enough to found a savings bank and start lending folk money at a legal rate of interest, and then of standing in front of destitute men and informing them that the depth of his poverty was such that soon he would have to sell the very soul from his body if he wished to escape imprisonment for debt? No, Ingolfur Arnarson Jonsson was by no means such a person; all his greatness came from his mother's side. Then was he the sort of person who owned a number of boats and made poverty-stricken men catch fish for him at the risk of their lives? Did he grab all the profit on the fish that others had caught and buy mahogany furniture, works of art, and electric lighting with it, while those who had caught all the fish received a pittance that barely allowed them to buy their wives a penny packet of hairpins by the way of a luxury? Or did he draw a fat income from Denmark and other distant countries for managing the sort of business that sold the necessities of existence to men who in strict reality could not afford to exist? Or did he run his own business and, while crawling in the dust before the richer farmers and allowing them to decide the value of their sheep themselves, because they could always threaten to take their custom elsewhere, did he rule like a tyrant over the unfortunate peasants who owed him money, starving them every spring and robbing them of every opportunity of advancement? No, Ingolfur Arnarson's road to honour and repute had been neither the miser's nor the merchant's bloody career, hitherto the sole paths to wealth and true dignity recognized as legal by the Icelandic community and its justice.

What made Ingolfur Arnarson a great man was first and foremost his ideals, his unquenchable love of mankind, his conviction that the people needed improved conditions of life and better facilities for cultural advancement, his determination to mitigate his fellow men's sufferings by establishing a better form of government in the country. This government, instead of being a helpless puppet in the hands of the peasant's ruthless oppressors, the merchants, would be the small producer's, especially the peasant's, most powerful ally in his struggle for existence. Middlemen and other parasites would no longer be allowed to batten on the farming classes. Ingolfur wanted to elevate the farmer's life to a position of honour and dignity, not in word alone, but in deed. Because of these ideals the farmers had chosen him to represent them in the Althingi and other places where their welfare was at stake. Now, so far this constituency had been completely neglected by the government. It was not that old Dr. Finsen, Bruni's mouthpiece, had been inactive in Parliament; merely that he had concentrated his endeavours upon one particular cause, that of persuading the Treasury to rebuild and extend quays and breakwaters which had been rebuilt and extended for the merchant the previous spring, but which high tides had washed away like so much spit as soon as completed. For upwards of twenty years he had pursued this recurring object with commendable zeal and undiminished vigour, producing his bill with such annual regularity that eventually it became known as a perpetual motion. But when Ingolfur took his seat in Parliament, he had the whole matter quietly shelved and the building of piers and breakwaters was never again mentioned in public. The time was not long, however, before he was having modern roads laid and fine bridges built to improve communications throughout his constituency. And this was only the beginning. He wanted now to have large-scale agriculture introduced and decent houses built for folk. The National Bank in Reykjavik, which hitherto had acted as a sort of horn of plenty for speculators in cod and herring, was to be

liquidated and placed under State control as an agricultural
bank, since the State already lay under heavy obligations as
surety for its debts. This agricultural bank would then lend
money to the farmers, at a low rate of interest, for building-
purposes and the better cultivation of the land. He proposed in
addition to direct a certain amount of public money into a special
fund that would help the farmers to purchase agricultural implements, everything from ploughs, harrows, tractors, mowers,
and mechanical rakes down to sewing-machines and separators.
Another subsidy would provide the farmers with sewers and
manure cisterns, for he was the sworn enemy of muck-heaps and
open cesspools. The provision of electric lighting in the country
district was also very close to his heart, but this plan, unfortunately, was still rather nebulous in form. Waking and sleeping he
worked upon the problems presented by the new era of rural
colonization and development, and though he was still co-
operative manager in name and still gave his permanent address
as Fjord, one could hardly say that he ever went there except on
a flying visit, for now that a deputy looked after the co-operative
society for him, he spent the greater part of the year in Reykjavik,
where he edited his party's newspaper, worked on parliamentary committees, and engaged in various other activities as
guardian of the farmer's interests. For his personal interests and
profit he had never a moment to spare. He was, in a word, the
Ingolfur Arnarson of the new era, the Icelandic pioneer of the
twentieth century, differing from his illustrious predecessor in
this respect only, that he was a Jonsson.

Then, now that spring was here and the general elections
approaching, surely one might have taken it for granted that
Ingolfur would have been returned unopposed and that no one
would have had the foolhardiness to offer himself as a rival
candidate? On the contrary. One must not assume that plutocracy
and merchant power had been altogether routed just because
they had suffered a set-back here and there, in those few, scattered places where the peasants had succeeded in forming consumers' societies in their own defence. Then again, the present
boom had strengthened rather than enfeebled the creed of egoism that was so popular in the towns; and this constituency had
two towns, Fjord and Vik, and egoism was especially rife among
the boat owners, craftsmen, and small traders in Vik, though
probably it received its strongest backing from the new merchant
who had suddenly appeared upon the scene in that town. This

person had rapidly surrounded himself with all the most prosperous men from town and country and had even gone and married the Fell King's daughter within a few months of his arrival, though some people maintained that originally he had been nothing more or less than a common swindler and speculator, even that he had spent a year or two in jail. Then, in the third place, the influence of a foreign doctrine named Socialism was rapidly growing more perceptible in Vik. The town was rarely free of paid agitators, specially sent from the south, who vied with one another in leading the poorer classes astray and inciting them to a hatred of both God and men, as if God and men were not sufficiently antagonistic towards such people already.

Ingolfur Arnarson: "Socialism is all lies. They puff destitute people up with endless promises that can never have any hope of fulfilment until man has reached the same stage of maturity as the gods; but their real aims are simply murder and rapine."

Fortunately Ingolfur Arnarson was in no great danger from this menace as yet. The danger threatened from the other side. The capitalists, it now appeared, had dug up a rival candidate with a whole bank behind him, the selfsame bank that Ingolfur had wanted to raze to the ground and rebuild as an agricultural bank run for the benefit of the peasantry, and with his own men in command, if he had any say in the matter. That swindlers in Reykjavik should send out one of their own kidney, the manager of a half-insolvent bank, to spread their gospel throughout the land, was in itself of course no great marvel. But what came of it? If this brass-faced missionary of a gang of capitalist criminals did not have the nerve, in his utter lack of ideals, originality, and elementary decency, to get up on his hind legs and offer the farmers not only everything that Ingolfur Arnarson had promised them, but a whole host of other things into the bargain! He offered to equip every croft in the constituency with electric lighting within the space of a year or two, and not only this constituency, but throughout the length and breadth of the land as well.

Ingolfur Arnarson: "Actually the difference between his and the Socialists' promises can only be regarded as a difference in forms of insanity, with this exception, that the bank manager does not propose that folks should be robbed and murdered, probably because he remembers only too well that he is the emissary of that fractional part of the nation's population which has robbed and murdered people without cease ever since Iceland was Iceland, though by different means and without preaching any form of Socialism."

Later, when the banker had promised the farming classes the whole of Ingolfur Arnarson's program and more if he were elected, all in a much shorter period of time than Ingolfur had planned, he turned his attention to the towns, which had so far never been accorded any definite place in the platform of the farmers' representative. Here again he was the very soul of generosity. To Vik he promised a bank and a big fishing company, to Fjord a bone-meal factory and a coal mine. The seaside electors lent ready ears to this sort of talk, as was only natural, and it was considered probable that these populous places would be solid in their support of the banker. Well, this was a fine kettle of fish. Things were looking pretty black for Ingolfur Arnarson. Where could he turn now? No, esteemed electors, Ingolfur was no turncoat on the field of political battle; he did not allow other men to take the promises out of his mouth. What did he do, then? He simply resurrected the famous parliamentary evergreen of his predecessor Finsen, the old breakwater. And, what was more, he promised Fjord not only a breakwater and a quay; he promised it a complete harbour costing no less than half a million crowns as well. An engineering scheme so vast, he said, would afford unlimited employment not only to the inhabitants of Fjord, but also to the working people of the neighbouring town of Vik; nor should one forget all these countless business undertakings which the State would establish in Fjord as a natural sequel to the construction of such a harbour. Never before, no, not even in old Finsen's time, had quays and breakwaters excited such burning and such opportune interest as they did now. Then, feeling, no doubt, that his generosity ought to be as impartial as it was large-hearted, he transferred the banker's bone-meal factory from Fjord to Vik, and instead of his opponent's big fishing company he promised the little fishing company in Vik a large subsidy from the State, together with numerous other privileges which would make it the most flourishing little fishing company in the whole country and would ensure for everyone in Vik, no matter what the depth of his present poverty, a prosperous and happy future as a member of the middle classes. There remained the coal mine. This he divided impartially between the two townships, though always on the proviso that the mine should be proved to contain real coal, and not lignite or just ordinary stones and earth. When this stage had

been reached, it was virtually impossible to determine whose
were the better promises, and it began to appear likely that the
issue would depend not so much on what was actually offered
as on the oratorical skill of the candidates, especially their ability
to play upon the electors' heart-strings. It was reported that
many working people had already discarded Socialism in favour
of the chance of securing permanent employment, prosperous
membership in the middle classes, and a share in a boat.

"One never knows how things are going to turn out, and that's
why I say it's essential never to lean too far to the one side,
especially in politics," observed the Fell King. "Ingolfur Arnarson
is a man of great ability, of course, like all the family, and you
couldn't wish for a finer speaker at a meeting, but when I saw
last year the importance that the people of Fjord and Vik attach
to private enterprise these days, I suspected immediately that
he would lose a great deal of his support. And that's why I
resigned immediately from the co-operative society; my private
affairs had nothing to do with it; politics are not private affairs,
and anyway I'm not talking as a private person now. And though
I left the co-operative society and transferred the whole of my
custom to my son-in-law's in Vik, which I am sure was only a
perfectly natural action that anyone would have done under
the circumstances, it doesn't follow that I think there's anything
wrong with the Rauthsmyri people as people. No one denies
their many virtues, and the promises Ingolfur makes are, of
course, very fine and very attractive. But what's going to happen
if he doesn't get in, may I ask? What if his party goes down, as
most people prophesy? I'm only afraid that some folk around
here are going to have a long wait for their sewing-machines and
their manure-cisterns if that happens. And that their new houses
aren't going to be quite so commodious as some of them may have
been led to expect. And what guarantee of security will the
people who voted for him have if he goes down? None at all, or
for just as long as the bank manager thinks fit. The big fellows in
the south aren't easily knocked off their perches, you know. And
it has never been considered foolish to be in well with the big
fellows."

So much was certain about this Fell King, that immediately on
transferring his custom to his son-in-law's in Vik he had launched
out on a venture he had never even dared to contemplate while
dealing with the co-op: he had begun building himself a house.
Load upon load of timber and cement had been delivered in

trucks; the house was to be ready by term-day. Bjartur eyed him askant for a few moments, then replied:

"Huh, it isn't everybody's daughter that's married into the merchant clique, you know."

"Well, if it comes to that, you can't very well say that you're married into the Rauthsmyri family either," retorted the Fell King. "So at least it isn't on the score of family connections that you have to vote on their side."

"My voting, like that of a few others I could mention, is determined not so much by family connections as by business interests," said Bjartur coldly. "I believe in voting for the people I deal with, though, of course, only as long as they steer clear of bankruptcy. And though you personally may have excellent reasons for hobnobbing with the big pots in the south that you're always bragging about, I for my part have never had anything to do with them, and don't see any reason why I should start now."

"Oh, I don't know," said the Fell King. "Someone was saying you were thinking of building yourself a house."

"What's that to you? And even if I was, what's it got to do with politics?"

"Nothing, nothing at all," replied the Fell King. "Except that if you're thinking of new buildings it's always wisest to be sure of your welcome at the banks."

"Oh, and what's to stop me from getting all my building stuff on credit at the co-op, if necessary? I should think my name's as good as anyone's there."

"Yes, but unfortunately there are other things to be considered besides building materials alone, my friend. You can't pay the men their wages on nothing nowadays, you know. And carpenters and masons don't let you have credit. It's best to have a few thousand in ready cash behind you if you intend building anything worthy of the name."

"Never you fear, old cock," said Bjartur confidently. "Money will be easy enough to come by. It isn't so very long since there passed this way a certain gentleman who's at least as important as yourself, and he gave me to understand that if ever I needed a loan there was welcome on the mat for me at the savings bank."

"The savings bank," said the Fell King, "yes, quite so. A most praiseworthy institution, as I've always been first to acknowledge. And as for Jon of Myri, we've sat together at the council board for many a long year, yes, since well before the war began, and never have I heard anyone hint that he was anything but a man of the most admirable and most outstanding qualities. And it isn't his fault, surely, if people of an untrustworthy character who made a habit of pestering him for money in and out of season should have ended up by joining forces and threatening to have the law on him, just because he insisted on a rate of interest that they themselves had agreed to in the first place. So personally I'm not in the least surprised that he should have decided to open a savings bank, where his money can always be in circulation, even if it's only at the statutory six per cent, instead of continuing to lend to unreliable folk, privately and behind the authorities' backs, at anything from twelve to twenty-five per cent, with the threat of jail always hanging over his head. A savings bank is always a safe, steady sort of business. And it's convenient to have a savings bank in the district, in case one should happen to require a small amount for a short period. But they're never anything more than small amounts, and never for more than a very short time. Because no one is fool enough to borrow a large sum at the rates the savings bank demands. Those who are thinking of building are wiser to go to the banks where a loan on a mortgage runs for forty years."

"Oh, I don't suppose I'd need more than a year or two before I was square with them again. Some people thought prices would collapse at the end of the war, but the wool touched record heights in the spring there, and I've heard from a responsible quarter that they'll be giving us more than ever for the lambs this autumn."

The Fell King sat deep in cerebration for a while, absent-mindedly stroking his beard this way and that; he was much given to tormenting his brains, this man, for in his view no thought was perfect unless it could be set down in writing, in a public document; he had been a public official for dogs, men, and parsons far too long to be so foolish as to rush to a hasty conclusion.

"Oh, well," he said at length, "it's no business of mine really, but I thought I'd make a suggestion for old friendship's sake. But you mustn't on any account get it into your head that I've come in any sort of public capacity, or as anyone's official agent in the matter. On the other hand, I can't declare with absolute truth that I came entirely in a private capacity. I've come as something more or less betwixt and between. As you know very well, I have never been able to give the co-operative movement my unqualified support, even though I discern much that is noble and beautiful in it as a movement, and have ever been first to acknowledge the virtues of the Rauthsmyrians, especially Madam, as people. The truth of the matter is that I've always tried to stick more or less to the

middle way, and that in consequence I have invariably been prepared to admit that both parties were in the right, at least until
there was conclusive proof that one or the other was in the wrong.
And now, to return to the matter in hand, I should like you to
know that my relations with various highly placed people are such
that I have the power, though not, unfortunately, the written
authority, to offer you a loan on exceptionally liberal terms, a
mortgage for forty years with a bank in the south, if you care to
start building this year. But naturally such a loan will only be
possible if we who nourish the love of independence in our bosoms
know where our political well-being lies and have sufficient common sense to transfer our custom to the proper quarter."

66.   THE RACEHORSE

GVENDUR of Summerhouses was on everyone's lips that spring, in
the first place because he had decided to go to America, in the
second place because he had decided not to go to America. In the
third place he had bought himself a horse; it was a racehorse and
he had bought it from someone living in a distant parish for an
enormous sum of money. Many people laughed. The young fool
had spent the night chasing Ingolfur Arnarson's only daughter over
the moors and had ended up by missing his ship; could anything
be more idiotic? Some people said the lad must be a half-wit.
Others said his horse was no more than an average horse, even that
it was getting on in years. What a dunderhead! Prior to this, no
one had noticed that Gvendur of Summerhouses so much as existed;
now, with startling suddenness, he was everywhere notorious as
an idiot and a dunderhead. If ever a meeting of any description
was to be held in the neighbourhood, he was sure to nose out all
the particulars so that he could put in an appearance on his horse.
Countrymen greeted him with a conservative grin. Townsmen
laughed heartily at this clodhopper who ranged the countryside
on an expensive horse after chasing the Althingi member's only
daughter from dusk till dawn. Horse-dealers stopped him on the
main road, poked at the horse's teeth, made a fool of the owner
when he had ridden away, and made up their minds to foist an
even worse horse on him as soon as they had swindled him out of
his present one.

It was one Sunday just before Midsummer Day and an election
meeting was to be held at Utirauthsmyri. The minister made use

of the opportunity to hold a service beforehand. One or two of the electors drifted on to the scene too early, timing their arrival so badly that they were let in for the service; otherwise the increasing interest in politics appeared to indicate that the public were beginning to believe that their affairs were governed from earth here, and not from heaven. Gvendur arrived at a gallop just as the service was about to begin. A small group of crofters standing outside the entrance to the horse-pen greeted him with a sly grin because he had not gone to America. Some of them looked the racehorse over coldly, with disapproval. He stole a quick glance at the big two-storeyed house with its third floor of gable attics, to see if anyone had noticed him when he rode in on his horse. But in a mansion so famous no one came to the windows to gaze on vanity; all he saw was the poetess's flowery plants spreading their lovely petals in the rays of the sun. He hoped that the Bailiff's family had already gone in to the service. He entered the church and, choosing a seat near the door, sat down and looked around to see if she were anywhere about. After a few moments of anxious search he caught sight of her, sitting in the front row, almost directly below the pulpit. She had a red hat on. There were a number of people between her and him, he could just make out the hat between all the heads. Through him there passed the sort of current that makes the lungs too big and the heart too small and the ear too sensitive for music; he felt as if the hymn would drive him mad; there was a mist before his eyes as well. Time passed and passed, and still the congregation went on braying away at the hymn as if they would never cease. How was he to get near her? What would be the best method of arranging a rendezvous so that the others would not notice? Ought he to wait until the end of the service, nudge her as she was passing him on her way out, and whisper: "Come round the corner with me, there's something I want to say to you?" No, to nudge a girl in church is an unseemly and wholly unpardonable act; especially if it is such a girl; and more especially still if it is to ask her to come round the corner. It would be a different story entirely if he were to invite her out to the horse-pen to take a look at a horse. But presently it occurred to him that probably people were not allowed to mention horses in church, for in all the Scriptures there is not one single reference to a horse, only an ass at the most. As if through a mist he saw the minister approach the altar and utter a loud cry. Then he began singing some long rigmarole, and everyone stood up, and she stood up, and he saw that she was wearing a blue coat. No girl in all the world had such lovely shoulders; anyone could see that they weren't intended for heavy burdens. Her golden curls peeped from under her hat, an expensive hat in keeping with the solemnity of the occasion. She looked proud and upright, as was only natural on a Sunday morning in church; if only she would look around, just for a second or two, so that he could transmit to her the current of his love. But what if she couldn't be bothered to look at other folk's horses, she who had a whole stable at her disposal? Unless he were to offer to make her a present of the horse? It was an expensive horse, pretty near a thousand crowns, and yet if she would accept it he would be ready and willing to return home on foot, yes, crawling on all fours even, if she liked. And this was the very thing he was longing to tell her most; he had been her devoted slave from the first moment he set eyes on her, she could command him to do anything she cared to think of — ride, walk, crawl on all fours. Already he had sacrificed to her the greatest country in the world, the land of infinite opportunity where one could be whatever one pleased and need not just keep on doing something in utter imbecility. Yes, and they had lain on the banks of the lake, and there had been two swans, a he and a she. But what could have happened to them? They had disappeared, surely it hadn't been illusion merely; no, no, no, she had loved him and then had ridden away from him, out into the blue —

"Dearly beloved Christian brethren, for I permit myself to call you my brethren, what word of six letters, yes, just six little letters, means something that ascends?" At last the minister had got himself into the pulpit, and God grant that he might preach a long sermon, so that the boy should have time to reach a conclusion, so that he might receive some inspiration. "And now, on the other hand, let us consider, my beloved brethren, what five letters, yes, just five little letters, mean something that descends?"

Yes, he was quite prepared to make her a present of the horse, or at least to make her the offer of it. She wasn't bound to accept, of course, but if she did, it wouldn't matter in the slightest; on the contrary it would make her indebted to him. True, she could always say: "I have plenty of horses, I have a whole stable full of horses," but he hoped she would add: "This horse is the loveliest horse I've ever seen, and I'm going to accept it because it is you that wants to give it me, and because you're so broad across here, but if I take it from you, you won't have any horse left and you'll have to go home on foot, won't you?" Then he would reply: "It doesn't matter. Even if I have to crawl home. Crawl on all fours. And what's more, you've only to say the word and I'll bark like a dog if you like. For I happen to be the future freeholder of Summerhouses, and soon we're going to start building; we're going to build a house at least as big as your house at Myri here, two storeys, and three with the attics, but whereas you built of wood and iron, we are going to build of stone. But Heaven help me, if people aren't allowed to mention horses, only asses — "

"Who was led out?" inquired the minister, bending over the edge of the pulpit and leaning in deep religious solemnity far out over the congregation. The lad from Summerhouses hoped and prayed with all his heart that it was a horse that had been led out.

"He was led out," announced the minister triumphantly, with great emphasis on the word "He." Unfortunately the object of discussion had evaded the boy.

"And who led Him out?" asked the minister, and prolonged the ensuing silence to inordinate length while he fixed every person in the church with a long, soul-searching gaze. Gvendur was stricken with immediate panic at the thought of being called upon to answer such a question. But finally the minister answered it himself: "Pilate's soldiers led Him out. And when did they lead Him out? They led Him out at five o'clock. And where did they lead Him? They led Him into the open. And why did they lead Him out? Because He wasn't allowed to remain inside." The boy heaved a huge sigh of relief.

Supposing he were to sneak out of the church in the middle of the service; it need not attract much attention, he could slip out backwards with his knees well bent, and once outside he could run across to the horse pen. He would lead his horse out. He would stand with it on the rein in front of the church door, waiting until the service was over. And as she stepped out of church he would place the reins in her hand and say: "From now on, this is yours." But then he recollected the people. They weren't alone. What would the parish say? Was it seemly that he, a peasant's son, should present Jon of Myri's grand-daughter with a horse? Would not the whole parish burst out into one great roar of laughter? And would not she herself be offended by this ignominy? A cold sweat started out upon him at the thought of becoming a nation-wide laughing-stock. His difficulties grew ever the more complicated and insoluble the more he racked his brains.

"Dearly beloved Christian brethren," said the minister, "time passes." And leaning out over the congregation, he gazed soul-deep into everyone present in the long silence that he allowed to ensue upon these words of deepest solemnity; but longest of all he gazed into Gvendur of Summerhouses. "Yes, time passes," he reiterated at length. "Yesterday was Saturday. Today it is Sunday. Tomorrow it is Monday. Then comes Tuesday. It was one o'clock only a short while ago. Now it's past two. Soon it will be three. Then it will be four." Gvendur felt that these words of grave warning were being directed at him in particular; the consciousness of having found no pretext, no solution to his problem, wrung his heart; the sweat streamed from his brow and ran in cold beads down his temples. Soon the end of the sermon was in sight, and the red hat still remained motionless, except that now it was tilted a trifle backward, for the girl was gazing steadfastly up at the minister, drinking into her soul every word that passed his lips, as if she were determined to live up to every single one of them, while poor Gvendur heard only a sentence here and there as his brain whirled in wilder and wilder confusion. "And the rocks were riven, my brethren; yes, there was little that could stand its ground in that hour, let me tell you. And the veil of the temple was rent in twain from top to bottom; yes, and that wasn't the only thing that was rent, either. Not by a long way. And there was a darkness over the whole of heaven and earth, yes there was little light in that hour, let me assure you — "

Yes there was darkness over everything indeed, and now the sermon was practically over, and now it was over altogether. There followed yet another hymn. By this time the lad was unable to hear or see. The people stood up. He stood up too. Ought he to wait until she came past, or ought he to go out ahead of her? He waited. Ought he to make an effort to look at her as she passed, and try to send her a current, for he believed in the current of love, or ought he to look down at his feet in resignation and utter despair? He looked at her with the current of love. And then he saw that it wasn't her at all, it was another person altogether, it was a middle-aged woman from up-country, a woman, moreover, who had had a baby to someone — it was Thorthur of Gilteig's middle daughter in a ghastly red hat. So the boy could breathe once more in a normal fashion. But he felt now as if everything was so dreadfully empty in and around his heart, and he had sat in the church all that length of time for nothing, and his spiritual torment during the hymns and the sermon had been altogether a waste.

At the end of the service the folk went crowding along to the meeting. A gleaming automobile was standing on the paving outside the Bailiff's windows. The visitors thronged inquisitively around this glittering portent, scrutinizing it from every angle possible. They rapped on the windshield and the side windows, then squeezed the tires to see how hard they were. Gvendur also rapped on the windows and squeezed the tires. The Althingi member had arrived during the service and was now sitting inside with his parents. Just at this moment the banker and his followers came driving along the road from Vik; they drew up at the other end of the enclosure. The Bailiff went walking across to meet them. He was clad in an old rag of a jacket so disreputable in appearance as to suggest that it had been slept on by one of the dogs for a twelve-month past, though only to be resurrected as a change of clothes to mark the importance of the present occasion. A safety-pin held his shirt together at the neck. His trouser bottoms were tucked into his socks, which had obviously been refooted. One could hardly have been surprised had the elegant and dignified gentlemen in overcoats and stiff collars had to curb a strong desire to slip him a copper or two as he bade them welcome. The visitors were told to accomodate themselves in the Moot Hall, whither the candidates would proceed as soon as they had partaken of coffee. Gvendur took a seat in a corner with his cap on his knees and someone gave him a pinch of snuff and he sneezed. Presently the candidates entered. Gvendur of Summerhouses saw only his candidate. Ingolfur Arnarson Jonsson, where was his peer? His splendour beggared invention. Tall, stalwart, and lion-hearted, he had had macadamized roads laid for penniless crofters in isolated valleys; his face with its compelling eyes behind their gold-rimmed glasses shone like a sun over the decrepit peasants assembled before him, and as he began to speak, in a voice sonorous and unforced, his small, snowy-cuffed hands moved in gestures so smooth and graceful that one did not need listen to his words, it was enough simply to watch his hands. The boy from Summerhouses was amazed that anyone should be so obtuse as to doubt the justice of his cause. With quivering heart he reflected that he had loved this man's daughter, wherever she was; that this great man, whose car stood outside the window, was in reality his father-in-law.

Soon the meeting was in full swing, and mankind's most urgent problems under discussion — co-operatives and the peasantry, merchant power and middlemen's profits, banking scandals, losses sustained by fishing companies, the rate of interest on farmers' loans, the Agricultural Bill, the implements' subsidy, the question of sewage, the sale of produce, roads, bridges, telephones, rural colonization, education, housing, the electrification of the country districts. And Ingolfur Arnarson stood up again and again and, puffing his chest and flourishing his hands with inimitable artistry, pointed to his opponent and proved conclusively and beyond a doubt that it was he who was directly responsible for the enormous losses incurred by the banks, which had allowed speculators to squander the savings of a whole nation, for the financial scandals that had brought the fishing companies into such widespread disrepute, for the ever increasing tuberculosis of a nation that was housed in hovels, for the fall of the crown, as barefaced and blatant an act of robbery as had ever been perpetrated on the working classes of any country, and for an educational policy that aimed at bringing the nation down to the same level as the Negroes of Darkest Africa. And now that the peasantry had united to defend their rights and to secure improved conditions, this man had risen up against them, with the foul intention of dragging into the mire the very class that had borne the nation on its shoulders through fire and ice and pestilence for a thousand years, preserving its culture intact through numberless perils.

Gvendur was in agreement with everything that Ingolfur Arnarson said, because he felt he was already his son-in-law. He was filled with an unbounded admiration for this great man who was not content simply with providing people with roads and bridges, but wanted in addition to see everyone living in a house. For the life of him he could not understand why anyone should bother to listen to Ingolfur's opponent, a fat little fellow with a poor delivery who maintained a shameless tranquillity in spite of all his crimes, who even smiled at every fresh accusation, who seemed the better pleased the more it grew obvious that he ought to have been locked up years ago. When at last each had finished describing how he proposed to save the country from the perils that beset her, and neither could be bothered to say any more, the meeting was declared over, and the rival candidates walked out side by side and strolled across the enclosure laughing loud and heartily, as if they had never been better friends than now; many people had enjoyed themselves, and some exceedingly well, but it was doubtful whether anyone had had such a good time of it as the candidates themselves. The people stood staring after them, amazed that they did not fly at each other's throat. They said good-bye at the gate, fondly clasped hands and gazing long and expressively into each other's eyes, like a pair of secret lovers, then the banker drove off, leaving the spectators to scratch their heads.

Shortly afterwards the voters also began to prepare for the road, led their horses out of the pen, rode off in little groups. Gvendur managed to find various pretexts for delay, with the result that when most of the others had departed he was still mooning about the house, keeping a watchful eye on the doors, and stealing an occasional glance up at the windows. He was even thinking of knocking at the back door and asking for the loan of a hammer and block to fasten a loose horseshoe with, or just for a drop of water to drink, perhaps. But it occurred to him that if he were to do this it was almost certain that one of the kitchen-maids would answer the door, and that of course would spoil everything completely. At last he had a brain-wave: he would hide his whip in the wall of the pen, as if he had lost it; then when he had ridden as far as the ridge, he would turn back, knock at the door, inform them of his loss, and ask them to look after the whip for him should they find it. Then possibly the news that he had been at Myri would spread through the house, possibly his name would be mentioned in the house, possibly someone would go out in secret to look for the whip, possibly she would find it. He stuck the whip deep between the stones of the pen wall and rode off. Half-way up the ridge he turned about and made his way back to Myri to ask them to keep the whip for him if they should find it. When he rode once more into the enclosure, the pen had long been empty, everyone gone. He dismounted and walked up to the house. But at that moment the hall door was opened and Ingolfur Arnarson, dressed in a huge overcoat, came out on the doorstep with his mother. He kissed her, opened the door of his car, and stepped in. Then there appeared a fair-haired young girl wearing a blue dress and carrying a coat slung over her arm; she threw her arms round her grandfather's neck and kissed him good-bye. A moment later and she had swept down the steps and was sitting by her father's side; she waved her bright hand to her grandfather and grandmother, and he saw her smile gleaming behind the glass; for him it held all the loveliness of life. There came the humming of the engine as it was started up, low and smoothly powerful. She smiled to her father as the car moved off, and as it drove past him, with the sun glinting on the enamel, the boy's senses were filled with the pleasing scent of gasoline; neither of them had noticed him. He was left standing alone in the empty enclosure, staring after the gleaming automobile as it receded into the distance. Never had he known such utter desolation, he retrieved his whip, mounted, rode off. The car was out of sight in a hollow. A few moments later he caught a glimpse of it on the skyline, right at the top of the ridge. Madness to have thought of giving her a horse. He lashed it with his whip and the horse snorted; probably it was just a nag anyway, a stupid, broken-down old beast that ought to have been pensioned off years ago. The best thing he could do with it would be to sell it to anyone fool enough to buy it.

"Wait here just a moment, love," said the Althingi member. "I think I'll pop over to the hut there for a word or two with the old man." He drew into the side of the road, applied the brakes, and switched off the engine. "Unless you'd care to come along with me?"

"No, thank you," she replied. "It would spoil my shoes."

She watched her father walk briskly away up the path, stalwart and broad-shouldered in thick overcoat.

Bjartur came down the home-field to meet the co-operative manager, called him Ingi lad, and asked him in. But Ingolfur Arnarson was pressed for time and wanted only to say how-d'you-do to his old friend and foster-brother and clap him on the back. When he asked why he hadn't been at the meeting, Bjartur replied that he had better things to do than sit and listen to their blasted squabbling.

"Oh, I don't know," said the Althingi member. "It makes things clearer for you farmers, clarifies your ideas, you know, to hear these vital questions thrashed out."

"Sending one another to hell on a fine Sunday morning, like you high-and-mighty aristocrats do nowadays, isn't my idea of arguing vital questions. Such muck-slinging wouldn't have been considered argument in the old days, when there were great deeds and glorious doings, and mighty men of famous valour walked the earth, men who challenged one another to single combat, or summoned their followers and fought in great armies until the corpses of the slain lay heaped higher than the tops of the hills."

But the Althingi member had no time to listen to ballad politics and replied only that he had heard the farmer of Summerhouses was going to start building, and if that was the case, when was he thinking of beginning?

"Oh, I'll begin when I think fit," said Bjartur.

"Well, if you're thinking of starting this summer, it would be just as well if we got it all settled now, because I'm going south to Reykjavik in the middle of the week, and I doubt if I shall be returning until after the elections."

"How do you know I can't get better terms elsewhere, Ingi lad?" asked Bjartur.

"You misunderstand me completely if you think I'm offering you terms," replied the co-operative manager. "The society is no haggling establishment, and we don't set out to attract custom with fine-sounding offers of bargain prices. The co-operative is your own store, man, where it is you that decide your own terms. There are no middlemen there to add their quota to the cost of the timber and the cement. Nor is there anyone to press you for payment except yourself. All I ask is, what are your orders? I am your servant. When do you want our stuff? And do you want me to work out for you the amount you'll require from the savings bank, or would you rather do it yourself?"

"The terms at the savings bank are hopeless. The ordinary banks are better."

"Yes, Bjartur, so much better that I shouldn't be surprised if your old friend the Fell King hadn't lost all he owns by Christmas and was living in an old shack down on the beach, where he rightly belongs, or was working his guts out as a stableman for his son-in-law, whom I can have put in prison whenever I care. I am the man who will rule the destiny of the National Bank before this summer is over, mark my words. And the whole of that infernal gang of swindlers shall be bankrupted or my name isn't Ingolfur Arnarson Jonsson. And in that day there will be little comfort for those who trusted the swindlers and laid their fate in their hands. Our savings bank, on the other hand, is a solid, trustworthy establishment, Bjartur; and though it may not grant a loan for a very long period, you're all the better off for that, because a farm saddled with a long mortgage isn't one's own property, except on paper."

This was high finance with a vengeance, and Bjartur was in two minds, hardly knowing what to believe. He was merely a simple up-country peasant who had fought nature and the country's monsters with his bare hands, and his higher culture was derived all from ballads and old sagas where men fought one another without any beating about the bush, hewed one another to pieces, and heaped the corpses of the slain one above another; this was the only higher politics he understood.

"Our building materials are as much as a third cheaper than the stuff you'll get in Vik," continued the co-operative manager. "We got a whole cargo of cement direct from abroad last summer. And, in addition, there's every prospect that we'll be giving as high as fifty crowns a head for the lambs this autumn."

"It's a pity one can never tell when you're lying and when you're not lying," said Bjartur. "Personally, I'm nearest to believing that you lie all the time."

At this the Althingi member clapped him on the shoulder and laughed.

Then he prepared to take his leave.

"So it will be in order for me to send you the first load of cement tomorrow," said he. "The rest will come of itself. My agent will show you all the architect's plans you need. And we've plenty of masons and joiners around the store. As far as the loan from the savings bank is concerned, we have a rough idea of what you'll be needing. Give us a look in tomorrow or the day after and we'll discuss the matter at great length."

The car was standing on the road opposite Summerhouses, and the racehorse was very frightened; it pricked its ears restively, refusing to advance in spite of its rider's efforts to urge it on. Finally he had to dismount and lead it by the reins. The strange, highly polished machine glittered in the rays of the evening sun, alien in the landscape, preternatural, but nevertheless he led his horse right up to it. From the open front window there rose, coiling in the tranquil air, a thin plume of blue smoke. The daughter was sitting alone there in the front seat; he saw her shoulder, her white neck, her golden curls, her cheek. She did not look at him, though he was only a few yards away, and the smoke went on rising from the window in graceful coils and loops. He went closer still and wished her good-evening. She gave a little start and made as if to hide the cigarette, then raised it once more to her lips.

"Why did you startle me like that?" she asked, in her singing, rather nasal voice.

"I thought I'd like to show you my horse," he said with a countrified smile.

"Horse?" she said vacantly, as if she had never heard of such a beast.

"Yes," he said, and pointed to the horse and told her the price, and it was one of the costliest horses in the district.

"Dear me," she said, without deigning to look at it. "Has it anything to do with me?"

"Don't you remember me, then?" he asked.

"Not that I know of," she answered tonelessly, gazing straight along the road through the windshield of her father's car, with the cigarette daintily held between her fingers. He went on staring at her. Finally she turned her head and, giving him a supercilious look, asked, as if he had done her some personal injury: "Why aren't you in America?"

"I missed the ship that night," he replied.

"Why didn't you go on the next one?"

"I wanted a h-horse instead."

"A horse?"

Then, plucking up courage, he said: "I felt I would be able to make good at home here after I'd g-got to know you."

"Wretch!" she said. "Spineless wretch!"

This stung him to a hint of temper: he flushed hotly, and the smile gave way to a quivering upper lip. "I'm no wretch," he cried. "I'll show you that. You'll see one day."

"The sort of people who set out to do something and give up before it's done are all wretches and weeds. I call them frightful wretches and weeds. I call them wretches and weeds and cowards. Yes, cowards. I'm ashamed of myself, ashamed of myself, for having set eyes on them, let alone spoken to them."

He hopped back a pace and there was a momentary glint in his eyes as he cried, matching provocation for provocation: "Maybe we shall build as big a mansion as you people at Rauths-myri. Or bigger."

She laughed contemptuously down her nose, and nothing more.

"You blasted Rauthsmyri gang," he cried, "you've always thought you could trample on us, yes, that's what you've always thought," and advancing a step nearer, he shook his clenched fist in her face. "But I'll show you!"

"I'm not talking to you," said she. "Why can't you leave me alone?"

"In a few years I shall be the owner of Summerhouses, and I'll be as big a farmer as your grandfather, maybe bigger. You'll see."

She puffed the smoke out of her mouth in a great cloud as she narrowed her eyes and measured him.

"My father will soon be master of the whole country," she told him. Then she opened her eyes and, leaning towards him, sharpened them on him as if in menace. "Of the whole of Iceland. All of it."

This took the shine out of him again, and he looked down at the ground. Then he asked:

"Why are you so cruel to me now? You who know that it was

only because of you that I didn't go to America. I thought you were fond of me."

"Fathead," she said. "Yes, maybe if you'd gone, just a little." She thought of a good joke and couldn't bear to suppress it: "And more especially if you'd never come back — then, perhaps. But there's Father coming now," and straightway she threw her cigarette into the ditch.

"So you've found someone to talk to, love," said Ingolfur Arnarson Jonsson. "That was fine." He got into the car and lit himself a cigar.

"It's only a country lad," she said. "He was going to America once."

"Oh, is it he?" asked the Althingi member as he trod on the self-starter and let the brakes off.

"You did right, mate, in giving up this idea of going to America. We must stay at home, contend with our own difficulties and overcome them. It pays to believe in one's own motherland. Everything for Iceland. By the way, how old are you?"

But the lad was only seventeen and too young to vote yet.

So the Althingi member put the car in gear without troubling more about him, and, as the car moved off, absent-mindedly raised a finger to his hat, as if in farewell, perhaps it was only to straighten it.

In a few moments they were away in the distance. There remained only a puff or two of dust swirling about in the air. Presently it had settled and there was no more dust in the air.

67.   MODERN POETRY

MANY a man may have his doubts for the moment, but when all comes to all and a long view is taken, one discovers usually that things have been making some sort of forward progress, some headway or other. And a man's dreams have a habit of coming true, more especially if he has made no particular effort to fulfil them — and there on the paving, before the crofter has quite waked up to the fact, lie the first loads of cement for building. It is popularly supposed that when a man has made himself worthy of living in a real house, he will be given a real house to live in; it sprouts out of the earth for him of its own accord, they say; life bestows on the individual all that he is worthy of, and the same is said to be true of the nation as a whole. The war raised many

people, and one or two countries, to positions of great worth, it
is, in fact, extremely doubtful whether any number of politicians,
however brilliant, however high-minded, can do more for Iceland
than one war accompanied by plenty of lively slaughter in foreign
parts. After Bjartur had become a person of great worth, even he
was prone to admit on occasion that life had sometimes been
pretty hard in Summerhouses in the old days, but one has to take
a few knocks if one wants to get on, surely, and anyway we never
ate other folk's bread. Other folk's bread is the most virulent form
of poison that a free and independent man can take; other folk's
bread is the only thing that can rob him of independence and the
one true freedom. Time was when certain persons had tried to
force upon him the gift of a cow, but he was most certainly not
the man to accept presents from his enemies; and when, in the
following year, he had slaughtered this same cow, it was because
he had had a distant goal in prospect in his husbandry, or, as he
had told the workmen in those far-off days, because he knew quite
well what he was going to do with his money, maybe he was going
to build himself a palace with it. And it was in very much the same
strain that he spoke down in the co-operative store now. "A big
house or nothing at all," he said, "two storeys and a third under
gables at the least." They managed, however, to persuade him
that it would be better to have a nice, well-built cellar and one
storey less, which would make three storeys just the same, base-
ment, ground floor, upper floor. He raised a loan in the savings
bank. The croft, with its lack of good buildings, was of course not
considered sufficient security for a long loan, so it was only granted
for a period of one year at a time. It was considered suitable to
lend thirty per cent on the strength of the first mortgage on the
land, though only provided that the co-operative society went
surety. The co-operative society accepted the responsibility immediately in exchange for a second mortgage on the land. The
savings bank then declared itself not unwilling to advance another
loan in the autumn, when the house was finished building, subject
to a further mortgage on the house and property together. From
this new loan the co-operative society was to be repaid the loan
they had advanced for building materials. Such are the workings
of higher finance, and in return for all this the crofter voted for
Ingolfur Arnarson Jonsson, that he might sit as his representative
in the Althingi and solve the nation's problems, and shortly afterwards the co-operative manager was declared elected, and merchant power had thereby suffered a second defeat on this particular

front. All those who had voted for the co-operative manager had
reason now to rejoice, whereas those who had voted for the banker
gnawed their knuckles and cursed themselves black in the face,
partly because the bank was in a pretty shaky condition and might,
indeed, be declared insolvent at any moment, partly because these
same people had shown themselves in open enmity of the Rauthsmyrians; and to whom could they look now in the midst of their
self-wrought destruction? Then, to make the outlook blacker still,
those idiotic foreigners didn't seem to have had the sense to keep
their precious war going for another twelve-month or so, and it
looked as if the bottom might fall out of the farmer's market any
day now.

The foundations were dug in the slope of the ground just
south of the old croft, and then masons and joiners came and made
the cellar, and it was a marvellous cellar; then they knocked off
for a week's breathing-space, and, at the end of it, set to work on
the ground floor, where there were to be four rooms and a scullery.
Yes, if only there had been one or two little children, young and
avid of novelty, to rejoice over the building, as there had been
years ago when the ewe-house was being built, for there was great
excitement and much afoot on the croft these days, the smell of
wood and cement, the tapping of hammers and the churning
rattle of the mixer, workmen by the score, carts and horses, sand
and gravel. At this date double walls and ferro-concrete were un-
heard of; single walls were made to suffice, but they were built
thick. Half-way through the meadow haymaking the upper storey
and the roof were still lacking, and as the money had all been spent
by this time, Bjartur went down to town to get a further advance
from the savings bank. But Ingolfur Arnarson happened to be in
Reykjavik and money was tight in the savings bank, though they
gave him to understand that there might be a chance in the
autumn. Nor was this his only difficulty, for the store was out of
corrugated iron for roofs and was also very short of window-glass,
there were so many folk building just now, but they expected a
fresh consignment of glass later in the summer and of corrugated
iron in the autumn. "We'll see what sort of price the lambs fetch,"
they said. So Bjartur's house stood in the moulds all that summer,
a most depressing object to meet the eye; travellers passing that
way missed the friendly old grass-grown turf cottage, for it lay out
of sight behind this formless, gaping monstrosity, which reminded
one of nothing so much as the havoc and devastation left in the
trail of a hurricane. But if anyone imagined that Bjartur's house

would be allowed to stay as it was indefinitely, he was sadly in error. For in the autumn it came to light that the heaven-sent blessings of war were still in operation as far as prices were concerned, though the fighting itself had been over and done with for almost a year now. Never had such prices been heard of before in Iceland; so much so that Madam of Myri spoke these winged words at the National Congress of Women's Institutes in Reykjavik that very autumn: "Iceland is a heavenly country." The lambs were bringing in as much as fifty crowns apiece, and naturally no words in the language were idyllic enough to praise the virtues of rural culture, past and present, in the southern newspapers. The merits of the peasantry were exalted above all other merits. Bjartur was able to obtain more money from the savings bank, and then both timber and window-panes and corrugated iron and workmen, so that the time was not long before the house was finished and complete with roof. But when they were busy moulding the upper floor, it was discovered that the cellar had begun to crack. When the foreman joiner and the foreman mason were summoned, they announced that these cracks must have been caused by the earthquakes that had occurred that summer. Bjartur said that no one had noticed any earthquakes that particular summer, not on the upper surface of the earth at least.

"There were earthquakes in Korea," said the foreman joiner.

Fortunately the cracks were comparatively small and it was easy to fill them up again and possible to see many an entrancing vision of the future in connection with the house in spite of them. Bjartur gazed at the building long and often, mumbling a variety of things to himself.

After the autumn round-up both father and son went down to Fjord with two carts, for there was still a good deal of smaller stuff needed for the house. Bjartur said not a word till they had crossed the heath and were descending its eastern declivity. Then he broke the silence:

"You told me in the spring there that Asta Sollilja thought my poetry was nothing but empty doggerel, didn't you?"

"Yes," replied Gvendur, "those were her words more or less."

"And that her friends down in Fjord were all in favour of this modern poetry?"

"Yes," said Gvendur, "she's engaged to a man who is a modern poet."

"Well, it's easy enough to write like these modern fellows," said Bjartur. "It's just like diarrhœa. End-rhymes and nothing more."

But Gvendur had not the poet's tongue and was therefore chary of words when such matters were the subject of discussion. After a short silence his father went on:

"If you should run across Asta Sollilja today, I'd like you to recite her these three modern verses of mine, so that no one shall say of me that I couldn't write in these simple modern measures, if need be."

"Very well, as long as I can learn them."

"For heaven's sake, lad, never let anyone hear you say you're such a blockhead as not to be able to learn three easy little verses first go."

He walked on for a while, mumbling under his breath, then said aloud: "They are three verses about the war."

> Ten million men and a half, I see,
> Were slaughtered in fun in that maniacs' spree.
> By now they're probably all in hell,
> But I mourn them not. God-speed. Farewell.
>
> There was, however, another war,
> Waged near a rock in the blind days of yore,
> And that was fought over one sweet flower
> That was torn away in disastrous hour.
>
> And that's why I'm lately so moody grown
> And pride myself little on what I own.
> For what are riches and houses and power
> If in that house blooms no lovely flower?"

"Wouldn't you rather go and see her yourself?" asked Gvendur.

"I?" asked the father, gaping. "No, I have nothing in common with such folk."

"What folk?"

"Folk who have betrayed my trust. It isn't I who must go and ask forgiveness of anyone. Let those who have betrayed my trust come to me and ask forgiveness. I ask forgiveness of no one. Besides," he added, "I'm no relation of hers anyway."

"You ought to go and see her all the same," said the lad. "I'm sure she must often have a pretty hard time of it. And it was you who kicked her out when she was pregnant."

"It's no business of yours whom I kick out. You can think yourself lucky that I don't kick you out; and I won't be long about it, either, let me tell you, if I have any more of your blasted lip."

"I'm sure Sola would love you to go and see her."

Bjartur gave his horse a mighty swipe and replied: "No, while there's a breath of life left in me, nothing will make me go to her." Then after a moment or two he added, looking over his shoulder at his son: "But if I die, you can tell her from me that she may gladly lay me out."

Asta Sollilja had just moved into her betrothed's house at Sandeyri, farther down the fjord. It was a little house. Actually it wasn't a house at all in the ordinary sense of the word, it was a turf hut roofed with rusty corrugated iron, reflecting much the same degree of civilization as those inhabited by the Negroes of Darkest Africa. There were two rusty tin bowls in the window, full of earth, and from one of them stuck the stem of some plant or other that was struggling to live. Two beds; one for Asta Sollilja and her fiancé, the other for his mother, who owned the hut. The fiancé was out of work. Asta Sollilja greeted her brother in not unfriendly fashion, though her left eye was very much more in evidence than the right. She was pale and strange and her decayed tooth had been extracted, leaving a gap. For the rest, she was not very talkative with her brother and did not even mention his old plan of emigrating to America. Obviously she did not consider it in any way remarkable that he should have abandoned the idea; she had not believed in America in the spring and did not believe in it now. He saw immediately that she was pregnant, and gazed at her long-fingered hands, in which there dwelt a wealth of human reality, and at her arms, which were too thin. She had a dry cough.

"You seem to have a bad cold," he remarked.

No, she hadn't a cold, but she was always coughing just the same; sometimes she spat a little blood in the mornings. He asked her then whether she was thinking of getting married, but it appeared that she was not looking forward to marriage now with quite the same pride as she had shown in the spring, when she had informed Bjartur of Summerhouses' son that she was engaged and that her fiancé was a modern poet. "What concern is it of anyone in Summerhouses what I do?" she asked.

"Father gave me a poem to learn this morning," said Gvendur. "It's about the war. A modern poem. Shall I recite it for you?"

"No," she said, "I can't be bothered to listen to it."

"I think I'll recite it all the same," he said, and recited the three verses.

She listened and her eyes grew strangely warm at the sound of it, and the lines in her face dissolved, as if she were about to burst out weeping, or about to fly into a rage, but she said not a word, or, rather, left all that she had intended saying unsaid, and turned away from him.

"The new house is almost ready now," he said. "We shall be moving into it shortly."

"Really," she said, "what's that to me?"

"Judging from the poem, I should say that Father has certain ideas of his own with regard to the house. I'm sure he'd give you the big room all to yourself if you came back to us."

"I," she replied with a proud toss of her head, "I am engaged to a young man, a gifted young man who loves me."

"You ought to come back all the same," said Gvendur.

"Do you think that I, I, would ever leave a man who loves me?"

But this was too much for the old woman, who, unable to contain herself any longer, burst out from the region of the stove: "It wouldn't be a bad idea if you were to show him a little more kindness, then. Poor lad, he never has a moment's peace with you when he's indoors here."

"It's a lie," cried Asta Sollilja passionately, turning to face the old woman. "I love him, yes, love him more than anything in the whole world, and you've no right to go telling strangers that I'm not good to him, when I'm at least twice as good to him as he deserves — it's his child I'm carrying, isn't it? And though Bjartur of Summerhouses were to come to me in person, and were to crawl across this floor here on hands and knees to beg forgiveness for all that he's done to me since I was born, I still wouldn't hear a word about his house, much less ever dream of moving a step in his direction. So you can tell him this from me: that while there's a breath of life left in me, nothing will ever make me go back to Bjartur of Summerhouses, but that when I'm dead he may gladly bury my carrion for all that I care."

68.   WHEN A MAN IS UNMARRIED

ONE has grown weary of one's house before it has finished building; strange that mankind should need to live in a house, instead of remaining content with the house of wishes. What news now of that much discussed concrete building in which Bjartur of Summerhouses proposed to take up his residence? As related above, there had been earthquakes in Korea, but what of that? — there were windows in the house now, and panes in the win-

dows, and the house had a roof, with a chimney sticking out of
it, and in the kitchen there was a range with three grates, bought
at a bargain price. And to improve matters still further, they even
went and built a concrete stairway up to the front door so that
people could get into the house, five steps high. Then came the
entrance hall, for naturally there was an entrance hall. The intention was to flit into the house at some time during the autumn.
The largest room on the ground floor had been panelled inside;
one person suggested that the panelling should be painted, another
that picture pages cut from foreign newspapers should be pasted
on it, to smarten it up as they did in the towns, but Bjartur didn't
want anything smartened up, he didn't want any trash in his house.
So far so good. But early in the autumn heavy gales sprang up,
with day after day of storm-driven rain and sleet, and then it came
to light that it was just as windy inside the house as out. Why was
this? It was because they had forgotten to put doors on the house.
No one had had the forethought to order them in time, and it was
too late now, for it takes a good while to make a door, and the
joiners in Fjord were all far too busy with jobs that people needed
doing before the winter set in.

"Oh, just knock a few old boards together," said Bjartur.

But this the joiner refused to do, saying that it would be useless
hanging ramshackle doors in a stone house, as the wind always
seemed twice as searching in a house build of stone. He was willing, however, to equip the house with first-class thresholds before
he left, but I'm telling you now that to match such thresholds
you'll need doors of the finest quality only, doors of special wood,
doors hung on proper hinges.

"Oh, the blacksmith won't be long in hammering out a few
hinges for me," said Bjartur.

"No," said the joiner. "That's where you're wrong. Ordinary
hinges, such as the blacksmith will make you, may be quite all
right on a box or chest, but they're no good for a decently made
door. What you want are proper door-hinges of the finest work-
manship and quality. In a boom year all doors must be hung on
proper hinges."

"Oh, to hell with it all," cried Bjartur angrily, for he was ex-
asperated beyond measure at the thought of how much this gaping
cement monster had already cost him in ready money.

But there were worse things than the mere absence of doors.
The house was no doubt finished as far as the builders were concerned, but nevertheless there was a total lack of all those things

which are indispensable in a house if it is properly to be worthy
of the name. There were no beds, for instance. The bedsteads in
the old croft had been built into the framework of the living-room,
and it was impossible to transfer them. The same thing applied to
tables. The table in the croft had in its time been knocked together
out of a few roughly planed boards, which had then been nailed
to the window-sill, and though it was true that time had long since
planed them smooth, it was equally true that time had done much
more: it had broken them in various places and rotted them
through and through. There were no cupboards that could be
moved either; the old shelves had been nailed to the wall and had
rotted away along with it. Nor were there any chairs; there had
never been any chairs in Summerhouses, had never been benches
either, much less any of the superior luxuries in the way of decorative furniture such as curtains, *God Bless Our Home, Hallgrimur
Pjetursson, The Czar of Russia,* china dogs. In short, throughout
all these years there had never existed in Summerhouses one
single object that could have served either for use or for ornament
in a real house. Such are the many problems that arise and con-
front a man when, having reached the highest peaks of culture,
he begins living in a house. It isn't doors alone that are needed.
Bjartur therefore decided to spend yet another winter in the old
turf croft, especially as the hard weather looked as if it would set
in early. He had the doors boarded up. And thus, for the time
being, the house remained, towering up from the slope in front
of the croft like any other advertisement of those boom years that
the man had experienced in his husbandry, a peculiar façade.

Now we turn to housekeepers. It is difficult to keep housekeepers. Housekeepers differ from married women in this respect:
that they insist on doing as they please, whereas married women
are required to do as they are told. Housekeepers are continually
demanding things, whereas married women may think themselves lucky for getting nothing at all. Housekeepers always need
everything for everything, whereas married women need nothing
for anything, and think it quite natural. Most things are considered by housekeepers as being beneath their dignity, but who
bothers listening to a married woman if she starts grumbling? No
one is any the worse for it but her. One needn't mention their fits
of sulks or the fact that they'll argue the head off a man if everything isn't exactly to their liking; and it's hard, surely, to have to
marry a woman just to be able to tell her to keep her trap shut.
"I'd rather be married to three women at once than have one house-

keeper," Bjartur was wont to say, but he was inconsistent enough in deed to keep on engaging the importunate termagants and to suffer a life of continual squabbling from one year's end to another.

During the first three years he had three housekeepers, each of whom stayed with him a twelve-month, one young, one middle-aged, one elderly. The young one was terrible, the middle-aged one worse, the old one worse still. Finally he engaged one without any age, and she proved to be the least objectionable of the lot; she was named Brynhildur, usually shortened to Brynja. She had stuck it out for two years now in spite of everything. One good quality that served to mark her out from the others was that she was interested in the farm and wished it well. But that was not the only point in her favour. She was not addicted, like the young one, to reserving the best of everything for the hired man, and to keeping him up at night with billing and cooing so that he was useless in the morning; she did not work herself up into a frenzy of rage against God and men, then roll about the floor in a fit of hysterics, like the middle one; and she did not seek to humiliate Bjartur by comparing the leaks in Summerhouses and her present life of misery with the superior roofing arrangements and the freedom from rheumatism of a youth spent happily in the service of clergymen, as the old one did. No, she went about her work quietly and efficiently and was truthful in all her dealings with her master. But she was by no means free from the minor failings of the sex for all that. She felt that she was never appreciated at her true worth, that her labours went unrecognized, her virtues unacknowledged. Everyone misunderstood her, she thought, even suspected her of various crimes, for they seemed always to be accusing her of something or other, though usually of thieving. For charges so manifestly unjust she maintained a perpetual watch, ready to meet them and ward them off with a steadfast and vigorous defence. "You seem to forget that the calf got the dregs," she would say if Bjartur ever suggested that what had been left of the morning's coffee might be heated up to quench his thirst. "You seem to think I go about the house stealing," she would grumble if Bjartur asked politely for the bite or two of fish he had left uneaten at dinner-time. "Perhaps you think I've been lying in bed coddling myself like a bailiff's daughter," would be her retort if Bjartur ever hinted that she was making a somewhat belated appearance out in the meadow after the morning milking. She had never married. She was supposed to have been friendly with a man in her youth, but apparently she had found out that he had a wife already, and she had never been able to get over it since. As she had worked for a wage all her life long and had saved it up and banked it all, she was generally considered to be pretty well off. She had also a horse of her own, an old roan mare which had never been broken in, but of which she was extremely fond. Most remarkable of all, however, was the fact that she was the possessor of a treasure that exalted her high above the majority of the working people in the country. What was this treasure? It was a bed, a bed that was independent of the framework of the house, a bed that could be taken to pieces and put together again at will, so that it could be moved from one place to another, a bed, in short, that was nothing less than a piece of furniture. She had her own mattress, which she always put out to air on the first day of summer, and she had an over-mattress and a coverlet of the finest-quality down, two sets of linen sheets, and a lovely pillow with "Good Night" embroidered on it. Actually she was a fine, dependable woman, uncommonly well built and a match for any man. Though she was clean as a cat and always in the right, she was no squeamish shirker who would shrink from the thought of carrying muck night or day, with her hands as big as hams and not altogether free from the marks of old chilblains, and dressed in a tight-fitting jacket and no corsets, so that she seemed as big in the girth as a good strong pack-horse. There was a pleasant, youthful rosiness in her weather-beaten cheeks, and perhaps just a tinge of blue about them when she was cold. She had the eyes of a realist, and a mouth that was set in coarse, hard-working lines, free from any suggestion of the modern spirit of captiousness in thought or feeling. She spoke usually in a strained voice and cold tones not unlike an unjustly accused person in front of a judge, always a little aggrieved, a little wounded in her inmost heart.

Now, Bjartur had been so certain of moving into the house that autumn that he had done nothing during the summer to patch up the old croft, and when, towards the end of October, the frosts suddenly gave way to thawing winds and heavy rain, it was soon made uncomfortably obvious that the roof was in a state of acute disrepair. Bjartur stood the leaks as long as he could, then moved downstairs, but the grandmother, being a conservative old creature, refused to move and, having had a sack spread over her, lay in bed there till it faired. Well, one evening Bjartur was sitting downstairs waiting for the housekeeper to bring him his porridge, and presently she set it down in front of him and he began eating. She stood for a while watching him out of the corner of her eye, as, busy with his spoon, he sat eating from the bowl on his knees, and when he was almost done she opened her mouth and addressed him. She had a habit of turning her back on him when speaking to him, and now it was almost as if she was grumbling away at the wall.

"I must say I can't see the point of building a fine big house if you intend sticking on in this leaky old hole the same afterwards as before. Folk would have had a lot to say about bad management if it had been I that was responsible for it."

"Oh, I don't think we'll take much harm though we have to put up with a few leaks here and there for one winter more. Leaks are healthy enough if they come from the skies. And anyway it wasn't my fault that the doors weren't ready."

"I would have been quite prepared to pay for a door for my room if I had been asked in time."

"Yes, but it happens that I intend having the doors in my own house hung at my own expense," retorted Bjartur. "And anyway, there were other things besides doors needed, and I wasn't prepared to go and buy all the furniture necessary for such a big house when winter was already upon us."

"You seem to have managed quite well without furniture so far," said the housekeeper, "but if it was really necessary I could always have bought two chairs with my own money. And I could always have lent you my bed, or at least shared it with others, if it had been possible to come to any sort of agreement with a living soul in this place."

"Huh," said Bjartur, and looked her over as she stood in front of him. No one could deny that she was a fine figure of a woman. And she was certainly good at her work, and intelligent; and free from any kind of vanity or extravagance. Possibly his best course would be to marry the bitch, so that he could have full leave to tell her to shut up; or at the least go to bed with her, as she herself was suggesting in her own starchy fashion. He felt that he could not be angry with this colossus, whom the years could not bend, or answer her roughly or haughtily, as she so rightly deserved, and he had to confess that it was both uneconomical and eccentric of him to be always paying her a wage instead of simply getting in beside her in that marvellous bed of hers, one of the best beds in the whole parish, one such as he himself had never before had the opportunity of sleeping in. And besides, didn't she have money in the savings bank?

"Oh, it wasn't because I was short of money that I didn't move into the house this autumn, Brynja lass," he continued. "I could have bought plenty of doors, plenty of beds, plenty of chairs if I had wanted to. And perhaps a picture of God, and one of the Czar too, if I'd felt like it."

"I don't have to ask why it was," she replied, still grumbling away at the wall. "Poetry is being written about those who have neither the nature nor the sense to understand it, but other folk never hear a friendly word spoken to them. All that other folk get are the leaks."

"The leak that comes from outside harms no one," he stated once more. "It is the leak that one finds indoors that is worst."

When one is unmarried, one must tell people to shut up in roundabout fashion.

69.   INTEREST

Was it surprising if most people considered that Bjartur of Summerhouses would have been much better off without the house he had built? Then what about the Fell King and his house? Did he fare any better, may I ask? No; the truth was that Bjartur's house, though innocent of furniture and so far uninhabitable, was a veritable fount of happiness compared with the house that the Fell King had built and fitted out at such expense. For whereas Bjartur's house continued to stand there by virtue of the loan he had raised in the savings bank, and his sheep to pay off the interest stipulated, the supports that sustained the Fell King's house collapsed completely, engulfing the owner in sudden ruin. It was a fine house, this of the Fell King's, so fine, in fact, and so well furnished that it might be designated, along with the mansion at Rauthsmyri itself, as a dwelling such as civilized human beings need not be ashamed of living in; but the lamentable outcome was that no sooner had the Fell King brought it to such a desirable pitch than he was thrown out neck and crop and forced to flee. People simply can't afford to live like civilized human beings, as has been so often demonstrated before and will be again; even middle-class farmers can't afford it, and in a boom year at that. The only sensible course for ordinary folk, the only one that pays, is to live in a little hut on the same cultural level as the Negroes of central Africa and to let the merchant keep a flicker of life going in them, as the Icelandic nation has been doing for a thousand years now. People take more upon themselves than they can manage if they aim higher. True, it had been quite usual in the old days for people to owe the merchant money and to be refused credit when the debt had grown too big. It had likewise been nothing uncommon for people thus denied sustenance to die of starvation, but such a fate, surely, was infinitely preferable to being ensnared by the banks, as people are nowadays, for at least they had lived like independent men, at least they had died of hunger like free people. The mistake lies in assuming that the helping hand proffered by the banks is as reliable as it is seductive, when in actual fact the banks may be relied upon only by those few exceptionally great men who can afford to owe anything from one to five millions. So about the same time as Bjartur sold his better cow to raise money for wages and paid a thousand crowns off the loan and six hundred as interest by making inroads on his stock of sheep, the Fell King sold his farm to a speculator for the amount of the mortgages with which it was encumbered and fled to live in a hovel in the town, yes, and thought himself lucky to escape. The National Bank had passed into Ingolfur Arnarson's control and had become a State bank on the basis of a huge government loan from England; remissions of and concessions on loans were out of the question now, unless it was a matter of millions, and the farmers' produce had fallen disastrously in price.

Yes, the bottom fell out of everything, the autumn that Bjartur's house was one year old. The war's blessings were no longer operative as far as trade and prices were concerned, for the foreigners had begun rearing sheep of their own again instead of killing men, worse luck. Icelandic mutton was once more one of the world's superfluous commodities. No one was asking for wool these days, the foreigners' sheep had started growing wool of their own again. Bjartur had to stand by and watch a hundred of these unwelcome Icelandic sheep melt away simply to pay the interest and the part payment of his loan. But this loss he took with the same unflinching fortitude as he had previously shown in the face of famine, spectres, and merchants, complaining to no one. The walls of his prison of debt were no doubt growing the thicker the lower his produce sank in price, but he was determined to keep on running his head against those walls as long as there was a drop of blood or a particle of brain left in it. This was a new phase in the crofter's eternal struggle for independence, this fight against the normal economic conditions that must of necessity return when the abnormal prosperity of war has passed away; when the unnatural optimism that has betrayed the hut-dwelling peasant into an act of folly so imbecile as to propose living in a house has evaporated and left not a trace behind. He returned to his senses, now that the boom years were over, to find himself stuck in the bog that, with infinite labour, he had managed to avoid in the hard years; the free man of the famine years had become the interest-slave of the boom years. It seemed after all that in their freedom from debt, their dead children, their dirt, their hunger, the lean years had been more dependable than the boom years with all their coquettish lending establishments, their house.

It was about the same time as Ingolfur Arnarson was appointed Governor, and the National Bank resuscitated by means of several millions in share capital from the Icelandic State, — that is to say, from a certain bank in London, — that there came a new manager to the co-operative society in Fjord. "Things have got into a hell of a mess here," growled the new manager angrily, and the deeper he probed into the books, the angrier he became; people's debts had been allowed to run far too high, things were in an awful state, precautionary measures of a most drastic nature would have to be taken immediately. Those people who owed more than they could ever pay were straightway declared bankrupt, and might thank their lucky stars for being let off so lightly, but all those who had anything in them at all were allowed to hang on in their halter of debt, with their toes barely touching the ground, in the hope that they might be able to scrape at least the interest together with their broken and bleeding nails — a misfortune even greater, perhaps, than that of being bankrupted and kicked out empty-handed. The big men arranged that the public should be put on rations in the co-operative society, so that they might go on keeping body and soul together — for the sake of the interest. People's most essential requirements were then doled out to them, in quantities varying with their means and circumstances so that they could go on slaving for the interest they had to pay. Many folk could only get essential provisions if a more prosperous person went security for them. Coffee and sugar were out of the question except for landed farmers; the wheat ration could be measured most conveniently with a thimble, though some unfortunates got none at all; small wares were cut down severely, and clothes were strictly forbidden, especially to those people who were really in need of them. On the other hand, the Government had made tremendous progress as regards tobacco, laws having recently been passed whereby a free grant of tobacco from public funds was to be made to every member of the farming community to aid him in defending his sheep against scab and lung-worm; this luxury might be administered either internally, as a medicine, or externally, as a dip. This tobacco was given a very warm welcome; it was christened Exchequer or Wormy and even the Bailiff chewed Wormy in the interests of economy in these difficult times.

"It's hard lines, surely," said Bjartur, on being informed of the rations allotted him for his subsistence in the second year of the new house, "if I'm no longer to be allowed to decide my purchases for myself, like a free man. And if I don't get what I want here, I'll take my custom elsewhere."

"Please yourself," was the reply. "But in that case we simply distrain on your property."

"What the hell am I supposed to be, a slave and a half-wit, or what?"

"I don't know," was the rejoinder, "we're only going according to the books."

He was allowed only half a sack of rye meal and the same of oats, but was given plenty of salt refuse fish, which the co-op seemed to have in cartloads, likewise lots of Wormy. It was the first time in all his life as a farmer that he was refused a handful or so of wheat flour with which to make pancakes should a visitor ride into the enclosure, and coffee and sugar were out of the question for such people as he, unless they paid in cash. Time was when he had not scrupled to say what he thought of those who held the peasants' lives in their grasp, but whom was he to rail at here? A few books?

However, they did not succeed in preventing his making the house habitable that autumn. There were still a good many things lacking, of course, but at least they had got the biggest room on the middle floor into some sort of order, and the kitchen had also been brought into use, and the house fitted with three doors, one outer and two inner, all hung with proper hinges, and complete with suitable knobs at that. He bought a second-hand bedstead for himself and Gvendur down in Fjord, and though no one had hitherto considered him much of a handy man, he hammered a few planks together to fashion a bed for the old woman, likewise a rough-and-ready sort of table and a little bench to sit on. The family then moved into the house, all into the one room. But no sooner had they got settled than they discovered that there was something wrong with the range; the smoke blew down incessantly whenever a fire was made, and the whole house filled with an incredible reek. Various people were called in, and many were the meetings held to discuss the matter, many the noteworthy theories propounded and conclusively demonstrated. Some held that the chimneypot wasn't high enough, others that the chimneypot was too high. Some people thought that the flue was too wide, while others considered that it must be too narrow, or even imperforate. Reference was made, moreover, to a scientific theory that had been published in a newspaper, to the effect that chimneys built during spring tides always gave a lot of trouble. Judging by this, Bjartur's chimney must have been built during spring tides. One thing was certain: the chimney went on smoking in spite of all their theorizing. Obviously, expensive repairs would be necessary to put the thing in order, and it was extremely doubtful whether it would pay to have them done, for the range was a glutton for firewood and other fuel with its three big grates. Finally an oil-stove was bought for cooking on, and the range allowed to stand untouched in the kitchen, as if for ornament.

70.   TROLLS IN AUTUMN

Now it was housekeeper Brynja's custom, once every autumn, to saddle her mare and take a trip to town on a shopping expedition. On these occasions she would be away for a week at a time, for this trip of hers was in the nature also of a holiday tour; probably she had friends the same as anyone else. She was wont to return ruddy of complexion and with a certain air of importance about her as she ambled along on her roan, with a large assortment of packages tied to the saddle, small wares, cotton remnants, sewing-thread, hard biscuits to gnaw at on festive occasions and to offer folk if they were of a reasonable way of thinking, a grain or so of coffee, a lump or two of sugar. This time, however, things were rather different, for she returned, not on horseback, but on foot, leading the roan behind her with saddle-packs filled to capacity. She was warm and cheerful in her mood as she asked the crofter if he would help her unhitch the packs and carry them in.

"What's all this you've been buying?" inquired Bjartur.

"Oh, nothing very much, really. Nothing worth talking about anyway," she replied, unwilling to tell him everything at once. Her manner was a trifle self-important, and perhaps just a trifle happy, just a trifle proud underneath; perhaps on her way over the moors she had been looking forward to his questioning her and trying to probe into every detail. But he closed up immediately in cold reserve and showed no further sign of curiosity. It was not his habit to cross-examine anyone about anything, he himself never permitted anyone to cross-examine him about anything, let her please herself about what she bought. He bundled her purchases into the entrance in silence, then let her mare loose in the marshes and gave it a kick, it was a pitch-dark autumn night. He found a few odd jobs to delay him outside and did not go in again before bedtime. He suspected that the housekeeper, following her usual autumn habit, would offer him a biscuit to eat if he went in before she was in bed, but on this occasion he cared less for biscuits than ever before, being afraid of what they might lead to, maybe hard words on both sides. Yet when at long length he entered with the intention of going to bed, he found that he could not restrain himself from striking a light in the passage and taking a closer look at the stuff she had bought. There was half a sack of wheat flour, a bag of rice, a whole loaf of sugar, and a box fragrant with the odours of colonial goods such as coffee, raisins, and who knows what else – all goods that the burden of debt forbade an independent man to buy in a free country. Prizing open one of the boards in the lid, he peered under. And what was the first thing that met his eyes? It was a roll of delightfully fragrant snuff-tobacco. No wonder he felt like losing his temper, a man who for a whole month past had had nothing but free Wormy to allay, or rather irritate, his craving for tobacco. Too disturbed to pursue his investigations further, he put out the light and went into the room.

The old woman asleep, Gvendur in bed too, his face turned to the wall. Only Brynja was still up, and she was sitting on her bed, still dressed in her best. She had unpacked some cloth to examine and had laid it aside again as if disappointed in it. She gazed down at the hands in her lap and did not look at him. It was only a short while since she had been so proud and so consequential, yet now she said nothing; no delight, no expectant cheerfulness left.

"Do we have to waste all this oil?" grumbled the farmer, screwing down the lamp by more than half.

She made no reply, something most unusual for her, but after a while she gave a slight sniff. He had begun unlacing his shoes. He hoped he would be able to get into bed and pull the clothes over his head before she found an opportunity of offering him a biscuit. He was careful not to look at her, but pondered all the more her behaviour. This sensible, hard-headed woman, who had long outgrown the years of youthful folly and frivolous excitement, this woman who had scraped and saved all her life long, never wasting a penny, except perhaps on a pound of biscuits once a year — had she taken leave of her senses? Was she sitting there sulking because the eyes had not popped out of his head with admiration when she had brought a horse-load of provisions into his house, his big new house? But she was a fine, dependable woman nevertheless, and rarely given to idle chatter, and he had had no complaints to make against her, except that once, last year it must have been, she had interfered in something that didn't concern her. And she was a fine figure of a woman, too, wherever one saw her, strong-looking and in good flesh, with the red blood of youth still in her cheeks; actually all she needed was the spectacles to be as imposing in presence as Madam of Myri a few years ago, when she was still at her best. And she was the very soul of cleanliness, never let anyone put anything on unless it had been mended, never allowed dirt to accumulate in the corners, knew how to make the most of the provisions, invested everything she cooked with an appetizing flavour. And she wasn't the one to spare herself either, or to turn her nose up at anything, for she was ready to carry muck by night or day, if necessary; no, she was most definitely not the type to lie coddling herself in bed, like a bailiff's daughter with nothing better to do. And she was a woman of substance, with a tidy little sum to her credit in the savings bank, and though her mare was a false stepper, a mare is always a mare nevertheless. And last but not least there was that magnificent bed of hers, the finest piece of furniture in the whole of the crofter's new house, the range not excepted; it was doubtful whether Madam of Myri herself slept between sheets that were softer.

No, she showed no signs of offering him a biscuit; probably it would never occur to her the way things stood now. For a good while she went on sitting on the bed with her hands in her lap — strange how helpless her hands could look when there was nothing in them — and he remained acutely conscious of her in the twilight of the room, there was a shadow lying across her face. Finally she took the stuff she had been inspecting and, rolling it up into a careless bundle as if it were some worthless rag, stuck it under the lid of her clothes-chest. Then she gave a little sigh. Then she took the counterpane off her bed, folded it with habitual neatness, laid back the red-chequered eiderdown and the snow-white sheet, sat down on the edge of the bed, and began undressing — unfastened her tie, unhooked her jacket, wriggled out of her skirt; and, having carefully folded all her outer clothes, put them, together with her best petticoat, under the lid of the chest. She was wearing thick, well-made woollen underclothes which she had worked herself, and her figure seemed to grow and burgeon and be set free as she peeled off the close-fitting outer garments; the strong, substantial haunches were so elastic still that it seemed incredible that she could be past the age of child-bearing yet. There dwelt a colossal strength in her knees and thighs, her neck was strong and youthful, her breasts the breasts of a girl, firm and tremulous, resilient, high in front, cupped even. She took her vest off altogether, she was a troll of a woman, but no more of a troll than he, for he too had the shoulders of a giant, a breast that could withstand anything. She put on her night-jacket. Then and not before did she put the light out. Her bed creaked as she lay down.

He found it impossible to get to sleep somehow, and lay twisting and turning from side to side, envying his son, who had been snoring for hours now. Time and time again he gave vent to his feelings in a stream of muttered curses, angry that foolish thoughts should be keeping him awake. The fact was that he was dying for a bit of decent tobacco — that damned Wormy, he thought, damned co-op, damned savings bank, damned house. The smell in this new place was enough to stifle anyone. Yes, if one only had some decent tobacco instead of that damned Wormy. How could he get himself off to sleep? It is an old belief that crafty verse is good for insomnia, but after mumbling through one or two favourite quatrains, he found, on searching his mind for more, that the only examples he could remember were the dirty ones. These uninvited verses stormed his mind in invincible hosts, banishing even the finest masterpieces of complex versification.

All the others were bound to be asleep long ago, and there he still lay tossing and turning, cursing, and with a mind now turgid with obscenity, now obsessed with the longing for tobacco — oh, to hell, I think the best thing, if I want any peace, will be to pop out and cut myself a nice plug from that snuff-tobacco. I can always stuff it in my mouth, for the want of something better.

He pulled up his pants, got out of bed, and put on his shoes, being wary to make as little noise as possible. But the autumn night was as black as pitch and he had to grope his way towards the door. As he was fumbling along, his hand passed over a round knob that he did not recognize at first. He felt at it again, then round about it, and his hand went groping over a face; it must have been the knob on her bed that he had touched at first.

"Who's that?" was heard whispered in the dark.

"Did I wake you up?" he said, for he had thought she was asleep.

"Is it you?" she whispered in reply, and the bed creaked as if she was moving over and raising her head.

"Huh," he said, "no."

He felt his way onward along by the side of the bed till he found the door. The fragrance of expensive colonial goods, delicious to the taste, assailed his nostrils, and he forgot his craving for tobacco and remembered one thing only: that this stranger had bought provisions and brought them into his house as if she thought he was a cur and a slave; luxuries; it was the first time that other people's bread had been borne into his house.

He walked out into the open air of the night. Flakes of snow were drifting lightly earthward and the air was piercing cold, but he paid no heed to it and made his way down to the foot of the home-field, barefooted in his shoes, and in his underwear. It was a relief to breathe fresh air again after the smells of cement and damp in the house. Probably it was an unhealthy house. What the devil had he been thinking of to go and build a house?

Oh, well, now that he'd had a breath of fresh air he'd probably get some sleep. He went back to the house, groped his way up the five steps and into the entrance, once more to encounter the seductive smell of her expensive groceries, delicious in taste, prodigal in quantity, paid on the nail. But nevertheless it would be the last time that into his house was borne other people's bread.

He was afoot early next morning, and when he had seen to some of his tasks he came in for his morning drink of water. But what did she do then but pour him out a big cup of coffee, the aromatic vapour from the curving jet filled his senses, neither of his wives had been able to make coffee like Brynja, in his opinion she made the best coffee in the parish, everything she touched in the way of food seemed to acquire an attractive and appetizing flavour of its own. She kept her back turned on him except for the moment or two when she was filling his cup — had she answered when he said good-morning, or had he perhaps not said good-morning? For a while he gazed at the coffee in the cup before him, yes, he had always been particularly fond of coffee. Finally he pushed the cup away without having touched the contents and, rising to his feet, said, without warning:

"Brynhildur, you'll have to go."

She looked at him then and said: "Go?" Her face was far from being old. And it wasn't ugly. There was a young woman in her face, and this young woman was looking at him, stricken with terror.

"You seem to think — " she said, and said no more.

It was as if this troll-woman had broken into fragments at one blow. Her features dissolved and she hid her eyes in the crook of her elbow in a deep quivering sob, like a little girl; he closed the door after him and went out to his work. All that day her face was swollen with weeping, but she said nothing.

Next day she was gone.

71.   IDEALS FULFILLED

THEN, were Ingolfur Arnarson's ideals nowhere put into practice? Yes, of course they were. They were put into practice everywhere. In all spheres. The land-development laws had come into force, and men were being rewarded with large sums of money for cultivating extensive tracts of land, yes, quite a few crowns for just a little patch even. Folk received prizes if they built nice stables and hay-barns of concrete, and they were allowed a grant if they wanted to buy costly agricultural machinery such as tractors, ploughs, harrows, mowers, rakes, in fact everything down to sewing-machines. The sewage scheme also was soon in going order; subsidies were granted for the construction of pits and cisterns provided they were substantial enough and sufficiently expensive. The Bank of Iceland opened a department for providing loans for rural house-building. Here the farmers could obtain long-term loans at a low rate of interest and with small capital repayments, but only on condition that good substantial houses were built, the regulations requiring double walls of reinforced concrete, cross-veneer on the panelling, linoleum on the floor, water on tap, sewers, central heating, and electricity if at all possible. Only really first-class houses could be considered, experience having shown that cheap, jerry-built houses were a risky proposition. Laws were also passed dealing with the systematic scaling-down of all large agricultural debts, so there was much rejoicing among those farmers whose property had been colossal enough for them to accumulate colossal debts upon it. And the co-operative society flourished, brotherhood's own commercial enterprise, into which no middleman or other sneak-thief might ever penetrate to batten on the small producer's just profits. If the times were prosperous they credited the farmer not only with the value of the produce he had sold them, but also with a bonus, which might be anything from a few crowns upwards, depending on the amount he had had for sale. The Bailiff of Myri's bonus ran into thousands. He won large cultivation prizes, for he brought extensive tracts of land under the plough and built most impressive stables. He also received a grant from the Implements Fund for the purchase of a tractor, modern ploughs, modern harrows, a modern mowing-machine, a modern raking-machine, and other valuable agricultural requisites, even a sewing-machine. A subsidy from the Sewage Fund was also granted him, and with its aid he built one of the finest manure-cisterns in the district. No sooner was this completed than it was discovered that the house was rotting away from beneath his feet, so he raised a big loan in the Rural Building Loans Department of the Bank of Iceland, and built, in accordance with that department's regulations, a fine first-class house, with a cellar, two floors, and a third of attics, all of reinforced concrete with double walls, veneered panelling, linoleum on the floors, a bathroom for Madam, central heating, hot and cold water, electric light. Such men are the flower of the nation. Men such as the Bailiff and the speculator who had saved the Fell King by buying his property. Speculator? It wasn't true he was a speculator, he was simply a modern financier who had decided to take up farming as a hobby. The Fell King had only himself to blame if he had lost all he possessed, anyway, because he had always been a duffer at farming and had never been able to keep within reasonable bounds, in spite of all his talk about the golden mean. He had never been a financier either, and now in his old age he was forced to work as a warehouse drudge down in the town, dependent for his existence on the charity of his son-in-law. No, the new man on the Fell King's croft was certainly no speculator, he had hardly been in the district a month before he was elected to the parish council, he received forthwith a grant for the purchase of modern agricultural implements, he built fine stables and was awarded a prize, he was given a sewage grant, he was given a big bonus on his produce, he fitted out the Fell King's house with electric light; the World War had not been fought in vain as far as he was concerned.

But what of Bjartur of Summerhouses and his friends? How did they fare?

Let us consider first Thorir of Gilteig, the father of sprightly daughters who at one time had had a weakness for silk stockings of inordinate length. Actually things had turned out much better

for them than had seemed likely; the youngest was even married
to a fellow of some means in town. And as for Thorir, he hadn't
owed so much that he could become a great man on the strength
of his debts, nor had he owed so little that there could be any
question of declaring him bankrupt. At the end of the war he could
describe himself as a middle-class farmer. He was chosen as Fell
King for the parish. The purging of the dogs fell to his lot, along
with the responsibilities and the emoluments pertaining thereto.
He was chosen parish clerk. He kept well in with both sides, ceased
complaining about the flightiness of women and was said to be
not averse to a seat on the parish council, if one should ever come
his way. Remarkable though it may seem, that which saved him
in these days of high wages was his erring daughters, who, com-
pelled by special circumstances to remain under their father's roof,
not only worked for him through the years of the war, but saw to
it that their children helped as well. Nor had he risked building
a house for the people on his croft; he had built only for the sheep,
and, as most people have bitter reason to agree, it is safest for
one's future welfare to do as little as possible for the people.

And the others? They slaved on now the same as before,
crushed beneath the burdens of parish rates, debt, worms, illness,
and death, while Ingolfur Arnarson's ideals achieved fulfilment,
and prizes and grants and subsidies and liberal terms were
showered on the well-to-do. Olafur of Yztadale had entered on a
contract to buy his croft, but he was still living in the same turf
hut that had been the death of his wife and all his children — human life isn't long enough for a peasant to become a man of means
— a fact that is said to have been conclusively proved in a book by
a famous foreign scientist. As for Hrollaugur of Keldur, he had
decided, at the end of the war and its concomitant prosperity, to
purchase the croft he had rented for so long from the Bailiff, and
now it was taking him all his time to keep up the interest. No, he
had not been able to build a house, that would have to wait till
next war. By that time, probably, the Bailiff would have taken the
hut from him again in settlement of unpaid interest; but the future
would have to take care of itself for the present, and Hrollaugur,
who had never learned to distinguish between the natural and the
supernatural, but always took everything in its turn, would take
that also in its turn when it came.

And what of Einar of Undirhlith? Though for the space of a
year or two he had been able to watch his debts slowly diminishing
in size, he had managed neither to buy his farm nor to renew his

buildings, and now his debts were once more piling up and he
would be lucky if the sheep he had for sale that autumn brought
in enough to pay the taxes and the fodder. The doctor's bill would
have to wait, likewise the refuse fish; human life is human life;
but he wrote nice memorial poems the same now as before whenever anyone died, and he was as steadfast as ever in his hope that
the Lord would be more favourably disposed towards the peasants in the next life than He was in this, and would allow them to
profit from the fact that they had immortal souls.

Then did all the grants and the subsidies, the benefits and the
bargain offers pass over these poverty-stricken peasants when
Ingolfur Arnarson's ideals were at last brought to fruition? What
is one to say? It so happens that it signifies little though a penniless
crofter be offered a grant from the Treasury towards the cost of
tractors and modern ploughs. Or a forty years' loan to build a concrete house with double walls, water on tap, linoleum, and electric
light. Or a bonus on his deposits. Or a prize for cultivating a large
expanse of land. Or a princely manure-cistern for the droppings
from one or one and a half cows. The fact is that it is utterly pointless to make anyone a generous offer unless he is a rich man; rich
men are the only people who can accept a generous offer. To be
poor is simply the peculiar human condition of not being able to
take advantage of a generous offer. The essence of being a poor
peasant is the inability to avail oneself of the gifts that politicians
offer or promise and to be left at the mercy of ideals that only
make the rich richer and the poor poorer.

Bjartur was now spending his second winter in the house he
had built. It was the worst house in the world and unbelievably
cold. Shortly before Advent the old woman began to keep to her
bed, though without being able to die, so Bjartur decided to move
her into the empty stall in the cow-shed, seeing that she couldn't
die of cold. Even Bjartur himself was so much affected by the
cold in the house that he began to have fears that he was growing
old, but there was comfort in the reflection that his son, in the
flower of life, could not stand it either. The walls of the room
sweated with damp and were covered with a veneer of ice during
frosty weather. The windows never thawed, the wind blew
straight through the house, upstairs there was snow lying on the
floors and swirling about in the air. Father and son saw to the
cooking themselves that winter, and in no spirit of great cheerfulness; there was not even a grumble to be heard on the farm these
days, no one seemed to be in the right about anything any longer.

The following summer Bjartur once more engaged work-people and once more made hay for his Icelandic sheep, even though no consumer in the world would degrade himself by touching Icelandic sheep, with the exception of foxes and lung-worms. The market fell still further that autumn. No one has any use for Icelandic sheep and never has had; and finally the Government was forced to sell the nation's right to its principal source of wealth, the fishing grounds, in return for the purchase by a foreign country of a few casks of foul salt mutton, which was then allowed to rot in distant harbours and finally taken out to sea and jettisoned. All that Bjartur felt he could spare for sale that autumn went in wages and taxes, leaving nothing for the interest and capital repayments on his loans — had he sold the whole lot it would have been but a drop in the ocean, anyway. He went down to the savings bank to see if he could come to some arrangement about his debt, but the only person to be found on the premises was a limp, consumptive-looking wretch who languidly turned the leaves of a ledger and informed him that he had no power to make any reduction. It had been decided to open a branch of the Bank of Iceland at Vik shortly and the Fjord savings bank was to be merged with it, so the only person who had power to modify existing terms of savings-bank loans was the governor of the bank himself, Ingolfur Arnarson. The manager listlessly advised Bjartur to go and see Ingolfur in Reykjavik and try to come to some arrangement with him there. Bjartur went home and thought the matter over. Perhaps he didn't even bother to think the matter over; it's all the same whether one thinks or doesn't think, they are all thieves, every one of them. And while he was busy thinking things over, there spread like wild-fire throughout the land the news that Ingolfur Arnarson Jonsson had temporarily given up his position as governor of the bank; he had been appointed Prime Minister of Iceland that autumn.

72. DOGS, SOULS, ETC.

MORTGAGEE'S SALE. Notice is hereby given that on the petition of the Vik Branch of the Bank of Iceland, the Farm of Summerhouses in the Parish of Rauthsmyri will be sold at auction on the 29th day of May next, in settlement of debts, interest on debts, and the cost of the sale. Sale to begin at 3 p.m. at the property to be sold.   JON SKULASON, *Sheriff*

This advertisement was pinned up in both Vik and Fjord and published in the *Gazette* from mid-winter onwards. Some time later, notification to the same effect reached Bjartur himself. He said nothing. It had never been a habit of his to lament over anything he lost; never nurture your grief, rather content yourself with what you have left, when you have lost what you had; and fortunately he had had the sense to hang on to the sheep as long as possible. Of these he still had something like a hundred left, as well as one cow, three old hacks, and a yellow bitch, the fourth generation in direct female line from his first bitch.

That evening, when Bjartur went into the cow-shed, he halted by the old woman's bedside and stood for a moment looking down at her.

"Perhaps you remember that hut of yours away up north on Sandgilsheath, Bera?" he asked at length.

Hut? She couldn't say really, her memory had given out ages ago, she remembered nothing about anything these days.

"Huh, I imagine it's still there in spite of that," he said.

"It was a good hut," she said. "I lived there for forty years and nothing ever happened. But here there always seems to be something happening."

"Oh, well, I'm leaving here now," he told her. "They're forcing me to sell up."

"And I'm not surprised," she replied. "It's that dirty old devil again, he who haunts Summerhouses and always has. And always will. Kolumkilli has rarely allowed anyone who lived on this croft to escape scot-free. I say for my part that I have never made this place my home. I have been nothing more than a lodger for the night."

But the crofter did not wish to discuss ghosts; he had never believed in ghosts, or on the whole in any form of superhuman being except those that one meets in poetry, so he came straight to the point and said:

"Would you like to lease me Urtharsel in the spring, Bera?"

"The sunsets were lovely at Urtharsel," she said, "when my dear husband Ragnar had put on his big coat and was riding northwards over the moors in search of his sheep, to clip them wherever he found them. And he had fine dogs too. We always did have fine dogs."

"Yes, you're right there, Bera," agreed Bjartur, "Ragnar's dogs were always good ones. I remember the time when he had a yellowy-brown one, a marvellous animal that could see in the dark as well as any other dog in the brightest day. It isn't often you're lucky enough to come across a creature like that, I can tell you. But I've had my share of good dogs too, you know, Bera; faithful animals, dogs that never let me down, and once I had a yellow bitch, the great-grandmother of my present one, that seemed for all the world to have power over life and death."

Come what may and go what may, a man always has the memories of his dogs. Of these at least no one can deprive him, though both the prosperity of world war and the fulfilment of important people's ideals have proved to be no more than a cloud of dust that has swirled up to obscure the lone worker's vision.

"Well, well, Bjartur, so this is how it's all ended," said Thorir of Gilteig with some compassion. It was early in the spring and he and several other peasants were sitting on the pen wall, blood-stained from the marking, with the lambs and their mothers bleating wildly around their legs.

"Oh, it will be your turn next," replied Bjartur. "There's no security in being dog-purger, as we've all seen."

"I don't know so much about that, Bjartur," said Thorir, not without a trace of temper, perhaps. "I don't swear by the dogs, of course, because to me the important thing seems to be to have faith, not in dogs, but in one's own children, whatever happens. That's what I've always done. Whatever happened to my children, I never kicked them out. And the result was that they went on working for me, bless their hearts, and for themselves at the same time. To believe in one's children is the same thing as believing in one's country."

Yes, he had graduated into a middle-class farmer, as was easily to be recognized from his tone. The secret of his success lay in the fact that his daughters had made him a grandfather in his own home and had stuck on there throughout the years along with their illegitimate children. He had thus been provided with unpaid female labour to help him all through the war, and had managed, at the end of it, to attain a position of some honour as well. In addition he had begun to believe in his country: Everything for Iceland.

"My children have never brought any shame upon their father," said Bjartur. "They have been independent children, my children."

The company saw immediately whither matters were heading, and that one short step farther in the same direction might result in personal insults. There followed an embarrassed silence, which seemed difficult to bridge, but fortunately our old friend Olafur of Yztadale was quick to seize the opportunity, for he knew from old experience that he who hesitates to seize his opportunity in any debate will never worm a word in edgeways.

"Well, personally," he said, "I've come to the conclusion that a fellow has no more chance of becoming an independent man these days than he had in the old days, if he goes and builds himself a house. Never in the whole history of the country, from the time of the Settlement onward, has an ordinary working man managed to build himself a house worthy of the name, so I don't see what good will come of it by starting now. We'll just have to let the old turf walls suffice. And anyway, what does it matter if a man has to live in a little mud hut all his life when his life, if you can really call it a life, is so short? It would be another matter altogether if folk had souls and were immortal. Only in that case would there be any point in trying to get oneself a house built."

Einar of Undirhlith: "Well, I'm not like Olafur, and I don't profess, on those rare occasions when I have anything to say, that my arguments are based on scientific theory. I just say what seems probable to myself and I don't bother about the opinions of scientists. And I must say on this occasion that it's simply because I know that the soul exists, and that it is immortal, that I don't mind though I live in a turf hut for the sort while that the soul lingers here on earth. And though life be miserable, one's house small, one's debts heavy, one's provisions inadequate, and illnesses long and inescapable, yet the fact remains that the soul is the soul. The soul is and always will be the soul and belongs to another and a higher world."

"Oh, go to the devil with all your bloody nonsense about souls," said Bjartur, jumping contemptuously down from the pen wall.

It was at this point that Hrollaugur of Keldur turned the conversation to worms.

PART III

Conclusion

73.   OTHER PEOPLE'S BREAD

THAT spring, at about the same time Bjartur finished rebuilding
the ruined farmhouse at Urtharsel — it was the same sort of farmhouse he had built once before, the sort of farmhouse that is built
by instinct — the Bailiff of Utirauthsmyri bought back his winter
sheep-cotes for the price of the mortgages with which they were
encumbered. Most people considered that he had made a good
bargain. His intention was to turn Summerhouses into a huge
fox-farm, because it was growing daily more and more obvious
that the country's worst enemy was no longer the fox, the country's
worst enemy was the sheep. Bjartur in the meantime had moved
his stock and his household goods away up north into Sandgilsheath, and there was now nothing of his left on the place except
the old woman, whom he proposed to convey to Urtharsel on his
return from town. He was making his first trip to town under the
name Bjartur of Urtharsel, his son in company with him. This man
was now so deeply in debt to the co-operative stores that he wasn't
allowed even a handful of rye meal on his own account. He was
allowed a horse-load of goods in the name of Hallbera Jonsdottir,
widow, after producing written authority. It was useless to indulge in threatening language, useless to revile anyone, for no
one had time to listen to threats or to hurl back abuse, unless
indeed some pack-horse boy told one to keep one's mouth shut.
And there was no point in punching anyone on the nose, because
somehow or other it was always the wrong nose that got punched.
He had sold his two better horses to buy timber for the new living-
room at Urtharsel, and now all he had left was a twenty-six-year-
old wreck called Blesi, whom we have met before. We remember
him from the old days, when we attended a funeral at Summerhouses, yes, a long time ago; he stood tied to the doorpost on **a**

winter's day and gazed in while old Thorthur of Nithurkot sang.
Many are the things that can befall a horse. This horse had lived
in Summerhouses for as long as Bjartur had farmed it, the only
horse in the lean years, one of several when times were good, but
now once more the only horse, bony, drooping, mangy, bald, and
with a cataract in one eye; poor old nag; but he had a stout heart
like Bjartur.

They were late in reaching Fjord, and the crofter felt that it
would be too much of a strain on Blesi to make him do the return
journey the same evening. They had put him out to graze, but
his teeth were few and he was slow in eating his fill, so they had
no other choice than to wait for early morning, when he might be
presumed to have eaten what he needed. It was late in the evening, the stores shut, their errands finished, and nothing to do
but wait for dawn; they walked off down the street. They were
both hungry, for they had eaten nothing all day, and as neither
had any money, they could not spend the night in lodgings. The
sky grew overcast and a cold breeze blew in from the sea, but
the rain kept off; they were both longing for coffee, neither mentioned it.

"I shouldn't think there's much risk of rain tonight," said
Bjartur, looking up at the sky. "We can lie down behind a garden
wall somewhere for an hour or two."

There had been trouble in the town, though Bjartur of Urtharsel had had more serious matters to occupy his mind. The fact
was that Ingolfur Arnarson's ideals were in process of being
realized in Fjord. A fortnight ago work had been started on the
great harbour scheme that the Prime Minister had once promised
this market town and then pushed through Parliament with all
his well-known drive; he was never the man to break a promise.
Besides the local inhabitants, a large number of people from Vik
had found work on this ambitious undertaking; they had left their
homes and were now living in some old baiting-sheds, which
were used as dormitories and were called barracks. It had been
agreed that the rates of pay should be in conformity with what is
usual in the remoter parts of the country. Work was begun by
once more rebuilding the far-famed breakwater, a task requiring
enormous quantities of stone and concrete. The men had worked
for a week at blasting and transporting the stones; then the first
pay-day arrived. It then came to light that their ideas of what
constituted normal rates of pay in the remoter parts of the country
had been much too rosy; they were being offered an amount that,

far from enabling them to become members of the middle class, was in their opinion insufficient to keep body and soul together for themselves and their families. They called such wages an attack by starvation on the workers and said they were against a Constitution which allowed working people to go hungry, as if such a Constitution was anything new! They demanded higher wages, but no one had authority to pay higher wages in these hard times. Who cares though your children have nothing to eat, the Icelandic Constitution is holy. They laid down their tools and came out on strike. There had never been a strike in Fjord before, but the Vik workmen, who were the leaders in the present affair, had once had one in their native town and had won, with the result that their dependents had been able to have rye bread with their refuse fish for quite a while afterwards. The people of Fjord, however, were divided on the question, and while many of them were enthusiastic supporters of the strike, a considerable number kept out of it, being not unwilling to make some sacrifice for Iceland's independence. The foreman gave a ready welcome to all those willing to accept the pay offered; the others could pack their traps and go. A number of small boat-owners and other members of the middle class even came forward and offered their services free of charge, with a view to preserving the nation's independence and the Icelandic Constitution. But the strikers refused to quit the job and, what was more, posted pickets who prevented those willing to work from entering. As a result there had been frequent clashes between those who could afford to protect the independence of Iceland and those who wanted their families to have something to eat. Many of the combatants had been sadly knocked about, some had had bones broken. Words and ideas unlike anything previously known in this locality were soon on everyone's lips; these people who had come here to disturb the peace were a set of vile, disreputable toughs who maintained quite openly that what they were after was a new system in which working people should have enough to eat. There was no police force in the place to suppress such crazy notions, and the Constitution stood helpless and unprotected, along with the country's independence, till the Sheriff wired the authorities and asked for police to be sent to protect those who wanted to work and to remove from the scene of operations a gang of villainous hooligans who didn't belong to Fjord anyway and who were illegally using force to prevent the work from being carried on. This request met with a ready response from the government; a squad of police was even now on its way and was expected to arrive by coastal steamer tomorrow morning. It was also reported that the strikers were well prepared for the police, and a big fight was expected. The whole town was in a state of apprehensive tension, so it was not surprising that no one had a thought to spare for Bjartur of Summerhouses when they were all wondering whether they would get a drubbing on the morrow. But now it was late in the evening; the turbulent voices of the working class had grown silent, giving way to the tern's untuneful screech. The night lay like a transparent veil over the town. The dale crofter and his son sat down at the edge of the road, in front of a sleeping house, and chewed straws and did not speak for a good while.

It was the son who at last broke the silence.

"Oughtn't we both to go along to our Asta Sollilja's and see how she's getting on?" he said. "I've heard she's ill."

No reply.

The son: "Don't you think we ought to go along and see our Asta Sollilja? They say her sweetheart has run away and left her."

Continued silence.

The son: "Father, I'm certain our Asta Sollilja would love us to look in and see her. I'm certain she would give us a drink of coffee."

Finally the father lost his patience, gave his son an angry look and said, "Oh, shut up before I slap your face. Won't you ever learn to behave like a man, you damned young milksop?"

There the matter ended.

They had been sitting there in silence for a good while when they espied a man loitering about on the road at no very great distance, dawdling slowly nearer, tall and thin, wearing blue nankeen trousers and a jersey, his cap on the back of his head. Now and then he halted and looked at the houses and turned around in a circle. Presently, catching sight of the pair, he stopped examining the houses and slouched up to them, halting at a few paces' distance. He fumbled in his pockets and produced a cigarette butt, then considered the two countrymen and the cigarette in turn. Then he smiled and, after lighting up, approached still nearer.

"Good evening, comrades," he said.

They answered his greeting stolidly and without any great enthusiasm, not moving, and still staring down into the ditch at the side of the road, with the grass stalks between their teeth.

The stranger hung about, shifting his feet and altering his

posture occasionally, but showing no signs of leaving. His gaze wandered about here and there, but fixed itself finally on the sky.

"It's clouded over with the coming of night," said he.

They made no reply.

"This is a rotten hole to be in anyway," said the stranger. "I wish I was back home. Not that it's any better there, of course."

"Where do you come from?" asked Bjartur.

He came from Vik, and had left that town because he had thought that things wouldn't be so bad in Fjord this summer, whereas actually they had turned out to be a good deal worse than they were at home even. The whole business had turned out to be nothing but a damned swindle. "Listen," he said all at once, looking at Bjartur as if he had just had a brain-wave, "I don't suppose you could sell me a loaf of bread, could you?"

"Sell you a loaf? Are you sure you're right in the head? No; I have no bread to sell."

"Oh well," replied the other, smiling aimlessly, "it doesn't matter. I can't pay for it anyway."

There was a short silence, then the stranger exclaimed: "God damn and blast it all, flaming hell and bloody corruption — what book is that in again?"

"In the Bible, I expect," replied Bjartur.

"Tut, what am I thinking of?" said the other; "of course it is."

"You're one of these fellows who have come out on strike, I suppose," said Bjartur. "You ought to be ashamed of yourselves and get back to work."

"What's the point, when we've been swindled?" said the man. "It's to be hoped that you aren't one of those who want to go on working?"

"Yes, I am," replied Bjartur. "I've always been a hard-working man. But I am no man's underling. I am an independent man — still."

"They're saying now that the police are coming tomorrow," said the stranger. "I hope you didn't vote for Ingolfur Jonsson, the damned bloodhound."

But on this point Bjartur preferred to remain silent.

"It's a crime not being able to get hold of some bread," observed the man. "The chaps sent me out to get some, you see. We were going to make some coffee."

Bjartur: "You said you hadn't any money."

The man looked up at the sky again, clicked his tongue, and smiled the same aimless smile as before. "Well, I wasn't actually thinking of buying it, you see. Not very seriously, anyway. I was just taking a look at the bakery."

"The bakery shut hours ago," Bjartur informed him.

"That doesn't matter so much, as long as they haven't hidden the bread," said the man.

"Hidden it?"

"Yes, yes, they've hidden it. I saw some damned fine loaves in the shop at seven o'clock, real monsters, you should have seen them, man."

He had finished his cigarette butt now. "Do you suppose it will rain?" he added, looking once more at the sky.

"I shouldn't think so," said Bjartur.

"Not that I mind," said the man. "It can rain as hard as it damned well likes for all I care. Listen, it's a hell of a long time since I was last with a woman, now that I come to think of it."

"Dear me," said Bjartur.

"Oh well, it doesn't matter anyway," said the other. "If the bastards send the police tomorrow, it will be just as well not to have been with a woman. I say, wouldn't you like to join in with us, comrades?"

"Against whom?"

"Against that big bastard Ingolfur Jonsson, of course," said the man.

Bjartur considered the matter for a while, then replied: "No, I'm afraid I wouldn't be much good in a scrap nowadays."

"We've a whole heap of pick-handles," said the man. "And all sorts of clubs."

"Really," said Bjartur.

"But if the bastards bring rifles, we'll just have to give in, of course. We're all agreed on that. Most of us have kids, you see. I wouldn't mind being shot if I didn't have any kids. I say, are you two waiting for anything special?"

"No," replied Bjartur. "I'm waiting for my horse to finish eating. He's twenty-five and has to take his time over it. We're going back home over the heath there, first thing in the morning."

The man: "But surely you're not going before the scrap, comrades? Listen, what the devil are you doing sitting there anyway? Why don't you come along and have some bread and hot coffee with us?"

"So you have some bread, have you?"

"Bread?" repeated the man wonderingly. "Why, of course, heaps of bread. Just come along with me."

He was so straightforward and disarming, so easy with his talk and so companionable, that they stood up and strolled along with him. He was not much given to walking in a straight line, rather followed some meandering path of his own; they walked straight. Twice he bade them wait for him while he popped round to the back of the house.

"Honestly, it's a hell of a joke," he said. "They're so scared that even the old women have gone and locked their kitchen doors." He seemed to think that this was something really funny and laughed at it, but neither of the others could see anything funny about it. In between he went on discussing the police, the weather, women, and anything else that happened to occur to him.

"I say," he said, "there's no point in getting married these days."

"No?" said Bjartur.

"No, none at all," said the other, clicking his tongue.

"All right, don't get married then," said Bjartur.

"I say," said the man. "I was talking to a very intelligent fellow the other day and do you know what he said? He said that letting people live was a much bigger crime on the part of the authorities than killing them."

"Damned nonsense," snorted Bjartur.

"No, no," said the man quite simply and calmly. "I think so too. I hold the very same opinion. I hold that people aren't big enough criminals to live under this system. People aren't big enough damned rogues for this system; that is, the masses, anyway. That's what's wrong."

Bjartur was too busy trying to fathom what the man was saying to make any reply.

"And we aren't armed either," said the man. "If we were only armed, it would be another matter altogether. We have to steal their own pick-handles from them to smash their blasted heads with. But if they bring fire arms, then of course — half a moment, there's an old woman lives here."

In a matter of seconds he was out of their sight behind a house, a medium-sized house with flowers in the windows and a tiny hen-coop. After a brief absence he returned with a large, uncut loaf of rye bread.

"I've skinned my hand," he said, licking the blood from a scratch, "but it's nothing much. Let's go now."

"I hope you haven't stolen that loaf," exclaimed Bjartur angrily.

"Pshaw," said the man, clicking his tongue. He pushed the

loaf down inside the front of his trousers and pulled his jersey over it. "It doesn't matter. She owns a lot of land. She's an archdeacon's widow."

Here Bjartur halted on the road and said: "That's enough; I, for one, am going no farther."

"Oh, but you must," persuaded the man. "Come along now, come and have some coffee. This is lovely bread. I don't think the old girl really needs all this bread."

"I have never been a thief," said Bjartur " — or a receiver either."

"No more have I," said the other. "But what is a man to do, when everything is stolen from him and he's probably going to be shot into the bargain? What difference will one loaf more or less make to the capitalism that murdered ten million men for fun in the war? Capitalism punishes people much more for not stealing than for stealing — so why shouldn't a fellow steal? All the people that I've talked to said that they were far better off in prison than anywhere else. The old woman I got the loaf from, all she does is sit on her backside and watch the rents rolling in from the farms she owns. But I'm sure that it's much better being in prison than owning a farm like you. I'm sure that a man is much more independent in prison. So come along, then, comrades. The coffee must be ready by now. And the only thief there is is capitalism."

There were ten or twelve workmen in this particular barrack. The oil-stove on which they were preparing coffee smoked abominably, but they had got the water boiled and a delicious smell of coffee pervaded the night air as the newcomers approached.

"Who are these two?"

"They were sitting at the side of the road taking snuff," replied their guide, a statement that was not altogether correct, as they had only been chewing grass stalks. "I asked them along for some coffee."

"Have you brought any bread back?"

"Yes, of course," said the guide in matter-of-fact tones, "heaps of bread. Step inside, won't you, comrades? It's quite safe to let them in, lads, they're against capitalism."

The hosts offered their guests a seat on one of the bunks, then began questioning them when they had made themselves comfortable. Several of them had heard of Bjartur of Summerhouses and knew that he had built a house and that his croft had been sold up by his creditors a few days beforehand; these wanted to know his story in greater detail, but he refused to divulge anything. They offered him a mug of coffee, which he was very thankful to accept, but when it came to the bread, his anger mounted once more, it was other people's bread. Yet he would have given much for bread to eat. Gvendur accepted a good thick slice and looked at his father.

"You do it on your own responsibility and not on mine," said Bjartur.

"Bjartur," asked one young fellow with a peculiar candid expression and living, sensitive features, "do you know what the Russian peasants have done?"

He made no reply.

"From time immemorial they had lived independent existences, like wild cats, or, more properly speaking, like Icelandic crofters such as you. Capitalism used them for stealing from and murdering, you see. Eight years ago capitalism started a war and for a period of three years had them murdered like dogs, for amusement's sake. On some days two hundred thousand were killed at once. At last the Russian peasants got tired of it, and joining force with their comrades, the workers in the towns, they overthrew capitalism and killed the Czar and took back all the wealth that the capitalists had stolen from them. Then they created a new society in which no one was allowed to make a profit on other people's work. Such a society is called a socialist society."

"Well, well," said Bjartur with a laugh, "so the Czar has fallen, has he."

He then told them something of his history, and explained to them also the present state of his affairs. "Maybe I'll have a bite of bread with you after all, lads," he said finally, for he saw that they were all eating the bread, and that their appetites were good, and that half the loaf had already gone. They cut him a good thick slice and it was lovely bread. "Oh, well, maybe they'll avenge me there then," he said with his mouth full of bread, " – like Grettir the Strong, who was avenged all the way east in Miklagard, for which reason he was accounted the greatest man in Iceland."

"You aren't dead yet," said one of them. "And you'll be fighting along with us tomorrow," said another.

"No," he said, "I've built myself another hut, on another holding, and I've no time for brawling down on the fjords."

"The day will come when the working class will throw off

these murderers and thieves," said one of the men. "And in that day you won't need to regret joining in with us."

"Sorry, but I've always been an independent sort of person. I want land of my own. I'm going over to Urtharsel first thing in the morning, as soon as the nag has had its fill, that's definite. But little Gvendur there can stay behind with you, and if he breaks a few of those Rauthsmyri bastards' heads, I don't think I'll let it worry me too much. So you'll stay behind with these fellows, Gvendur, do you hear? Who knows whether some day they may not give you the America you were seeking not so long ago."

When they had drunk their coffee, some of them started singing while others prepared themselves for sleep. They did not undress, but threw themselves into bed as they were, two or three to each bunk. In most of them there were one or two rags of blankets by way of bedclothes. Two of the men offered Gvendur a third of their bunk. "He shall be found work if we win," they said. "We'll make him one of the union straight away."

After a short space of time most of them had lain down and things were comparatively quiet. Room had been found for Bjartur also in one of the bunks; he was lying on the outside. He was feeling sick, as if he might vomit at any moment. It must have been the bread, of course; but, strange as it may seem, he managed to keep it down. It seemed as if he would never get to sleep; this night's lodging put him in too great a quandary. Was it a gang of thieves he had fallen in with? Of hooligans and robbers who intended to beat up the authorities and pillage the country? Had he not gone too far when he had decided that his son should remain here in the company of thieves? What had he, the free man, or his children, in common with such a crew? Why the devil had he had to go and fall in with them, of all people; he, an independent man who had just taken over a new holding? Or was it, on the other hand, possible that these were the just men? If such was the case, they were the only just men he had ever met. For there were only two things to choose from now; either the authorities were the officers of justice and these men criminals, or these men were the officers of justice and the authorities criminals. It was no easy problem to solve in the space of one short night, and he bitterly regretted having accepted the invitation to come here. He still had pains in the stomach from the stolen bread. He felt that he had sustained the greatest defeat of his life. So great was his sense of shame that the blood mounted to his cheeks, and there were moments when he was on the point of getting out of bed and vomiting the bread of humiliation out of the door. But nevertheless he did not get up, rather lay where he was. The others had long been snoring around him.

74. THE CZAR FALLEN

So he had fallen asleep, after all. When he opened his eyes it was broad daylight in the hut, the morning sun shining in through the open door. He got out of bed and looked at the sun, to find that the time must be about six o'clock; he had slept three hours or so. The men were still asleep. The bread and the talk from the night before had lost something of their reality but none of their guilt, as if he had dreamed something that was unworthy of him; it was strange that he should have landed in this mess. His back was aching and he was feeling stiff. The talk wouldn't have mattered, one hears so many things at one time and another — if only he hadn't eaten that accursed bread. Then he remembered that he had given them his son, too. Surely they hadn't put something in his coffee, to deprive him of every vestige of common sense? He stood on the threshold of the barrack, looking alternately in and out of doors, and wondering how he could get Gvendur away from them again. After a few moments' indecision he tiptoed across the room, intending to nudge him and wake him as quietly as possible. There lay the lad, fast asleep between his two mates, big, powerful men all three of them, broad in the chest and with resolute jaws, their hands thick and big-boned; while above them lay several pick-handles. And he felt that his son showed up so well in his sleep among these strong, well-built fellows that he had not the heart to wake him and take him away; he would show up just as well among them when he was awake. He felt that in reality such men deserved to own the land and govern it. But if Ingolfur Arnarson's men should bring rifles and kill them, his son included — what then? Wouldn't it be safer to wake the boy and take him away up-country rather than let him be shot like a dog on the street here? He had always thought a lot of the lad, though he had concealed it well. To be sure, he had once been on the very point of sneaking off to America, but his love of independence had won the day and he had decided to overcome the difficulties of life at home here along with his father. "Ah, well," reflected Bjartur, "what does it matter? I suppose I've lost boys before." For a moment he cast his memory back to the boys he had carried off in a box to bury in the Rauthsmyrians' churchyard; and to those others that he had lost in his struggle for independence. Maybe it's just as well that this one should go the same way, then, he thought. A man is not independent unless he has the courage to stand alone. Grettir Asmundarson was an oulaw on Iceland's mountains for nineteen years, until he was vanquished in Drangey; but he was avenged in Miklagard for all that, the biggest city in the world. Possibly I too will be avenged, with the passing of the years. Possibly in some big city even. All at once he remembered that the Czar had fallen, and the thought cheered him greatly — what would old Jon of Myri have to say to that? So, having abandoned the idea of waking his son, he left the barrack as quietly as possible.

It was time to fetch the horse from pasture and to make ready for departure, but he showed no signs of wishing to fetch the horse, rather loitered here and there about the sleeping village for a while, answering absently-mindedly the morning greetings of the few old fishermen who were already afoot. After a good deal of this aimless wandering he turned his steps with more purpose seaward along the fjord, towards that part of the town where the worst hovels were congregated. This part was called Sandeyri. He had never had occasion to go there before, but he knew various people who lived there. One or two women were up and out of doors, dusting sacks against the wall. A group of working men stood deep in conversation in a garden at the side of one of the huts; none of them paid any attention to Bjartur, it was some sort of meeting.

By the side of the road sat a thin-faced little girl making mud-cakes early in the morning. As he passed her by, she stood up and wiped her hands on her stomach; yes, she had long legs for her years, poor child, and long-knuckled hands as well, and her face, her face was not the face of a child, but full of character and experience; and she looked at him by chance and he knew her eyes immediately, both the good eye and the cross-eye, and coming abruptly to a halt in the middle of the road, he stared at her fixedly — it was little Asta Sollilja.

"What?" he said, staring at the child, for it had seemed to him that she said something as she looked up at him.

"I didn't say anything," she said.

"What are you doing out of bed at this hour, little girl?" he asked. "It's barely six o'clock."

"I couldn't sleep," she replied. "I have whooping cough. My mother said I would be best outside."

"Oh, dear," he said, "so you've a bad cough, have you? No wonder you've a bad cough when that thing you're wearing is so terribly thin."

She made no reply, but sat down to see her cakes again. He scratched his head.

"Well, well, Sola girl," he said, "poor lass."

"They don't call me Sola," she said.

"What do they call you, then?"

"They call me Bjort," she replied proudly.

"Well, well, Bjort my girl," he said, "I don't suppose it makes much difference."

He sat down at the side of the road and went on looking at her.

She ladled the mud into an old enamel mug, then placed the mug on a stone for baking.

"It's a Christmas cake," she said, giving him a little smile to keep the conversation going.

He said nothing, but still went on gazing at her.

Finally she stood up again and asked:

"What are you sitting there for? What are you looking at me for?"

"Your mother ought to be making the breakfast coffee by now, oughtn't she?" he asked.

"There isn't any coffee," she said, "only water."

"Oh, lots of people have had to content themselves with water before today."

She was seized with a fit of coughing. It turned her face blue. She lay down on the ground until the fit was over.

"What are you doing there?" she asked when she began to recover from the coughing. "Why don't you go away?"

"I was thinking of coming in with you for a cup of breakfast water," he answered in matter-of-fact tones.

After looking at him searchingly for a moment or two, she said: "All right, come on, then."

He had eaten other people's bread last night, bread, moreover, that had been stolen by thieves, so what did it matter if he had his breakfast water with this little girl. He straddled the barbed-wire fence and followed the child home to the hut. Never had his moral fortitude ebbed so low as the night that was passing and the morning of sunshine that was succeeding it; yes, it was doubt-

ful whether he could really call himself an independent man any
longer.

There was a window made for four panes in the gable, with
sacks stuffed into two of the openings, the third nailed over with
pieces of wood, and only in the fourth a whole pane of glass.
Bjort led the way. At one time the hut had been papered inside,
in town fashion, but the paper was now black with damp and
hanging from the clincher roof in tatters. There were two beds;
in one of them lay the owner of the house, the old woman, and in
the other Asta Sollilja with her younger child. There was an oil-
stove on a table by the window, a box, and a broken chair.

"Are you back already?" said Asta Sollilja when she saw her
daughter in the doorway. She sat up in bed, her breasts pendulous
under her open vest, her hair in disorder; she was very thin, very
pale. But when she saw Bjartur following the child inside, her
eyes began to stare. She shook her head as if to break some optical
illusion, but it was no illusion, he was standing there on the floor,
it was he.

"Father," she cried, gasping for breath.

Open-mouthed she stared at him, her eyes growing bigger and
bigger, the pupils more and more dilated. Her features drooped,
as if she had lost control of her facial muscles, but seemed at the
same time to fill out and grow younger, all in the twinkling of an
eye, and then again she shouted, completely beside herself:
"Father!"

Grabbing her petticoat, she pulled it hastily over her head and
smoothed it down over her hips as she sprang barefooted out of
bed, ran to the door, and flung herself into his embrace. With her
arms round his neck she pressed her mouth to his throat, under
the beard.

Yes, it was he. Her mouth was resting once more in its old
place, it was he, he had come. At last she lifted her head, looked
into his face again, and sighed:

"I thought you would never come."

"Listen, lass," he said, "hurry up and heat some water and
dress the kids. I'm taking you back with me today."

"Father," was all she could say, with her eyes still glued on
his face. She stood as if rooted to the spot. "No, I can't believe
it's you."

He went over to her bed and she pivoted round on the floor
and continued to stare at him, overwhelmed. He stood contem-

plating the infant that lay sleeping on the bed before him, and was, as always when he saw a living babe, filled with compassion.

"Heavens, what a helpless-looking object!" he said. "Yes, mankind is rather a pitiful sight when you come to look at it as it is in actual fact."

"I don't believe it yet," said Asta Sollilja, as she pressed herself against him once more.

"Run along and put your things on, lass," he said. "We've a long way before us."

At that she began dressing herself. She had a cough.

"You ought to have come home again before your chest grew so bad," he said. "I built you a house, as I told you I would, but there's no pleasure in it left, it's all gone. Old Hallbera has leased me Urtharsel."

"Father," she said, and nothing else.

"My opinion has always been this," he said, "that you ought never to give up as long as you live, even though they have stolen everything from you. If nothing else, you can always call the air you breathe your own, or at any rate you can claim that you have it on loan. Yes, lass, last night I ate stolen bread and left my son among men who are going to use pick-handles on the authorities, so I thought I might just as well look you up this morning."

75.   BLOOD IN THE GRASS

"Heaven's, what a time you've been away, girl!" said the grandmother when Asta was left alone with her on their last day in Summerhouses, Bjartur having gone off to Urtharsel with the provisions. "I thought you were dead."

"Yes, I was dead, Grandmother," said the girl.

The Grandmother: "Isn't it funny how everyone manages to die except me?"

"Yes, but now I've risen up from the dead, Grandmother," said Asta Sollilja.

"Eh?" said the grandmother.

"I've risen from the dead."

"Oh no, wench," replied the grandmother, "no one rises from the dead. And a good thing too."

Then she turned away and, once more fixing her peering gaze

on the knitting she was busy with, began mumbling to herself an old hymn about the Resurrection.

In the evening Asta took her children down to the brook and stood staring in wonder at this ugly house with the sharp corners, the impressions left on the concrete by the boards in the moulds, the dabs of cement on some of the windows, the broken panes of others, and the holes that had been dug in the earth all around. New though it was, it reminded one of the ruins of a building shelled in the war. Such was the palace he had built in the dream that she would return. She, too, had once upon a time dreamed of a bright house in a green meadow by the sea. Now she missed only the little cottage of Summerhouses with its rounded lines and agreeable proportions, where she had experienced her holiest sufferings, her dearest longings. Still, it was a great comfort to see the old hills at home, to find that, though so many centuries seemed to have passed, they were still in their places; as was also the lake, and the marsh, and the smoothly flowing river in the marsh. Once there had been a Midsummer Eve, and she had been going out to view the world for the first time; once there had been the glance of a stranger's eyes, and she had longed to rest her soul there to all eternity; her life had been laid waste before it had begun, like Bjartur Jonsson's house and his independence, and now she was a mother with two children, perhaps three, though no one need know of that. She showed these two her old croft brook and said, "Look, there's my old brook," and kissed them. She was like defenceless nature, that withers in the blast because it has shelter neither of God nor of men; human beings do not give one another shelter; and God? We shall see, when in the end we are dead of consumption. Perhaps the Almighty had made a note of all that she had had to suffer. All the same, she felt that evening that she was not too old once more to view the future in a dream; in a new dream. To be able to look forward is to live.

On the day following, Bjartur took the last load of his belongings up to Urtharsel. He had fitted old Blesi out with two peat-boxes, and in one box he seated the old woman, who was over ninety now, while in the other he put the two children. Then he set off, leading the horse on its way. Asta Sollilja walked by his side over the ridge. The bitch loitered along in the rear, carelessly nosing this and that, as dogs are wont to do on fragrant days of spring. There was nothing said. They were like people on a long journey leaving a poor night-lodging on the moors. They were the moors of life. The road lies towards moors even more remote. No lamentations — never harbour your grief, never mourn what you have lost. He did not even turn around and give his old valley a parting glance when they reached the top of the ridge. But when they were passing Gunnvor's cairn he halted and left the road. Seizing hold of the headstone that he had placed there to her memory a few years back, he rolled it over the brink of the ravine. He knew now for certain that it was impossible to cleanse her of Kolumkilli; she had always lain there with him, in hard times and in good alike; she was lying there with him still. Once again had they laid waste the lone worker's farm; they are always the same from century to century, for the simple reason that the lone worker remains the same from century to century. A war on the Continent may bring some relief, for a year or so, but it is only a seeming help, an illusion. The lone worker will never escape from his life of poverty for ever and ever; he will go on existing in affliction as long as man is not man's protector, but his worst enemy. The life of the lone worker, the life of the independent man, is in its nature a flight from other men, who seek to kill him. From one night-lodging into another even worse. A peasant family flits, four generations of the thirty that have maintained life and death in this country for a thousand years — for whom? Not for themselves anyway, nor for anyone of theirs. They resembled nothing so much as fugitives in a land devastated by year after year of furious warfare; hunted outlaws — in whose land? Not in their own at least. In foreign books there is a holy story that tells of a man who was fulfilled by sowing his enemy's field one night. Bjartur of Summerhouses' story is the story of a man who sowed his enemy's field all his life, day and night. Such is the story of the most independent man in the country. Moors; more moors. From the ravine there came an eerie echoing rumble as the headstone crashed its way down, and the bitch sprang to the brink and stood there barking wildly.

A little farther along the ridge, at a point from which it was possible to see down to Utirauthsmyri, the man left the highroad and began heading north, over old, untrodden footpaths from the past, in the direction of Sandgilsheath. The peat-boxes kept up a continual creaking; the children were asleep in the one on the other side of the horse, but the old woman sat in hers holding on to the pack-saddle peg with her withered blue hands. She was on her way home, home from her night's lodging.

The going grew heavier and heavier the farther they progressed northwards over the moors; landslides, gullies, bogs, boulders, all kinds of obstacles; finally moorland watercourses rising higher and always higher. A mile or so of this and Asta Sollilja had come to the end of her strength. She threw herself down on a grassy slope, coughing violently; some blood appeared. When at length the fit was over she sank back with a groan and lay there in a state of collapse. Bjartur took the boxes down and allowed the horse to graze. He helped the children and the old creature out of the boxes. Little Bjort stood some yards away with her finger in her mouth, gazing at her mother, but the old woman sat down at her head, with the infant sleeping in her lap, as it says in the old poem:

> *Running blood reddens the blade*
> *And lullababalulla.*

All that it says in the poem had come true, there was blood in the grass. They waited a while for Asta Sollilja to recover her strength. Bjartur stood at a loss some distance away; the little girl asked her mother whether it hurt a lot, but it didn't hurt her much, she was just exhausted and she didn't think she could walk yet. She lay there in the grass, feebly groaning, her eyes shut, blood in the corner of her mouth. The old woman bent over her and peered at her closely for a moment or two, her head on the slant.

"Yes," she mumbled, "and I'm not surprised. One more corpse shall I live to kiss."

Eventually Bjartur gave up all hope of the girl as being able to walk any farther. Seating the children and the old woman in the boxes again, he lifted them on to the peg. Then he took Asta Sollilja up into his arms, told her to keep a good hold of his neck, and led the horse off once more. When they had got well up the hillside, she whispered:

"At last I'm with you again."

And he replied:

"Keep a good hold round my neck, my flower."

"Yes," she whispered. "Always — as long as I live. Your one flower. The flower of your life. And I shan't die yet awhile; no, not for a long while yet."

Then they went on their way.

A NOTE ON THE TYPE IN WHICH THIS BOOK IS SET

The text of this book is set in Caledonia, a Linotype face which belongs to the family of printing types called "modern face" by printers — a term used to mark the change in style of type-letters that occurred about 1800. Caledonia borders on the general design of Scotch Modern, but is more freely drawn than that letter.

The book was composed by The Plimpton Press, Norwood, Massachusetts, and printed and bound by H. Wolff, New York. The typography and binding design are by W. A. Dwiggins.